F-105 Thunderchiefs

F-105 Thunderchiefs

A 29-Year Illustrated Operational History, with Individual Accounts of the 103 Surviving Fighter Bombers

W. Howard Plunkett

McFarland & Company, Inc., Publishers
Jefferson, North Carolina, and London

The present work is a reprint of the illustrated casebound edition of F-105 Thunderchiefs: A 29-Year Illustrated Operational History, with Individual Accounts of the 103 Surviving Fighter Bombers, *first published in 2001 by McFarland.*

Library of Congress Cataloguing-in-Publication Data

Plunkett, W. Howard.
F-105 Thunderchiefs : a 29-year illustrated operational history, with individual accounts of the 103 surviving fighter bombers / W. Howard Plunkett.
p. cm.
Includes index.

ISBN 978-0-7864-3885-3
softcover : 50# alkaline paper ♾

1. Thunderchief (Fighter plane)—History. I. Title.
UG1242.F5 P58 2008 358.4'383—dc21 00-48961

British Library cataloguing data are available

Front cover: F-105D-5RE 61-0107 at the Atomic Museum at Albuquerque, New Mexico (from a photograph by W. Howard Plunkett).
Back cover: F-105D-5RE 59-1739 at the Confederate Air Force's American Airpower Heritage Museum at Midland, Texas (photograph by W. Howard Plunkett).

Manufactured in the United States of America

McFarland & Company, Inc., Publishers
Box 611, Jefferson, North Carolina 28640
www.mcfarlandpub.com

For Dad, Bill, and Frank,
who couldn't wait to read it

Table of Contents

Part II. The Survivors 25

Preface

Aviation museums are grazing pastures for retired war horses. This book is about a herd of winged war horses called Thunderchief. It is a respectful tribute to the retired F-105 Thunderchiefs that are in pastures and stables around the world. It depicts the ones lovingly kept by caretakers who really care—and have the means to groom the Thunderchief in the way this noble steed deserves. It also shows the faded hides and bedraggled bodies of some that are less fortunate.

This book also traces the careers of each of the surviving Thunderchiefs to show how they earned their keep and found their way to pasture. These war horses lived through four periods in their lives.

- *Breaking In (1955–1964)* when the broncobusters and stable hands at flying units around the world tamed their supersonic steeds to be saddled and harnessed and trained for riding the range.
- *War (1964–1973)* when the cavalry mounted their war horses and rode from their forts to battle in the skies over Southeast Asia.
- *Peace (1973–1983)* when the steeds that survived were horse-traded to the Guard and Reserve—and sent to the scrub pasture in Arizona and on to the glue factories that rendered them to aluminum and titanium scrap.
- *Retirement (1983 and beyond)* when the remaining war horses were let out to pasture to graze in museum grounds and city parks as memorials to fallen war heroes and mementos to patriotism.

As you view the pictures of these mounts and read their stories, remember how much these steeds meant to the men who once rode them—no less than life itself—for these are the war horses that survived. With fire in their bellies, they always brought their riders home. Their fire now quenched, they truly deserve to be out to pasture.

Acknowledgments

I am deeply indebted to the many people who shared their time and information for this book. In addition to putting up with my obsession, my wife Wray and friend Richard Feldman edited early drafts. Friend and neighbor and retired Wild Weasel pilot, John J. Revak helped me throughout the project in ways too numerous to list. Dutch aviation journalist and historian, Theodore W. Van Geffen, Jr. provided a much-needed critique of the manuscript's historical accuracy.

Former F-105 maintenance people who shared their memories and memorabilia were Jerry Arruda, CMSgt Charlie Ashley, Charles Byler, Bobby Dean, Don Doty, David A. Hansen, David Gurtner, Gabby Hays, Mary Head, William Oliver, Michael R. Osier, Sr., Harold Seibel, and John Taylor. Although, most F-105 pilots were too busy making history to document it, those who helped were Michael P. Cooper, Henry Crescibene, Bob Kronebusch, Ed Mackett, Leo Marquez, Gene Cirillo, and Russ Temperly. Two 100-mission F-105 EWOs, Stan Goldstein, and Ralph Stearman, also shared their experiences.

Historians who contributed information from their files were Sgt. Judge Burns, McClellan AFB, California; Archie DiFante and Essie Roberts who furnished F-105 microfilms from the archives at Maxwell AFB, Alabama; TSgt. Edward Kelleher of the Virginia ANG; MSgt. David A. Levin from Spangdahlem AB, Germany; and Rick Versteeg from the Netherlands who maintains a World Wide Web site devoted to keeping alive the combat history of the F-105. I'm also indebted for inspiration and advice from aviation authors and researchers John M. Campbell, Robert Dorr, Jeff Glasser, Mike Hill, David Menard, Frank Strnad, Ron Thurlow, and David Wilton.

People associated with museums displaying F-105s and in restoring Thunderchiefs for display shared historical records and other information about their planes. They were: Mike Bianucci, Dan Bissell, Tom Brewer, Dick Cole, Darwin G. Edwards, Rebecca Garza, Craig Hannah, Bob Harper, Benjamin Kristy, Russell E. Lee, Brian Merideth, Kirsten Oftedahl, John J. Penoski, Ed Petrushka, Al Reddick, Jim Snyder, John Swihart, James Till, Enrique Flores Tritschler, CMSgt. Brian Wasko, and MSgt John White.

The photo contributors, many of whom went out of their way to photograph a specific plane at my request, were: MSgt James A. Allender, Ron Alley, James Babineaux, Mike Benolkin, Lt Col Judith Breeding, Jack W. Brothers, Dr. Carroll Brown, John Coon, Jay Finch, Norman Hamrah, SSgt. Gregory S. Henneman, Steve Hester, Donald L. Hilburn, Kyle Kirby, Donald Kuenn, William E. Malerba, Marianne McNelly, Robert L. North, Wray Pardy, Pamela Robbins, Larry Rogers, Walter W. Saeger, Jr., Pete A. Sanders, Jr., Leslie Sargent, Jo Ann Schuler, Ronald L. Shepard, J. Paul Siffre, Joshua Stoff, Hansel "Turk" Turley, Dwight W. Tuttle, Stan Williams, and Peter Yearsley.

Finally, others who helped in various ways, were Phil D'Alessio, Jack Britton, Ted Fandel, Chris Halverson, and my brother, Lynn M. Plunkett.

Introduction

Looking back over a 20-year Air Force career in aircraft maintenance, my two years with the F-105, nearly 35 years ago, remain some of my most vivid memories. I learned first-hand what working with a front-line jet fighter really meant when world events in August 1964 woke me from a sound sleep in Kansas and sent me, with no warning, half-way around the world to Japan. For the next four months, I helped care for a squadron of Thunderchiefs that deployed to Yokota Air Base north of Tokyo after the clash of ships in the Gulf of Tonkin. A year later, I supported another Thunderchief squadron, this time in Thailand, with the planes and their pilots flying combat missions over North Vietnam. During these four months in 1965, I felt the immense sadness of knowing men and their machines who didn't return; suffered the inescapable, stifling heat and humidity of the South East Asian climate; and contended with the dust, noise, and confusion of the rapid military build-up of one of the major air bases of the Vietnam war.

Years later, in an effort to better understand the events that kick-started my Air Force career, I began to compile information on the first and most remarkable plane I encountered in my 20 years of service. My initial goal was to track down what happened to each of the 833 Thunderchiefs that the Air Force had bought from Republic Aviation. This early approach was like studying a forest by examining each of its trees. Much to my satisfaction, and with help from numerous people, I succeeded in my obsession.

After completing a full accounting of the F-105 fleet, I shared my work with two aviation authors who had compiled a book of F-105 photographs. (*Roll Call: THUD*, published in 1996 by Schiffer Publishing). I then continued digging into the histories of the planes, concentrating initially on the ones that were on public display around the country and in other parts of the world. The longer I worked, the more I realized that there were more survivors than I had originally thought, and, for planes that hadn't flown in over 15 years, the fleet was surprisingly mobile. Planes that used to be in one location had been trucked to another. Planes that I thought had been scrapped, had been patched up and put on display. And, sadly, a few that used to be displayed were junked when their caretakers could no longer care for them.

This book, resulting from over five years of research, details the histories of the one hundred-three F-105s that have survived and are displayed around the world. These survivors—over twelve percent of all the F-105s produced—represent the full range of the airplanes' operational history and are a comprehensive sample of the original F-105 fleet. Except for the two "A" models, they include at least one of every type of Thunderchief built, and their individual histories involve every unit that flew the airplane throughout its nearly 30 years of operation.

The book is divided into two main parts. To enhance an understanding of the details of each surviving aircraft's history, Part I summarizes F-105 operations at the planes' locations in Europe and the Far East as well as across the United States. This historical summary focuses on events, aircraft configurations, units, and bases mentioned in the individual aircraft histories in Part II. Part I also discusses the planes' retirement activities, including some of the factors involved in putting an F-105 on static display.

Part II contains the individual histories of each surviving F-105 from the time it was produced to the time it went on static display. Each aircraft record tells where the plane was throughout its history. When historical sources identified them, the records describe combat and other operational events and name pilots and crew chiefs associated with the plane. The records are in aircraft serial number sequence and include a recent photograph of each plane.

Appendix 1 is a listing of the 103 surviving planes sequenced by geographic location to help the true fan plan a "Thud Tour." As you can see, however, some planes are less accessible to the general public than others.

Appendix 2 identifies the fate of the 118 F-105s that survived their operational career only to end up in scrap yards where a few still await their ultimate fate while others have been sold for pennies a pound.

During the years of compiling the information for this book, many of the 103 planes on display were relocated. Despite my efforts to keep track of their current locations, by the time the book is published some of the planes may have moved from the places identified in their histories.

As you page through this book, I think you'll find it contains detail not usually found in aircraft histories or in books on aviation museums. The detail, though often tedious, chronicles what happened to each plane throughout its life. Taken together, the records illustrate the F-105 program and document the development, operational uses, and inevitable march to obsolescence of one of the Air Force's most historic fighter bombers. I hope it whets your appetite to see each of these distinguished war horses for yourself. They are all that's left of a fleet of once-magnificent machines.

W. H. Plunkett
Lt. Col. USAF (Ret.)
Albuquerque, New Mexico
August 2000

Part I

F-105 Operational History

Initial Production

Production of all 833 Thunderchiefs took place at a single location—Republic Aviation Corporation at Farmingdale on Long Island, New York. This was the same aircraft factory that produced the P-47 Thunderbolts during World War II and the F-84 Thunderjets of the Korean War era—the plant that one historian appropriately named the "Thunder Factory." Production lasted a little less than ten years until the last F-105 was completed in December 1964 and delivered in January 1965.

Initial deliveries started in 1955 with fifteen test planes—two F-105As and 13 F-105Bs—whose six-digit serial numbers began with "54," referring to the government fiscal year for the contract. All of these initial planes were involved in test programs for Republic and the USAF, primarily at three locations: Edwards AFB, California, Eglin AFB, Florida, and the Republic plant on Long Island.

When the USAF considered buying a reconnaissance version of the F-105, Republic produced three of these fifteen planes with a "photo nose" that had camera windows instead of a Gatling gun. After the Air Force bought the McDonnell RF-101 Voodoo instead of an "RF-105," Republic sealed the windows with metal plates and delivered the three as part of the test fleet.

This book includes the histories of the four survivors

The "B" model featured a short radome forward of the gun port that covered the E-34 ranging radar, part of the MA-8 fire control system. F-105B 57-5837 is one of the survivors in Part II of this book on display at Castle Air Force Base, California. (USAF photograph, 1965.)

A Republic exhibit of the first F-105D, 58-1146, displayed the avionics that gave the F-105 a weapons delivery capability that far surpassed any previous USAF fighter-bomber. The Autonetics R-14 search and ranging radar behind the radome was the central portion of the ASG-19 Thunderstick fire control system. It was integrated with the Doppler navigation system and the air data and bombing computers. This plane was scrapped following a takeoff accident at Eglin Air Force Base on 26 September 1960. (Republic Aviation photograph, 1959.)

of this initial group of test planes including the one remaining "photo nose."

The "Bs" Make Their Mark

Deliveries of operational F-105Bs (all of whose serial numbers began with "57") started in 1958 when the 335 Tactical Fighter Squadron (TFS), received their first aircraft at Eglin AFB, Florida. This squadron, the first operational unit to convert to the Thunderchief, was tasked with "Phase II" testing to help speed the introduction of the new fighter into the fleet of the Tactical Air Command. The squadron's parent organization, the 4 Tactical Fighter Wing (TFW) based at Seymour Johnson AFB, North Carolina, began receiving their complement of F-105Bs in 1959. These planes eventually equipped the other three squadrons of the 4th (the 333 TFS, 334 TFS and 336 TFS) while the 335 TFS continued testing the F-105B at Eglin.

In December 1959, the Commander of the 4 TFW, Brigadier General Joe Moore, demonstrated the potential of the F-105 when he flew a "B" to set a world record of 1,878.67 kilometers per hour over a 100-kilometer closed course at Edwards AFB, California.

For a short while in early 1964, the Thunderbirds demonstration team flew the F-105B, until May 1964 when one of their planes broke apart, killing its pilot.

In all, Republic built 65 operational "B" models. Sixteen have survived to be illustrated in this book, including one of the nine used by the Thunderbirds and possibly (as described in Appendix 2) the one flown by General Moore on his record-breaking flight.

The "D" Model

The 4 TFW operated their F-105Bs until 1964, but began replacing them at Eglin with F-105Ds in June 1960. The "D" had a more powerful engine, a navigation radar, and could carry more bombs than the "B." The 4th began Phase II testing of the "D" with the 335 TFS at Eglin and turned over most of their obsolete "Bs" to the 141 TFS of the Air National Guard at McGuire AFB, New Jersey. Some "Bs" went to Nellis AFB, Nevada, to support F-105 pilot training.

Starting in 1959, Republic produced 610 F-105Ds the serial numbers of which began with the fiscal years "58," "59," "60," "61," and "62." These "Ds" were distributed from factory production to eight fighter wings at nine bases over the next four years. The first organization was the 4 TFW's 335 TFS at Eglin AFB, Florida, to begin Category II testing followed shortly by the 4520 Combat Crew Training Wing at Nellis to support initial pilot training. Two bases in Germany, under the United States Air Forces In Europe (USAFE), were next. They were followed by two more bases in the Tactical Air Command (TAC) in the United States, and two in the Pacific Air Forces (PACAF) in the far east. The last delivery destination was McConnell AFB, Kansas, which was to host the F-105 for the next sixteen years. Fifty-four "Ds" survived to be included in this book.

The table at the top of page 7 lists the units receiving initial F-105D deliveries.

A Two-Seat Trainer

In December 1963, Republic began deliveries to operational units of the two-seat Thunderchief, the F-105F. The factory produced 143 of the "Fs" that replaced the last "D"

Fighter Wings That Received F-105Ds from Production

Wing & Air Command	Base	F-105D Initial Delivery
4 TFW TAC	Eglin AFB FL	June 1960
4520 CCTW TAC	Nellis AFB NV	August 1960
36 TFW USAFE	Bitburg AB, Germany	May 1961
49 TFW USAFE	Spangdahlem AB, Germany	October 1961
4 TFW TAC	Seymour Johnson AFB NC	November 1961
355 TFW TAC	George AFB CA	July 1962
18 TFW PACAF	Kadena AB, Okinawa	October 1962
8 TFW PACAF	Itazuke AB, Japan	May 1963
388 TFW TAC	McConnell AFB KS	November 1963

models in the production line. The "Fs" were assigned serial numbers beginning with "62" and "63." They were the last of the Thunderchiefs and were distributed as trainers to the original F-105 operational units around the world. Twenty-nine two-seat Thunderchiefs survived and are illustrated in this book.

Flying Organizations

The wings were the parent organizations of the fighter squadrons that flew the F-105. Most F-105 operations centered around activities of the fighter squadrons. Each wing had three or four squadrons that usually consisted of 18 planes, but this number varied from 12 to 25 or more. The table below identifies the 27 squadrons assigned to the original eight F-105 wings.

Initial F-105 Squadrons Assigned to Original F-105 Wings

Wing	F-105 Squadron	Squadron Name
4520 CCTW	4520 ADS	Thunderbirds
	4523 CCTS	Hornets
	4526 CCTS	Cobras
36 TFW	22 TFS	
	23 TFS	Hawks
	53 TFS	Tigers
49 TFW	7 TFS	
	8 TFS	Black Sheep
	9 TFS	Iron Knights
4 TFW	333 TFS	Lancers
	334 TFS	Fighting Eagles
	335 TFS	Chiefs
	336 TFS	Rocketeers
355 TFW	354 TFS	Fighting Bulldogs
	357 TFS	Dragons
	421 TFS	
	469 TFS	
18 TFW	12 TFS	
	44 TFS	Vampires
	67 TFS	Fighting Cocks
8 TFW	35 TFS	Black Panthers
	36 TFS	Flying Fiends
	80 TFS	Headhunters
388 TFW	560 TFS	
	561 TFS	
	562 TFS	
	563 TFS	

While the wings normally remained at their home bases, the squadrons deployed with their pilots and support people. These people included personal equipment technicians who maintained oxygen masks and parachutes, intelligence specialists who prepared target folders for the pilots, and operations specialists who posted flying schedules and kept track of pilot training. Deployments often included a flight surgeon—the doctor who kept the pilots healthy and who sometimes flew in the rear seat of the "Fs" to better understand the environment of their "patients."

Squadron deployments also included several hundred maintenance technicians. Initially, these people came from the wing's maintenance squadrons and were assigned to a fighter squadron for deployments. Experience during early deployments showed that F-105s in squadrons with their own maintenance people had higher reliability and could fly more sorties than they could at their home base. By the late 1960s, this experience led the Air Force to break up the fighter wings' maintenance squadrons and assign maintenance people directly to the fighter squadrons.

The initial depot for F-105s was at Brookley AFB, near

Mobile, Alabama. Most of the early production aircraft were first flown from the Republic factory to the Mobile Air Materiel Area (MOAMA) at Brookley to have modifications installed before they were delivered to the operational units. Production-delivery flights were scheduled by the 4440 Aircraft Delivery Group at Langley AFB, Virginia. This organization arranged for a pilot from an F-105 organization to pick up the aircraft from the factory and deliver it to MOAMA. For deliveries from the depot to the initial units, the 4440th would also schedule the in-flight refueling tankers as well as the delivery pilots.

Most pilots in squadrons initially receiving the F-105 were trained at Nellis. Nearly all of the initial units converted from F-100s, and their pilots, experienced in jet fighters, cycled through Nellis for "Upgrade Training." After pilots completed their Nellis training, they often picked up their aircraft at Republic's factory or at the depot and flew them to their home bases.

Growing Pains

For the initial units receiving aircraft from the factory, the early years of the F-105 program were extremely unstable. The planes required corrections to a series of deficiencies that plagued their pilots and maintenance crews. Early aircraft were delivered from the factory with unsealed fuselage panels that leaked water into the avionics bays, a problem particularly bad for those planes delivered to Germany. To seal water leaks, the depots coated the planes with aluminized acrylic paint. The "F" models were delivered from the factory with this coating.

Production shortages due to a labor strike at the Republic factory delayed scheduled deliveries. Pilot training was further aggravated by a rash of crashes in early 1964 that frequently grounded the planes until fixes could be installed.

The major problems were engine bay fires and explosions caused by fuel trapped in the aft fuselage. The deficiency was corrected by a series of depot-level modifications called Safety Pack I and II. This work, begun in early 1964, dirtied the sleek lines of the Thunderchief by adding air scoops to both sides of the aft fuselage and elongating the engine cavity drain tube.

In-flight fires and explosions caused many F-105 accidents. During the years 1964 through 1968, the Thunderchief had one of the highest accident rates of any USAF fighter. In 1964 it ranked first, above all twelve types of fighters in its category, with a rate of 27.5 accidents per 100,000 flying hours. In 1966, it again led all fighters with an accident rate of 20.6. In 1965, 1967 and 1968, the F-105 had the fourth highest fighter accident rate.

Organizational changes also interrupted USAF efforts in learning to use this highly advanced warplane. Shortly after getting their F-105s, three of the wings changed designation or location. In February 1964, the 388 TFW at McConnell became the 23 TFW ("Flying Tigers") while, between July and October 1964, the 355 TFW moved from George AFB, California, to join the 23 TFW at McConnell. In May 1964, under "Project Clearwater," the three fighter squadrons in the 8 TFW at Itazuke AB, Japan, moved north with their F-105s to the 41st Air Division at Yokota AB near Tokyo. Soon, the war in South East Asia produced more changes to these original organizations. The 355 TFW moved from McConnell to Takhli Royal Thai Air Base (RTAB), Thailand, in November 1965. In April 1966, the Air Force assigned the 388 TFW to oversee the F-105 squadrons at Korat RTAB, Thailand. Many other squadron assignments and locations changed as well, particularly those squadrons associated with the two bases in Thailand during the war in Vietnam.

Enforcing the Peace

Starting with the "B" models, Thunderchiefs became the Air Force's first-line fighter with its range, speed and firepower exceeding all other fighters of the time. Immediately after receiving the first of their "Bs" and "Ds," and despite the aircraft's growing pains, the Tactical Air Command (TAC) sent their Thunderchiefs on numerous firepower demonstrations and "show-the-force" deployments to other countries. For example, during the summer

Air scoops added to the F-105's fuselage during the Safety Pack II modification in 1965 solved the problem of in-flight fires and explosions. However, the scoops "resulted in a 5 percent performance loss in miles per pound of fuel burned in cruise condition." (Photograph by author, 12 October 1996.)

of 1961, the "Bs" from the 4 TFW deployed for firepower demonstrations to Spain, Germany, and England under "Operation Thunder East." They spent a week at home in North Carolina, then leaped across the Pacific for further exercises in Okinawa under "Operation Thunder West." Later the wing operated F-105s from Spain and Turkey on NATO alert rotations.

Thunderchiefs from the 4 TFW deployed for a real crisis in October 1962 when President John F. Kennedy announced a blockade of Cuba after reconnaissance photos confirmed Russian missiles were being shipped to that island 90 miles from Florida. On a Sunday morning, the 4 TFW launched its F-105s from Seymour Johnson to McCoy AFB, Florida, where the planes sat on one-hour air-defense alert for over a month. The wing had 57 of its 72 F-105s grounded for modifications when the deployment was ordered so the 4520 Combat Crew Training Wing from Nellis contributed twenty F-105s with pilots and maintenance crews to the deployment.

After receiving their F-105s, the two wings in Europe continued the exercises from their F-100 days with air forces of other NATO countries. They also frequently rotated planes from their home bases in Germany to Wheelus AB, Libya, where the pilots practiced weapons delivery on the El Uotia range in the Sahara Desert.

However, the Thunderchief's primary function in Europe was to be loaded with nuclear weapons and parked in alert shelters as part of NATO's massive retaliation strategy during this Cold War period. When the Soviet Union walled off East Berlin in September 1961, the Thunderchiefs in Europe were temporarily relieved from nuclear alert to fly patrols with hot guns and sit cocked with rockets and GAR-8 missiles.

The maintenance depot in Europe was an Air Force Logistics Command (AFLC) contract facility run by Construcciones Aeronauticas S.A. (CASA), at Getafe, Spain, south of Madrid. The European-based F-105s were flown to this facility periodically to receive heavy maintenance and modifications.

World events kept the two F-105 bases in the Far East even busier than their counterparts in Europe and the United States. A year after receiving their Thunderchiefs, the three F-105 squadrons at Itazuke (the 35 TFS, 36 TFS, and 80 TFS) moved to the 41st Air Division at Yokota AB. As in Europe, the primary mission of the two F-105 wings in the Pacific was nuclear retaliation. Aircraft in the squadrons in Japan, where nuclear weapons were banned by post-World War II treaties, were rotated to Osan Air Base near Seoul, Korea, to sit "Victor Alert" loaded with hydrogen bombs and a requirement to scramble within 15 minutes. F-105s of the 18 TFW at Kadena Air Base on the island of Okinawa had similar alert duties at their home station.

The overhaul depot in the Pacific was also an AFLC contract operation run by Air Asia at Tainan Airport, Taiwan, where F-105s from Yokota and Kadena cycled in and out for major maintenance and modifications.

Combat Over Vietnam

For units flying F-105s, the war in Vietnam began in August 1964 immediately after the infamous "Gulf of Tonkin Resolution" when U.S. President Lyndon B. Johnson directed a build up of forces in Vietnam and Thailand to conduct retaliatory air strikes against North Vietnamese forces in Laos and South Vietnam. The initial F-105 engagement in the war occurred when the 36 TFS deployed F-105s from their home base at Yokota to Korat Royal Thai Air Base (RTAB), Thailand. They conducted strikes on targets in Laos. These initial strikes were the forerunner of four years of bombing missions over North Vietnam named "Rolling Thunder."

On 5 August 1964, TAC launched the 357 TFS from McConnell to Yokota to fill in for Yokota's F-105s deployed to Korat. This squadron had recently moved with the 355 TFW from George AFB, California, to McConnell and was only partially manned and equipped. To support the short deployment notice for the 357th, the 23 TFW, the sister F-105 wing at McConnell, contributed aircraft, support equipment, and people. This was the first TAC F-105 deployment in response to the growing war in South East Asia. While at Yokota, 357 TFS pilots sat nuclear alert at Osan AB, Korea, and flew training sorties, but were not allowed to help with missions "Down South," the term used at Yokota to refer to their classified combat operations over Laos and North Vietnam from Korat in Thailand.

These deployments in August 1964 started a turbulent 16-month period during which F-105 squadrons from Japan and Okinawa rotated on temporary duty for two to four months to the two bases in Thailand while squadrons from the two TAC bases at McConnell and Seymour Johnson, moved in and out of Japan and Okinawa and eventually directly into Thailand. With their frequent deployments, the squadrons were seldom home. Some of the busiest were the four squadrons of the 4 TFW. In addition to rotations to Asia, the squadrons from Seymour Johnson were still supporting their commitment to NATO nuclear alerts at Incirlik Air Base, Turkey, as well as conducting numerous firepower demonstrations and participating in weapons competitions in Florida and Nevada. The 4 TFW historian expressed his frustration in his 1965 annual report when he declared, "Getting material from the wing's four tactical fighter squadrons for historical purposes was something like trying to pin a diaper on a flea. Just about the time you had him pinned down, he was somewhere else." The 18 TFW historian at Kadena AB, Okinawa, "solved" the problem by simply not including the squadron histories in the wing's histories of this period.

Ready to take the runway loaded with practice bomb dispensers and rocket launchers, two F-105Ds from the 357 TFS were on temporary duty at Yokota Air Base, Japan. Both aircraft survived their careers and are shown in Part II of this book. In the foreground, 61-0056 is at Seymour Johnson AFB, North Carolina, while 62-4347 is on a pylon at Hill AFB, Utah. (Photograph by author, October 1964.)

In 1965, Takhli became a forward operating base for Yokota while Korat was the forward base for Kadena. Each of the main operating bases supplied aircraft, pilots and maintenance technicians for combat missions from their forward bases and performed scheduled maintenance when the planes rotated home.

The 16 months of turmoil for the pilots and support people involved in these rotations began to ease in November 1965, when the 355 TFW moved permanently to Takhli. Also in November, F-105 squadrons began being assigned permanently to Korat under the interim 6234 TFW that was replaced by the 388 TFW in April 1966.

Combat Takes Its Toll

During the next eight years, the heavy F-105 combat operations over North Vietnam and Laos, launched from Takhli and Korat, devastated not only the bridges and factories of North Vietnam but also the F-105 fleet. Between 1965 and the end of the air war in 1972, 397 F-105s were lost to combat and accidents in South East Asia. In 1966 and 1967, F-105 combat attrition at Takhli and Korat was so extensive that only a few planes survived from this era. For example, on 30 June 1967, the 355 TFW at Takhli possessed sixty-four F-105s. By the end of that year, twenty-seven of these planes had been lost in combat—forty-two percent attrition in six months. By 1972, only 14 of these planes were still flying. Of the 64 combat veterans that were at Takhli in June 1967, four made it into this book.

F-105 operations outside of South East Asia (SEA) centered around attrition replacements of both pilots and aircraft for the two Thai bases. Pilot replacements were especially needed, not only because of combat attrition, but also due to the USAF policy of reassigning aircrews after they had flown 100 missions over North Vietnam. Many pilots completed this requirement in only seven months.

Supporting the War

After gaining F-105 combat experience during their deployments to SEA in 1964 and 1965, the squadrons

At Takhli, Thailand, a load crew from the 562 TFS fuze a 750-pound bomb to load on the centerline rack of an F-105D. In 1965, the 562nd from the 23 TFW at McConnell AFB, Kansas, flew four months of combat from Takhli dropping over 3,375 tons of ordnance. (Photograph by author, November 1965.)

of the 23 TFW at McConnell became Replacement Training Units (RTUs) in January 1966. Their combat-experienced aircrews, nearly all with 100 missions, were the instructors for pilots en route to F-105 combat duty at Takhli and Korat. After a short period conducting similar RTU training, the squadrons of the 4 TFW at Seymour Johnson replaced their F-105s with F-4Ds and distributed their Thunderchiefs to units at McConnell or in SEA. By September 1967, both wings in Europe had converted to F-4Ds and transferred their F-105s to units in the U.S.

Initially, F-105 students coming to the RTUs at McConnell were experienced pilots. Each class was five months long. However, by the end of 1967, the demand for replacement Thunderchief pilots for Korat and Takhli was so great that RTU classes began including second lieutenants directly from undergraduate pilot training. For these students with little flying experience, RTU class length increased to six months. To practice firing Bullpup and Sidewinder missiles and the 20 mm gun at aerial targets, each of McConnell's RTU classes deployed for two weeks to George AFB, California. George offered an air-to-air gunnery range larger than the air-to-ground range in Kansas. For this phase of training, each class deployed with 18 to 25 F-105s and was "chaperoned" by one of the 23 TFW's four F-105 squadrons with their instructor pilots.

By the start of the war in SEA, the Air Force Logistics Command (AFLC) had transferred their F-105 support depot from Brookley AFB, Alabama, to the Sacramento Air Materiel Area (SMAMA) at McClellan AFB, California. (In 1972, the AFLC depots were renamed "Air Logistics Centers" so the Sacramento depot abbreviation became "SM-ALC"). In addition to the contract depot at Tainan, AFLC operated repair teams from SMAMA at the two combat bases in Thailand. Comprised mostly of civilian technicians, these "RAM teams" (for Rapid Area Maintenance) repaired the frequent combat damage the F-105s received during their missions over North Vietnam and Laos. For heavy repair beyond the capability of the field teams, some aircraft were patched up for a flight to Air Asia. However, many aircraft that limped

A pilot from the 562 TFS on temporary duty at Takhli, Thailand, climbs into the cockpit of his F-105D while his crew chief waits to remove the ladder. (Photograph by author, September 1965.)

Heading to North Vietnam, a 562 TFS F-105D lifts off the runway at Takhli, Thailand. From August to December 1965, the 562nd flew 1,740 sorties with their eighteen F-105s. In these four months, they lost seven planes and two pilots to combat and accidents. (Photograph by author, September 1965.)

"Texas Humpbacks" was the name painted on the fuselage of F-105D 61-0110 by the Air Force Reserve's 457 TFS from Carswell AFB, Texas. After its retirement, the plane was used for battle-damage repair training. The student metal workers avoided patching over the artwork. This plane's history is included in Part II of this book. (Photogaph by author, 4 August 1997.)

back to Takhli and Korat from North Vietnam and Laos were so badly shot up they were disassembled and shipped in C-124 or C-5 cargo planes to the depots at Taiwan and McClellan.

Starting in mid–1965, depot overhaul included covering the planes in camouflage paint to reduce sun-glint from their silver metal or aluminum paint. The jungle camouflage scheme with tan and two tones of green was initially applied to planes in South East Asia but soon covered all F-105s including the "B" models which were not directly involved with combat in SEA. Beginning in 1967, the planes' paint scheme included two-letter tail codes that designated their base and squadron.

Many pilots and crew chiefs in SEA gave their planes nicknames that were painted on the fuselage sides or engine air intakes. These names were often accompanied by cartoon drawings that added a bit of color to the dull camouflage. With the rapid turnover of pilots, many planes received numerous names in the course of their service. The Air National Guard and Air Force Reserve units who flew Thunderchiefs after the war continued the practice of giving nicknames to their planes. The aircraft histories in Part II of this book include many of the names given to the individual planes over their careers.

Wild Weasels and Other Beasts

The war changed the role of the two-seat F-105F. Initially assigned as trainers, the "Fs" found their place as hunters and killers of the radar stations that guided the North Vietnamese SA-2 and SA-3 surface-to-air missiles (SAMs). Dubbed "Wild Weasel III," the first of these modified "Fs" arrived at Korat in May 1966 after three months of testing at Eglin AFB, Florida. These Wild Weasels supported strike aircraft by alerting them to SAMs and by suppressing SAM sites ahead of the main strike force. The pilot and his Electronic Warfare Officer (EWO) worked as a team. The EWO in the back seat operated the electronic equipment to identify and locate the missile radars so that the crew could attack with its own weapons or direct the attack by others in the strike force. As more became available, Wild Weasel IIIs were also deployed

A MiG-17 kill, claimed on 12 March 1966 but not officially credited, is captured in this frame of gun camera film from F-105D 62-4278 while flying from Korat, Thailand. This F-105 was shot down by anti-aircraft fire on 12 August 1967. (USAF photograph via William Oliver, former crew chief of 62-4278.)

to Takhli. Their electronic warfare equipment was frequently upgraded so that the "Fs" had several configurations throughout the war, taking on the unofficial designation "EF-105F."

Some "Fs" had unique configurations that complicated mission scheduling at Korat, where they were initially based. Starting in April 1967, eight "Fs" were modified under "Commando Nail" with improved radar bombing systems, but with rear cockpit flight controls removed. This modification provided a night bombing capability for the operation called "Ryan's Raiders."

A second configuration was named "Combat Martin." By April 1968, Korat had received five of the ten "Fs" modified under this program. Five more went to Takhli. These aircraft had the rear seat removed and QRC-128 UHF jamming equipment installed to block the radio signals that directed North Vietnamese MiGs defending areas around Hanoi. However, on 1 April 1968, when President Johnson imposed bombing restrictions above the 18th parallel, the Combat Martin gear served little purpose since MiGs were not a threat in the southern areas of North Vietnam. Without using it, the 388 TFW removed the QRC-128 equipment and flew the planes as single-seat bombers.

Yet a third configuration of the "F" was tested at Korat beginning in August 1968. Four of their twelve Wild Weasel IIIs were modified for a test of the Bistatic Aided Strike System (BASS). The BASS modifications to electronic warfare equipment in the "F's" were intended to operate with a specially-equipped EC-121K, named "Rivet Top." The sensitive receivers on the EC-121 were able to detect the weak signals from a radar site that was transmitting into a dummy load, a tactic used to foil the Weasels. By displaying on its radar scope a coded IFF signal from the F-105F along with the signal from the SAM radar, the EC-121 could vector the Wild Weasel to the radar site. The system failed to work and, after several tests and ten unsuccessful missions, the program was stopped in November 1968.

The most successful conversion of the "F" was the upgrade of the Wild Weasel III configuration under T. O. 1F-105-1133, dated 23 February 1970. This modification added additional equipment, including Electronic Counter Measures (ECM) pods scabbed to both sides of the lower fuselage, and changed the aircraft's designation to "F-105G." Between 1969 and 1971, a total of 61 "Fs" were converted to "Gs." Of the twenty-nine surviving two-seat Thunderchiefs illustrated in this book, twenty are "Gs."

MiG Killers

Even though their aircraft was not designed as an air-superiority fighter, F-105 pilots were officially credited with shooting down 27½ MiG-17s in air-to-air combat over North Vietnam. (The half a MiG was a kill shared with an F-4D). Unfortunately, due to the Air Force's poor record keeping, serial numbers are known for only 24 F-105s credited with destroying a MiG and four of these are not certain. Of the known MiG killers, two survived to be placed on display and are illustrated in this book.

Major John Revak, pilot (top), and Major Stanley Goldstein, EWO, were one of the Wild Weasel crews of the 44 TFS at Korat in 1968. They graduated from Wild Weasel training at Nellis in January 1968 but were sent to Osan Air Base, Korea, for nearly three months in response to the U.S.S. Pueblo incident. After arriving at Korat in April, they flew their 100th mission over North Vietnam on 25 November 1968. (USAF photograph via John Revak.)

Many F-105 pilots reported MiG kills but, based on evidence presented, as well as other intelligence data, the Seventh Air Force Enemy Aircraft Claims Evaluation Board did not validate their claims. For example, the F-105G at the Air Force Museum had three claimed MiG kills in 1967 and flew for years with three red stars on its fuselage. As you can see from its history in Part II of this book, none of these claims was officially credited. Nevertheless, the Museum still displays it with its three red stars, a case where the plane's lore has become part of its history.

The U.S.S. Pueblo Diversion

For some F-105 units and aircrews, the war in Vietnam was temporarily interrupted in January 1968 when North Korea captured a US Navy intelligence ship, the U.S.S. Pueblo. As part of the United States' response, F-105s from Kadena AB, Okinawa, flew to Osan Air Base in South Korea under an operation named "Combat Fox." F-105 crews from Takhli, Korat and Yokota as well as from McConnell and Nellis were also ordered to Osan to help guard against an escalation in the tense situation. This deployment was reminiscent of the start of the air war over North Vietnam that began three and a half years earlier after a confrontation with Navy ships in the Gulf of Tonkin. The Pueblo incident started a series of F-105 rotations from Okinawa to Korea that lasted over three years and included two other air bases in South Korea—Kwangju and Taegu.

Winding Down

When President Johnson halted the Rolling Thunder bombing of North Vietnam on 1 November 1968, combat missions from Takhli and Korat were restricted to

Getting a thumbs-up from their crew chief, the Wild Weasel crew of F-105F 62-4416 from the 6010 Wild Weasel Squadron taxis out for a mission from Korat, Thailand in early 1971. They are carrying Standard Arm and Shrike missiles. The plane also appears as a survivor in Part II of this book. (Donald Doty photograph, April/May 1971.)

interdicting North Vietnamese supply routes in Laos and South Vietnam. From this date, the combat role of the F-105 began its gradual decline. A week after the start of the bombing restriction, Korat began equipping their squadrons with the more versatile F-4E, redistributing the Thunderchiefs and pilots of the 469 TFS to the remaining F-105 squadrons at Korat and Takhli. Six months later, in May 1969, Korat's 34 TFS followed the same route, leaving only the 44 TFS at Korat equipped with Thunderchiefs. In October 1969, the 44th transferred to the 355 TFW making Takhli the only base in South East Asia flying F-105s.

With the lessening demand for F-105 pilots in Thailand, three of the four Replacement Training Units at McConnell's 23 TFW reverted to combat-capable squadrons. The first to drop their training role was the 561 TFS, beginning in March 1970, when they were chosen to fly F-105G Wild Weasels. The 562 TFS was next. Most of the thirteen graduates of the 562 TFS's last RTU class in August 1970 were assigned to the three F-105 squadrons at McConnell instead of receiving orders to Takhli or Korat.

In September 1967, McConnell had received F-105Bs from Nellis when the 4520 CCTW began instructing aircrews in the F-111A and dropped their F-105 training. These "Bs," used by McConnell's RTU instructor pilots, were transferred to the 119 TFS of the New Jersey Air National Guard based at Atlantic City, the second New Jersey Guard unit to get the Air Force's cast-off "B" models. By August 1970, the 419 Tactical Fighter Training Squadron, added to the 23rd wing in January 1968 as the 4519 Combat Crew Training Squadron, remained the sole squadron training F-105 pilots at McConnell. Its last class of eight students graduated in November 1970 and the squadron deactivated in May 1971.

One Last Configuration

In March 1970, the first of a new configuration of F-105Ds began arriving at McConnell. In an attempt to provide the single-seat "D" with a night and bad-weather bombing capability, the USAF selected thirty for a modification called "Thunderstick II." This conversion packed additional avionics into the plane, including a LORAN receiver and an inertial navigation system more accurate than the F-105's Doppler navigator. To house the additional equipment, a large turtle deck was added along the top of the fuselage.

Unfortunately, by the time the modified planes were completed, single-seat Thunderchiefs were no longer needed in South East Asia. After being tested at Eglin AFB, using the LORAN ground transmitters in Florida, the aircraft ended up with the 563 TFS at McConnell. For the next two years, the squadron struggled to keep the unique "T-Stick II" systems operational in the face of too-few spare parts and no LORAN signals over Kansas. When the 563 TFS was inactivated in 1972, the planes were passed to the Air Force Reserve in Fort Worth, Texas, where they served for the next ten years. Five of these T-Stick II F-105Ds have survived to be illustrated in this book.

Bringing the "Ds" Home

The 355 TFW flew their last F-105 combat mission from Takhli on 6 October 1970. Shortly thereafter forty-eight of the wing's F-105s were flown to McConnell, the main Air Force base in the States still using the Thunderchief. There were more of these combat veterans than the 23 TFW needed and so, under a program named "Coronet Bighorn," McConnell placed them in flyable storage. They used some for weapons load training until the planes could be refurbished and dispersed to the Air National Guard units scheduled to receive them.

The Wild Weasels Fight On

In December 1970, the USAF deactivated the 355 TFW and shut down Takhli. By this time the only Thunderchiefs flying in South East Asia were the Wild Weasel F-105Fs that had earlier gathered at Korat. After arriving at Korat, these planes had been initially assigned to Detachment 1 of the 12 TFS, whose parent organization was the 18 TFW at Kadena. On 1 November 1970, this organization was absorbed by the newly-activated 6010 Wild Weasel Squadron (WWS) and placed under the 388 TFW. Later, in 1971, this 388 TFW unit received a third name, the 17 WWS.

On 20 November 1970, when the unit was the 6010 WWS, five of its aircraft were abruptly pressed into service as decoys during the raid to rescue American POWs believed to be at the Son Tay prison camp west of Hanoi. The five Wild Weasel F-105Gs, with radio call signs "Firebird," struck SAM sites around Son Tay to divert the attention of the North Vietnamese missile operators from the rescue helicopters landing at the prison. The raiders successfully returned from the raid after finding that the prisoners were no longer at the camp. However, Firebird 5 (F-105G 62-4436) was hit over North Vietnam and the crew bailed out in Laos. They were rescued by two of the helicopters returning from Son Tay. Of the four remaining Firebirds, only one survives and its history is in this book.

Joining the Guard and Reserves

By January 1971, the USAF had withdrawn all F-105 units from Thailand except the 6010 WWS with their F-105Fs and "Gs" at Korat. The remaining Air Force units operating Thunderchiefs were the 18 TFW at Kadena, the 23 TFW at McConnell, and the 57 Fighter Weapons Wing at Nellis.

By this time, of the original 833 F-105s, only 264 were still flying and 45 of these were the surviving F-105Bs in the two units of the New Jersey ANG. The other 569 planes had been retired, scrapped, lost in combat or had accidentally crashed. Furthermore, many of the surviving planes were approaching or had exceeded the F-105's design life of 4,000 flying hours. The problem for the Air Force became what to do with the 139 "Ds" and the 80 "Fs" and "Gs" remaining in their aging F-105 inventory.

Except for the Wild Weasel "Gs," for which they had no replacement, the Air Force was well into equipping their former F-105 units with F-4s or A-7Ds. The machine that, six years earlier, had been the Air Force's front-line fighter-bomber and the mainstay of Rolling Thunder, was now past its prime, its combat-stressed airframe an expensive burden to maintain. It was time to pass on the remaining Thunderchiefs to the Air National Guard and Air Force Reserves.

Over the next year, McConnell turned over their F-105Ds and "Fs" to three Air National Guard units, starting with the 184 Tactical Fighter Group across the runway from the 23 TFW. This unit inherited McConnell's legacy for F-105 pilot training and changed its name to the 184 Tactical Fighter Training Group. At the same time, the Virginia ANG at Richmond picked up its F-105s from McConnell after its pilots were some of the last to be trained by the 23 TFW. Three months later, in April 1971, the Washington DC ANG unit at Andrews AFB, Maryland, became the third ANG squadron to take on the D-model Thunderchief.

Three Air Force Reserve units were next in line to receive the aging "Ds" and "Fs," starting with the "Sooners" of the 465 TFS at Tinker AFB, Oklahoma, who inherited F-105s from Kadena in May 1972.

In July 1972, the 23 TFW left its F-105s at McConnell and relocated to England AFB, Louisiana, to fly new A-7D Corsair IIs. Before the wing left McConnell, they turned over their thirty unique T-Stick II F-105Ds to the Reserve's 457 TFS at Carswell AFB, Texas.

Starting in September 1972, after keeping their "Bs" for a little more than two years, the Air National Guard unit at Atlantic City turned some of them over to their sister unit at McGuire and the rest to the Reserves at Hill AFB, Utah. This Utah unit later acquired F-105Ds and "Fs" and was destined to be the last organization to fly the Thunderchief.

The table below summarizes the Guard and Reserve squadrons that received F-105s during this period.

Air National Guard and USAF Reserve Squadrons That Operated F-105s

Squadron	Base	Beginning	Ending
141 TFS ANG	McGuire AFB NJ	April 1964	May 1981
119 TFS ANG	Atlantic City NJ	June 1970	January 1973
127 TFTS ANG	McConnell AFB KS	January 1971	November 1979
149 TFS ANG	Byrd Field VA	January 1971	February 1982
121 TFS ANG	Andrews AFB MD	April 1971	July 1981
465 TFS AFRES	Tinker AFB OK	May 1972	October 1980
457 TFS AFRES	Carswell AFB TX	June 1972	June 1982
466 TFS AFRES	Hill AFB UT	September 1972	February 1984
128 TFS ANG	Dobbins AFB GA	October 1978	May 1983

Last Combat for the Wild Weasels

When they left McConnell in July 1972, the 23 TFW abandoned the 561 TFS with its collection of Wild Weasel F-105Fs and "Gs," that, except for a few at Nellis, were the only ones remaining outside of Korat. Operating from McConnell during the next year, this squadron was assigned directly under the 832 Air Division.

However, by the time their parent wing had left McConnell, many of the crews and planes of the 561st had been called on to support the last campaigns of the Vietnam War. In April 1972, President Richard M. Nixon renewed the bombing of North Vietnam in an effort to counter the North Vietnamese Spring offensive in South Vietnam. On 12 April, under "Constant Guard I," twelve F-105Gs from the 561st deployed from McConnell as "Detachment Alpha" to Korat, Thailand. This detachment joined the thinly-stretched 17 WWS in flying missions over Laos, Cambodia, and North Vietnam in the series of bombing campaigns named "Freedom Train," "Linebacker I," and "Linebacker II."

Between February and July 1973, while Detachment Alpha of the 561st was at Korat, the Air Force relocated the squadron's home base from McConnell to the 35 TFW at George AFB, California.

The Weasels Come Home

F-105G combat operations in South East Asia ceased at the end of April 1973, but Detachment Alpha of the 561st did not begin returning home until June. Leaving their planes at Korat, squadron crews arrived at McConnell and immediately began relocating to George. The detachment parked their 12 "Gs" at Korat under the care of one pilot and 180 maintenance technicians. In September 1973, the "Constant Guard I" deployment officially ended and the 35 TFW sent twelve aircrews to Korat to retrieve the 561st's aircraft. The return of these twelve "Gs" marked the end of Tactical Air Command's nine-year participation in the Vietnam war.

In October 1974, the last of the "Gs" belonging to the 17 WWS at Korat arrived at George where they equipped the resurrected 562 TFS. The 35 TFW was the last active-duty unit to operate the Thunderchief.

To the Boneyard

In July 1973, the Guard and Reserves began flying their F-105s to the "Boneyard," then officially known as the Military Aircraft Storage and Disposition Center (MASDC) at Davis-Monthan AFB, Arizona. Over the next ten years, 94 Thunderchiefs, including eleven F-105Gs from the 35 TFW in 1980, were delivered to desert storage as shown in the following table.

F-105 Retirements to MASDC at Davis-Monthan AFB, Arizona.

Year	1973	1975	1976	1980	1981	1982	1983	Total
Quantity	4	4	3	16	47	19	1	94

Peace Time Operations

F-105 operations during the years after the war in Vietnam consisted of firepower demonstrations and deployments similar to those during the pre-war days but with far less intensity. In August 1976, F-105s began participating in a series of European deployments, code-named "Coronet," when six of the 35 TFW's "Gs" deployed from George AFB to Spangdahlem AB, Germany, for "Coronet Yankee." Guard and Reserve units flying the F-105 also participated in these late-summer European exercises until the last Thunderchief deployment to Denmark for "Coronet Rudder" in August 1981.

During this same period, the Air Force Logistics Command overhauled aging Thunderchiefs using contract depot facilities in Crestview, Florida, and Moultrie, Georgia. Also, contract teams from companies such as Dynalectron Corporation and General Dynamics did depot maintenance at Guard and Reserve bases that flew the planes.

Final Phase Out

The 35 TFW at George remained the only unit operating the Wild Weasel Thunderchiefs until October 1978, when they began turning over their "Gs" to the 128 TFS of the Georgia Air National Guard at Dobbins AFB, north of Atlanta. This conversion was completed on 12 July 1980 when the 562 TFS hosted a "Sawadee Party" at George to commemorate the retirement of the last F-105 from the active-duty Air Force. During this event an example of every production model of the F-105 flew in the ceremony that also memorialized an F-105G placed on static display at George. After the base's closure in 1992, this aircraft was stored at George, now called the Southern California International Airport, and was moved six years later to nearby Palmdale, California.

The 128th operated their "Gs" from Dobbins until May 1983 when they flew the last 15 planes to Patuxent River Naval Air Station for delivery to the U.S. Army. The Army loaded the planes on barges and towed them by tugboat up Chesapeake Bay, parking them in a field on Aberdeen Proving Grounds. Over the next ten years, the Army's Ballistic Missile Research Laboratory used some of the planes as

One of 47 F-105s retired to MASDC in 1981, F-105B 57-5792, here in its protective plastic coating, was from the New Jersey Air National Guard. Stenciled on its nose gear door is its MASDC storage number—FK028. It arrived at MASDC on 7 January 1981, the 28th F-105 sent to the Boneyard. In Part II of this book, the plane is shown displayed at Anderson, South Carolina. (Michael Benolkin photograph, December 1981.)

targets for testing missiles such as the Shapparal—an ironic end to these missile-hunting Wild Weasels.

The Air Force Reserve's 419 TFW at Hill AFB, Utah, was the last unit to fly the F-105. The unit conducted a series of bitter-sweet ceremonies marking the end of the plane's operational career. In June 1983, they flew the last F-105 mission when they launched 24 Thunderchiefs (the 25th ground aborted) for a base fly-over and flight to the bombing range. Flying in the rear cockpit of one of the F-105Fs on this final mission was retired Col. Leo Thorsness, who had won the Medal of Honor for a Wild Weasel mission over North Vietnam on 19 April 1967. Eleven days later, he was shot down to become a prisoner-of-war for the next six years.

The F-105's retirement culminated in a ceremonial flight and the "Thud Out" party on 25 February 1984 hosted by the 419th in their hanger at Hill. The 419th invited nearly everyone they could track down who had been associated with the F-105. Afterwards, over the next month, the unit unceremoniously flew their remaining three Thunderchiefs to retirement at museums and static displays at military bases.

After Retirement

Most aircraft histories end with the plane's last flight. However, many surviving F-105s have continued to see action in the fifteen years since the last one flew—albeit action of a different type than during their flying years. By the time of the last flight, 612 of the original 833

Crowded on their miniature "flattop," these six F-105Gs from the Georgia Air National Guard are tugged up Chesapeake Bay to the Army's Aberdeen Proving Grounds for use as missile targets. (Bill Malerba archive photograph.)

F-105G 63-8313 heads a row of Wild Weasels, parked at Aberdeen Proving Ground, awaiting their fate as targets for missile tests. (Bill Malerba photograph, 14 October 1987.)

Five of the ten F-105Ds on a mock flightline used by the 343 Training Squadron at Lackland Air Force Base, Texas, to teach Security Police recruits how to guard parked airplanes. (Photograph by author, 4 August 1997.)

This portion of the aircraft graveyard in the hills behind the New Mexico Institute of Mining & Technology in Socorro, New Mexico, shows a variety of fuselage carcasses including a TF-102, several T-38s, and a number of CH-47 helicopters. However, when the photo was taken, all thirty-two F-105s that had been shipped to Socorro in 1985 had been scrapped. (Photograph by author, 7 October 1995.)

Thunderchiefs had been lost in accidents and combat. The remaining 221 surviving planes, the subject of this book, were used in a variety of ways.

In early 1985, thirty-two of the ninety-four planes that had been at the Boneyard at Davis-Monthan AFB, Arizona, were shipped to Socorro, New Mexico, to support a U.S. Navy program called "TERA" (Terminal Effects Research and Analysis) run by the New Mexico Institute of Mining and Technology. The planes served as targets for weapons where high-speed cameras filmed the effects of projectiles on airframes. The fuselage carcasses (eighteen of them T-Stick II F-105Ds) were stored like cordwood in canyons in the rugged hills above the college until they were sold as scrap in the early 1990s. Some parts from the planes, particularly ejection seats and instruments, found their way to collectors through advertisements in publications such as "Trade-A-Plane."

Many of the planes stored at Davis-Monthan, and others that retired directly from their last units, were used for training sheet metal technicians in repairing battle damage. Some were crated and shipped in cargo planes to bases in Europe and the far east to be used for this program. During their Aircraft Battle Damage Repair (ABDR) training, technicians bashed holes in the planes and then patched them up. Many of these F-105s were sold as scrap metal after they could be patched no more. However, several of the aircraft on static display illustrated in Part II of this book survived ABDR training and were restored at bases and museums by people who didn't have the heart to scrap the historic planes.

Over the years of storage at MASDC (since 1985 named the "Aerospace Maintenance and Regeneration Center" [AMARC]), many of the planes have been sold as scrap metal. Two of these were bought in 1996 for 40 cents a pound by an aviation enthusiast from St. Louis, Missouri, with the intent of restoring and displaying them in his aircraft collection. However, before trucking them from the Boneyard, he was required by Air Force regulations to cut their wing spars and fuselage frame to prevent their being restored to flying condition.

Not all retirement activities destroyed the planes. After their final mission at Hill AFB, Utah, in June 1983, seven of the Thunderchiefs flew to Lackland AFB, Texas, where they were placed in a row on a simulated flightline to train USAF Security Police recruits in guarding parked aircraft. This fleet has grown to ten F-105Ds and is the largest col-

The Battleship Museum in Mobile, Alabama, previously displayed F-105B 54-0102 in these markings depicting its history as a test aircraft at Edwards Air Force Base. Compare its appearance in this photo with a more current picture in Part II. (Photograph by author, 19 March 1995.)

lection of restored Thunderchiefs in existence today. Each is illustrated in this book.

Lively Static Displays

Surprisingly, nearly half of the 221 Thunderchiefs that survived to retire are still around. The reason has as much to do with coincidence as with the desire of individuals to preserve a highly-regarded fighter. In the late 1970s and early 1980s, when the F-105 began retiring, the Air Force kicked off a program called "Project Warrior" that emphasized the Air Force's aviation heritage. One element of the program involved collecting historic aircraft in static displays at Air Force bases around the world. With Thunderchiefs becoming readily available, the many bases from which these planes flew (and several bases that probably never saw an F-105) were eager to acquire one for their heritage collections.

Most (but not all) of the survivors in this book are still the property of the U.S. Air Force and are loaned to the organizations displaying them. The Air Force has two programs that provide aircraft for static display. Planes that are

The Air Force Museum provided these fiberglass replicas of the speed brake actuator covers to replace the radioactive magnesium thorium panels on F-105D 61-0107 at the National Atomic Museum, Kirtland Air Force Base, New Mexico. (Photograph by author, 16 April 1996.)

displayed at Air Force bases or established museums are administered by the USAF Museum at Wright-Patterson AFB, Ohio, while AMARC at Davis-Monthan AFB,

Sanding off old paint prior to repainting F-105D 61-0107 at the National Atomic Museum, Kirtland Air Force Base, New Mexico. (Photograph by author, 13 March 1997.)

Arizona, controls planes displayed by cities and veterans organizations. Both programs issue formal agreements on how the planes will be displayed and maintained and require their caretakers to submit an annual status report including a recent photograph.

Restoring Thunderchiefs has its risks. For several years, the Air Force Museum sent crews with Geiger counters to survey static-display aircraft and to remove radioactive panels and cockpit instruments with radium dials that could be a health hazard to people involved in fixing up these planes. Their surveys have determined that the F-105 has approximately twenty panels made of a magnesium thorium alloy that the museum says is harmless "... unless attempts are made which would alter the physical, chemical, or metallurgical state of the alloy by grinding, sanding, drilling, or cutting ...," all common practices for aircraft being refurbished. Four of the potentially radioactive panels are the formed covers for the speed brake actuators. To replace these panels the Museum developed molded fiberglass replicas that its crews installed during their visits.

With the military draw-down of recent years, many Air Force bases with static aircraft displays were closed. Some aircraft were relocated but, surprisingly, many communities have managed to retain the displays despite their

Not all repainting work is tedious. While restoring F-105G 63-8300, the Le Bourget Museum near Paris, France, had some fun with their Thunderchief and a propeller from an airplane of an earlier era. (Photograph from Musee de l'Air et de l'Espace/Le Bourget, 1993.)

bases shutting down. For example, in September 1994, the Air Force closed Lowry AFB with its large aviation museum in Denver, Colorado. Instead of closing the museum, the Air Force transferred Lowry's aircraft collection (including their F-105D) to a volunteer group that formed the Wings Over the Rockies Air & Space Museum. Other closed Air Force Bases that have retained F-105s are Chanute AFB, Illinois; March and Mather AFBs in California; and England AFB, Louisiana.

Museum Foibles

Organizations displaying a Thunderchief do not always depict it with historical accuracy. Many aircraft displayed at museums and air bases have markings and paint schemes that are not historically accurate for the specific plane. Some F-105s in this book have erroneous serial numbers and several more are painted in paint schemes or tail codes inappropriate for the plane's history. In some cases incorrect markings are a result of careless research. Others commemorate an honored pilot who flew an F-105 with those markings in Vietnam. However, in some, the aircraft markings reflect a museum's philosophy for displaying historic artifacts.

For example, the Battleship Museum in Mobile, Alabama, has an early F-105B (the fifth F-105 produced) that was used only for testing at Edwards AFB, California. Interestingly, its records show that it was flown at Edwards by test pilot Captain Deke Slaton, who would become one of the original NASA Mercury astronauts. After its test days, the plane languished for years at nearby Mobile AFB before the museum acquired it. The museum originally displayed the plane in an historically accurate natural silver metal with high-visibility orange markings from its Edwards test days.

However, in recent years the museum grouped their aircraft and other artifacts into displays illustrating historic periods, such as World War II and Vietnam. Even though their F-105B never left the country, the museum repainted it in camouflage colors and marked it (complete with two MiG-kill stencils) as an F-105 used in the Vietnam war. Displayed in this way, the history of this specific aircraft was subordinated to the museum's larger goal of illustrating a type of plane used during this war. To put it less politely, show business won out over history.

The museum's choice in displaying their F-105 was based on economics not history. This private museum is a business and, to stay open, must entice paying customers (its only source of revenue) through attractive displays – the most enticing of which is the restored battleship U.S.S. Alabama.

However, despite the lack of historical accuracy in its Thunderchief's current paint scheme, the museum shouldn't be criticized too strongly. The plane is well maintained, marked with its correct serial number, and is now protected from the Alabama sun and humidity inside the museum's aircraft pavilion.

Historically inaccurate markings on F-105s at other museums and Air Force bases cannot be defended so easily. Incorrect tail numbers are on Thunderchiefs at Dyess AFB, Texas; Hill AFB, Utah; Langley AFB, Virginia; Dobbins AFB, Georgia, and Eglin AFB, Florida.

Even museums with free admission sometimes disregard, for no apparent reason, the histories of their aircraft. An example is the F-105D at the USAF Armament Museum at Eglin. This plane is also well-maintained, stored inside, and is one of the few that still has its engine and gun (displayed in its open gun bay). Its original serial number is 58-1155, the only one remaining of the "58-" series and the oldest surviving "D."

Admittedly, the plane had an unspectacular operational career. It began service as a test support aircraft at Eglin in 1961 and stayed there for eight years. It then served at McConnell and Andrews Air Force Bases until it returned to Eglin for the museum in 1981.

Like the Battleship Museum, the Armament Museum has organized some of its exhibits around the Vietnam war. However, rather than simply displaying their F-105D with its original serial number, the Armament Museum chose to paint it with the serial number, tail code, and colorful fuselage markings of an F-105D that had a South East Asia combat record. Their phony "Foley's Folly/Ohio Express" illustrates the F-105D (59-1771) flown from Korat on 10 August 1968 by Capt. Peter K. Foley for his 200th mission over North Vietnam. The museum treated its Thunderchief as if it were decorating a plastic scale model, copying the plane's art work from a modeler's reference book.

Ironically, in June 1981, about the time the Armament Museum acquired its Thunderchief, the Air Force flew the original "Foley's Folly" to the Boneyard at Tucson, Arizona. In December 1997, 59-1771 was removed from storage for display by the AMVETS post in Circleville, Ohio, as a memorial to an F-105 pilot from Circleville killed in the Vietnam war.

The F-105D at Circleville is one of ten Thunderchiefs displayed outside of museums and military bases. These ten are at city parks and airport entrances or in front of veterans' halls. Usually kept up only through small groups of dedicated individuals, these planes are the ones most at risk for deterioration and destruction. One of them has been transferred four times from community to community and, at one of its homes, was damaged by vandals and carelessness. Each succession of sponsors ran out of interest and money. Another community, using volunteers, "fixed up" their Thunderchief in front of their veteran's post with a new paint job just in time for a Memorial Day remembrance. Three months later, in the heat of summer, the paint was already peeling.

Even established museums with access to more resources than most civic organizations, have difficulty affording the cost of repainting an F-105. It's a large airplane that requires many labor hours of surface preparation. In 1997, as an example, the National Atomic Museum in Albuquerque, New Mexico, completed repainting their camouflaged F-105D. The work was done by a professional painter retained by the museum. It took more than a year of part-time work, and cost nearly $16,000, most of which was for labor to completely strip its badly deteriorated paint to bare metal.

Despite their foibles, the organizations preserving a Thunderchief deserve our appreciation for providing retirement pastures for this distinguished war-horse.

Part II

The Survivors

Introduction

Part II of this book presents the individual histories of each of the 103 surviving F-105s. The planes are presented in aircraft serial number sequence. Each plane is illustrated with a recent photograph showing how it is displayed. The reports give each plane's original production block number, Republic's factory production number, the production sequence number, the plane's current location, and the organization responsible for the aircraft. Each detailed history is a chronology of the plane's assignments and major events from the time the aircraft was manufactured to when it retired and sometimes beyond. For reading convenience, photo captions summarize each detailed chronology. The histories also include nicknames given to a plane over the years by its succession of pilots or crew chiefs.

Historical Research

For those interested in the research for this book, here is a brief summary of the sources used.

The aircraft chronologies predominately reflect a maintenance point of view since their primary source was the series of USAF aircraft records called the GO-33 Report preserved on 16 mm microfilms. These records are computer-printed reports by aircraft type and serial number generated from data entered by the maintenance organization of each unit that possessed the aircraft. The reports are snapshots made at odd intervals listing an aircraft's location, possessing organization, and status.

The reports have their limitations. They are not always accurate and often skip individual aircraft. They are coded with numbers and letters that are difficult to interpret since the meaning of many of the codes is not obvious. The formats for the reports and their contents changed over time so that codes in earlier reports don't always match the ones in later reports. To help other researchers, the chronologies that follow include many of these codes and their meanings.

To capture the twenty-nine years of F-105 operational histories required twenty-nine microfilm reels. Each reel included only a portion of the range of F-105 serial numbers for a year or less. Copies of these aircraft history microfilms are available for a fee from the Air Force Historical Research Agency (AFHRA) at Maxwell AFB, Montgomery, Alabama.

The table on page 26 identifies the specific aircraft microfilms used in these histories.

From one year to the next, the reports added additional data, reflecting progress in computer memory and storage technology. Up through 1964, the records were printed on one or more index cards for a single aircraft. Beginning in 1965, the reports were formatted for full-page paper printouts listing multiple aircraft. Starting in 1976, they included each aircraft's accumulated flying hours, at first in whole numbers, and, later, to the tenth of an hour. In 1979, with further progress in computer technology, the USAF stopped microfilming the paper printouts and began dumping the reports directly from the computer to acetate microfiche cards.

USAF Microfilms and Microfiche Used for F-105 Histories

Period	S/N Range	Microfilm	Period	S/N Range	Microfilm
1955–Jun 1964	54-0098 – 54-0112	ACA-53	Jan–Dec 1969	57-5776 – 63-8366	AVH-12
	57-5776 – 57-5840	ACA-79	Jan–Dec 1970	57-5776 – 63-8366	AVH-14
	58-1146 – 58-1173	ACA-82	Jan–Dec 1971	57-5776 – 63-8366	AVH-16
	59-1717 – 59-1826	ACA-84	Jan–Dec 1972	57-5776 – 63-8366	AVH-18
	60-0409 – 60-0427	ACA-85	Jan–Dec 1973	57-5776 – 63-8366	AVH-20
	60-0428 – 60-5385	ACA-86	Jan–Dec 1974	57-5776 – 57-5840	AVH-21
	61-0041 – 61-0220	ACA-87		58-1146 – 63-8366	AVH-22
	62-4217 – 62-4447	ACA-88	Jan–Dec 1975	57-5776 – 63-8366	AVH-23
	63-8260 – 63-8310	ACA-89	Jan–Dec 1976	57-5776 – 63-8366	AVH-24
Jul–Sep 1964	57-5782 – 63-8350	AVH-1	Jan–Dec 1977	57-5776 – 63-8366	AVH-25
Oct–Dec 1964	57-5776 – 63-8365	AVH-2	Jan–Dec 1978	57-5776 – 63-8366	AVH-26
Jan–Dec 1965	54-0098 – 61-0220	AVH-3	Jan–Dec 1979	57-5776 – 63-8366	AVH-27
	62-4217 – 63-8366	AVH-4	Jan–Dec 1980	57-5776 – 63-8366	GO33B Jan 81*
Jan–Dec 1966	57-5776 – 63-8366	AVH-5	Jan–Dec 1981	57-5776 – 63-8366	GO33B Dec 81*
Jan–Dec 1967	57-5776 – 61-0220	AVH-7	Jan–Dec 1982	57-5776 – 63-8366	GO33B Feb 83*
	62-4217 – 63-8366	AVH-8	Jan–Dec 1983	57-5776 – 63-8366	GO33B Feb 84*
Jan–Dec 1968	57-5776 – 63-8366	AVH-10			

**Documents on microfiche available at the USAF Historical Research Agency.*

Unfortunately, these microfiche do not have a "master" from which duplicates can be made. Getting aircraft data from these reports required a visit to AFHRA in Montgomery.

In addition to aircraft status reports, information in the aircraft chronologies was pulled from recently-declassified histories of F-105 wings and squadrons. These histories are also on microfilms obtained from AFHRA. Other data came from aircraft maintenance records, particularly the Air Force Technical Order (AFTO) Form 95, Significant Historical Data. Unfortunately, only a few planes still had maintenance records available. Documentation from some combat missions was found in the gun and strike camera film descriptions in the records of the National Archives at their Internet Web site. Finally, blended into these reports are bits of information on specific F-105s extracted from published books, newspaper stories, and magazine articles along with recollections and personal records of many F-105 aircrews and crew chiefs. The chronologies identify the source of each entry.

To organize and control this collected information, a custom-designed computerized database captured most of the data gathered during the years of research. The aircraft chronologies started as reports generated from this database.

YF-105B–1RE 54-0102

Republic Production No: B-5 Production Sequence No: 5

Location: Displayed inside the U.S.S. Alabama Battleship Museum, Mobile, Alabama.

Aircraft Chronology

29 Apr 1957 First flight from Republic Aircraft, Farmingdale NY to Calverton NY. Flown by Republic test pilot Hank Beaird. First F-105 flown from the Republic factory. Aircraft flew for 60 minutes and had erratic

trailing edge flap operation and fuel venting on deceleration. (Frank Strnad record & Republic flight log).

30 Apr 1957 USAF production acceptance after second sixty-minute flight from Republic Aviation, Farmingdale NY. Pilot was Hank Beaird. Aircraft had a canopy seal leak. (ACA-53 & Republic flight log).

2 May 1957 On third flight, returned from Calverton NY to Farmingdale NY. Pilot was Hank Beaird. Flight lasted 35 minutes. Aircraft had fuel venting at noseover, slight right roll at 1.5 Mach, and cockpit pressurization malfunction.

28 May 1957 Assignment of aircraft transferred to Air Force Flight Test Center, Edwards AFB CA.

26 Jul 1957 The seventh flight, flown from Farmingdale NY to Andrews AFB MD en route to Edwards AFB CA by Republic pilot, Lindell Hendrix. Flight time was 45 minutes. First F-105 flown away from Republic factory.

28 Jul 1957 Its eighth flight, a fly-over of Andrews AFB MD by Republic Aviation test pilot Lindell Hendrix, the aircraft was the first F-105 to be demonstrated to the public. The aircraft recovered at Wright Patterson AFB OH en route to Edwards AFB CA. Flight time was 80 minutes. (Republic Aviation News, August 2, 1957).

29 Jul 1957 Its ninth flight, flown from Wright Patterson AFB OH to Tinker AFB OK by Lindell Hendrix. Flight time to Tinker was 85 minutes with 10 minutes more spent burning off fuel prior to landing.

31 Jul 1957 Tenth and eleventh flights by Lindell Hendrix from Tinker AFB OK to Albuquerque NM for refueling and final leg to AFFTC, Edwards AFB CA. Aircraft had a J-75 P5 engine and instrumentation installed at Edwards and was used for engine tests. (Republic flight log and AFFTC History, Jul–Dec 57, Vol. 2, USAF microfilm M2287).

26 Aug 1957 Flown by Republic test pilot Hank Beaird for 45 minutes on first test flight at Edwards AFB CA.

30 Aug 1957 Aircraft flew two test flights with J-75 P5 engine for functional testing and engine check. Pilot was Hank Beaird. During first flight of 60 minutes, aircraft "engine stalled with slightest throttle advance." On second flight of 40 minutes, maximum speed was 1.67 Mach but aircraft porpoised above 1.4 Mach. (AFFTC History, Jul–Dec 1957, Vol. 2, USAF microfilm M2287 & Republic flight log).

10 Sep 1957 Sixteenth flight was first one in this aircraft flown by a USAF pilot who was Capt. Deke Slayton. Test was for supersonic engine stall checks and lasted 80 minutes. Second flight of the day, also for engine checks, was by USAF Captain Robert M. White, F-105 project test pilot, who flew for 65 minutes and wrote-up unsatisfactory afterburner lights at 35,000 feet altitude. (Republic flight log).

15 Oct 1957 At Edwards AFB CA, during aircraft's 25th flight flown by Republic pilot Hank Beaird, aircraft was damaged due to hard landing and dragging tail during a simulated dead stick landing on test flight for engine air inlet duct stability. Required repair to aft fuselage. (Republic flight log & AFFTC History, Jul–Dec 1957, Vol. 2, USAF microfilm M2287).

25 Nov 1957 First functional check flight by Republic test pilot, Rusty Roth, after aircraft was repaired. Aircraft malfunctions were: "Lateral control bumps when going thru neutral, excessive fuel venting, and cabin pressure relief valve failed."

10 Dec 1957 While at Edwards AFB CA, the aircraft was flown on a test flight that required dropping both wing fuel tanks and venting water from the liquid pressure vent valve on a wing pylon. (National Archives motion picture film shot list control No. NWDNM(m)-342-USAF-27908).

31 Dec 1957 While at Edwards AFB CA, aircraft had accumulated 34:40 flying hours. (AFFTC History, Jul–Dec 1957, USAF microfilm M2287).

17 Feb 1958 On aircraft's 46th sortie, flown for 45 minutes by USAF Col. Cowalt on F-105 familiarization flight. (Republic flight log).

28 Feb 1958 On aircraft's 50th sortie, flown for 60 minutes by USAF Capt. Satterfield to investigate afterburner light problem and for pilot transition. The lower speed brake was scraped on landing.

19 Mar 1958 While at Edwards AFB CA, the aircraft was flown on a test flight that required air-to-air refueling from a KB-50 tanker. (National Archives motion picture film shot list control No. NWDNM(m)-342-USAF-27908).

10 Apr 1958 On aircraft's 73rd sortie, flown for 45 minutes by USAF Col. Ritchie for pilot familiarization. Total aircraft time was 67:40 flying hours.

The fifth F-105 was an Edwards test bird but unlike earlier prototypes was the first Thunderchief flown to Edwards from the Republic factory, arriving after a six-day journey on the last day of July 1957. The first Air Force pilot to fly the plane was Capt. Donald K. "Deke" Slaton who, two years later, became one of NASA's original astronauts. During 1959 the plane tested the heavier wheel brakes and other improved parts being installed in the first "D"-models rolling off Republic's production line. Its three-year flying career ended in 1960 when it was stored at the depot at Mobile, Alabama. Rather than being scrapped, it was displayed for years as a gate guard at the base before being given to the Battleship museum in the early 1980s. (Photograph by author, 5 August 1997.)

8 July 1958	On aircraft's 115th sortie, flown for 45 minutes by Republic test pilot Carlton Ardery for pilot familiarization. Second sortie of day was flown for 55 minutes by USAF Capt. Carman also for pilot familiarization. Total aircraft time was 101:55 flying hours.
20 Nov 1958	On aircraft's 149th sortie, flown for 45 minutes by Republic test pilot Jack Bade for Variable Air Inlet checks and high altitude afterburner lights with the P-19 engine.
26 Feb 1959	On aircraft's 179th sortie, flown for 45 minutes by Republic test pilot Rusty Roth to test performance takeoff and climb using the schedule for the Variable Air Inlet ducts established for the F-105D.
17 Mar 1959	On aircraft's 180th sortie, flown for 30 minutes by Republic test pilot Hank Beaird to evaluate F-105D wheel brakes.
Oct 1959	Assigned to NASA Flight Research Center, Edwards AFB CA, so that NASA pilots could familiarize themselves with the high-speed flight characteristics of the F-105B. (NASA Dryden Flight Research Center Web site).
Jan 1960	Departed NASA Flight Research Center.
21 Mar 1960	At MOAMA, Brookley AFB AL for storage (ACA-53).
1 Sep 1962	Reclamation approved at Brookley AFB AL. Aircraft put on display at Brookley AFB AL.
6 Mar 1977	Aircraft still displayed at Broad Street entrance on Brookley AFB AL. (Letter to Editor of Mobile Press Register newspaper by Joe McDonald).
5 Feb 1985	F-105 nose gear strut and one main landing gear needed for restoration of aircraft arrived at Mobile AL from MASDC, Tucson AZ. Parts had been removed from F-105D 60-0493 and were shipped aboard the B-52 being flown to Mobile for display at the Battleship Museum. (DD Form 1149, Requisition and Invoice/Shipping Document).

Mar 1986 Put on outside display at the Battleship Museum, Mobile AL.

6 May 1995 Aircraft moved inside to newly-opened Aircraft Pavilion at Battleship Museum, Mobile AL.

F-105B–5RE 54-0104

Republic Production No: B-7 Production Sequence No: 7

Location: Displayed on ramp at Octave Chanute Aerospace Museum, Rantoul, Illinois.

Aircraft Chronology

14 Mar 1958 Available from production at the Republic plant, Farmingdale NY (ACA-53).

24 Apr 1958 First flight from Republic plant, Farmingdale NY. Republic pilot (Frank Strnad record).

28 May 1958 First flight from Farmingdale NY by USAF pilot (9th flight).

5 Jun 1958 Flown to Republic Aircraft at Edwards AFB CA for USAF acceptance.

7 Jul 1958 USAF production acceptance at Edwards AFB CA.

7 Jul 1958 Transferred to AFFTC, Edwards AFB CA.

13 May 1959 At MOAMA, Brookley AFB AL.

22 Oct 1959 Transferred to Amarillo AFB TX. Aircraft had accumulated 81 flights and 90 flying hours. (RAC Memo 3 Mar 60 "F-105 Statistical Report for period ending 29 February 1960").

30 Jun 1962 Assigned to 3320 MSG Amarillo AFB TX as UF-105B.

24 Oct 1962 At 3320 MSG Amarillo AFB TX as GF-105B.

Mar 1968 Relocated to 3345 MSG, Chanute AFB IL.

31 Oct 1975 At CTTC, Chanute AFB IL as GF-105B. Assignment status "TX." (AVH-23 & AV-24).

After a brief period of testing at Edwards Air Force Base in 1958, the seventh F-105 spent most of its career as a maintenance trainer at two Air Force technical schools, first at Amarillo Air Force Base, Texas, and finally at Chanute Air Force Base, Illinois. Today, the museum at Chanute displays it in Thunderbird colors. (Photograph by author, 9 August 1995.)

JF-105-1RE 54-0105

Republic Production No: JF-1 Production Sequence No: 13

Location: Displayed at Lackland AFB Annex, San Antonio, Texas.

Designated a "JF-105," this is the only remaining example of the three F-105s produced with a "photo nose." When the Air Force did not buy a reconnaissance version of their fighter-bomber, Republic sealed over the camera windows and the plane spent most of its flying career at the Republic factory. It accumulated 100 flights before being flown to Amarillo Air Force Base, Texas, to be used as a maintenance trainer. It has been displayed for years at Lackland Air Force Base, Texas, where it was decked out in Vietnam colors and given the "WW" tail code of Korat's 17th Wild Weasel Squadron. (Photograph by author, 3 August 1997.)

Aircraft Chronology

18 Jul 1957	First flight from Republic, Farmingdale NY. Pilot: Lindell Hendrix.
30 Aug 1957	USAF production acceptance on 37th flight from Republic. (ACA-53 & Frank Strnad record).
30 Aug 1957	Bailed to Republic Aviation, Farmingdale NY.
20 Nov 1958	Emergency landing at Calverton Airport NY on 56th flight.
6 Nov 1959	100th flight (106 cumulative flying hours) from Republic plant, Farmingdale NY. Flown by Capt. Robb Satterfield for delivery to Amarillo AFB TX. (Frank Strnad record).
11 May 1962	Transferred to 3320 MSG, Amarillo AFB TX as UJF-105B.
24 Oct 1962	At 3320 MSG, Amarillo AFB TX as GJF-105B.
	Displayed at Lackland AFB Annex, San Antonio, Texas.
	Declared "excess" at History and Traditions Museum, Lackland AFB, San Antonio TX.

F-105B-5RE 54-0107

Republic Production No: B-9 Production Sequence No: 9

Location: Displayed by the Sabre Society at Hickory Municipal Airport, Hickory, North Carolina.

The last of the surviving pre-production F-105s, this plane's contribution was cold-weather testing at the climatic hanger at Eglin Air Force Base, Florida, and at Eielson Air Force Base, Alaska. After accumulating nearly 200 flying hours, it retired in the early 1960s to Lackland Air Force Base, Texas, where it became the mascot for a basic training squadron. In 1992, it was given to the city of Hickory, North Carolina, joining this city's airport-museum collection maintained by the Sabre Society, a group of volunteer aviation buffs. (Photograph by Kyle Kirby, 17 August 1996.)

Aircraft Chronology

9 Sep 1957	USAF production acceptance from Republic Aviation, Farmingdale NY (ACA-53).
10 Nov 1957	Delivered to Wright-Patterson AFB OH for testing in climatic hanger at Eglin AFB FL.
Feb 1958	At Eielson AFB AK for cold-weather testing.
Mar 1958	Returned from Eielson AFB.
3 Jun 1958	Redesignated JF-105B.
9 Jan 1959	To USAF Museum for Lackland AFB TX. Aircraft had accumulated 156 flights and 193 flying hours.
17 Sep 1959	In depot maintenance, Wright-Patterson AFB OH.
5 Oct 1959	Depot maintenance completed at Wright-Patterson AFB OH.
1 Sep 1962	To Reclamation.
2 Jan 1972	Displayed at Lackland AFB, Texas, in front of the barracks of the 3727 Basic Military Training Squadron. (Journal of Military Aviation, Vol. 1, No 2).
1992	The city of Hickory NC requested an F-105 from AMARC for static display. After a couple of months, AMARC offered 54-0107 from Lackland AFB TX. (Kyle Kirby, Historian, The Sabre Society).
5 Dec 1992	The mayor of Hickory NC signed the conditional deed of gift for the aircraft.

24 Feb 1993 A Sabre Society volunteer group arrived at Lackland AFB TX from Hickory NC to assist a USAF volunteer crew from Randolph AFB TX in dismantling the F-105. the USAF crew, working during a week's permissive TDY, consisted of SMSgt Steve Haskins, SSgt Rodrick B. "Rick" Bolick (from Hudson NC), SSgt Larry Wellfel, Sra Brian Hedley, and Sra Brett Holbrook.

28 Feb 1993 The disassembled F-105 was loaded onto two flatbed trucks that departed San Antonio TX for NC.

3 Mar 1993 The two trucks with the F-105 arrived at Hickory NC. The aircraft was off-loaded and placed on tires on the ground until it could be reassembled.

May 1993 The Sabre Society completed the reassembly of the F-105 and placed it on display with their other aircraft at the Hickory NC airport.

F-105B–10RE 57-5776

Republic Production No: B-13 Production Sequence No: 16

Location: Displayed on a pedestal in the ANG area at McGuire AFB, Trenton, New Jersey.

The first production "B" model was delivered in October 1958 to the 335 Tactical Fighter Squadron that was responsible for testing the F-105 for the Tactical Air Command at Eglin Air Force Base, Florida. During one of its test flights, its landing gear popped out, an occurrence that had plagued early F-105s during tests at Edwards. The pilot successfully landed the plane allowing engineers to find and fix this F-105 design problem. After six years with the 4 Tactical Fighter Wing, the plane transferred in 1964 to the New Jersey Air National Guard. In July 1980, it flew in the ceremony at George Air Force Base, California commemorating the retirement of the Thunderchief from the active-duty Air Force. Less than a year later, 23 years after it first flew, the plane finally retired and was placed on a pedestal at its last home in the Air National Guard area at McGuire Air Force Base, New Jersey. (Photograph by author, 30 August 1995.)

Aircraft Chronology

3 Apr 1958	Aircraft ready for flight test after production at Republic Aviation. (ACA-79).
18 May 1958	Flown by a Republic pilot on its first test flight from the Republic plant, Farmingdale NY. (Frank Strnad record).
15 Sep 1958	Emergency landing at Calverton Airport NY by USAF pilot (4th flight).
22 Sep 1958	Returned to Republic plant from Calverton NY by Republic pilot (5th flight).
5 Oct 1958	USAF production acceptance from Republic Aviation. Delivered to the 335 TFS, 4 TFW, Eglin AFB FL by a USAF pilot. (ACA-79).
Mar 1959	"During a transition flight by Col. O'Keefe (4 TFW Commander), … the right main landing gear extended in flight after take-off at an estimated speed of 350 knots. Damage to the aircraft was minor. Since this was the first aircraft to successfully land after inadvertent gear extension, Republic Aviation Corporation engineers and the Air Force were afforded the opportunity to find the cause and obtain a fix. All F-105 aircraft were immediately restricted to 350 KIAS until completion of an inspection of the gear. All (4 TFW) aircraft had been inspected by 31 March." (History of the 4 TFW, Jan 59—30 Jun 59, USAF Microfilm MO289).
9 Jun 1959	At WADC, Wright Patterson AFB OH. (ACA-79).
13 Jan 1960	At MOAMA, Brookley AFB AL.
14 Jan 1960	At Republic Aviation, Farmingdale NY for "Project Optimize."
29 Feb 1960	In modification at Republic plant. Aircraft had accumulated 76 flights and 91 flying hours. (RAC Memo 3 Mar 60 "F-105 Statistical Report for period ending 29 February 1960").
2 Sep 1960	First test flight from Republic plant, Farmingdale NY after completion of "Project Optimize" modifications to F-105Bs.
18 Oct 1960	Flown from Republic plant by USAF delivery pilot to 4 TFW, Seymour Johnson AFB NC. (9th flight).
10 Jan 1961	At MOAMA, Brookley AFB AL. (ACA-79).
7 Feb 1961	Returned to 4 TFW, Seymour Johnson AFB NC.
15 May 1962	In depot work (WZ) by MOAMA at Seymour Johnson AFB NC.
6 Jun 1962	At 336 TFS, 4 TFW, Seymour Johnson AFB NC. (RAC record).
22 Jun 1962	At 4 TFW, Seymour Johnson AFB NC. (ACA-79).
7 Feb 1964	In depot work (WO) at MOAMA, Brookley AFB AL.
29 Oct 1964	Transferred to the 108 TFG ANG, McGuire AFB NJ. (AVH-2).
17 May 1965	In contract depot maintenance (WM) by General Dynamics (DYNFW) at McGuire AFB NJ. (AVH-3).
26 Jun 1965	At 108 TFG ANG, McGuire AFB NJ.
22 Aug 1967	In contract depot maintenance (WK) by Fairchild Engine and Aircraft Corporation (FACCF) at Crestview FL. (AVH-7).
9 Dec 1967	At 108 TFW ANG, McGuire AFB NJ.
29 Dec 1967	In contract depot maintenance (WK) by Fairchild Engine and Aircraft Corporation (FACCF) at Crestview FL.
30 Dec 1967	Returned to 108 TFG ANG, McGuire AFB NJ. (AVH-10).
25 Feb 1971	In contract depot work (WK) by Fairchild Engine and Aircraft Corporation (FACCF) at Bob Sikes Airport, Crestview FL. (AVH-16).
24 Mar 1971	Returned (PL) to 108 TFG ANG, McGuire AFB NJ.
30 Mar 1971	At 108 TFG (CC), McGuire AFB NJ.
14 Oct 1972	In contract depot work (WK) by Fairchild Engine and Aircraft Corporation (FACCF) at Bob Sikes Airport, Crestview FL. (AVH-18).
10 Nov 1972	Returned to 108 TFG ANG, McGuire AFB NJ.

13 Apr 1973	In contract depot work (WK) by Fairchild Engine and Aircraft Corporation (FACCF) at Bob Sikes Airport, Crestview FL. (AVH-20).
19 Dec 1973	Returned to 108 TFG, 141 TFS, ANG, McGuire AFB NJ.
12 Jul 1980	Flown by the 141 TFS from the NJ ANG during the ceremony retiring the F-105 from active duty hosted by the 562 TFS at George AFB CA. (Warbirds Illustrated No 49 by Robert Dorr).
30 Apr 1981	At 108 TFG ANG, McGuire AFB NJ. Being processed to museum (ZW). 3,969.1 flying hours.

F-105B-10RE 57-5778

Republic Production No: B-15 Production Sequence No: 18

Location: Inside New England Air Museum, Windsor Locks, Connecticut.

This "B" was another early operational test airplane delivered in January 1959 to the 335 Tactical Fighter Squadron at Eglin Air Force Base, Florida. Six months later it was one of the first four F-105s to join its parent wing at Seymour Johnson Air Force Base in North Carolina. Being one of the Air Force's most advanced fighters of the time, it was displayed at the annual Air Force Association Convention in Miami Beach, Florida. For the display it was towed down McArthur Boulevard and set up inside the Miami Beach Convention Hall. After leaving the 4 Tactical Fighter Wing, the plane spent the remainder of its career with the New Jersey Air National Guard at McGuire Air Force Base. It retired to the New England Air Museum in September 1981. (Photograph from Robert L. North, Curator, New England Air Museum, November 1992.)

Aircraft Chronology

1 May 1958	Production complete at Republic Aviation, Farmingdale NY. (ACA-79).
23 Jan 1959	USAF production acceptance from Republic Aviation, Farmingdale NY.
25 Jan 1959	Delivered to 335 TFS, 4 TFW, Eglin AFB FL.
16 Jun 1959	Moved to 4 TFW, Seymour Johnson AFB NC. One of the first four F-105s to arrive at Seymour Johnson.
31 Aug 1959	Flown from Seymour Johnson AFB NC to Miami International Airport FL and towed to Miami Beach Convention Hall via McArthur Causeway for Republic Aviation display at Air Force Association Convention. (Air Force Magazine, Oct 1959).
3 Sep 1959	Displayed for three days at the Air Force Association Convention in Miami Beach FL. (Miami Herald, 4 Sep 1959).
29 Feb 1960	At 336 TFS, 4 TFW, Seymour Johnson AFB NC. Aircraft had accumulated 157 flights and 211 flying hours. (RAC Memo 3 Mar 60 "F-105 Statistical Report for Period Ending 29 February 1960").
8 Apr 1960	At Republic Aviation, Farmingdale NY for factory modification to F-105Bs ("Project Optimize").
30 Jun 1960	Aircraft belonged to the 336 TFS, 4 TFW at Seymour Johnson AFB NC. In modification for "Project Optimize." (4 TFW History, Jan—Jun 60, USAF microfilm MO290).
15 Nov 1960	First test flight by Republic pilot after factory modification (Frank Strnad record).
25 Nov 1960	First test flight by USAF pilot after factory modification (4th test flight).
22 Dec 1960	Flown by USAF pilot from Republic factory to 4 TFW, Seymour Johnson AFB NC (10th flight).
26 Dec 1960	At 4 TFW, Seymour Johnson AFB NC. (ACA-79).
7 Dec 1961	At MOAMA, Brookley AFB AL for depot work.
26 Dec 1961	Returned to 4 TFW, Seymour Johnson AFB NC.
6 Jun 1962	At 336 TFS, 4 TFW, Seymour Johnson AFB NC. (RAC record).
15 Jan 1964	At MOAMA, Brookley AFB AL for depot work.
5 Jan 1965	At 108 TFG ANG, McGuire AFB NJ. (AVH-3).
3 Feb 1967	In depot maintenance (WO) at MOAMA, Brookley AFB AL. (AVH-7).
10 Mar 1967	Returned to 108 TFG ANG, McGuire AFB NJ.
14 Apr 1971	In contract depot work (WK) by Fairchild Engine and Aircraft Corporation (FACCF) at Bob Sikes Airport, Crestview FL. (AVH-16).
6 May 1971	Returned (PL) to 108 TFG ANG, McGuire AFB NJ.
8 May 1971	At 108 TFG ANG (CC), McGuire AFB NJ.
12 Apr 1972	In contract depot maintenance (WK) by Fairchild Engine and Aircraft Corporation (FACCF) at Bob Sikes Municipal Airport, Crestview FL. (AVH-18).
22 Jul 1972	Returned (PL) to 108 TFG ANG, McGuire AFB NJ.
23 Aug 1973	In contract depot maintenance (WK) by Fairchild Engine and Aircraft Corporation (FACCF) at Bob Sikes Municipal Airport, Crestview FL. (AVH-20).
29 Apr 1981	At 108 TFG ANG, McGuire AFB NJ. Being processed to museum (ZW). 4,000.9 flying hours.
23 Sep 1981	Relocated to New England Air Museum, Windsor Locks CT.

F-105B–10RE 57-5783

Republic Production No: B-20 Production Sequence No: 23

Location: Inside Hanger 4 at Cradle of Aviation Museum, Mitchel Field, Long Island, New York.

Aircraft Chronology

14 Jun 1958	Production complete. (ACA-79).
1 Feb 1959	USAF production acceptance from Republic Aviation, Farmingdale NY.
5 Feb 1959	Delivered to 335 TFS, 4 TFW, Eglin AFB, FL.
18 Jul 1959	Moved to 4 TFW, Seymour Johnson AFB NC.
Jan 1960	Aircraft involved in an accident at Seymour Johnson AFB NC. "A crew chief started the aircraft for a run-up check. The fuel control was stuck at full military causing the engine to reach ninety-five percent of rpm before the crewman could stopcock the throttle. The aircraft jumped its chocks dragging with it the MA-2 used for starting. Before the aircraft could be stopped, it collided with two other parked F-105 aircraft. Damage to the parked aircraft, 57-5831 and 57-5781, was minor and (the aircraft were) back in commission in a short time. Aircraft 57-5783, however, was rather badly damaged and was not in commission until mid-April 1960." (4 TFW History, Jan–Jun 60, USAF microfilm MO290).

Following the path of most early "Bs," this plane began its career in operational testing at Eglin Air Force Base, Florida. In January 1960, six months after it transferred to its parent base at Seymour Johnson, it was damaged in a ground accident that sidelined it for three months. It spent its last seven years with the Air National Guard's F-105B fleet at McGuire Air Force Base, New Jersey. It's last flight was in April 1981 when one of the most experienced F-105 pilots, Lieutenant Colonel Russell Schoonover, returned it to the Republic factory on Long Island where it was turned over to the Cradle of Aviation Museum. (Photograph from Joshua Stoff, Curator, Cradle of Aviation Museum.)

29 Feb 1960	At 336 TFS, 4 TFW, Seymour Johnson AFB NC. Aircraft had accumulated 95 flights and 118 flying hours. (RAC Memo 3 Mar 60 "F-105 Statistical Report for Period Ending 29 February 1960").
13 Apr 1960	At Republic Aviation, Farmingdale NY for factory modification to F-105Bs. (ACA-79).
30 Jun 1960	Aircraft belonged to the 336 TFS, 4 TFW, at Seymour Johnson AFB NC. In modification for "Project Optimize." (4 TFW History, Jan–Jun 60, USAF microfilm MO290).
31 Jan 1961	First test flight by Republic Aviation pilot after factory modification to F-105Bs. (Frank Strnad record).
26 Feb 1961	Redelivered to 4 TFW, Seymour Johnson AFB NC after factory modification.
7 Apr 1961	Returned to the Republic factory, Farmingdale NY for radio test program.
12 Apr 1961	Radio test flight.
14 Apr 1961	Redelivered to 4 TFW, Seymour Johnson AFB NC after radio test.
6 Jun 1962	At 336 TFS, 4 TFW, Seymour Johnson AFB NC. (RAC record).
27 Dec 1963	At Brookley AFB AL for depot work. (ACA-79).
31 Oct 1964	Transferred to 108 TFG, McGuire AFB, NJ ANG. (AVH-2).
1 Mar 1965	In contract depot maintenance (WM) by General Dynamics (DYNFW) at McGuire AFB NJ. (AVH-3).
9 Apr 1965	At 108 TFG ANG, McGuire AFB NJ.
12 Jul 1965	In contract depot maintenance (WM) by General Dynamics (DYNFW) at McGuire AFB NJ.
29 Jul 1965	At 108 TFG, McGuire AFB NJ ANG.
12 Jan 1966	At Crestview FL for contract depot work (FK). (AVH-5).
4 Feb 1966	Returned to 108 TFG ANG, McGuire AFB NJ.
31 May 1967	At 108 TFG ANG, McGuire AFB NJ. (AVH-7).
12 Sep 1967	In contract depot maintenance (WK) by Fairchild Engine and Aircraft Corporation (FACCF) at Crestview FL.
16 Dec 1967	At 108 TFG ANG, McGuire AFB NJ.
29 Dec 1967	In contract depot maintenance (WK) by Fairchild Engine and Aircraft Corporation (FACCF) at Crestview FL.
30 Dec 1967	Returned to 108 TFG ANG, McGuire AFB NJ. (AVH-10).
2 Jun 1971	In contract depot maintenance (WK) by Fairchild Engine and Aircraft Corporation (FACCF) at Bob Sikes Municipal Airport, Crestview FL. (AVH-16).
28 Jun 1971	Returned (PL) to 108 TFG ANG, McGuire AFB NJ.
1 Jul 1971	At 108 TFG ANG (CC), McGuire AFB NJ.
28 Dec 1972	In contract depot maintenance (WK) by Fairchild Engine and Aircraft Corporation (FACCF) at Bob Sikes Municipal Airport, Crestview FL. (AVH-18).
18 May 1973	At 108 TFG ANG (CC), McGuire AFB NJ. (AVH-20).
2 Oct 1973	In contract depot maintenance (WK) by Fairchild Engine and Aircraft Corporation (FACCF) at Bob Sikes Municipal Airport, Crestview FL.
3 Apr 1979	At 108 TFW, McGuire AFB NJ. 3,675.8 flying hours. (AVH-27).
29 May 1979	At Byrd Field VA for depot maintenance by Dynalectron Corporation (DYNZZ). 3,675.8 flying hours.
15 Jun 1979	Returned to 108 TFW, McGuire AFB NJ. 3,724.1 flying hours.
29 Apr 1981	At 108 TFG ANG, McGuire AFB NJ. Being processed for museum (ZW). 3,988.8 flying hours. (GO33B Dec 81 & GO33B 1 Feb 83).
29 Apr 1981	Flown by USAF pilot, Lt. Col. Russell R. Schoonover, to Fairchild-Republic factory on Long Island on its way to Cradle of Aviation Museum.

F-105B-10RE 57-5784

Republic Production No: B-21 Production Sequence No: 24

Location: Displayed outside at Planetario Severo Diaz Galindo, Guadalajara, Mexico.

Aircraft Chronology

23 Jun 1958	Production complete. (ACA-79).
23 Mar 1959	USAF production acceptance at Republic Aviation, Farmingdale NY.
23 Mar 1959	Delivered to 335 TFS, 4 TFW, Eglin AFB FL as part of the F-105B Category II test program.
30 Jul 1959	Moved to 4 TFW, Tactical Air Command (TAC), Seymour Johnson AFB NC.
29 Feb 1960	At 336 TFS, 4 TFW, Seymour Johnson AFB NC. Aircraft had accumulated 116 flights and 154 flying hours. (RAC Memo 3 Mar 60 "F-105 Statistical Report for Period Ending 29 February 1960").
30 Jun 1960	Aircraft belonged to the 336 TFS, 4 TFW at Seymour Johnson AFB NC. In modification for "Project Optimize." (4 TFW History, Jan–Jun 60, USAF microfilm MO290).

This aircraft was the 21st "B" model Republic Aviation built. It was delivered in March 1959 to Eglin Air Force Base, Florida where it, too, was involved in early testing. In July 1959 it moved to its home base in North Carolina with the 4 Tactical Fighter Wing. In April 1965, it transferred to the New Jersey Air National Guard along with most of the other F-105Bs when the 4 Tactical Fighter Wing received new "D" models. It spent the rest of its career in New Jersey and accumulated over 3,700 flying hours before retiring in 1981. It is the oldest of seven F-105s displayed outside the United States. Its new paint job in November 1996 was funded by the Crayola company, a fact that no one who visits the plane can miss. (Photograph by Marianne McNelly, 29 October 1997.)

4 Aug 1960	At Republic Aviation, Farmingdale NY for modification to F-105Bs.
8 Jan 1961	First test flight by Republic Aviation pilot after factory modification to F-105Bs. (Frank Strnad record).
19 Feb 1961	Re-delivered to 4 TFW, Seymour Johnson AFB NC by USAF pilot after factory modification.
6 Jun 1962	At 336 TFS, 4 TFW (TAC), Seymour Johnson AFB NC. (RAC record).
5 May 1964	At Brookley AFB AL for depot work (WO).
13 Apr 1965	At 108 TFG NJ ANG, McGuire AFB NJ. (AVH-3).
7 Jun 1965	In contract depot maintenance (WM) by General Dynamics (DYNFW) at McGuire AFB NJ.
29 Jun 1965	At 108 TFG NJ ANG, McGuire AFB NJ.
19 Jan 1966	In contract depot maintenance (WK) by Fairchild Engine and Aircraft Corporation (FACCF) at Crestview FL. (AVH-5).
18 Feb 1966	Returned to 108 TFG NJ ANG, McGuire AFB NJ.
15 May 1969	At 108 TFG ANG, McGuire AFB NJ. (AVH-12).
24 Apr 1970	In contract depot maintenance (WK) by Fairchild Engine and Aircraft Corporation (FACCF) at Crestview FL. (AVH-14).
12 Aug 1970	At 177 TFW ANG, Atlantic City Airport NJ.
18 Aug 1970	At 108 TFG ANG, McGuire AFB NJ.
16 Feb 1971	In contract depot maintenance (WK) by Fairchild Engine and Aircraft Corporation (FACCF) at Bob Sikes Municipal Airport, Crestview FL. (AVH-16).
16 Mar 1971	Returned (PL) to 108 TFG ANG, McGuire AFB NJ.
18 Mar 1971	At 108 TFG ANG (CC), McGuire AFB NJ.
22 May 1971	In contract depot maintenance (WK) by Fairchild Engine and Aircraft Corporation (FACCF) at Bob Sikes Municipal Airport, Crestview FL.
25 May 1971	At 108 TFG ANG (CC), McGuire AFB NJ.
4 Jun 1971	In contract depot maintenance (WK) by Fairchild Engine and Aircraft Corporation (FACCF) at Bob Sikes Municipal Airport, Crestview FL.
5 Jun 1971	At 108 TFG ANG (CC), McGuire AFB NJ.
13 Jun 1972	In contract depot maintenance (WK) by Fairchild Engine and Aircraft Corporation (FACCF) at Bob Sikes Municipal Airport, Crestview FL. (AVH-18).
8 Jul 1972	Returned (PL) to 108 TFG ANG, McGuire AFB NJ.
11 Jul 1972	At 108 TFG ANG (CC), McGuire AFB NJ.
7 Jun 1973	At 108 TFG ANG (WQ), McGuire AFB NJ. (AVH-20).
2 Jul 1973	In contract depot maintenance (WK) by Fairchild Engine and Aircraft Corporation (FACCF) at Bob Sikes Municipal Airport, Crestview FL.
28 Apr 1975	In contract depot maintenance (WK) by Fairchild Engine and Aircraft Corporation (FACCF) at Bob Sikes Municipal Airport, Crestview FL. (AVH-23).
28 Oct 1975	At 108 TFW ANG (CC), McGuire AFB NJ.
22 Jan 1979	At Sacramento ALC, McClellan AFB CA for ground test (EJ). 3,334.8 flying hours. (AVH-27).
27 Jan 1979	Returned to 108 TFW NJ ANG, McGuire AFB NJ. 3,334.8 flying hours.
23 Apr 1981	Sent to MASDC ("Storage, low probability of withdrawal"—XX), Davis-Monthan AFB AZ. 3,721.7 flying hours. (GO33B Dec 81).
23 Apr 1981	At MASDC ("ZW" Inventory Account—School or Museum), Davis-Monthan AFB AZ. 3,721.7 flying hours. (GO33B 1 Feb 83).
3 Jun 1981	Transferred from MASDC to Pima Air Museum, Tucson AZ. (DD Form 1149).
May 1983	Shipped by rail from Pima Air Museum to Planetario Severo Diaz Galindo, Guadalajara, Mexico. (E. Flores Tritschler, Director, e-mail, 30 Aug 1996).
Jun 1983	Placed on display at Planetario Severo Diaz Galindo.

Oct 1984 Officially transferred by direction of USAF Museum to Guadalajara Museum of Science and Technology, Guadalajara, Mexico. USAF Museum deeded aircraft as a gift to Guadalajara. (Pima Air Museum letter signed by Mary Gentry, Collections Manager, 21 Mar 89).

Nov 1996 Aircraft refurbished and repainted at Planetario Severo Diaz Galindo, Guadalajara, Mexico. (E. Flores Tritschler, Director).

F-105B–15RE 57-5789

Republic Production No: B-26 Production Sequence No: 29

Location: At USAF Detachment 1, 343 Training Squadron, Camp Bullis, San Antonio, Texas.

Aircraft Chronology

29 Jan 1959 Aircraft production completed at Republic Aviation, Farmingdale, New York. (ACA-79).

27 May 1959 USAF production acceptance at Republic Aviation, Farmingdale, New York.

28 May 1959 Delivered to the 335 TFS, 4 TFW at Eglin AFB FL.

16 Sep 1959 While assigned to Category II testing by 335 TFS at Eglin AFB FL, aircraft was slightly damaged "...when the cartridge starter failed during a pneumatic starting cycle. The turbine wheel split causing the drive shaft to shear. One half of the wheel was thrown through the starter scroll and fell to the ramp. Damage to the aircraft was negligible." ("History of The 4 TFW, 1 Jul 59–30 Dec 59," USAF microfilm MO289).

29 Feb 1960 At 335 TFS, 4 TFW, Eglin AFB FL. Aircraft had accumulated 57 flights and 99 flying hours (RAC Memo 3 Mar 60 "F-105 Statistical Report for Period Ending 29 February 1960").

This F-105B was produced in January 1959 and delivered to Eglin Air Force Base, Florida, where it was also used in the F-105B Category II testing program conducted by the 335 Tactical Fighter Squadron. After finishing its testing in April 1960, it returned home to the 4 Tactical Fighter Wing at Seymour Johnson Air Force Base, North Carolina. In 1964, it transferred, along with most of the 4 Tactical Fighter Wing's F-105Bs, to the 141 Tactical Fighter Squadron of the New Jersey Air National Guard at McGuire Air Force Base. It served with this Air Guard unit until early 1981 when it was allocated to the Aircraft Battle Damage Repair program at Kelly Air Force Base, Texas. Unrestored, it is one of three F-105s being used by Lackland Air Force Base's 343 Training Squadron in their combat arms training courses. (Photograph by author, 4 August 1997.)

10 Apr 1960	At 4 TFW, Seymour Johnson AFB NC but assigned to Brookley AFB AL. (ACA-79).
30 Jun 1960	Aircraft belonged to the 333 TFS, 4 TFW, in modification for "Project Optimize" at Seymour Johnson AFB NC. (4 TFW History, Jan–Jun 60, USAF microfilm MO290).
10 Mar 1961	At 4 TFW, Seymour Johnson AFB NC. (ACA-79).
23 Apr 1961	At MOAMA, Brookley AFB AL.
18 Aug 1961	Returned to 4 TFW, Seymour Johnson AFB NC.
26 Jan 1962	At MOAMA, Brookley AFB AL.
31 Jul 1962	Returned to 4 TFW, Seymour Johnson AFB NC.
3 Jun 1964	At MOAMA, Brookley AFB AL.
12 Aug 1965	At 108 TFG ANG, McGuire AFB NJ. (AVH-3).
17 Aug 1965	In contract depot maintenance (WM) by General Dynamics (DYNFW) at McGuire AFB NJ.
21 Oct 1965	At 108 TFG ANG, McGuire AFB NJ.
18 Feb 1971	In contract depot maintenance (WK) by Fairchild Engine and Aircraft Corporation (FACCF) at Bob Sikes Airport, Crestview FL (AVH-16).
18 Mar 1971	Returned (PL) to 108 TFG ANG, McGuire AFB NJ.
10 Aug 1971	In contract depot maintenance (WK) by Fairchild Engine and Aircraft Corporation (FACCF) at Bob Sikes Airport, Crestview FL.
9 Nov 1971	Returned (PL) to 108 TFG ANG, McGuire AFB NJ.
21 Jun 1972	In contract depot maintenance (WK) by Fairchild Engine and Aircraft Corporation (FACCF) at Bob Sikes Airport, Crestview FL. (AVH-18).
15 Jul 1972	At Fairchild Engine and Aircraft Corporation (FACCF), Bob Sikes Airport, Crestview FL being prepared for transfer (PL).
19 Jul 1972	Returned (PL) to 108 TFG ANG, McGuire AFB NJ.
23 Jul 1972	Combat capable (CC) at 108 TFG ANG, McGuire AFB NJ.
16 Aug 1973	In contract depot maintenance (WK) by Fairchild Engine and Aircraft Corporation (FACCF) at Bob Sikes Airport, Crestview FL (AVH-20).
30 Apr 1981	At 108 TFG ANG, McGuire AFB NJ. Combat capable (CC) but in Inventory Account: "ZD." 3,599.7 flying hours. (GO33B Dec 81 & 1 Feb 83).
9 Nov 1983	Possessed by 2954 CLSS, Kelly AFB TX for ABDR training under deployment conditions at the Army's Camp Bullis TX. (HQ 2852 ABG/DADF Letter 9 Nov 83).
22 May 1985	Possessed by 2954 CLSS, Kelly AFB TX for ABDR training. (HQ 2852 ABG/DADF Letter 22 May 85).
	Transferred to the 343 Training Squadron from Lackland AFB TX but remained at Camp Bullis for Security Police Combat Arms Training.

F-105B-15RE 57-5792

Republic Production No: B-29 Production Sequence No: 32

Location: At the Municipal Airport, Zanesville, Ohio.

Aircraft Chronology

12 Feb 1959	Production complete. (ACA-79).
30 Mar 1959	USAF production acceptance from Republic Aviation, Farmingdale NY.

14 May 1959	Delivered to the 335 TFS, 4 TFW, Eglin AFB FL. Aircraft was one of six F-105Bs assigned to the F-105B Category II Nuclear Weapons Test Team. (Air Proving Ground Center History, Jan–Jun 1961, USAF microfilm K2762).
29 Feb 1960	At 335 TFS, 4 TFW, Eglin AFB FL. Aircraft had accumulated 103 flights and 104 flying hours (RAC Memo 3 Mar 60 "F-105 Statistical Report for Period Ending 29 February 1960").
2 Apr 1960	At MOAMA, Brookley AFB AL for depot work. (ACA-79).
1 May 1960	Returned to 4 TFW, Eglin AFB FL.
2 Nov 1960	Moved to 4 TFW, Seymour Johnson AFB NC after termination of F-105B Air Superiority Cat II follow-on testing by 335 TFS.
4 May 1961	At MOAMA, Brookley AFB AL for depot work.
11 May 1961	Returned to 4 TFW, Seymour Johnson AFB NC.
11 Sep 1961	At MOAMA, Brookley AFB AL for depot work.
6 Jun 1962	At 336 TFS, 4 TFW, Seymour Johnson AFB NC. (RAC record).
27 Dec 1963	At MOAMA, Brookley AFB AL for depot work.
31 Oct 1964	Transferred to 108 TFG ANG, McGuire AFB NJ. (AVH-2).
22 Jan 1965	At 108 TFG, McGuire AFB NJ ANG. (AVH-3).
11 May 1965	In AFLC contract depot maintenance (WM) by General Dynamics (DYNFW) at McGuire AFB NJ.
2 Jun 1965	At 108 TFG ANG, McGuire AFB NJ.
7 Apr 1970	In contract depot maintenance (WK) by Fairchild Engine and Aircraft Corporation (FACCF) at Crestview FL. (AVH-14).
28 Jul 1970	Returned to 108 TFG ANG, McGuire AFB NJ.
6 Aug 1970	At 108 TFG ANG, McGuire AFB NJ.
28 Jun 1971	In contract depot maintenance (WK) by Fairchild Engine and Aircraft Corporation (FACCF) at Crestview FL. (AVH-16).
27 Jul 1971	Returned (PL) to 108 TFG ANG, McGuire AFB NJ.
29 Jul 1971	At 108 TFG ANG (CC), McGuire AFB NJ.
2 Dec 1972	In contract depot maintenance (WK) by Fairchild Engine and Aircraft Corporation (FACCF) at Bob Sikes Municipal Airport, Crestview FL. (AVH-18).
25 Dec 1972	At 108 TFG ANG (CC), McGuire AFB NJ.
12 Sep 1979	In contract depot maintenance by Dynalectron Corporation (DYNZZ) at Byrd Field VA. 3,995.8 flying hours. (AVH-27).
4 Oct 1979	Returned to 108 TFW, McGuire AFB NJ. 4,003.8 flying hours.
7 Jan 1981	Placed in storage at MASDC, Davis-Monthan AFB AZ. (MASDC Acft. Status Directory 30 Jun 1984).
5 Jul 1982	In storage at MASDC. (Inventory account "ZJ"). 4,254.3 flying hours. (GO33B 1 Feb 83).
22 Jul 1985	Departed MASDC for Kings Mountain, NC. (AMARC Inventory List 24 Mar 87).
19 Sep 1989	Anderson County Council, Anderson SC, unanimously voted to approve requesting the aircraft from the Air Force. (Wayne Gaskins, Manager Anderson County Airport, interview 7 Aug 1997).
4 Dec 1989	AMARC transfer documents for AF Static Display Program signed by Anderson County SC. (AMARC/LG-3 Static Report 5/3/96).
26 Aug 1991	Transferred from Kings Mountain NC to Blue Ridge Air Group, Anderson SC. (John Coon).
	Placed on display at Anderson County airport by Blue Ridge Air Group headed by Mr. Bill Eck.
	Blue Ridge Air Group disbanded and aircraft turned back over to Anderson County SC.
1993	Anderson County commissioners disapproved $500 request from Anderson County Airport for a security fence around the aircraft.
1994	Hole punched in canopy by vandals. Horizontal stabilator damaged by mowing tractor. (Wayne Gaskins, Manager Anderson County Airport, interview 7 Aug 1997).

This F-105B 57-5792 began life in 1959 with delivery to the 335 Tactical Fighter Squadron at Eglin Air Force Base, Florida. It was one of six "Bs" assigned to the Category II test team that tested the F-105's nuclear weapon delivery capability. It transferred to the New Jersey Air National Guard in October 1964 where it remained until January 1981 when it was stored at Davis-Monthan Air Force Base, Arizona. It was initially displayed at Kings Mountain, North Carolina, but was moved to Anderson, South Carolina, in 1991 (its location in the photo). The plane was damaged at Anderson and the local county government was not willing to support repairs. In February 1999, the Air Force reassigned the plane to the city of Zanesville, Ohio, that wanted a Vietnam Veteran's memorial. (Photograph by author, 7 August 1997.)

1995 Anderson County commissioners struck $3,000 from budget for erecting a fence to secure the aircraft at the Anderson County Airport.

1997 Anderson County airport manager requested that the Air Force relocate the aircraft.

8 Feb 1999 AMARC transferred the aircraft to the city of Zanesville, Ohio, for display as a memorial to Vietnam Veterans at the city's municipal airport. (MSgt. John White, restoration volunteer, e-mail, 24 July 1999).

F-105B–15RE 57-5793

Republic Production No: B-30 Production Sequence No: 33

Location: At Yankee Air Museum, Willow Run Airport, Belleville, Michigan.

Aircraft Chronology

18 Feb 1959 Production complete. (ACA-79).

27 May 1959 USAF production acceptance from Republic Aviation, Farmingdale NY.

28 May 1959 Delivered to 335 TFS, 4 TFW, Eglin AFB, FL. One of two F-105Bs used in F-105B Category II testing of air-to-air gunnery. During testing, the M61 gun had to be replaced three times due to numerous malfunctions. Unreliable gun installation required frequent gun boresighting during the last five months of the test program. (Air Proving Ground Center History, Jan–Jun 61, USAF microfilm K2762).

The 30th F-105B built was also delivered in May 1959 to the 335 Tactical Fighter Squadron at Eglin Air Force Base, Florida, and was assigned to Category II testing of air-to-air gunnery. A month after delivery, while being flown by the commander of the 4 Tactical Fighter Wing, a broken oil line nearly ended its budding career. However, the engine ran without oil long enough for the pilot to successfully land. Four years later, the plane was one of nine "Bs" selected as the new mount for the Thunderbirds demonstration team. It flew the "Slot" position and received a stainless tail so it could withstand the heat from flying in the leader's jet exhaust. After only six performances, the Thunderbirds gave up their F-105s when one of their planes broke up in the air killing its pilot. For nearly six months the plane was assigned to train pilots at Nellis Air Force Base, Nevada, but, in March 1966, it went to the New Jersey Air National Guard where it spent the remainder of its career. In 1982, it flew to the Air Force Museum, remaining parked in front of the museum's restoration hangers (its location in the photo) until June 1996 when it was given to the Yankee Air Museum in Michigan. (Photograph by author, 10 August 1995.)

25 Jun 1959 At Eglin AFB FL with 4 TFW. "During his second transition mission, Col. Graham (4 TFW Commander) experienced total loss of oil pressure.... Conditions of flight were left bank at 23,000 feet and a speed of Mach 1.2. The aircraft was turned toward the home base approximately 70 miles away. While descending from the contrail level, the chase pilot noted a discharge of colored fluid from the aircraft. Col. Graham arrived over Eglin and set up a forced landing pattern. Smoke was noted in the cockpit during the pattern, approach and landing. The aircraft was stopped on the runway and engine shut down. A grinding noise was heard as the engine decelerated through 32 per cent. The engine ran for 12 minutes from time of zero oil pressure to landing and 2 minutes after landing. Preliminary investigation revealed a broken oil line in the lower engine compartment, aft." (History of the 4 TFW, 1 Jan 59–30 Jun 59, Microfilm MO289).

29 Feb 1960 At 335 TFS, 4 TFW, Eglin AFB FL. Aircraft had accumulated 64 flights and 84 flying hours. (RAC Memo 3 Mar 60 "F-105 Statistical Report for period ending 29 February 1960").

26 Mar 1960 Moved to 4 TFW, Seymour Johnson AFB NC. (ACA-79).

11 Apr 1960 At 335 TFS, 4 TFW, Eglin AFB, FL for F-105B Category II follow-on testing.

2 Jun 1960 At MOAMA, Brookley AFB AL for depot work.

2 Nov 1960 Moved to 4 TFW, Seymour Johnson AFB NC after termination of F-105B Air Superiority Category II follow-on testing by the 335 TFS.

6 Jun 1962 At 334 TFS, 4 TFW, Seymour Johnson AFB NC. (RAC record).

Apr 1963 One of nine F-105Bs assigned to USAF Thunderbird Demonstration Team. Slot aircraft with stainless steel tail.

May 1964 The Thunderbirds gave up their F-105Bs.

1 Jun 1964 At MOAMA, Brookley AFB AL for depot work (WO). (Possibly the Thunderbird demodification). (AVH-1).

3 Jun 1965	Transferred to 4520 CCTW, Nellis AFB NV for "student and combat crew training" (TF). (AVH-3).
1 Aug 1965	At 4520 CCTW, Nellis AFB NV for "other activities" (ZA).
1 Nov 1965	At 4520 CCTW, Nellis AFB NV for "student and combat crew training" (TF).
15 Dec 1965	At MOAMA Brookley AFB AL for depot work (WO).
1 Mar 1966	At 108 TFG ANG, McGuire AFB NJ. (AVH-5).
3 Dec 1966	In contract depot maintenance (WK) by Fairchild Engine and Aircraft Corporation (FACCF) at Crestview FL (WK).
19 Apr 1967	At 108 TFG ANG, McGuire AFB NJ. (AVH-7).
16 Mar 1968	In contract depot maintenance (WK) by Fairchild Engine and Aircraft Corporation (FACCF) at Crestview FL. (AVH-10).
8 Jul 1968	Returned to 108 TFG ANG, McGuire AFB NJ.
6 May 1971	In contract depot maintenance (WK) by Fairchild Engine and Aircraft Corporation (FACCF) at Crestview FL. (AVH-16).
1 Jun 1971	Returned (PL) to 108 TFG ANG, McGuire AFB NJ.
2 Jun 1971	At 108 TFG ANG (CC), McGuire AFB NJ.
24 Jun 1972	In contract depot maintenance (WK) by Fairchild Engine and Aircraft Corporation (FACCF) at Bob Sikes Municipal Airport, Crestview FL. (AVH-18).
27 Sep 1972	Returned to 108 TFG ANG (CC), McGuire AFB NJ.
5 Jun 1973	At 108 TFG ANG (WQ), McGuire AFB NJ. (AVH-20).
21 Aug 1973	In contract depot maintenance (WK) by Fairchild Engine and Aircraft Corporation (FACCF) at Bob Sikes Municipal Airport, Crestview FL.
8 Jan 1981	At 108 TFG ANG, McGuire AFB NJ. Being processed to museum (ZW). 3,573.0 flying hours. (GO33B Dec 81).
4 Jul 1982	Delivered to Air Force Museum. Crew Chief: SMSgt. Robert F. Hardy.
10 Aug 1995	Parked outside restoration hanger at the Air Force Museum, Wright-Patterson AFB, Dayton OH. (Personal visit).
12 Jun 1996	Moved on two trucks from USAF Museum, Ohio, to Yankee Air Museum at Willow Run Airport, Belleville MI. (Bill Lary, Display Manager, phone interview 30 Nov 96).
15 Jul 1996	Reassembled after move and placed on display at Yankee Air Museum.

F-105B-20RE 57-5803

Republic Production No: B-40 Production Sequence No: 43

Location: Displayed at March Field Museum, March Air Reserve Base, Riverside, California.

Aircraft Chronology

19 Aug 1959	First production test flight from Republic Aviation, Farmingdale NY. (Frank Strnad record).
29 Aug 1959	USAF production acceptance from Republic Aviation, Farmingdale NY. (ACA-79).
11 Sep 1959	Emergency landing at Calverton Airport (3rd test flight).
12 Sep 1959	Returned from Calverton NY to Republic factory, Farmingdale NY.
15 Sep 1959	Delivered to Edwards AFB CA by Republic test pilot, Mr. Carlton B. Ardery, Jr.

For the first two years of its career, this "B" bounced between the Republic plant on Long Island, Edwards Air Force Base in California, Eglin Air Force Base in Florida, and Wright Patterson Air Force Base, Ohio, while it was used for testing F-105 air-to-air refueling. After spending three years with the 4 Tactical Fighter Wing in North Carolina, it began a five year period where it was flown by F-105 instructor pilots, first at Nellis Air Force Base, Nevada, and then at McConnell Air Force Base, Kansas. In June 1970 it was one of the "Bs" used to equip the second New Jersey Air National Guard unit at Atlantic City. Two years later it went to the Air Force Reserve unit at Hill Air Force Base, Utah. Its last flight in 1980 was from Hill to the museum at March Air Force Base, California. (Photograph by author, 31 October 1996.)

29 Feb 1960	At Edwards AFB with Republic Aviation. Aircraft had accumulated 67 flights and 57 flying hours. (RAC Memo 3 Mar 60 "F-105 Statistical Report for Period Ending 29 February 1960").
1 Apr 1960	At Republic Aviation, Farmingdale NY. (ACA-79).
10 Jun 1960	At APGC, Eglin AFB FL.
22 Jun 1960	At Wright Patterson AFB OH.
23 Jun 1960	Aircraft redesignated "JF-105B" at Wright Patterson AFB OH.
3 Mar 1961	At MOAMA, Brookley AFB AL.
24 Jan 1962	Aircraft redesignated "F-105B" at MOAMA, Brookley AFB AL.
6 Jun 1962	Assigned to APGC but at Brookley AFB AL for modification. (RAC record).
31 Jul 1962	Transferred to 4 TFW, Seymour Johnson AFB NC.
5 Oct 1962	At MOAMA, Brookley AFB AL for depot work.
9 Jun 1964	At MOAMA, Brookley AFB AL for depot work (WO). (AVH-1).
23 Jun 1965	At 4520 CCTW, Nellis AFB NV for F-105 instructor pilot support. (AVH-3).
4 Jan 1966	At MOAMA, Brookley AFB AL for depot work (WO). (AVH-5).
29 Mar 1966	Returned to 4520 CCTW, Nellis AFB NV for combat crew training (TF).
31 Mar 1967	In depot work (WM) by SMAMA field team at Nellis AFB NV. (AVH-7).
4 Apr 1967	At 4520 CCTW, Nellis AFB NV for combat crew training (TF).
13 Sep 1967	In depot work (WM) by SMAMA field team at Nellis AFB NV.
16 Sep 1967	At 4520 CCTW, Nellis AFB NV for combat crew training (TF).
4 Oct 1967	Being prepared for transfer (PL) from 4520 CCTW, Nellis AFB NV.

11 Oct 1967	Transferred to 23 TFW, McConnell AFB KS.
13 Nov 1967	At 23 TFW, McConnell AFB KS for instructor pilots conducting replacement aircrew training (TF).
27 Nov 1967	In contract depot work (WK) by Fairchild Engine and Aircraft Corporation at Bob Sikes Airport (FACCF), Crestview FL.
1 Oct 1967	Assigned to the 23 TFW for F-105 RTU instructor pilot support. (23 TFW History, Jul–Dec 67, USAF microfilm MO554).
1 Mar 1968	At 23 TFW, McConnell AFB KS. (AVH-10).
7 Mar 1968	Assigned to combat crew training (TF) at 23 TFW, McConnell AFB KS.
23 May 1968	At 23 TFW, McConnell AFB KS being prepared for transfer (PL).
28 May 1968	In depot work (WO) at SMAMA, McClellan AFB CA.
30 Aug 1968	Returned (PL) to 23 TFW, McConnell AFB KS for combat crew training (TF).
23 Apr 1969	In depot maintenance (WM) by SMAMA at McConnell AFB KS. (AVH-12)
24 Apr 1969	Returned to 23 TFW, McConnell AFB KS for student and combat crew training (TF).
Sep 1969	While at the 23 TFW, McConnell AFB KS, one of four aircraft modified in July 1969 with positive limb restraint system for TAC Test 68-228 that was completed during Sep 1969. (23 TFW History, Jul–Sep 69, USAF microfilm MO555).
28 May 1970	At 23 TFW, McConnell AFB KS. (AVH-14).
5 Jun 1970	Transferred to 177 TFG ANG, Atlantic City Airport NJ.
12 Dec 1970	At 177 TFG ANG, Atlantic City Airport NJ.
20 Jan 1971	In contract depot maintenance (WK) by Fairchild Engine and Aircraft Corporation (FACCF) at Crestview FL. (AVH-16).
19 Feb 1971	Returned (PL) to 177 TFG ANG, Atlantic City Airport NJ.
20 Feb 1971	At 177 TFG ANG (CC), Atlantic City Airport NJ.
2 Mar 1972	In depot maintenance (WK) by Fairchild Engine and Aircraft Corporation at Bob Sikes Municipal Airport, Crestview FL. (AVH-18).
6 Jun 1972	Returned to 177 TFG ANG, Atlantic City Airport NJ.
31 Jul 1972	In contract depot maintenance (WK) by Fairchild Engine and Aircraft Corporation (FACCF) at Bob Sikes Municipal Airport, Crestview FL.
25 Aug 1972	Returned (PL) to 177 TFG ANG, Atlantic City Airport NJ.
29 Nov 1972	Transferred to 945 MALGp AFRES, Hill AFB UT.
1 Jan 1973	At 508 TFG AFRES, Hill AFB UT. (AVH-20).
15 Aug 1973	In contract depot maintenance (WK) by Fairchild Engine and Aircraft Corporation (FACCF) at Bob Sikes Municipal Airport, Crestview FL.
15 Nov 1975	In depot work (WO) by 508 CLMSQ at Hill AFB UT. (AVH-23).
21 Sep 1976	In contract depot maintenance (WK) by Fairchild Engine and Aircraft Corporation (FACCF) at Bob Sikes Municipal Airport, Crestview FL. (AVH-24).
5 Apr 1977	At 508 TFG, AFRES, Hill AFB UT. 2,539.0 flying hours. (AVH-25 & AVH-26).
19 Apr 1978	At 508 TFG, AFRES, Hill AFB UT. 2,751.0 flying hours.
12 Jul 1978	In depot maintenance by DYNFW at Hill AFB UT. 2,781.0 flying hours.
13 Jan 1979	Returned to 466 TFS, Hill AFB UT. 2,781.0 flying hours. (AVH-27).
28 Nov 1979	In depot maintenance at Ogden ALC, Hill AFB UT. 3,105.0 flying hours.
4 Jan 1980	At 466 TFS, Hill AFB UT. 3,135.5 flying hours. (GO33B 24 Jun 80).
17 Oct 1980	AFLC/LOACA authorized one of nine AFRES/NGB F-105Bs for transfer to Air Force Museum for loan as static display by 22 BMW at March AFB CA. (AFLC Form 1032).
22 Oct 1980	Aircraft scheduled for transfer and delivery by 508 TFG, Hill AFB UT to 22 BMW, March AFB CA on or about 11 Dec 1980. (508 TFG/MA TWX 222215Z Oct 80).

31 Oct 1980 At 466 TFS AFRES, Hill AFB UT. 3,340.4 flying hours. Being transferred to museum (ZW). (GO33B 22 Jan 81).

Nov 1980 Aircraft flown from Hill AFB UT to March AFB CA for delivery to the March Field Museum by 466 TFS AFRES pilot, Capt. Wayne Conroy. (Lt. Col. Wayne Conroy, interview 25 Mar 1997).

F-105B-20RE 57-5817

Republic Production No: B-54 Production Sequence No: 57

Location: At municipal airport entrance, Chillicothe, Missouri.

Aircraft Chronology

29 Jul 1959 USAF production acceptance from Republic Aviation, Farmingdale NY. (ACA-79).

2 Oct 1959 Delivered to 334 TFS, 4 TFW, Seymour Johnson AFB NC.

29 Feb 1960 At 334 TFS, 4 TFW, Seymour Johnson AFB NC. Aircraft had accumulated 51 flights and 67 flying hours. (RAC Memo 3 Mar 60 "F-105 Statistical Report for Period Ending 29 February 1960").

In October 1959, this "B" arrived at the first Air Force unit to become operational in the F-105, the 334 Tactical Fighter Squadron at Seymour Johnson Air Force Base, North Carolina. In the summer of 1960, the plane was used at Williams Air Force Base, Arizona, for the F-105B Category III testing that was described by the 4 Tactical Fighter Wing commander as "... a complete flop due to difficulties with the ... Fire Control System and to an almost total lack of supply support." In 1965 the plane transferred to the New Jersey Air National Guard at McGuire Air Force Base and then, five years later, was one of the "Bs" that equipped the second New Jersey Guard unit at Atlantic City. Its last seven years were with the Reserves at Hill Air Force Base, Utah. In October 1980, it was the 25th F-105 retired to Davis-Monthan Air Force Base, Arizona. Five years later it was shipped from the Boneyard to Chillicothe, Missouri, where it was painted in Thunderbird colors to serve as an attraction at the entrance to the town's airport. (Photograph by author, 7 August 1995.)

11 Apr 1960	At MOAMA, Brookley AFB AL for contract work. (ACA-79).
19 Jun 1960	Returned to 4 TFW, Seymour Johnson AFB NC.
16 Jul 1960	At Williams AFB AZ with 4 TFW for F-105B Category III armament testing.
15 Aug 1960	Returned to 4 TFW, Seymour Johnson AFB NC.
6 Jun 1962	Assigned to 334 TFS but at Brookley AFB AL for modification. (RAC record).
5 Oct 1962	At MOAMA, Brookley AFB AL for depot work.
6 Oct 1962	Returned to 4 TFW, Seymour Johnson AFB NC.
15 Apr 1964	At MOAMA, Brookley AFB AL for depot work (WO). (AVH-1).
19 Mar 1965	Transferred to the 108 TFG NJ ANG, McGuire AFB. (AVH-3).
16 Apr 1965	In contract depot maintenance (WM) by General Dynamics at McGuire AFB NJ.
14 May 1965	At 108 TFG NJ ANG, McGuire AFB.
8 May 1970	In contract depot work (WK) by Fairchild Engine and Aircraft Corporation at Bob Sikes Airport (FACCF), Crestview FL. (AVH-14).
28 Aug 1970	Transferred to 177 TFG ANG, Atlantic City Airport NJ.
10 Sep 1970	At 177 TFG ANG, Atlantic City Airport NJ.
1 Apr 1971	In contract depot work (WK) by Fairchild Engine and Aircraft Corporation at Bob Sikes Airport (FACCF), Crestview FL. (AVH-16).
20 Apr 1971	Returned (PL & CC) to 177 TFG ANG, Atlantic City Airport NJ.
1 Nov 1972	In contract depot maintenance (WK) by Fairchild Engine and Aircraft Corporation (FACCF) at Bob Sikes Municipal Airport, Crestview FL. (AVH-18).
7 Dec 1972	In depot work (WO) by SM-ALC, McClellan AFB CA.
2 May 1973	Transferred (PL) to 508 CMTSq AFRES, Hill AFB UT. (AVH-20).
9 Oct 1973	At (CC) 508 CMTSq AFRES, Hill AFB UT.
18 Apr 1975	At 508 CLMSQ AFRES, Hill AFB UT. (AVH-23 & AVH-24).
25 Oct 1975	In depot maintenance (WM) by OC-ALC, Tinker AFB OK.
8 Dec 1975	Returned to 508 CLMSQ AFRES, Hill AFB UT. 2,686 flying hours.
12 Jul 1978	In contract depot maintenance (DYNFW) at Hill AFB UT. 3,194.0 flying hours. (AVH-26).
28 Feb 1979	In depot maintenance at Ogden ALC, Hill AFB UT. 3,194.0 flying hours. (AVH-27).
5 Apr 1979	At 466 TFS AFRES, Hill AFB UT. 3,194.0 flying hours.
6 Nov 1979	Assigned to depot at Ogden ALC, Hill AFB UT. 3,391.1 flying hours.
27 Nov 1979	Returned to 466 TFS AFRES, Hill AFB UT. 3,433.6 flying hours.
10 Oct 1980	Sent to storage at MASDC ("Low probability of withdrawal"—XX), Davis-Monthan AFB AZ. 3,691.4 flying hours. (GO33B 22 Jan 1981).
5 Jul 1982	In storage at MASDC, (Inventory account "ZJ"), Davis-Monthan AFB AZ. 3,693.0 flying hours.
31 Jan 1985	Delegation from Chillicothe MO visited AMARC to select aircraft for display at their city airport. Delegation consisted of Mayor Robert J. Posch and Mr. Robert Staton, Chillicothe Airport Board member.
15 Mar 1985	AMARC transfer documents signed with city of Chillicothe MO for Air Force Static Display Program.
9 May 1985	Removed from MASDC storage for delivery to Chillicothe MO. (AMARC Report 24 Mar 87).
Jul 1985	Aircraft arrived at Chillicothe MO from Tucson AZ. Transported by Western International Aviation from Tucson to Chillicothe in two trucks.
Aug 1985	Aircraft placed on display atop pylons constructed by Mr. Robert Staton at entrance to municipal airport on U.S. Route 36, Chillicothe MO.

F-105B-20RE 57-5819

Republic Production No: B-56 Production Sequence No: 59

Location: Displayed at Poinsett Electronic Combat Range, Shaw AFB, Sumpter, South Carolina.

Aircraft Chronology

5 Oct 1959	USAF production acceptance from Republic Aviation, Farmingdale NY. (ACA-79).
20 Oct 1959	Delivered to 334 TFS, 4 TFW, Seymour Johnson AFB NC.
29 Feb 1960	At 334 TFS, 4 TFW, Seymour Johnson AFB NC. Aircraft had accumulated 46 flights and 68 flying hours. (RAC Memo 3 Mar 60 "F-105 Statistical Report for Period Ending 29 February 1960").
1 Apr 1960	At 4 TFW but operating from Brookley AFB AL due to runway repairs at Seymour Johnson AFB NC. (ACA-79 & 4 TFW History, Jan–Jun 60, microfilm MO290).
19 Jun 1960	Returned to 4 TFW, Seymour Johnson AFB NC. (ACA-79).
2 Aug 1960	With the 334 TFS, 4 TFW at Williams AFB AZ for F-105B Cat III testing.
16 Aug 1960	Returned to 4 TFW, Seymour Johnson AFB NC after completion of Cat III testing.
8 Dec 1961	At MOAMA, Brookley AFB AL for depot work (WO).
22 Dec 1961	Returned to 4 TFW, Seymour Johnson AFB NC.
1 Apr 1963	At Moron AB, Spain with the 336 TFS, 4 TFW. (British Aviation Review, Dec 1995 & ACA-79).

At the beginning of its 24-year career, this "B" was assigned in 1959 to Seymour Johnson Air Force Base in North Carolina where it remained for five years. For the next five years it supported pilot training, first at Nellis Air Force Base, Nevada, then at McConnell Air Force Base, Kansas. After a short time at Atlantic City with the New Jersey Air National Guard, it went to the Air Force Reserve at Hill Air Force Base, Utah. It ended up at Robins Air Force Base, Georgia, where it was used for Aircraft Battle Damage Repair training. It went to the scrap yard at Robins in 1985 but survived to be placed on static display at the Electronic Combat Range outside Shaw Air Force Base, South Carolina. (Photograph by author, 8 August 1997.)

9 Jan 1964	Returned from Spain to the 4 TFW, Seymour Johnson AFB NC.
9 Jun 1964	At MOAMA, Brookley AFB AL for depot work (WO). (ACA-79 & AVH-1).
11 Jun 1965	At 4520 CCTW, Nellis AFB NV for combat crew training (TF). (AVH-3).
17 Nov 1965	At MOAMA, Brookley AFB AL for depot work (WO).
29 Dec 1965	Returned to 4520 CCTW, Nellis AFB NV for combat crew training (TF). (AVH-5).
12 Oct 1965	At MOAMA, Brookley AFB AL for depot work (WO).
4 Jan 1967	At 4520 CCTW, Nellis AFB NV for combat crew training (TF). (AVH-7).
28 Mar 1967	In depot maintenance by SMAMA field team at Nellis AFB NV.
29 Mar 1967	At 4520 CCTW, Nellis AFB NV for combat crew training (TF).
25 Sep 1967	In depot maintenance by SMAMA field team at Nellis AFB NV.
27 Sep 1967	At 4520 CCTW, Nellis AFB NV for combat crew training (TF).
4 Oct 1967	Being prepared for transfer (PL) from 4520 CCTW, Nellis AFB NV.
11 Oct 1967	Transferred to 23 TFW, McConnell AFB KS.
13 Nov 1967	At 23 TFW, McConnell AFB KS for instructor pilots conducting replacement aircrew training (TF).
15 May 1968	At 23 TFW, McConnell AFB KS. (AVH-10).
4 Jun 1968	In depot maintenance (WM) by team from Tinker AFB OK at McConnell AFB KS.
8 Jul 1968	At 23 TFW, McConnell AFB KS for combat crew training (TF).
14 Mar 1969	At 23 TFW, McConnell AFB KS being prepared for depot (PL). (AVH-12).
16 Mar 1969	In depot maintenance (WO) at SMAMA, McClellan AFB CA.
21 Apr 1969	Returned to 23 TFW, McConnell AFB KS for student and combat crew training (TF).
12 May 1969	In depot maintenance (WM) by SMAMA at McConnell AFB KS.
13 May 1969	Returned to 23 TFW, McConnell AFB KS for student and combat crew training (TF).
17 Jun 1970	At 23 TFW TAC, McConnell AFB KS. (AVH-14).
19 Jun 1970	In contract depot work (WK) by Fairchild Engine and Aircraft Corporation (FACCF) at Bob Sikes Airport, Crestview FL.
23 Mar 1971	Transferred (PL) to 177 TFG ANG, Atlantic City Airport NJ. (AVH-16).
15 Dec 1971	At 177 TFG ANG, Atlantic City Airport NJ.
2 Feb 1972	In contract depot maintenance (WK) by Fairchild Engine and Aircraft Corporation (FACCF) at Bob Sikes Municipal Airport, Crestview FL. (AVH-18).
9 Aug 1972	Returned (PL) to the 177 TFG ANG, Atlantic City Airport NJ.
6 Dec 1972	Transferred (PL) to 945 MALGp AFRES, Hill AFB UT.
1 Jan 1973	At 508 TFG AFRES, Hill AFB UT. (AVH-20).
28 Nov 1973	In contract depot maintenance (WK) by Fairchild Engine and Aircraft Corporation (FACCF) at Bob Sikes Municipal Airport, Crestview FL.
10 Jan 1975	At 508 CLMSQ AFRES, Hill AFB UT. (AVH-23).
14 Jan 1975	In contract depot maintenance (WK) by Fairchild Engine and Aircraft Corporation (FACCF) at Bob Sikes Municipal Airport, Crestview FL.
16 May 1975	Returned to 508 CLMSQ AFRES, Hill AFB UT.
9 Dec 1975	At 508 CLMSQ AFRES, Hill AFB UT.
9 Feb 1976	At 508 TFG, AFRES, Hill AFB UT. 2,983 flying hours. (AVH-24).
1 Aug 1978	At 466 TFS AFRES, Hill AFB UT. 3,601.0 flying hours. (AVH-26).
14 Dec 1978	At 466 TFS AFRES, Hill AFB UT. 3,695.3 flying hours. (AVH-27).
11 Jun 1979	In depot maintenance at Odgen ALC, Hill AFB UT. 3,861.9 flying hours.
22 Jun 1979	Returned to 466 TFS AFRES, Hill AFB UT. 3,861.9 flying hours.
3 Jul 1979	Assigned to Ogden ALC, Hill AFB UT. 3,861.9 flying hours.

9 Jul 1979	At 466 TFS AFRES, Hill AFB UT. 3,861.9 flying hours.
1 Oct 1980	At 466 TFS AFRES, Hill AFB UT. 4,152.4 flying hours. (GO33B 22 Jan 81).
9 Nov 1983	At 2955 CLSS, Robins AFB GA for ABDR training. (HQ 2852 ABG/DADF letter, 9 Nov 83).
22 May 1985	At 2955 CLSS, Robins AFB GA. Turned over to "Local Property Disposal Office IAW AFM 67-1." (2852 ABG/DAFD letter, 22 May 85).

F-105B-20RE 57-5820

Republic Production No: B-57 Production Sequence No: 60

Location: At the Florida Military Aviation Museum, Fort Meade, Florida.

Aircraft Chronology

11 Nov 1959	USAF production acceptance from Republic Aviation, Farmingdale NY. (ACA-79).
14 Nov 1959	Delivered to 4 TFW, Seymour Johnson AFB NC.
29 Feb 1960	At 336 TFS, 4 TFW, Seymour Johnson AFB NC. Aircraft had accumulated 34 flights and 50 flying hours. (RAC Memo 3 Mar 60 "F-105 Statistical Report for Period Ending 29 February 1960").
25 Apr 1960	At MOAMA, Brookley AFB AL for contract depot work (WK).
19 Jun 1960	Returned to 4 TFW, Seymour Johnson AFB NC.
26 Sep 1960	At Eglin AFB FL with 4 TFW.
15 Dec 1960	Returned to 4 TFW, Seymour Johnson AFB NC.
10 Jan 1961	At MOAMA, Brookley AFB AL for depot work (WO).
4 Feb 1961	Returned to 4 TFW, Seymour Johnson AFB NC.
6 Jun 1962	At 336 TFS, 4 TFW, Seymour Johnson AFB NC. (RAC record).
1 Apr 1963	At Moron AB, Spain, with the 4 TFW. (British Aviation Review, Dec 1995).
9 Jan 1964	Returned from Spain to Seymour Johnson AFB NC.
3 Jun 1964	At MOAMA, Brookley AFB AL for depot work (WO). (AVH-1).
4 Jun 1965	At 4520 CCTW, Nellis AFB NV for student and combat crew training (TF). (AVH-3).
19 Jun 1965	At MOAMA, Brookley AFB AL for depot work (WO).
7 Jan 1966	At 4520 CCTW, Nellis AFB NV for combat crew training (TF). (AVH-5).
27 Mar 1967	In depot work (WO) at SMAMA, McClellan AFB CA. (AVH-7).
17 Oct 1967	Transferred to 23 TFW, McConnell AFB KS.
13 Nov 1967	At 23 TFW, McConnell AFB KS for use by instructor pilots conducting replacement aircrew training (TF).
21 Mar 1968	At 23 TFW, McConnell AFB KS. (AVH-10).
22 Mar 1968	At SMAMA, McClellan AFB CA for test (EI).
16 Apr 1968	Returned (PL) to 23 TFW, McConnell AFB KS for combat crew training (TF).
22 Apr 1969	In depot maintenance (WM) by SMAMA at McConnell AFB KS. (AVH-12).
27 Jul 1968	At 23 TFW, McConnell AFB KS (WQ).
2 Aug 1968	At 23 TFW, McConnell AFB KS for combat crew training (TF).
10 Jun 1970	At 23 TFW TAC, McConnell AFB KS. (AVH-14).

This plane followed the path of many other "Bs" with initial delivery in November 1959 to the 4 Tactical Fighter Wing at Seymour Johnson Air Force Base, North Carolina, the first wing to operate F-105s. The 4th used the plane for their first NATO deployment to Spain in 1963. This initial assignment was followed by a transfer in 1965 to Nellis Air Force Base, Nevada, where it was used to train F-105 pilots. A second pilot-training assignment in 1967 brought it to McConnell Air Force Base, Kansas. Starting in 1970, the plane spent two years with the New Jersey Air National Guard at Atlantic City and then transferred to the Air Force Reserve unit at Hill Air Force Base, Utah, the last unit to fly the F-105. After being consigned to the Aircraft Battle Damage Repair training program at Robins Air Force, Georgia, it escaped the scrap yard when it was given to the aviation museum in Clearwater, Florida, its location in the photograph. Unfortunately, the plane deteriorated severely in the Florida climate and the museum closed in 1996. In the summer of 2000, the aircraft was to be moved to the museum's new location south of Fort Meade, Florida. (Photograph by John Coon, 22 August 1996.)

15 Jun 1970 Transferred to 177 TFG ANG, Atlantic City Airport NJ.

4 Jul 1970 At 177 TFG ANG, Atlantic City Airport NJ.

21 May 1971 In contract depot maintenance (WK) by Fairchild Engine and Aircraft Corporation (FACCF) at Bob Sikes Municipal Airport, Crestview FL. (AVH-16).

8 Jun 1971 Returned to 177 TFG ANG, Atlantic City Airport NJ.

22 Jun 1971 In contract depot maintenance (WK) by Fairchild Engine and Aircraft Corporation (FACCF) at Bob Sikes Municipal Airport, Crestview FL.

29 Oct 1971 Returned to 177 TFG ANG, Atlantic City Airport NJ.

20 Sep 1972 In contract depot maintenance (WK) by Fairchild Engine and Aircraft Corporation (FACCF) at Bob Sikes Municipal Airport, Crestview FL. (AVH-18).

13 Oct 1972 Returned to 177 TFG ANG, Atlantic City Airport NJ.

7 Dec 1972 Transferred (PL) to 945 MALGp AFRES, Hill AFB UT.

1 Jan 1973 Aircraft reassigned from the 945 MALGp to the 508 TFG AFRES, Hill AFB UT. (AVH-20).

1 Apr 1973 At 508 CMTSq AFRES, Hill AFB UT.

30 Jun 1973 In contract depot maintenance (WK) by Fairchild Engine and Aircraft Corporation (FACCF) at Bob Sikes Municipal Airport, Crestview FL.

Jan 1974 Returned to 508 TFG AFRES, Hill AFB UT. (John Coon).

25 Oct 1975 In depot maintenance (WM) by SM-ALC at Tinker AFB OK. (AVH-23 & AVH-24).

31 Dec 1975 Returned to 508 TFG AFRES, Hill AFB UT. 3,007 flying hours.

18 Jul 1978 In contract depot maintenance (DYNFW) at Hill AFB UT. 3,546.0 flying hours. (AVH-26).

27 Jul 1978 At 466 TFS AFRES, Hill AFB UT. 3,601.0 flying hours.

14 Dec 1978	At 466 TFS AFRES, Hill AFB UT. 3,712.1 flying hours. (AVH-27).
11 Apr 1979	In depot maintenance at Ogden ALC, Hill AFB UT. 3,773.4 flying hours.
23 Apr 1979	At 466 TFS AFRES, Hill AFB UT. 3,773.4 flying hours.
17 Mar 1980	At Odgen ALC, Hill AFB UT for depot maintenance. 3,948.4 flying hours. (GO33B 24 Jun 80).
1 Apr 1980	At 466 TFS AFRES, Hill AFB UT. 3,953.1 flying hours. (GO33B 22 Jan 81).
11 Jul 1980	At 466 TFS AFRES, Hill AFB UT. 4,045.8 flying hours. (AFTO Form 781)
2 Oct 1980	At 466 TFS AFRES, Hill AFB UT. 4,055.3 flying hours. Assigned to ABDR program at Robins AFB GA. Test to destruction (ZD). (GO33B 22 Jan 81).
9 Nov 1983	At 2955 CLSS, Robins AFB GA for ABDR training. (HQ 2852 ABG/DADF Letter 9 Nov 83).
22 May 1985	At 2955 CLSS, Robins AFB GA for ABDR training. (HQ 2852 ABG/DADF Letter 22 May 85).
22 May 1988	Transported to Florida Military Aviation Museum at St. Petersburg-Clearwater International Airport FL by Alabama Army National Guard CH-54 helicopter. (John Coon).
24 May 1988	Shipping document signed by Robins AFB Museum to Yesterday's Air Force and Museum, Pinellas Park FL. Attn: Dennis Cole. (DD Form 1348-1, "DOD Single Line Item Release/Receipt Document").
Summer 2000	The plane was to be disassembled and moved by B&B Aircraft Services from the St. Petersburg-Clearwater Airport to the Florida Military Aviation Museum's new location at Fort Meade, Florida, on highway 175. (John Coon, phone interview 26 Mar 00).

F-105B-20RE 57-5823

Republic Production No: B-60 Production Sequence No: 63

Location: Displayed at the Heritage Museum, Fairchild AFB, Spokane, Washington.

Shortly after delivery to the 4 Tactical Fighter Wing at Seymour Johnson Air Force Base, North Carolina, this plane went to Edwards Air Force Base, California, where it was one of four F-105Bs the 4th used in its successful attempt to set a world speed record. One of its companions, F-105B 57-5812, a less fortunate survivor listed in Appendix 2 of this book, was the plane flown on the record-setting flight. 57-5823 remained with the 4th until it transferred in June 1965 to Nellis Air Force Base, Nevada, where it supported F-105 pilot training. Two years later, when Nellis began training pilots in the new F-111A, it sent this "B" (and seven others) to McConnell Air Force Base, Kansas, where it continued to support pilot training. After training pilots for the second New Jersey Air National Guard unit, McConnell transferred the plane to that unit at Atlantic City. From September 1972 to its retirement in October 1980, the plane was with the Air Force Reserve at Hill Air Force Base, Utah. Its last flight was in March 1981 from Hill to the aviation museum at Fairchild Air Force Base, Washington. (Photograph from Fairchild Heritage Museum, November 1995.)

Aircraft Chronology

7 Oct 1959	USAF production acceptance from Republic Aviation, Farmingdale NY. (ACA-79).
25 Oct 1959	Delivered to the 4 TFW, Seymour Johnson AFB NC.
11 Dec 1959	While assigned to the 4 TFW, the aircraft was one of four F-105Bs and one F-100F the 4th deployed to Edwards AFB CA under "Operation Fast Wind" for its successful attempt to reclaim a world speed record for the United States. BG Joseph H. Moore, the 4 TFW Commander, flew F-105B 57-5812 1,878.67 KPH over a 100 km closed course to take the speed record from a French Nord Griffon II. ("Aerospace Safety" Mar 61 & M. R. Pablo, National Aeronautic Association, e-mail, 5 Jan 00).
29 Feb 1960	At 334 TFS, 4 TFW, Seymour Johnson AFB NC. Aircraft had accumulated 27 flights and 37 flying hours. (RAC Memo 3 Mar 60 "F-105 Statistical Report for Period Ending 29 February 1960").
19 Apr 1960	At MOAMA, Brookley AFB AL. (ACA-79).
19 Jun 1960	Returned to 4 TFW, Seymour Johnson AFB NC.
10 Apr 1962	At MOAMA, Brookley AFB AL for depot work.
6 Jun 1962	Assigned to 336 TFS but at MOAMA, Brookley AFB AL for modification. (RAC record).
31 Jul 1962	Returned to 4 TFW, Seymour Johnson AFB NC.
10 Oct 1962	At MOAMA, Brookley AFB AL for depot work.
10 Oct 1962	At 4 TFW, Seymour Johnson AFB NC.
1 Apr 1963	At Moron AB, Spain, with the 4 TFW. (British Aviation Review, Dec 1995).
8 Jan 1964	Returned from Spain and assigned to 336 TFS, 4 TFW, Seymour Johnson AFB NC.
9 Jun 1964	At MOAMA, Brookley AFB AL for depot work (WO). (AVH-1).
21 Jun 1965	Transferred to 4520 CCTW, Nellis AFB NV for combat crew training (TF). (AVH-3).
6 Jan 1966	At MOAMA, Brookley AFB AL for depot work (WO). (AVH-5).
29 Mar 1966	Returned to 4520 CCTW, Nellis AFB NV for student and combat crew training (TF).
11 Apr 1967	In depot work (WM) by SMAMA field team at Nellis AFB NV. (AVH-7).
12 Apr 1967	At 4520 CCTW, Nellis AFB NV for aircrew training.
6 Sep 1967	In depot work (WM) by SMAMA field team at Nellis AFB NV.
8 Sep 1967	At 4520 CCTW, Nellis AFB NV for aircrew training.
25 Sep 1967	Being prepared for transfer (PL) from 4520 CCTW, Nellis AFB NV.
30 Sep 1967	One of eight F-105Bs transferred to 23 TFW, McConnell AFB KS when Nellis AFB ended their F-105 training program and began F-111A aircrew training.
13 Nov 1967	At 23 TFW, McConnell AFB KS for use by instructor pilots conducting replacement aircrew training (TF).
2 Apr 1968	At 23 TFW, McConnell AFB KS being prepared for transfer (PL). (AVH-10).
3 Apr 1968	At SMAMA, McClellan AFB CA for depot work (WO).
27 Aug 1968	Returned (PL) to 23 TFW, McConnell AFB KS for combat crew training (TF).
29 Apr 1969	In depot maintenance (WM) by SMAMA at McConnell AFB KS. (AVH-12).
1 May 1969	At 23 TFW, McConnell AFB KS for combat crew training (TF).
10 Jun 1970	Transferred to 177 TFG ANG, Atlantic City Airport NJ. (AVH-14).
20 Apr 1971	In contract depot work (WK) by Fairchild Engine and Aircraft Corporation at Bob Sikes Airport (FACCF), Crestview FL. (AVH-16).
12 May 1971	Returned to 177 TFG ANG, Atlantic City Airport NJ.
6 Apr 1972	In contract depot maintenance (WK) by Fairchild Engine and Aircraft Corporation (FACCF) at Bob Sikes Municipal Airport, Crestview FL. (AVH-18).
19 Jul 1972	Returned to 177 TFG ANG, Atlantic City Airport NJ.
29 Sep 1972	Transferred (PL) to 945 MALGp AFRES, Hill AFB UT.

1 Jan 1973	At 508 TFG AFRES, Hill AFB UT. (AVH-20).
21 Mar 1975	At 508 CLMSQ AFRES, Hill AFB UT. (AVH-23).
1 Nov 1975	In depot maintenance (WM) by SM-ALC at Tinker AFB OK.
31 Dec 1975	Returned to 508 TFG AFRES, Hill AFB UT. 2,947 flying hours. (AVH-24).
1 Oct 1977	At 466 TFS AFRES, Hill AFB UT. 3,493.8 flying hours. (AVH-26).
19 Apr 1978	At 508 TFG AFRES, Hill AFB UT. 3,397.0 flying hours.
14 Dec 1978	At 466 TFS AFRES, Hill AFB UT. 3,618.2 flying hours. (AVH-27).
24 Apr 1979	In depot maintenance at Ogden ALC, Hill AFB UT. 3,660.0 flying hours.
15 May 1979	At 466 TFS AFRES, Hill AFB UT. 3,722.1 flying hours.
6 Sep 1979	At OC ALC AFLC, Tinker AFB OK for special project (DO). 3,743.6 flying hours.
28 Nov 1979	At OC ALC AFLC, Tinker AFB OK. 3,780.8 flying hours.
30 Nov 1979	Returned to 466 TFS AFRES, Hill AFB UT. 3,780.8 flying hours.
17 Oct 1980	One of nine AFRES/NGB F-105Bs that AFLC/LOACA authorized for transfer to Air Force Museum for loan as static displays. (AFLC Form 1032).
22 Oct 1980	Aircraft scheduled for transfer and delivery by 508 TFG, Hill AFB UT to 92 BMW, Fairchild AFB WA on or about 30 Oct 1980. (508 TFG/MA TWX 222215Z Oct 80).
3 Dec 1980	At 466 TFS AFRES, Hill AFB UT. 3,993.5 flying hours. Marked for museum (ZW). (GO33B 22 Jan 1981).
16 Mar 1981	Aircraft signed for by Lt. Col. Paul C. Patrick, 92 BMW, Fairchild AFB WA on Voucher Number 1982-719, 3 Feb 81. (DD Form 1149, Requisition and Invoice/Shipping Document, 3 Feb 1981).
6 May 1981	Conditioned for static display by 92 BMW/MAS, Fairchild AFB WA, under loan agreement number LA3175. Inert condition inspection certified by William H. Deering. (AFM Museum Form 0-36).

F-105B-20RE 57-5835

Republic Production No: B-72 Production Sequence No: 75

Location: At USAF Detachment 1, 343 Training Squadron at Camp Bullis, San Antonio, Texas.

Aircraft Name(s)	Crew	Unit	Date	Description
Brooks Barnstormer		Brooks AFB AL	Aug 81	Name stenciled in black on right side of fuselage below wing. Yellow and white cloud.

Aircraft Chronology

5 Dec 1959	USAF production acceptance from Republic Aviation, Farmingdale NY. (ACA-79).
11 Dec 1959	Delivered to 4 TFW, Seymour Johnson AFB NC.
29 Feb 1960	At 336 TFS, 4 TFW, Seymour Johnson AFB NC. Aircraft had accumulated 18 flights and 26 flying hours. (RAC Memo 3 Mar 60 "F-105 Statistical Report for Period Ending 29 February 1960").
9 Mar 1960	At 4 TFW, Seymour Johnson AFB NC. (ACA-79).
19 Apr 1960	Assigned to Brookley AFB AL for depot work at Seymour Johnson AFB NC.
18 Jun 1960	At 4 TFW, Seymour Johnson AFB NC.
13 Jul 1960	In depot work (WK) at 4 TFW, Seymour Johnson AFB NC.

F-105B 57-5835 arrived from production in late 1959 at the 4 Tactical Fighter Wing, Seymour Johnson Air Force Base, North Carolina. It deployed to Spain for the Wing's NATO commitment in 1963 and, in 1965, transferred to Nellis Air Force Base, Nevada, where it was used for F-105 pilot training. It continued serving in this role after it was sent to the 23 Tactical Fighter Wing at McConnell Air Force Base, Kansas, in October 1967. In 1970, it was assigned to the New Jersey Air National Guard unit at Atlantic City, relocating two years later to its sister organization at McGuire. In January 1973 it went to the Air Force Reserve's 466 Tactical Fighter Squadron at Hill Air Force Base, Utah, the last unit to fly the Thunderchief. It remained at Hill until 1981 when it was allocated to the Aircraft Battle Damage Repair program at Kelly Air Force Base, Texas. Despite not being restored, it still serves as a training aid for Lackland's 343 Training Squadron's combat arms training course. (Photograph by author, 4 August 1997.)

15 Jul 1960	At Williams AFB AZ with the 334 TFS, 4 TFW, for F-105B Cat III testing.
15 Aug 1960	Returned to 4 TFW, Seymour Johnson AFB NC after termination of F-105B Cat III testing.
9 Nov 1960	At Eglin AFB FL with 4 TFW from Seymour Johnson AFB NC.
13 Feb 1962	At 4 TFW, Seymour Johnson AFB NC.
1 Apr 1963	Deployed to Moron AB, Spain with 4 TFW. (British Aviation Review, Dec 1995).
9 Jan 1964	Returned from Spain to 4 TFW, Seymour Johnson AFB NC. (ACA-79).
5 Jun 1964	At MOAMA, Brookley AFB AL for depot work (WO). (ACA-79 & AVH-1).
12 Jun 1965	At 4520 CCTW, Nellis AFB NV for combat crew training (TF). (AVH-3).
4 Jan 1966	In depot work (WO) at MOAMA, Brookley AFB AL. (AVH-5).
24 Mar 1966	Returned to 4520 CCTW TAC for aircrew training (TF).
28 Mar 1967	In depot maintenance (WM) by SMAMA at Nellis AFB NV. (AVH-7).
29 Mar 1967	At 4520 CCTW TAC for aircrew training (TF).
16 Aug 1967	In depot maintenance (WM) by SMAMA at Nellis AFB NV.
18 Aug 1967	At 4520 CCTW TAC for aircrew training (TF).

2 Oct 1967	In depot maintenance (WM) by SMAMA at Nellis AFB NV.
3 Oct 1967	At 4520 CCTW TAC for aircrew training (TF).
4 Oct 1967	At 4520 CCTW TAC being prepared for transfer (PL).
11 Oct 1967	Transferred (PL) to the 23 TFW TAC, McConnell AFB KS.
13 Oct 1967	Combat capable (CC) at 23 TFW, McConnell AFB KS.
13 Nov 1967	At 23 TFW, McConnell AFB KS for combat crew training (TF).
2 Aug 1968	At 23 TFW, McConnell AFB KS being prepared for transfer (PL) to depot. (AVH-10).
4 Aug 1968	In depot work (WO) by SMAMA at McClellan AFB CA.
5 Sep 1968	Returned (PL) to 23 TFW, McConnell AFB KS.
9 Sep 1968	At 23 TFW, McConnell AFB KS for combat crew training (TF).
24 Jan 1969	At 23 TFW, McConnell AFB KS being prepared for transfer (PL) to depot. (AVH-12).
28 Jan 1969	In contract depot work (WK) by Fairchild Engine and Aircraft Corporation (FACCF), Crestview FL.
15 May 1969	Returned (PL) to 23 TFW, McConnell AFB KS.
19 May 1969	In depot maintenance (WM) by SMAMA at McConnell AFB KS.
20 May 1969	At 23 TFW, McConnell AFB KS for combat crew training (TF).
3 Jun 1970	At 23 TFW, McConnell AFB KS being readied for transfer (PL). (AVH-14).
10 Jun 1970	Transferred (PL) to the 177 TFG ANG, Atlantic City Airport NJ.
22 Mar 1971	In contract depot work (WK) by Fairchild Engine and Aircraft Corporation (FACCF), Bob Sikes Airport, Crestview FL. (AVH-16).
14 Apr 1971	Returned (PL) to 177 TFG ANG, Atlantic City Airport NJ.
1 Oct 1971	At 177 TFG ANG, Atlantic City Airport NJ.
29 Sep 1972	At 108 TFG ANG, McGuire AFB NJ. (AVH-18).
1 Nov 1972	In contract depot work (WK) by Fairchild Engine and Aircraft Corporation (FACCF), Bob Sikes Airport, Crestview FL.
2 Dec 1972	Returned to 108 TFG ANG, McGuire AFB NJ.
30 Jan 1973	Transferred (PL) to 508 TFG AFRES, Hill AFB UT. (AVH-20).
5 Feb 1973	Combat capable (CC) at 508 TFG AFRES, Hill AFB UT.
31 May 1973	At 508 TFG AFRES, Hill AFB UT being prepared for transfer.
4 Jun 1973	In contract depot work (WK) by Fairchild Engine and Aircraft Corporation (FACCF), Bob Sikes Airport, Crestview FL.
20 Dec 1973	Returned to 508 TFG, Hill AFB UT. Assigned to an "Instructional Project" (PJ).
2 Jan 1974	Combat capable (CC) at 508 TFG AFRES, Hill AFB UT.
6 Mar 1975	Possession changed to 508 CLMSq AFRES, Hill AFB UT. (AVH-23).
1 Dec 1975	At 508 CLMSq AFRES, Hill AFB UT.
19 Mar 1976	Organization assignment changed to 508 TFG AFRES, Hill AFB UT. (AVH-24).
12 Jul 1978	In depot maintenance (DM) by General Dynamics (DYNFW) at Hill AFB UT. 3,591.0 flying hours. (AVH-26).
28 Feb 1979	In depot maintenance (DM) by Ogden ALC at Hill AFB UT. 3,591.0 flying hours. (AVH-27).
22 Aug 1979	Operational (CC) at 466 TFS AFRES, Hill AFB UT. 3,658.5 flying hours.
1 Oct 1980	At 466 TFS AFRES, Hill AFB UT. 3,836.8 flying hours. Inventory account: ZD. (GO33B 22 Jan 81).
9 Nov 1983	At 2954 CLSS, Kelly AFB TX for ABDR training. (HQ 2852 ABG/DADF Letter 9 Nov 83).
22 May 1985	At 2954 CLSS, Kelly AFB TX for ABDR training. (HQ 2852 ABG/DADF Letter 22 May 85).

F-105B-20RE 57-5837

Republic Production No: B-74 Production Sequence No: 77

Location: At Castle Air Museum, Atwater, California.

Aircraft Chronology

23 Dec 1959 USAF production acceptance from Republic Aviation, Farmingdale NY. (ACA-79).
5 Jan 1960 Delivered to 4 TFW, Seymour Johnson AFB NC.
29 Feb 1960 At 336 TFS, 4 TFW, Seymour Johnson AFB NC. Aircraft had accumulated 14 flights and 18 flying hours. (RAC Memo 3 Mar 60 "F-105 Statistical Report for Period Ending 29 February 1960").
28 Apr 1960 At MOAMA, Brookley AFB AL for depot work (WK). (ACA-79).
19 Jun 1960 Returned to 4 TFW, Seymour Johnson AFB NC.
16 Jul 1960 At Williams AFB AZ with 334 TFS, 4 TFW, for F-105B Cat III armament testing.
15 Aug 1960 Returned to 4 TFW, Seymour Johnson AFB NC.
6 Jun 1962 At 334 TFS, 4 TFW, Seymour Johnson AFB NC. (RAC record).
1 Apr 1963 Deployed to Moron AB, Spain with 4 TFW. (British Aviation Review, Dec 1995).
8 Jan 1964 Returned from Spain and assigned to 336 TFS, 4 TFW, Seymour Johnson AFB NC.
4 Jun 1964 At MOAMA, Brookley AFB AL for depot work (WO). (AVH-1).
25 May 1965 At 4520 CCTW, Nellis AFB NV for combat crew training (TF). (AVH-3).
18 Jan 1966 At MOAMA, Brookley AFB AL for depot work (WO). (AVH-5).
25 Mar 1966 At 4520 CCTW, Nellis AFB NV for student and combat crew training (TF).
10 Apr 1967 In depot work (WM) by SMAMA field team at Nellis AFB NV. (AVH-7).
12 Apr 1967 At 4520 CCTW, Nellis AFB NV for aircrew training (TF).
3 Nov 1967 At SMAMA, McClellan AFB CA for depot work (WO).

Seymour Johnson Air Force Base, North Carolina, got this "B" in January 1960 and, six months later, used it in its aborted Category III armament testing at Williams Air Force Base, Arizona. The 4 Tactical Fighter Wing also flew the plane on its first NATO deployment to Moron Air Base, Spain. The plane followed a common "B" model assignment pattern to Nellis Air Force Base, Nevada, and McConnell Air Force Base, Kansas, then to the Air National Guard at Atlantic City, ending up with the Air Force Reserve's 466 Tactical Fighter Squadron at Hill Air Force Base, Utah. The plane stayed at Hill until the end of 1980 when it was flown to the museum at Castle Air Force Base, California. (Photograph by Hansel "Turk" Turley, December 1998.)

4 Mar 1968	Transferred to (PL) to 23 TFW, McConnell AFB KS for combat crew training (TF). (AVH-10).
8 Oct 1968	At McConnell AFB KS being prepared (PL) for transfer to depot.
16 Oct 1968	At SMAMA, McClellan AFB CA for depot work (WO).
22 Nov 1968	Returned (PL) to 23 TFW, McConnell AFB KS for combat crew training (TF).
7 May 1969	In depot maintenance (WM) by SMAMA at McConnell AFB KS. (AVH-12).
9 May 1969	At 23 TFW, McConnell AFB KS for combat crew training (TF).
5 Jun 1970	Transferred to 177 TFG ANG, Atlantic City Airport NJ. (AVH-14).
13 Apr 1971	In contract depot work (WK) by Fairchild Engine and Aircraft Corporation at Bob Sikes Airport (FACCF), Crestview FL. (AVH-16).
6 May 1971	Returned to 177 TFG ANG, Atlantic City Airport NJ.
6 Oct 1971	In contract depot work (WK) by Fairchild Engine and Aircraft Corporation at Bob Sikes Airport (FACCF), Crestview FL.
26 Jan 1973	At 177 TFG ANG, Atlantic City Airport NJ. (AVH-20).
30 Jan 1973	Transferred (PL) to 508 TFG AFRES, Hill AFB UT.
15 Aug 1973	In contract depot maintenance (WK) by Fairchild Engine and Aircraft Corporation (FACCF) at Bob Sikes Municipal Airport, Crestview FL.
25 Feb 1975	At 508 CLMSQ AFRES, Hill AFB UT. (AVH-23).
18 Feb 1976	At 508 TFG AFRES, Hill AFB UT. 3,085 flying hours. (AVH-24).
12 Jul 1978	In contract depot maintenance (DYNFW) at Hill AFB UT. 3,549.0 flying hours. (AVH-26).
22 Jul 1978	At 466 TFS AFRES, Hill AFB UT. 3,635.0 flying hours.
14 Dec 1978	At 466 TFS AFRES, Hill AFB UT. 3,727.4 flying hours. (AVH-27).
16 Jul 1979	In depot maintenance at Ogden ALC, Hill AFB UT. 3,865.9 flying hours.
20 Aug 1979	At 466 TFS AFRES, Hill AFB UT. 3,902.3 flying hours.
17 Oct 1980	One of nine AFRES/NGB F-105Bs that AFLC/LOACA authorized for transfer to the Air Force Museum for loan as static displays. (AFLC Form 1032).
22 Oct 1980	Aircraft scheduled for transfer and delivery by 508 TFG, Hill AFB UT to 93 BMW, Castle AFB CA on or about 18 Dec 1980. (508 TFG/MA TWX 222215Z Oct 80).
23 Dec 1980	At 466 TFS AFRES, Hill AFB UT. Being processed to museum (ZW). 4,182.8 flying hours. (GO33B Dec 81 & GO33B 1 Feb 83).

F-105B-20RE 57-5838

Republic Production No: B-75 Production Sequence No: 78

Location: At the Wisconsin ANG Museum, Volk Field, Wisconsin.

Aircraft Name(s)	Crew	Unit	Date	Description
Xanadu		466 TFS		

Aircraft Chronology

29 Dec 1959	USAF production acceptance from Republic Aviation, Farmingdale NY. (ACA-79).
8 Jan 1960	Delivered to 4 TFW, Seymour Johnson AFB NC.

When the 4 Tactical Fighter Wing received this "B" in January 1960, they sent it to Eglin Air Force Base where the 335 Tactical Fighter Squadron used it in testing improved systems for later F-105s. In April 1963, the plane was one of 18 that deployed to Spain with the 334 Tactical Fighter Squadron for the Tactical Air Command's first NATO air-defense alert with their new Thunderchief. By June 1964, the 4th was receiving "D" models to replace their initial fleet of "Bs" and so the plane transferred to Nellis Air Force Base, Nevada, and then to McConnell Air Force Base, Kansas, where it helped train pilots learning to fly F-105s for the war in Southeast Asia. In 1970, it became one of the "Bs" that equipped the Air National Guard unit at Atlantic City, New Jersey. The last unit to fly F-105s, the Air Force Reserve's 466 Tactical Fighter Squadron at Hill Air Force Base, Utah, got it in January 1973. Its last flight was from Hill to the Wisconsin Air National Guard Museum in early 1981. (Photograph by Donald Kuenn, October 1989.)

10 Jan 1960 At Eglin AFB FL with 4 TFW. Aircraft used to test DX2 tow reel installed on the fuselage center line pylon. It was also used to test a modified fuel control and throttle quadrant to give extended range to afterburner thrust modulation during air-to-air refueling. (Air Proving Ground Center History, Jan–Jun 61, USAF microfilm K2762).

29 Feb 1960 At 335 TFS, 4 TFW, Eglin AFB FL. Aircraft had accumulated 40 flights and 56 flying hours. (RAC Memo 3 Mar 60 "F-105 Statistical Report for Period Ending 29 February 1960").

11 Apr 1960 Returned to 4 TFW, Seymour Johnson AFB NC. (ACA-79).

20 Apr 1960 At MOAMA, Brookley AFB AL for depot work.

19 Jun 1960 Returned to 4 TFW, Seymour Johnson AFB NC.

24 Apr 1962 The 336 TFS placed aircraft on static display at McGhee-Tyson Airport TN. (4 TFW History, Jan–Jun 1962, USAF microfilm MO290).

6 Jun 1962 At 336 TFS, 4 TFW, Seymour Johnson AFB NC. (RAC record).

1 Apr 1963 Deployed to Moron AB, Spain, with the 4 TFW under "Fox Able 147" with the 334 TFS. (British Aviation Review, Dec 1995).

10 Jan 1964 Returned from Spain, and assigned to 336 TFW, 4 TFW, Seymour Johnson AFB NC.

5 Jun 1964 At MOAMA, Brookley AFB AL for depot work (WO). (AVH-1).

25 Jun 1965 At 4520 CCTW, Nellis AFB NV for combat crew training (TF). (AVH-3).

19 Oct 1965 At MOAMA, Brookley AFB AL for depot work (WO).

29 Nov 1965 At 4520 CCTW, Nellis AFB NV for combat crew training (TF).

12 Apr 1967	In depot work (WM) by SMAMA field team at Nellis AFB NV. (AVH-7).
14 Apr 1967	At 4520 CCTW, Nellis AFB NV for aircrew training (TF).
17 May 1967	In depot work (WO) by SMAMA at McClellan AFB CA.
3 Nov 1967	Transferred to 23 TFW, McConnell AFB KS.
14 Nov 1967	At 23 TFW, McConnell AFB KS for use by instructor pilots conducting replacement aircrew training (TF).
18 Jun 1968	At 23 TFW, McConnell AFB KS for combat crew training (TF). (AVH-10).
19 Dec 1968	At SMAMA, McClellan AFB CA for depot work (WO).
26 Feb 1969	Returned to (PL) 23 TFW, McConnell AFB KS. (AVH-12).
2 Mar 1969	At 23 TFW, McConnell AFB KS for combat crew training (TF).
15 Jun 1970	Transferred to 177 TFG ANG, Atlantic City Airport NJ. (AVH-14).
16 Apr 1971	At 177 TFG ANG, Atlantic City Airport NJ. (AVH-16).
17 Jun 1971	In contract depot work (WK) by Fairchild Engine and Aircraft Corporation at Bob Sikes Airport (FACCF), Crestview FL.
10 Jul 1971	Returned to 177 TFG ANG, Atlantic City Airport NJ.
26 Jan 1973	At 177 TFG ANG, Atlantic City Airport NJ. (AVH-20).
30 Jan 1973	Transferred to 508 TFG AFRES, Hill AFB UT.
15 Mar 1973	In contract depot maintenance (WK) by Fairchild Engine and Aircraft Corporation (FACCF) at Bob Sikes Municipal Airport, Crestview FL.
8 Nov 1973	Returned (PL) to 508 CMTSq AFRES, Hill AFB UT.
13 May 1975	At 508 CLMSQ AFRES, Hill AFB UT. (AVH-23).
17 Feb 1976	At 508 TFG AFRES, Hill AFB UT. 3,059 flying hours. (AVH-24).
4 Aug 1977	In depot work (DR) at SM-ALC, McClellan AFB CA. 3,246.0 flying hours. (AVH-25 & AVH-26).
24 May 1978	In depot project work (DO) at SM-ALC, McClellan AFB CA. 3,391.0 flying hours.
5 Sep 1978	In depot work (DR) at SM-ALC, McClellan AFB CA. 3,392.0 flying hours.
7 Sep 1978	At 466 TFS AFRES, Hill AFB UT. 3,392.0 flying hours.
20 Nov 1978	At 466 TFS AFRES, Hill AFB UT. 3,417.2 flying hours.
14 Dec 1978	At 466 TFS AFRES, Hill AFB UT. 3,438.9 flying hours. (AVH-27).
17 Dec 1979	At Odgen ALC, Hill AFB UT for depot maintenance. 3,782.2 flying hours. (GO33B 24 Jun 80).
4 Jan 1980	At 466 TFS, Hill AFB UT. 3,782.2 flying hours.
17 Oct 1980	One of nine AFRES/NGB F-105Bs that AFLC/LOACA authorized for transfer to Air Force Museum for loan as static displays. (AFLC Form 1032).
22 Oct 1980	Aircraft scheduled for transfer and delivery by 508 TFG, Hill AFB UT to PFTS, Volk Field WI on or about 18 Dec 1980. (508 TFG/MA TWX 222215Z Oct 80).
15 Jan 1981	At 466 TFS ANG, Hill AFB UT. Being processed to museum (ZW). 4,020.3 flying hours. (GO33B Dec 81 & GO33B 1 Feb 83). Flown to Volk Field in 1981.

F-105B-20RE 57-5839

Republic Production No: B-76 Production Sequence No: 79

Location: At the South Dakota Air and Space Museum, Ellsworth AFB, Rapid City, South Dakota.

Aircraft Chronology

30 Dec 1959	USAF production acceptance from Republic Aviation, Farmingdale NY. (ACA-79).
30 Dec 1959	Delivered to 4 TFW, Seymour Johnson AFB, NC.
29 Feb 1960	At 335 TFS, 4 TFW, Eglin AFB FL. Aircraft had accumulated 40 flights and 56 flying hours (RAC Memo 3 Mar 60 "F-105 Statistical Report for Period Ending 29 February 1960").
2 Mar 1960	At Eglin AFB FL with 4 TFW. (ACA-79).
10 Mar 1960	Returned to 4 TFW, Seymour Johnson AFB, NC.
11 Apr 1960	In depot work at MOAMA, Brookley AFB AL.
19 Jun 1960	Returned to 4 TFW, Seymour Johnson AFB, NC.
26 Sep 1960	At Eglin AFB FL with 4 TFW.
15 Dec 1960	Returned to 4 TFW, Seymour Johnson AFB, NC.
4 Jan 1961	In depot work at MOAMA, Brookley AFB AL.
30 Jan 1961	Returned to 4 TFW, Seymour Johnson AFB, NC.
13 Nov 1961	At Republic Aviation, Farmingdale NY.
6 Jun 1962	At Republic Aviation, Farmingdale NY but assigned to 334 TFS, Seymour Johnson AFB NC. (RAC record).
8 Jun 1962	Returned to 4 TFW, Seymour Johnson AFB, NC.
1 Apr 1963	Deployed to Moron AB, Spain, with 4 TFW. (British Aviation Review, Dec 1995).
9 Jan 1964	Returned from Spain and assigned to 336 TFS, 4 TFW at Seymour Johnson AFB, NC.
5 Jun 1964	At MOAMA, Brookley AFB AL for depot work (WO). (AVH-1).
21 Jun 1965	At 4520 CCTW, Nellis AFB NV for student and combat crew training (TF). (AVH-3).
18 Nov 1965	At MOAMA, Brookley AFB AL for depot work (WO).
5 Jan 1966	Returned to 4520 CCTW, Nellis AFB NV for student and combat crew training (TF). (AVH-5).
23 Jul 1966	In depot work (WO) at MOAMA, Brookley AFB AL.
3 Oct 1966	Returned to 4520 CCTW, Nellis AFB NV for student and combat crew training (TF).
19 Oct 1966	In depot maintenance (WM) by SMAMA at Nellis AFB NV.
26 Oct 1966	At 4520 CCTW, Nellis AFB NV for student and combat crew training (TF).
30 Mar 1967	In depot work (WM) by SMAMA field team at Nellis AFB NV. (AVH-7).
31 Mar 1967	At 4520 CCTW, Nellis AFB NV for aircrew training (TF).
12 Oct 1967	Being prepared for transfer (PL) from 4520 CCTW, Nellis AFB NV.
18 Oct 1967	Transferred to 23 TFW, McConnell AFB KS.
14 Nov 1967	At 23 TFW, McConnell AFB KS for use by instructor pilots conducting replacement aircrew training (TF).
19 Jun 1968	In depot maintenance (WM) by field team from Tinker AFB OK at 23 TFW, McConnell AFB KS. (AVH-10).
3 Jul 1968	At 23 TFW, McConnell AFB KS for combat crew training (TF).
7 Apr 1969	In depot maintenance (WM) by SMAMA at McConnell AFB KS. (AVH-12).
9 Apr 1969	At 23 TFW, McConnell AFB KS for combat crew training (TF).
5 Jun 1970	In contract depot work (WK) by Fairchild Engine and Aircraft Corporation at Bob Sikes Airport (FACCF), Crestview FL. (AVH-14).
29 Oct 1970	Transferred to 177 TFG ANG, Atlantic City Airport NJ.
2 Dec 1970	At 177 TFG ANG, Atlantic City Airport NJ.
6 May 1971	In contract depot work (WK) by Fairchild Engine and Aircraft Corporation at Bob Sikes Airport (FACCF), Crestview FL. (AVH-16).
28 May 1971	Returned to 177 TFG ANG, Atlantic City Airport NJ.

This was the next to the last "B" produced and its career followed the path of many earlier ones starting service with the 4 Tactical Fighter Wing in December 1959 where it joined the test force at Eglin Air Force Base, Florida. It moved to Nellis Air Force Base, Nevada, McConnell Air Force Base, Kansas, joined the New Jersey Air National Guard at Atlantic City, and finished with the Air Force Reserve at Hill Air Force Base, Utah. It flew from Utah to the South Dakota Air And Space Museum in December 1980. (Photograph from Ron Alley, Curator, South Dakota Air And Space Museum, 26 July 1996.)

19 Dec 1972 In contract depot maintenance (WK) by Fairchild Engine and Aircraft Corporation (FACCF) at Bob Sikes Municipal Airport, Crestview FL. (AVH-18).

16 Jan 1973 Transferred to 508 TFG AFRES, Hill AFB UT. (AVH-20).

29 Jun 1973 In contract depot maintenance (WK) by Fairchild Engine and Aircraft Corporation (FACCF) at Bob Sikes Municipal Airport, Crestview FL.

14 Mar 1975 In contract depot maintenance (WK) by Fairchild Engine and Aircraft Corporation (FACCF) at Bob Sikes Municipal Airport, Crestview FL. (AVH-23).

8 Jul 1975 Returned to 508 CLMSQ AFRES, Hill AFB UT.

9 Dec 1975 At 508 CLMSQ AFRES, Hill AFB UT.

27 Feb 1976 At 508 TFG AFRES, Hill AFB UT. 2,936 flying hours. (AVH-24).

21 Jun 1977 In depot work (DO) at Ogden ALC, Hill AFB UT. 3,179.0 flying hours. (AVH-25 & AVH-26).

1 Jul 1977 At 508 TFG AFRES, Hill AFB UT. 3,177.0 flying hours.

12 Jul 1978 In contract depot maintenance (DYNFW) at Hill AFB UT. 3,339.0 flying hours.

28 Feb 1979 In depot maintenance at Ogden ALC, Hill AFB UT. 3,358.0 flying hours. (AVH-27).

21 Mar 1979 At 466 TFS AFRES, Hill AFB UT. 3,358.0 flying hours.

16 May 1979 At Ogden ALC AFLC, Hill AFB UT. 3,393.9 flying hours.

11 Jun 1979 At 466 TFS AFRES, Hill AFB UT. 3,393.9 flying hours.

11 Jul 1979 At Ogden ALC AFLC, Hill AFB UT. 3,463.7 flying hours.

12 Jul 1979 At 466 TFS AFRES, Hill AFB UT. 3,463.7 flying hours.

11 Aug 1979 At 466 TFS AFRES, Hill AFB UT. 3,476.8 flying hours.

17 Oct 1980 One of nine AFRES/NGB F-105Bs that AFLC/LOACA authorized for transfer to Air Force Museum for loan as static displays. (AFLC Form 1032).

22 Oct 1980	Aircraft scheduled for transfer and delivery by 508 TFG, Hill AFB UT to 28 BMW, Ellsworth AFB SD on or about 11 Dec 1980. (508 TFG/MA TWX 222215Z Oct 80).
11 Dec 1980	At 466 TFS AFRES, Hill AFB UT. 3,839.0 flying hours. Marked for museum (ZW). (GO33B 22 Jan 81).
Dec 1980	Aircraft received at South Dakota Air and Space Museum. (Ron Ally, Museum Director, letter, 26 July 1996).
1982	Aircraft put on display at South Dakota Air and Space Museum.

F-105D-5RE 58-1155

Republic Production No: D-10 Production Sequence No: 90

Location: At the USAF Armament Museum, Eglin AFB, Shalimar, Florida.

Of the initial twenty-eight F-105Ds produced with "58-" serial numbers, this is the only one that remains and is the oldest "D" that still exists. It was the tenth "D" delivered and went to Eglin Air Force Base, Florida, in April 1960 as a test plane with the Air Force Systems Command. It supported testing at Eglin for the next nine years and, beginning in August 1969, spent two years with the 23 Tactical Fighter Wing at McConnell Air Force Base, Kansas. Its last unit was the Washington DC Air National Guard at Andrews Air Force Base, Maryland. It remained at Andrews until 1980 when it found its way back to Eglin and retirement in the Armament Museum. With its "JV" tail code for the 469 Tactical Fighter Squadron at Korat, Thailand, and its colorful "*Ohio Express*" markings, the museum displays it as the combat veteran, 59-1771, that carried Captain Peter K. Foley on his 200th mission over North Vietnam on 10 August 1968. (Photograph by author, 7 June 1995.)

Aircraft Chronology

9 Mar 1960	First test flight by Republic Aviation Department S-17, Final Assembly, from Farmingdale NY. Structural integrity flight test program. (Frank Strnad record).
27 Apr 1960	USAF production acceptance. Assigned to Republic Aviation Corporation at Eglin AFB FL as test support aircraft. (ACA-82).
21 Apr 1961	First test flight by Republic Aviation Department S-43, Experimental Shop, from Farmingdale NY. Seventh test flight in structural integrity flight test program.
12 July 1961	Delivered to PGCC, Eglin AFB FL after 12 structural integrity test flights by Republic Aviation from Farmingdale NY.
15 Jan 1962	Assigned to Republic Aviation at Eglin AFB as bailment test aircraft (EB). (ACA-82).
6 Jun 1962	Still bailed to Republic at Eglin AFB FL. (RAC record).
26 Nov 1963	Assigned to 3201 Maintenance Group AFSC, Eglin AFB FL as JF-105D for test support (EH). (ACA-82).
20 Feb 1964	Reassigned to APGC AFSC as F-105D for test support (EH).
17 Apr 1964	Placed in storage (XT) at MOAMA, Brookley AFB AL. (ACA-82 and AVH-1).
1 Sep 1964	At MOAMA, Brookley AFB AL for depot work (WO). (AVH-3).
13 Apr 1965	At PGCC Eglin AFB FL for test support (EH).
26 Apr 1965	In depot maintenance (WM) by "LASON" at Eglin AFB FL.
19 May 1965	At PGCC, Eglin AFB FL for test support (EH).
1 Oct 1965	In contract depot maintenance (WK) by Fairchild Engine and Aircraft Corporation (RACFA) at Bob Sikes Municipal Airport, Crestview FL.
28 Oct 1965	Returned to PGCC Eglin AFB FL for test support (EH).
16 Mar 1966	Redesignated JF-105D at PGCC, Eglin AFB FL. (AVH-5).
29 Sep 1966	In depot maintenance (WO) at MOAMA, Brookley AFB AL.
17 Dec 1966	Returned to PGCC, Eglin AFB FL for test support (EH).
6 Jun 1967	At PGCC, Holloman AFB NM as JF-105D for test support (EH). (AVH-7).
8 Sep 1967	At PGCC, Eglin AFB FL for test support (EH).
Nov 1968	Redesignated F-105D.
30 Nov 1968	At ADTC, Eglin AFB FL for test support (EH). (AVH-10).
13 Aug 1969	At ADTC, Eglin AFB FL being processed for transfer (PL). (AVH-12).
26 Aug 1969	Transferred to 23 TFW TAC, McConnell AFB KS.
10 Dec 1969	In depot work (WO) at SMAMA, McClellan AFB CA.
24 Mar 1970	At 23 TFW TAC, McConnell AFB KS. (AVH-14).
2 Jun 1971	In contract depot maintenance (WK) by Fairchild Engine and Aircraft Corporation (FACCF) at Bob Sikes Municipal Airport, Crestview FL. (AVH-16).
30 Jun 1971	Transferred to 113 TFG ANG, Andrews AFB MD.
20 Apr 1972	In contract depot maintenance (WK) by Fairchild Engine and Aircraft Corporation (FACCF) at Bob Sikes Municipal Airport, Crestview FL. (AVH-18).
19 May 1972	Returned to 113 TFG ANG, Andrews AFB MD for further depot work (WM) by Dynalectron Corporation (DYNZZ).
6 Jun 1972	Combat capable (CC) at 113 TFG ANG, Andrews AFB MD.
5 Oct 1973	In contract depot work (WM) by Dynalectron Corporation (DYNZZ) at Andrews AFB MD. (AVH-20).
15 Oct 1973	Combat capable (CC) at 113 TFG ANG, Andrews AFB MD.
6 Dec 1973	In contract depot work (WM) by Dynalectron Corporation (DYNZZ) at Andrews AFB MD.
10 Dec 1973	Combat capable (CC) at 113 TFG ANG, Andrews AFB MD.

3 Jan 1974	In contract depot work (WM) by Dynalectron Corporation (DYNZZ) at Andrews AFB MD.
8 Jan 1974	Combat capable (CC) at 113 TFG ANG, Andrews AFB MD. (AVH-22).
22 Apr 1974	In contract depot work (WM) by Dynalectron Corporation (DYNZZ) at Andrews AFB MD.
23 Apr 1974	Combat capable (CC) at 113 TFG ANG, Andrews AFB MD.
14 May 1974	In contract depot maintenance (WK) by Fairchild Engine and Aircraft Corporation (FACCF) at Bob Sikes Municipal Airport, Crestview FL.
20 Sep 1974	Combat capable (CC) at 113 TFG ANG, Andrews AFB MD.
30 Nov 1974	Assigned organization redesignated 113 TFW ANG, Andrews AFB MD.
14 Apr 1975	In contract depot maintenance (WM) by Dynalectron Corporation (DYNZZ) at Andrews AFB MD. (AVH-23 & AVH-24).
28 Apr 1975	At 113 TFW ANG, Andrews AFB MD.
25 Jan 1977	In depot maintenance by SM-ALC at Andrews AFB MD. 1,808.0 flying hours. (AVH-25 & AVH-26).
7 Feb 1977	At 113 TFW ANG, Andrews AFB MD. 1,808.0 flying hours.
22 Jan 1980	In contract depot maintenance by Dynalectron Corporation (DYNZZ) at Andrews AFB MD. 2,531.3 flying hours. (GO33B 24 Jun 80).
28 Feb 1980	At 113 TFW, Andrews AFB MD. 2,575.0 flying hours.
25 Sep 1981	At ADTC, Eglin AFB FL. Declared "Excess to command" (XJ). 2,793.7 flying hours. (GO33B Dec 81 & GO33B 1 Feb 83).
31 Oct 1981	At ADTC, Eglin AFB FL. 2,811.8 flying hours. Inventory account "ZJ."

F-105D-5RE 59-1738

Republic Production No: D-50 Production Sequence No: 130

Location: Displayed as "60-0517" at Linear Air Park, Dyess AFB, Abilene, Texas.

Aircraft Chronology

9 Nov 1960	USAF production acceptance from Republic Aviation, Farmingdale NY. (ACA-84).
12 Nov 1960	Delivered to 4520 CCTW, Nellis AFB NV.
1 Aug 1961	At 4520 CCTW, Nellis AFB NV for combat crew training (TF).
9 Jan 1962	Transferred to APGC AFSC, Eglin AFB FL.
15 Jan 1962	Bailed to Republic Aviation at Eglin AFB FL.
6 Jun 1962	Bailed to Republic Aviation at APGC Eglin AFB FL. (RAC record).
13 Mar 1963	At AFSC, Eglin AFB FL for test support (EH). (ACA-84).
31 Jul 1964	At AFSC, Eglin AFB FL as JF-105D for test support (EH). (AVH-1).
9 Apr 1965	In depot maintenance (WM) by "LASON" at Eglin AFB FL. (AVH-3).
25 May 1965	At PGCC Eglin AFB FL as JF-105D for test support (EH).
23 Dec 1965	At MOAMA, Brookley AFB AL for depot maintenance (WO).
23 Mar 1966	At PGCC AFSC, Eglin AFB FL as JF-105D for test support (EH). (AVH-5).
3 Feb 1967	At PGCC AFSC, for test and test support (EH) at Eglin AFB FL. (AVH-7).
9 Feb 1967	Assigned to AFLC for test and test support and bailed (EB) to Republic Aviation at Eglin AFB FL.
25 Jun 1968	At SMAMA, McClellan AFB CA for test (EI). (AVH-10).

26 Aug 1968	At Eglin AFB FL bailed (EB) to Republic Aviation.
6 Sep 1968	At SMAMA, McClellan AFB CA for test (EI).
22 Oct 1968	At Eglin AFB FL bailed (EB) to Republic Aviation.
1 Oct 1968	At SMAMA, McClellan AFB CA for test (EI).
21 Nov 1968	At SMAMA, McClellan AFB CA for depot work (WO).
7 Apr 1969	Transferred to 23 TFW, McConnell AFB KS. (AVH-12).
28 Apr 1969	In depot maintenance (WM) by SMAMA at McConnell AFB KS.
28 Apr 1969	At 23 TFW, McConnell AFB KS.
29 Jun 1969	In depot work (WO) at SMAMA, McClellan AFB CA.
7 Oct 1969	Returned to 23 TFW, McConnell AFB KS.
8 May 1970	At 23 TFW, McConnell AFB KS. (AVH-14).
17 Jun 1971	In contract depot maintenance (WK) by Fairchild Engine and Aircraft Corporation (FACCF) at Bob Sikes Municipal Airport, Crestview FL. (AVH-16).
13 Jul 1971	Transferred to 113 TFG ANG, Andrews AFB MD.
13 Apr 1972	In depot work (WM) by Dynalectron Corporation (DYNZZ) at Andrews AFB MD. (AVH-18).
27 Apr 1972	Returned to 113 TFG ANG, Andrews AFB MD.
25 May 1972	In contract depot maintenance (WK) by Fairchild Engine and Aircraft Corporation (FACCF) at Bob Sikes Municipal Airport, Crestview FL.
21 Jun 1972	Returned to 113 TFG ANG, Andrews AFB MD.
24 Feb 1973	In contract depot work (WM by Dynalectron Corporation (DYNZZ) at Andrews AFB MD. (AVH-20).
14 Mar 1973	Combat capable (CC) at 113 TFG ANG, Andrews AFB MD.
26 Apr 1973	In contract depot work (WM by Dynalectron Corporation (DYNZZ) at Andrews AFB MD.
4 May 1973	Combat capable (CC) at 113 TFG ANG, Andrews AFB MD.
25 Sep 1973	In contract depot work (WM by Dynalectron Corporation (DYNZZ) at Andrews AFB MD.
5 Oct 1973	Combat capable (CC) at 113 TFG ANG, Andrews AFB MD.
14 Dec 1973	In contract depot maintenance (WK) by Fairchild Engine and Aircraft Corporation (FACCF) at Bob Sikes Municipal Airport, Crestview FL.
6 Jun 1974	At 113 TFG ANG, Andrews AFB MD. (AVH-22).
25 Sep 1974	In contract depot maintenance (WM) by Dynalectron Corporation (DYNZZ) at Andrews AFB MD.
19 Oct 1974	Combat capable (CC) at 113 TFG ANG, Andrews AFB MD.
30 Nov 1974	Assigned organization redesignated 113 TFW ANG, Andrews AFB MD.
24 Mar 1975	In contract depot maintenance (WM) by Dynalectron Corporation (DYNZZ) at Andrews AFB MD. (AVH-23).
28 Mar 1975	At 113 TFW ANG, Andrews AFB MD.
12 Nov 1975	In contract depot maintenance (WM) by Dynalectron Corporation (DYNZZ) at Andrews AFB MD. (AVH-23 & AVH-24).
14 Nov 1975	At 113 TFW ANG , Andrews AFB MD.
26 Nov 1979	At General Dynamics, Ft. Worth TX (DYNFW) for contract depot maintenance. 2,551.1 flying hours. (GO33B 24 Jun 80).
19 Dec 1979	At 113 TFW, Andrews AFB MD. 2,551.1 flying hours.
28 Aug 1981	At 113 TFG ANG, Andrews AFB MD. Being processed for museum (ZW). 2,835.7 flying hours. (GO33B Dec 81 & GO33B 1 Feb 83).
28 Aug 1981	Arrived at Dyess AFB TX for static display. Gun removed but engine remained installed. Aircraft sponsored by Cooper High School Jr. ROTC until 1993. Instructor: Lt. Col. John C. Wright, USAF Ret., an F-105 pilot who flew 140 missions in SEA in F-105D 60-0517, "The Yellow Rose." (Richard A. Warner, Director, Linear Air Park in letter, 17 Sep 1996).

This F-105D 59-1738 had a relatively peaceful career remaining within the United States while many of its sisters contended with the rigors of combat in South East Asia. After a short stay training pilots to fly F-105s at Nellis Air Force Base, Nevada, it became a test bird for six years at Eglin Air Force Base, Florida. As did most F-105s, it spent some time with the 23 Tactical Fighter Wing at McConnell Air Force Base, Kansas, and then, beginning in 1971, went to the Washington DC Air National Guard at Andrews Air Force Base, Maryland. Ten years later it retired to Dyess Air Force Base, Texas, with only 2,800 hours on its airframe, one of the lowest-time surviving Thunderchiefs. It is displayed with the serial number and markings of another F-105D that was flown over Vietnam by one of its original sponsors at Dyess. (Photograph by author, 13 October 1996.)

F-105D-5RE 59-1739

Republic Production No: D-51 Production Sequence No: 131

Location: Displayed at the American Airpower Heritage Museum, Midland, Texas.

Aircraft Name(s)	Crew	Unit	Date	Description
Queen of the Fleet		388 TFW		Witch with broom
Bulldog I		354 TFS 355 TFW		Bulldog with beer mug
Queen of the Fleet		149 TFS VA ANG		Nude woman with pistol wearing holster, vest, boots and hat next to saloon with "Sierra Hotel" on sign. Name in white letters on red banner
Rum Runner		34 TFS 388 TFW	Jun 67	
Peanuts	Capt. Donald W. Kilgus	44 TFS 355 TFW	Oct 70	

Aircraft Chronology

14 Sep 1960 USAF production acceptance from Republic Aviation, Farmingdale NY. (ACA-84).

16 Sep 1960 Delivered to 4526 CCTS, 4520 CCTW, Nellis AFB NV.

14 Apr 1961	At Republic Aviation, Farmingdale NY for depot work (WK).
9 Aug 1961	Returned to 4520 CCTW, Nellis AFB NV for combat crew training (TF).
28 Feb 1962	While assigned to the 4520 CCTW, Nellis AFB NV, the aircraft flew 11:20 hours for the month of February 1962 and had accumulated 201:45 flying hours. (4520 CCTW History, Jan–Jun 62, USAF microfilm M2197).
17 Apr 1962	In depot work (WZ) by MOAMA at Nellis AFB NV. (ACA-84).
2 May 1962	At 4520 CCTW, Nellis AFB NV for combat crew training (TF).
9 Oct 1962	At MOAMA Brookley AFB AL for depot work.
27 Nov 1962	Returned to 4520 CCTW, Nellis AFB NV.
24 Sep 1963	At Republic Aviation, Farmingdale NY for contract work (WK).
15 Apr 1964	At Eglin AFB FL for depot work (WK). (AVH-1).
25 Apr 1964	Transferred to the 23 TFW, McConnell AFB KS. (AVH-1).
24 Apr 1965	Deployed on TDY to Yokota AB with 561 TFS, 23 TFW from McConnell AFB KS under "Operation One Buck Nine." (AVH-3).
16 Jul 1965	At 23 TFW, McConnell AFB KS.
25 Oct 1965	At Republic Aviation, Crestview FL (RACFA) for contract depot work (WK).
19 Nov 1965	Returned to 23 TFW, McConnell AFB KS.
21 Jan 1966	Transferred to 6234 TFW, Korat RTAB, Thailand. (AVH-5)
6 Nov 1966	At Air Asia, Tainan, Taiwan for contract depot work (WK).
31 Dec 1966	At 388 TFW, Korat RTAB, Thailand.
3 Jul 1967	Assigned to 355 TFW, Takhli RTAB, Thailand. (AVH-7).
7 Jul 1967	As "Rum Runner," the aircraft flew a combat mission from Takhli RTAB, Thailand. Its load was 750-pound bombs on the center line rack and a Shrike missile on an outboard pylon. Chaplain Maj. Philip E. Grimmett, Jr. gave the pilot a departing "thumbs-up" send-off in the arming area. (National Archives motion picture film shot list, control No. NWDNM(m)-342-USAF-43022).
29 Sep 1967	At 355 TFW, Takhli RTAB, Thailand.
3 Oct 1967	Flown by Maj. Donald M. Russell (333 TFS, 355 TFW) on a combat mission that lasted 3.6 hours from Takhli RTAB, Thailand. (Maj. Russell's Individual Flight Record as of 31 Dec 67).
17 Nov 1967	Flown by Capt. Gene I. Basel (354 TFS, 355 TFW) on a mission lasting 2.5 hours from Takhli RTAB, Thailand. (Capt. Basel's Individual Flight Record as of 31 Dec 67).
22 Nov 1967	Flown by Capt. Gene I. Basel (354 TFS, 355 TFW) on a mission lasting 1.9 hours from Takhli RTAB, Thailand.
27 Nov 1967	Flown by Capt. Gene I. Basel (354 TFS, 355 TFW) on a mission lasting 2.6 hours from Takhli RTAB, Thailand.
14 Dec 1967	While flown by the 355 TFW from Takhli RTAB, Thailand, during a strike on the Hanoi Railroad and Highway Bridge, the aircraft received battle damage from AAA consisting of a 2 3/4" X 1 1/4" hole in the left leading edge of the horizontal stabilator. (355 TFW History, Oct–Dec 67, USAF microfilm NO463).
26 Feb 1968	In depot work (WM) by SMAMA at Takhli RTAB, Thailand. (AVH-10).
28 Feb 1968	At 355 TFW, Takhli RTAB, Thailand.
23 Apr 1968	In depot work (WM) by SMAMA at Takhli RTAB, Thailand.
27 Apr 1968	At 355 TFW, Takhli RTAB, Thailand.
12 Jul 1968	While assigned to the 355 TFW, Takhli RTAB, aircraft received battle damage when a M-117 bomb being dropped struck the fuselage in panel FF44. The panel was torn 16 inches by 5 inches. (355 TFW History, Jul–Sep 68, USAF microfilm NO465).
7 Sep 1968	In depot work (WM) by SMAMA at Takhli RTAB, Thailand. (AVH-10).
11 Sep 1968	At 355 TFW, Takhli RTAB, Thailand.

Six years after it was produced, following peaceful periods at Nellis Air Force Base, Nevada, and McConnell Air Force Base, Kansas, this plane found itself flying combat missions over North Vietnam, first from Korat then from Takhli air bases in Thailand. During its years with the 355 Tactical Fighter Wing at Takhli, the plane was damaged at least twice, patched up and sent back for more. When its combat tour ended just before Takhli closed in late 1970, the plane returned to McConnell for a short while before going to the Air National Guard at Andrews Air Force Base, Maryland. For its last nine years, it served as "*Queen of the Fleet*" with the Virginia Air National Guard and was then displayed at Gila Bend, Arizona. In 1994, it moved to the Confederate Air Force's American Airpower Heritage Museum at Midland, Texas. (Photograph by author, 12 October 1996.)

23 Sep 1968	In depot work (WM) by SMAMA at Takhli RTAB, Thailand.
25 Sep 1968	At 355 TFW, Takhli RTAB, Thailand.
26 Oct 1968	At Air Asia, Tainan, Taiwan, for contract depot work (WK).
1 Nov 1968	While in the depot from the 355 TFW, Takhli RTAB, Thailand, the aircraft had accumulated 2,644.2 flying hours. (355 TFW History, Oct–Dec 68, USAF microfilm NO466).
6 Dec 1968	Returned to 355 TFW, Takhli RTAB, Thailand.
28 Feb 1969	While assigned to the 355 TFW, Takhli RTAB, Thailand, the aircraft flew 57.9 hours during the month of February 1969 and had accumulated 2,767.2 flying hours. (355 TFW History, Jan–Mar 69, Vol. II, USAF Microfilm NO467).
17 Mar 1969	At 355 TFW, Takhli RTAB, Thailand. (AVH-12).
27 Apr 1969	At 355 TFW, Takhli RTAB, Thailand being prepared for transfer (PL).
11 May 1969	In depot work (WO) at SMAMA, McClellan AFB CA.
13 Feb 1970	At 355 TFW, Takhli RTAB, Thailand. (AVH-14).
19 Apr 1970	In depot maintenance (WM) by SMAMA at Takhli RTAB, Thailand.
4 May 1970	At 355 TFW, Takhli RTAB, Thailand.
19 Oct 1970	Transferred to 23 TFW, McConnell AFB KS.

17 Jun 1971	In contract depot maintenance (WK) by Fairchild Engine and Aircraft Corporation (FACCF) at Bob Sikes Municipal Airport, Crestview FL. (AVH-16).
13 Jul 1971	Transferred to 113 TFG ANG, Andrews AFB MD.
28 Jul 1971	At 113 TFG ANG, Andrews AFB MD.
11 Feb 1972	Transferred to 192 TFG ANG, Byrd Field, Richmond VA. (AVH-18).
4 Aug 1972	In contract depot maintenance (WK) by Fairchild Engine and Aircraft Corporation (FACCF) at Bob Sikes Municipal Airport, Crestview FL.
29 Aug 1972	Returned to 192 TFG ANG, Byrd Field VA.
7 Mar 1973	In contract depot maintenance (WM) by Dynalectron Corporation (DYNZZ) at Byrd Field VA. (AVH-20).
10 Mar 1973	At 192 TFG ANG, Byrd Field VA.
15 Jan 1974	In contract depot maintenance (WM) by Dynalectron Corporation (DYNZZ) at Byrd Field VA. (AVH-22).
1 Feb 1974	At 192 TFG ANG, Byrd Field VA.
24 Oct 1974	In contract depot maintenance (WM) by Dynalectron Corporation (DYNZZ) at Byrd Field VA.
8 Jan 1975	At 192 TFG ANG, Byrd Field VA. (AVH-23).
22 Jul 1977	In contract depot maintenance (WM) by Dynalectron Corporation (DYNZZ) at Byrd Field, Richmond VA. 3,834.0 flying hours. (AVH-25 & AVH-26).
9 Aug 1977	At 192 TFG ANG, Byrd Field, Richmond VA. 3,836.0 flying hours.
6 Apr 1978	At 192 TFG ANG, Byrd Field, Richmond VA. 3,919.0 flying hours.
2 Jun 1978	At 192 TFG ANG, Byrd Field, Richmond VA. 3,983.0 flying hours.
2 Oct 1979	In depot maintenance (WM) by Dynalectron Corporation (DYNZZ) at Byrd Field, Richmond VA. 4,120.1 flying hours. (AVH-27).
7 Nov 1979	At 192 TFG ANG, Byrd Field, Richmond VA. 4,120.1 flying hours.
24 Sep 1981	At 192 TFG ANG, Byrd Field, Richmond VA. Being processed for museum (ZW). 4,419.7 flying hours. (GO33B Dec 81 & GO33B 1 Feb 83).
23 Sep 1986	Displayed as "Queen of The Fleet" at Gila Bend Air Field AZ.
May 1994	Moved from Gila Bend AZ to Midland TX for display by the Confederate Air Force.

F-105D-5RE 59-1743

Republic Production No: D-55 Production Sequence No: 135

Location: Displayed outside of Aerospace Museum, Hill AFB, Ogden, Utah.

Aircraft Name(s)	Crew	Unit	Date	Description
Darn Dago		13 TFS 388 TFW	Jun 67	
Arkansas Traveler	Col. Paul P. Douglas, Jr.	34 TFS 388 TFW	Dec 68	Two figures riding on bomb. "Arkansas Traveler" in arc below. Eight swastikas below cockpit on port side.
Lead Zeppelin	1Lt Glen Cloes	354 TFS 355 TFW	Jan 70	Name on intake, artwork on fuselage.
Hanoi Express		149 TFS VA ANG	Jun 79	100 mission patch, River Rats emblem and Yankee Air Pirates flag above name.

This "D" spent the first five years of its life as a trainer. On its initial assignment in 1960 to the growing Thunderchief fleet at Nellis Air Force Base, Nevada, it trained early F-105 pilots, one of whom landed the plane without its canopy when he failed to lock it down. The plane then moved to the 4 Tactical Fighter Wing and its F-105 training program at Seymour Johnson Air Force Base, North Carolina. The increasing loss rate of F-105s in South East Asia sent the plane to combat in mid-1966 with the 388 Tactical Fighter Wing at Korat, Thailand. Throughout 1968, as the "*Arkansas Traveler*," it was the personal mount of the 388th wing commander, Colonel Paul P. Douglas, Jr. Colonel Douglas was a World War II fighter ace in Europe where he had eight swastikas, representing the German planes he shot down, painted on his P-47D Thunderbolt, also named "*Arkansas Traveler.*" Over 30 years later, he painted the same swastikas on the Thunderchief that carried him to a different war. After the plane returned home in 1970, it spent the last eight years of service with the Air National Guard at Richmond, Virginia. It retired in 1981 to the Aerospace Museum at Hill Air Force Base, Utah, where it was redecorated with an erroneous serial number, "61-1743," and Colonel Douglas' eight swastikas. (Photograph by author, 25 March 1997.)

Aircraft Chronology

30 Nov 1960 USAF production acceptance from Republic Aviation, Farmingdale NY. (ACA-84).

1 Dec 1960 Delivered to 4520 CCTW, Nellis AFB NV for combat crew training (TF).

19 May 1961 While assigned to 4520 CCTW, Nellis AFB, NV, the aircraft lost its canopy shortly after takeoff when the pilot failed to secure the canopy locks. (4520 CCTW History, Jan–Jun 61, USAF microfilm MO2195).

17 Aug 1961 At Republic Aviation, Farmingdale NY.

12 Nov 1961 Returned to 4520 CCTW, Nellis AFB NV.

28 Feb 1962 While assigned to the 4520 CCTW, Nellis AFB NV, the aircraft flew 4:00 hours for the month of February 1962 and had accumulated 180:30 flying hours. (4520 CCTW History, Jan–Jun 62, USAF microfilm M2197).

9 Oct 1962 At MOAMA, Brookley AFB AL for depot work.

19 Nov 1962 Returned to 4520 CCTW, Nellis AFB NV.

21 Apr 1964 Transferred to 4 TFW, Seymour Johnson AFB NC. (AVH-1).

31 Dec 1964 While assigned to the 4 TFW at Seymour Johnson AFB NC, the aircraft had 473.3 total flying hours. Assigned crew chief: SSgt. Collins. (4 TFW History, Jul–Dec 64, Vol. II, USAF microfilm MO292).

20 Apr 1965 At SMAMA, McClellan AFB CA for depot work (WO). (AVH-3).

13 May 1965 At 4 TFW, Seymour Johnson AFB NC.

20 Aug 1965 At MOAMA, Brookley AFB AL for depot work (WO).

28 Nov 1965 Returned to 4 TFW, Seymour Johnson AFB NC.

30 Nov 1965 While assigned to the 4 TFW, Seymour Johnson AFB NC, the aircraft flew 1.9 hours for the month of

	November 1965 and had 640.9 total flying hours. Assigned crew chief: SSgt. McKinley. (4 TFW History, Jul–Dec 65, Vol. II, USAF microfilm MO292).
31 Dec 1965	While assigned to the 4 TFW, Seymour Johnson AFB NC, the aircraft flew 25.5 hours for the month of December 1965 and had 666.3 total flying hours. Assigned crew chief: SSgt. Medlin. (4 TFW History, Jul–Dec 65, Vol. II, USAF microfilm MO292).
14 Jun 1966	Transferred to the 388 TFW, Korat RTAB, Thailand. (AVH-5).
21 May 1967	At the 388 TFW, Korat RTAB, Thailand. (AVH-7).
1 Jun 1967	Combat damaged (VO) at the 388 TFW, Korat RTAB, Thailand.
29 Jun 1967	In depot maintenance (WM) by SMAMA field team at Korat RTAB, Thailand.
2 Jul 1967	Combat damaged (VO) at the 388 TFW, Korat RTAB, Thailand.
3 Aug 1967	At the 388 TFW, Korat RTAB, Thailand.
27 Sep 1967	Flown on a Rolling Thunder mission (RT56A-147) by Maj Stanley H. Horne from the 469 TFS, 388 TFW, Korat RTAB, Thailand. The target was at coordinates 17-22-40N and 106-13-30E near the Ban Karai pass in RP-1, North Vietnam. (National Archives strike camera film shot list, item 42649B).
6 Oct 1967	One of three F-105Ds flown on a Rolling Thunder mission (RT56A-156) by pilots from the 469 TFS, 388 TFW, Korat RTAB, Thailand. They struck the Mo Trong railroad bridge NE of Hanoi, North Vietnam, at coordinates 21-30N and 106-07E. The pilot was Capt Frederick.
11 Oct 1967	One of two F-105Ds flown on a Rolling Thunder mission (RT56A-161) by pilots from the 469 TFS, 388 TFW, Korat RTAB, Thailand. They struck an underground storage area NE of Hanoi, North Vietnam, at coordinates 21-26N and 106-09E. The pilot was Capt Burney.
18 Oct 1967	Flown on a Rolling Thunder mission (RT56A-168) by Lt Col William N. Reed from the 469 TFS, 388 TFW, Korat RTAB, Thailand. He dropped M-117 750-lb bombs on the target, the Lang Dang railroad complex, at coordinates 21-38N and 106-35E in North Vietnam.
25 Oct 1967	Flown on a Rolling Thunder mission (RT56A-175) by Maj Blakeslee from the 34 TFS, 388 TFW, Korat RTAB, Thailand. The target was at 21-02-31N and 105-54-30E in Hanoi, North Vietnam.
27 Oct 1967	One of five F-105Ds flown on a Rolling Thunder mission (RT56A-177) by pilots from the 469 TFS and 44 TFS, 388 TFW, Korat RTAB, Thailand. They struck a storage area in Hanoi, North Vietnam, at coordinates 20-59-06N and 105-50-35E. The pilot was Lt Col William N. Reed from the 469 TFS. The plane received combat damage (VO) during the mission. (AVH-7).
28 Oct 1967	In depot maintenance (WM) by SMAMA field team at Korat RTAB, Thailand.
31 Oct 1967	At 388 TFW, Korat RTAB, Thailand.
22 Dec 1967	Being prepared (PL) for flight to depot by 388 TFW from Korat RTAB, Thailand.
23 Dec 1967	At Air Asia, Tainan, Taiwan, for contract depot work (WK).
5 Mar 1968	Returned to 388 TFW, Korat RTAB, Thailand. (AVH-10).
31 Oct 1968	Aircraft had accumulated 2,195.2 flying hours while assigned to the 388 TFW, Korat RTAB, Thailand. (388 TFW History, Oct–Dec 68, USAF microfilm NO585).
31 Jan 1969	At Takhli RTAB, Thailand, with the 388 TFW during runway repair at Korat RTAB, Thailand.
31 Jan 1969	At Takhli RTAB, Thailand, with the 388 TFW during runway repair at Korat RTAB, Thailand. Aircraft was flown by a pilot from the 44 TFS on a strike mission in the Barrel Roll region of Laos. (AVH-12 & 388 TFW History, Jan–Mar 69, USAF microfilm NO586).
23 Feb 1969	Aircraft was flown by a pilot from the 44 TFS, 388 TFW, on a strike mission in the Steel Tiger region of Laos while operating from Takhli RTAB, Thailand. (388 TFW History, Jan–Mar 69, USAF microfilm NO586).
25 Feb 1969	Aircraft was flown by a pilot from the 44 TFS, 388 TFW, on a strike mission in the Steel Tiger region of Laos while operating from Takhli RTAB, Thailand.
5 Mar 1969	At Air Asia, Tainan, Taiwan, for contract depot work (WK). (AVH-12).
24 Apr 1969	Returned to 388 TFW, Korat RTAB, Thailand.
30 Apr 1969	While assigned to the 34 TFS, 388 TFW, Korat RTAB, Thailand, the aircraft had accumulated 2,436.1 flying hours. (388 TFW History, Apr–Jun 69, USAF microfilm NO586).

8 May 1969	Transferred from the 34 TFS at Korat RTAB to the 355 TFW, Takhli RTAB, Thailand, when the 34 TFS converted to F-4Es. (AVH-12).
1 Dec 1969	In depot maintenance (WM) by SMAMA at Takhli RTAB, Thailand.
13 Dec 1969	At 355 TFW, Takhli RTAB, Thailand.
19 Oct 1970	Transferred (PL) to 23 TFW, McConnell AFB KS. (AVH-14).
27 Oct 1970	Place in flyable storage (PR) at 23 TFW, McConnell AFB KS.
4 Jan 1971	At 23 TFW, McConnell AFB KS being prepared for transfer (PL).
28 Jan 1971	Transferred to 192 TFG ANG (CC), Byrd Field, Richmond VA. (AVH-16).
26 May 1971	At SMAMA, McClellan AFB CA for depot work (WO).
11 Feb 1972	Returned to 192 TFG ANG (CC), Byrd Field, Richmond VA. (AVH-18).
18 Aug 1972	In depot maintenance (WM) by Dynalectron Corporation (DYNZZ) at Byrd Field, Richmond VA.
12 Sep 1972	At 192 TFG ANG (CC), Byrd Field, Richmond VA.
27 Sep 1972	In contract depot maintenance (WK) by Fairchild Engine and Aircraft Corporation (FACCF) at Bob Sikes Municipal Airport, Crestview FL.
25 Oct 1972	Returned to 192 TFG ANG (CC), Byrd Field, Richmond VA.
29 Mar 1973	In depot maintenance (WM) by Dynalectron Corporation (DYNZZ) at Byrd Field, Richmond VA. (AVH-20).
31 Mar 1973	At 192 TFG ANG (CC), Byrd Field, Richmond VA.
13 Apr 1973	In depot maintenance (WM) by Dynalectron Corporation (DYNZZ) at Byrd Field, Richmond VA.
17 Apr 1973	At 192 TFG ANG (CC), Byrd Field, Richmond VA.
28 Aug 1973	In depot maintenance (WM) by Dynalectron Corporation (DYNZZ) at Byrd Field, Richmond VA.
31 Aug 1973	At 192 TFG ANG (CC), Byrd Field, Richmond VA.
14 Dec 1973	In contract depot maintenance (WM) by Dynalectron Corporation (DYNZZ) at Byrd Field, Richmond VA.
28 Dec 1973	At 192 TFG ANG (CC), Byrd Field, Richmond VA.
19 Mar 1975	In contract depot maintenance (WM) by Dynalectron Corporation (DYNZZ) at Byrd Field, Richmond VA. (AVH-23).
9 Apr 1975	At 192 TFG ANG (CC), Byrd Field, Richmond VA.
13 May 1976	In depot work (DK) by Aero Corporation (ARDLF) at Moultrie GA. 3,919 flying hours. (AVH-24).
21 Jul 1976	Returned to 192 TFG ANG (CC), Byrd Field, Richmond VA. 3,953 flying hours.
1 Oct 1976	In contract depot maintenance (WM) by Dynalectron Corporation (DYNZZ) at Byrd Field, Richmond VA. 3,953 flying hours.
3 Dec 1976	At 192 TFG ANG (CC), Byrd Field, Richmond VA. 3,974 flying hours.
9 Jul 1977	In contract depot maintenance (WM) by Dynalectron Corporation (DYNZZ) at Byrd Field, Richmond VA. 4,033.0 flying hours. (AVH-25 & AVH-26).
18 Jul 1977	At 192 TFG ANG, Byrd Field, Richmond VA. 4,033.0 flying hours.
3 Oct 1979	In depot maintenance (WM) by Dynalectron Corporation (DYNZZ) at Byrd Field, Richmond VA. 4,321.3 flying hours. (AVH-27).
7 Nov 1979	At 192 TFG ANG, Byrd Field, Richmond VA. 4,327.3 flying hours.
27 Feb 1981	At 192 TFG ANG, Byrd Field, Richmond VA. Being processed for museum (ZW). 4,499.9 flying hours. (GO33B Dec 81 & GO33B 1 Feb 83). Flown to Hill AFB Museum.
25 Feb 1984	On static display in the 419 TFW hangar for Thud Out Ceremony at Hill AFB UT. Had "JJ" tail code for 34 TFS at Korat RTAB, Thailand. (Photo from Ronald H. "Gabby" Hays, retired F-105 crew chief).

F-105D–6RE 59-1771

Republic Production No: D-83 Production Sequence No: 163

Location: Displayed outside AMVETS Post 2256, Circleville, Ohio.

Aircraft Name(s)	Crew	Unit	Date	Description
Foley's Folly/Ohio Express	Capt. Peter K. Foley	469 TFS 388 TFW	Sep 68	River Rats Shield & first name on fuselage left side below wing, second name on right.
Underdog II	Capt. Al Adams	357 TFS 355 TFW	Jan 70	On both intakes. Underdog cartoon on left side. 357 TFS crest on left side.
Dynamic Duo		149 TFS 192 TFG	Sep 79	Red letters with Rocky and Bullwinkle under wing.

Aircraft Chronology

16 Dec 1960	USAF production acceptance from Republic Aviation, Farmingdale NY. (ACA-84)
20 Dec 1960	Delivered to the 4520 CCTW, Nellis AFB, NV for combat crew training (TF).
28 Feb 1962	While assigned to the 4520 CCTW, Nellis AFB NV, the aircraft had accumulated 204:00 flying hours. (4520 CCTW History, Jan–Jun 62, USAF microfilm M2197).
16 Apr 1962	In depot work (WO) at MOAMA, Brookley AFB AL.
17 Nov 1962	Returned to the 4520 CCTW, Nellis AFB, NV for combat crew training (TF).
17 Oct 1963	Completed contract work (WK) by Republic Aviation at Farmingdale NY and transferred to the 355 TFW, George AFB CA.
24 Jul 1964	Transferred with the 355 TFW to McConnell AFB KS when the 355th moved from George AFB CA. (AVH-1).
7 Apr 1965	Deployed on TDY to Kadena AB, Okinawa, with the 421 TFS, 355 TFW, from McConnell AFB KS under "Operation Two Buck 3." Assigned crew chief: SSgt. Lawrence. (18 TFW History, Jan–Jun 65, USAF microfilm MO497).
29 Jun 1965	In depot work (WO) by MOAMA at Brookley AFB AL. (AVH-3).
23 Sep 1965	Returned to the 355 TFW, McConnell AFB KS.
19 Oct 1965	In depot work (WO) by SMAMA at McClellan AFB CA.
17 Nov 1965	Transferred to the 23 TFW, McConnell AFB KS when the 355 TFW moved to Takhli RTAB, Thailand.
7 Dec 1966	Transferred to the 6441 TFW, Yokota AB, Japan. (AVH-5).
28 Feb 1966	Deployed from the 6441 TFW for combat operations at Takhli RTAB, Thailand, as an attrition replacement aircraft.
20 May 1966	At Osan AB, Korea for nuclear alert with the 6441 TFW.
12 Jul 1966	In depot work (WO) by SMAMA at McClellan AFB CA.
22 Nov 1966	Transferred (PL) to the 23 TFW, McConnell AFB KS.
28 Nov 1966	Combat capable (CC) at the 23 TFW, McConnell AFB KS.
29 Nov 1966	In depot maintenance (WM) by SMAMA at McConnell AFB KS.
7 Dec 1966	Combat capable (CC) at the 23 TFW, McConnell AFB KS.
12 Jun 1967	At the 23 TFW, McConnell AFB KS being prepared for transfer (PL). (AVH-7).
17 Jun 1967	Transferred (PL) to the 388 TFW, Korat RTAB, Thailand, as an attrition replacement aircraft.
22 Jun 1967	Transferred (PL) to the 41 AD, Yokota AB, Japan.

This plane bounced around the United States and in and out of the Far East for its first seven years of service beginning with a short stay at the pilot training program at Nellis Air Force Base, Nevada. It then joined the 355 Tactical Fighter Wing in October 1963 at George Air Force Base, California, and moved nine months later when the wing transferred to McConnell Air Force Base, Kansas. After at least three trips from McConnell to Japan, Korea, and Thailand in 1966 and 1967, it settled down with the 388 Tactical Fighter Wing at Korat, Thailand. On 10 August 1968, as "*Foley's Folly/Ohio Express*," it carried its pilot, Captain Peter K. Foley, on his 200th combat mission over North Vietnam. It spent its last year in South East Asia with the 355 Tactical Fighter Wing at Takhli, Thailand. When Takhli began closing down at the end of 1970, the plane came home to McConnell and then transferred to the Virginia Air National Guard at Byrd Field in Richmond. By the time it joined the Guard, the plane had accumulated over 3,800 hours in ten years of flying – nearly four of them in combat. The Guardsmen added only 980 more hours before wing cracks doomed the plane to retirement. Its last flight was in June 1981, when it flew to desert storage in Arizona where it sat for sixteen years. Removed from retirement in 1998, it is now a memorial at the American Veterans post in Circleville, Ohio. The plane honors Captain William J. Barthelmas, Jr., an F-105 pilot from Circleville who was killed on a combat mission from Takhli in July 1965. (Photograph by author, 5 June 1998.)

5 Jul 1967	Combat capable (CC) at the 41 AD, Yokota AB, Japan.
27 Aug 1967	In depot maintenance (WM) by SMAMA field team at Kadena AB, Okinawa.
31 Aug 1967	Returned to the 41 AD, Yokota AB, Japan.
7 Sep 1967	At Osan AB, Korea for nuclear alert with the 41 AD.
3 Oct 1967	Returned to the 41 AD, Yokota AB, Japan.
20 Nov 1967	Transferred (PL) to the 388 TFW, Korat RTAB, Thailand.
24 Nov 1967	Combat capable (CC) at the 388 TFW, Korat RTAB, Thailand.
13 Dec 1967	Aircraft flown on a combat mission over North Vietnam by Dennis Jarvi from the 469 TFS, 388 TFW, Korat RTAB, Thailand. (Dennis Jarvi letter to Dick Cole, 19 May 1998).
26 Dec 1967	Aircraft flown on a combat mission over North Vietnam by Dennis Jarvi from the 469 TFS, 388 TFW, Korat RTAB, Thailand.
6 Mar 1968	In depot maintenance (WM) by SMAMA at Korat RTAB, Thailand.
8 Mar 1968	Combat capable (CC) at the 388 TFW, Korat RTAB, Thailand.
18 Apr 1968	Aircraft flown on a combat mission over North Vietnam by Dennis Jarvi from the 469 TFS, 388 TFW, Korat RTAB, Thailand. This mission was led by Capt. Peter K. Foley. (Dennis Jarvi letter to Dick Cole, 19 May 1998).

20 Apr 1968	In contract depot work (WK) by Air Asia at Tainan Airport, Taiwan.
9 Jun 1968	Returned (PL) to the 388 TFW, Korat RTAB, Thailand.
21 Jun 1968	Combat capable (CC) at the 388 TFW, Korat RTAB, Thailand.
10 Aug 1968	While assigned to the 469 TFS, 388 TFW, Korat RTAB, Thailand, the aircraft, named "Foley's Folly/ Ohio Express," was flown by Capt. Peter K. Foley on his 200th mission over North Vietnam. Capt. Foley was the third F-105 pilot to complete 200 missions. Other pilots in the flight, each completing his 100th mission, were: Maj. Ford H. Smart, Capt. Christopher H. Brown (469 TFS), and Maj. Bryant Heston. (Thunderchief Worldwide Report, Vol. IV, No. 1, September, 1968). "... I considered my decision to return to combat, under the circumstances (in 1968) to be 'an act or example of foolishness'—hence the name 'Foley's Folly' on 771. SSgt. John Lewis was 771's crew chief and asked me to have 'Ohio Express' placed on the right side of the aircraft." (Peter K. Foley in letter to Richard Cole, 13 January 1998).
10 Oct 1968	In depot maintenance (WM) by SMAMA at Korat RTAB, Thailand.
13 Oct 1968	Combat capable (CC) at the 388 TFW, Korat RTAB, Thailand.
29 Jan 1969	Operated with the 388 TFW from Takhli RTAB, Thailand, during runway repairs at Korat RTAB, Thailand. (AVH-12).
1 Mar 1969	Returned to Korat RTAB, Thailand with the 388 TFW.
20 Apr 1969	While assigned to the 388 TFW, Korat RTAB, Thailand, the aircraft's drag chute failed to deploy during landing. (388 TFW History, Apr–Jun 69, USAF microfilm NO586).
30 Apr 1969	While assigned to the 44 TFS, 388 TFW, Korat RTAB, Thailand, the aircraft flew 51 hours in the month of April 1969 and had accumulated 2,396.4 total flying hours. (388 TFW History, Apr–Jun 1969, USAF microfilm NO586).
3 May 1969	At 388 TFW, Korat RTAB, Thailand, being prepared for transfer (PL) to the depot. (AVH-12).
5 May 1969	In contract depot work (WK) by Air Asia (AAITT) at Tainan Airport, Taiwan. Aircraft time: 2,409.7 flying hours. Work included replacing left and right main landing gears and overhaul of nose gear. (AFTO Form 95 Significant Historical Data, entry dated 24 Jun 69).
25 Jun 1969	At Air Asia, Tainan Airport, Taiwan, being prepared for transfer (PL).
30 Jun 1969	Transferred (PL) to the 355 TFW, Takhli RTAB, Thailand.
15 Jul 1969	Combat capable (CC) at 355 TFW, Takhli RTAB, Thailand.
12 Jan 1970	In depot maintenance (WM) by SMAMA field team at Takhli RTAB, Thailand. (AVH-14).
26 Jan 1970	Combat capable (CC) at 355 TFW, Takhli RTAB, Thailand. Assigned crew chief was Gerald Urango. Aircraft was named "Underdog II."
22 Mar 1970	In battle damage repair (VO) at 355 TFW, Takhli RTAB, Thailand.
23 Mar 1970	Combat capable (CC) at 355 TFW, Takhli RTAB, Thailand.
5 Jun 1970	In battle damage repair (VJ) at Nakhon Phanom RTAB, Thailand.
10 Jun 1970	Returned to the 355 TFW, Takhli RTAB, Thailand.
19 Oct 1970	Transferred (PL) to 23 TFW, McConnell AFB KS when the 355 TFW was being deactivated and Takhli RTAB, Thailand closed.
27 Oct 1970	Placed in flyable storage (PR) under "Coronet Bighorn" at 23 TFW, McConnell AFB KS.
4 Jan 1971	At 23 TFW, McConnell AFB KS being prepared for transfer (PL).
2 Apr 1971	Transferred to the 192 TFG Virginia Air National Guard at Byrd Field, VA. (AVH-16).
8 Apr 1971	In depot work (WO) by SMAMA at McClellan AFB CA for Project A-17112-SM "Speedline" modification at 3,813.8 flying hours. (AFTO Form 95 Significant Historical Data, entry dated 25 May 71).
27 May 1971	Returned (PL) to 192 TFG VA ANG, Byrd Field VA.
29 Sep 1971	In contract depot maintenance (WM) by Dynalectron Corporation at Byrd Field VA.
25 Oct 1971	Combat capable (CC) at 192 TFG VA ANG, Byrd Field VA.
24 Apr 1972	In depot work (WO) by SMAMA at McClellan AFB CA for Project A-2-7036-SM at 3,237.0 flying hours. (AVH-18 & AFTO Form 95 Significant Historical Data, entry dated 17 Aug 72).

24 Aug 1972	Returned (PL) to 192 TFG VA ANG, Byrd Field VA.
21 Mar 1973	In contract depot maintenance (WM) by Dynalectron Corporation at Byrd Field VA. (AVH-20).
24 Mar 1973	Combat capable (CC) at 192 TFG VA ANG, Byrd Field VA.
28 Feb 1974	In contract depot maintenance (WM) by Dynalectron Corporation at Byrd Field VA. (AVH-22).
12 Mar 1974	Combat capable (CC) at 192 TFG VA ANG, Byrd Field VA.
27 May 1975	In contract depot maintenance (WM) by Dynalectron Corporation at Byrd Field VA. (AVH-23 & AVH-24).
3 Jul 1975	Combat capable (CC) at 192 TFG VA ANG, Byrd Field VA.
8 July 1975	The 192 TFG deactivated the Stablock system, the Fire Extinguisher system, and the VAI system (AFTO Form 95 Significant Historical Data, entry dated 8 July 75).
13 Feb 1976	In contract depot work (WK) (Analytical Condition Inspection) by Aero Corporation (AROLF) at Moultrie GA. Aircraft time was 3,902.6 flying hours. (AVH-24 & AFTO Form 95 Significant Historical Data, entry dated 20 May 76).
9 Jun 1976	Returned to 192 TFG VA ANG, Byrd Field VA. 3,969 flying hours.
18 Jul 1976	The 192 TFG VA ANG at Byrd Field VA discovered cracks in the right bottom forward wing side plate forging. (AFTO Form 95 Significant Historical Data, entry dated 18 July 76).
4 Jan 1977	In contract depot maintenance (DM) by Dynalectron Corporation at Byrd Field VA. 4,018 flying hours. (AVH-25 & AVH-26).
20 Jan 1977	At 192 TFG VA ANG, Byrd Field VA. 4,018 flying hours.
12 Feb 1977	The 192 TFG VA ANG at Byrd Field VA replaced the left and right main landing gear struts with overhauled struts received from Ogden ALC. Aircraft flying time: 4,029.9 hours. (AFTO Form 95 Significant Historical Data, entries dated 12 Feb 77).
2 Apr 1977	The aircraft's wings were removed for inspection at the 192 TFG VA ANG, Byrd Field VA. 4,067.3 flying hours. (AFTO Form 95 Significant Historical Data, entry dated 2 April 1977).
7 Apr 1977	In contract depot maintenance (DM) by Dynalectron Corporation at Byrd Field VA. 4,025 flying hours. (AVH-25 & AVH-26).
26 Apr 1977	Aircraft flown on a functional check flight by the 192 TFG VA ANG at Byrd Field VA after its wings were reinstalled. (AFTO Form 95 Significant Historical Data, entry dated 2 April 1977).
24 Feb 1978	The 192 TFG ANG at Byrd Field, Richmond VA, found and repaired cracks in both main landing gear ribs. (AFTO Form 95 Significant Historical Data, entry dated 24 Feb 1978).
11 Sep 1978	The aircraft's wings were removed for the third 400-hour inspection of the wing lugs at the 192 TFG ANG at Byrd Field, Richmond VA. No cracks were found. Aircraft flying time: 4,317.5 flying hours. (AFTO Form 95 Significant Historical Data, entry dated 12 Oct 1978).
12 Oct 1978	Aircraft flown on a functional check flight by the 192 TFG VA ANG at Byrd Field VA after its wings were reinstalled. (AFTO Form 95 Significant Historical Data, entry dated 12 Oct 1978).
4 Oct 1979	In depot maintenance (DO) at SM-ALC at McClellan AFB CA. 4,491.6 flying hours. (AVH-27). Aircraft received treatment for surface corrosion and was repainted.
3 Dec 1979	Returned to the 192 TFG ANG, Byrd Field, Richmond VA. 4,504.7 flying hours.
4 Jan 1980	The 192 TFG ANG at Byrd Field, Richmond VA installed an ARC-164 UHF radio as a modification to the aircraft per T.O. 1F-105-1291. (AFTO Form 95 Significant Historical Data, entry dated 4 Jan 80).
3 May 1980	The 192 TFG ANG at Byrd Field, Richmond VA installed a self-contained standby attitude indicator as a modification to the aircraft per T.O. 1F-105-1287. (AFTO Form 95 Significant Historical Data, entry dated 3 May 80).
3 Feb 1981	The aircraft's wing lugs were inspected by the 192 TFG ANG at Byrd Field, Richmond VA. No cracks were found and the aircraft was flown on a "Wing Off Inspection" functional check flight. Aircraft flying time: 4,717.5 flying hours. (AFTO Form 95 Significant Historical Data, entry dated 3 Feb 81).
9 Feb 1981	The 192 TFG ANG at Byrd Field, Richmond VA inspected the aircraft's wings under safety TCTO 1F-105-1316 and found two cracks in the front inboard spar cap tangs of each wing. Aircraft flying time: 4,711.0 hours. (AFTO Form 95 Significant Historical Data, entry dated 9 Feb 1981).

5 Mar 1981	Due to wing cracks, the F-105 depot at SM-ALC, McClellan AFB CA authorized an "… unrestricted flight … to (aircraft) retirement from service or the end of FY 1981 whichever is earliest." (SM-ALC/MMSRBA msg. 052227Z Mar 81 to 192 TFG).
12 May 1981	The aircraft ground aborted for the AC generator not staying on line during an attempted flight by the 192 TFG ANG at Byrd Field, Richmond VA. (AFTO Form 781A entry dated 12/05/1).
25 Jun 1981	The 192 TFG ANG flew the aircraft from Byrd Field, Richmond VA to Davis-Monthan AFB AZ for MASDC storage. The aircraft had accumulated 4,795.7 flying hours. Lt. Col. James R. "Ralph" Shaw was the pilot who made the last flight. His final entry in the aircraft's maintenance record said "INFO—GOOD BYE AND THANKS FOR A SIERRA HOTEL TOUR—." TSgt. Thomas R. Dean, the aircraft's crew chief for the past 10 years, prepared it for its final flight. (AFTO Form 781A Maintenance Discrepancy and Work Document, and TSgt. Edward M. Kelleher, 192 FW Historian, Virginia Air National Guard, e-mails, 9 Aug 98 and 5 Nov 98).
22 Mar 1982	In MASDC storage, inventory account "ZD" (Test to Destruction) at Davis-Monthan AFB AZ. 4,752.7 flying hours. (GO33B 1 Feb 1983).
Aug 1997	Aircraft selected for transfer from AMARC for static display at AMVETS Post 2256, Circleville OH. (Dick Cole, phone interview 29 Nov 1997).
20 Jan 1998	Aircraft released from storage and placed in work at AMARC to prepare it for shipment to Circleville OH. ("AMARC Aircraft Disposition Activity for FY 96" report).
23 Feb 1998	AMARC preparation work completed.
12 Mar 1998	AMARC replaced the nose landing gear with one taken from F-105D 60-5385 that was being scrapped. Aircraft ready for shipment from AMARC. (AFTO Form 95 Significant Historical Data, entry dated 12 Mar 98).
24 Apr 1998	Aircraft arrived at Circleville Ohio from AMARC. To be assembled and painted by the 121 ARW ANG from Rickenbacker Airport, Columbus, Ohio, and volunteers from AMVETS Post 2256. Marked with "JV" tail code for the 469 TFS at Takhli. (Dick Cole, phone interview, 25 Apr 98).
6 Jun 1998	Dedication ceremony to Vietnam Veterans at AMVETS Post 2256, Circleville, Ohio. Displayed as a memorial to the first Circleville native to die in the Vietnam war, Capt. William J. Barthelmas, Jr., who was killed in the combat loss of F-105D 61-0177 on 27 July 1965. (The Herald, Circleville, Ohio, 9 June 1998).

F-105D-10RE 60-0445

Republic Production No: D-133 Production Sequence No: 213

Location: Stored at the National Air & Space Museum, Bldg. 22, at Silver Hill, Maryland.

Aircraft Name(s)	Crew	Unit	Date	Description
Entropy Machine		44 TFS 388 TFW	Jun 67	
Skipper Ship	Capt. Boyd	333 TFS 355 TFW	Jan 70	On both intakes
Spartan		333 TFS 355 TFW	Jan 70	On both intakes

Aircraft Chronology

31 Mar 1961	USAF production acceptance from Republic Aviation, Farmingdale NY. (ACA-86).
5 Apr 1961	At MOAMA, Brookley AFB AL for depot work.
13 May 1961	Delivered to 22 TFS, 36 TFW, Bitburg AB, Germany. Piloted by 1Lt Gary Retterbush, this was the first F-105 to land on European soil.

23 Jun 1961	At Ramstein AB, Germany with 36 TFW.
5 Jul 1961	Returned to 36 TFW, Bitburg AB, Germany.
6 Jun 1962	At 22 TFS, 36 TFW, Bitburg AB, Germany. (RAC record).
6 Jun 1963	At MOAMA, Brookley AFB for depot work. "Operation Look Alike," Phase II.
8 Jun 1963	Returned to 36 TFW, Bitburg AB, Germany.
4 Oct 1964	At Wheelus AB, Libya ,with 36 TFW. (AVH-2).
9 Oct 1964	At 36 TFW, Bitburg AB, Germany.
11 Oct 1964	At Wheelus AB, Libya, with 36 TFW.
17 Dec 1964	At 36 TFW, Bitburg AB, Germany.
8 Jan 1965	At 36 TFW, Bitburg AB, Germany. Assigned crew chief: A1C Robert C. Renparger. (36 OMS Special Order 31, signed by Maj. Hoyt S. Vandenberg, Jr., Commander).
7 Apr 1965	At Wheelus AB, Libya, with 36 TFW. (AVH-3).
1 May 1965	At 36 TFW, Bitburg AB, Germany.
4 May 1965	At Wheelus AB, Libya, with 36 TFW.
7 May 1965	At 36 TFW, Bitburg AB, Germany.
10 May 1965	At Wheelus AB, Libya, with 36 TFW.
2 Jun 1965	At 36 TFW, Bitburg AB, Germany.
21 Jun 1965	At Construcciones Aeronautics S.A. (CASA), Getafe, Spain, for contract depot work (WK).
7 Jul 1965	Returned to 36 TFW, Bitburg AB, Germany.
1 Sep 1965	At Wheelus AB, Libya, with 36 TFW.
2 Oct 1965	At 36 TFW, Bitburg AB, Germany.
28 Apr 1966	Transferred to 4 TFW, Seymour Johnson AFB NC. (AVH-5).
29 Apr 1966	At MOAMA, Brookley AFB AL for depot work (WO).
22 Jul 1966	Returned to 4 TFW, Seymour Johnson AFB NC.
31 Jul 1966	While assigned to the 4 TFW, Seymour Johnson AFB NC, the aircraft flew 2.3 hours for the month of July 1966 and had accumulated 1,187.7 flying hours. Assigned crew chief: SSgt. D. L. Drake. (4 TFW History, Jul–Dec 66, USAF microfilm MO293).
6 Sep 1966	Transferred to the 18 TFW, Kadena AB, Okinawa. (AVH-5).
31 Dec 1966	While assigned to the 18 TFW, Kadena AB, Okinawa, the aircraft flew 16 hours during the month of December 1966 and had accumulated 1,291 flying hours. (18 TFW History, Jul–Dec 66, USAF microfilm MO498).
28 Jan 1967	At 18 TFW, Kadena AB, Okinawa. Assigned to the 67 TFS. (AVH-7).
29 Apr 1967	Transferred to 388 TFW, Korat RTAB, Thailand. 1,339 flying hours. (18 TFW History, Apr–Jun 67, USAF microfilm MO498).
2 Aug 1967	Combat damaged (VO) at 388 TFW, Korat RTAB, Thailand. (AVH-7).
8 Aug 1967	At 388 TFW, Korat RTAB, Thailand.
22 Aug 1967	In depot maintenance (WM) by SMAMA field team at Korat RTAB, Thailand.
24 Aug 1967	At 388 TFW, Korat RTAB, Thailand.
14 Oct 1967	Flown on Rolling Thunder mission RT56A-164 by Maj King from the 34 TFS, 388 TFW, Korat RTAB, Thailand. The target was the Dap Cau railroad by-pass bridge NE of Hanoi, North Vietnam, at coordinates 17-22-40N and 106-13-30E. (National Archives strike camera film shot list, item 42649C).
20 Oct 1967	In depot maintenance (WM) by SMAMA field team at Korat RTAB, Thailand.
21 Oct 1967	At 388 TFW, Korat RTAB, Thailand.
9 Dec 1967	One of three F-105Ds flown on Rolling Thunder mission RT56A-220 by pilots from the 34 TFS, 388 TFW, Korat RTAB, Thailand. The target was NW of Dien Bien Phu, North Vietnam, at coordinates 21-31-16N and 102-54-47E. The pilot was Capt Robert M. Elliot. (National Archives strike camera film shot list, item 42649B).

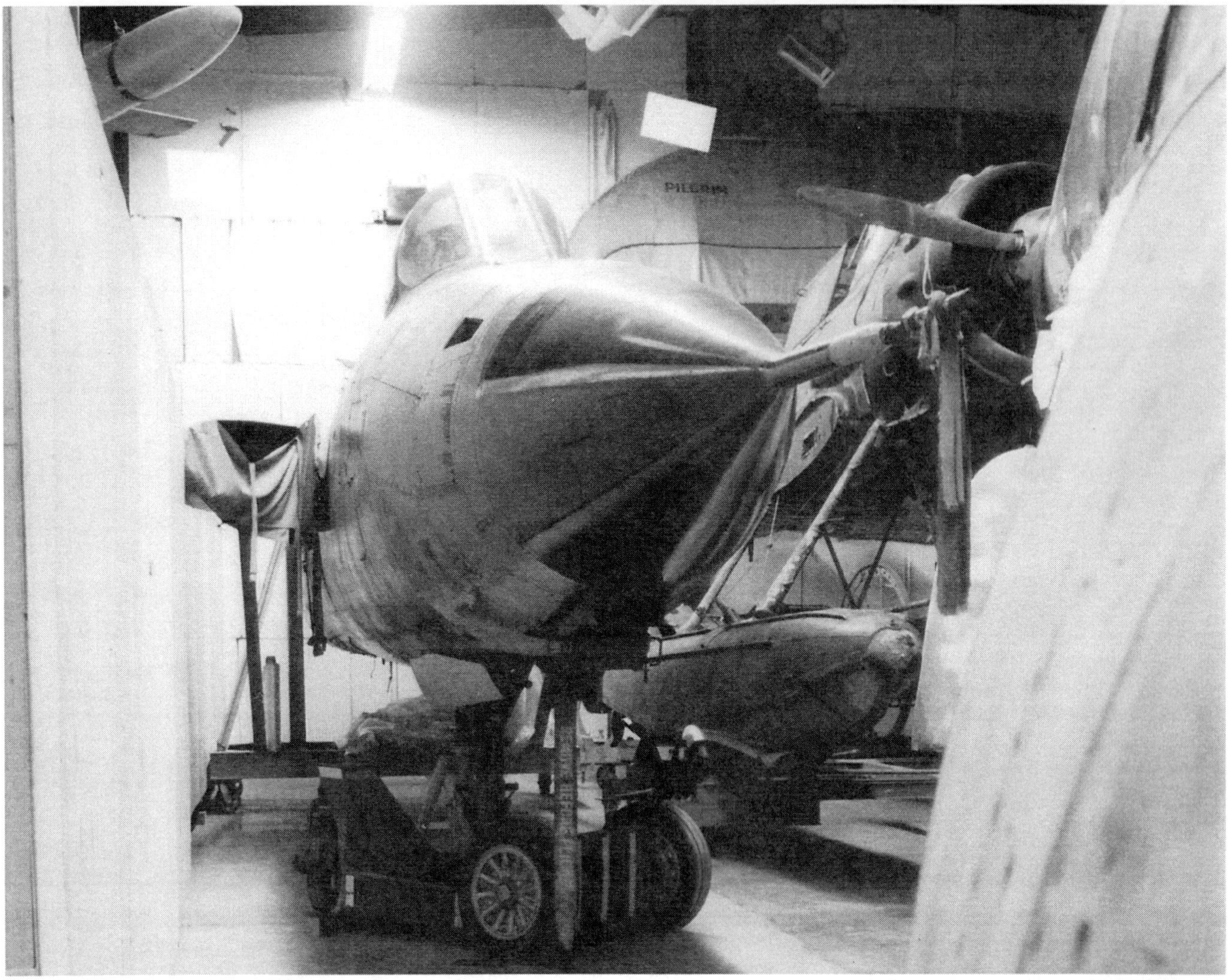

This plane achieved early fame as the first F-105 to land in Europe when it arrived in May 1961 at the 36 Tactical Fighter Wing at Bitburg Air Base, Germany. After five years in Europe, it had brief assignments to the 4 Tactical Fighter Wing in North Carolina and the 18 Tactical Fighter Wing in Okinawa before its transfer to the 388 Tactical Fighter Wing at Korat, Thailand. It spent a year flying combat missions from Korat then moved in April 1968 to the 355 Tactical Fighter Wing at Takhli, Thailand. The plane completed its combat tour after two years with the 355th. Following short stays back in Okinawa and at McConnell Air Force Base in Kansas, it ended up in 1971 with the Washington DC Air National Guard at Andrews Air Force Base, Maryland. Its ten years of service at Andrews came to an end when cracks in its wings grounded the plane. It became available at the time the National Air and Space Museum was looking for an F-105 for its collection. Initially, during its tour at Korat, the plane was thought to be the one flown by Maj Ralph L. Kuster on 3 June 1967 when he shot down a MiG-17 and so the Museum acquired it from the DC Air National Guard. However, research for this book revealed the plane was not the one flown by Maj Kuster. As shown in the photograph, the museum has stored the plane dissembled in a warehouse with other aviation artifacts at Silver Hill, Maryland. They plan to restore and display it at its new facility at Dulles Airport. (Photograph by author, 28 April 1997.)

6 Feb 1968	In depot work (WM) by SMAMA at Korat RTAB, Thailand. (AVH-10).
9 Feb 1968	At the 388 TFW, Korat RTAB, Thailand.
14 Apr 1968	Transferred to the 355 TFW, Takhli RTAB, Thailand.
29 Jun 1968	In depot work (WM) by SMAMA at Takhli RTAB, Thailand.
30 Jun 1968	At 355 TFW, Takhli RTAB, Thailand.
5 Aug 1968	At Air Asia, Tainan, Taiwan, for contract depot work (WK).
27 Sep 1968	Returned to 355 TFW, Takhli RTAB, Thailand.
30 Nov 1968	While assigned to the 355 TFW, Takhli RTAB, Thailand, aircraft had accumulated 2,563.7 flying hours. (355 TFW History, Oct–Dec 68, USAF microfilm NO466).

28 Feb 1969	While assigned to the 355 TFW, Takhli RTAB, Thailand, the aircraft flew 83.8 hours during the month of February 1969 and had accumulated 2,798.3 flying hours. (355 TFW History, Jan–Mar 69, Vol. II, USAF Microfilm NO467).
17 Mar 1969	In depot maintenance (WM) by SMAMA at Takhli RTAFB, Thailand. (AVH-12).
18 Mar 1969	At 355 TFW, Takhli RTAB, Thailand.
6 Jul 1969	In depot maintenance (WM) by SMAMA at Takhli RTAFB, Thailand.
28 Jul 1969	At 355 TFW, Takhli RTAB, Thailand (CC).
8 Dec 1969	Combat damaged (VO) at 355 TFW, Takhli RTAB, Thailand.
9 Dec 1969	At 355 TFW, Takhli RTAB, Thailand (CC).
24 Mar 1970	In depot maintenance (WM) by SMAMA at Takhli RTAB, Thailand. (AVH-14).
27 Mar 1970	At 355 TFW, Takhli RTAB, Thailand.
28 Oct 1970	Transferred to 18 TFW, Kadena AB, Okinawa.
4 Jan 1971	At Air Asia, Tainan, Taiwan, for contract depot work (WK).
5 Mar 1971	Returned to 18 TFW, Kadena AB, Okinawa. (AVH-16).
10 Mar 1971	Placed in flyable storage (PR) by 18 TFW at Kadena AB, Okinawa.
19 Mar 1971	Transferred (PL) to 23 TFW, McConnell AFB KS.
30 Mar 1971	Placed in flyable storage (PR) by the 23 TFW at McConnell AFB KS.
26 Jul 1971	Transferred (PL) to 113 TFG ANG, Andrews AFB MD.
9 Aug 1971	At 113 TFG ANG (CC), Andrews AFB MD.
24 Sep 1972	In depot work (WO) by SM-ALC at McClellan AFB CA. (AVH-18).
16 Mar 1973	Returned (PL) to 113 TFG ANG (CC), Andrews AFB MD. (AVH-20).
8 Jan 1974	In contract depot maintenance (WM) by Dynalectron Corporation (DYNZZ) at Andrews AFB MD. (AVH-22).
14 Jan 1974	At 113 TFG ANG (CC), Andrews AFB MD.
26 Jun 1974	In contract depot maintenance (WM) by Dynalectron Corporation (DYNZZ) at Andrews AFB MD.
24 Jul 1974	At 113 TFG ANG (CC), Andrews AFB MD.
1 Aug 1974	In depot maintenance (WM) by SM-ALC at Andrews AFB MD.
30 Sep 1974	At 113 TFG ANG (CC), Andrews AFB MD.
30 Nov 1974	Assigned unit redesignated 113 TFW ANG, Andrews AFB MD.
31 Dec 1974	At 113 TFW ANG (CC), Andrews AFB MD.
28 Mar 1975	In contract depot maintenance by Dynalectron Corporation (DYNZZ) at Andrews AFB MD. (AVH-23).
14 Apr 1975	At 113 TFW ANG (CC), Andrews AFB MD. (AVH-23 & AVH-24).
19 Nov 1976	In depot maintenance by SM-ALC at Andrews AFB MD. 4,841.0 flying hours. (AVH-25 & AVH-26).
2 Dec 1976	At 113 TFW ANG, Andrews AFB MD. 4,841 flying hours.
2 May 1980	In contract depot maintenance (WM) by Dynalectron Corporation (DYNZZ) at Andrews AFB MD. 5,518.6 flying hours. (GO33B 24 Jun 80).
10 May 1980	At 113 TFG ANG, Andrews AFB MD. 5,518.6 flying hours. (GO33B Dec 80).
3 Jun 1981	Aircraft grounded for wing cracks and allocated to the National Air and Space Museum. (LOG1F-91 as reported in NASM Memorandum 6 Aug 81 by Robert Mikesh, Curator).
5 Aug 1981	Engine and vertical fin removed from aircraft by personnel from the 113 TFW ANG in preparation for moving aircraft to the Paul Garber Facility at Silver Hill MD.
11 Aug 1981	At 113 TFW ANG, Andrews AFB MD. Being processed to museum (ZW). 5,688.6 flying hours. (GO33B Dec 81 & GO33B 1 Feb 83).
24 Sep 1981	Aft section of the aircraft removed, placed on aft section dolly, and transported to the Paul E. Garber Facility in Suitland MD. (NASM Memo 8 Oct 81 by William Reese).
30 Sep 1981	Aircraft placed onto a lowboy trailer.

1 Oct 1981	Wings removed from aircraft and transferred to the NASM's Garber Facility by a flatbed trailer.
2 Oct 1981	Fuselage transported to the NASM's Garber Facility for indoor storage. Aircraft assigned Account Number NASM-6780 and Catalog Number 1982-0064.

F-105D–10RE 60-0455

Republic Production No: D-143 Production Sequence No: 223

Location: In front of Harry H. Graves American Legion Post 1, Jackson, Mississippi.

Aircraft Name(s)	Crew	Unit	Date	Description
Matzoh Ball Special		357 TFS 355 TFW	Jun 69	On intake
Kay's Baby		357 TFS 355 TFW	Jan 70	On both intakes
Carolina Thunder		357 TFS 355 TFW	Oct 70	

This "D" spent the first five years of its life in Europe—first with the 36 Tactical Fighter Wing at Bitburg Air Base, Germany, and then with the 49 Tactical Fighter Wing at neighboring Spangdahlem Air Base. In 1966, when F-105s were withdrawn from Europe due to the demands for more Thunderchiefs in South East Asia, the plane transferred to McConnell Air Force Base, Kansas, where it supported the F-105 Replacement Training Unit of the 23 Tactical Fighter Wing. In the two years it was at McConnell, it deployed five times for gunnery training to George Air Force Base, California. In October 1968, the war in Vietnam caught up with it when the plane arrived at the 355 Tactical Fighter Wing at Takhli, Thailand. After its combat tour, it became one of 30 "Ds" selected to receive the Thunderstick II modification with improved blind-bombing avionics. The modification added a turtle deck to the back of the fuselage to house the electronic equipment. By the time the modification was completed, "D" models were no longer needed for the war and so the plane returned to McConnell for a year with the 563 Tactical Fighter Squadron. The plane transferred in 1972 with the other "T-Sticks" to the Air Force Reserve at Carswell Air Force Base, Texas. It retired to the "Boneyard" nine years later with nearly 5,000 flying hours on its airframe. In 1986, the American Legion Post in Jackson, Mississippi, after being assured this plane had been a "killer" and not a trainer during the Vietnam war, selected it as a war memorial for the front of their Legion hall. (Photograph by author, 26 March 1995.)

Aircraft Chronology

8 May 1961	USAF production acceptance from Republic Aviation, Farmingdale NY. (ACA-86).
24 May 1961	Picked up by pilot assigned to 4440 Delivery Group, Langley AFB VA and delivered to MOAMA, Brookley AFB AL for depot work (WO).
9 Jun 1961	Delivered to 22 TFS, 36 TFW, Bitburg AB, Germany, by pilot assigned to 4440 DG.
21 Jul 1961	At Wheelus AB, Libya, with 36 TFW.
30 Aug 1961	Returned to 36 TFW, Bitburg AB, Germany.
21 Apr 1962	At Chateauroux AB, France, for contract depot work (WK).
11 May 1962	Returned to 36 TFW, Bitburg AB, Germany.
6 Jun 1962	At 22 TFS, 36 TFW, Bitburg AB, Germany. (RAC record).
6 Apr 1963	At MOAMA, Brookley AFB AL for depot work (WO). "Operation Look Alike," Phase II.
1 Aug 1963	Returned to 36 TFW, Bitburg AB, Germany.
18 Sep 1964	At 36 TFW, Bitburg AB, Germany. (AVH-1).
8 Nov 1964	At Wheelus AB, Libya, with 36 TFW. (AVH-2).
15 Nov 1964	At 36 TFW, Bitburg AB, Germany.
16 Nov 1964	At Wheelus AB, Libya, with 36 TFW.
21 Nov 1964	At 36 TFW, Bitburg AB, Germany.
22 Nov 1964	At Wheelus AB, Libya, with 36 TFW.
12 Dec 1964	At 36 TFW, Bitburg AB, Germany.
8 Jan 1965	At 36 TFW, Bitburg AB, Germany. Assigned crew chief: A1C Charlie W. Reams. (36 OMS Special Order 31, signed by Maj. Hoyt S. Vandenberg, Jr., Commander).
15 Mar 1965	At Wheelus AB, Libya, with 36 TFW. (AVH-3).
7 Apr 1965	At 36 TFW, Bitburg AB, Germany.
17 May 1965	At CASA, Getafe, Spain, for contract depot work (WK).
8 Jun 1965	At 36 TFW, Bitburg AB, Germany.
8 Oct 1965	At CASA Getafe, Spain, for contract depot work (WK).
5 Jan 1966	At 36 TFW, Bitburg AB, Germany. (AVH-5).
16 Feb 1966	Transferred to 49 TFW, Spangdahlem AB, Germany.
17 Mar 1966	At Wheelus AB, Libya, with 49 TFW.
25 Mar 1966	At 49 TFW, Spangdahlem AB, Germany.
9 Jul 1966	At Wheelus AB, Libya, with 49 TFW.
11 Aug 1966	At 49 TFW, Spangdahlem AB, Germany.
6 Dec 1966	Transferred to 23 TFW, McConnell AFB KS.
7 Dec 1966	At MOAMA, Brookley AFB AL for depot work (WO).
9 Mar 1967	At 23 TFW, McConnell AFB KS. (AVH-7).
25 May 1967	Deployed to George AFB CA with the 563 TFS, 23 TFW, for air-to-air gunnery training for RTU Class 67IR.
16 Jun 1967	Returned to 23 TFW, McConnell AFB KS.
26 Jun 1967	In depot maintenance (WM) by SMAMA field team at McConnell AFB KS.
28 Jun 1967	At 23 TFW, McConnell AFB KS.
29 Sep 1967	Deployed to George AFB CA with the 562 TFS, 23 TFW, for air-to-air gunnery training for RTU Class 68BR.
13 Oct 1967	Returned to 23 TFW, McConnell AFB KS.
1 Dec 1967	Deployed to George AFB CA with the 560 TFS, 23 TFW, for air-to-air gunnery training for RTU Class 68ER.

22 Dec 1967	Returned to 23 TFW, McConnell AFB KS.
12 Mar 1968	Deployed to George AFB CA with the 562 TFS, 23 TFW, for air-to-air gunnery training for RTU Class 68HR. (AVH-10).
28 Mar 1968	Returned to 23 TFW, McConnell AFB KS.
14 May 1968	Deployed to George AFB CA with the 560 TFS, 23 TFW, for air-to-air gunnery training for RTU Class 68JR.
29 May 1968	Returned to 23 TFW, McConnell AFB KS.
15 Aug 1968	At SMAMA, McClellan AFB CA for depot work (WO).
23 Sep 1968	At 23 TFW, McConnell AFB KS.
18 Oct 1968	Transferred to 355 TFW, Takhli RTAB, Thailand.
30 Nov 1968	While assigned to the 357 TFS, 355 TFW, Takhli RTAB, Thailand, aircraft had accumulated 1,917.5 flying hours. (355 TFW History, Oct–Dec 68, USAF microfilm NO466).
3 Dec 1968	At 355 TFW, Takhli RTAB, Thailand.
28 Feb 1969	While assigned to the 355 TFW, Takhli RTAB, Thailand, the aircraft flew 67.5 hours during the month of February 1969 and had accumulated 2,134.2 flying hours. (355 TFW History, Jan–Mar 1969, Vol. II, USAF Microfilm NO467).
7 Mar 1969	In depot maintenance (WM) by SMAMA at Takhli RTAB, Thailand. (AVH-12).
8 Mar 1969	At 355 TFW, Takhli RTAB, Thailand.
21 Oct 1969	At 355 TFW, Takhli RTAB, Thailand being prepared for transfer (PL).
23 Oct 1969	At Air Asia, Tainan, Taiwan for contract depot work (WK).
9 Jan 1970	Returned to 355 TFW, Takhli RTAB, Thailand. (AVH-14).
25 Feb 1970	In depot maintenance (WM) by SMAMA at Takhli RTAB, Thailand.
27 Feb 1970	At 355 TFW, Takhli RTAB, Thailand.
19 Oct 1970	In depot work (WO) at SMAMA, McClellan AFB CA, for T-Stick II Modification.
4 Mar 1971	Transferred (PL) to 563 TFS, 23 TFW, McConnell AFB KS. (AVH-16).
5 Apr 1971	In contract depot maintenance (WK) by Fairchild Engine and Aircraft Corporation (FACCF) at Bob Sikes Municipal Airport, Crestview FL. (AVH-18).
1 Mar 1972	Carried on assignment roster with the 563 TFS, 23 TFW, at McConnell AFB KS. (Master 23 TFW Aircraft Assignment as of 1 March 1972).
1 May 1972	Returned to the 23 TFW, McConnell AFB KS.
1 Aug 1972	Transferred to 506 TFG, 457 TFS AFRES, Carswell AFB TX.
1 Apr 1973	At 506 CMTSq AFRES, Carswell AFB TX. (AVH-20).
22 Feb 1974	In contract depot maintenance (WK) by Fairchild Engine and Aircraft Corporation (FACCF) at Bob Sikes Municipal Airport, Crestview FL. (AVH-22).
23 Jul 1974	Returned to 506 CMTSq AFRES, Carswell AFB TX.
1 Dec 1974	Unit assignment changed to 506 CLMSq AFRES, Carswell AFB TX.
6 Oct 1975	At 506 CLMSQ AFRES, Carswell AFB TX. (AVH-23 & AVH-24).
18 Dec 1975	In depot maintenance (WM) by SM-ALC at Tinker AFB OK.
23 Jan 1976	At 457 TFS AFRES, Carswell AFB TX. 3,885 flying hours. (AVH-24).
18 Jan 1977	In depot maintenance by SM-ALC at Carswell AFB TX. 3,941.8 flying hours. (AVH-25 & AVH-26).
27 Jan 1977	At 457 TFS AFRES, Carswell AFB TX. 3,941.0 flying hours.
10 Feb 1978	In contract depot maintenance (DYNFW) at Carswell AFB TX. 4,090.0 flying hours.
22 Mar 1978	At 457 TFS AFRES, Carswell AFB TX. 4,176.0 flying hours.
25 Oct 1978	In contract depot maintenance (DYNFW) at Carswell AFB TX. 4,283.8 flying hours.
2 Nov 1978	At 457 TFS AFRES, Carswell AFB TX. 4,283.0 flying hours.

5 Feb 1979	In contract depot maintenance at General Dynamics ("DYNFW"), Carswell AFB TX. 4,328.1 flying hours. (AVII-27).
21 Feb 1979	At 457 TFS AFRES, Carswell AFB TX. 4,341.7 flying hours.
12 May 1979	Deployed under "Coronet Palomino" with 457 TFS to Gioia Del Colle, Italy, from Carswell AFB TX. (British Aviation Review, Dec 1995).
24 May 1979	Returned from Italy to the 457 TFS AFRES, Carswell AFB TX.
31 May 1979	During the month of May 1979, while assigned to the 457 TFS AFRES, the aircraft flew 45.6 hours and had accumulated a total of 4,433.3 flying hours. (301 TFW History, Apr–Jun 1979, USAF microfilm 34382).
30 Jun 1979	While assigned to the 457 TFS AFRES, Carswell AFB TX, the aircraft flew 17.1 hours during the month of June 1979 and had accumulated 4,450.4 flying hours. (301 TFW History, Apr–Jun 1979, USAF microfilm 34382).
30 Jul 1979	In contract depot maintenance at General Dynamics ("DYNFW"), Carswell AFB TX. 4,450.4 flying hours.
9 Aug 1979	At 457 TFS AFRES, Carswell AFB TX. 4,450.4 flying hours.
22 Aug 1979	At 457 TFS AFRES, Carswell AFB TX. 4,495.3 flying hours.
14 Jan 1980	In contract depot maintenance at General Dynamics, Carswell AFB TX. 4,577.6 flying hours. (GO33B 24 Jun 80).
13 Jun 1980	At 457 TFS AFRES, Carswell AFB TX. 4,650.8 flying hours. (GO33B Dec 80).
23 Jun 1980	At 457 TFS AFRES, Carswell AFB TX. 4,674.4 flying hours.
25 Aug 1981	Placed in storage at MASDC, Davis-Monthan AFB AZ. 4,961 flying hours. (MASDC Aircraft Status Directory, 30 Jun 84).
4 Sep 1981	Stored at MASDC, Davis-Monthan AFB AZ. 4,951.8 flying hours. ("Low probability of withdrawal"—XX). (GO33B Dec 81 & GO33B 1 Feb 83).
22 Jul 1986	Donation documents signed to release the aircraft for display at Jackson MS.
28 Nov 1986	Transfer document signed by James W. Till, Commander, American Legion Post 1, Jackson MS.
19 Mar 1987	Aircraft placed on display at American Legion Post 1, Jackson MS. Placed into position by CH-54 Sky Crane helicopter from the 252 Transportation Company, Alabama ANG. Restoration done by Mississippi ANG at Thompson Field, Jackson MS.

F-105D-10RE 60-0482

Republic Production No: D-169 Production Sequence No: 250

Location: The NE corner of the quadrangle at the Air Force Academy, Colorado Springs, Colorado.

Aircraft Name(s)	Crew	Unit	Date	Description
The Salty Dog	1 Lt. Salty Roark	357 TFS 355 TFW		
Iron Butterfly		388 TFW	Sep 66	Red letters with yellow butterfly on fuselage side below cockpit.

Aircraft Chronology

23 Jun 1961	USAF production acceptance from Republic Aviation, Farmingdale NY. (ACA-86).
20 July 1961	Delivered to 23 TFS, 36 TFW, Bitburg AB, Germany.

This F-105D is better known for being a static display than for its flying career. After spending its first five years with the 36 Tactical Fighter Wing at Bitburg, Germany, it found its way to the 355 Tactical Fighter Wing at Takhli, Thailand. Its combat history in 1966 is not well documented, but it was apparently severely damaged in combat and shipped to a contract depot in Florida where it was written off as beyond repair. At the depot at Sacramento, California, it was restored for static display by the 2951 Combat Logistics Support Squadron. Men of this squadron reassembled it at the Air Force Academy. It was dedicated during the 1968 Memorial Day ceremony still legendary at the Academy for a supersonic flyover of a flight of F-105s that blew out most of the windows around the quadrangle. It has been an historic fixture on the Academy quadrangle since. (Photograph by author, 5 April 1996.)

13 Sep 1961	At Wheelus AB, Libya, with 36 TFW.
12 Oct 1961	Returned to 36 TFW, Bitburg AB, Germany.
6 Jun 1962	At 23 TFS, 36 TFW, Bitburg AB, Germany. (RAC record).
11 Oct 1962	At MOAMA, Brookley AFB AL for depot work. "Operation Look Alike," Phase II.
31 Aug 1964	At 36 TFW, Bitburg AB, Germany. (AVH-1).
8 Oct 1964	At MOAMA, Brookley AFB AL for depot work. (AVH-2).
26 Feb 1965	At 36 TFW, Bitburg AB, Germany. (AVH-3).
1 Apr 1965	At Wheelus AB, Libya, with 36 TFW.
2 Apr 1965	Returned to 36 TFW, Bitburg AB, Germany.
5 Apr 1965	At Wheelus AB, Libya, with 36 TFW.
25 Apr 1965	Returned to 36 TFW, Bitburg AB, Germany.
24 Jul 1965	At CASA, Madrid, Spain, for contract depot work (WK).
30 Nov 1965	Returned to 36 TFW, Bitburg AB, Germany.
13 Jan 1966	At 36 TFW, Bitburg AB, Germany. (AVH-5).
2 Feb 1966	Transferred to 23 TFW, McConnell AFB KS.
Feb 1966	Flying combat missions from Takhli RTAB. ("Profile 226" by Van Geffin, page 89).
15 Mar 1966	At Air Asia, Tainan, Taiwan, from 6441 TFW for contract depot work (WK). (AVH-5).
Sep 1966	Received severe combat damage. ("Profile 226" by Van Geffin, page 89).
18 Oct 1966	At St. Augustine FL for contract depot repair of crash damage (WR). (AVH-5).
20 Apr 1967	At Crestview FL. "Attritted" from crash damage (WR). (AVH-7).
31 May 1968	Aircraft was placed on static display during a dedication ceremony at the USAF Academy, Colorado Springs, Colorado. During the dedication ceremony, a flyby of four F-105's from McConnell smashed

windows when the flight's lead aircraft broke the sound barrier at low level. Flying glass injured 15 people. ("F-105 Thunderchief" by J. C. Scutts, Page 89).

"During the special ceremonies .. [the] Thunderchief was put on permanent display ... and a scholarship was dedicated in honor of Lt. Karl W. Richter, an F-105 pilot who was killed over North Vietnam after completing 198 missions. The Thunderchief, built from parts salvaged from ten F-105s which had been battle-damaged in Vietnam, was presented to the cadets prior to the scholarship dedication. The F-105 was put together at Sacramento Air Materiel Area, McClellan AFB, California, by members of the 2951st Combat Logistics Support Squadron. Cadet Second Class Terry L. Balven, chairman of the Cadet Heritage Committee, dedicated the aircraft. ... Richter, who graduated from the Academy in 1964, was the first Air Force Academy graduate to be so honored.

"... Attending the ceremony were: "Lt. Gen. Thomas S. Moorman, Academy Superintendent; Donald J. Strait, General Manager, Republic Aviation; Maj. Gen. George B. Simler, Director of Operations, Hq. USAF; Brig. Gen. Robert F. McDermott, Academy Dean of Faculty; Brig. Gen. William S. Chairsell, Asst. for Southeast Asia, Air Force Systems Command (who was Richter's wing commander in SEA); Col. Robin Olds, Cadet Commandant; Col. Robert R. Scott, who commanded the first Air Force F-105 squadron and later the 355th TFW at Takhli; Col. Frank Merritt, Athletics Director, Air Force Academy; Maj. Merlyn H. Dethlefsen, a former F-105 pilot and Medal of Honor recipient; and Capts. Leonard 'Lucky' Ekman and Howard Bodenhamer, both academy graduates ... who have completed 100 combat missions or more over North Vietnam.

"... The nine members of the 2951st Combat Logistics Support Squadron who reassembled the Thunderchief at the Air Force Academy ... were ... Lt. Richard A. Follett, M. Sgt. Jack D. Jones, T. Sgt. Walter B. Hill, Sgt. John H. Russell, S. Sgt. Carl Dyer and Airmen 1. C. Marty Quattlegaum, Raymond E. Granstrand, Creighton P. Wong and Joseph D. Ayotte." (Fairchild Hiller Corporation "Thunderchief World Wide Report," Vol. III, No. 10, June, 1968).

F-105D–10RE 60-0500

Republic Production No: D-187 Production Sequence No: 268

Location: Displayed outside at the Pate Museum of Transportation, Cresson, Texas.

Aircraft Chronology

20 Jul 1961	USAF production acceptance from Republic Aviation, Farmingdale NY. (ACA-86).
25 Jul 1961	Picked up from Republic Aviation by pilot assigned to 4440 Delivery Group, Langley AFB VA and delivered to MOAMA, Brookley AFB AL for depot work (WO).
18 Oct 1961	Delivered to 36 TFW, Bitburg AB, Germany, by pilot assigned to 4440 DG.
26 Oct 1961	At Wheelus AB, Libya, with 36 TFW.
21 Nov 1961	Returned to 36 TFW, Bitburg AB, Germany.
6 Jun 1962	At 53 TFS, 36 TFW, Bitburg AB, Germany. (RAC record).
4 Jun 1963	At MOAMA, Brookley AFB AL for depot work. "Operation Look Alike," Phase II.
18 Oct 1963	Returned to 36 TFW, Bitburg AB, Germany.
25 Sep 1964	At 36 TFW, Bitburg AB, Germany. (AVH-1).
8 Jan 1965	At 36 TFW, Bitburg AB, Germany. Assigned crew chief: A1C William N. Graham. (36 OMS Special Order 31, signed by Maj. Hoyt S. Vandenberg, Jr., Commander).
24 Jan 1965	At Wheelus AB, Libya, with 36 TFW. (AVH-3).
29 Jan 1965	Returned to 36 TFW, Bitburg AB, Germany.

This is one of the thirty F-105Ds modified with the Thunderstick II bombing system that added a turtle deck on top of the fuselage. It started its career with the two fighter wings in Germany, spending its first four years at Bitburg Air Base before transferring for a year to Spangdahlem Air Base. Both units used it for weapons delivery training at Wheelus Air Base in Libya. In November 1966, it transferred to the 23 Tactical Fighter Wing at McConnell Air Force Base, Kansas, where it supported pilot training for the next three years. In early 1970, it was modified at the depot with the Thunderstick II system and returned to McConnell for two more years before transferring with the rest of the Thunderstick II fleet to the Air Force Reserve at Fort Worth, Texas. It was one of the planes the Reserve used for their 1977 NATO summer deployment to Germany. It retired in late 1981. (Photograph by author, 13 July 1995.)

2 Feb 1965	At Wheelus AB, Libya, with 36 TFW.
5 Feb 1965	Returned to 36 TFW, Bitburg AB, Germany.
7 Feb 1965	At Wheelus AB, Libya, with 36 TFW.
17 Feb 1965	Returned to 36 TFW, Bitburg AB, Germany.
14 Apr 1965	At Wheelus AB, Libya, with 36 TFW.
15 Apr 1965	Returned to 36 TFW, Bitburg AB, Germany.
17 Apr 1965	At Wheelus AB, Libya, with 36 TFW.
25 Apr 1965	Returned to 36 TFW, Bitburg AB, Germany.
27 Apr 1965	At Wheelus AB, Libya, with 36 TFW.
7 May 1965	Returned to 36 TFW, Bitburg AB, Germany.
20 May 1965	At CASA, Madrid, Spain, for contract depot work (WK).
22 Jun 1965	Transferred to 49 TFW, Spangdahlem AB, Germany.
22 Dec 1965	At CASA, Madrid, Spain, for contract depot work.
27 Jan 1966	Returned to 49 TFW, Spangdahlem AB, Germany. (AVH-5).
11 Mar 1966	At Wheelus AB, Libya, with 49 TFW.
9 Apr 1966	At 49 TFW, Spangdahlem AB, Germany.
6 Sep 1966	At Wheelus AB, Libya, with 49 TFW.
17 Sep 1966	At 49 TFW, Spangdahlem AB, Germany.
11 Oct 1966	At Wheelus AB, Libya, with 49 TFW.
21 Oct 1966	At 49 TFW, Spangdahlem AB, Germany.
7 Nov 1966	Transferred to 23 TFW McConnell AFB KS.

21 Nov 1966	At MOAMA, Brookley AFB AL for depot work (WO).
30 Jan 1967	At 23 TFW, McConnell AFB KS. (AVH-7).
22 Feb 1967	In depot work (WM) by SMAMA field team at McConnell AFB KS.
27 Feb 1967	At 23 TFW, McConnell AFB KS.
12 Oct 1967	In depot work (WM) by SMAMA field team at McConnell AFB KS.
13 Oct 1967	At 23 TFW, McConnell AFB KS.
1 Dec 1967	Deployed to George AFB CA with the 560 TFS, 23 TFW, for air-to-air gunnery training for RTU Class 68ER.
22 Dec 1967	Returned to 23 TFW, McConnell AFB KS.
12 Mar 1968	Deployed to George AFB CA with the 562 TFS, 23 TFW, for air-to-air gunnery training for RTU Class 68HR. (AVH-10).
28 Mar 1968	Returned to 23 TFW, McConnell AFB KS.
14 May 1968	Deployed to George AFB CA with the 560 TFS, 23 TFW, for air-to-air gunnery training for RTU Class 68JR.
29 May 1968	Returned to 23 TFW, McConnell AFB KS.
2 Jul 1968	At SMAMA, McClellan AFB CA for depot work (WO).
13 Aug 1968	Returned to 23 TFW, McConnell AFB KS.
23 Sep 1968	At SMAMA, McClellan AFB CA for depot work (WO).
14 Oct 1968	Returned to 23 TFW, McConnell AFB KS.
3 May 1969	In depot maintenance (WM) by SMAMA at McConnell AFB KS. (AVH-12).
4 May 1969	At 23 TFW, McConnell AFB KS for combat crew training (TF).
15 Dec 1969	At SMAMA, McClellan AFB CA for depot work (WO). T-Stick II modification.
27 Apr 1970	Returned to 563 TFS, 23 TFW, McConnell AFB KS. (AVH-14).
1 Oct 1970	At 563 TFS, 23 TFW, McConnell AFB KS.
4 Mar 1971	In contract depot maintenance (WK) by Fairchild Engine and Aircraft Corporation (FACCF) at Bob Sikes Municipal Airport, Crestview FL. (AVH-16).
29 Mar 1971	Returned to 563 TFS, 23 TFW, McConnell AFB KS.
29 Oct 1971	In depot work (WO) by SMAMA at McClellan AFB CA.
17 Jan 1972	Placed in flyable storage (PR) at McClellan AFB CA. (AVH-18).
1 Mar 1972	Carried on assignment roster with the 563 TFS, 23 TFW at McConnell AFB KS. (Master 23 TFW Aircraft Assignment as of 1 March 1972).
18 Apr 1972	Returned to 23 TFW, McConnell AFB KS.
1 Jul 1972	Assigned directly to 561 TFS, McConnell AFB KS after the 23 TFW moved to England AFB LA.
7 Aug 1972	Transferred to 506 TFG, 457 TFS AFRES, Carswell AFB TX.
18 Aug 1972	In depot work (WO) by SM-ALC at McClellan AFB CA.
12 Mar 1973	At 506 TFG AFRES, Carswell AFB TX. (AVH-20).
1 Apr 1973	Assigned to 506 CMTSq AFRES, Carswell AFB TX.
4 Jan 1974	At 506 CMTSq AFRES, Carswell AFB TX.
25 Mar 1974	At 506 CMTSq AFRES (CC), Carswell AFB TX. (AVH-22).
1 Dec 1974	Assigned unit redesignated 506 CLMSQ AFRES (CC), Carswell AFB TX.
26 Mar 1975	In contract depot maintenance (WK) by Fairchild Engine and Aircraft Corporation (FACCF) at Bob Sikes Municipal Airport, Crestview FL. (AVH-23).
19 Aug 1975	Returned to 506 CLMSQ AFRES, Carswell AFB TX. (AVH-23 & AVH-24).
7 Jun 1976	At 457 TFS AFRES, Carswell AFB TX. 3,142 flying hours. (AVH-24).
20 Jun 1977	At 457 TFS AFRES, Carswell AFB TX. 3,322.0 flying hours. (AVH-25 & AVH-26).

14 Aug 1977	Deployed under "Coronet Poker" with 457 TFS to Norvenich, Germany, from Carswell AFB TX. (British Aviation Review, Dec 1995).
27 Aug 1977	Returned from Germany to Carswell AFB TX.
30 Jan 1978	At 457 TFS AFRES, Carswell AFB TX. 3,369.0 flying hours. (AVH-26).
30 Mar 1978	At 457 TFS AFRES, Carswell AFB TX. 3,385.0 flying hours.
31 Jul 1978	In contract depot maintenance (DYNFW) at Carswell AFB TX. 3,493.0 flying hours.
28 Aug 1978	At 457 TFS AFRES, Carswell AFB TX. 3,577.3 flying hours. (AVH-27).
19 Mar 1979	In depot maintenance (DYNFW) at Carswell AFB TX. 3,602.4 flying hours.
1 May 1979	At 457 TFS AFRES, Carswell AFB TX. 3,605.4 flying hours.
30 Jun 1979	While assigned to the 457 TFS AFRES, Carswell AFB TX, the aircraft flew 40.9 hours during the month of June 1979 and had accumulated 3,710.5 flying hours. (301 TFW History, Apr–Jun 1979, USAF microfilm 34382).
22 Aug 1979	At 457 TFS AFRES, Carswell AFB TX. 3,712.0 flying hours. (AVH-27).
19 Oct 1979	At 457 TFS AFRES, Carswell AFB TX. 3,765.1 flying hours.
19 May 1980	In depot maintenance (DYNFW) at Carswell AFB TX. 3,883.3 flying hours. (GO33B Dec 80).
16 Jul 1980	At 457 TFS AFRES, Carswell AFB TX. 3,901.2 flying hours.
8 Oct 1981	At 457 TFS AFRES, Carswell AFB TX. Inventory account "ZJ." 4,101.2 flying hours. (GO33B Dec 81 & GO33B 1 Feb 83).

F-105D-10RE 60-0504

Republic Production No: D-191 Production Sequence No: 272

Location: Inside Air Force Museum, Wright-Patterson AFB, Dayton, Ohio.

Aircraft Name(s)	Crew	Unit	Date	Description
Patience My Ass I'm Gonna Kill Something		121 TFS DC ANG		Two blue and red buzzards on yellow radar reflector.
Andrews AFB		121 TFS DC ANG		
Memphis Bell II	Maj. Buddy Jones	357 TFS 355 TFW	Jan 70	On both intakes, pinup on fuselage below
Beats Walking		357 TFS 355 TFW	Oct 70	

Aircraft Chronology

26 Sep 1961	USAF production acceptance from Republic Aviation, Farmingdale NY. (ACA-86).
27 Sep 1961	Picked up from Republic Aviation by pilot, Maj. Walter S. Bruce, 335 TFS, assigned to 4440 Delivery Group, Langley AFB VA and delivered to MOAMA, Brookley AFB AL for depot work (WO). "Maj. ... Bruce landed ... at Eglin AFB FL enroute to Brookley AFB AL. (4 TFW History, Jul–Dec 61, USAF microfilm MO290).
27 Sep 1961	Maj. Walter S. Bruce took off from Eglin AFB configured with one BDU-3B bomblet for Brookley AFB. Enroute to Brookley, Maj. Bruce made a bomb run on Range 75 (Eglin West complex) and expended the BDU-3B in the BTIP mode. This portion of the ferry mission was conducted as part of the F-105D Aircraft Sampling Program in accordance with Hq. TAC ...."

Named after the B-17 from World War II, the "*Memphis Belle II*" had a three-year combat tour with the 355 Tactical Fighter Wing during the Vietnam war. Inconclusive evidence indicates it carried Lt. Col. Arthur Dennis when he shot down a MiG-17 over North Vietnam on 28 April 1967. Before its wartime career it served for five years with the 36 Tactical Fighter Wing in Germany and was then briefly assigned to the wings at Seymour Johnson Air Force Base, North Carolina, McConnell Air Force Base, Kansas, and Kadena Air Base in Okinawa. When it came home from war, it returned to McConnell, this time with the Kansas Air National Guard. It spent a few months training pilots at Nellis Air Force Base, Nevada, and finally settled down with the Air National Guard at Andrews Air Force Base, Maryland. It retired to storage in Arizona in 1981 until, nine years later, the Air Force Museum found it worthy of its collection. (Photograph by author, 7 June 1998.)

30 Oct 1961	Delivered to 36 TFW, Bitburg AB, Germany by pilot assigned to 4440 DG.
8 Nov 1961	At Wheelus AB, Libya, with 36 TFW.
14 Dec 1961	Returned to 36 TFW, Bitburg AB, Germany.
6 Jun 1962	At 53 TFS, 36 TFW, Bitburg AB, Germany. (RAC record).
31 Oct 1963	At MOAMA, Brookley AFB AL for depot work. "Operation Look Alike," Phase II.
8 Mar 1964	Returned to 36 TFW, Bitburg AB, Germany.
26 Oct 1964	At Wheelus AB, Libya, with 36 TFW. (AVH-2).
15 Nov 1964	Returned to 36 TFW, Bitburg AB, Germany.
16 Nov 1964	At Wheelus AB, Libya, with 36 TFW.
21 Nov 1964	Returned to 36 TFW, Bitburg AB, Germany.
22 Nov 1964	At Wheelus AB, Libya, with 36 TFW.
8 Jan 1965	At 36 TFW, Bitburg AB, Germany. Assigned crew chief: A2C Barton T. Rembert. (36 OMS Special Order 31, signed by Maj. Hoyt S. Vandenberg, Jr., Commander).
25 Feb 1965	At Wheelus AB, Libya, with 36 TFW. (AVH-3).
19 Mar 1965	Returned to 36 TFW, Bitburg AB, Germany.
21 Mar 1965	At Wheelus AB, Libya, with 36 TFW.
26 Mar 1965	Returned to 36 TFW, Bitburg AB, Germany.
12 May 1965	At CASA, Madrid, Spain, for contract depot work (WK).
7 Jun 1965	Returned to 36 TFW, Bitburg AB, Germany.
19 Jun 1965	At Wheelus AB, Libya, with 36 TFW.
22 Jun 1965	Returned to 36 TFW, Bitburg AB, Germany.
19 Jul 1965	At Wheelus AB, Libya, with 36 TFW.
30 Jul 1965	Returned to 36 TFW, Bitburg AB, Germany.

31 Jul 1965	At Wheelus AB, Libya, with 36 TFW.
11 Aug 1965	Returned to 36 TFW, Bitburg AB, Germany.
30 Dec 1965	At CASA, Madrid, Spain, for contract depot work (WK).
30 Jan 1966	Returned to 36 TFW, Bitburg AB, Germany. (AVH-5).
19 Feb 1966	Transferred to 4 TFW, Seymour Johnson AFB NC. Assigned crew chief: SSgt. Miracle. (4 TFW History, Jan–Jun 66, USAF microfilm MO293).
31 Mar 1966	At MOAMA, Brookley AFB AL for depot work. (AVH-5)
6 Apr 1966	Returned to 4 TFW, Seymour Johnson AFB NC.
23 May 1966	Transferred to 23 TFW, McConnell AFB KS.
31 May 1966	At MOAMA, Brookley AFB AL for depot work (WO).
31 May 1966	Transferred back to 4 TFW, Seymour Johnson AFB NC.
30 Aug 1966	At 4 TFW, Seymour Johnson AFB NC.
31 Aug 1966	At MOAMA, Brookley AFB AL for depot work (WO).
6 Sep 1966	Transferred to 18 TFW, Kadena AB, Okinawa.
31 Dec 1966	While assigned to the 67 TFS, 18 TFW, Kadena AB, Okinawa, the aircraft flew 17 hours during the month of December 1966 and had accumulated 1,224 flying hours. (18 TFW History, Jul–Dec 66, USAF microfilm MO498).
20 Jan 1967	At 18 TFW, Kadena AB, Okinawa. (AVH-7).
16 Mar 1967	Transferred from the 67 TFS, 18 TFW, Kadena AB, Okinawa to the 355 TFW, Takhli RTAB, Thailand. Aircraft had accumulated 1,268 flying hours. (AVH-7 & 18 TFW History, Jan–Mar 67, USAF microfilm MO498).
28 Apr 1967	Pilot Lt. Col. Arthur F. Dennis, 357 TFS, 355 TFW, shot down a MiG-17 while on a strike mission against the Han Phong causeway. Call sign: "Atlanta 01." (Tail number not certain). "I closed on the MIG-17, and when I obtained a missile tone in my headset I fired the AIM-9. The firing was normal; however, the missile did not guide. I continued closing until about 3,000 to 4,000 feet and began firing 20-mm, but realized I was still too far out for a good firing pass.... The MIG at this time was in a shallow right turn, level, and apparently did not see me because he did not attempt evasive action. I continued closing to approximately 1,500 feet, began firing, closing to about 700 feet, and the MIG burst into a large ball of flame. It continued to burn and trail smoke as it went into a steeper turn to the right and nosed over into a wide spiral toward the ground. I continued to watch it in its spiral near the ground, but I had to reverse my turn to move out of the target area because I was receiving SAM launch indications. When I rolled back to the left toward my egress route, the MIG impact with the ground should have been in my 7-8 o'clock position but I was unable to see it." (Aces & Aerial Victories, Page 50).
31 May 1967	At 355 TFW, Takhli RTAB, Thailand. (AVH-7).
May/Jun 1967	While assigned to the 355 TFW at Takhli RTAB, Thailand, its pilot, Capt. Thomas C. Lesan, claimed a MiG kill that was not officially credited. (Tom Brewer, USAF Museum).
23 Aug 1967	In depot maintenance (WM) by SMAMA field team at Takhli RTAB, Thailand.
26 Aug 1967	At 355 TFW, Takhli RTAB, Thailand.
7 Oct 1967	One of four F-105Ds flown on a Rolling Thunder mission (RT56A-157) by pilots from the 357 TFS, 355 TFW, Takhli RTAB, Thailand. They strafed the Hoa Lac helicopter dispersal area in North Vietnam at coordinates 21-05-00N and 105-23-50E. The pilot was named Jewett. (National Archives gun camera film shot list, item 42718A).
31 Oct 1967	While assigned to the 357 TFS, 355 TFW, Takhli RTAB, Thailand, the aircraft flew 35 sorties, the highest number of any F-105 in the squadron for the month. (355 TFW History, Oct–Dec 67, USAF microfilm NO463).
22 Nov 1967	Being prepared (PL) for flight to depot at 355 TFW, Takhli RTAB, Thailand.
24 Nov 1967	At Air Asia, Tainan, Taiwan, for contract depot work (WK).
27 Jan 1968	Returned to 355 TFW, Takhli RTAB, Thailand. (AVH-10).

11 Mar 1968	In depot maintenance (WM) by SMAMA at Takhli RTAB, Thailand.
13 Mar 1968	At 355 TFW, Takhli RTAB, Thailand.
18 Jun 1968	In depot maintenance (WM) by SMAMA at Takhli RTAB, Thailand.
20 Jun 1968	At 355 TFW, Takhli RTAB, Thailand.
17 Aug 1968	While assigned to the 355 TFW, Takhli RTAB, Thailand, the aircraft received major combat damage to the bomb bay frame at the left center locking position with holes in the skin on the left side. (355 TFW History, Jul–Sep 68, USAF microfilm NO465).
25 Sep 1968	In depot maintenance (WM) by SMAMA at Takhli RTAB, Thailand. (AVH-10).
27 Sep 1968	At 355 TFW, Takhli RTAB, Thailand.
30 Nov 1968	While assigned to the 357 TFS, 355 TFW, Takhli RTAB, Thailand, aircraft had accumulated 2,776.7 flying hours. (355 TFW History, Oct–Dec 68, USAF microfilm NO466).
28 Feb 1969	While assigned to the 355 TFW, Takhli RTAB, Thailand, the aircraft flew 68.7 hours during the month of February 1969 and had accumulated 2,971.3 flying hours. (355 TFW History, Jan–Mar 69, Vol. II, USAF Microfilm NO467).
3 Mar 1969	At Air Asia, Tainan, Taiwan, for contract depot work (WK). (AVH-12).
24 Apr 1969	Returned to 355 TFW, Takhli RTAB, Thailand.
16 Nov 1969	In depot maintenance (WM) by SMAMA at Takhli RTAB, Thailand.
27 Nov 1969	Combat capable (CC) at 355 TFW, Takhli RTAB, Thailand.
10 May 1970	In depot maintenance (WM) by SMAMA at Takhli RTAB, Thailand. (AVH-14).
13 May 1970	At 355 TFW, Takhli RTAB, Thailand.
24 Oct 1970	At 355 TFW, Takhli RTAB, Thailand, being prepared for transfer (PL).
27 Oct 1970	Transferred (PL) to 23 TFW (TAC), McConnell AFB KS.
4 Nov 1970	Placed in flyable storage (PR) at the 23 TFW (TAC), McConnell AFB KS.
4 Jan 1971	At 23 TFW, McConnell AFB KS being prepared for transfer (PL).
22 Jan 1971	Transferred to 184 TFG ANG, McConnell AFB KS. (AVH-16).
22 Apr 1971	In depot work (WO) by SMAMA at McClellan AFB CA.
28 Sep 1971	Returned (PL) to 184 TFG ANG, McConnell AFB KS.
12 Dec 1972	In contract depot maintenance (WK) by Fairchild Engine and Aircraft Corporation (FACCF) at Bob Sikes Municipal Airport, Crestview FL. (AVH-18).
9 Jan 1973	Returned (CC) to 184 TFG ANG, McConnell AFB KS. (AVH-20).
23 Jul 1973	Transferred (PL) to 57 FWW TAC, Nellis AFB NV for combat crew training (TF).
10 Sep 1973	In depot maintenance (WM) by SM-ALC at Nellis AFB NV.
24 Sep 1973	At 57 FWW TAC, Nellis AFB NV for combat crew training (TF).
5 Dec 1973	Transferred back (PL) to 184 TFG ANG, McConnell AFB KS.
3 Jan 1974	At 184 TFG ANG, McConnell AFB KS for combat crew training (TF).
21 Jun 1974	In contract depot maintenance (WM) by Dynalectron Corporation (DYNZZ) at McConnell AFB KS. (AVH-22).
12 Jul 1974	At 184 TFG ANG, McConnell AFB KS for combat crew training (TF).
4 Feb 1975	In contract depot maintenance (WM) by Dynalectron Corporation (DYNZZ) at McConnell AFB KS. (AVH-23).
18 Feb 1975	At 184 TFG ANG, McConnell AFB KS for combat crew training (TF).
11 Mar 1975	In contract depot maintenance (WK) by Fairchild Engine and Aircraft Corporation (FACCF) at Bob Sikes Municipal Airport, Crestview FL.
12 Aug 1975	Returned to 184 TFG ANG, McConnell AFB KS for combat crew training (TF). (AVH-23 & AVH-24).
8 Mar 1976	Transferred to 113 TFG ANG, Andrews AFB MD. (AVH-24).
9 Mar 1976	At 113 TFG ANG, Andrews AFB MD. 5,052 flying hours.

23 Oct 1976	Deployed to Lakenheath AB, England, with the 121 TFS ANG from Andrews AFB MD. (British Aviation Review, Dec 1995).
6 Nov 1976	Returned from England to the 113 TFG ANG, Andrews AFB MD.
15 Nov 1976	In depot maintenance by SM-ALC at Andrews AFB MD. 5,085.0 flying hours. (AVH-25 & AVH-26).
18 Nov 1976	At 113 TFW ANG, Andrews AFB MD. 5,085.0 flying hours.
28 Feb 1978	In depot maintenance by OC-ALC at Andrews AFB MD. 5,272.0 flying hours.
30 Mar 1978	At 113 TFW ANG, Andrews AFB MD. 5,272.0 flying hours.
10 Jul 1979	In contract depot maintenance by Dynalectron Corporation (DYNZZ) at Andrews AFB MD. 5,634.0 flying hours. (AVH-27).
4 Aug 1979	At 113 TFW ANG, Andrews AFB MD. 5,663.4 flying hours.
12 Jun 1981	Placed in storage at MASDC ("Low probability of withdrawal"—XX), Davis- Monthan AFB AZ. 5,934.6 flying hours. (GO33B Dec 81 & GO33B 1 Feb 83).
17 Feb 1983	Still stored at MASDC, Davis-Monthan AFB AZ. 5,934.6 flying hours. (GO33B 9 Feb 84).
7 Apr 1990	Removed from AMARC storage and shipped to USAF Museum, Dayton OH. (AMARC Report D003A/B, 3 Aug 90).
13 Apr 1990	Arrived at USAF Museum from storage.
Jul 1991	Put on display at the USAF Museum.

F-105D-10RE 60-0508

Republic Production No: D-195 Production Sequence No: 276

Location: In Wings Over Rockies Air & Space Museum at former Lowry AFB, Denver, Colorado.

This plane has the shortest flying history of any of the surviving F-105Ds. It flew for five years with its first and only operational unit, the 49 Tactical Fighter Wing at Spangdahlem Air Base in Germany. In 1965 it was assigned as a maintenance trainer to the technical school at Lowry Air Force Base in Denver, Colorado, where it remained for the rest of its service. After training hundreds of weapons loaders and other technicians, it was added to the large collection of static display aircraft at Lowry. When the base closed in 1994, a museum foundation inherited the collection and its hanger. The plane is unique in that it is the surviving "D" closest to its original production configuration. As a non-flying maintenance trainer, it missed the modifications installed during the middle to late 1960s that added air scoops to the F-105's aft fuselage and installed other safety and combat-required improvements. (Photograph by author, 6 April 1996.)

Aircraft Chronology

8 Nov 1961	USAF production acceptance from Republic Aviation, Farmingdale NY. (ACA-86).
10 Nov 1961	Picked up from Republic Aviation by pilot assigned to 4440 Delivery Group, Langley AFB VA and delivered to MOAMA, Brookley AFB AL for depot work (WO).
22 Dec 1961	Delivered to 49 TFW, Spangdahlem AB, Germany, by pilot assigned to 4440 DG.
29 Oct 1962	At MOAMA, Brookley AFB AL for depot work.
31 Aug 1964	At 49 TFW, Spangdahlem AB, Germany. (AVH-1).
13 Jul 1965	At CASA, Getafe, Spain, for contract depot work. (AVH-3).
14 Aug 1965	Transferred to 3415 MSGp ATC, Lowry AFB CO.
28 Feb 1966	At 3415 MSGP, Lowry AFB, CO as ground instructional aircraft (TJ). (AVH-5).
31 Oct 1975	At Lowry Technical Training Center as GF-105D, Lowry AFB CO. Assignment status code "TX." Inventory account "GF." (AVH-23 & AVH-24).
18 Mar 1976	At Lowry Technical Training Center as GF-105D, Lowry AFB CO. Assignment status code "TX." Inventory account "TW." (AVH-24)
30 Sep 1994	USAF closed Lowry AFB. Aircraft transferred to Wings Over the Rockies Air & Space Museum that took over the base's aircraft collection.

F-105D-10RE 60-0535

Republic Production No: D-223 Production Sequence No: 303

Location: Displayed on a pedestal at Keesler AFB, Biloxi, Mississippi.

Aircraft Chronology

23 Oct 1961	USAF production acceptance at Republic Aviation, Farmingdale NY. (ACA-86).
24 Oct 1961	Picked up from Republic Aviation by pilot assigned to 4440 Delivery Group, Langley AFB VA and delivered to MOAMA, Brookley AFB AL for depot work (WO).
2 Dec 1961	Delivered to 49 TFW, Spangdahlem AB, Germany, by pilot from 4440 Delivery Group.
29 Oct 1962	At MOAMA, Brookley AFB AL for depot work. "Operation Look Alike," Phase II.
12 Mar 1963	Returned to 49 TFW, Spangdahlem AB, Germany.
28 Jul 1965	At CASA, Madrid, Spain, for contract depot work (WK). (AVH-3).
13 Sep 1965	At 49 TFW, Spangdahlem AB, Germany.
27 Jan 1966	At CASA, Madrid, Spain, for contract depot work (WK). (AVH-5).
23 Feb 1966	Returned to 49 TFW, Spangdahlem AB, Germany.
23 May 1966	Transferred to 23 TFW, McConnell AFB KS.
27 May 1966	At MOAMA, Brookley AFB AL for depot work (WO).
23 Aug 1966	At 23 TFW, McConnell AFB KS.
13 Nov 1966	In depot work (WM) by SMAMA field team at McConnell AFB KS.
30 Nov 1966	At 23 TFW, McConnell AFB KS.
5 Jul 1967	In depot work (WM) by SMAMA field team at McConnell AFB KS. (AVH-7).
6 Jul 1967	At 23 TFW, McConnell AFB KS.

This "D" belonged to only three units in its career. It started in December 1961 with the 49 Tactical Fighter Wing in Germany, moved to the 23 Tactical Fighter Wing in Wichita in 1966 and transferred to the Air National Guard at Andrews Air Force Base, Maryland in 1971. It retired in 1976 and, a year later, was put on the pedestal at Keesler Air Force Base, Mississippi. (Photograph by author, 5 August 1997.)

30 Sep 1967	Deployed to George AFB CA with the 562 TFS, 23 TFW, for air-to-air gunnery training for RTU Class 68BR.
13 Oct 1967	Returned to 23 TFW, McConnell AFB KS.
23 Jan 1968	Deployed to George AFB CA with the 561 TFS, 23 TFW, for air-to-air gunnery training for RTU Class 68FR. (AVH-10).
8 Feb 1968	Returned to 23 TFW, McConnell AFB KS.
15 Mar 1968	Deployed to George AFB CA with the 562 TFS, 23 TFW, for air-to-air gunnery training for RTU Class 68HR.
28 Mar 1968	Returned to 23 TFW, McConnell AFB KS.
3 Sep 1969	At SMAMA, McClellan AFB CA for depot work (WO). (AVH-12).
31 Dec 1969	Returned to 23 TFW, McConnell AFB KS.
29 Apr 1971	At 23 TFW, McConnell AFB KS being prepared (PL) for transfer to depot. (AVH-16).
3 May 1971	In contract depot maintenance (WK) by Fairchild Engine and Aircraft Corporation (FACCF) at Bob Sikes Municipal Airport, Crestview FL.
24 May 1971	Returned to 23 TFW, McConnell AFB KS.
7 Jul 1971	Transferred (PL) to 113 TFG ANG, Andrews AFB MD.
14 Jul 1971	At 113 TFG ANG (CC), Andrews AFB MD.
5 Apr 1972	In contract depot work (WM) by Dynalectron Corporation (DYNZZ) at Andrews AFB MD. (AVH-18).
19 Apr 1972	Returned to 113 TFG ANG (CC), Andrews AFB MD.

27 Apr 1972	Back in depot work (WM) by Dynalectron Corporation (DYNZZ) at Andrews AFB MD.
11 May 1972	Returned to 113 TFG ANG (CC), Andrews AFB MD.
16 Nov 1972	In contract depot maintenance (WK) by Fairchild Engine and Aircraft Corporation (FACCF) at Bob Sikes Municipal Airport, Crestview FL.
13 Dec 1972	Returned (PL) to 113 TFG ANG, Andrews AFB MD.
8 May 1973	In contract depot work (WM) by Dynalectron Corporation (DYNZZ) at Andrews AFB MD. (AVH-20).
16 May 1973	At 113 TFG ANG, Andrews AFB MD.
14 Jan 1974	In contract depot maintenance (WK) by Fairchild Engine and Aircraft Corporation (FACCF) at Bob Sikes Municipal Airport, Crestview FL. (AVH-22).
12 Jun 1974	Returned (CC) to 113 TFG ANG, Andrews AFB MD.
30 Nov 1974	Unit designation and assignment changed to 113 TFW ANG, Andrews AFB MD.
31 Dec 1974	At 113 TFW ANG, Andrews AFB MD.
15 Sep 1975	In contract depot work (WM) by Dynalectron Corporation (DYNZZ) at Andrews AFB MD. (AVH-23).
19 Sep 1975	At 113 TFW ANG, Andrews AFB MD. (AVH-23 & AVH-24).
20 Jan 1976	In storage (XX) at 113 TFW ANG, Andrews AFB MD. Inventory Account: GB. (AVH-24).
30 Mar 1976	In storage (XX) at 113 TFW ANG, Andrews AFB MD. 3,127.0 flying hours. Inventory Account: TW. (AVH-24 & AVH-26).
Aug 1977	Aircraft placed on display at Keesler AFB MS. The Keesler runway was too short for an F-105 to land, so the aircraft flew to Gulfport MS. It was then picked up by a CH-54 Sky Crane helicopter from the U.S. Army National Guard Transportation Aircraft Repair Shop at Gulfport, MS and lifted to the runway at Keesler. (Air Force Times, 5 Sept 1977).

F-105D–15RE 61-0041

Republic Production No: D-236 Production Sequence No: 316

Location: Displayed by the 113 FW, Washington DC ANG, at Andrews AFB, Maryland.

Aircraft Name(s)	Crew	Unit	Date	Description
Kordel-Eden	Col. Wilbur J. Grumbles	49 TFW	Nov 61	On nose below gun port with map of Texas

Aircraft Chronology

4 Oct 1961	Picked up from production at Republic Aviation, Farmingdale NY by USAF pilot from 4440 Delivery Group. (ACA-87).
10 Oct 1961	Delivered to MOAMA, Brookley AFB AL for depot work (WO).
26 Oct 1961	Picked up from MOAMA by USAF pilot from 4440 Delivery Group.
30 Oct 1961	The first F-105D delivered to the 49 TFW, Spangdahlem AB, Germany. It was piloted by Col. Wilbur J. Grumbles, 49 TFW Commander, who named it "Kordel-Eden" after Kordel, Germany, and his hometown of Eden, Texas.
31 Jul 1962	At 49 TFW, Spangdahlem AB, Germany. (ACA-87).
25 May 1963	At MOAMA, Brookley AFB AL for depot maintenance (WO). "Operation Look Alike," Phase II.

26 May 1963	Returned to 49 TFW, Spangdahlem AB, Germany.
23 Oct 1964	At MOAMA, Brookley AFB AL for depot maintenance (WO). (AVH-2).
22 Apr 1965	Returned to 49 TFW, Spangdahlem AB, Germany. (AVH-3).
24 Nov 1965	Transferred to 4 TFW, Seymour Johnson AFB NC.
30 Nov 1965	While assigned to the 4 TFW, Seymour Johnson AFB NC, the aircraft flew 4.6 hours for the month of November 1965 and had 940.4 total flying hours. Assigned crew chief: SSgt. Rush. (4 TFW History, Jul–Dec 65, Vol. II, USAF microfilm MO292).
31 Dec 1965	While assigned to the 4 TFW, Seymour Johnson AFB NC, the aircraft flew 25.6 hours for the month of December 1965 and had 865.9 total flying hours. Assigned crew chief: TSgt. Schumate. (4 TFW History, Jul–Dec 65, Vol. II, USAF microfilm MO292).
25 Mar 1966	In test (EI) by SMAMA at McClellan AFB CA. (AVH-5).
8 Apr 1966	Returned to 4 TFW, Seymour Johnson AFB NC.
31 Jul 1966	While assigned to the 4 TFW, Seymour Johnson AFB NC, the aircraft flew 41.6 hours for the month of July 1966 and had accumulated 1,101.1 flying hours. Assigned crew chief: SSgt. J. L. Nyland. (4 TFW History, Jul–Dec 66, USAF microfilm MO293).
22 Nov 1966	Transferred to 4520 CCTW, Nellis AFB NV for combat crew training (TF). (AVH-5).
9 Jun 1967	At 4520 CCTW, Nellis AFB NV for combat crew training (TF). (AVH-7).
21 Dec 1967	Transferred to 23 TFW, McConnell AFB KS for combat crew training (TF).
21 Apr 1968	At SMAMA, McClellan AFB CA for depot maintenance (WO). (AVH-10).
25 Jun 1968	Returned to 23 TFW, McConnell AFB KS.
23 Oct 1968	At SMAMA, McClellan AFB CA for depot maintenance (WO).
12 Nov 1968	Returned to 23 TFW, McConnell AFB KS.
16 Dec 1970	In contract depot maintenance (WK) by Fairchild Engine and Aircraft Corporation (FACCF) at Bob Sikes Municipal Airport, Crestview FL. (AVH-14).
18 Jan 1971	Returned (PL) to 23 TFW, McConnell AFB KS. (AVH-16).
6 Apr 1971	Assigned to AFLC (WQ) at 23 TFW, McConnell AFB KS.
7 Jun 1971	In depot work (WO) by SMAMA, McClellan AFB CA.
11 Apr 1972	Transferred to 113 TFG ANG, Andrews AFB MD. (AVH-18).
18 Oct 1972	In contract depot maintenance (WK) by Fairchild Engine and Aircraft Corporation (FACCF) at Bob Sikes Municipal Airport, Crestview FL.
8 Nov 1972	Returned (PL) to 113 TFG ANG, Andrews AFB MD.
11 Mar 1973	In contract depot maintenance (WO) by Dynalectron Corporation (DYNZZ) at Andrews AFB MD. (AVH-20).
14 Mar 1973	At 113 TFG ANG, Andrews AFB MD.
21 Jan 1974	In contract depot maintenance (WM) by Dynalectron Corporation (DYNZZ) at Andrews AFB MD. (AVH-22).
25 Jan 1974	At 113 TFG ANG, Andrews AFB MD.
6 Nov 1974	In contract depot maintenance (WM) by Dynalectron Corporation (DYNZZ) at Andrews AFB MD.
14 Nov 1974	At 113 TFG ANG, Andrews AFB MD.
30 Nov 1974	Assigned organization changed to 113 TFW ANG, Andrews AFB MD.
31 Dec 1974	At 113 TFW ANG, Andrews AFB MD.
3 Mar 1975	In contract depot maintenance (WM) by Dynalectron Corporation (DYNZZ) at Andrews AFB MD. (AVH-23).
7 Mar 1975	At 113 TFW ANG, Andrews AFB MD.
10 Dec 1975	In storage, low probability of withdrawal (XX), at 113 TFW ANG, Andrews AFB MD. Inventory. Account: GB. (AVH-23 & AVH-24).

This F-105D 61-0041 was the first F-105 delivered to the 49 Tactical Fighter Wing in Germany. The 49th wing commander who flew the plane to Germany named it "*Kordel-Eden*" after Kordel, Germany, a town south of Spangdahlem Air Base, and his home town of Eden, Texas. The plane left Spangdahlem in 1965 and trained pilots at Seymour Johnson Air Force Base, North Carolina, Nellis Air Force Base, Nevada, and McConnell Air Force Base, Kansas. In 1972 it joined the Air National Guard at Andrews Air Force Base, Maryland. After the Guard retired it in 1975, they placed it on display at Andrews. (Photograph by Jay Finch, November 1996.)

21 May 1976 In storage at 113 TFW ANG, Andrews AFB MD. 3,263.0 flying hours. Possession Code: XX. Inventory Account: TL. (AVH-24, AVH-25 & AVH-26).

F-105D–15RE 61-0050

Republic Production No: D-245 Production Sequence No: 325

Location: Mounted on a column at Byrd Field, Richmond, Virginia.

Aircraft Name(s)	Crew	Unit	Date	Description
The 'Boss'		149 TFS VA ANG	Jan 79	F-105 with dragster tires. Pilot with scarf and rebel flag on helmet.

Aircraft Chronology

1 Dec 1961 USAF production acceptance from Republic Aviation, Farmingdale NY. (ACA-87).

6 Dec 1961 At MOAMA, Brookley AFB AL for depot work.

21 Dec 1961 Delivered to 49 TFW, Spangdahlem AB, Germany.

21 May 1963 At MOAMA, Brookley AFB AL for depot work. "Operation Look Alike," Phase II.

17 Sep 1963 Returned to 49 TFW, Spangdahlem AB, Germany.

1 Apr 1965 At CASA, Madrid, Spain, for contract depot work (WK). (AVH-3).

6 May 1965 At 49 TFW, Spangdahlem AB, Germany.

Sep 1965	At Wheelus AB, Libya, with 49 TFW.
12 Apr 1966	At CASA, Madrid, Spain, for contract depot work (WK). (AVH-5).
16 May 1966	At 49 TFW, Spangdahlem AB, Germany.
19 Aug 1966	At Wheelus AB, Libya, with 49 TFW.
10 Sep 1966	Returned to 49 TFW, Spangdahlem AB, Germany.
13 Oct 1966	Transferred to 23 TFW, McConnell AFB KS.
28 Oct 1966	At MOAMA, Brookley AFB AL for depot work (WO).
16 Jan 1967	At 23 TFW, McConnell AFB KS. (AVH-7).
31 Jan 1967	In depot maintenance (WM) by SMAMA field team at McConnell AFB KS.
6 Feb 1967	At 23 TFW, McConnell AFB KS.
1 Jun 1967	Deployed to George AFB CA with the 563 TFS, 23 TFW, for air-to-air gunnery training for RTU Class 67IR.
16 Jun 1967	Returned to 23 TFW, McConnell AFB KS.
8 Oct 1967	In depot maintenance (WM) by SMAMA field team at McConnell AFB KS.
9 Oct 1967	At 23 TFW, McConnell AFB KS.
3 Nov 1967	Deployed to George AFB CA with the 563 TFS, 23 TFW, for air-to-air gunnery training for RTU Class 68DR.
22 Nov 1967	Returned to 23 TFW, McConnell AFB KS.
16 Apr 1968	Deployed to George AFB CA with the 563 TFS, 23 TFW, for air-to-air gunnery training for RTU Class 68IR. (AVH-10).
9 May 1968	Returned to 23 TFW, McConnell AFB KS.
22 Jul 1968	At SMAMA, McClellan AFB CA for depot work (WO).
30 Aug 1968	Returned to 23 TFW, McConnell AFB KS.
20 Oct 1968	Transferred to 388 TFW, Korat RTAB, Thailand.
31 Oct 1968	Aircraft had accumulated 1,656.5 flying hours while assigned to the 388 TFW, Korat RTAB, Thailand. (388 TFW History, Oct–Dec 68, USAF microfilm NO585).
10 Nov 1968	Transferred to 18 TFW, Kadena AB, Okinawa.
23 Nov 1968	At 18 TFW, Kadena AB, Okinawa.
29 Apr 1969	At Kwangju AB, Korea, with 18 TFW. (AVH-12).
15 May 1969	Returned to 18 TFW, Kadena AB, Okinawa.
13 Jun 1969	At Kwangju AB, Korea, with 18 TFW.
26 Jun 1969	Returned to 18 TFW, Kadena AB, Okinawa.
9 Aug 1969	At Air Asia, Tainan, Taiwan, for contract depot work (WK).
14 Oct 1969	Returned to 18 TFW, Kadena AB, Okinawa.
27 Aug 1970	At Kwangju AB, Korea, with 18 TFW. (AVH-14).
7 Sep 1970	Returned to 18 TFW, Kadena AB, Okinawa.
3 Nov 1970	Transferred to 23 TFW, McConnell AFB KS.
4 Jan 1971	At 23 TFW, McConnell AFB KS.
2 Feb 1971	In depot work (WO) by SMAMA, McClellan AFB CA. (AVH-16).
19 Mar 1971	Transferred (PL) to 192 TFG ANG, Byrd Field, Richmond VA.
17 Feb 1972	At 192 TFG ANG, Byrd Field, Richmond VA. (AVH-18).
18 Dec 1972	In depot work (WO) by SM-ALC, McClellan AFB CA.
10 Apr 1973	At 192 TFG ANG, Byrd Field, Richmond VA. (AVH-20).
15 Aug 1973	In contract depot work (WM) by Dynalectron Corporation (DYNZZ) at Byrd Field, Richmond VA.
17 Aug 1973	At 192 TFG ANG, Byrd Field, Richmond VA.

This F-105D 61-0050 was one of the production F-105Ds that replaced the F-100D Super Sabers of the 49 Tactical Fighter Wing at Spangdahlem Air Base, Germany, in 1961. When F-4Ds replaced Thunderchiefs at Spangdahlem in 1966, the plane went to McConnell Air Force Base, Kansas, where it trained pilots for the next two years. It then spent the next two years in the Pacific, primarily at Kadena Air Base, Okinawa. After a short stay back at McConnell, it went to the Virginia Air National Guard at Richmond who named it *"The Boss."* However, in 1976 the Guard retired it early when it developed a tendency to roll at speeds above 500 knots. They traced the problem to a depot wing change that resulted in wings with slight aeronautical differences from two different manufacturers. *"The Boss,"* keeping below 500 knots, has since guarded the entrance to the Air National Guard's side of the Richmond airport. (Photograph by author 9 August 1997.)

9 Apr 1974	In contract depot work (WM) by Dynalectron Corporation (DYNZZ) at Byrd Field, Richmond VA. (AVH-22).
30 Apr 1974	At 192 TFG ANG, Byrd Field, Richmond VA.
17 Dec 1974	In contract depot work (WM) by Dynalectron Corporation (DYNZZ) at Byrd Field, Richmond VA.
25 Jan 1975	At 192 TFG ANG, Byrd Field, Richmond VA. (AVH-23).
23 Oct 1975	In contract depot work (WM) by Dynalectron Corporation (DYNZZ) at Byrd Field, Richmond VA. (AVH-23 & AVH-24).
9 Jan 1976	In depot maintenance (WM) by SM-ALC at Byrd Field, Richmond VA. (AVH-24).
6 Feb 1976	At 192 TFG ANG, Byrd Field, Richmond VA. Inventory Account: TW.

F-105D–15RE 61-0056

Republic Production No: D-251 Production Sequence No: 331

Location: Displayed on a steel pylon at Seymour Johnson AFB, Goldsboro, North Carolina.

Aircraft Chronology

	Delivered from production to 4 TFW, Seymour Johnson AFB NC.
13 Apr 1962	At 4 TFW, Eglin AFB FL. (ACA-87).
14 Apr 1962	At 4 TFW, Seymour Johnson AFB NC.
6 Jun 1962	At 333 TFS, 4 TFW, Seymour Johnson AFB NC. (RAC record).

20 Dec 1962	At Republic Aviation, Farmingdale NY.
2 May 1963	Transferred to 355 TFW, George AFB CA.
15 Jul 1964	Moved with 355 TFW to McConnell AFB KS. (AVH-1)
5 Aug 1964	Deployed on TDY to Yokota AB, Japan, with the 357 TFS from the 355 TFW, McConnell AFB KS.
5 Dec 1964	Returned from Japan to the 355 TFW, McConnell AFB KS.
Jan 1965	Deployed on TDY to Kadena AB, Okinawa, with 469 TFS, 355 TFW, from McConnell AFB KS. Assigned crew chief: SSgt. Davis. (18 TFW History, Jan–Jun 65, USAF microfilm MO497).
Mar 1965	Transferred on TDY to Kadena AB, Okinawa, with the 354 TFS, 355 TFW, from McConnell AFB KS. Assigned crew chief: SSgt. Bacon. (18 TFW History, Jan–Jun 65, USAF microfilm MO497).
11 Jul 1965	At 355 TFW, McConnell AFB KS. (AVH-3).
27 Jul 1965	At MOAMA, Brookley AFB AL for depot work (WO).
27 Oct 1965	At Crestview FL for contract depot work (WK).
23 Nov 1965	Transferred to the 23 TFW, McConnell AFB KS when the 355 TFW moved to Takhli RTAB, Thailand.
27 Aug 1966	At 23 TFW, McConnell AFB KS. (AVH-5).
11 Feb 1967	In depot maintenance by SMAMA field team at McConnell AFB KS. (AVH-7).
17 Feb 1967	At 23 TFW, McConnell AFB KS.
30 Jun 1967	Deployed to George AFB CA with the 560 TFS, 23 TFW, for air-to-air gunnery training for RTU Class 67JR.
14 Jul 1967	Returned to 23 TFW, McConnell AFB KS.
29 Sep 1967	Deployed to George AFB CA with the 562 TFS, 23 TFW, for air-to-air gunnery training for RTU Class 68BR.
13 Oct 1967	Returned to 23 TFW, McConnell AFB KS.
2 Dec 1967	Deployed to George AFB CA with the 560 TFS, 23 TFW, for air-to-air gunnery training for RTU Class 68ER.
14 Dec 1967	Returned to 23 TFW, McConnell AFB KS.
17 Dec 1967	Returned to George AFB CA to continue with the 560 TFS, 23 TFW, for air-to-air gunnery training for RTU Class 68ER.
22 Dec 1967	Returned to 23 TFW, McConnell AFB KS.
14 May 1968	Deployed to George AFB CA with the 560 TFS, 23 TFW, for air-to-air gunnery training for RTU Class 68JR. (AVH-10).
29 May 1968	Returned to 23 TFW, McConnell AFB KS for combat crew training (TF).
9 Dec 1968	Transferred to the 4525 FWW, Nellis AFB NV for combat tactics development (CB).
16 May 1969	At 4525 FWW TAC, Nellis AFB NV being readied for transfer (PL). (AVH-12).
19 May 1969	In depot maintenance (WO) at SMAMA, McClellan AFB CA.
2 Sep 1969	Returned to 4525 FWW, Nellis AFB NV for combat tactics development (CB).
15 Oct 1969	Transferred to 57 FWW TAC, Nellis AFB NV for combat tactics development (CB).
9 Jun 1970	In depot work (WM) by SMAMA at McClellan AFB CA. (AVH-14).
29 Jun 1970	Returned to 57 FWW, Nellis AFB NV.
21 Apr 1971	Transferred to 23 TFW, McConnell AFB KS. (AVH-16).
4 May 1971	In contract depot maintenance (WK) by Fairchild Engine and Aircraft Corporation (FACCF) at Bob Sikes Municipal Airport, Crestview FL.
26 May 1971	While assigned to the 23 TFW, McConnell AFB KS, the aircraft was damaged due to a failed clamp on hot air ducting. Electrical wire bundles in the ATM compartment were overheated from 15th stage engine bleed air that ported through an open hot air duct near the rain removal valve. (23 TFW History, Apr–Jun 71, USAF microfilm MO556).
14 Jul 1971	At 23 TFW, McConnell AFB KS. (AVH-16).

Since the 4 Tactical Fighter Wing was the first Air Force unit to fly the Thunderchief it is fitting that their home at Seymour Johnson Air Force Base in North Carolina has one on display. This plane was briefly assigned to Seymour Johnson in 1962 but it spent most of its career at McConnell Air Force Base, Kansas, arriving there with the 355 Tactical Fighter Wing in July 1964. A month later, it was one of 18 Thunderchiefs that deployed after a 24-hour notice with the 357 Tactical Fighter Squadron to Yokota Air Base, Japan. This deployment was part of President Johnson's initial response to the Gulf of Tonkin crisis. As the Vietnam war escalated over the next year, the plane stayed in the Pacific for deployments of two more 355th squadrons from McConnell to Kadena Air Base, Okinawa. However, when the 355th wing moved to Takhli, Thailand, in November 1965, the plane returned to McConnell to train pilots with the 23 Tactical Fighter Wing. It spent a year and a half at Nellis Air Force Base, Nevada, before moving back to McConnell in 1971. In 1972 the plane transferred to the Washington DC Air National Guard who flew it for the next ten years. The Guard retired it in 1982 after 20 years of service. (Photograph by author, 9 August 1997.)

10 Sep 1971 The aircraft had two engine bay fire extinguisher initiators inadvertently fired due to personnel error while on the ramp at the 23 TFW, McConnell AFB KS. (23 TFW History, Jul–Sep 71, USAF microfilm MO556).

1 Mar 1972 Carried on assignment roster for the 562 TFS, 23 TFW, at McConnell AFB KS. (Master 23 TFW Aircraft Assignment as of 1 March 1972).

1 Jul 1972 Assigned directly to the 561 TFS, McConnell AFB KS when the 23 TFW moved to England AFB LA. (AVH-18).

28 Jul 1972 In contract depot maintenance (WK) by Fairchild Engine and Aircraft Corporation (FACCF) at Bob Sikes Municipal Airport, Crestview FL.

22 Aug 1972 Transferred (PL) to 113 TFG ANG, Andrews AFB MD.

17 Feb 1973 In contract depot work (WM) by Dynalectron Corporation (DYNZZ) at Andrews AFB MD. (AVH-20).

1 Mar 1973 At 113 TFG ANG, Andrews AFB MD.

1 Apr 1974 In contract depot maintenance (WM) by Dynalectron Corporation (DYNZZ) at Andrews AFB MD. (AVH-22).

19 Apr 1974 At 113 TFG ANG, Andrews AFB MD.

30 Nov 1974 Assigned organization changed to 113 TFW ANG, Andrews AFB MD.

31 Dec 1974 At 113 TFW ANG, Andrews AFB MD.

13 Jan 1975 In contract depot work (WM) by Dynalectron Corporation (DYNZZ) at Andrews AFB MD. (AVH-23).

31 Jan 1975 At 113 TFW ANG, Andrews AFB MD.

1 Nov 1976 In depot maintenance by SM-ALC at Andrews AFB MD. 3,589.0 flying hours. (AVH-25 & AVH-26).

27 Dec 1976 At 113 TFW ANG, Andrews AFB MD. 3,663 flying hours.

14 Aug 1978	At SM-ALC depot, McClellan AFB CA. 3,943.0 flying hours.
29 Aug 1978	At 113 TFW ANG, Andrews AFB MD. 3,971.0 flying hours.
15 Dec 1979	In contract depot maintenance (DM) by General Dynamics (DYNFW) at Andrews AFB MD. 4,274.7 flying hours. (GO33B. 24 Jun 1980).
29 Dec 1979	At 113 TFW, Andrews AFB MD. 4,274.7 flying hours.
19 Apr 1980	In contract depot maintenance by Dynalectron Corporation (DYNZZ) at Andrews AFB MD. 4,306.1 flying hours.
23 Apr 1980	At 113 TFW ANG, Andrews AFB MD. 4,318.3 flying hours. (GO33B 22 Jan 81).
12 Feb 1982	At 113 TFW ANG, Andrews AFB MD. Inventory account "ZW"—School or Museum. 4,463.7 flying hours. (GO33B 1 Feb 83).

F-105D-15RE 61-0069

Republic Production No: D-264 Production Sequence No: 344

Location: At the Strategic Air Command Museum, Ashland, Nebraska.

Aircraft Name(s)	Crew	Unit	Date	Description
Cherry Girl			Oct 83	Naked female with legs open around refueling receptacle. Special restoration.

Aircraft Chronology

5 Jan 1962	USAF production acceptance from Republic Aviation, Farmingdale NY. (AFTO Form 95).
9 Jan 1962	Delivered to APGC, Eglin AFB FL. (ACA-87).
12 Jan 1962	Bailed (EB) to Republic Aviation at Eglin AFB FL.
6 Jun 1962	At APGC, Eglin AFB FL bailed to Republic. (RAC record).
21 Sep 1962	At MOAMA, Brookley AFB AL for depot work (WO).
19 Nov 1962	Transferred to the 355 TFW, George AFB CA.
3 May 1963	At Republic Aviation, Farmingdale NY for depot work (WK).
4 May 1963	Returned to 355 TFW, George AFB CA.
8 Jul 1964	Moved with the 355 TFW to McConnell AFB KS. (AVH-1)
28 Dec 1964	At MOAMA, Brookley AFB AL for depot work (WO). (AVH-2).
27 Apr 1965	At SMAMA, McClellan AFB CA for depot work (WO). (AVH-3).
9 May 1965	At 355 TFW, McConnell AFB KS.
2 Sep 1965	At McClellan AFB CA for depot work (WO).
10 Oct 1965	Returned to 355 TFW, McConnell AFB KS.
20 Oct 1965	Transferred to 23 TFW, McConnell AFB KS when the 355 TFW moved to Takhli, Thailand.
21 Nov 1965	At SMAMA, McClellan AFB CA for depot work (WO).
8 Apr 1966	At 388 TFW, Korat RTAB, Thailand. (AVH-5).
27 Jan 1967	At Air Asia, Tainan, Taiwan, for contract depot work (WK). (AVH-7).
22 Mar 1967	Depot work completed. Consisted of IRAN, MOD/TCTO, corrosion control and repainting. 1,538.9 flying hours. (AFTO Form 95).

"069" had a somewhat unusual career. It spent much of its active-duty service as a test airplane starting in 1962 at Eglin Air Force Base, Florida. However, it had one brief but glorious year of flying combat from Korat, Thailand. In June 1967, it was the plane Capt. Larry Wiggins flew when he shot down a North Vietnamese MiG-17. A little over a month later, the plane returned home and resumed test duties at McClellan Air Force Base, California, and Nellis Air Force Base, Nevada. The Air Force Reserve in Oklahoma inherited it in 1972 and flew it for the next eight years. In 1978, it was one of 18 F-105s they flew on their NATO summer deployment to Great Britain. After the Reserve unit at Hill Air Force Base, Utah, received it they took it on their NATO deployment to Denmark in 1981. It's last flight was to Norton Air Force Base, California, in 1983 where it was dedicated on Veterans Day 1984 at the county museum in nearby Redlands, its location in the photo. In January 2000, the plane was relocated to the SAC Museum in Nebraska. (Photograph by author, 31 October 1996.)

23 Mar 1967 Returned to 388 TFW, Korat RTAB, Thailand.

12 May 1967 Flown on Rolling Thunder mission RT56C-078 by Capt James S. Walbridge from the 388 TFW, Korat RTAB, Thailand. The target was in Hanoi, North Vietnam, at coordinates 20-59-05N and 105-47-57E. (National Archives strike camera film shot list, item 41720B).

13 May 1967 Flown by 388 TFW pilots on two combat sorties during Rolling Thunder mission RT56C-079. In the morning it was flown by Maj. Robert B. Bennett from the 13 TFS, one of four F-105Ds in "Ozark" flight. The flight dropped 24 750-pound bombs on a truck park in RP-3, North Vietnam. In the afternoon it was flown as "Ragtop 3" by Maj. Ralph Lloyd Kuster from the 469 TFS. The flight was one of four flights of F-105Ds from the 388 TFW that bombed the Vinh Yen Army barracks. Each flight encountered several MiG-17s one of which was shot down by Maj. Maurice E. Seaver, a pilot in "Tamale" flight. (National Archives strike camera film shot list, item 41720B and 388 TFW/DOI JOPREP message 131208Z May 67).

19 May 1967 One of two F-105Ds flown on Rolling Thunder mission RT56C-085 to attack a target NE of Phu Lang Thuong, North Vietnam, at coordinates 21-21-35N and 106-16-00E. The pilot was Maj Wray C. Lasswell from the 13 TFS, 388 TFW, Korat RTAB, Thailand.

31 May 1967 One of three F-105Ds flown on Rolling Thunder mission RT56A-027 to attack Kep Airfield, North Vietnam, at coordinates 21-23N and 106-16E. The pilot was Maj Peter H. Karalus from the 44 TFS, 388 TFW, Korat RTAB, Thailand, who bombed barracks at the airfield. (National Archives strike camera film shot list, item 41720D).

3 Jun 1967 One of five F-105Ds flown on Rolling Thunder mission RT56A-030 to attack the Bac Giang railroad and highway bridge and the adjacent railroad yards NE of Hanoi, North Vietnam, at coordinates 21-16-30N and 106-11-18E. Flown by Capt Larry D. Wiggins (469 TFS 388 TFW) who shot down a MiG 17 with an AIM-9 missile and the 20mm gun. Call sign: "Hambone 03." " ... Approximately 6 miles from the target the flight leader saw three MIG-17's at 10 o'clock low at a range of 2 miles. ... The three MIG's went into a tight left-hand orbit at about 500 feet altitude. The U.S. and enemy flights completed a circle and a half before Wiggins was able to fire his AIM-9B at the third MIG. The enemy plane attempted to evade the missile but was damaged. Wiggins' film showed that the missile went alongside the MIG's tailpipe and exploded. The aircraft began trailing a heavy white vapor. Continuing to close on the MIG as it rolled over and started down, Wiggins fired 376 rounds of 20-mm at a high angle-off. The MIG exploded in flame and crashed." (National Archives strike camera film shot list, item 41720C and "Aces & Aerial Victories," page 62).

6 Jun 1967	One of seven F-105Ds flown on Rolling Thunder mission RT56A-033 to attack railroad and highway bridges in North Vietnam. The pilot was Maj Richard E. Moser from the 44 TFS, 388 TFW, Korat RTAB, Thailand, who bombed a target NE of Hanoi at coordinates 21-30-30N and 106-07-50E. (National Archives strike camera film shot list, item 41720D).
9 Jun 1967	One of two F-105Ds flown on Rolling Thunder mission RT56A-036 to attack a target NE of Hanoi, North Vietnam, at coordinates 21-24N and 106-17-30E. The pilot was Capt James E. Chambers from the 44 TFS, 388 TFW, Korat RTAB, Thailand. (National Archives strike camera film shot list, item 41720C).
11 Jun 1967	Flown on Rolling Thunder mission RT56A-038 by a pilot named Haggard from the 388 TFW, Korat RTAB, Thailand.
12 Jun 1967	Flown on Rolling Thunder mission RT56A-039 by a pilot named Majors from the 13 TFS, 388 TFW, Korat RTAB, Thailand. The target was at coordinates 21-18-50N and 107-52-35E.
14 Jun 1967	Flown on Rolling Thunder mission RT56A-042 by Maj Robert B. Bennett from the 13 TFS, 388 TFW, Korat RTAB, Thailand. The target was NE of Kep airfield in North Vietnam at coordinates 21-28-21N and 106-22-58E.
19 Jun 1967	One of two F-105Ds flown on Rolling Thunder mission RT56A-047 to attack a target NE of Kep airfield in North Vietnam at coordinates 21-26-15N and 106-20-35E. The pilot was Maj Maurice E. Seaver from the 44 TFS, 388 TFW, Korat RTAB, Thailand.
18 Jul 1967	At the 388 TFW, Korat RTAB, Thailand, being prepared for transfer (PL) to the depot.
23 Jul 1967	Transferred to SMAMA, McClellan AFB CA.
17 Aug 1967	In storage (XW) at SMAMA, McClellan AFB CA.
5 Dec 1967	Bailed (EB) to Republic Aviation, Farmingdale NY for installation of TCTOs. 1,849.8 flying hours. (AFTO Form 95).
21 Dec 1968	Aircraft departed Republic Aviation, Farmingdale NY. 1,852.6 flying hours. (AFTO Form 95).
23 Dec 1968	At 2750 ABW, Wright-Patterson AFB OH for transient maintenance (WL). (AVH-12).
16 Jan 1969	Bailed (EB) to Fairchild Republic factory, Farmingdale NY for test.
17 Jan 1969	Assigned to SMAMA, McClellan AFB CA for instructional project (PJ) and depot work (WO).
8 May 1969	At SMAMA, McClellan AFB CA. Transfer and Twelfth Phase Inspections completed, engine changed and modifications accomplished. 1,863.0 flying hours. (AFTO Form 95).
19 May 1969	Transferred to 4525 FWW TAC, Nellis AFB NV for combat tactics development (CB).
15 Oct 1969	At 4525 FWW, Nellis AFB NV.
13 Apr 1970	Transferred to 57 FWW, Nellis AFB NV. (AVH-14).
15 Apr 1970	In depot maintenance (WO) at SMAMA, McClellan AFB CA.
17 Jul 1970	IRAN/MOD completed at SMAMA, McClellan AFB CA. 2,143.9 flying hours. (AFTO Form 95).
31 Jul 1970	Returned to 66 FWS, 57 FWW, Nellis AFB NV for combat tactics development (CB). (AVH-14).
7 Aug 1970	Class 2 modification for Bomb Tone completed at SMAMA, McClellan AFB CA. (AFTO Form 95).
15 Mar 1971	At 66 FWS, 57 FWW, Nellis AFB NV. Aircraft prepared for transfer to Crestview FL for wing modification. (AFTO Form 95).
1 Apr 1971	In contract depot maintenance (WK) by Fairchild Engine and Aircraft Corporation (FACCF) at Bob Sikes Municipal Airport, Crestview FL. Wing pylon fitting and doubler modification completed so that Category 3 flight restriction was lifted. 2,380.2 flying hours. (AVH-16 & AFTO Form 95).
8 Apr 1971	Aircraft returned to 66 FWS, 57 FWW, Nellis AFB NV. Completed acceptance inspection. (AFTO Form 95).
19 Apr 1971	Flown by Maj. Gene I. Basel as member of F-105 Operational Test and Evaluation team at Nellis AFB NV. (Letter from G. I. Basel in Air Classics Magazine).
20 Apr 1971	Transferred to 23 TFW, McConnell AFB KS (AVH-16).
22 Apr 1971	At 562 TFS, 23 TFW (CC), McConnell AFB KS.
1 Mar 1972	Carried on assignment roster for the 562 TFS, 23 TFW, at McConnell AFB KS. (Master 23 TFW Aircraft Assignment as of 1 March 1972).

11 Mar 1972	While assigned to 562 TFS, 23 TFW, McConnell AFB KS, the variable air inlet ramps were deactivated per Class A modification as directed in TAC message, 10 Mar 1972. (AFTO Form 95).
27 Jun 1972	In contract depot maintenance (WK) by Fairchild Engine and Aircraft Corporation (FACCF) at Bob Sikes Municipal Airport, Crestview FL. (AVH-18).
21 Jul 1972	AIMS and Flap Track Modifications (T.O.s 1F-105-1127 and 1F-105-1172) completed at Bob Sikes Municipal Airport, Crestview FL. 2,784.1 flying hours. (AFTO Form 95).
26 Jul 1972	Transferred to 507 TFG AFRES, Tinker AFB OK.
8 Mar 1973	In depot maintenance (WM) by SM-ALC at Tinker AFB OK. (AVH-20).
31 Mar 1973	Assigned to 507 CMTSq AFRES, Tinker AFB OK.
7 Mar 1974	In depot maintenance (WM) by SM-ALC at Tinker AFB OK. (AVH-22).
14 Mar 1974	At 507 CMTSq AFRES, Tinker AFB OK.
9 May 1974	In depot maintenance (WM) by SM-ALC at Tinker AFB OK.
16 May 1974	At 507 CMTSq AFRES, Tinker AFB OK.
31 Jul 1974	In contract depot work (WK) by Fairchild Engine and Aircraft Corporation (FACCF) at Bob Sikes Municipal Airport, Crestview FL.
14 Nov 1974	Depot work completed at Crestview FL. 3,115.3 flying hours. (AFTO Form 95).
21 Nov 1974	Returned to 507 CLMSq AFRES, Tinker AFB OK.
29 Jan 1975	In contract depot maintenance (WK) by Fairchild Engine and Aircraft Corporation (FACCF) at Bob Sikes Municipal Airport, Crestview FL. (AVH-23).
4 Feb 1975	At 507 CLMSq AFRES, Tinker AFB OK.
19 May 1975	In contract depot maintenance (WK) by Fairchild Engine and Aircraft Corporation (FACCF) at Bob Sikes Municipal Airport, Crestview FL. (AVH-23 & AVH-24).
2 Jun 1975	At 507 CLMSq AFRES, Tinker AFB OK.
21 Jul 1975	In depot maintenance (WM) by SM-ALC at Tinker AFB OK.
8 Aug 1975	At 507 CLMSq AFRES, Tinker AFB OK.
6 Oct 1975	In depot maintenance (WM) by SM-ALC at Tinker AFB OK.
6 Oct 1975	At 507 CLMSq AFRES, Tinker AFB OK.
16 Dec 1975	In depot maintenance (WM) by SM-ALC at Tinker AFB OK.
14 Jan 1976	At 507 CLMSq AFRES, Tinker AFB OK (AVH-24).
7 Jun 1976	In depot maintenance (WM) by SM-ALC at Tinker AFB OK. 3,337 flying hours.
11 Jun 1976	At 507 TFG AFRES, Tinker AFB OK. 3,337 flying hours.
10 Nov 1976	In depot maintenance (WM) by SM-ALC at Tinker AFB OK. 3,442 flying hours.
22 Nov 1976	At 507 TFG AFRES, Tinker AFB OK. 3,442 flying hours.
28 Oct 1977	At 465 TFS AFRES, Tinker AFB OK. 3,743.0 flying hours. (AVH-26).
2 Mar 1978	In depot maintenance by SM-ALC at Tinker AFB OK. 3,761.0 flying hours.
14 Mar 1978	At 465 TFS AFRES, Tinker AFB OK. 3,784.0 flying hours.
12 May 1978	On display at Randolph AFB TX. (Dan Hagedorn photo, letter 29 Apr 97).
10 Jun 1978	Deployed under "Coronet Oriole" with 465 TFS to Sculthorpe, England from Tinker AFB OK. (British Aviation Review, Dec 1995).
23 Jun 1978	Returned from England to Tinker AFB OK.
25 Jun 1978	In depot maintenance by SM-ALC at Tinker AFB OK. 3,929.0 flying hours. (AVH-26).
18 Jul 1978	At 465 TFS AFRES, Tinker AFB OK. 3,965.0 flying hours.
27 Apr 1979	While assigned to the 465 TFS AFRES, Tinker AFB OK, the aircraft ground aborted due to a high EGT reading caused by a misadjusted fuel control. (301 TFW History 1 Apr–30 Jun 1979, USAF microfilm 343832).
30 Jun 1979	While assigned to the 465 TFS AFRES, Tinker AFB OK, the aircraft flew 12.0 hours during the month

of June 1979 and had accumulated a total of 4,166.3 flying hours. The assigned crew chief was SSgt. Chester E. Gooden. (301 TFW History, Apr–Jun 1979, USAF microfilm 34382).

10 Jul 1979 In depot maintenance (FACBM) at Tinker AFB OK. 4,104.3 flying hours. (AVH-27)

20 Jul 1979 At 465 TFS AFRES, Tinker AFB OK. 4,104.3 flying hours.

3 Mar 1980 In depot maintenance by Fairchild Baltimore (FACBM) at Tinker AFB OK. 4,297.6 flying hours. (GO33B 24 Jun 80).

27 Mar 1980 At 465 TFS AFRES, Tinker AFB OK. 4,314.3 flying hours.

28 Mar 1980 While assigned to 507 TFG AFRES, Tinker AFB OK, the aircraft had a replacement M-61 20mm gun installed. (Previous gun, S/N 1621, had fired a total of 26,609 rounds). (AFTO Form 95).

1 Oct 1980 Transferred to 508 CAM Sq AFRES, Hill AFB UT. 4,434.8 flying hours. (GO33B 22 Jan 81 & AFTO Form 95).

15 Aug 1981 Deployed under "Coronet Rudder" with 466 TFS to Skrydstrup, Denmark, from Hill AFB UT. (British Aviation Review, Dec 1995).

29 Aug 1981 Returned from Denmark to Hill AFB UT.

16 Feb 1982 While assigned to 508 CAM Sq., Hill AFB UT, the AN/ALT-34 System was removed from the aircraft per HQ 10 AF message 27 Oct 1981. (AFTO Form 95).

23 Mar 1982 At 466 TFS, Hill AFB UT. Inventory account "ZW"—School or Museum. 4,611.8 flying hours. (GO33B 1 Feb 83).

11 Nov 1984 Veterans Day presentation of the aircraft on static display at the San Bernardino County Museum. "The presentation … culminated a project begun in 1978, when the museum requested a display aircraft. After working numerous possibilities, one of three F-105's being retired from service was flown to Norton AFB from Hill AFB, Utah on 23 March 1982, its last flight. It took two years of volunteer labor to get the bird stripped of its engine and as much internal equipment as possible, sand it down, and repaint it to its Vietnam colors. The mounting and heavy internal beef-up were based on designs used at other air bases. The San Bernardino Associated Contractors contributed the mounting and the big crane needed to lift the plane. The local Redlands police helped us tow the plane the two miles to the museum. … Among the speakers at the dedication were Capt. Wiggins, who described his gun kill of a MiG-17 near Hanoi on 3 Jun 1967; and Capt. Jim Sehorne, who was shot down in an F-105 near Hanoi, and spent five years as a POW. The presentation concluded an arduous and very satisfactory project by Flight 30, Order of Daedalians (The National Fraternity of Military Pilots)." (Theodore M. Fite, Lt. Col. USAF (Ret), letter to Air Classics Magazine).

30 Nov 1997 San Bernardino County Museum has announced they no longer want to display the aircraft. (Tom Brewer, USAF Museum, telephone interview, 30 Nov 1997).

22 Jan 2000 Moved to the SAC Museum near Ashland, Nebraska, for restoration and eventual display. The museum anticipates replacing about 35 percent of the plane's skin due to corrosion. (Dennis Haun, museum Deputy Director, telephone interview, 7 Apr 00).

F-105D-15RE 61-0073

Republic Production No: D-268 Production Sequence No: 348

Location: Displayed at Airpower Park and Museum, Hampton, Virginia.

Aircraft Chronology

29 Jan 1962 USAF production acceptance from Republic Aviation, Farmingdale NY. (ACA-87).

31 Jul 1962 Delivered to 49 TFW, Spangdahlem AB, Germany.

In its 18 years of flying, this "D" was one of the few that escaped a combat tour over Vietnam. It began life in 1962 as a cold-war warrior with nuclear weapon alerts at the 49 Tactical Fighter Wing in Germany. In the later 1960s through the mid-1970s, it trained pilots with the 23 Tactical Fighter Wing in Kansas and the 57 Fighter Weapons Wing at Nellis Air Force Base, Nevada. Beginning in 1974, it served with the Air National Guard, first in Kansas and then Washington DC. In 1981, it retired and was put on display near Langley Air Force Base, Virginia, the headquarters home of the Tactical Air Command that owned the aircraft for much of its career. (Photograph by James Babineaux, 16 November 1996.)

4 Jun 1963	At MOAMA, Brookley AFB AL for depot work. "Operation Look Alike," Phase II.
4 Nov 1963	Returned to 49 TFW, Spangdahlem AB, Germany.
17 Mar 1965	At CASA, Madrid, Spain, for contract depot work (WK). (AVH-3).
30 Apr 1965	Returned to 49 TFW, Spangdahlem AB, Germany.
2 Dec 1965	At CASA, Madrid, Spain, for contract depot work (WK).
19 Jan 1966	At 49 TFW, Spangdahlem AB, Germany. (AVH-5).
16 Mar 1966	At Wheelus AB, Libya, with 49 TFW.
20 May 1966	At 49 TFW, Spangdahlem AB, Germany.
29 Jul 1966	At Wheelus AB, Libya, with 49 TFW.
11 Aug 1966	At 49 TFW, Spangdahlem AB, Germany.
13 Aug 1966	At Wheelus AB, Libya, with 49 TFW.
27 Aug 1966	At 49 TFW, Spangdahlem AB, Germany.
6 Jan 1967	Transferred to 23 TFW, McConnell AFB KS. (AVH-7).
9 May 1967	At 23 TFW, McConnell AFB KS being prepared (PL) for transfer to depot.
11 May 1967	At SMAMA, McClellan AFB CA.
15 May 1967	In storage (XT) at SMAMA, McClellan AFB CA.
23 May 1967	Storage code changed to "XW" at SMAMA, McClellan AFB CA.
18 Sep 1967	Place in depot work (WO) at SMAMA, McClellan AFB CA.
13 Dec 1967	Returned to 23 TFW, McConnell AFB KS.
12 Mar 1968	Deployed to George AFB CA with the 562 TFS, 23 TFW, for air-to-air gunnery training for RTU Class 68HR. (AVH-10).
28 Mar 1968	Returned to 23 TFW, McConnell AFB KS for combat crew training (TF).
18 Jun 1968	Assigned to fighter duties (CC) at 23 TFW, McConnell AFB KS.
28 Mar 1969	At SMAMA, McClellan AFB CA for depot work (WO). (AVH-12).
30 Apr 1969	Returned to 23 TFW, McConnell AFB KS.
2 Apr 1971	At 23 TFW, McConnell AFB KS being prepared for transfer to depot (PL). (AVH-16).
7 Apr 1971	In depot work (WO) by SMAMA, McClellan AFB CA.
2 Aug 1971	Returned to 23 TFW, McConnell AFB KS.
1 Mar 1972	Carried on assignment roster for the 562 TFS, 23 TFW, at McConnell AFB KS. (Master 23 TFW Aircraft Assignment as of 1 March 1972).
1 Jul 1972	Assigned directly to the 561 TFS at McConnell AFB KS when the 23 TFW moved to England AFB LA. (AVH-18).

24 Jul 1972 Transferred (PL) to 57 FWW, Nellis AFB NV for Combat Crew Training (TF).

21 Aug 1972 In contract depot maintenance (WK) by Fairchild Engine and Aircraft Corporation (FACCF) at Bob Sikes Municipal Airport, Crestview FL.

14 Sep 1972 Returned to 57 FWW, Nellis AFB NV for Combat Crew Training (TF).

20 Aug 1973 In depot maintenance (WM) by 916 CLSS SM-ALC at Nellis AFB NV. (AVH-20).

30 Aug 1973 At 57 FWW, Nellis AFB NV for Combat Crew Training (TF).

16 Jan 1974 In depot maintenance (WM) by 916 CLSS SM-ALC at Nellis AFB NV. (AVH-22).

19 Jan 1974 At 57 FWW TAC, Nellis AFB NV for Combat Crew Training (TF).

9 Sep 1974 Transferred to 184 TFG ANG, McConnell AFB KS for Combat Crew Training (TF).

13 Mar 1975 In contract depot work (WM) by Dynalectron Corporation (DYNZZ) at Andrews AFB MD (AVH-23).

27 Mar 1975 At 184 TFG ANG, McConnell AFB KS for Combat Crew Training (TF).

7 Oct 1975 In depot work (WQ) by SM-ALC at McConnell AFB KS. (AVH-23 & AVH-24).

18 Nov 1975 At 184 TFG ANG, McConnell AFB KS for Combat Crew Training (TF).

2 Dec 1975 In depot work (WQ) at 184 TFG at McConnell AFB KS. (AVH-24).

6 Jan 1976 At 184 TFG ANG, McConnell AFB KS for Combat Crew Training (TF).

11 Nov 1976 In depot maintenance by SM-ALC at McConnell AFB KS. 3,369.0 flying hours. (AVH-25 & AVH-26).

21 Nov 1976 At 184 TFTG ANG for student and combat crew training (TF), McConnell AFB KS. 3,369.0 flying hours.

18 Jul 1979 At 113 TFW ANG, Andrews AFB MD. 4,095.8 flying hours. (AVH-27).

22 Nov 1981 Assigned to 1 TFW TAC, Langley AFB, Hampton VA for static display. (Inventory account "ZW"). 4,473.6 flying hours. (GO33B Dec 81 & GO33B 1 Feb 83).

Jul 1994 Ownership of aircraft transferred from Air Force Museum to AMARC's Air Force Static Display Program. Location remained at Hampton VA. (Tom Brewer, AFM staff).

26 Jan 1996 AMARC transferred the aircraft to the city of Hampton VA.

F-105D–15RE 61-0086

Republic Production No: D-281 Production Sequence No: 361

Location: Displayed as "Big Sal" at the Pima Air Museum, Tucson, Arizona.

Aircraft Name(s)	Crew	Unit	Date	Description
Don't Tread on Me		44 TFS 388 TFW	May 68	American flag. Left side.
Betty Lou		34 TFS 388 TFW	Sep 68	Name under left wing in red and gold.
Big Sal	Capt. John Hoffman	44 TFS 355 TFW	May 70	In black on the engine inlets.
Lucky Linda		44 TFS 355 TFW	Sep 70	
Yankee Dood It!		149 TFS VANG	Jan 79	American flag with yellow cord and tassel under wing.
Keep 'em Flyin		149 TFS VA ANG	Jul 81	American flag with yellow cord and tassel under wing. Left side.

Aircraft Chronology

19 Jan 1962 USAF production acceptance from Republic Aviation, Farmingdale NY. (AFTO Form 95).

23 Jan 1962 Delivered to 333 TFS, 4 TFW, Seymour Johnson AFB NC. (ACA-87).

This Thunderchief had a distinguished 19-year flying career. Shortly after its delivery to the 4 Tactical Fighter Wing in early 1962, it flew in a firepower demonstration for President John F. Kennedy at Eglin Air Force Base, Florida. It served at George, Nellis, Yokota, and Kadena, before beginning a combat tour at Korat, Thailand, in November 1967. When Korat replaced its F-105Ds with F-4Es in 1969 the plane went to nearby Takhli where it was flown by Capt. John Hoffman who gave it the best known of its many nicknames, "*Big Sal*," after his wife Sally. When Takhli closed at the end of 1970, the plane came home to Wichita, Kansas, and within a year began serving with the Virginia Air National Guard. As the plane's maintenance record shows, the Virginia Guard nursed it in its declining years through a number of cracked fuselage parts, wing ribs, and even a couple of wing changes until retiring it in 1981. After sitting in desert storage in Tucson, Arizona, for two years, the plane was towed to the neighboring Pima County Museum who has given it the retirement care it deserves. (Photograph by author, 2 May 1996.)

13 Apr 1962 At Eglin AFB FL with the 4 TFW for firepower demonstration, "Silk Hat/Eglin 1-62," attended by President John F. Kennedy.

6 May 1962 At 4 TFW, Seymour Johnson AFB NC.

6 Jun 1962 At 335 TFS, 4 TFW, Seymour Johnson AFB NC. (RAC record).

17 Sep 1962 In depot maintenance (WM) ("Look-Alike," Phase I) by MOAMA at Seymour Johnson AFB NC.

20 Dec 1962 At Republic Aviation, Farmingdale NY for contract work (WK). ("Look-Alike," Phase II).

29 Apr 1963 Transferred to 355 TFW, George AFB CA.

2 May 1963 At 355 TFW, George AFB CA.

28 Oct 1964 Transferred with 355 TFW to McConnell AFB KS. (AVH-2).

13 Apr 1965 At SMAMA, McClellan AFB CA for depot work. (AVH-3).

1 May 1965 Returned to 355 TFW, McConnell AFB KS.

12 May 1965 Transferred to 4520 CCTW, Nellis AFB NV.

29 Nov 1965 At 4520 CCTW, Nellis AFB NV for student and combat crew training (TF).

13 Jan 1966 At MOAMA, Brookley AFB AL for depot work (WO). (AVH-5).

4 Apr 1966 Returned to 4520 CCTW, Nellis AFB NV for combat crew training (TF).

22 Aug 1966 Reassigned to 6441 TFW, Yokota AB, Japan.

6 Sep 1966 Transferred to 18 TFW, Kadena AB, Okinawa.

31 Dec 1966 While assigned to the 18 TFW, Kadena AB, Okinawa, the aircraft flew 17 hours during the month of December 1966 and had accumulated 785 flying hours. (18 TFW History, Jul–Dec 66, USAF microfilm MO498).

23 Jan 1967 At 18 TFW, Kadena AB, Okinawa . (AVH-7).

13 Jul 1967 In depot maintenance (WM) by SMAMA at Kadena AB, Okinawa.

20 Jul 1967 At 18 TFW, Kadena AB, Okinawa.

11 Sep 1967 In depot maintenance (WM) by SMAMA at Kadena AB, Okinawa.

12 Sep 1967 At 18 TFW, Kadena AB, Okinawa.

1 Nov 1967 At 18 TFW, Kadena AB, Okinawa, being prepared for transfer (PL).

2 Nov 1967 Transferred to 388 TFW, Korat RTAB, Thailand, as a combat attrition replacement.

6 Nov 1967	In depot maintenance (WM) by SMAMA field team at Korat RTAB, Thailand.
9 Nov 1967	At 388 TFW, Korat RTAB, Thailand.
3 Feb 1968	In depot maintenance (WM) by SMAMA at Korat RTAB, Thailand. (AVH-10).
7 Feb 1968	At 388 TFW, Korat RTAB, Thailand.
18 May 1968	In depot maintenance ()WM) by SMAMA at Korat RTAB, Thailand.
21 May 1968	At 388 TFW, Korat RTAB, Thailand.
26 Jun 1968	At Air Asia in Tainan, Taiwan for contract depot work (WK).
30 Aug 1968	Returned to 388 TFW, Korat RTAB, Thailand.
31 Oct 1968	Aircraft had accumulated 1,522.0 flying hours while assigned to the 388 TFW, Korat RTAB, Thailand. (388 TFW History, Oct–Dec 68, USAF microfilm NO585).
10 Nov 1968	At 388 TFW, Korat RTAB, Thailand.
20 Jan 1969	During a combat mission from the 388 TFW, Korat RTAB, Thailand, aircraft was damaged by ordnance from the C/L MER. Right rear portion of the left 450 tank dented and tank fin knocked off. Left horizontal slab tip was bent upwards and cracked in several places. Required 99 man hours to repair. Aircraft was flown by 1Lt David T. Dinan, 34 TFS, who was killed in action in F-105D 61-0104 on 17 March 1969. (AFTO Form 95 & 388 TFW History, Jan–Mar 69, USAF microfilm NO585).
29 Jan 1969	At Takhli RTAB, Thailand with the 44 TFS, 388 TFW during runway repairs at Korat RTAB, Thailand. Enroute to Takhli from Korat, aircraft was flown on a strike mission in the Steel Tiger region of Laos. (AVH-12 & 388 TFW History, Jan–Mar 69, USAF microfilm NO586).
2 Feb 1969	Flown on a strike mission in the Steel Tiger region of Laos by 44 TFS pilot, 388 TFW, while operating from Takhli RTAB, Thailand. (388 TFW History, Jan–Mar 69, USAF microfilm NO586).
22 Feb 1969	Flown on a strike mission in the Steel Tiger region of Laos by 44 TFS pilot, 388 TFW, while operating from Takhli RTAB, Thailand.
2 Mar 1969	Returned to 388 TFW, Korat RTAB, Thailand.
30 Apr 1969	While assigned to the 44 TFS, 388 TFW, Korat RTAB, Thailand, the aircraft flew 78 hours in the month of April 1969 and had accumulated 1,871.7 total flying hours. (388 TFW History, Apr–Jun 69, USAF microfilm NO586).
15 Jun 1969	In depot maintenance (WM) by SMAMA at Takhli RTAB, Thailand. (AVH-12).
30 Jun 1969	While assigned to the 44 TFS, 388 TFW, Korat RTAB, Thailand, the aircraft flew 32.9 hours in the month of June 1969 and had accumulated 1,968.5 total flying hours. (388 TFW History, Apr–Jun 69, USAF microfilm NO586).
11 Jul 1969	Returned to 388 TFW, Korat RTAB, Thailand. (AVH-12).
14 Sep 1969	While assigned to the 388 TFW, Korat RTAB, Thailand, the aircraft drag chute failed due to the door not opening. (388 TFW History, Jul–Sep 69, Vol. III, USAF microfilm NO587).
30 Sep 1969	While assigned to the 44 TFS, 388 TFW, Korat RTAB, Thailand the aircraft ground aborted due to AC power falling off the line caused by a faulty Air Turbine Motor. (388 TFW History, Jul–Sep 69, Vol. III, USAF microfilm NO587).
10 Oct 1969	Transferred with the 44 TFS to the 355 TFW, Takhli RTAB, Thailand. Pilot: Capt. John Hoffman. Crew Chief: Sgt. Mike Nadworny.
24 Oct 1970	At 355 TFW, Takhli RTAB, Thailand. (AVH-14).
27 Oct 1970	Transferred to the 23 TFW, McConnell AFB KS.
4 Jan 1971	At 23 TFW, McConnell AFB KS.
18 Mar 1971	In depot work (WO) by SMAMA, McClellan AFB CA. (AVH-16).
5 May 1971	Depot work completed for "Speedline" modification. (SMAMA Project A-1-7112-SM). 2,676.9 flying hours. (AFTO Form 95).
4 Jun 1971	Transferred (PL) to 192 TFG ANG, Byrd Field, Richmond VA. (AVH-16).
23 Jun 1972	In depot work (WO) by SM-ALC, McClellan AFB CA. (AVH-18).
2 Oct 1972	Depot work at SMAMA, McClellan AFB CA completed (Project A-2-7036-SM). 2,774.3 flying hours. (AFTO Form 95).

6 Oct 1972	Returned (PL) to 192 TFG ANG, Byrd Field, Richmond VA. (AVH-18).
10 Apr 1973	In contract depot maintenance (WM) by Dynalectron Corporation (DYNZZ) at Byrd Field, Richmond VA. (AVH-20).
13 Apr 1973	At 192 TFG ANG, Byrd Field, Richmond VA.
13 Aug 1973	In contract depot maintenance (WM) by Dynalectron Corporation (DYNZZ) at Byrd Field, Richmond VA.
15 Aug 1973	At 192 TFG ANG, Byrd Field, Richmond VA.
21 Sep 1973	In contract depot maintenance (WM) by Dynalectron Corporation (DYNZZ) at Byrd Field, Richmond VA.
4 Oct 1973	At 192 TFG ANG, Byrd Field, Richmond VA.
18 Sep 1974	Stabilizer found to be cracked beyond limits IAW TO 1F-105-1207. Replacement stabilizer installed by 192 TFG ANG, Byrd Field VA. (AFTO Form 95).
18 Jun 1975	In contract depot maintenance (WM) by Dynalectron Corporation (DYNZZ) at Byrd Field, Richmond VA. (AVH-23 & AVH-24).
30 Jul 1975	At 192 TFG ANG, Byrd Field, Richmond VA.
12 May 1976	Overhauled left strut received from Ogden ALC and installed by 192 TFG ANG, Byrd Field VA. 3,513.4 flying hours. (AFTO Form 95).
19 Sep 1976	Florescent inspection revealed a 1.25 inch crack in the fuselage's Right Side Plate Radius aft of F.S. 442.78 at 192 TFG ANG, Byrd Field VA. (AFTO Form 95).
22 Sep 1976	In depot maintenance (BQ) by SM-ALC at Byrd Field, Richmond VA. 3,580 flying hours. (AVH-24).
25 Sep 1976	At 192 TFG ANG, Byrd Field VA. 3,649.0 flying hours. (AVH-25 & AVH-26).
23 Oct 1976	Deployed to Lakenheath AB, England under "Coronet Fife" with 149 TFS VA ANG. (British Aviation Review, Dec 1995).
6 Nov 1976	Returned from England to Byrd Field, Richmond VA.
13 Nov 1976	Second wing change at 192 TFG ANG, Byrd Field VA. 3,620.0 flying hours. (AFTO Form 95).
6 Dec 1976	FCF flown for second wing change.
20 Jan 1977	Nose gear strut changed due to roughness inside strut that continually cut seals. (AFTO Form 95).
15 Aug 1977	In depot maintenance at SM-ALC, McClellan AFB CA. 3,690.0 flying hours.
2 Sep 1977	Crack discovered on 19 Sep 1976 in fuselage Right Side Plate Radius repaired during depot maintenance. 3,691.6 flying hours. (AFO Form 95).
24 Feb 1978	Aircraft flight restricted due to cracks found in right wing main landing gear rib by 192 TFG ANG, Byrd Field VA. 3,750.3 flying hours. (AFTO For 95).
30 Mar 1978	At 192 TFG ANG, Byrd Field VA. 3,770.9 flying hours. (AFTO Form 95).
10 Apr 1978	Flight restrictions removed after completion of T.O. 1F-105-1281 at 192 TFG ANG, Byrd Field VA. (AFTO Form 95).
19 Aug 1978	Third wing change at 192 TFG ANG, Byrd Field VA. (AFTO Form 95).
19 Sep 1978	Functional check flight for third wing change. 3,864 flying hours.
22 Oct 1978	Aircraft grounded for cracks in right wing main landing gear rib found during 100-hour inspection by 192 TFG ANG, Byrd Field VA. (AFTO Form 95).
26 Oct 1978	At 192 TFG ANG, Byrd Field VA. 3,866.0 flying hours.
15 Dec 1978	192 TFG ANG, Byrd Field VA. 3,888.4 flying hours.
16 Dec 1978	Right wing changed. Wing swapped with F-105D 62-4411. 3,891.4 flying hours. (AFTO Form 95).
11 Oct 1979	During NDI inspection at 192 TFG ANG, Byrd Field VA, a crack was found in left wing in 'A' hole. "Aircraft now Cat 2." (AFTO Form 95).
9 Jan 1980	In contract depot maintenance (DYNZZ) at Byrd Field VA. 4,097.1 flying hours. (GO-33. 24 Jun 1980).
15 Jan 1980	At 192 TFG ANG, Byrd Field, Richmond VA. 4,097.1 flying hours.

4 Mar 1980	In contract depot maintenance (Analytic Condition Inspection) by Dynalectron Corp (DYNZZ) at Byrd Field VA. 4,143.7 flying hours.
14 Mar 1980	Depot maintenance complete.
1 Apr 1980	At 192 TFG ANG, Byrd Field, Richmond VA. 4,165.9 flying hours.
24 Sep 1981	Sent to storage at MASDC ("Low probability of withdrawal"—XX), Davis- Monthan AFB AZ. 4,452.7 flying hours. (GO33B Dec 81 & GO33B 1 Feb 83).
8 Jul 1983	Air Force Museum transferred aircraft from MASDC to Pima Air Museum, Tucson AZ. (DD Form 1149).
3 Apr 1984	Aircraft received from MASDC by Pima Air Museum, Tucson AZ. (DD Form 1149).
29 Apr 1994	At Pima Air Museum. Name on canopy: "Col. Al Mattox." (John Revak visit with River Rats).
Jun 1995	Aircraft refurbished and repainted by Pima Air Museum. Restored to markings as flown during 1969 -70 at 44 TFS, 355 TFW, by Capt. John Hoffman. Name on intakes: "Big Sal." (A reference to Capt. Hoffman's wife, Sally). (Kirsten Oftedahl, Pima Curator of Collections, 3 May 1996).

F-105D-15RE 61-0088

Republic Production No: D-283 Production Sequence No: 363

Location: Displayed at the Heritage Museum Park, Grissom ARB, Peru, Indiana.

Aircraft Name(s)	Crew	Unit	Date	Description
Balls 88		563 TFS 23 TFW	Jul 72	

Aircraft Chronology

14 Mar 1962	Delivered from MOAMA, Brookley AFB AL to 49 TFW, Spangdahlem AB, Germany. (ACA-87).
31 Jul 1962	At Wheelus AB, Libya, with 49 TFW.
6 Jul 1963	At 49 TFW, Spangdahlem AB, Germany.
7 Jul 1963	At MOAMA, Brookley AFB AL for depot work. "Operation Look Alike," Phase II.
9 Nov 1963	Returned to 49 TFW, Spangdahlem AB, Germany.
28 Jun 1965	At CASA, Getafe, Spain, for contract depot work (WK). (AVH-3).
19 Jul 1965	Returned to 49 TFW, Spangdahlem AB, Germany.
16 Mar 1966	At Wheelus AB Libya, with 49 TFW. (AVH-5).
27 Apr 1966	At CASA, Getafe, Spain for contract depot work (WK).
31 May 1966	Returned to 49 TFW, Spangdahlem AB, Germany.
23 Oct 1966	At Wheelus AB Libya, with 49 TFW.
28 Oct 1966	At 49 TFW, Spangdahlem AB, Germany.
16 Nov 1966	At Wheelus AB Libya, with 49 TFW.
9 Dec 1966	At 49 TFW, Spangdahlem AB, Germany.
24 Jan 1967	At 49 TFW, Spangdahlem AB, Germany, being prepared for transfer (PL). (AVH-7).
4 Feb 1967	Transferred to 23 TFW, McConnell AFB KS.
4 Feb 1967	At 23 TFW, McConnell AFB KS.
11 Apr 1967	At 23 TFW, McConnell AFB KS being prepared for transfer to depot (PL).

Known as "*Balls 88*" when it served at McConnell Air Force Base, Kansas, this "D" was first delivered to Spangdahlem Air Base, Germany in 1962. When the 49 Tactical Fighter Wing converted to F-4Ds in 1967, the plane relocated to the 23 Tactical Fighter Wing at McConnell where it trained pilots heading to war in South East Asia. The Air Force Reserve unit at Tinker Air Force Base, Oklahoma, picked it up in 1972. It was one of 18 F-105s the Reserves flew during their NATO summer deployment to Italy in 1979. In 1980, the plane transferred to the Reserve unit at Hill Air Force Base, Utah, for its last two years of service. (Photograph by author, 9 August 1995.)

20 Apr 1967	Transferred to SMAMA, McClellan AFB CA.
1 May 1967	Placed in storage (XT) at SMAMA, McClellan AFB CA.
23 May 1967	Storage code changed to "XM" at SMAMA, McClellan AFB CA.
13 Jul 1967	Placed in depot work (WO) at SMAMA, McClellan AFB CA.
23 Oct 1967	Returned to 23 TFW, McConnell AFB KS.
27 Nov 1967	Assigned to aircrew training (TF) at 23 TFW, McConnell AFB KS.
23 Mar 1968	Deployed to George AFB CA with the 562 TFS, 23 TFW, for air-to-air gunnery training for RTU Class 68HR. (AVH-10).
28 Mar 1968	Returned to 23 TFW, McConnell AFB KS.
16 Apr 1968	Deployed to George AFB CA with the 563 TFS, 23 TFW for air-to-air gunnery training for RTU Class 68IR.
9 May 1968	Returned to 23 TFW, McConnell AFB KS.
17 May 1968	Deployed to George AFB CA with the 560 TFS, 23 TFW for air-to-air gunnery training for RTU Class 68JR.
22 May 1968	At 23 TFW, McConnell AFB KS.
26 Mar 1969	At SMAMA McClellan AFB CA for depot work (WO). (AVH-12).
6 May 1969	Returned to 23 TFW, McConnell AFB KS.
15 May 1969	At 23 TFW, McConnell AFB KS.
4 Jun 1970	At 23 TFW, McConnell AFB KS. (AVH-14).
4 May 1971	At 23 TFW, McConnell AFB KS being prepared for transfer (PL). (AVH-16).
6 May 1971	In depot work (WO) by SMAMA at McClellan AFB CA.
5 Nov 1971	Returned (PL) to 23 TFW, McConnell AFB KS.
10 Nov 1971	At 23 TFW (CC), McConnell AFB KS.
1 Mar 1972	Carried on assignment roster for the 562 TFS, 23 TFW at McConnell AFB KS. (Master 23 TFW Aircraft Assignment as of 1 March 1972).
1 Jul 1972	Assigned directly to the 562 TFS, McConnell AFB KS, when the 23 TFW relocated to England AFB LA. (AVH-18).
17 Jul 1972	In contract depot maintenance (WK) by Fairchild Engine and Aircraft Corporation (FACCF) at Bob Sikes Municipal Airport, Crestview FL.

11 Aug 1972	Transferred (PL) to 507 TFG AFRES, Tinker AFB OK.
31 Mar 1973	At 507 CMTSq AFRES, Tinker AFB OK. (AVH-20).
12 Apr 1973	In depot maintenance by SM-ALC at Tinker AFB OK.
18 Apr 1973	At 507 CMTSq AFRES, Tinker AFB OK.
12 Nov 1973	In depot maintenance by SM-ALC at Tinker AFB OK.
5 Dec 1973	At 507 CMTSq AFRES, Tinker AFB OK.
30 Apr 1974	At 507 CMTSq AFRES, Tinker AFB OK. (AVH-22).
16 Oct 1974	Organization and assignment changed to 507 CLMSq AFRES, Tinker AFB OK.
21 Oct 1974	In depot maintenance (WM) by SM-ALC at Tinker AFB OK.
25 Nov 1974	At 507 CLMSq AFRES, Tinker AFB OK.
5 Oct 1975	At 507 CLMSq AFRES, Tinker AFB OK. (AVH-23 & AVH-24).
6 Oct 1975	In depot maintenance (WM) by SM-ALC at Tinker AFB OK.
6 Oct 1975	At 507 CLMSq AFRES, Tinker AFB OK.
28 Jan 1976	In depot maintenance (WM) by SM-ALC at Tinker AFB OK. (AVH-24).
21 Feb 1976	At 507 CLMSq AFRES, Tinker AFB OK.
7 Jun 1976	In depot maintenance (WM) by SM-ALC at Tinker AFB OK. 2,953 flying hours.
17 Oct 1976	At 507 TFG AFRES, Tinker AFB OK. 2,953 flying hours.
25 Mar 1978	In depot maintenance by SM-ALC at Tinker AFB OK. 3,249.0 flying hours. (AVH-26).
22 Oct 1978	At 465 TFS AFRES, Tinker AFB OK. 3,280.0 flying hours.
12 May 1979	Deployed under "Coronet Palomino" with 465 TFS to Gioia Del Colle, Italy from Tinker AFB OK. (British Aviation Review, Dec 1995).
24 May 1979	Returned from Italy to Tinker AFB OK.
31 May 1979	While assigned to the 465 TFS AFRES, Tinker AFB OK, the aircraft flew 49.0 hours during the month of May 1979 and had accumulated 3,482.4 flying hours. The assigned crew chief was Bragg.
31 May 1979	In programmed depot maintenance at McClellan AFB (AFLC) CA. 3,433.4 flying hours. (AVH-27).
30 Jun 1979	While assigned to the 465 TFS AFRES, Tinker AFB OK, the aircraft was in depot maintenance and did not fly during the month of June 1979 but had accumulated a total of 3,482.4 flying hours. The assigned crew chief was Bragg. (301 TFW History, Apr–Jun 1979, USAF microfilm 34382).
28 Sep 1979	At McClellan AFB (AFLC) CA. 3,482.4 flying hours. (AVH-27).
11 Oct 1979	At 465 TFS AFRES, Tinker AFB OK. 3,482.4 flying hours.
3 Mar 1980	In depot maintenance by Fairchild Baltimore at Tinker AFB OK. 3,565.4 flying hours. (GO33B 24 Jun 80).
17 Mar 1980	At 465 TFS, Tinker AFB, OK. 3,565.4 flying hours.
30 Jul 1980	Transferred to the 466 TFS AFRES, Hill AFB UT. 3,679.3 flying hours. (GO33B 22 Jan 81).
27 Oct 1980	In depot maintenance at Ogden ALC, Hill AFB UT. 3,705.8 flying hours.
10 Nov 1980	At 466 TFS AFRES, Hill AFB UT. 3,711.9 flying hours.
24 Mar 1982	At 466 TFS AFRES, Hill AFB UT. 3,909.9 flying hours. Inventory account "ZW"—School or Museum. (GO33B 1 Feb 83).

F-105D-15RE 61-0093

Republic Production No: D-288 Production Sequence No: 368

Location: Displayed outside at the Texas Air Museum, Caprock Chapter, Slaton, Texas.

Aircraft Name(s)	Crew	Unit	Date	Description
The Nurd Bird		113 TFG		
Honey Babe	Lt. Col. Jack Gaudion	469 TFS 388 TFW		Bee cartoon.
Honey Bee				
Jumpin' Jack	Lt. Col. Jack Gaudion	44 TFS 388 TFW	Jul 69	In blue script on left side.
Good Vibrations	Capt. Pete Brakeley	44 TFS 355 TFW	Jul 70	On intakes. Silver letters shadowed in red.

Aircraft Chronology

20 Feb 1962	USAF production acceptance from Republic Aviation, Farmingdale NY. (ACA-87).
13 Mar 1962	In depot work (WO) at MOAMA, Brookley AFB AL.
22 Mar 1962	Delivered to 49 TFW, Spangdahlem AB, Germany.
31 Jul 1962	At Wheelus AB, Libya, for nuclear weapons delivery training with the 49 TFW.
6 Jul 1963	At 49 TFW, Spangdahlem AB, Germany.
7 Jul 1963	In depot work (WO) at MOAMA, Brookley AFB AL. "Operation Look Alike," Phase II.
22 Nov 1963	Returned to 49 TFW, Spangdahlem AB, Germany.
19 Jan 1966	At 49 TFW, Spangdahlem AB, Germany. (AVH-5).
15 Apr 1966	At Wheelus AB, Libya, with the 49 TFW.
17 May 1966	Returned to 49 TFW, Spangdahlem AB, Germany.
29 Sep 1966	At Wheelus AB, Libya, with the 49 TFW.
7 Oct 1966	Returned to 49 TFW, Spangdahlem AB, Germany.
12 Nov 1966	Transferred to 4520 CCTW, Nellis AB NV for combat crew training (TF).
10 Apr 1967	At Brookley AFB AL for depot work. (AVH-7).
19 Apr 1967	At 4520 CCTW, Nellis AFB NV.
7 Aug 1967	At SMAMA, McClellan AFB CA.
14 Aug 1967	At 18 TFW, Kadena AB, Okinawa.
21 Aug 1967	At Air Asia, Tainan AB, Taiwan, for contract depot work.
20 Oct 1967	Transferred to 41 AD, Yokota AB, Japan.
30 Nov 1967	At Osan AB, Korea on nuclear alert with 41 AD.
12 Dec 1967	Returned to 41 AD, Yokota AB, Japan.
18 Jan 1968	Reassigned to 347 TFW, Yokota AB, Japan. (AVH-10).
29 Jan 1968	At Osan AB, Korea, with the 18 TFW, Kadena AB, Okinawa, in response to the capture of the U.S.S. Pueblo by North Korea on 24 January 1968.
1 Apr 1968	Transferred to the 18 TFW, Kadena AB, Okinawa.
4 Apr 1968	Returned to Osan AB, Korea, with the 18 TFW.
14 May 1968	At 18 TFW, Kadena AB, Okinawa.
22 May 1968	Returned to Osan AB, Korea, with the 18 TFW.
31 May 1968	At 18 TFW, Kadena AB, Okinawa.
1 Jun 1968	Transferred to the 388 TFW, Korat RTAB, Thailand, as a combat attrition replacement aircraft. (AVH-10 & 388 TFW History, Apr–Jun 68, USAF microfilm NO584).
3 Jun 1968	In depot maintenance (WM) by SMAMA field team at Korat RTAB, Thailand.
9 Jun 1968	At 388 TFW, Korat RTAB, Thailand.
13 Jun 1968	Aircraft damaged while assigned to 388 TFW, Korat RTAB, Thailand, due to material failure of a hot air line. The pilot was Maj. Richard D. Matthews. Aircraft was placed in depot maintenance (WM) by SMAMA field team at Korat. (388 TFW History, Apr–Jun 68, USAF microfilm NO584 & AVH-10).

F-105D 61-0093 served in a variety of units, particularly in the Far East. It began its career in 1962 as one of the F-105s that equipped the fleet of the 49 Tactical fighter Wing in Germany. When it arrived in the Far East in 1967, it hit all the bases—Kadena, Yokota, Korat, and Takhli, with excursions to Osan in Korea. It flew combat missions from Thailand with both the 388th and 355th wings between June 1968 and June 1970. During these two years, President Johnson had halted most bombing in North Vietnam and so the plane was used for interdiction missions in Laos and Cambodia. It last served with the Air National Guard units in Kansas and Washington DC. When it retired in November 1981, its airframe had accumulated 4,974 flying hours. After being used as a battle damage repair trainer in San Antonio, Texas, it was slated for the scrap yard in 1996. At the last minute, however, the Texas Air Museum arranged to add it to its growing collection and moved it to their small museum at Slaton outside Lubbock. (Photograph by author, 16 May 1998.)

27 Jul 1968 Combat ready (CC) at 388 TFW, Korat RTAB, Thailand.

28 Dec 1968 Being prepared for transfer (PL) to depot by 388 TFW, Korat RTAB, Thailand.

2 Jan 1969 In contract depot maintenance (WK) by Air Asia (AAITT), Tainan, Taiwan.

12 Feb 1969 Returned to 388 TFW, Korat RTAB, Thailand. (AVH-12).

13 Feb 1969 Began operating from Takhli RTAB, Thailand, with the 388 TFW on combat missions over Laos while the runway at Korat RTAB, Thailand, was being repaired.

1 Mar 1969 Returned to Korat RTAB, Thailand, with the 388 TFW.

7 Apr 1969 While assigned to the 388 TFW, Korat RTAB, Thailand, the aircraft's drag chute failed to deploy during landing. (388 TFW History, Apr–Jun 69, USAF microfilm NO586).

30 Apr 1969 While assigned to the 34 TFS, 388 TFW, Korat RTAB, Thailand, the aircraft flew 85.5 hours for the month of April 1969 and had accumulated 1,941.6 total flying hours. (388 TFW History, Apr–Jun 69, USAF microfilm NO586).

16 Jul 1969 At 388 TFW, Korat RTAB, Thailand, being prepared for transfer (PL). (AVH-12).

18 July 1969 Transferred to Takhli RTAB, Thailand, for depot-level modifications (WM) by SMAMA field team.

28 July 1969 Returned (PL) to 388 TFW, Korat RTAB, Thailand.

20 Aug 1969 While assigned to the 44 TFS, 388 TFW, Korat RTAB, Thailand, the aircraft air aborted due to an inoperative ARC-70 UHF radio. (388 TFW History, Jul–Sep 69, Vol. III, USAF microfilm NO587).

10 Oct 1969 Transferred with the 44 TFS to the 355 TFW, Takhli RTAB, Thailand, when the squadron was reassigned from the 388 TFW. (AVH-12).

May 1970 Aircraft assigned to C Flight, 44 TFS, 355 TFW, Takhli RTAB. Pilot: Capt. Peter Brakeley. (44 TFS Aircraft Assignment Roster).

19 Oct 1970 Transferred (PL) to the 23 TFW, McConnell AFB KS shortly before the 355 TFW was discontinued and Takhli RTAB, Thailand, closed. (AVH-14).

27 Oct 1970 Under "Project Bighorn," aircraft was placed in flyable storage (PR) at McConnell AFB KS and used as a trainer for weapons loaders.

4 Jan 1971 At 23 TFW, McConnell AFB KS being prepared for transfer (PL).

14 Jan 1971	In depot work (WO) by SMAMA, McClellan AFB CA. (AVH-16).
26 Feb 1971	Transferred (PL) to 184 TFG ANG, McConnell AFB KS.
12 Mar 1971	Combat capable (CC) at 184 TFG ANG, McConnell AFB KS.
14 May 1971	In depot work (WO) by SMAMA, McClellan AFB CA.
30 Nov 1971	Returned to 184 TFG ANG, McConnell AFB KS.
11 Oct 1972	In contract depot maintenance (WK) by Fairchild Engine and Aircraft Corporation (FACCF) at Bob Sikes Municipal Airport, Crestview FL. (AVH-18).
2 Nov 1972	Returned to 184 TFG ANG, McConnell AFB KS.
10 Sep 1973	In contract depot maintenance (WM) by Dynalectron Corporation (DYNZZ) at McConnell AFB KS. (AVH-20).
19 Sep 1973	At 184 TFG ANG, McConnell AFB KS.
3 Jan 1974	Assigned to combat crew training (TF) at 184 TFG ANG, McConnell AFB KS.
22 Jul 1974	In contract depot maintenance (WM) by Dynalectron Corporation (DYNZZ) at McConnell AFB KS. (AVH-22).
30 Jul 1974	At 184 TFG ANG, McConnell AFB KS for combat crew training (TF).
4 Oct 1974	In contract depot maintenance (WM) by Dynalectron Corporation (DYNZZ) at McConnell AFB KS.
18 Oct 1974	At 184 TFG ANG, McConnell AFB KS for combat crew training (TF).
9 Apr 1975	In contract depot maintenance (WM) by Dynalectron Corporation (DYNZZ) at McConnell AFB KS. (AVH-23 & AVH-24).
18 Apr 1975	At 184 TFG ANG, McConnell AFB KS for combat crew training (TF).
15 Oct 1975	In depot work (WO) by SM-ALC at McConnell AFB KS.
7 Jun 1976	Transferred to 113 TFG ANG, Andrews AFB MD. 4,091 flying hours. (AVH-24).
23 Oct 1976	Deployed for a NATO exercise to Lakenheath AB, England, under "Coronet Fife" with the 121 TFS ANG from Andrews AFB MD. (British Aviation Review, Dec 1995).
6 Nov 1976	Returned from England to Andrews AFB MD.
7 Mar 1977	In depot maintenance (DM) by SM-ALC at Andrews AFB MD. 4,190 flying hours. (AVH-25 & AVH-26).
9 Mar 1977	At 113 TFG ANG, Andrews AFB MD. 4,190 flying hours.
18 Jan 1979	In depot at OC-ALC, Tinker AFB OK for "domestic project" (DO & DR) . 4,558.2 flying hours. (AVH-27).
30 Apr 1979	Returned to 113 TFG ANG, Andrews AFB MD. 4,558.2 flying hours.
6 Nov 1981	Sent to MASDC storage, Davis-Monthan AFB AZ. "Inviolate Storage." 4,974 flying hours. (MASDC Aircraft Status Directory 30 Jun 84 & GO33B Dec 81 & GO33B 1 Feb 83).
13 Aug 1985	Removed from MASDC storage for use as ABDR trainer at Kelly AFB TX. (John Coon's list, 24 Mar 87).
20 May 1996	At Brooks AFB TX. Expected to be scrapped within a year. (John Coon letter).
Jun 1996	Aircraft sent to scrap yard at Kelly AFB TX. (Steve Hester via John Coon, 2 Apr 97).
30 May 1997	Airlifted under control of the Texas Air Museum, Caprock Chapter, from Brooks AFB TX to Stinson Field in San Antonio TX for disassembly and transportation to Slaton TX. (E-mail from Craig Hannah, Texas Air Museum Volunteer).
26 Oct 1997	Disassembled and moved from Stinson Field, San Antonio TX to Slaton TX by three members of the Texas Air Museum, Caprock Chapter. "The plane at Stinson … left Sunday on two trailers. Three guys took it apart under rather austere circumstances. I really couldn't believe they were able to do it all let alone so quickly. For the most part, they did well. However, there were some significant casualties. The straps slipped on the front, caught the radar unit and ripped everything off the plane. The straps cut a large gash in one wing. They got everything disconnected in the wings except for a couple of impossible things they had to saw into. …" (E-mail from Dr. Carroll Brown, Brooks AFB TX, 27 Oct 1997).

F-105D–15RE 61-0099

Republic Production No: D-294 Production Sequence No: 374

Location: Displayed by the Air Classics Museum at Sugar Grove Airport, Aurora, Illinois.

Aircraft Name(s)	Crew	Unit	Date	Description
The Mad Bomber		465 TFS AFRES	Jun 78	

Aircraft Chronology

9 Feb 1962	USAF acceptance from production at Republic Aviation, Farmingdale NY. (ACA-87).
20 Feb 1962	At MOAMA, Brookley AFB AL for depot work (WO).
3 Mar 1962	Delivered to 49 TFW, Spangdahlem AB, Germany.
6 Jun 1962	At Wheelus AB Libya, with 49 TFW for weapons delivery practice. (RAC record).
31 Jul 1962	At 49 TFW, Spangdahlem AB, Germany. (ACA-87).
30 Jul 1963	At MOAMA, Brookley AFB AL for "Operation Look Alike," Phase II modification.
22 Nov 1963	Returned to 49 TFW, Spangdahlem AB, Germany.
27 Apr 1965	At 49 TFW, Spangdahlem AB, Germany. (AVH-3).
29 Apr 1965	At CASA, Getafe, Spain, for contract depot work (WK).
20 May 1965	Returned to 49 TFW, Spangdahlem AB, Germany.
19 Mar 1966	At Wheelus AB, Libya, with the 49 TFW. (AVH-5)
15 Apr 1966	At 49 TFW, Spangdahlem AB, Germany.
24 Jun 1966	At CASA, Getafe, Spain, for contract depot work (WK).
27 Jul 1966	Returned to 49 TFW, Spangdahlem AB, Germany.
7 Oct 1966	At Wheelus AB, Libya, with the 49 TFW.
14 Oct 1966	At 49 TFW, Spangdahlem AB, Germany.
17 Oct 1966	At Wheelus AB, Libya, with the 49 TFW.
21 Oct 1966	At 49 TFW, Spangdahlem AB, Germany.
5 Jan 1967	At 49 TFW, Spangdahlem AB, Germany, being prepared for transfer (PL). (AVH-7).
8 Jan 1967	Transferred to 4520 CCTW, Nellis AFB NV for aircrew training (TF).
8 May 1967	At MOAMA, Brookley AFB AL for depot work (WO).
21 Jul 1967	Returned to 4520 CCTW, Nellis AFB NV for aircrew training (TF).
28 Dec 1967	Transferred to 23 TFW, McConnell AFB KS for Southeast Asia F-105 replacement aircrew training (TF).
16 Apr 1968	Deployed to George AFB CA with the 563 TFS, 23 TFW, for air-to-air gunnery training for RTU Class 68IR. (AVH-10).
9 May 1968	Returned to 23 TFW, McConnell AFB KS for combat crew training (TF).
18 Jun 1968	Reassigned from training to combat readiness (CC) at 23 TFW, McConnell AFB KS.
26 Sep 1968	At SMAMA, McClellan AFB CA for depot maintenance (WO).
3 Nov 1968	Returned to 23 TFW, McConnell AFB KS.
22 Apr 1969	In depot maintenance (WM) by SMAMA at McConnell AFB KS. (AVH-12).
30 Apr 1969	At 23 TFW, McConnell AFB KS.
Sep 1969	While at the 23 TFW, McConnell AFB KS, one of four aircraft modified in July 1969 with positive limb restraint system for TAC Test 68-228 that was completed during Sep 1969. (23 TFW History, Jul–Sep 69, USAF microfilm MO555).

The career of "0099" paralleled that of its sister ship "0088" described earlier. Its initial assignment in 1962 was to Spangdahlem, Germany, followed, in 1967, by a brief pilot-training assignment at Nellis Air Force Base, Nevada, before settling down to continue pilot training at McConnell Air Force Base, Kansas. In 1972, it began its Air Force Reserve duty at Tinker Air Force Base, Oklahoma, down the road from McConnell. It transferred in 1980 to the last unit to fly the Thunderchief, the 466 Tactical Fighter Squadron at Hill Air Force Base, Utah. They flew it to Denmark for their NATO deployment in 1981 and, less than a year later, turned it over to battle damage repair training. Instead of scrapping it, the Air Force donated it to the Chicago suburb of Aurora, Illinois, where it sat in Phillips Park for over ten years slowly sinking into the grass near a family picnic area and children's playground (its location in the photograph). In September 1997 it was added to the collection of the Air Classics Museum at Aurora's Sugar Grove Airport. (Photograph by author, 24 August 1997.)

4 Jun 1970	At 23 TFW, McConnell AFB KS. (AVH-14).
1 Mar 1971	In depot work (WO) by SMAMA, McClellan AFB CA. (AVH-16).
27 Jul 1971	Returned (PL) to 23 TFW, McConnell AFB KS.
30 Jul 1971	At 23 TFW (CC), McConnell AFB KS.
1 Mar 1972	Carried on assignment roster for the 562 TFS, 23 TFW at McConnell AFB KS. (Master 23 TFW Aircraft Assignment as of 1 March 1972).
2 Jun 1972	In contract depot maintenance (WK) by Fairchild Engine and Aircraft Corporation (FACCF) at Bob Sikes Municipal Airport, Crestview FL. (AVH-18).
28 Jun 1972	Transferred (PL) to 507 TFG AFRES, Tinker AFB OK.
31 Mar 1973	At 507 CMTSq AFRES, Tinker AFB OK. (AVH-20).
11 Apr 1973	In depot maintenance by SM-ALC at Tinker AFB OK.
17 Apr 1973	At 507 CMTSq AFRES, Tinker AFB OK.
30 Aug 1973	In depot maintenance by SM-ALC at Tinker AFB OK.
24 Sep 1973	At 507 CMTSq AFRES, Tinker AFB OK.
25 Mar 1974	In depot maintenance by SM-ALC at Tinker AFB OK. (AVH-22).
4 Apr 1974	At 507 CMTSq AFRES, Tinker AFB OK.
16 Oct 1974	Assigned organization changed to 507 CLMSq AFRES, Tinker AFB OK.
27 Feb 1975	In depot work (WM) by SM-ALC at Tinker AFB OK. (AVH-23 & AVH-24).
17 Mar 1975	At 507 CLMSQ AFRES, Tinker AFB OK.
6 Oct 1975	In depot work (WM) by SM-ALC at Tinker AFB OK.
6 Oct 1975	At 507 CLMSQ AFRES, Tinker AFB OK. Possession code: WQ.
28 Jan 1976	Combat ready (CC) at 507 TFG AFRES, Tinker AFB OK. 3,414 flying hours. (AVH-24).
27 Jul 1977	At 507 TFG AFRES, Tinker AFB OK. 3,458.0 flying hours. (AVH-25 & AVH-26).
3 Oct 1978	In contract depot maintenance (DYNFW) at Tinker AFB OK. 3,748.0 flying hours.

16 Oct 1978 At 465 TFS AFRES, Tinker AFB OK. 3,780.8 flying hours.

27 Nov 1978 In contract depot maintenance (DYNFW) at Tinker AFB OK. 3,780.8 flying hours.

4 Dec 1978 At 465 TFS AFRES, Tinker AFB OK. 3,805.5 flying hours.

19 Jun 1979 While assigned to the 465 TFS AFRES, Tinker AFB OK, the aircraft ground aborted due to an inoperative anti skid caused by a bad harness. (301 TFW History 1 Apr–30 Jun 1979, USAF microfilm 343832).

30 Jun 1979 While assigned to the 465 TFS AFRES, Tinker AFB OK, the aircraft flew 25.5 hours during the month of June 1979 and had accumulated a total of 3,928.0 flying hours. The assigned crew chief was SSgt. John W. Glover. (301 TFW History, Apr–Jun 1979, USAF microfilm 34382).

24 Mar 1980 In depot maintenance by Fairchild Baltimore (FACBM) at Tinker AFB OK. 4,031.1 flying hours. (GO33B 24 Jun 80).

1 Apr 1980 At 465 TFS, Tinker AFB OK. 4,031.1 flying hours.

30 Jul 1980 Transferred to the 466 TFS AFRES, Hill AFB UT. 4,144.5 flying hours. (GO33B 22 Jan 81).

6 Oct 1980 At 466 TFS AFRES, Hill AFB UT. 4,173.0 flying hours.

19 Nov 1980 At SM-ALC, McClellan AFB CA for depot maintenance. 4,2141 flying hours.

15 Aug 1981 Deployed under "Coronet Rudder" with 466 TFS to Skrydstrup, Denmark, from Hill AFB UT. (British Aviation Review, Dec 1995).

29 Aug 1981 Returned from Denmark to Hill AFB UT.

21 Apr 1982 At 466 TFS AFRES, Hill AFB UT. 4,532.7 flying hours. Inventory account "ZD"–Test to destruction. Assigned to aircraft battle damage repair training. (GO33B 1 Feb 83).

13 Jul 1984 Declared by 2955 Combat Logistic Support Squadron (AFLC), Robins AFB GA as " ... excess to our Aircraft Battle Damage Repair (ABDR) training requirements" and offered to the USAF Museum for "... static display purposes." (2955 CLSS/CC letter).

2 Apr 1985 AMARC transfer document signed to donate aircraft to city of Aurora, Illinois. (Becky Garza, AMARC records). Displayed at Phillips Park inside 8' chain-link fence enclosure.

April 1997 Decision made to transfer aircraft from the city of Aurora to the Air Classics Museum. (E-mail, Michael Bianucci, museum director, 20 Dec 97).

8 Sep 1997 Moved from Phillips Park to hanger 5 at the Sugar Grove Municipal Airport, Sugar Grove, Illinois. Aircraft disassembled, moved on three semi-trucks, and reassembled by World Wide Aircraft Moving.

10 Dec 1997 New tires, donated by Goodyear Tire and Rubber Company, were installed on the aircraft.

F-105D-15RE 61-0100

Republic Production No: D-295 Production Sequence No: 375

Location: Displayed at NAS Ft. Worth Joint Reserve Base, Ft. Worth, Texas.

Aircraft Name(s)	Crew	Unit	Date	Description
Hot Stuff		357 TFS 355 TFW	Jan 70	On both intakes.

Aircraft Chronology

28 Mar 1962 USAF production acceptance from Republic Aviation, Farmingdale NY. (ACA-87).

2 Apr 1962 At MOAMA, Brookley AFB AL for depot work (WO).

13 Apr 1962 Delivered to 49 TFW, Spangdahlem AB, Germany.

22 Nov 1963 At MOAMA, Brookley AFB AL for "Operation Look Alike," Phase II.

7 Apr 1964 Returned to 49 TFW, Spangdahlem AB, Germany. (AVH-1).

23 Apr 1965 At CASA, Getafe, Spain, for contract depot work (WK). (AVH-3).

14 May 1964 Returned to 49 TFW, Spangdahlem AB, Germany.

11 Oct 1965 At CASA, Getafe, Spain, for contract depot work.

5 Jan 1966 Returned to 49 TFW, Spangdahlem AB, Germany. (AVH-5).

22 Jul 1966 At Wheelus AB, Libya, with the 49 TFW.

11 Aug 1966 At 49 TFW, Spangdahlem AB, Germany.

13 Aug 1966 At Wheelus AB, Libya, with the 49 TFW.

19 Aug 1966 At 49 TFW, Spangdahlem AB, Germany.

20 Dec 1966 Being prepared for transfer (PL) at 49 TFW, Spangdahlem AB, Germany.

6 Jan 1967 Transferred to 23 TFW, McConnell AFB KS. (AVH-7).

27 Feb 1967 At MOAMA, Brookley AFB AL for depot work (WO).

25 May 1967 Returned to 23 TFW, McConnell AFB KS.

1 Jun 1967 Deployed to George AFB CA to join the 563 TFS, 23 TFW, for air-to-air gunnery training for RTU Class 67IR.

16 Jun 1967 Returned to 23 TFW, McConnell AFB KS.

16 Nov 1967 Deployed to George AFB CA to join the 563 TFS, 23 TFW, for air-to-air gunnery training for RTU Class 68DR.

23 Nov 1967 Returned to 23 TFW, McConnell AFB KS.

27 Nov 1967 Assigned to aircrew training (TF) at 23 TFW, McConnell AFB KS.

16 Apr 1968 Deployed to George AFB CA with the 563 TFS, 23 TFW, for air-to-air gunnery training for RTU Class 68IR. (AVH-10).

9 May 1968 Returned to 23 TFW, McConnell AFB KS for combat crew training (TF).

5 Jul 1968 Transferred to 355 TFW, Takhli RTAB, Thailand.

30 Nov 1968 While assigned to the 357 TFS, 355 TFW, Takhli RTAB, Thailand, the aircraft had accumulated 1,993.6 flying hours. (355 TFW History, Oct–Dec 68, USAF microfilm NO466).

28 Feb 1969 While assigned to the 355 TFW, Takhli RTAB, Thailand, the aircraft flew 74.6 hours during the month of February 1969 and had accumulated 2,182.3 flying hours. (355 TFW History, Jan–Mar 69, Vol. II, USAF Microfilm NO467).

19 Mar 1969 In depot maintenance (WM) by SMAMA at Takhli RTAB, Thailand. (AVH-12).

20 Mar 1969 At 355 TFW, Takhli RTAB, Thailand.

3 May 1969 At Air Asia, Tainan, Taiwan, for contract depot work (WK).

24 Jun 1969 Returned to 355 TFW, Takhli RTAB, Thailand.

13 Dec 1969 At 355 TFW, Takhli RTAB, Thailand.

16 Apr 1970 At Air Asia, Tainan, Taiwan, for contract depot work (WK). (AVH-14).

23 Jun 1970 Returned to 355 TFW, Takhli RTAB, Thailand.

19 Oct 1970 Transferred to 23 TFW, McConnell AFB KS.

28 Dec 1970 In depot work (WO) at SMAMA, McClellan AFB CA for the T-Stick II modification.

8 Apr 1971 Returned (PL) to 563 TFS, 23 TFW, McConnell AFB KS. (AVH-16).

24 Sep 1971 Placed in flyable storage (PR) at 23 TFW, McConnell AFB KS for use as a source of spare parts for other T-Stick II F-105s.

1 Mar 1972 Carried on assignment roster with the 563 TFS, 23 TFW, at McConnell AFB KS. (Master 23 TFW Aircraft Assignment as of 1 March 1972).

8 Mar 1972 Combat capable (CC) at 23 TFW, McConnell AFB KS. (AVH-18).

10 May 1972 Transferred to 916 Maint. & Log Gp. AFRES, Carswell AFB TX.

This is the third of the surviving "Ds" modified with the Thunderstick II blind-bombing system. It began its career in Germany in 1962 with the 49 Tactical Fighter Wing who flew it for the next four years. It then transferred to the 23 Tactical Fighter Wing at McConnell Air Force Base where it trained pilots headed to the war in South East Asia. It accompanied three F-105 Replacement Training Unit classes to George Air Force Base, California, for gunnery training and then, in July 1968, went to war itself when it was assigned to the 355 Tactical Fighter Wing at Takhli, Thailand. When Takhli closed at the end of 1970, it was one of the thirty "Ds" that entered the T-Stick II modification line at the depot in Sacramento, California. For the next year and a half, the 563 Tactical Fighter Squadron at McConnell struggled to keep its T-Stick II fleet flying despite having too few spare parts for the unique systems. This plane was deliberately grounded for six months so that its parts could be used to keep others flying. Finally, in 1972, the T-Sticks were turned over to the Air Force Reserve's 457 Tactical Fighter Squadron at Carswell Air Force, Texas, who flew them for nine years. When the 457th began converting to F-4Ds in 1981, they selected 61-0100 and lovingly restored it as a memento of their Thunderchief years. (Photograph by author, 12 July 1995.)

8 Jul 1972	Assigned to the 506 TFG, 457 TFS AFRES, Carswell AFB TX.
2 Nov 1972	In contract depot maintenance (WK) by Fairchild Engine and Aircraft Corporation (FACCF) at Bob Sikes Municipal Airport, Crestview FL.
5 Dec 1972	Being transferred (PL) from Bob Sikes Municipal Airport, Crestview FL.
29 Dec 1972	Arrived at 506 TFG AFRES, Carswell AFB TX. (AVH-20).
1 Apr 1973	Transferred to 506 CMTSq AFRES, Carswell AFB TX.
20 Jun 1974	In contract depot maintenance (WK) by Fairchild Engine and Aircraft Corporation (FACCF) at Bob Sikes Municipal Airport, Crestview FL. (AVH-22).
17 Oct 1974	Returned to 506 CMTSq AFRES, Carswell AFB TX.
1 Dec 1974	Assigned organization changed to 506 CLM Sq. AFRES, Carswell AFB TX.
6 Oct 1976	At 506 CLMSQ AFRES, Carswell AFB TX. Possession code: WQ. (AVH-24).
29 Jan 1976	In depot work by SM-ALC at Carswell AFB TX.
29 Jan 1976	At 506 CLMSQ AFRES, Carswell AFB TX. Possession code: CC.
2 Mar 1976	Assigned organization changed to 457 TFS AFRES, Carswell AFB TX. 2,137 flying hours.
25 Jan 1977	In depot work by SM-ALC at Carswell AFB TX. 3,920.0 flying hours. (AVH-25 & AVH-26).

14 Aug 1977	Deployed under "Coronet Poker" with 457 TFS to Norvenich, Germany, from Carswell AFB TX. (British Aviation Review, Dec 1995).
27 Aug 1977	Returned from Germany to Carswell AFB TX.
27 Jan 1978	At 457 TFS AFRES, Carswell AFB TX. 3,920.0 flying hours. (AVH-26).
12 Apr 1978	At 457 TFS AFRES, Carswell AFB TX. 4,108.0 flying hours.
25 Apr 1978	In contract depot maintenance (DYNFW) at Carswell AFB TX. 4,122.0 flying hours.
19 May 1978	At 457 TFS AFRES, Carswell AFB TX. 4,096.0 flying hours.
12 Jan 1979	In contract depot maintenance (DYNFW) at Carswell AFB TX. 4,294.4 flying hours. (AVH-27).
23 Jan 1979	At 457 TFS AFRES, Carswell AFB TX. 4,320.9 flying hours.
9 Apr 1979	In contract depot maintenance (DYNFW) at Carswell AFB TX. 4,347.1 flying hours.
18 Apr 1979	At 457 TFS AFRES, Carswell AFB TX. 4,380.0 flying hours.
12 May 1979	Deployed under "Coronet Palomino" with 457 TFS to Gioia Del Colle, Italy, from Carswell AFB TX. (301 TFW History, Apr–Jun 1979, USAF microfilm 34382).
24 May 1979	Returned from Italy to Carswell AFB TX.
31 May 1979	During the month of May 1979, while assigned to the 457 TFS AFRES, the aircraft flew 43.4 hours and had accumulated a total of 4,480.4 flying hours.
30 Jun 1979	While assigned to the 457 TFS AFRES, Carswell AFB TX, the aircraft flew 38.4 hours during the month of June 1979 and had accumulated 4,518.8 flying hours. (301 TFW History, Apr–Jun 1979, USAF microfilm 34382).
18 Jul 1979	At OC-ALC AFLC, Tinker AFB OK. 4,518.5 flying hours. (AVH-27).
20 Sep 1979	At OC-ALC AFLC, Tinker AFB OK. 4,530.0 flying hours.
27 Sep 1979	At 457 TFS AFRES, Carswell AFB TX. 4,530.0 flying hours.
15 Sep 1981	At 457 TFS AFRES, Carswell AFB TX. Marked for museum ("ZW"). 4,921.3 flying hours. (GO33B Dec 81 & GO33B 1 Feb 83).

F-105D–15RE 61-0106

Republic Production No: D-301 Production Sequence No: 381

Location: At Security Police Flightline Training Area #7, Lackland AFB, San Antonio, Texas.

Aircraft Chronology

22 Mar 1962	USAF production acceptance from Republic Aviation, Farmingdale NY. (ACA-87).
4 Apr 1962	At MOAMA, Brookley AFB AL for depot work.
13 Apr 1962	Delivered to 49 TFW, Spangdahlem AB, Germany.
6 Jun 1962	At Wheelus AB, Libya, with 49 TFW. (RAC record).
20 Nov 1963	At MOAMA, Brookley AFB AL for depot work. Phase II of "Operation Look Alike."
16 Mar 1964	Returned to 49 TFW, Spangdahlem AB, Germany.
24 Jun 1965	At 49 TFW, Spangdahlem AB, Germany. (AVH-3).
28 Feb 1966	At Wheelus AB, Libya, with 49 TFW. (AVH-5).
4 Apr 1966	At CASA, Madrid, Spain, for contract depot work (WK).
7 May 1966	At 49 TFW, Spangdahlem AB, Germany.

During its active-duty days, this F-105D served at only two Air Force bases. It started with the 49 Tactical Fighter Wing at Spangdahlem Air Base, Germany, in April 1962. To help with the 49th's NATO commitment, the plane rotated periodically to Wheelus Air Base, Libya, where its pilots practiced bombing at the El Uotia range in the Sahara desert. In February 1967, it transferred to McConnell Air Force Base, Kansas. For the next five years it supported the 23 Tactical Fighter Wing's mission to train replacement pilots for Southeast Asia. When the plane left active duty in 1972, it moved across the McConnell runway to the Kansas Air National Guard where it continued to train pilots. It then spent a year as a maintenance trainer in the Georgia Air National Guard before it went to the Reserve at Tinker Air Force Base, Oklahoma, and, finally, Hill Air Force Base, Utah. In June 1983, it was one of seven F-105Ds flown directly to Lackland where it continues its life-long career as a trainer, this time for security police flight line guards. (Photograph by author, 4 August 1997.)

9 Jul 1966 At Wheelus AB, Libya, with 49 TFW.

11 Aug 1966 At 49 TFW, Spangdahlem AB, Germany.

15 Feb 1967 At 49 TFW, Spangdahlem AB, Germany, being prepared for transfer (PL). (AVH-7).

24 Feb 1967 Transferred to 23 TFW, McConnell AFB KS.

22 Mar 1967 At MOAMA, Brookley AFB AL for depot work (WO).

29 Mar 1967 Returned to 23 TFW, McConnell AFB KS.

5 May 1967 In depot work by SMAMA field team at McConnell AFB KS.

10 May 1967 At 23 TFW, McConnell AFB KS.

1 Jun 1967 Deployed to George AFB CA to join the 563 TFS, 23 TFW, for air-to-air gunnery training for RTU Class 67IR.

16 Jun 1967 Returned to 23 TFW, McConnell AFB KS.

30 Jun 1967 Deployed to George AFB CA with the 560 TFS, 23 TFW, for air-to-air gunnery training for RTU Class 67JR.

14 Jul 1967 Returned to 23 TFW, McConnell AFB KS.

17 Jul 1967 In depot work by SMAMA field team at McConnell AFB KS.

18 Jul 1967 At 23 TFW, McConnell AFB KS.

30 Sep 1967 Assigned to 563 TFS. Crew Chief, SSgt. Douglas R. McAnaugh, awarded 23 TFW Crew Chief of Month. Aircraft flew 52.8 hours. (23 TFW History, Jun 64- Jun 68, USAF microfilm MO554)

3 Nov 1967 Deployed to George AFB CA with the 563 TFS, 23 TFW, for air-to-air gunnery training for RTU Class 68DR. (AVH-7).

20 Nov 1967 At SMAMA, McClellan AFB CA for depot work (WO).

23 Feb 1968 Returned to 23 TFW, McConnell AFB KS. (AVH-10).

16 Apr 1968 Deployed to George AFB CA with the 563 TFS, 23 TFW, for air-to-air gunnery training for RTU Class 68IR.

9 May 1968 Returned to 23 TFW, McConnell AFB KS.

14 May 1968 Deployed to George AFB CA with the 560 TFS, 23 TFW, for air-to-air gunnery training for RTU Class 68JR.

15 May 1968 Returned to 23 TFW, McConnell AFB KS.

27 Feb 1969	At 23 TFW, McConnell AFB KS. (AVH-12).
28 Feb 1969	At SMAMA, McClellan AFB CA for depot work (WO).
10 Apr 1969	Returned to 23 TFW, McConnell AFB KS.
29 Apr 1969	At 23 TFW, McConnell AFB KS.
31 Jan 1970	At 563 TFS, 23 TFW, McConnell AFB KS. Crew Chief, SSgt. Thomas J. McGibbons, selected Wing Crew Chief of the Month. Aircraft flew 22 sorties and 34.8 hours. (23 TFW History, Jan–Mar 70, USAF microfilm MO555).
6 Jun 1970	At 23 TFW, McConnell AFB KS. (AVH-14).
7 Oct 1970	While assigned to the 23 TFW, McConnell AFB KS, the aircraft landed short of Runway 18 Right and broke off the nose wheel gear assembly. (23 TFW History, Oct–Dec 70, USAF microfilm MO556).
30 Dec 1970	In depot maintenance (WM) by OCAMA at McConnell AFB KS.
4 Mar 1971	At 23 TFW, McConnell AFB KS. (AVH-16).
12 Mar 1971	In contract depot maintenance (WK) by Fairchild Engine and Aircraft Corporation (FACCF) at Bob Sikes Municipal Airport, Crestview FL.
31 Mar 1971	Returned to 23 TFW, McConnell AFB KS.
30 Aug 1971	In depot work (WO) by SMAMA at McClellan AFB CA.
9 Feb 1972	Returned to 23 TFW TAC, McConnell AFB KS. (AVH-18).
29 Feb 1972	Transferred to 184 TFG ANG, McConnell AFB KS.
9 Nov 1972	In contract depot maintenance (WK) by Fairchild Engine and Aircraft Corporation (FACCF) at Bob Sikes Municipal Airport, Crestview FL.
13 Dec 1972	Returned to 184 TFG ANG, McConnell AFB KS.
3 Jan 1974	At 184 TFG ANG, McConnell AFB KS. (AVH-20).
1 Jul 1974	In contract depot maintenance (WM) by Dynalectron Corporation (DYNZZ) at McConnell AFB KS. (AVH-22).
5 Jul 1974	At 184 TFG ANG, McConnell AFB KS for combat crew training (TF).
21 Oct 1974	In contract depot maintenance (WM) by Dynalectron Corporation (DYNZZ) at McConnell AFB KS.
11 Nov 1974	At 184 TFG ANG, McConnell AFB KS for combat crew training (TF).
28 Feb 1975	In contract depot maintenance (WM) by Dynalectron Corporation (DYNZZ) at McConnell AFB KS. (AVH23).
13 Mar 1975	At 184 TFTG ANG, McConnell AFB KS for combat crew training (TF).
7 Oct 1975	In depot maintenance (WM) by SM-ALC at McConnell AFB KS. (AVH-23 & AVH-24).
7 Oct 1975	At 184 TFTG ANG, McConnell AFB KS. Assignment code: WQ.
12 Nov 1975	At 184 TFTG ANG, McConnell AFB KS for combat crew training (TF).
12 Apr 1976	In depot work (DK) by Aero Corporation (ARDLF) at Moultrie GA. (AVH-24).
20 Sep 1976	Returned to 184 TFTG ANG, McConnell AFB KS for combat crew training (TF). 3,351 flying hours.
1978	At 116 TFW, GANG, Dobbins AFB GA. On loan from 149 TFS VA ANG. (History of the 116 TFW, 1941–1983).
15 Jun 1979	At 116 TFW ANG, Dobbins AFB GA. 4,090.9 flying hours. Used as maintenance trainer. (AVH-27 & History of the 116 TFW, 1941–1983).
9 Nov 1979	At 465 TFS AFRES, Tinker AFB OK. 4,168.1 flying hours.
18 Dec 1979	In contract depot maintenance (FACBM), Tinker AFB OK. 4,168.1 flying hours.
6 Jan 1980	At 465 TFS Tinker AFB OK. 4,170.8 flying hours. (GO33B 24 Jun 80).
14 Mar 1980	At McClellan AFB CA for depot maintenance. 4,170.8 flying hours.
22 May 1980	At 465 TFS AFRES, Tinker AFB OK. 4,213.1 flying hours. (GO33B 22 Jan 81).
30 Jul 1980	At 466 TFS AFRES, Hill AFB UT. 4,249.4 flying hours.
18 Nov 1980	In depot maintenance at Odgen ALC, Hill AFB UT. 4,294.2 flying hours.

4 Dec 1980 At 466 TFS AFRES, Hill AFB UT. 4,294.2 flying hours.

14 Sep 1982 In depot maintenance by Sacramento ALC at Hill AFB UT. 4,565.6 flying hours. (GO33B 1 Feb 83).

4 Jun 1983 One of 24 F-105s flown on ceremonial final mission at Hill AFB UT. After mission, aircraft was one of seven delivered to 3280 TTA Group (ATC), Lackland AFB TX for security police flightline training. (Possession code: TX. Inventory account: GB). 4,657.1 flying hours. (Kirtland Focus, 24 June 1983, page 9, & GO33B 9 Feb 84).

5 Jun 1983 Redesignated GF-105D at 3280 TTA Group (ATC), Lackland AFB TX. (Possession code: TX. Inventory account: GC). 4,657.1 flying hours.

F-105D-20RE 61-0107

Republic Production No: D-302 Production Sequence No: 382

Location: At the National Atomic Museum, Kirtland AFB, Albuquerque, New Mexico.

Aircraft Chronology

7 Mar 1962 USAF production acceptance from Republic Aviation, Farmingdale NY. (ACA-87).

19 Mar 1962 At MOAMA, Brookley AFB AL for depot work.

9 April 1962 Delivered to 49 TFW, Spangdahlem AB, Germany.

6 Jun 1962 At Wheelus AB, Libya, with 49 TFW (RAC record).

After it was produced in March 1962, this F-105D was sent to the 49 Tactical Fighter Wing in Germany to provide a NATO nuclear retaliation capability during the depths of the cold war. After pilot-training assignments to McConnell Air Force Base, Kansas, and Nellis Air Force Base, Nevada, it joined the Kansas Air National Guard at McConnell. It transferred to the Washington DC Air National Guard in 1979. In 1981, when it was being flown to the "Boneyard" at Tucson, Arizona, it stopped to refuel at Kirtland Air Force Base, New Mexico. On its final takeoff from Kirtland, it lost power and the pilot snagged the barrier at the end of the runway. The barrier cable sliced off the tip of the aft ventral fin and damaged the plane's tail hook. The plane was patched up and placed on a pedestal at the Atomic Museum. The tail hook is missing and the ventral fin squared off. It was repainted in the summer of 1997. (Photograph by author, 15 December 1999.)

11 Sep 1963	At MOAMA, Brookley AFB AL for depot work. "Operation Look Alike," Phase II.
27 Jan 1964	Returned to 49 TFW, Spangdahlem AB, Germany.
23 Apr 1965	At CASA, Madrid, Spain, for contract depot work. (AVH-3).
18 May 1965	Returned to 49 TFW, Spangdahlem AB, Germany.
24 Feb 1966	At CASA, Madrid, Spain, for contract depot work (WK). (AVH-5).
22 Mar 1966	At 49 TFW, Spangdahlem AB, Germany.
22 Apr 1966	At Wheelus AB, Libya, with 49 TFW.
23 May 1966	Returned to 49 TFW, Spangdahlem AB, Germany.
14 July 1966	Transferred to the 23 TFW, McConnell AFB KS.
27 Jul 1966	At MOAMA, Brookley AFB AL for depot work (WO).
5 Aug 1966	Returned to the 23 TFW, McConnell AFB KS.
14 Apr 1967	At SMAMA, McClellan AFB CA for storage (XT & XW) and depot work (WO). (AVH-7).
19 Jun 1967	Depot work completed at SMAMA, McClellan AFB CA.
20 Sept 1967	At 23 TFW, McConnell AFB KS.
3 Nov 1967	Deployed to George AFB CA with the 563 TFS, 23 TFW, for air-to-air gunnery training for RTU Class 68DR.
22 Nov 1967	Returned to 23 TFW, McConnell AFB KS.
27 Nov 1967	Assigned to aircrew training (TF) at 23 TFW, McConnell AFB KS.
16 Apr 1968	Deployed to George AFB CA with the 563 TFS, 23 TFW, for air-to-air gunnery training for RTU Class 68IR. (AVH-10).
9 May 1968	Returned to 23 TFW, McConnell AFB KS for combat crew training (TF).
8 Jan 1969	At SMAMA, McClellan AFB CA for depot work (WO). (AVH-12).
25 Feb 1969	Returned to 23 TFW, McConnell AFB KS.
24 Nov 1970	At 23 TFW, McConnell AFB KS for combat crew training (TF). (AVH-14).
12 Dec 1970	At 23 TFW, McConnell AFB KS assigned to combat duties (CC).
9 Mar 1971	In depot work (WO) by SMAMA at McClellan AFB CA. (AVH-16).
15 Sep 1971	Returned (PL) to 23 TFW, McConnell AFB KS.
1 Mar 1972	Carried on assignment roster for the 562 TFS, 23 TFW, at McConnell AFB KS. (Master 23 TFW Aircraft Assignment as of 1 March 1972).
22 Jun 1972	In contract depot maintenance (WK) by Fairchild Engine and Aircraft Corporation (FACCF) at Bob Sikes Municipal Airport, Crestview FL. (AVH-18).
18 Jul 1972	Assigned to 561 TFS, McConnell AFB KS, after 23 TFW relocated to England AFB, LA.
25 July 1972	Transferred (PL) to 57 FWW Nellis AFB, NV for combat crew training (TF).
27 Feb 1973	In depot maintenance (WM) by SM-ALC at Nellis AFB NV. (AVH-20).
1 Mar 1973	At 57 FWW TAC, Nellis AFB, NV for combat crew training (TF).
23 Jan 1974	In depot maintenance (WM) by SM-ALC at Nellis AFB NV. (AVH-22).
28 Jan 1974	At 57 FWW TAC, Nellis AFB, NV for combat crew training (TF).
9 Sep 1974	Transferred to 184 TFG ANG, McConnell AFB KS.
14 Feb 1975	In contract depot maintenance (WM) by Dynalectron Corporation (DYNZZ) at McConnell AFB KS. (AVH-23).
5 Mar 1975	At 184 TFTG, McConnell AFB KS for combat crew training (TF).
7 Oct 1975	In depot maintenance (WQ) by SM-ALC at McConnell AFB KS. (AVH-23 & AVH-24).
23 Oct 1975	At 184 TFTG, McConnell AFB KS for combat crew training (TF).
24 Oct 1975	In depot maintenance (WQ) by SM-ALC at McConnell AFB KS.
8 Dec 1975	At 184 TFTG, McConnell AFB KS for combat crew training (TF).

10 Dec 1976	In depot maintenance by SM-ALC at McConnell AFB KS. 3,283.0 flying hours. (AVH-25 & AVH-26).
20 Dec 1976	At 184 TFG ANG, McConnell AFB KS. 3,283.0 flying hours.
18 July 1979	Assigned to 113 TFW ANG, Andrews AFB, MD. 3,974.4 flying hours. (AVH-27).
12 Jun 1981	Damaged on takeoff at Kirtland AFB NM. Aircraft was one of four F-105D's from 121 TFS, Andrews AFB MD enroute to storage at MASDC, Davis-Monthan AFB AZ. " Capt. David W. Kelsey can credit a steel cable for saving his life Friday. The one-inch cable stretched across the runway at Albuquerque International Airport stopped his aging F-105 jet fighter after it was unable to attain enough power to take off about 3:10 p.m. Kelsey was not injured. ... Air Force officials said that as he was trying to take off, he was unable to obtain enough power, and he dropped an emergency hook from the back of the plane to catch the steel cable. ... A crane was used to lift the aircraft onto a long blue Air Force trailer, to haul it to another spot where it could be examined. ... " (Albuquerque Journal, June 13, 1981, Page B1).
26 Jun 1981	Atomic Museum at Kirtland AFB requested the USAF Museum provide the aircraft for static display. (TWX 261610Z Jun 81).
21 Jul 1981	Assigned to museum inventory account (ZW) by 113 TFW ANG, Andrews AFB MD. 4,348.9 flying hours. (GO33B Dec 81 & GO33B 1 Feb 83).
28 Feb 1983	Mounted on pylon after restoration by 1550 ATTW, Kirtland AFB NM.
17 May 1983	Display dedication ceremony at National Atomic Museum, Kirtland AFB NM to the memory of the pilots who flew the aircraft in combat in Southeast Asia. " Maj. Gen. James A. Young, USAF, Ret., who commanded the first F-105 unit in Southeast Asia, presented the dedication address. He described the 'Thud' as a pilot's airplane that fully loaded could outrun a MiG at low altitudes. Maj. Gen. Young flew 100 combat missions in the F-105 and 105 missions in an F-4. He said that the F-105 was the best strike fighter in the Air Force inventory then—and now, even though the aircraft type is being retired from service. Several members of the Red River Rats, an organization of pilots who flew combat missions over North Vietnam, attended the ceremony." (Air Classics magazine).
Jul 1996	Atomic Museum began work to completely strip and repaint aircraft. Painting contractor was Ray Bouffard, Museum Services Company.
Oct 1997	Aircraft repainting completed.

F-105D-20RE 61-0108

Republic Production No: D-303 Production Sequence No: 383

Location: At Security Police Flightline Training Area #7, Lackland AFB, San Antonio, Texas.

Aircraft Name(s)	Crew	Unit	Date	Description
Kombat Kathy		466 TFS		Woman in bikini riding bomb. Letters in yellow above and below figure..

Aircraft Chronology

19 Mar 1962	USAF production acceptance from Republic Aviation, Farmingdale NY. (ACA-87).
27 Apr 1962	At MOAMA, Brookley AFB AL for depot work.
18 May 1962	Delivered to 49 TFW, Spangdahlem AB, Germany.
2 Jul 1963	At MOAMA, Brookley AFB AL for depot work. "Operation Look Alike," Phase II.
6 Jan 1964	Returned to 49 TFW, Spangdahlem AB, Germany.
18 May 1965	At CASA, Madrid, Spain, for contract depot work (WK). (AVH-3).

F-105D 61-0108 followed the same Air Force service as its sister 61-0106 described previously—initial delivery to the 49 Tactical Fighter Wing at Spangdahlem Air Base, Germany, in 1962 with reassignment to the 23 Tactical Fighter Wing's Replacement Training Unit at McConnell Air Force Base, Kansas, in 1967. In August 1972, it transferred to the Air Force Reserve at Tinker Air Force Base, Oklahoma, where it flew on two NATO summer deployments, the first to England in 1978 and then to Italy in 1979. It continued its Reserve duty with the 466 Tactical Fighter Squadron at Hill Air Force Base, Utah, where, in the summer of 1981, it deployed to Denmark for its last NATO exercise. It was one of the F-105Ds that participated in the "Thudout" at Hill in June 1983, after which it was flown to Lackland for service at the Security Police training "flightline." (Photograph by Pete A. Sanders, Jr., 16 June 1996.)

16 Jun 1965	Returned to 49 TFW, Spangdahlem AB, Germany.
28 Feb 1966	At Wheelus AB, Libya, with 49 TFW. (AVH-5).
7 May 1966	Returned to 49 TFW, Spangdahlem AB, Germany.
16 May 1966	At CASA, Madrid, Spain, for contract depot work (WK).
17 Jun 1966	Returned to 49 TFW, Spangdahlem AB, Germany.
23 Sep 1966	At Wheelus AB, Libya, with 49 TFW.
7 Oct 1966	Returned to 49 TFW, Spangdahlem AB, Germany.
26 Jan 1967	At 49 TFW, Spangdahlem AB, Germany being prepared for transfer (PK). (AVH-7).
4 Feb 1967	Transferred to 23 TFW, McConnell AFB KS.
11 Apr 1967	At 23 TFW, McConnell AFB KS being prepared for transfer to depot (PL).
14 Apr 1967	At SMAMA, McClellan AFB CA for storage (XT & XW) and depot work (WO).
28 Jun 1967	Returned from depot to 23 TFW, McConnell AFB KS.
4 Oct 1967	At 23 TFW, McConnell AFB KS.
2 Dec 1967	Deployed to George AFB CA with the 560 TFS, 23 TFW, for air-to-air gunnery training for RTU Class 68ER.
22 Dec 1967	Returned to 23 TFW, McConnell AFB KS.
23 Jan 1968	Deployed to George AFB CA with the 561 TFS, 23 TFW, for air-to-air gunnery training for RTU Class 68FR. (AVH-10).
7 Feb 1968	Returned to 23 TFW, McConnell AFB KS.
14 May 1968	Deployed to George AFB CA with the 560 TFS, 23 TFW, for air-to-air gunnery training for RTU. Class 68JR.
29 May 1968	Returned to 23 TFW, McConnell AFB KS.
18 Jun 1968	Assigned to combat crew training (TF) at 23 TFW, McConnell AFB KS.

5 Feb 1969	At SMAMA, McClellan AFB CA for depot work (WO). (AVH-12).
25 Mar 1969	Returned to 23 TFW, McConnell AFB KS.
16 Nov 1970	At 23 TFW, McConnell AFB KS for combat crew training (TF). (AVH-14).
12 Dec 1970	At 23 TFW, McConnell AFB KS assigned to combat duties (CC).
1 Apr 1971	In depot work (WO) by SMAMA at McClellan AFB CA. (AVH-16).
2 Aug 1971	Returned (PL) to 23 TFW, McConnell AFB KS.
4 Aug 1971	At 23 TFW (CC), McConnell AFB KS.
1 Mar 1972	Carried on assignment roster for the 562 TFS, 23 TFW at McConnell AFB KS. (Master 23 TFW Aircraft Assignment as of 1 March 1972).
1 Jul 1972	Assigned to 561 TFS, McConnell AFB KS, after 23 TFW transferred to England AFB LA to fly A-7Ds. (AVH-18).
19 Jul 1972	In contract depot maintenance (WK) by Fairchild Engine and Aircraft Corporation (FACCF) at Bob Sikes Municipal Airport, Crestview FL.
21 Aug 1972	Transferred to 507 TFG AFRES, Tinker AFB OK.
13 Mar 1973	In depot maintenance (WM) by SM-ALC at Tinker AFB OK. (AVH-20).
15 Mar 1973	At 507 TFG AFRES, Tinker AFB OK.
31 Mar 1973	Assigned to 507 CMTSq AFRES, Tinker AFB OK.
20 Nov 1973	In depot maintenance (WM) by SM-ALC at Tinker AFB OK.
7 Dec 1973	At 507 CMTSq AFRES, Tinker AFB OK.
27 Feb 1974	In depot maintenance (WM) by SM-ALC at Tinker AFB OK. (AVH-22).
7 Mar 1974	At 507 CMTSq AFRES, Tinker AFB OK.
16 Oct 1974	Assigned organization changed to 507 CLMSq AFRES, Tinker AFB OK.
17 Mar 1975	In depot maintenance (WM) by SM-ALC at Tinker AFB OK. (AVH-23).
4 Apr 1975	At 507 CLMSq AFRES, Tinker AFB OK.
6 Oct 1975	In depot maintenance (WM) by SM-ALC at Tinker AFB OK. (AVH-23 & AVH-24).
17 Feb 1976	At 507 TFG AFRES, Tinker AFB OK. 2,137 flying hours.
4 Jan 1977	In depot maintenance by SM-ALC at Tinker AFB OK. 3,286.0 flying hours. (AVH-25 & AVH-26).
27 Jan 1977	At 507 TFG AFRES, Tinker AFB OK. 3,286.0 flying hours.
10 Jun 1978	Deployed under "Coronet Oriole" with 465 TFS to Sculthorpe, England, from Tinker AFB OK. (British Aviation Review, Dec 1995).
23 Jun 1978	Returned from England to Tinker AFB OK.
17 Aug 1978	In depot maintenance by SM-ALC at Tinker AFB OK. 3,573.0 flying hours. (AVH-26).
30 Aug 1978	At 507 TFG AFRES, Tinker AFB OK. 3,573.0 flying hours.
6 Dec 1978	In depot maintenance by SM-ALC at Tinker AFB OK. 3,686.5 flying hours.
12 Feb 1979	At 465 TFS AFRES, Tinker AFB OK. 3,686.5 flying hours. (AVH-27).
1 Mar 1979	In contract depot maintenance (FACBM), Tinker AFB OK. 3,686.5 flying hours.
25 Apr 1979	At 465 TFS AFRES, Tinker AFB OK. 3,686.5 flying hours.
12 May 1979	Deployed under "Coronet Palomino" with 465TFS to Gioia Del Colle, Italy, from Tinker AFB OK. (British Aviation Review, Dec 1995).
24 May 1979	Returned from Italy to Tinker AFB OK.
31 May 1979	While assigned to the 465 TFS AFRES, Tinker AFB OK, the aircraft flew 39.3 hours during the month of May 1979 and had accumulated 3,667.0 flying hours. The assigned crew chief was Rufus Cleveland. (301 TFW History 1 Apr–30 Jun 1979, USAF microfilm 343832).
9 Jun 1979	While assigned to the 465 TFS AFRES, Tinker AFB OK, the aircraft ground aborted due to split trailing edge flaps caused by a bad potentiometer. (301 TFW History 1 Apr–30 Jun 1979, USAF microfilm 343832).

30 Jun 1979	While assigned to the 465 TFS AFRES, Tinker AFB OK the aircraft flew 43.6 hours during the month of June 1979, the highest time for the month of any of the squadron's F 105s. The aircraft's total flying time was 3,710.6 hours. The crew chief was Rufus Cleveland. (301 TFW History 1 Apr–30 Jun 1979, USAF microfilm 343832).
7 Apr 1980	In depot maintenance (FACBM) at Tinker AFB OK. 3,899.4 flying hours. (GO33B 24 Jun 80).
6 May 1980	At 465 TFS, Tinker AFB OK. 3,922.0 flying hours.
24 Oct 1980	Transferred to 466 TFS AFRES, Hill AFB UT. 3,951.5 flying hours. (GO33B 22 Jan 81).
15 Aug 1981	Deployed under "Coronet Rudder" with 466 TFS AFRES to Skrydstrup, Denmark, from Hill AFB UT. (British Aviation Review, Dec 1995).
29 Aug 1981	Returned from Denmark to Hill AFB UT.
13 Jul 1982	In depot maintenance at Ogden ALC, Hill AFB UT. 4,316.0 flying hours. (GO33B 1 Feb 83).
4 Jun 1983	One of 24 F-105s flown on ceremonial final mission at Hill AFB UT. After mission, aircraft was one of seven delivered to 3280 TTA Group (ATC), Lackland AFB TX for security police flightline training. (Possession code: TX. Inventory account: GC). 4,407.1 flying hours. (GO33B 9 Feb 84).
5 Jun 1983	Redesignated GF-105D at 3280 TTA Group (ATC), Lackland AFB TX. (Possession code: TX. Inventory account: GC). 4,407.1 flying hours.

F-105D–20RE 61-0110

Republic Production No: D-305 Production Sequence No: 385

Location: At USAF Detachment 1, 343 Training Squadron, Camp Bullis, San Antonio, Texas.

Aircraft Name(s)	Crew	Unit	Date	Description
Texas Humpbacks		457 TFS AFRES	Nov 80	Cowboy riding bull while shooting pistols in each hand. Brown gloves with fringe. Hat with yellow star. Brown vest and red shirt. Red letters below art outlined in black. On fuselage below left wing.

Aircraft Chronology

7 Mar 1962	USAF production acceptance from Republic Aviation, Farmingdale, New York. (ACA-87).
7 Apr 1962	At MOAMA, Brookley AFB AL for depot work (WO).
1 May 1962	Delivered to 49 TFW, Spangdahlem AB, Germany.
22 Nov 1963	At MOAMA, Brookley AFB AL for depot work (WO).
25 Nov 1963	Returned to 49 TFW, Spangdahlem AB, Germany.
3 Jul 1965	In contract depot work (WK) at CASA, Getafe, Spain . (AVH-3).
19 Jul 1965	Returned to 49 TFW, Spangdahlem AB, Germany.
7 Oct 1965	In contract depot work (WK) at CASA, Getafe, Spain.
13 Dec 1965	Returned to 49 TFW, Spangdahlem AB, Germany.
15 Nov 1966	At 49 TFW, Spangdahlem AB, Germany, USAFE, being readied for transfer (PL). (AVH-5).
5 Dec 1966	Transferred (PL) to 23 TFW TAC, McConnell AFB KS.
8 Dec 1966	Combat ready (CC) at 23 TFW, McConnell AFB KS.
2 Feb 1967	At 23 TFW, McConnell AFB KS being prepared for transfer (PL) to depot. (AVH-7).

This is the third of the 343 Training Squadron's F-105Ds that started service with the 49 Tactical Fighter Wing at Spangdahlem Air Base, Germany, followed by transfer to McConnell Air Force Base, Kansas. However, in 1968, 61-0110 transferred briefly to the 355 Tactical Fighter Wing at Takhli, Thailand, where it flew combat missions over North Vietnam. Within a month it relocated to the 18 Tactical Fighter Wing at Kadena Air Base, Okinawa, where it rotated periodically to Kwangju Air Base, Korea, an alert site for the 18th after the U.S.S. Pueblo incident. In 1970, 61-0110 was one of thirty F-105Ds modified with additional avionics housed in a raised turtle deck along the aircraft spine. This Thunderstick Two (T-Stick II) modification added a LORAN receiver and an inertial navigation system that gave the planes an improved blind-bombing capability needed for the Vietnam war. However, by the time the aircraft were modified, F-105Ds had been withdrawn from South East Asia and the T-Stick IIs were assigned to the 23 Tactical Fighter Wing at McConnell Air Force Base, Kansas. In 1972, when the 23rd moved to England Air Force Base, Louisiana, and gave up F-105s, the 30 T-Sticks were transferred to the Air Force Reserve's 457 Tactical Fighter Squadron at Carswell Air Force Base, Texas. This aircraft, badly needing restoration, is one of five T-Stick IIs that have survived. (Photograph by author, 4 August 1997.)

3 Feb 1967	At MOAMA, Brookley AFB AL for depot work (WO).
10 Feb 1967	Returned to the 23 TFW, McConnell AFB KS.
3 Apr 1967	At MOAMA, Brookley AFB AL for depot work (WO).
23 Jun 1967	Returned to the 23 TFW, McConnell AFB KS.
21 Jul 1967	In depot maintenance (WM) by SMAMA at McConnell AFB KS.
23 Jul 1967	At 23 TFW, McConnell AFB KS.
29 Sept 1967	Deployed to George AFB CA with the 562 TFS, 23 TFW, from McConnell AFB KS to support F-105 RTU Class 68BR, "The Many Splendored Studs."
13 Oct 1967	Returned to 23 TFW, McConnell AFB KS.
15 Oct 1967	In depot maintenance (WM) by SMAMA at McConnell AFB KS.
16 Oct 1967	At the 23 TFW, McConnell AFB KS.
7 Nov 1967	In depot maintenance (WM) by SMAMA at McConnell AFB KS.
7 Nov 1967	At the 23 TFW, McConnell AFB KS.
12 Mar 1968	Deployed to George AFB CA with the 562 TFS, 23 TFW, from McConnell AFB KS to support F-105 RTU Class 68HR. (AVH-10).
28 Mar 1968	Returned to 23 TFW, McConnell AFB KS for combat crew training (TF).
2 Aug 1968	At 23 TFW, McConnell AFB KS being prepared for transfer to depot (PL).
5 Aug 1968	In depot work (WO) by SMAMA at McClellan AFB CA.
10 Sep 1968	Returned (PL) to 23 TFW, McConnell AFB KS.
16 Sep 1968	At 23 TFW, McConnell AFB KS for combat crew training (TF).
23 Sep 1968	At 23 TFW, McConnell AFB KS being prepared for transfer (PL).
1 Oct 1968	Transferred (PL) to 355 TFW, Takhli RTAB, Thailand.
26 Oct 1968	Transferred (PL) to 18 TFW, Kadena AB, Okinawa.

2 Nov 1968	Combat capable (CC) at 18 TFW, Kadena AB, Okinawa.
3 Feb 1969	Deployed to Kwangju AB, Korea, with the 18 TFW. (AVH-12).
20 Feb 1969	Returned to the 18 TFW, Kadena AB, Okinawa.
7 Jun 1969	Deployed to Kwangju AB, Korea, with the 18 TFW.
10 Jun 1969	Returned to the 18 TFW, Kadena AB, Okinawa.
26 Jun 1969	Deployed to Kwangju AB, Korea, with the 18 TFW.
13 Sep 1969	Returned to the 18 TFW, Kadena AB, Okinawa.
13 Oct 1969	At the 18 TFW, Kadena AB, Okinawa, being prepared for transfer (PL).
14 Oct 1969	Arrived (PL) at Air Asia (AAITT), Tainan, Taiwan.
22 Oct 1969	In contract depot work (WK) by Air Asia (AAITT) at Tainan, Taiwan.
26 Dec 1969	At Air Asia (AAITT) at Tainan, Taiwan, being prepared for transfer (PL).
27 Dec 1969	Returned (PL) to the 18 TFW, Kadena AB, Okinawa.
1 Jan 1970	At Kadena AB, Okinawa, being prepared for transfer (PL) by SMAMA.
2 Jan 1970	In depot maintenance (WM) by SMAMA at Kadena AB, Okinawa. (AVH-14).
4 Jan 1970	At 18 TFW, Kadena AB, Okinawa.
28 Apr 1970	In depot maintenance (WM) by SMAMA at Kadena AB, Okinawa.
3 May 1970	At 18 TFW, Kadena AB, Okinawa.
3 Nov 1970	Transferred (PL) to the 23 TFW, McConnell AFB KS.
12 Nov 1970	In flyable storage (PR) at the 23 TFW, McConnell AFB KS.
18 Nov 1970	At 23 TFW, McConnell AFB KS being prepared for transfer (PL).
27 Nov 1970	In depot work (WO) by SMAMA, McClellan AFB CA for the T-Stick II modification.
28 Mar 1971	Returned (PL) to 23 TFW, McConnell AFB KS. (AVH-16).
1 Apr 1971	Combat capable (CC) at 563 TFS, 23 TFW, McConnell AFB KS.
1 Mar 1972	Carried on assignment roster with the 563 TFS, 23 TFW, at McConnell AFB KS. (Master 23 TFW Aircraft Assignment as of 1 March 1972).
1 Jul 1972	Reassigned to 561 TFS, McConnell AFB KS when 23 TFW relocated to England AFB LA to fly A-7Ds. (AVH-18).
11 Jul 1972	At 561 TFS, McConnell AFB KS being prepared for transfer (PL).
20 Jul 1972	One of 30 T-Stick II F-105Ds reassigned (PL) to 506 TFG, 457 TFS AFRES, Carswell AFB TX.
21 Jul 1972	Combat capable (CC) at 506 TFG AFRES, Carswell AFB TX.
1 Oct 1972	At 506 TFG AFRES, Carswell AFB TX being prepared for transfer to depot (PL).
2 Oct 1972	In contract depot work (WK) by Fairchild Engine and Aircraft Corporation (FACCF), Bob Sikes Airport, Crestview FL.
26 Oct 1972	Returned (PL) to 506 TFG AFRES, Carswell AFB TX.
7 Nov 1972	Combat capable (CC) at 506 TFG AFRES, Carswell AFB TX.
14 Jun 1973	In depot work (WO) by SMAMA, McClellan AFB CA. (AVH-20).
14 Sep 1973	Returned to 506 CMTSq AFRES, Carswell AFB TX.
6 Oct 1975	In depot work (WO) at 506 CLMSq AFRES, Carswell AFB TX. (AVH-23 & AVH-24).
7 Feb 1976	In depot work (WQ) at 507 CLMSQ AFRES, Tinker AFB OK. (AVH-24).
10 Feb 1976	Returned to 506 CLMSq AFRES, Carswell AFB TX for further depot work (WQ).
10 Mar 1976	Combat capable (CC) at 506 CLMSq AFRES, Carswell AFB TX.
11 Mar 1976	Assigned unit changed to 457 TFS AFRES, Carswell AFB TX. 3,342 flying hours.
19 May 1978	In depot maintenance (DM) by General Dynamics (DYNFW) at Carswell AFB TX. 3,814.0 flying hours. (AVH-26).
11 Jul 1978	At 457 TFS AFRES, Carswell AFB TX. 3,837.0 flying hours.

19 Mar 1979	At 457 TFS AFRES, Carswell AFB TX. 3,974.3 flying hours. (AVH-27).
12 May 1979	Deployed under "Coronet Palomino" with 457 TFS to Gioia Del Colle, Italy, from Carswell AFB TX. (British Aviation Review, Dec 95).
24 May 1979	Returned from Italy to Carswell AFB TX.
30 Jun 1979	While assigned to the 457 TFS AFRES, Carswell AFB TX, the aircraft flew 17.4 hours during the month of June 1979 and had accumulated 4,033.2 flying hours. (301 TFW History, Apr–Jun 1979, USAF microfilm 34382).
10 Sep 1979	At 457 TFS AFRES, Carswell AFB TX. 4,043.3 flying hours. (AVH-27).
14 Jan 1982	At 457 TFS, AFRES, Carswell AFB TX. Inventory account: ZD, Test to Destruction. 4,588.5 flying hours. (GO33B 1 Feb 83).
9 Nov 1983	Assigned to 2954 CLSS, Kelly AFB TX for ABDR training. (HQ 2852 ABG/DADF Letter 9 Nov 83).
22 May 1985	At 2954 CLSS, Kelly AFB TX for ABDR training. (HQ 2852 ABG/DADF Letter 22 May 85).

F-105D–20RE 61-0115

Republic Production No: D-310 Production Sequence No: 390

Location: At Security Police Flightline Training Area #7, Lackland AFB, San Antonio, Texas.

Aircraft Chronology

27 Mar 1962	USAF production acceptance from Republic Aviation, Farmingdale NY. (ACA-87).
6 Jun 1962	At MOAMA, Brookley AFB AL for depot work.
8 Jul 1962	Delivered to 49 TFW, Spangdahlem AB, Germany.
31 Jul 1962	At Wheelus AB, Libya, with 49 TFW.
1 Jan 1964	At MOAMA, Brookley AFB AL for depot work. "Operation Look Alike," Phase II.
6 May 1964	Returned to 49 TFW, Spangdahlem AB, Germany. (AVH-1).
22 Mar 1965	At CASA, Spain, for contract depot work (WK). (AVH-3).
30 Apr 1965	Returned to 49 TFW, Spangdahlem AB, Germany.
16 Mar 1966	At Wheelus AB, Libya, with 49 TFW. (AVH-5).
7 May 1966	At CASA, Spain, for contract depot work (WK).
20 May 1966	Returned to 49 TFW, Spangdahlem AB, Germany.
14 Oct 1966	At Wheelus AB, Libya, with 49 TFW.
28 Oct 1966	Returned to 49 TFW, Spangdahlem AB, Germany.
7 Feb 1967	At 49 TFW, Spangdahlem AB, Germany, being prepared for transfer (PL). (AVH-7).
11 Feb 1967	Transferred to the 23 TFW, McConnell AFB KS.
25 Apr 1967	At 23 TFW, McConnell AFB KS being prepared for transfer to depot (PL).
27 Apr 1967	At SMAMA, McClellan AFB CA for storage (XT & XW) and depot work (WO).
13 Aug 1967	Returned from the depot to McConnell AFB KS.
31 Oct 1967	At 23 TFW, McConnell AFB KS.
1 Dec 1967	Deployed to George AFB CA with the 560 TFS, 23 TFW, for air-to-air gunnery training for RTU Class 68ER.
22 Dec 1967	Returned to 23 TFW, McConnell AFB KS.

F-105D 61-0115 is the fourth of the 343 Training Squadron's Thunderchiefs that started its service with the 49 Tactical Fighter Wing at Spangdahlem Air Base, Germany, in 1962. It transferred to the 23 TFW at McConnell Air Force Base, Kansas, in 1967 when the 49th converted to F-4Ds. It supported the 23rd's Replacement Training Unit with three gunnery-training deployments to George Air Force Base, California. In 1972, it began its service with the Air Force Reserve at the 465 Tactical Fighter Squadron, Tinker Air Force Base, Oklahoma, and deployed with them to Germany and England for NATO summer exercises in 1977 and 1978. When the 465th acquired F-4Ds, their F-105s were sent to the 466 Tactical Fighter Squadron at Hill Air Force Base, Utah, who flew 61-0115 on their NATO deployment to Denmark in 1981. The 466th kept their Thunderchiefs until they became the first Air Force Reserve unit to be equipped with F-16As. 61-0155 was one of seven F-105s flown to Lackland in June 1983. (Photograph by Pete A. Sanders, Jr., 16 June 1996.)

23 Jan 1968	Deployed to George AFB CA with the 561 TFS, 23 TFW, for air-to-air gunnery training for RTU Class 68FR. (AVH-10).
7 Feb 1968	Returned to 23 TFW, McConnell AFB KS for combat crew training (TF).
14 May 1968	Deployed to George AFB CA with the 560 TFS, 23 TFW, for air-to-air gunnery training for RTU Class 68JR.
29 May 1968	Returned to 23 TFW, McConnell AFB KS for combat crew training (TF).
4 Apr 1969	At 4519 CCTS, 23 TFW, McConnell AFB KS. Aircraft flown on 100th consecutive mission without an abort. Pilot: Col. Harry Schurr, 4519 CCTS commander. Crew chief: SSgt. Roy Dudley. (23 TFW Unit History).
19 May 1969	At SMAMA, McClellan AFB CA for depot work (WO). (AVH-12).
23 Jun 1969	Returned to 23 TFW, McConnell AFB KS.
17 Apr 1971	In depot work (WO) by SMAMA at McClellan AFB CA. (AVH-16).
1 Sep 1971	Returned (PL) to 23 TFW, McConnell AFB KS.
3 Sep 1971	Operational (CC) at 23 TFW, McConnell AFB KS.
1 Mar 1972	Carried on assignment roster for the 562 TFS, 23 TFW, at McConnell AFB KS. (Master 23 TFW Aircraft Assignment as of 1 March 1972).
1 Jul 1972	Assigned to the 561 TFS, McConnell AFB KS, when the 23 TFW relocated to England AFB LA to fly A-7Ds. (AVH-18).
28 Jul 1972	In contract depot maintenance (WK) by Fairchild Engine and Aircraft Corporation (FACCF) at Bob Sikes Municipal Airport, Crestview FL.

1 Sep 1972	Transferred to 507 TFG AFRES, Tinker AFB OK.
31 Mar 1973	Assigned to 507 CMTSq AFRES, Tinker AFB OK. (AVH-20).
15 Oct 1973	In depot maintenance (WM) by SM-ALC at Tinker AFB OK.
26 Oct 1973	At 507 CMTSq AFRES, Tinker AFB OK.
18 Mar 1974	In depot maintenance (WM) by SM-ALC at Tinker AFB OK. (AVH-22).
22 Mar 1974	At 507 CMTSq AFRES, Tinker AFB OK.
20 May 1974	In depot maintenance (WM) by SM-ALC at Tinker AFB OK.
24 May 1974	At 507 CMTSq AFRES, Tinker AFB OK.
16 Oct 1974	Assigned organization changed to 507 CLMSq AFRES, Tinker AFB OK.
22 Jan 1975	In depot maintenance (WM) by SM-ALC at Tinker AFB OK. (AVH-23).
13 Feb 1975	At 507 CLMSq AFRES, Tinker AFB OK.
6 Oct 1975	In depot maintenance (WM) by SM-ALC at Tinker AFB OK. (AVH-23 & AVH-24).
6 Oct 1976	At 507 CLMSq AFRES, Tinker AFB OK. Assignment code: WQ. (AVH-24).
28 Jan 1976	In depot maintenance (WM) by SM-ALC at Tinker AFB OK.
12 Feb 1976	At 507 CLMSq AFRES, Tinker AFB OK.
29 Dec 1976	In depot maintenance by SM-ALC at Tinker AFB OK. 3,421.8 flying hours. (AVH-25 & AVH-26).
12 Jan 1977	At 507 TFG AFRES, Tinker AFB OK. 3,460.0 flying hours.
14 Aug 1977	Deployed under "Coronet Poker" with 465 TFS to Norvenich, Germany, from Tinker AFB OK. (British Aviation Review, Dec 1995).
27 Aug 1977	Returned from Germany to Tinker AFB OK.
3 Feb 1978	At 465 TFS AFRES, Tinker AFB OK. 3,678.0 flying hours. (AVH-26).
15 Feb 1979	In contract depot maintenance (FACBM), Tinker AFB OK. 3,751.8 flying hours. (AVH-27).
5 Mar 1979	At 465 TFS AFRES, Tinker AFB OK. 3,926.1 flying hours.
1 Apr 1979	In contract depot maintenance (FACBM), Tinker AFB OK. 3,935.6 flying hours.
9 Apr 1979	While assigned to the 465 TFS AFRES, Tinker AFB OK the aircraft ground aborted due to the Mechanical Advantage Shifter being inoperative. (301 TFW History 1 Apr–30 Jun 1979, USAF microfilm 343832).
14 May 1979	In contract depot maintenance (FACBM), Tinker AFB OK. 3,937.3 flying hours.
4 Jun 1979	At 465 TFS AFRES, Tinker AFB OK. 3,986.3 flying hours.
10 Jun 1978	Deployed under "Coronet Oriole" with 465 TFS to Sculthorpe, England from Tinker AFB OK. (British Aviation Review, Dec 1995).
23 Jun 1978	Returned from England to Tinker AFB OK.
31 May 1979	While assigned to the 465 TFS AFRES, Tinker AFB OK, the aircraft did not fly during the month of May 1979 but had accumulated a total of 3,970.6 flying hours. The assigned crew chief was Mackey. (301 TFW History, Apr–Jun 1979, USAF microfilm 34382).
12 Jun 1979	While assigned to the 465 TFS AFRES, Tinker AFB OK, the aircraft ground aborted for the nose wheel steering turning hard right due to a bad servo. (301 TFW History 1 Apr–30 Jun 1979, USAF microfilm 343832).
30 Jun 1979	While assigned to the 465 TFS AFRES, Tinker AFB OK, the aircraft flew 15.7 hours during the month of June 1979 and had accumulated a total of 3,986.3 flying hours. The assigned crew chief was Mackey. (301 TFW History, Apr–Jun 1979, USAF microfilm 34382).
30 Oct 1979	At SM-ALC AFLC, McClellan AFB CA. 4,085.9 flying hours. (AVH-26).
4 Jan 1980	At 465 TFS, Tinker AFB OK. 4,120.0 flying hours. (GO33B 24 Jun 80).
1 Oct 1980	Transferred to 466 TFS AFRES, Hill AFB UT. 4,265.4 flying hours. (GO33B 22 Jan 81).
15 Aug 1981	Deployed under "Coronet Rudder" with 466 TFS to Skrydstrup, Denmark from Hill AFB UT. (British Aviation Review, Dec 1995).

29 Aug 1981	Returned from Denmark to Hill AFB UT.
4 Jun 1983	One of 24 F-105s flown on ceremonial final mission at Hill AFB UT. After mission, aircraft was one of seven delivered to 3280 TTA Group (ATC), Lackland AFB TX for security police flightline training. (Possession code: TX. Inventory account: GB). 4,708.8 flying hours. (GO33B 9 Feb 84).
5 Jun 1983	Redesignated GF-105D at 3280 TTA Group (ATC), Lackland AFB TX. (Possession code: TX. Inventory account: GC). 4,708.8 flying hours.

F-105D-20RE 61-0138

Republic Production No: D-333 Production Sequence No: 413

Location: Displayed on a pedestal near the main gate at Bolling AFB, Washington DC.

Aircraft Name(s)	Crew	Unit	Date	Description
Chipmonk		121 TFS DC ANG	Aug 72	

Aircraft Chronology

31 Jul 1962	USAF production acceptance from Republic Aviation, Farmingdale NY. (ACA-87).
24 Nov 1962	At MOAMA, Brookley AFB AL for depot work. "Operation Look Alike," Phase I.
9 Dec 1962	Delivered to 36 TFW, Bitburg AB, Germany.
27 Feb 1964	At MOAMA, Brookley AFB AL for depot work. "Operation Look Alike," Phase II.
9 Aug 1964	Transferred to 23 TFW, McConnell AFB, KS. (AVH-1).

"One Three Eight" entered service at the end of 1962 with the 36 Tactical Fighter Wing in Germany where it stayed for less than two years. Its next assignment in 1964 with the "Flying Tigers" of the 23 Tactical Fighter Wing at McConnell Air Force Base, Kansas, lasted seven years. In late 1964, it deployed with five other F-105s to Hawaii for an Army exercise that was the first opportunity for Thunderchiefs to sport the Flying Tigers' shark's mouth. After a four-month deployment to Japan in 1965, it settled down at McConnell's Replacement Training Unit to train pilots heading to the war in South East Asia. The Air National Guard at Andrews Air Force Base, Maryland, flew it for its last five years of service. The Guard retired it in 1976. The plane sat around collecting bird's nest before Pentagon generals in the early 1990s decided it would be a fitting display at nearby Bolling Air Force Base in Washington DC. During much of its ten months of rework, its restoration progress was briefed each week to the Air Force Chief of Staff. (Photograph by Jay Finch, November 1996.)

30 Oct 1964	Deployed to Hickam AFB, HI with the 560 TFS, 23 TFW, from McConnell AFB KS, for exercise "Tropic Lightning." Aircraft had 23 TFW shark's mouth painted on nose over its natural metal finish. (Photo in *National Geographic Magazine*, Sep 65, pages 344-345).
14 Dec 1964	Returned from Hawaii to the 23 TFW, McConnell AFB, KS. (AVH-2).
6 Mar 1965	Deployed from McConnell AFB KS to Yokota AB, Japan, with the 561 TFS, 23 TFW, on "Operation One Buck 9."
30 Apr 1965	Still on temporary duty with the 561 TFS from the 23 TFW, McConnell AFB KS, to the 6441 TFW, Yokota AB, Japan, under "Operation One Buck Nine." Assigned Crew Chief: SSgt. Farmer. (6441 History Apr–Jun 65, USAF microfilm PO231).
12 May 1965	Still at Yokota AB, Japan, with the 23 TFW. (AVH-3).
23 Jun 1965	Returned to the 23 TFW, McConnell AFB KS.
13 Aug 1965	Transferred to the 355 TFW, McConnell AFB KS.
28 Aug 1965	At SMAMA, McClellan AFB CA for depot work (WO).
28 Oct 1965	At SMAMA, McClellan AFB for test support (EH) of the Wild Weasel IA DPN-61-Maxson System.
8 Jan 1966	At SMAMA, McClellan AFB CA for depot work (WO). (AVH-5).
13 Jan 1966	Reassigned to the 23 TFW, McConnell AFB KS.
11 Feb 1966	At SMAMA, McClellan AFB CA for depot work (WO).
31 Mar 1966	At 23 TFW, McConnell AFB KS.
6 Oct 1966	In depot maintenance (WM) by SMAMA field team at McConnell AFB KS.
12 Oct 1966	At 23 TFW, McConnell AFB KS.
11 May 1967	In depot maintenance (WM) by SMAMA field team at McConnell AFB KS. (AVH-7).
1 Jun 1967	Deployed to George AFB CA for the 563 TFS, 23 TFW, for air-to-air gunnery training for RTU Class 67IR.
16 Jun 1967	Returned to 23 TFW, McConnell AFB KS.
4 Aug 1967	Deployed to George AFB CA with the 561 TFS, 23 TFW, for air-to-air gunnery training for RTU Class 68AR.
16 Aug 1967	Returned to 23 TFW, McConnell AFB KS.
3 Nov 1967	Deployed to George AFB CA with the 563 TFS, 23 TFW, for air-to-air gunnery training for RTU Class 68DR.
22 Nov 1967	Returned to 23 TFW, McConnell AFB KS.
26 Dec 1967	At 23 TFW, McConnell AFB KS being prepared for transfer to depot (PL).
28 Dec 1967	At SMAMA, McClellan AFB CA for depot work (WO).
23 Mar 1968	Returned (PL) to 23 TFW, McConnell AFB KS. (AVH-10).
16 Apr 1968	Deployed to George AFB CA with the 563 TFS, 23 TFW, for air-to-air gunnery training for RTU Class 68IR.
9 May 1968	Returned to 23 TFW, McConnell AFB KS for combat crew training (TF).
18 Jun 1968	Assigned to combat duties (CC) at 23 TFW, McConnell AFB KS.
3 Apr 1969	At SMAMA, McClellan AFB CA for depot work (WO). (AVH-12).
12 May 1969	Returned to 23 TFW, McConnell AFB KS.
21 Nov 1970	At 23 TFW, McConnell AFB KS. (AVH-14).
9 Mar 1971	In contract depot maintenance (WK) by Fairchild Engine and Aircraft Corporation (FACCF) at Bob Sikes Municipal Airport, Crestview FL. (AVH-16).
31 Mar 1971	Returned to 23 TFW, McConnell AFB KS.
16 Aug 1971	At 23 TFW, McConnell AFB KS being prepared for transfer (PL).
20 Aug 1971	Transferred (PL) to 113 TFG ANG, Andrews AFB MD.
22 Aug 1971	At (CC) 113 TFG ANG, Andrews AFB MD.

8 Apr 1972 In depot maintenance by SM-ALC at McClellan AFB CA. (AVH-18).
15 Aug 1972 Returned (PL) to 113 TFG ANG, Andrews AFB MD.
23 Mar 1973 In contract depot maintenance (WM) by Dynalectron Corporation (DYNZZ) at Andrews AFB MD. (AVH-20).
29 Mar 1973 At 113 TFG ANG, Andrews AFB MD.
30 Jan 1974 In contract depot maintenance (WM) by Dynalectron Corporation (DYNZZ) at Andrews AFB MD. (AVH-22).
7 Feb 1974 At 113 TFG ANG, Andrews AFB MD.
27 Aug 1974 In contract depot maintenance (WM) by Dynalectron Corporation (DYNZZ) at Andrews AFB MD.
25 Sep 1974 At 113 TFG ANG, Andrews AFB MD.
30 Nov 1974 Assigned organization redesignated 113 TFW ANG, Andrews AFB MD.
31 Dec 1974 At 113 TFW ANG, Andrews AFB MD.
17 Mar 1975 In contract depot maintenance (WM) by Dynalectron Corporation (DYNZZ) at Andrews AFB MD. (AVH-23).
20 Mar 1975 At 113 TFW ANG, Andrews AFB MD.
1 Mar 1976 Placed in storage (XX) At 113 TFW ANG, Andrews AFB MD. Inventory account: GB. (AVH-24).
8 Jul 1976 In storage (XX) at 113 TFW ANG, Andrews AFB MD. Assigned to museum inventory account: ZW. 3,267 flying hours.
Oct 1992 Under restoration at Bolling AFB, Washington DC. Restoration progress briefed every Thursday to the Air Force Chief of Staff, General McPeak, at the Pentagon. (CMSgt. Bryan Wasko, restoration project officer, letter 21 January 1994).
Aug 1993 Restoration completed at Bolling AFB, Washington DC.

F-105D–20RE 61-0145

Republic Production No: D-340 Production Sequence No: 420

Location: Displayed at Veteran's Square, Holloman AFB, Alamogordo, New Mexico.

Aircraft Name(s)	Crew	Unit	Date	Description
My Honey Pot		149 TFS 192 TFG		Woman in gold bathing suit with legs open sitting next to pot of gold under rainbow.

Aircraft Chronology

27 Apr 1962 USAF production acceptance from Republic Aviation, Farmingdale NY. (ACA-87).
6 Jun 1962 At MOAMA, Brookley AFB AL for depot work.
8 Jul 1962 Delivered to 49 TFW, Spangdahlem AB, Germany.
31 Jul 1962 At Wheelus AB, Libya, with 49 TFW.
10 Sep 1963 At 49 TFW, Spangdahlem AB, Germany.
11 Sep 1963 At MOAMA, Brookley AFB AL for depot work. "Operation Look Alike," Phase II.
6 Jan 1964 Returned to 49 TFW, Spangdahlem AB, Germany.
16 Jun 1965 At CASA, Getafe, Spain, for contract depot work (WK). Safety Package I. (AVH-3).

8 Jul 1965	Returned to 49 TFW, Spangdahlem AB, Germany.
11 Mar 1966	At CASA, Getafe, Spain, for contract depot work (WK). Safety Package II. (AVH-5).
12 Apr 1966	Returned to 49 TFW, Spangdahlem AB, Germany.
22 Jul 1966	At Wheelus AB, Libya, with 49 TFW.
11 Aug 1966	Returned to 49 TFW, Spangdahlem AB, Germany.
13 Aug 1966	At Wheelus AB, Libya, with 49 TFW.
19 Aug 1966	At 49 TFW, Spangdahlem AB, Germany.
10 Dec 1966	Transferred to the 23 TFW, McConnell AFB KS.
1 May 1967	At 23 TFW, McConnell AFB KS being prepared for transfer to depot (PL). (AVH-7).
2 May 1967	At MOAMA, Brookley AFB AL for depot work (WO).
10 May 1967	Returned to 23 TFW, McConnell AFB KS.
1 Jun 1967	Deployed to George AFB CA with the 563 TFS, 23 TFW, for air-to-air gunnery training for RTU Class 67IR, "The Reluctant Hog Herders."
16 Jun 1967	Returned to 23 TFW, McConnell AFB KS.
3 Nov 1967	Deployed to George AFB CA with the 563 TFS, 23 TFW, for air-to-air gunnery training for RTU Class 68DR.
22 Nov 1967	Returned to 23 TFW, McConnell AFB KS.
13 Dec 1967	Deployed to George AFB CA with the 560 TFS, 23 TFW, for air-to-air gunnery training for RTU Class 68ER.
22 Dec 1967	Returned to 23 TFW, McConnell AFB KS.
24 Mar 1968	At 23 TFW, McConnell AFB KS being prepared for transfer to depot (PL). (AVH-10).
25 Mar 1968	At SMAMA, McClellan AFB CA for depot work (WO).
13 May 1968	Returned (PL) to 23 TFW, McConnell AFB KS.
25 May 1970	At 23 TFW, McConnell AFB KS. (AVH-14).
12 Mar 1971	In contract depot maintenance (WK) by Fairchild Engine and Aircraft Corporation (FACCF) at Bob Sikes Municipal Airport, Crestview FL. (AVH-16).
2 Apr 1971	Returned (PL) to 23 TFW, McConnell AFB KS.
30 Jun 1971	While assigned to the 23 TFW, McConnell AFB KS, aircraft incurred a damaged right flap and outboard right flap screw jack assembly due to failure of the screw jack. (23 TFW History, Apr–Jun 71, USAF microfilm MO556).
15 Nov 1971	Placed in flyable storage (PR) at 23 TFW, McConnell AFB KS. (AVH-16).
30 Nov 1971	Operational (CC) at 23 TFW, McConnell AFB KS.
30 Dec 1971	At 23 TFW, McConnell AFB KS being prepared for transfer (PL).
3 Jan 1972	In depot work (WO) by SM-ALC, McClellan AFB CA.
1 Mar 1972	Assigned to 561 TFS, 23 TFW, at McConnell AFB KS. (Master 23 TFW Aircraft Assignment as of 1 March 1972).
16 May 1972	Returned (PL) to 23 TFW, McConnell AFB KS. (AVH-18).
24 May 1972	In contract depot maintenance (WK) by Fairchild Engine and Aircraft Corporation (FACCF) at Bob Sikes Municipal Airport, Crestview FL.
21 Jun 1972	Returned (PL) to 23 TFW, McConnell AFB KS.
1 Jul 1972	Assigned directly to the 561 TFS, McConnell AFB KS, when the 23 TFW relocated to England AFB LA.
12 Jul 1972	Reassigned to 184 TFG ANG, McConnell AFB KS.
3 Jan 1974	At 184 TFG ANG for combat crew training (TF), McConnell AFB KS. (AVH-20).
12 Dec 1974	In contract depot maintenance (WM) by Dynalectron Corporation (DYNZZ) at Andrews AFB MD. (AVH-22).
30 Dec 1974	At 184 TFG ANG for combat crew training (TF) at McConnell AFB KS.

During its seventeen-year career, this F-105D 61-0145 served at only three bases. It began in 1962 as a NATO nuclear bomber with the 49 Tactical Fighter Wing in Germany then, four years later, transferred to the 23 Tactical Fighter Wing at McConnell Air Force Base, Kansas. In 1972, it moved across the base to the Kansas Air National Guard where it stayed for six years. In August 1979, it went to the Virginia Air National Guard who flew it for only eighteen months—long enough for the plane to be adorned with one of this unit's famous paintings showing *My Honey Pot*. In 1981, the Air Force Museum, allocated it as a static display (without its colorful art work) to its original unit, the 49th Wing now at Holloman Air Force Base, New Mexico. (Photograph by author, 2 May 1996.)

17 Mar 1975	In contract depot maintenance (WK) by Fairchild Engine and Aircraft Corporation (FACCF) at Bob Sikes Municipal Airport, Crestview FL. (AVH-23).
5 Aug 1975	Returned to 184 TFG ANG for combat crew training (TF) at McConnell AFB KS. (AVH-23 & AVH-24).
3 Nov 1976	In depot maintenance by SM-ALC at McConnell AFB KS. 3,717.0 flying hours. (AVH-25 & AVH-26).
10 Nov 1976	At 184 TFG ANG for student and combat crew training (TF), McConnell AFB KS. 3,717.0 flying hours.
13 Jul 1979	In contract depot maintenance by General Dynamics (DYNFW), McConnell AFB KS. 4,432.8 flying hours. (AVH-27).
2 Aug 1979	At 184 TFG ANG, McConnell AFB KS. 4,462.7 flying hours.
15 Aug 1979	Transferred to 192 TFG ANG, Byrd Field VA. 4,462.7 flying hours.
27 Feb 1981	Assigned to museum inventory account (ZW) by 192 TFG ANG, Byrd Field Richmond VA. 4,672.9 flying hours. (GO33B Dec 81 & GO33B 1 Feb 83).
5 Mar 1981	Due to wing cracks, the F-105 depot at SM-ALC, McClellan AFB CA authorized an "... unrestricted flight ... to aircraft retirement from service or the end of FY 1981 whichever is earliest." (SM-ALC/MMSRBA msg. to 192 TFG 052227Z Mar 81).
17 Apr 1981	USAF Museum directed shipment of aircraft to 49th Combat Support Group, Holloman AFB NM. (DD Form 1149, Requisition and Invoice/Shipping Document).
24 Nov 1981	Aircraft received at Holloman AFB NM for static display. Receipt signed by Col. Robert A. Downs, Deputy Commander, 833 CSG.

F-105D–20RE 61-0146

Republic Production No: D-341 Production Sequence No: 421

Location: At South Base for AFFTC Museum, Edwards AFB, Rosamond, California.

Aircraft Chronology

8 Jun 1962	USAF production acceptance from Republic Aviation, Farmingdale NY. (ACA-87).
23 Aug 1962	At MOAMA, Brookley AFB AL for depot work.
30 Sep 1962	Delivered to 49 TFW Spangdahlem AB, Germany.
2 Oct 1963	At MOAMA, Brookley AFB AL for depot work. "Operation Look Alike," Phase II.
27 Jan 1964	Returned to 49 TFW Spangdahlem AB, Germany.
19 Jun 1965	At CASA, Getafe, Spain, for contract depot work (WK). (AVH-3).
30 Jun 1965	"Safety Package I" completed at CASA, Getafe, Spain. 791.5 flying hours. (AFTO Form 95).
3 Jul 1965	Returned to 49 TFW, Spangdahlem AB, Germany. (AVH-3).
16 Mar 1966	At Wheelus AB, Libya, with 49 TFW. (AVH-5).
19 Apr 1966	At CASA, Getafe, Spain, for contract depot work (WK).
13 May 1966	"Safety Package II" completed at CASA, Getafe, Spain. 971.4 flying hours. (AFTO Form 95).
16 May 1966	Returned to 49 TFW, Spangdahlem AB, Germany. (AVH-5).
11 Oct 1966	At Wheelus AB, Libya, with the 49 TFW.
21 Oct 1966	Returned to 49 TFW, Spangdahlem AB, Germany.
15 Feb 1967	At 49 TFW, Spangdahlem AB, Germany, being prepared for transfer (PL). (AVH-7).
24 Feb 1967	Transferred to the 4520 CCTW, Nellis AFB NV for aircrew training (TF).
2 May 1967	At MOAMA, Brookley AFB AL for depot work (WO).
13 May 1967	Returned to 4520 CCTW, Nellis AFB NV for combat crew training (TF).
4 Jun 1967	In depot work (WM) by SMAMA field team at Nellis AFB NV.
10 Jun 1967	At 4520 CCTW, Nellis AFB NV for combat crew training (TF).
27 Oct 1967	In depot work (WM) by SMAMA field team at Nellis AFB NV.
28 Oct 1967	At 4520 CCTW, Nellis AFB NV for combat crew training (TF).
28 Dec 1967	Transferred to 23 TFW, McConnell AFB KS for combat crew training (TF). 1367.4 flying hours. (AFTO Form 95).
31 Jan 1968	Deployed to George AFB CA with the 561 TFS, 23 TFW, for air-to-air gunnery training for RTU Class 68FR. (AVH-10).
8 Feb 1968	Returned to 23 TFW, McConnell AFB KS.
14 May 1968	At McClellan AFB CA for depot work (WO).
28 Jun 1968	IRAN and modifications completed at SMAMA, McClellan AFB CA. 1497.7 flying hours. (AFTO Form 95).
2 Jul 1968	Returned (PL) to 23 TFW TAC, McConnell AFB KS for combat crew training (TF).
14 Aug 1969	On loan (XY) to Air Force Systems Command at Dulles Airport MD from the 23 TFW, McConnell AFB KS. (AVH-12).
19 Aug 1969	Returned to 23 TFW TAC, McConnell AFB KS.
15 Jun 1970	While assigned to 419 TFTS, 23 TFW, McConnell AFB KS, cracks in left and right wings discovered and treated. Aircraft released for flight under Category 3 restrictions. 2,213.6 flying hours. (AFTO Form 95).
22 Dec 1970	At 23 TFW, McConnell AFB KS. (AVH-14).
23 Dec 1970	In contract depot maintenance (WK) by Fairchild Engine and Aircraft Corporation (FACCF) at Bob Sikes Municipal Airport, Crestview FL. (AVH-16 & AFTO Form 95).
19 Jan 1971	While at contract depot, aircraft was modified with wing pylon and doubler. Category 3 flight restrictions lifted. 2,030.5 flying hours. (AFTO Form 95).
2 Feb 1971	Returned (PL) to 23 TFW, McConnell AFB KS. Assigned to combat crew training (TF). (AVH-26).
10 May 1971	At 23 TFW, McConnell AFB KS. Assigned to combat duties (CC).

After accumulating over 5,100 flying hours in 22 years, this was one of the last Thunderchiefs to take to the air when it flew on 11 January 1984 from Hill Air Force Base, Utah, to Edwards Air Force Base, California. Its career started with the 49 Tactical Fighter Wing in Germany where it stayed from 1962 to 1967. It then trained pilots at Nellis and McConnell for four years. During an inspection at McConnell, maintenance technicians discovered cracks in its wings which restricted its flying until the cracks were repaired at a depot in Florida in 1971. A year later it was damaged by fire at the depot in Sacramento, California. When it was again repaired, it went to the Air Force Reserve unit at Tinker Air Force Base, Oklahoma. They flew it on their NATO deployment to England in the summer of 1978. Two years later it moved again to its final Reserve unit, the "Diamondbacks" at Hill Air Force Base, Utah. (Photograph by author, 1 November 1996.)

1 Mar 1972	Carried on assignment roster for the 562 TFS, 23 TFW, at McConnell AFB KS. (Master 23 TFW Aircraft Assignment as of 1 March 1972).
21 Apr 1972	In depot work (WO) by SM-ALC, McClellan AFB CA. (AVH-18).
14 July 1972	Nose section damaged by fire at McClellan AFB CA.
21 Aug 1972	In storage (XW—Limited probability of withdrawal) at McClellan AFB CA. (AVH-18).
1 Oct 1972	Returned to depot work (WO) by SM-ALC, McClellan AFB CA.
9 Nov 1972	Fire damage repaired under direction of SM-ALC engineers. 2,284.0 flying hours. (AFTO Form 95).
8 Dec 1972	IRAN/MOD completed at SM-ALC, McClellan AFB CA. 2,285.0 flying hours
20 Dec 1972	Transferred to 507 TFG AFRES, Tinker AFB OK. (AVH-18).
10 Jan 1973	At 507 TFG AFRES, Tinker AFB OK. (AVH-20).
31 Mar 1973	Reassigned to 507 CMTSQ AFRES, Tinker AFB OK.
28 Aug 1973	In depot maintenance (WM) by SM-ALC at Tinker AFB OK.
30 Aug 1973	At 507 CMTSQ AFRES, Tinker AFB OK.
8 Mar 1974	In depot maintenance (WM) by SM-ALC at Tinker AFB OK. (AVH-22).
18 Mar 1974	At 507 CMTSQ AFRES, Tinker AFB OK.
10 Jun 1974	In depot maintenance (WM) by SM-ALC at Tinker AFB OK.
13 Jun 1974	At 507 CMTSQ AFRES, Tinker AFB OK.
16 Oct 1974	Assigned organization redesignated 507 CLMSQ AFRES, Tinker AFB OK.
26 Nov 1974	In depot maintenance (WM) by SM-ALC at Tinker AFB OK.
3 Jan 1975	At 507 CLMSQ AFRES, Tinker AFB OK. (AVH-23).
27 Jun 1975	In contract depot maintenance (WK) by Fairchild Engine and Aircraft Corporation (FACCF) at Bob Sikes Municipal Airport, Crestview FL for modifications. Aircraft also stripped and repainted. (AVH-23, AVH-24, & AFTO Form 95).
9 Dec 1975	Contract depot work completed. 3,394.1 flying hours. (AFTO Form 95).
16 Dec 1975	Returned to 507 CLMSQ AFRES, Tinker AFB OK. (AVH-23).
5 Jan 1976	In depot work (WM) by SM-ALC at Tinker AFB OK. (AVH-24).
16 Mar 1976	At 507 TFG AFRES, Tinker AFB OK. 3,494 flying hours.

20 Dec 1976 In depot maintenance (DM) by SM-ALC at Tinker AFB OK. 3,559 flying hours.

5 Jan 1977 At 507 TFG AFRES, Tinker AFB OK. 3,595.0 flying hours. (AVH-25 & AVH-26).

13 Mar 1978 In OC-ALC depot at Tinker AFB OK. 3,877.0 flying hours.

26 May 1978 In OC-ALC depot at Tinker AFB OK. 3,983.0 flying hours.

30 May 1978 At 465 TFS AFRES, Tinker AFB OK. 3,983.0 flying hours.

10 Jun 1978 Deployed under "Coronet Oriole" with the 465 TFS to Sculthorpe, England, from Tinker AFB OK. (British Aviation Review, Dec 1995).

23 Jun 1978 Returned from England to Tinker AFB OK.

1 Apr 1979 In contract depot maintenance (FACBM), Tinker AFB OK. 4,148.6 flying hours. (AVH-27).

6 Apr 1979 At 465 TFS AFRES, Tinker AFB OK. 4,148.6 flying hours.

20 Jun 1979 While assigned to the 465 TFS AFRES, Tinker AFB OK, the aircraft ground aborted when the fuel inlet pressure light stayed on with the engine running. The fuel control box was changed. (301 TFW History, 1 Apr–30 Jun 1979, USAF microfilm 343832).

30 Jun 1979 While assigned to the 465 TFS AFRES, Tinker AFB OK, the aircraft flew 27.5 hours during the month of June 1979 and had accumulated a total of 4,216.5 flying hours The assigned crew chief was SSgt. Joseph D. Heil. (301 TFW History, Apr–Jun 1979, USAF microfilm 34382).

30 Jul 1980 Transferred to 466 TFS AFRES, Hill AFB UT. 4,560.6 flying hours. (GO33B 22 Jan 81 & AFTO Form 95).

18 Aug 1980 In depot maintenance at Odgen ALC, Hill AFB UT. 4,562.7 flying hours.

2 Jun 1981 In depot maintenance at Odgen ALC, Hill AFB UT. 4,702.4 flying hours. (GO33B Dec 81 & GO33B 1 Feb 83).

21 Jul 1981 At 466 TFS AFRES, Hill AFB UT. 4,831.8 flying hours. (GO33B 1 Feb 83).

26 Jan 1983 At 419 TFW AFRES, Hill AFB UT. 4,921.2 flying hours. (GO33B 9 Feb 84).

11 Jan 1984 Aircraft flown from Hill AFB UT to Edwards AFB CA for display at AFFTC Museum. 5,120.3 flying hours. (AFTO Form 95, Significant Historical Data).

F-105D–20RE 61-0159

Republic Production No: D-354 Production Sequence No: 434

Location: Displayed at Warrior Park, Davis-Monthan AFB, Tucson, Arizona.

Aircraft Name(s)	Crew	Unit	Date	Description
Have Gun Will Travel		149 TFS VA ANG		
Honeypot II/ Have Gun Will Travel	1Lt Robert B. Goodman	354 TFS 355 TFW	Jan 70	Letters on left side of fuselage below cockpit.

Aircraft Chronology

30 Sep 1962 At MOAMA, Brookley AFB AL for depot work after production from Republic Aviation. (ACA-87).

17 Oct 1962 Delivered to 36 TFW, Bitburg AB, Germany.

10 Feb 1964 At MOAMA, Brookley AFB AL for depot work (WO). "Operation Look Alike," Phase II.

26 Jun 1964 Transferred to 4 TFW, Seymour Johnson AFB NC. (ACA-87 & AVH-1).

17 Nov 1964 Deployed to Incirlik AB, Turkey, with the 335 TFS, 4 TFW for "Operation Cross Switch." (AVH-3).

30 Apr 1965 — On temporary duty (TDY) at Incirlik AB, Turkey, with the 334 TFS from the 4 TFW, Seymour Johnson AFB NC. (4 TFW History, Jan–Jun 65, Vol. II, USAF microfilm MO292).

28 May 1965 — Returned to 4 TFW, Seymour Johnson AFB NC. (AVH-3).

4 July 1965 — Aircraft at Yokota AB, Japan, assigned to 335 TFS, 4 TFW, on TDY from Seymour Johnson AFB NC. Crew Chief: SSgt. Davis. (6441 TFW History, Jul–Dec 65, USAF microfilm PO232).

1 Dec 1965 — At Takhli RTAB, Thailand, with the 6441 TFW from Yokota AB, Japan.

29 Jan 1966 — At Air Asia, Tainan, Taiwan, for contract depot work (WK). (AVH-5).

18 Feb 1966 — Reassigned to the 355 TFW, Takhli RTAB, Thailand.

19 Jun 1966 — While assigned to the 355 TFW at Takhli RTAB, Thailand, the aircraft received combat damage that required 100 labor hours to repair. The centerline fuel tank was damaged so the pilot jettisoned it. As the tank left the aircraft, it struck the bomb bay doors, causing minor damage to the left one and major damage to the right one. The tank struck the right landing gear fairing door and the right wing undersurface and the right horizontal stabilator, tearing away approximately 25% of its surface and supporting structural members. The right bomb bay door and the horizontal stabilator were replaced. Other damage was repaired locally. (355 TFW History, Jan–Jun 1966, USAF microfilm NO461).

19 Jan 1967 — At Air Asia, Tainan, Taiwan, for contract depot work (WK). (AVH-7).

31 Jan 1967 — While assigned to the 355 TFW at Takhli RTAB, Thailand, aircraft had accumulated 1,625 flying hours. (355 TFW History, Jan–Jun 67, USAF microfilm NO462).

23 Mar 1967 — Returned from Tainan to the 355 TFW, Takhli RTAB, Thailand. (AVH-7).

12 May 1967 — Flown by Capt. Jacques A. Suzanne (333 TFS, 355 TFW) who shot down a MiG 17 with the 20mm gun. Call sign: "Crossbow 01." "As the lead aircraft in a flak suppression flight of four F-105's approached the target area, five MiG-17's intercepted the strike group. … Suzanne recalls: 'At this time I turned into the MiGs and tracked the two that broke off to the right. Closing to 4,000 feet of range, I fired one burst of about 200 rounds. The MiGs then reversed to the left and at 800 to 1,000 feet, I fired another burst until minimum range. Then I broke off as one MiG went under my left wing in a 70 (degree) dive, trailing white smoke. The MiG continued in this descent and disappeared under a shelf of clouds at approximately 1,000 feet of altitude. Crossbow 02 (Capt. Lawrence D. Cobb) observed the MiG on the way down and saw a bright flash on the ground in the position that the MiG disappeared.' " (Aces & Aerial Victories, page 53).

2 Jul 1967 — At 355 TFW, Takhli RTAB, Thailand.

30 Aug 1967 — At Udorn RTAB, Thailand, for depot repair of battle damage (VM) by SMAMA field team.

8 Oct 1967 — Returned to 355 TFW, Takhli RTAB, Thailand.

14 Dec 1967 — While flown by the 355 TFW from Takhli RTAB, Thailand, during a strike on the Hanoi Railroad and Highway Bridge, the aircraft received battle damage consisting of an 8" X 1 1/2" hole in the right side of the fuselage and two holes in the right drop tank. (355 TFW History, Oct–Dec 67, USAF microfilm NO463).

19 Feb 1968 — In depot work (WM) by SMAMA at 355 TFW, Takhli RTAB, Thailand. (AVH-10).

22 Feb 1968 — At 355 TFW, Takhli RTAB, Thailand.

25 Apr 1968 — In depot work (WM) by SMAMA at 355 TFW, Takhli RTAB, Thailand.

27 Apr 1968 — At 355 TFW, Takhli RTAB, Thailand.

1 Nov 1968 — While assigned to the 355 TFW, Takhli RTAB, Thailand, the aircraft had accumulated 3,161.2 flying hours. (355 TFW History, Oct–Dec 68, USAF microfilm NO466).

18 Nov 1968 — At Air Asia, Tainan, Taiwan, for contract depot work (WK). (AVH-10).

27 Dec 1968 — Returned to (PL) 355 TFW, Takhli RTAB, Thailand.

28 Feb 1969 — While assigned to the 355 TFW, Takhli RTAB, Thailand, the aircraft flew 87.2 hours during the month of February 1969 and had accumulated 3,345.6 flying hours. (355 TFW History, Jan–Mar 69, Vol. II, USAF Microfilm NO467).

16 Nov 1969 — At Air Asia, Tainan, Taiwan, for contract depot work (WK). (AVH-12).

24 Jan 1970 — Returned to 355 TFW, Takhli RTAB, Thailand. (AVH-14).

The plaque near this display honors the Red River Valley Fighter Pilots Association (the "River Rats") and says the aircraft is painted in the markings of Col. "Scrappy" Johnson, the founder of the River Rats. Not mentioned is the MiG-kill star below the canopy. On 12 May 1967, Captain Jacques A. Suzanne, flying this F-105D from Takhli, Thailand, shot down a MiG-17 with the plane's Gatling gun. During its long career, the plane flew from a number of other bases including Bitburg, Seymour Johnson, and McConnell. It last served with the Virginia Air National Guard at Richmond who retired it in 1981 after it accumulated 6,094 hours (2,000 hours over the F-105's design limit), making it one of the high-time Thunderchiefs. (Photograph by author, 2 May 1996.)

Feb 1970	Aircraft accumulated 4,000 flying hours, the F-105 design limit, the first F-105 to reach this time. Pilot: 1Lt Robert B. Goodman, 354 TFS, 355 TFW, Takhli RTAB, Thailand. (Takhli Times, Feb 14, 1970).
28 Apr 1970	In depot work (WM) by SMAMA at Takhli RTAB, Thailand. (AVH-14).
1 May 1970	At 355 TFW, Takhli RTAB, Thailand.
28 Apr 1970	In depot maintenance (WM) by SMAMA at Takhli RTAB, Thailand.
1 May 1970	At 355 TFW, Takhli RTAB, Thailand.
24 Oct 1970	At 355 TFW, Takhli RTAB, Thailand, being prepared for transfer (PL).
27 Oct 1970	Transferred (PL) to 23 TFW, McConnell AFB KS.
12 Nov 1970	In flyable storage (PR) at 23 TFW, McConnell AFB KS.
4 Jan 1971	At 23 TFW, McConnell AFB KS being prepared for transfer (PL).
20 Jan 1971	Transferred (PL) to 192 TFG ANG, Byrd Field, Richmond VA. (AVH-16).
30 Apr 1971	In depot work (WO) by SMAMA at McClellan AFB CA.
21 Jun 1971	Returned to 192 TFG ANG, Byrd Field, Richmond VA.
22 Feb 1972	In contract depot work (WM) by Dynalectron Corp (DYNZZ) at Byrd Field, Richmond VA. (AVH-18).
13 Mar 1972	Returned to 192 TFG ANG, Byrd Field, Richmond VA.
7 Sep 1972	In contract depot maintenance (WK) by Fairchild Engine and Aircraft Corporation (FACCF) at Bob Sikes Municipal Airport, Crestview FL.
4 Oct 1972	Returned to 192 TFG ANG, Byrd Field, Richmond VA.
4 Apr 1973	In contract depot maintenance (WM) by Dynalectron Corporation (DYNZZ) at Byrd Field, Richmond VA. (AVH-20).
6 Apr 1973	At 192 TFG ANG, Byrd Field, Richmond VA.
25 Apr 1973	In contract depot maintenance (WM) by Dynalectron Corporation (DYNZZ) at Byrd Field, Richmond VA.
26 Apr 1973	At 192 TFG ANG, Byrd Field, Richmond VA.
4 May 1973	In contract depot maintenance (WM) by Dynalectron Corporation (DYNZZ) at Byrd Field, Richmond VA.

16 May 1973	At 192 TFG ANG, Byrd Field, Richmond VA.
1 Nov 1973	In contract depot maintenance (WK) by Fairchild Engine and Aircraft Corporation (FACCF) at Bob Sikes Municipal Airport, Crestview FL.
17 Jun 1974	At 192 TFG ANG, Byrd Field, Richmond VA. (AVH-22).
12 Apr 1975	In contract depot maintenance (WM) by Dynalectron Corporation (DYNZZ) at Byrd Field, Richmond VA. (AVH-23 & AVH-24).
23 Apr 1975	At 192 TFG ANG, Byrd Field, Richmond VA.
11 Jun 1975	In contract depot maintenance (WK) by Fairchild Engine and Aircraft Corporation (FACCF) at Bob Sikes Municipal Airport, Crestview FL.
25 Jul 1975	Returned to 192 TFG ANG, Byrd Field, Richmond VA.
21 Oct 1975	At 113 TFG ANG, Andrews AFB MD.
23 Dec 1975	At 192 TFG ANG, Byrd Field, Richmond VA. (AVH-24).
24 Feb 1976	At 192 TFG ANG, Byrd Field, Richmond VA.
6 Nov 1979	In contract depot maintenance by Dynalectron Corp (DYNZZ) at Byrd Field, Richmond VA. 5,775.3 flying hours. (AVH-27).
9 Nov 1979	At 192 TFG ANG, Byrd Field, Richmond VA. 5,775.3 flying hours.
25 Jun 1981	Placed in storage at MASDC, Davis-Monthan AFB AZ. 6,094 flying hours. (MASDC Aircraft Status Directory, 30 Jun 84).
22 Feb 1982	Stored at MASDC, Davis-Monthan AFB AZ. Inventory account "ZW"–School or Museum. 6,048.4 flying hours. (GO33B 1 Feb 83).
5 Mar 1985	Removed from AMARC storage for display at Davis-Monthan AFB, Tucson AZ. (AMARC D003A/B Report, 19 Feb 86, page 22).

F-105D–25RE 61-0164

Republic Production No: D-359 Production Sequence No: 439

Location: Displayed as "59-1746" at Hunter Park in the city of Douglasville, Georgia.

Aircraft Name(s)	Crew	Unit	Date	Description
Golden Gun		149 TFS VA ANG		Cowboy sheriff in front of saloon. Arrow in hat.

Aircraft Chronology

10 Jan 1964	Delivered from production as JF-105D for test support (EH) to Air Force Systems Command, Eglin AFB FL. (ACA-87).
20 Feb 1964	Assigned to Proving Ground Center (PGC) at Eglin AFB FL.
31 Jul 1964	At PGCC as JF-105D at Eglin AFB FL. (AVH-1).
4 Sep 1964	In depot work (WO) at MOAMA, Brookley AFB AL.
28 Dec 1964	At PGCC as JF-105D at Eglin AFB FL. (AVH-2).
13 Jul 1966	In depot work (WO) by MOAMA at Brookley AFB AL. (AVH-5).
20 Sep 1966	At PGCC as JF-105D for test support (EH) at Eglin AFB FL
27 May 1968	At PGCC, Eglin AFB FL as F-105D being prepared for transfer (PL). (AVH-10).
29 May 1968	In depot work (WO) by SMAMA at McClellan AFB CA.

This plane didn't have an exciting career. It spent the first half of its life as a test bird at Eglin Air Force Base, Florida, and the second half with the Virginia Air National Guard. The Virginia Guard took it on a NATO deployment to England in 1976, the plane's only trip outside the United States, and retired it in 1981. At 2,880 flying hours, it is one of the surviving Thunderchiefs with the lowest time on its airframe. In 1998, it was withdrawn from storage at Davis-Monthan to become a veteran's memorial in a city park named after an F-105 pilot from Douglasville, Georgia, who was killed in the Vietnam war. The plane is marked with serial number 59-1746, the F-105D in which 1st Lieutenant Robert G. "Jerry" Hunter was shot down over Laos on 25 May 1966. (Photograph by Wray Pardy, 6 June 1998.)

22 Jul 1968 Returned (PL) to PGCC at Eglin AFB FL as F-105D.

27 Jul 1968 At PGCC at Eglin AFB FL for test support (EH).

30 Nov 1968 Reassigned to ADTC at Eglin AFB FL.

2 Jul 1970 At ADTC, Eglin AFB FL. (AVH-14).

19 Mar 1971 In contract depot maintenance (WK) by Fairchild Engine and Aircraft Corporation (FACCF) at Bob Sikes Municipal Airport, Crestview FL (AVH-16).

9 Apr 1971 Returned (PL) to ADTC, Eglin AFB FL.

12 Apr 1971 At ADTC, Eglin AFB FL for test support (EH).

27 Sep 1971 In contract depot maintenance (WK) by Fairchild Engine and Aircraft Corporation (FACCF) at Crestview FL.

14 Oct 1971 At ADTC, Eglin AFB FL for test support (EH).

17 Nov 1971 At ADTC, Eglin AFB FL being prepared for transfer (PL).

30 Nov 1971 In depot work (WO) by SMAMA at McClellan AFB CA.

7 Apr 1972 Returned (PL) to ADTC, Eglin AFB FL. (AVH-18).

12 Apr 1972 At ADTC, Eglin AFB FL for test support (EH).

17 May 1972 In contract depot maintenance (WK) by Fairchild Engine and Aircraft Corporation (FACCF) at Crestview FL.

12 Jun 1972 Transferred to SMAMA at McClellan AFB CA for storage (PR & XW) and depot work (WO).

30 Nov 1972	Transferred to the 192 TFG ANG, Byrd Field VA.
3 May 1973	In depot maintenance (WM) by Dynalectron Corporation (DYNZZ) at Byrd Field, Richmond VA (AVH-20).
8 May 1973	At the 192 TFG ANG, Byrd Field VA.
12 Jun 1973	In depot maintenance (WM) by Dynalectron Corporation (DYNZZ) at Byrd Field, Richmond VA.
13 Jun 1973	At the 192 TFG ANG, Byrd Field VA.
16 Aug 1973	In depot maintenance (WM) by Dynalectron Corporation (DYNZZ) at Byrd Field, Richmond VA.
17 Aug 1973	At the 192 TFG ANG, Byrd Field VA.
2 Jan 1974	In depot maintenance (WM) by Dynalectron Corporation (DYNZZ) at Byrd Field, Richmond VA.
18 Jan 1974	At the 192 TFG ANG, Byrd Field VA. (AVH-22).
9 Oct 1974	In depot maintenance (WM) by Dynalectron Corporation (DYNZZ) at Byrd Field, Richmond VA.
1 Nov 1974	At the 192 TFG ANG, Byrd Field VA.
24 Feb 1976	At the 192 TFG ANG, Byrd Field VA. (AVH-24).
28 Jun 1976	In depot maintenance (WM) by Dynalectron Corporation (DYNZZ) at Byrd Field, Richmond VA.
22 Jul 1976	At the 192 TFG ANG, Byrd Field VA. 1,784 flying hours.
23 Oct 1976	Deployed to Lakenheath AB, England, under "Coronet Fife" with the 149 TFS Virginia ANG. (British Aviation Review, Dec 1995).
6 Nov 1976	Returned from England to Byrd Field, Richmond VA.
8 Feb 1977	In depot maintenance (WM) by Dynalectron Corporation (DYNZZ) at Byrd Field, Richmond VA. 1,982 flying hours. (AVH-25 & AVH-26).
22 Feb 1977	At the 192 TFG ANG, Byrd Field VA. 1,984 flying hours.
17 Jun 1981	Sent to storage at MASDC, Davis-Monthan AFB AZ. 2,880 flying hours. Assigned storage code FK046. (MASDC Aircraft Status Directory, 30 Jun 84 & GO33B Dec 81).
13 Dec 1997	Placed in work at AMARC after being allocated for static display at the city of Douglasville, Georgia. ("AMARC Aircraft Disposition Activity for FY 96" report).
5 Jan 1998	AMARC preparation work complete.
13 Jan 1998	Aircraft ready for shipment from AMARC to Douglasville, Georgia.
23 Feb 1998	Aircraft arrived at Douglasville, Georgia, on a flatbed trailer truck. (Bob Harper, e-mail, 23 Feb 1998).
25 May 1998	Aircraft dedicated to all Veterans in a public ceremony at Hunter Park, Douglasville, Georgia. The park is named for 1Lt Robert G. Hunter who was killed in Laos on 25 May 1966 when his F-105D, 59-1746, was shot down.

F-105D-25RE 61-0165

Republic Production No: D-360 Production Sequence No: 440

Location: Displayed near the main gate at Pope AFB, Fayetteville, North Carolina.

Aircraft Name(s)	Crew	Unit	Date	Description
Jake's Jewel		12 TFS 18 TFW	Jan 62	Black lettering on tail.
Suzi Baby	Capt. Tom Coady/ Col. R. Wayne	357 TFS 355 TFW	Feb 69	Yellow letters under cockpit over Eastern Airline logo.
The Little Harem		357 TFS 355 TFW	Apr 70	Three scantily-clad dark-haired girls within a white cloud outline. On gun door.

Aircraft Chronology

4 Oct 1962	At MOAMA, Brookley AFB AL for depot work (WO) after production from Republic Aviation. (ACA-87).
30 Oct 1962	One of the first three F-105's delivered to 67 TFS, 18 TFW, Kadena AB, Okinawa. (18 TFW Unit History, 1 Jul–31 Dec 62, Microfilm MO494).
19 Aug 1963	At 18 TFW, Kadena AB, Okinawa. (ACA-87).
21 Sep 1963	At Air Asia, Tainan, Taiwan, for contract depot work (WK).
5 Dec 1963	Returned to 18 TFW, Kadena AB, Okinawa.
31 Jul 1964	At 4 TFW, Seymour Johnson AFB NC. 404.0 total flying hours. (4 TFW History, Jul–Dec 64, Vol. II, USAF microfilm MO292).
31 Dec 1964	While assigned to the 4 TFW, Seymour Johnson AFB NC, the aircraft flew 26.8 hours for the month of December 1964 and had 488.6 total flying hours. Assigned crew chief: TSgt. Bentz. (4 TFW History, Jul–Dec 64, Vol. II, USAF microfilm MO292).
1 Mar 1965	At SMAMA, McClellan AFB CA for depot work (WO). (AVH-3).
25 Mar 1965	Returned to 4 TFW, Seymour Johnson AFB NC.
Apr 1965	Transferred to 18 TFW, Kadena AB, Okinawa.
28 Aug 1965	One of two F-105Ds from the 67 TFS at Korat RTAB, Thailand, that bombed a road in the Steel Tiger area (SL-3) of Laos. Flown by Capt. Edward Nowokunski. Flight lead was Lt. Col. Fair in F-105D 61-0195. The bombs "started a landslide creating a choke point" on Route 12. (67 TFS History, 1 Jul 65–31 Dec 65).
30 Sep 1965	At Air Asia, Tainan, Taiwan (AAITT), for contract depot work (WK).
17 Dec 1965	Returned to 18 TFW, Kadena AB, Okinawa.
17 Apr 1966	At Udorn RTAB, Thailand, from the 469 TFS, 388 TFW. (AVH-5).
25 Jun 1966	At 18 TFW, Kadena AB, Okinawa.
31 Dec 1966	While assigned to the 18 TFW, Kadena AB, Okinawa, the aircraft flew 17 hours during the month of December 1966 and had accumulated 982 flying hours. (18 TFW History, Jul–Dec 66, USAF microfilm MO498).
7 Feb 1967	At 18 TFW, Kadena AB, Okinawa. (AVH-7).
4 May 1967	While assigned to the 18 TFW, Kadena AB, Okinawa, the aircraft's drag chute fell out in flight due to failure of the drag chute door actuating crank. (18 TFW History, Apr–Jun 67, USAF microfilm MO499).
11 May 1967	While assigned to the 18 TFW, Kadena AB, Okinawa, the aircraft's fiberglass skin and UHF antenna on the ventral fin separated in flight. The cause was "maintenance error"—the forward support brackets had been installed with the wrong type of bolts.
6 Jul 1967	Transferred to 355 TFW, Takhli RTAB, Thailand. (AVH-7).
6 Jul 1967	At 355 TFW, Takhli RTAB, Thailand.
12 Jul 1967	In depot maintenance (WM) by SMAMA field team at Takhli RTAB, Thailand.
13 Jul 1967	At 355 TFW, Takhli RTAB, Thailand.
10 Aug 1967	While on a strike on the Thai Nguyen Railroad Station Yards with call sign "Dolphin Lead," aircraft received a hit which put a one inch hole in outboard side of the AIM-9 missile pylon. The pilot from the 355 TFW did not know his aircraft had been hit until after he landed at Takhli RTAB, Thailand. (355 TFW History, Jul–Sep 67, USAF microfilm NO463).
2 Sep 1967	In depot maintenance (WM) by SMAMA field team at Takhli RTAB, Thailand. (AVH-7).
5 Sep 1967	Combat capable (CC) at 355 TFW, Takhli RTAB, Thailand.
18 Sep 1967	Flown by Maj. Donald M. Russell (333 TFS, 355 TFW) on a combat mission that lasted 3.0 hours from Takhli RTAB, Thailand. (Maj. Russell's Individual Flight Record as of 31 Dec 67).
24 Sep 1967	Flown by Maj. Donald M. Russell (333 TFS, 355 TFW) on a combat mission that lasted 2.9 hours from Takhli RTAB, Thailand.

Except for short stays at Seymour Johnson and McConnell Air Force Bases, this "D" spent its active-duty career in the Pacific including more than three years with the 355 Tactical Fighter Wing at Takhli, Thailand, where it was damaged in combat at least three times. After returning to McConnell from the war zone in October 1970, it transferred six months later to the Virginia Air National Guard. The plane does not appear in official Air Force aircraft records after 1975 but does pop up on the museum account at George Air Force Base, California, in 1986. It is now parked along the main road at Pope Air Force Base, North Carolina, in a collection of static-display aircraft flown over the years by the "Flying Tigers" of the 23 Tactical Fighter Wing. (Photograph by author, 8 August 1997.)

26 Dec 1967	Flown by Capt. Gene I. Basel (354 TFS, 355 TFW) on a combat mission lasting 2.7 hours from Takhli RTAB, Thailand. (Capt. Basel's Individual Flight Record as of 31 Dec 67)
17 Feb 1968	In depot maintenance (WM) by SMAMA at 355 TFW, Takhli RTAB, Thailand. (AVH-10).
19 Feb 1968	At 355 TFW, Takhli RTAB, Thailand.
4 Mar 1968	At Air Asia, Tainan, Taiwan, for contract depot work (WK).
9 May 1968	Returned to 355 TFW, Takhli RTAB, Thailand.
15 Jul 1968	While assigned to the 355 TFW, Takhli, Thailand, the aircraft was damaged during a combat mission when the aircraft's gun ruptured as the result of a cartridge exploding in the barrel. Three panels of the gun compartment were blown from the aircraft. The boresight collar and muzzle clamp and the end of the barrel disintegrated into projectiles, causing a hole 2 1/2 inches by 2 1/2 inches through the aircraft blast panel and continuing through the inner panels to the ammunition drum compartment. The engine was damaged beyond limits as a result of the gun explosion. Also, the right horizontal stabilizer leading edge was damaged when it was struck by a bomb dropped by the aircraft. (355 TFW History, Jul–Sep 68, USAF microfilm NO465).
20 Sep 1968	While assigned to the 355 TFW, Takhli, Thailand, the aircraft received major battle damage to the left outboard and inboard pylons. The left leading edge flap was bent. It also received a hole in the wing tip and a small hole in the under side aft, and the inboard trailing edge. Panel W-7 was also damaged. Skin under the ventral fin was bent. There was also a bent fuselage former and the former aft of the bomb bay door was bent. (355 TFW History, Jul–Sep 68, USAF microfilm NO465).
27 Oct 1968	At 355 TFW, Takhli RTAB, Thailand. (AVH-10).
30 Nov 1968	While assigned to the 357 TFS, 355 TFW, Takhli RTAB, Thailand, the aircraft had accumulated 2,189.5 flying hours. (355 TFW History, Oct–Dec 68, USAF microfilm NO466).
10 Feb 1969	While assigned to the 355 TFW, Takhli RTAB, Thailand, the aircraft flew 29.3 hours during the month of February 1969 and had accumulated 2,409.1 flying hours before departing for IRAN depot maintenance. (355 TFW History, Jan–Mar 69, Vol. II, USAF Microfilm NO467).
11 Feb 1969	At Air Asia, Tainan, Taiwan, for contract depot work (WK). (AVH-12).
4 Apr 1969	Returned to 355 TFW, Takhli RTAB, Thailand. (AVH-12).
24 Sep 1969	In depot maintenance (WM) by SMAMA at Takhli RTAB, Thailand.
26 Sep 1969	At 355 TFW, Takhli RTAB, Thailand.
24 Oct 1970	At 355 TFW, Takhli RTAB, Thailand, being prepared for transfer (PL). (AVH-14).
27 Oct 1970	Transferred (PL) to 23 TFW, McConnell AFB KS.

4 Nov 1970	In flyable storage (PR) at 23 TFW, McConnell AFB KS.
4 Jan 1970	At 23 TFW, McConnell AFB KS being prepared for transfer (PL).
1 Mar 1971	In depot work (WO) by SMAMA at McClellan AFB CA. (AVH-16).
9 Apr 1971	Transferred to 192 TFG ANG, Byrd Field, Richmond VA.
10 Mar 1972	In depot work (WO) by SM-ALC at McClellan AFB CA. (AVH-18).
18 Jul 1972	Returned to 192 TFG ANG, Byrd Field, Richmond VA.
12 Oct 1972	In contract depot maintenance (WK) by Fairchild Engine and Aircraft Corporation (FACCF) at Bob Sikes Municipal Airport, Crestview FL.
9 Nov 1972	Returned to 192 TFG ANG, Byrd Field, Richmond VA.
9 Mar 1973	In contract depot maintenance (WM) by Dynalectron Corporation at Byrd Field, Richmond VA. (AVH-20).
15 Mar 1973	At 192 TFG ANG, Byrd Field, Richmond VA.
14 Aug 1973	In contract depot maintenance (WM) by Dynalectron Corporation at Byrd Field, Richmond VA.
16 Aug 1973	At 192 TFG ANG, Byrd Field, Richmond VA.
7 Dec 1973	In contract depot maintenance (WM) by Dynalectron Corporation (DYNZZ) at Byrd Field, Richmond VA.
11 Jan 1974	At 192 TFG ANG, Byrd Field, Richmond VA. (AVH-22).
23 Jun 1974	In contract depot maintenance (WM) by Dynalectron Corporation (DYNZZ) at Byrd Field, Richmond VA.
30 Sep 1974	At 192 TFG ANG, Byrd Field, Richmond VA.
30 Mar 1975	At 192 TFG ANG, Byrd Field, Richmond VA. Inventory account: TW. (AVH-23 & AVH-24).
Oct 1978	Preserved at George AFB, California.
23 Sep 1986	In USAF Museum account at George AFB CA. (AMARC Letter, 23 Sep 86).
Prior to Apr 1993	Transferred for display at Pope AFB NC.

F-105D-25RE 61-0175

Republic Production No: D-370 Production Sequence No: 450

Location: Displayed on a pedestal at Sheppard AFB, Wichita Falls, Texas.

Aircraft Chronology

24 Oct 1962	At MOAMA, Brookley AFB AL for depot work (WO) after production by Republic Aviation. (ACA-87).
4 Nov 1962	Delivered to 67 TFS, 18 TFW, Kadena AB, Okinawa.
26 Nov 1963	At Air Asia, Tainan, Taiwan, for contract depot work (WK).
31 Jan 1964	Returned to 18 TFW, Kadena AB, Okinawa.
31 Jul 1964	At the 4 TFW, Seymour Johnson AFB NC. (4 TFW History, Jul–Dec 64, Vol. II, USAF microfilm MO292).
31 Dec 1964	While assigned to the 4 TFW, Seymour Johnson AFB NC, the aircraft flew 22.4 hours for the month of December 1964 and had 450.5 total flying hours. Assigned crew chief: SSgt. Ramsey. (4 TFW History, Jul–Dec 64, Vol. II, USAF microfilm MO292).

7 Mar 1965	In depot maintenance by SMAMA at McClellan AFB CA. (AVH-3).
2 Apr 1965	Returned to 4 TFW, Seymour Johnson AFB NC.
30 Apr 1965	While assigned to the 4 TFW, Seymour Johnson AFB NC, the aircraft flew 33.3 hours for the month of April 1965 and had 538.4 total flying hours. Assigned crew chief: SSgt. Beane. (4 TFW History, Jan–Jun 65, Vol. II, USAF microfilm MO292).
30 May 1965	On TDY at Incirlik AB, Turkey, with the 336 TFS, 4 TFW, from Seymour Johnson AFB NC.
30 Aug 1965	Returned to 4 TFW, Seymour Johnson AFB NC.
9 Sep 1965	Transferred to 23 TFW, McConnell AFB KS. (AVH-3).
9 Oct 1965	In depot maintenance by SMAMA at McClellan AFB CA.
23 Nov 1965	Returned to 23 TFW, McConnell AFB KS.
11 Dec 1965	Transferred to 6441 TFW, Yokota AB, Japan.
31 Jan 1966	Transferred to the 355 TFW, Takhli RTAB, Thailand. (AVH-5).
25 Feb 1966	At Air Asia, Tainan, Taiwan, for contract depot work (WK).
28 Feb 1966	At Yokota AB, Japan, from the 355 TFW.
20 May 1966	Returned to the 355 TFW, Takhli RTAB, Thailand.
19 Jul 1966	At Air Asia, Tainan, Taiwan, for contract depot work (WK).
29 Sep 1966	Transferred to the 6441 TFW, Yokota AB, Japan.
13 Oct 1966	In depot maintenance by SMAMA field team at Yokota AB, Japan.
19 Oct 1966	At the 6441 TFW, Yokota AB, Japan.
15 Nov 1966	At Osan AB, Korea, for nuclear weapon alert from the 41 AD, Yokota AB, Japan.
18 Mar 1967	At 41 AD, Yokota AB, Japan. (AVH-7).
19 May 1967	At Osan AB, Korea, for nuclear weapon alert from the 41 AD, Yokota AB, Japan.
21 Jul 1967	At 41 AD, Yokota AB, Japan.
10 Aug 1967	At Osan AB, Korea, for nuclear weapon alert from the 41 AD, Yokota AB, Japan.
31 Aug 1967	At 41 AD, Yokota AB, Japan.
15 Nov 1967	At Osan AB, Korea, for nuclear weapon alert from the 41 AD, Yokota AB, Japan.
16 Dec 1967	At 41 AD, Yokota AB, Japan.
17 Jan 1968	Assigned unit redesignated 347 TFW, Yokota AB, Japan. (AVH-10).
29 Jan 1968	At Osan AB, Korea, with the 18 TFW in response to the U.S.S Pueblo incident.
19 May 1968	At 18 TFW, Kadena AB, Okinawa.
23 May 1968	At Osan AB, Korea, with the 18 TFW.
2 Jun 1968	At 18 TFW, Kadena AB, Okinawa.
3 Jun 1968	Transferred to 388 TFW, Korat RTAB, Thailand, as a combat attrition replacement.
22 Jun 1968	In depot maintenance (WM) by SMAMA at Korat RTAB, Thailand.
30 Jun 1968	At 388 TFW, Korat RTAB, Thailand.
4 Oct 1968	In depot maintenance (WM) by SMAMA at Korat RTAB, Thailand.
7 Oct 1968	At 388 TFW, Korat RTAB, Thailand.
9 Oct 1968	At Air Asia, Tainan, Taiwan, for contract depot maintenance (WK).
31 Oct 1968	Aircraft had accumulated 1,859.0 flying hours while assigned to the 388 TFW, Korat RTAB, Thailand. (388 TFW History, Oct–Dec 68, USAF microfilm NO585).
23 Nov 1968	At 388 TFW, Korat RTAB, Thailand. (AVH-10).
29 Apr 1969	At Kwangju AB, Korea, with 18 TFW. (AVH-12).
21 May 1969	Returned to 18 TFW, Kadena AB, Okinawa.
11 Jun 1969	At Kwangju AB, Korea, with 18 TFW.
15 Jun 1969	Returned to 18 TFW, Kadena AB, Okinawa.

This plane bounced around several units during its career. It was first delivered to the 18 Tactical Fighter Wing at Kadena Air Base, Okinawa, in November 1962. In 1964 it transferred to the 4 Tactical Fighter Wing at Seymour Johnson Air Force Base, North Carolina. It accompanied the 4th's 336 Tactical Fighter Squadron for its deployment to Turkey in May 1965. It stayed for short periods at McConnell Air Force Base, Kansas, and Yokota Air Base, Japan, and then, in January 1966, began six months with the 355 Tactical Fighter Wing flying combat missions from Takhli, Thailand. It returned to Yokota for the next year and a half before moving back to it's first unit at Kadena for the next six months. During the latter half of 1968, it again flew combat missions over North Vietnam, this time with the 388 Tactical Fighter Wing at Korat, Thailand. In early 1969 it returned once again to Kadena where it stayed until it moved to McConnell at the end of the year. Beginning in May 1971, the plane finally settled down with the Kansas Air National Guard at McConnell, who retired it in April 1976. (USAF Photograph from Dwight W. Tuttle, Historian, 82nd Training Wing, August 1996.)

11 Jul 1969	At Air Asia, Tainan, Taiwan, for contract depot work (WK).
22 Sep 1969	Returned to 18 TFW, Kadena AB, Okinawa.
8 Oct 1969	At Kwangju AB, Korea, with 18 TFW.
31 Oct 1969	Returned to 18 TFW, Kadena AB, Okinawa.
8 Dec 1969	In depot maintenance (WM) by SMAMA at Kadena AB, Okinawa.
9 Dec 1969	At 18 TFW, Kadena AB, Okinawa.
5 Nov 1970	Transferred (PL) to 23 TFW, McConnell AFB KS. (AVH-14).
12 Nov 1970	In flyable storage (PR) at 23 TFW, McConnell AFB KS.
4 Jan 1971	At 23 TFW, McConnell AFB KS being prepared for transfer (PL).
16 Jan 1971	In depot work (WO) by SMAMA at McClellan AFB CA. (AVH-16).
3 Mar 1971	Transferred (PL) to 184 TFG ANG, McConnell AFB KS.
24 Mar 1971	At 184 TFG ANG (CC), McConnell AFB KS.
17 May 1972	In contract depot maintenance (WK) by Fairchild Engine and Aircraft Corporation (FACCF) at Bob Sikes Municipal Airport, Crestview FL.
13 Jun 1972	At 184 TFG ANG (CC), McConnell AFB KS.
29 Jul 1973	In contract depot maintenance (WM) by Dynalectron Corp at McConnell AFB KS. (AVH-20).
17 Aug 1973	At 184 TFG ANG, McConnell AFB KS.
2 Oct 1973	In contract depot maintenance (WK) by Fairchild Engine and Aircraft Corporation (FACCF) at Bob Sikes Municipal Airport, Crestview FL.
5 Apr 1974	At 184 TFG ANG, McConnell AFB KS. (AVH-22).
5 Aug 1974	In contract depot maintenance (WM) by Dynalectron Corporation (DYNZZ) at McConnell AFB KS.
7 Aug 1974	At 184 TFTG ANG, McConnell AFB KS.
30 Apr 1975	In contract depot maintenance (WM) by Dynalectron Corporation (DYNZZ) at McConnell AFB KS. (AVH-23 & AVH-24).

14 May 1975	At 184 TFTG ANG, McConnell AFB KS for combat crew training (TF).
7 Oct 1975	In depot maintenance (WQ) by SM-ALC at McConnell AFB KS.
7 Nov 1975	In depot maintenance (WQ) at 184 TFTG at McConnell AFB KS.
18 Dec 1975	At 184 TFTG ANG, McConnell AFB KS for combat crew training (TF).
4 Feb 1976	In depot maintenance (WQ) at 184 TFTG at McConnell AFB KS. (AVH-24).
22 Apr 1976	At 184 TFTG ANG, McConnell AFB KS for combat crew training (TF). 3,338 flying hours. Inventory account: ZW (School or Museum).
23 Sep 1986	In USAF Museum account at Sheppard AFB TX. (AMARC Letter, 23 Sep 86).

F-105D-25RE 61-0176

Republic Production No: D-371 Production Sequence No: 451

Location: Displayed with the Maxwell AFB Collection, Montgomery, Alabama.

Aircraft Name(s)	Crew	Unit	Date	Description
Patience My Ass		357 TFS 355 TFW	Apr 69	Buzzard on bomb with name in red with white outline on fuselage below cockpit.
The Max Beak		357 TFS 355 TFW	Jun 69	On intake.
The Jolly Roger	Maj. R. Rogers	357 TFS 355 TFW	Jan 70	On both intakes. Skull and crossbones.

Aircraft Chronology

13 Oct 1962	USAF production acceptance from Republic Aviation, Farmingdale NY. (ACA-87).
13 Oct 1962	At MOAMA, Brookley AFB AL for depot work (WO).
Nov 1962	Delivered to 67 TFS, 18 TFW, Kadena AB, Okinawa.
20 Aug 1963	At 18 TFW, Kadena AB, Okinawa. (ACA-87).
3 Dec 1963	At Air Asia, Tainan, Taiwan, for contract depot work (WK).
5 Feb 1964	Returned to 18 TFW, Kadena AB, Okinawa.
Aug 1964	Transferred to the 4 TFW, Seymour Johnson AFB NC.
31 Aug 1964	While assigned to the 4 TFW, Seymour Johnson AFB NC, the aircraft flew 22.9 hours for the month of August 1964 and had 456.7 total flying hours. Assigned crew chief: A1C Godfrey. (4 TFW History, Jul–Dec 64, Vol. II, USAF microfilm MO292).
23 Oct 1964	At 333 TFS, 4485 TW, Eglin AFB FL. (AVH-2)
4 Dec 1964	Returned to 4 TFW, Seymour Johnson AFB NC.
31 Dec 1964	While assigned to the 4 TFW, Seymour Johnson AFB NC, the aircraft flew 20.7 hours for the month of December 1964 and had 541.0 total flying hours. Assigned crew chief: A1C Godfrey. (4 TFW History, Jul–Dec 64, Vol. II, USAF microfilm MO292).
9 Mar 1965	At SMAMA, McClellan AFB CA, for depot work. (AVH-3).
5 Apr 1965	Returned to the 4 TFW, Seymour Johnson AFB NC.
30 Apr 1965	While assigned to the 4 TFW, Seymour Johnson AFB NC, the aircraft flew 40.0 hours for the month of April 1965 and had 621.7 total flying hours. Assigned crew chief: SSgt. Ramsey. (4 TFW History, Jan–Jun 65, Vol. II, USAF microfilm MO292).

This "D" is another combat veteran that began its career with the 18 Tactical Fighter Wing at Kadena Air Base, Okinawa. Starting in November 1962, it stayed with the 18th for a little over a year before transferring to the 4 Tactical Fighter Wing at Seymour Johnson Air Force Base, North Carolina. In July 1965, the plane went with the 335 Tactical Fighter Squadron from Seymour to Yokota Air Base, Japan. This deployment, called "One Buck Thirteen," was to replace a squadron from McConnell. Beginning in December 1965, and lasting for the next two years, the plane moved at least five times, first to Takhli, Thailand, then to McConnell Air Force Base, Kansas. In June 1966 it returned to its initial home at Kadena, spent a brief time at Korat, Thailand, replacing a plane lost in combat, then returned to Kadena. Finally, in November 1967, the plane was an attrition replacement to the 355 Tactical Fighter Wing at Takhli where it stayed for the next three years. While at Takhli, it was damaged in combat at least twice. When Takhli closed at the end of 1970, the plane transferred to McConnell. It remained with the Kansas Air National Guard at McConnell for the next eight years, moved briefly to the Air Force Reserve unit at Carswell Air Force Base, Texas, and then ended up at Hill Air Force Base, Utah. The Reserve's 466 Tactical Fighter Squadron at Hill retired it in April 1982 with 5,800 flying hours on its airframe. (Photograph by author, 6 August 1997.)

3 July 1965	Aircraft deployed to Yokota AB, Japan, with the 335 TFS, 4 TFW, from Seymour Johnson AFB NC. Crew Chief: SSgt. Collins. (6441 TFW History, Jul–Dec 65, USAF microfilm PO232).
1 Dec 1965	At Takhli RTAB, Thailand, with the 6441 TFW. (AVH-3).
15 Dec 1965	Transferred to the 23 TFW, McConnell AFB KS.
23 Dec 1965	At MOAMA, Brookley AFB AL for depot work.
9 Mar 1966	At 23 TFW, McConnell AFB KS. (AVH-5).
31 May 1966	In depot maintenance (WM) by SMAMA field team at 23 TFW, McConnell AFB KS.
25 Jun 1966	Transferred to the 67 TFS, 18 TFW, Kadena AB, Okinawa.
22 Jul 1966	Temporarily transferred to 388 TFW, Korat RTAB, Thailand, as a combat attrition replacement.
29 Aug 1966	In depot maintenance (WM) by SMAMA field team at 18 TFW, Kadena AB, Okinawa.
31 Dec 1966	While assigned to the 18 TFW, Kadena AB, Okinawa, the aircraft flew 16 hours during the month of December 1966 and had accumulated 1,216 flying hours. (18 TFW History, Jul–Dec 66, USAF microfilm MO498).
4 Feb 1967	At 18 TFW, Kadena AB, Okinawa. (AVH-7).
24 Mar 1967	While assigned to the 18 TFW, Kadena AB, Okinawa, the aircraft lost its left 450-gallon wing tank during flight due to a failure of the rear bulkhead attachment fitting. (18 TFW History, Jan–Mar 67, USAF microfilm MO498).
16 Jul 1967	In depot maintenance (WM) by SMAMA field team at Kadena AB, Okinawa. (AVH-7).
23 Jul 1967	At 18 TFW, Kadena AB, Okinawa.
1 Nov 1967	Transferred to 355 TFW, Takhli RTAB, Thailand as a combat attrition replacement.
1 Dec 1967	In depot maintenance by SMAMA field team at Takhli RTAB, Thailand.
5 Dec 1967	Flown by Capt. Gene I. Basel (354 TFS, 355 TFW) on a mission lasting 2.4 hours from Takhli RTAB, Thailand. (Capt. Basel's Individual Flight Record as of 31 Dec 67)

10 Jan 1968	In depot maintenance (VM) for combat damage at 355 TFW, Takhli RTAB, Thailand. (AVH-10).
24 Jan 1968	At 355 TFW, Takhli RTAB, Thailand.
29 May 1968	In depot maintenance (WM) by SMAMA field team at Takhli RTAB, Thailand.
1 Jun 1968	At 355 TFW, Takhli RTAB, Thailand.
22 Jun 1968	At Air Asia, Tainan, Taiwan, for contract depot work (WK).
10 Sep 1968	At 355 TFW, Takhli RTAB, Thailand.
17 Sep 1968	In depot maintenance (WM) by SMAMA field team at Takhli RTAB, Thailand.
19 Sep 1968	At 355 TFW, Takhli RTAB, Thailand.
20 Sep 1968	In depot maintenance (WM) by SMAMA field team at Takhli RTAB, Thailand.
24 Sep 1968	At 355 TFW, Takhli RTAB, Thailand.
30 Nov 1968	While assigned to the 357 TFS, 355 TFW, Takhli RTAB, Thailand, aircraft had accumulated 2,120.0 flying hours. (355 TFW History, Oct–Dec 68, USAF microfilm NO466).
28 Feb 1969	While assigned to the 355 TFW, Takhli RTAB, Thailand, the aircraft flew 73.2 hours during the month of February 1969 and had accumulated 2,328.4 flying hours. (355 TFW History, Jan–Mar 69, Vol. II, USAF Microfilm NO467).
10 Mar 1969	In depot maintenance (WM) by SMAMA at Takhli RTAB, Thailand. (AVH-12).
11 Mar 1969	At 355 TFW, Takhli RTAB, Thailand.
3 May 1969	While assigned to the 355 TFW, Takhli RTAB, Thailand, the aircraft was damaged in combat. It "… received one round of 12.7 mm through the tail fin of the right 450 gal external fuel tank … . The pilot had delivered six M-117 bombs and two LAU-3A rocket pods on military structures in the 'C' Sector of Laos and reported no defenses observed in the target area. The damage was discovered during post-strike inspection and required only one man-hour to repair." (355 TFW History, Apr–Jun 69, Vol. III, USAF microfilm NO468).
8 May 1969	In depot maintenance (WM) by SMAMA at Takhli RTAB, Thailand. (AVH-12).
23 May 1969	While assigned to the 355 TFW, Takhli RTAB, Thailand, the aircraft was damaged in combat. It "… was hit by one round of 12.7 mm in the right aileron … . The pilot had delivered six M-117 bombs and two CBU-24s on a storage area in the 'C' sector of Laos. The flight reported light and random ZPU fire in the target area. The damage was discovered during post-flight inspection and required only one man-hour to repair." (355 TFW History, Apr–Jun 69, Vol. III, USAF microfilm NO468)
31 Mar 1970	In depot maintenance (WM) by SMAMA at Takhli RTAB, Thailand (AVH-14).
1 Apr 1970	At 355 TFW, Takhli RTAB, Thailand.
24 Oct 1970	At 355 TFW, Takhli RTAB, Thailand, being prepared for transfer (PL).
27 Oct 1970	Transferred (PL) to 23 TFW, McConnell AFB KS.
4 Nov 1970	In flyable storage (PR) at 23 TFW, McConnell AFB KS.
4 Jan 1971	At 23 TFW TAC, McConnell AFB KS being prepared for transfer (PL).
24 Mar 1971	Transferred to 184 TFG ANG, McConnell AFB KS. (AVH-16).
17 May 1971	In depot maintenance (WO) by SMAMA at McClellan AFB CA.
7 Jul 1971	Returned to 184 TFG ANG, McConnell AFB KS.
18 Jan 1972	In depot maintenance (WO) by SM-ALC at McClellan AFB CA. (AVH-18).
18 May 1972	Returned to 184 TFG ANG, McConnell AFB KS.
14 Nov 1972	In contract depot maintenance (WK) by Fairchild Engine and Aircraft Corporation (FACCF) at Bob Sikes Municipal Airport, Crestview FL.
15 Dec 1972	Returned to 184 TFG ANG, McConnell AFB KS.
31 May 1973	In contract depot maintenance (WM) by Dynalectron Corporation (DYNZZ) at McConnell AFB KS. (AVH-20).
6 Jun 1973	At 184 TFTG ANG, McConnell AFB KS. Assigned to combat duties (CC).
3 Jan 1974	At 184 TFTG ANG, McConnell AFB KS. Assigned to combat crew training (TF).

27 Jun 1974	In contract depot maintenance (WK) by Fairchild Engine and Aircraft Corporation (FACCF) at Bob Sikes Municipal Airport, Crestview FL. (AVH-22).
28 Jan 1975	At 184 TFTG ANG, McConnell AFB KS for combat crew training (TF). (AVH-23).
29 Oct 1975	In contract depot maintenance (WM) by Dynalectron Corporation (DYNZZ) at McConnell AFB KS. (AVH-23 & AVH-24).
12 Nov 1975	At 184 TFTG ANG, McConnell AFB KS for combat crew training (TF).
6 Mar 1979	In contract depot maintenance (DYNFW) at McConnell AFB KS. 5,344.7 flying hours. (AVH-27).
10 Apr 1979	At 184 TFG ANG, McConnell AFB KS for combat crew training (TF). 5,344.7 flying hours.
14 Aug 1979	In contract depot maintenance (DYNFW) at McConnell AFB KS. 5,410.3 flying hours.
21 Aug 1979	At 184 TFG ANG, McConnell AFB KS for combat crew training (TF). 5,410.3 flying hours.
21 Aug 1979	At 184 TFG ANG, McConnell AFB KS. 5,4695 flying hours. (GO33B 24 Jun 80).
19 Feb 1980	Transferred to 457 TFS AFRES, Carswell AFB TX. 5,4941 flying hours. (GO33B 22 Jan 81).
1 Aug 1981	At 457 TFS AFRES, Carswell AFB TX. 5,708.2 flying hours. (GO33B Dec 81).
6 Jan 1982	At 466 TFS AFRES, Hill AFB UT. 5,783.6 flying hours. (GO33B 1 Feb 83).
13 Apr 1982	At 466 TFS AFRES, Hill AFB UT. 5,813.1 flying hours. Inventory account "ZW'—School or Museum.
23 Sep 1986	In USAF Museum account at Maxwell AFB AL. (AMARC Letter, 23 Sep 86).

F-105D-25RE 61-0188

Republic Production No: D-383 Production Sequence No: 463

Location: Displayed as "61-0217" at TAC Memorial Park, Langley AFB, Hampton, Virginia.

Aircraft Name(s)	Crew	Unit	Date	Description
Stephanie Allison	1Lt. Bruce N. Cox	354 TFS 355 TFW	Jan 70	In white script on both sides of fuselage below cockpit.

Aircraft Chronology

13 Nov 1962	USAF production acceptance from Republic Aviation, Farmingdale NY. (ACA-87).
12 Dec 1962	At MOAMA, Brookley AFB AL for depot work after production (WO).
20 Dec 1962	Delivered to 18 TFW, Kadena AB, Okinawa.
15 Feb 1964	At Air Asia, Tainan, Taiwan, for contract depot work (WK).
8 Apr 1964	Returned to 18 TFW, Kadena AB, Okinawa. (ACA-87 & AVH-1).
30 Sep 1964	At 18 TFW, Kadena AB, Okinawa. Assigned crew chief: SSgt. J. Yahr. (18 TFW History, Jul–Dec 64, USAF microfilm MO496).
20 Dec 1964	Due to pilot error, the aircraft blew a tire on landing and engaged the barrier at Kadena AB, Okinawa. Pilot: Maj. James W. Mathews. (18 TFW History, Jul–Dec 64, USAF microfilm MO496).
31 Jan 1965	At 18 TFW, Kadena AB, Okinawa. Assigned crew chief: SSgt. J. Yahr. (18 TFW History, Jan–Jun 65, USAF microfilm MO497).
17 Aug 1965	Deployed to Korat RTAB, Thailand, with the 67 TFS from Kadena AB, Okinawa. (67 TFS History, 1 July–31 December 1965).
12 Sep 1965	Flown as "Elm 3" by Capt. Jack L. Francisco, 67 TFS, from Korat RTAB, Thailand, on a combat mission against the Yen Khoai barracks in North Vietnam. The aircraft was hit in the radome by flak.

From December 1962, this combat veteran spent nine years in the Pacific beginning with the 18 Tactical Fighter Wing at Kadena Air Base, Okinawa. In 1965, it deployed to Korat, Thailand, where, on one of its combat missions, it flew rescue cover for Lt. Col. Robinson Risner when he was shot down. It returned to Kadena by the end of 1965 and stayed until July 1967 when it transferred to the 355 Tactical Fighter Wing at Takhli, Thailand. In its three years of flying from Takhli it was combat-damaged and repaired at least twice. The plane was at the overhaul depot in Taiwan when Takhli closed at the end of 1970 so, in January 1971, it once again returned to Kadena where it was stored for three months. It returned to the States in March 1971 for storage at McConnell until July when it found a home with the Washington DC Air National Guard at Andrews Air Force Base, Maryland. The Guard retired it in December 1975. A little over a year later it became a static display at Luke Air Force Base, Arizona, where it was painted silver and given the tail number of F-105D 61-0217 that Lt. Col. Robinson Risner flew on the day in September 1965 he was shot down and became a prisoner in North Vietnam. In 1983, still marked with the tail number of Col. Risner's plane, it was placed on a pedestal at Langley Air Force Base, Virginia. (USAF photograph from SSgt. Gregory S. Henneman, Historian, 1st Fighter Wing.)

Flight lead was the 67 TFS commander, Lt. Col. Robinson Risner, flying F-105D 61-0191. His plane was hit in the canopy. Both aircraft returned safely to Korat. (67 TFS History, 1 Jul–31 Dec 65).

16 Sep 1965 Flown as "Oak 2" by Capt. Goode, 67 TFS, from Korat RTAB, Thailand, on an Iron Hand mission against a SAM site in RP-4, North Vietnam. "Oak 1," Maj. Raymond James Merritt, was shot down by flak and became a POW. He, too, was from the 67 TFS flying F-105D 61-0189. Lt. Col. Robinson Risner, 67 TFS commander, flying as "Pepper 1" in F-105D 61-0127, was also shot down and became a POW. Capt. Goode flew rescap for both Maj Merritt and Lt. Col. Risner, then landed at Da Nang AB, South Vietnam, when he ran short of fuel.

17 Sep 1965 Capt. Goode, 67 TFS, returned to Korat RTAB, Thailand, from Da Nang AB, South Vietnam, using call sign "Soup 1."

9 Dec 1965 Returned to 18 TFW, Kadena AB, Okinawa. Assigned Crew Chief: A1C A. Jones.

8 Jul 1966 Flown to Korat RTAB, Thailand, from the 18 TFW, Kadena AB, Okinawa. (AVH-5).

21 Nov 1966 Returned to the 18 TFW, Kadena AB, Okinawa.

31 Dec 1966 While assigned to the 67 TFS, 18 TFW, Kadena AB, Okinawa, the aircraft flew 16 hours during the month of December 1966 and had accumulated 966 flying hours. (18 TFW History, Jul–Dec 66, USAF microfilm MO498).

11 Jun 1967 In depot work (WM) by SMAMA field team at 18 TFW, Kadena AB, Okinawa. (AVH-7).

20 Jun 1967 At 18 TFW, Kadena AB, Okinawa.

15 Jul 1967 Transferred to 355 TFW, Takhli RTAB, Thailand.

2 Sep 1967	While flying with the 355 TFW from Takhli RTAB, Thailand, the aircraft received combat damage consisting of inboard pylons damaged beyond repair and six feet of leading edge flap broken off.. (355 TFW History, Oct–Dec 67, USAF microfilm NO463).
3 Sep 1967	In depot work to repair combat damage (WV) by SMAMA field team at Takhli RTAB, Thailand. (AVH-7).
8 Sep 1967	At 355 TFW, Takhli RTAB, Thailand.
13 Sep 1967	Flown by Maj. Donald M. Russell (333 TFS, 355 TFW) on a mission that lasted 5.0 hours from Takhli RTAB, Thailand. (Maj. Russell's Individual Flight Record, as of 31 Dec 67).
18 Dec 1967	At Air Asia, Tainan, Taiwan, for contract depot work (WK).
27 Feb 1968	Returned to 355 TFW, Takhli RTAB, Thailand. (AVH-10).
18 Jun 1968	At 355 TFW, Takhli RTAB, Thailand.
29 Jun 1968	On a combat mission over North Vietnam from the 355 TFW at Takhli RTAB, Thailand, the aircraft received battle damage when two M-117 bombs struck the lower left and right side of the fuselage causing damage between stations 513 and 610.25. (355 TFW History, Apr–Jun 68, USAF microfilm NO464).
30 Nov 1968	While assigned to the 357 TFS, 355 TFW, Takhli RTAB, Thailand, the aircraft had accumulated 2,054.0 flying hours. (355 TFW History, Oct–Dec 68, USAF microfilm NO466).
28 Feb 1969	While assigned to the 355 TFW, Takhli RTAB, Thailand, the aircraft flew 60.5 hours during the month of February 1969 and had accumulated 2,235.1 flying hours. (355 TFW History, Jan–Mar 69, Vol. II, USAF Microfilm NO467).
3 May 1969	At 355 TFW, Takhli RTAB, Thailand. (AVH-12).
6 May 1969	At Air Asia, Tainan, Taiwan, for contract depot work (WK).
15 Jul 1969	Returned to 355 TFW, Takhli RTAB, Thailand.
22 Oct 1969	Flown on a combat mission lasting 2.2 hours by 1Lt Bruce N. Cox, 354 TFS, 355 TFW, Takhli RTAB, Thailand. Call sign: Red Dog. He named the plane "Stephanie Allison" after his daughter. (E-mail from Bruce Cox, 22 Dec 99).
9 Nov 1969	In depot maintenance (WM) by SMAMA field team at Takhli RTAB, Thailand.
16 Nov 1969	Combat ready (CC) at the 355 TFW, Takhli RTAB, Thailand.
19 Jan 70	Flown on a combat mission lasting 2.2 hours by 1Lt Bruce N. Cox, 354 TFS, 355 TFW, from Takhli RTAB, Thailand. Call sign: Dolphin. (E-mail from Bruce Cox, 22 Dec 99).
21 Jan 1970	Flown on a mission lasting 2.4 hours by 1Lt Bruce N. Cox, 354 TFS, 355 TFW. Call sign: Dolphin.
23 Jan 1970	Flown on a combat mission lasting 2.3 hours by 1Lt Bruce N. Cox, 354 TFS, 355 TFW. Call sign: Barracuda.
24 Jan 1970	Flown on a mission lasting 2.6 hours by 1Lt Bruce N. Cox, 354 TFS, 355 TFW. Call sign: Dolphin.
14 Feb 1970	Flown on a mission lasting 2.7 hours by 1Lt Bruce N. Cox, 354 TFS, 355 TFW. Call sign: Basket.
16 Feb 1970	Flown on a mission lasting 2.5 hours by 1Lt Bruce N. Cox, 354 TFS, 355 TFW, Call sign: Dallas.
17 Feb 1970	Flown on a mission lasting 2.6 hours by 1Lt Bruce N. Cox, 354 TFS, 355 TFW. Call sign: Basket.
25 Feb 1970	Flown on a mission lasting 2.4 hours by 1Lt Bruce N. Cox, 354 TFS, 355 TFW. Call sign: Alamo.
26 Feb 1970	Flown on a mission lasting 2.3 hours by 1Lt Bruce N. Cox, 354 TFS, 355 TFW. Call sign: Mantis.
2 Mar 1970	Flown on a mission lasting 2.3 hours by 1Lt Bruce N. Cox, 354 TFS, 355 TFW. Call sign: Raccoon.
3 Mar 1970	Flown on a mission lasting 2.5 hours by 1Lt Bruce N. Cox, 354 TFS, 355 TFW. Call sign: Ashcan.
4 Mar 1970	Flown on a mission lasting 2.7 hours by 1Lt Bruce N. Cox, 354 TFS, 355 TFW. Call sign: Dino.
23 Mar 1970	Flown on his 100th combat mission over North Vietnam by 1Lt Bruce N. Cox, 354 TFS, 355 TFW, from Takhli RTAB, Thailand. The mission lasted 2.8 hours. Call sign: Cosmic.
29 Mar 1970	Flown on a mission lasting 2.2 hours by 1Lt Bruce N. Cox, 354 TFS, 355 TFW. Call sign: Swanny.
10 Apr 1970	Flown on a mission lasting 2.2 hours by 1Lt Bruce N. Cox, 354 TFS, 355 TFW. Call sign: Madman.
19 Apr 1970	Flown on a mission lasting 2.3 hours by 1Lt Bruce N. Cox, 354 TFS, 355 TFW. Call sign: Firebird.

21 Apr 1970	Flown on a mission lasting 2.1 hours by 1Lt Bruce N. Cox, 354 TFS, 355 TFW. Call sign: Carrot.
23 Apr 1970	Flown on a mission lasting 2.5 hours by 1Lt Bruce N. Cox, 354 TFS, 355 TFW. Call sign: Bear.
6 May 1970	Flown on a mission lasting 2.4 hours by 1Lt Bruce N. Cox, 354 TFS, 355 TFW, from Takhli RTAB, Thailand. Call sign: Basket. Plane recovered at Korat RTAB, Thailand, and then returned to Takhli later in the day in a sortie that lasted .7 hours.
12 May 1970	Flown on a mission lasting 2.4 hours by 1Lt Bruce N. Cox, 354 TFS, 355 TFW. Call sign: Carrot.
19 May 1970	Flown on a mission lasting 2.1 hours by 1Lt Bruce N. Cox, 354 TFS, 355 TFW. Call sign: Raccoon.
27 May 1970	In depot maintenance (WM) by SMAMA at Takhli RTAB, Thailand. (AVH-14).
31 May 1970	Combat ready (CC) at the 355 TFW, Takhli RTAB, Thailand.
5 Jun 1970	Flown on a mission lasting 2.8 hours by 1Lt Bruce N. Cox, 354 TFS, 355 TFW. Call sign: Bear. (E-mail from Bruce Cox, 22 Dec 99).
12 Jun 1970	Flown on a mission lasting 2.3 hours by 1Lt Bruce N. Cox, 354 TFS, 355 TFW. Call sign: Beanie.
30 Jun 1970	Flown on a local sortie lasting 1.4 hours from Takhli RTAB, Thailand, by 1Lt Bruce N. Cox, 354 TFS, 355 TFW, to support the Air Force Academy's Operation 3rd Lieutenant.
17 Aug 1970	At 355 TFW, Takhli RTAB, Thailand, being prepared for transfer (PL).
20 Aug 1970	At Air Asia, Tainan, Taiwan, for contract depot work (WK).
12 Jan 1971	Transferred to 18 TFW, Kadena AB, Okinawa. (AVH-16).
10 Mar 1971	Placed in flyable storage (PR) at 18 TFW, Kadena AB, Okinawa.
18 Mar 1971	At 18 TFW, Kadena AB, Okinawa, being prepared for transfer (PL).
19 Mar 1971	Transferred (PL) to 23 TFW TAC, McConnell AFB KS.
31 Mar 1971	Placed in flyable storage (PR) at 23 TFW TAC, McConnell AFB KS.
24 May 1971	Operationally ready (CC) at 23 TFW TAC, McConnell AFB KS.
26 Jul 1971	Transferred (PL) to 113 TFG ANG, Andrews AFB MD.
6 Aug 1971	Operationally ready (CC) at 113 TFG ANG, Andrews AFB MD.
21 Aug 1972	In contract depot maintenance (WK) by Fairchild Engine and Aircraft Corporation (FACCF) at Bob Sikes Municipal Airport, Crestview FL. (AVH-18).
13 Sep 1972	Returned (PL) to 113 TFG ANG, Andrews AFB MD.
14 Mar 1973	In contract depot maintenance (WM) by Dynalectron Corporation (DYNZZ) at Andrews AFB MD. (AVH-20).
16 Mar 1973	At 113 TFG ANG, Andrews AFB MD.
13 Sep 1973	In contract depot maintenance (WM) by Dynalectron Corporation (DYNZZ) at Andrews AFB MD.
25 Sep 1973	At 113 TFG ANG, Andrews AFB MD.
17 Dec 1973	In contract depot maintenance (WM) by Dynalectron Corporation (DYNZZ) at Andrews AFB MD.
20 Dec 1973	At 113 TFG ANG, Andrews AFB MD.
21 May 1974	In contract depot maintenance (WK) by Fairchild Engine and Aircraft Corporation (FACCF) at Bob Sikes Municipal Airport, Crestview FL. (AVH-22).
30 Sep 1974	At 113 TFG ANG, Andrews AFB MD.
30 Nov 1974	Assigned unit redesignated 113 TFW ANG, Andrews AFB MD.
31 Dec 1974	At 113 TFW ANG, Andrews AFB MD.
24 Feb 1975	In contract depot maintenance (WM) by Dynalectron Corporation (DYNZZ) at Andrews AFB MD. (AVH-23 & AVH-24).
3 Mar 1975	At 113 TFW ANG, Andrews AFB MD.
10 Dec 1975	At 113 TFW ANG, Andrews AFB MD. In storage (XX) with a low probability of withdrawal.
7 Jan 1976	At 113 TFW ANG, Andrews AFB MD. In storage (XX) with a low probability of withdrawal. Inventory account: GB. (AVH-24).
6 Feb 1977	At 58 TFTW TAC, Luke AFB AZ. In storage (Possession Code: XX). Inventory account: TW. 3,9150 flying hours. (AVH-25 & AVH-26).

Sep 1977	Displayed at Luke AFB AZ as F-105D 61-0217, painted silver and in the 67 TFS markings of Lt. Col. Robinson Risner's aircraft in which he was shot down over North Vietnam on 16 September 1965. (Mike Benolkin photo).
	Moved from Luke AFB AZ to be displayed at Langley AFB VA.
26 Aug 1983	Placed on display at newly-opened TAC Memorial Park, Langley AFB VA. (E-mail, 15 Aug 1996, from SSgt. Greg Henneman, 1 FW/HO).

F-105D-25RE 61-0199

Republic Production No: D-394 Production Sequence No: 474

Location: At Security Police Flightline Training Area #7, Lackland AFB, San Antonio, Texas.

Aircraft Chronology

11 May 1964	At MOAMA, Brookley AFB AL for depot work after production at Republic Aviation. (ACA-87 & AVH-1).
22 Sep 1964	Delivered to 4 TFW, Seymour Johnson AFB NC. (AVH-1).
17 Nov 1964	Deployed to Incirlik AB, Turkey, with the 335 TFS, 4 TFW from Seymour Johnson AFB NC. (AVH-3).
30 Apr 1965	On TDY to Incirlik AB, Turkey, with the 334 TFS from the 4 TFW, Seymour Johnson AFB NC. (4 TFW History, Jan–Jun 65, Vol. II, USAF microfilm MO292).
16 May 1965	Returned to 4 TFW, Seymour Johnson AFB NC. (AVH-3).
4 Jul 1965	Aircraft at Yokota AB, Japan, assigned to the 335 TFS, 4 TFW, deployed under "One Buck 13" from Seymour Johnson AFB NC. Crew Chief: SSgt. Steadings. (6441 TFW History, Jul–Dec 65, USAF microfilm PO232).

This plane started its service with the 4 Tactical Fighter Wing at Seymour Johnson Air Force Base, North Carolina, during a period when this wing was heavily tasked with squadron deployments. In 1964 and early 1965, 61-0199 spent six months in Turkey on NATO alert during the successive rotations of two fighter squadrons from the 4th. After returning home, the plane deployed in the summer of 1965 with the 4th's 335 Tactical Fighter Squadron to Yokota Air Base, Japan, to support that base's nuclear alert in South Korea while many of Yokota's F-105s were in Thailand. In November 1965, with the expanding war in Vietnam, 61-0199 was itself in Thailand, moving with the 335th from Japan to Takhli to participate in the bombing of North Vietnam. After a short combat tour, the plane transferred in December 1965 to McConnell Air Force Base, Kansas, to support F-105 pilot training. During its seven years with the 23 Tactical Fighter Wing at McConnell, the plane deployed five times to George AFB, California, for gunnery training. In 1972 it began eight years of service with the Air Force Reserve unit at Tinker Air Force Base, Oklahoma, transferring to its sister unit at Hill Air Force Base, Utah, in July 1980. A year later it deployed with the 466 Tactical Fighter Squadron from Hill to Denmark for a NATO summer exercise. Its final flight was to Lackland Air Force Base, Texas, in June 1983 when it began its service with the Air Force's security police flight line training program. (Photograph by author, 4 August 1997.)

1 Dec 1965	At Takhli RTAB, Thailand, with the 335 TFS, 4 TFW, that deployed from Yokota AB, Japan to Takhli. (AVH-3).
21 Dec 1965	Transferred to 23 TFW, McConnell AFB KS.
19 Jan 1966	At 23 TFW, McConnell AFB KS. (AVH-5).
16 Sep 1966	In depot maintenance (WM) by SMAMA field team at 23 TFW, McConnell AFB KS.
23 Sep 1966	At 23 TFW, McConnell AFB KS.
20 Dec 1966	At MOAMA, Brookley AFB AL for depot maintenance (WO).
28 Apr 1967	Returned to the 23 TFW, McConnell AFB KS. (AVH-7).
1 Jul 1967	Deployed to George AFB CA with the 560 TFS, 23 TFW, for air-to-air gunnery training for RTU Class 67JR, the "Roaring 20 + 1."
14 Jul 1967	Returned to 23 TFW, McConnell AFB KS.
4 Aug 1967	Deployed to George AFB CA with the 561 TFS, 23 TFW, for air-to-air gunnery training for RTU Class 68AR.
16 Aug 1967	Returned to 23 TFW, McConnell AFB KS.
29 Sep 1967	Deployed to George AFB CA with the 562 TFS, 23 TFW, for air-to-air gunnery training for RTU Class 68BR, "The Many Splendored Studs."
1 Nov 1967	At 23 TFW, McConnell AFB KS.
23 Jan 1968	Deployed to George AFB CA with the 561 TFS, 23 TFW, for air-to-air gunnery training for RTU Class 68FR. (AVH-10).
7 Feb 1968	Returned to 23 TFW, McConnell AFB KS.
12 Mar 1968	Deployed to George AFB CA with the 562 TFS, 23 TFW, for air-to-air gunnery training for RTU Class 68HR.
28 Mar 1968	Returned to 23 TFW, McConnell AFB KS.
24 Oct 1968	At SMAMA, McClellan AFB CA for depot work (WO).
5 Dec 1968	Returned to 23 TFW, McConnell AFB KS.
6 May 1969	At 23 TFW, McConnell AFB KS. (AVH-12).
15 Jul 1970	At SMAMA, McClellan AFB CA for depot work (WO). (AVH-14).
17 Dec 1970	Returned (PL) to 23 TFW, McConnell AFB KS for combat crew training.
1 Mar 1972	Carried on assignment roster for the 562 TFS, 23 TFW, at McConnell AFB KS. (Master 23 TFW Aircraft Assignment as of 1 March 1972).
28 Jun 1972	In contract depot maintenance (WK) by Fairchild Engine and Aircraft Corporation (FACCF) at Bob Sikes Municipal Airport, Crestview FL. (AVH-18).
26 Jul 1972	Transferred (PL) to 507 TFG AFRES, Tinker AFB OK.
31 Jul 1972	At 507 TFG AFRES, Tinker AFB OK (CC).
31 Mar 1973	Assigned to 507 CMTSQ AFRES, Tinker AFB OK (CC). (AVH-20).
4 Apr 1973	In depot maintenance by SM-ALC at Tinker AFB OK.
18 Apr 1973	At 507 CMTSQ AFRES, Tinker AFB OK (CC).
2 Jun 1973	In depot maintenance by SM-ALC at Tinker AFB OK.
14 Jun 1973	At 507 CMTSQ AFRES, Tinker AFB OK (CC).
2 Oct 1973	In depot maintenance by SM-ALC at Tinker AFB OK.
17 Oct 1973	At 507 CMTSQ AFRES, Tinker AFB OK (CC).
29 Nov 1973	In contract depot maintenance (WK) by Fairchild Engine and Aircraft Corporation (FACCF) at Bob Sikes Municipal Airport, Crestview FL.
24 Apr 1974	At 507 CMTSQ AFRES, Tinker AFB OK (CC). (AVH-22).
16 Oct 1974	Assigned unit redesignated 507 CLMSQ AFRES, Tinker AFB OK.
3 Mar 1975	In depot maintenance (WM) by SM-ALC at Tinker AFB OK. (AVH-23).

25 Mar 1975	At 507 CLMSQ AFRES, Tinker AFB OK.
6 Oct 1975	In depot maintenance (WM) by SM-ALC at Tinker AFB OK. (AVH-23 & AVH-24).
23 Jan 1976	At 507 TFG AFRES, Tinker AFB OK. 3,381 flying hours. (AVH-24).
30 Aug 1976	In depot maintenance (DM) by SM-ALC at Tinker AFB OK. 3,381 flying hours.
22 Sep 1976	At 507 TFG AFRES, Tinker AFB OK. 3,381 flying hours.
1 Dec 1976	In depot maintenance (DM) by SM-ALC at Tinker AFB OK. 3,419 flying hours.
29 Dec 1976	At 507 TFG AFRES, Tinker AFB OK. 3,439.0 flying hours. (AVH-25 & AVH-26).
8 May 1978	In depot maintenance by SM-ALC at Tinker AFB OK. 3,762.0 flying hours.
17 May 1978	At 465 TFS AFRES, Tinker AFB OK. 3,827.0 flying hours.
9 Apr 1979	In contract depot maintenance by Fairchild Aircraft Corporation (FACBM) at Tinker AFB OK. 3,958.1 flying hours. (AVH-27).
19 Apr 1979	At 465 TFS AFRES, Tinker AFB OK. 3,958.1 flying hours.
19 Jun 1979	While assigned to the 465 TFS AFRES, Tinker AFB OK, the aircraft ground aborted due to the rudder kicking when the stability augmentation was engaged. The control assembly was changed. (301 TFW History 1 Apr–30 Jun 1979, USAF microfilm 343832).
23 Jun 1979	While assigned to the 465 TFS AFRES, Tinker AFB OK, the aircraft ground aborted due to an inoperative CIN power blower. (301 TFW History 1 Apr–30 Jun 1979, USAF microfilm 343832).
30 Jun 1979	While assigned to the 465 TFS AFRES, Tinker AFB OK, the aircraft flew 26.7 hours during the month of June 1979 and had accumulated a total of 4,041.4 flying hours. The assigned crew chief was Walton. (301 TFW History, Apr–Jun 1979, USAF microfilm 34382).
26 Mar 1980	In contract depot maintenance (FACBM) at Tinker AFB OK. 4,246.4 flying hours. (GO33B 24 Jun 80).
16 Apr 1980	At 465 TFS, Tinker AFB OK. 4,254.0 flying hours.
30 Jul 1980	Transferred to 466 TFS AFRES, Hill AFB UT. 4,277.1 flying hours. (GO33B 22 Jan 81).
25 Nov 1980	In depot maintenance at McClellan AFB CA. 4,323.1 flying hours.
15 Aug 1981	Deployed under "Coronet Rudder" with 466 TFS to Skrydstrup, Denmark, from Hill AFB UT. (British Aviation Review, Dec 1995).
29 Aug 1981	Returned from Denmark to Hill AFB UT.
4 Jun 1983	One of 24 F-105s flown on ceremonial final mission at Hill AFB UT. After mission, aircraft was one of seven delivered to 3280 TTA Group (ATC), Lackland AFB TX for security police flightline training. (Possession code: TX. Inventory account: GB). 4,786.6 flying hours. (GO33B 9 Feb 84).
5 Jun 1983	Redesignated GF-105D at 3280 TTA Group (ATC), Lackland AFB TX. (Possession code: TX. Inventory account: GC). 4,786.6 flying hours.

F-105D-25RE 62-4228

Republic Production No: D-427 Production Sequence No: 507

Location: At Security Police Flightline Training Area #7, Lackland AFB, San Antonio, Texas.

Aircraft Name(s)	Crew	Unit	Date	Description
Papa Thud/"Mutt's Man-O-War"		354 TFS 355 TFW	Jan 70	"Pappa Thud" On intake. Other name on fuselage below cockpit.
Silver Tongue Devil		466 TFS AFRES	May 83	Smiling red devil in diaper. "Silver" in front and "Tongue" behind figure. Below left wing.

This F-105D spent most of its service in the Far East, starting with the 18 Tactical Fighter Wing at Kadena Air Base, Okinawa, in 1963. Beginning in 1964, the 18th supported the war in Vietnam with short deployments to Korat, Thailand, and Danang Air Base, South Vietnam, so 62-4228 probably saw combat duty during this period. In 1967 it went to the 355 Tactical Fighter Wing at Takhli, Thailand, where it's pilots flew it in combat over North Vietnam. With the closure of Takhli at the end of 1970, the plane transferred back to the 18th at Okinawa. In March 1971, it was sent to storage at McConnell Air Force Base, Kansas, until the Washington DC Air National Guard accepted it at Andrews Air Force Base, Maryland. Like the other nine F-105s on the security police training "flightline," the plane's last unit was the Air Force Reserve's 466 Tactical Fighter Squadron at Hill Air Force Base, Utah, where it served from 1981 to 1983. (Photograph by Pete A. Sanders, Jr., 16 June 1996.)

Aircraft Chronology

4 Jan 1963	At MOAMA, Brookley AFB AL for depot work after production from Republic Aviation. (ACA-88).
12 Jan 1963	Delivered to 18 TFW, Kadena AB, Okinawa.
29 May 1964	At Air Asia, Tainan, Taiwan, for contract depot work (WK). (AVH-1).
24 Aug 1964	Returned to 18 TFW, Kadena AB, Okinawa.
30 Sep 1964	At 18 TFW, Kadena AB, Okinawa. Assigned crew chief: SSgt. J. Whitely. (18 TFW History, Jul–Dec 64, USAF microfilm MO496).
18 Nov 1964	At Air Asia, Tainan, Taiwan, for contract depot work (WK). (AVH-2).
21 Dec 1964	At 18 TFW, Kadena AB, Okinawa.
31 Jan 1965	At 18 TFW, Kadena AB, Okinawa. Assigned crew chief: A1C E. Guddendorf. (18 TFW History, Jan–Jun 65, USAF microfilm MO497).
30 Jun 1965	At Air Asia, Tainan, Taiwan, for contract depot work (WK). (AVH-4).
9 Jul 1965	At 18 TFW, Kadena AB, Okinawa.
30 Nov 1965	At 18 TFW, Kadena AB, Okinawa. Assigned crew chief: A1C D. Lewonczyk. (18 TFW History, Jul–Dec 65, USAF microfilm MO497).

14 Dec 1965	At Air Asia, Tainan, Taiwan, for contract depot work (WK).
4 Jan 1966	At 18 TFW, Kadena AB, Okinawa . (AVH-5).
23 Apr 1966	At Korat RTAB, Thailand with 18 TFW.
11 May 1966	At 18 TFW, Kadena AB, Okinawa.
25 May 1966	At Air Asia, Tainan, Taiwan, for contract depot work (WK).
2 Aug 1966	Returned to 18 TFW, Kadena AB, Okinawa.
8 Aug 1966	In depot maintenance (WM) by SMAMA field team at 18 TFW, Kadena AB, Okinawa.
31 Dec 1966	While assigned to the 18 TFW, Kadena AB, Okinawa, the aircraft flew 7 hours during the month of December 1966 and had accumulated 1,007 flying hours. (18 TFW History, Jul–Dec 66, USAF microfilm MO498).
16 Apr 1967	At 18 TFW, Kadena AB, Okinawa. (AVH-8).
31 May 1967	At 12 TFS, 18 TFW, Kadena AB, Okinawa. Aircraft had accumulated 1,044 flying hours. (18 TFW History, Apr–Jun 67, USAF microfilm MO499).
10 Oct 1967	In depot maintenance (WM) by SMAMA field team at Takhli RTAB, Thailand. (AVH-8).
11 Oct 1967	Transferred to 355 TFW, Takhli RTAB, Thailand.
1 Nov 1967	At 355 TFW, Takhli RTAB, Thailand.
6 Feb 1968	In depot maintenance (WM) by SMAMA at Takhli RTAB, Thailand. (AVH-10).
9 Feb 1968	At 355 TFW, Takhli RTAB, Thailand.
16 Feb 1968	At Air Asia, Tainan, Taiwan, for contract depot maintenance (WK).
26 Apr 1968	Returned to 355 TFW, Takhli RTAB, Thailand.
24 May 1968	In depot maintenance (WM) by SMAMA at Takhli RTAB, Thailand.
30 May 1968	At 355 TFW, Takhli RTAB, Thailand.
1 Nov 1968	While assigned to the 354 TFS, 355 TFW, Takhli RTAB, Thailand, the aircraft had accumulated 2,047.5 flying hours. (355 TFW History, Oct–Dec 68, USAF microfilm NO466).
28 Feb 1969	While assigned to the 355 TFW, Takhli RTAB, Thailand, the aircraft flew 32.3 hours during the month of February 1969 and had accumulated 2,257.2 flying hours. (355 TFW History, Jan–Mar 69, Vol. II, USAF Microfilm NO467).
20 Mar 1969	At Air Asia, Tainan, Taiwan, for contract depot maintenance (WK). (AVH-12).
10 May 1969	Returned to 355 TFW, Takhli RTAB, Thailand.
19 Nov 1969	In depot maintenance (WM) by SMAMA at Takhli RTAB, Thailand.
26 Nov 1969	At 355 TFW, Takhli RTAB, Thailand.
24 May 1970	In depot maintenance (WM) by SMAMA at Takhli RTAB, Thailand. (AVH-14).
28 May 1970	At 355 TFW, Takhli RTAB, Thailand.
24 Oct 1970	At 355 TFW, Takhli RTAB, Thailand being prepared for transfer (PL).
27 Oct 1970	Transferred (PL) to 18 TFW, Kadena AB, Japan.
28 Oct 1970	Place in flyable storage (PR) at 18 TFW, Kadena AB, Japan.
6 Nov 1970	Place in storage with limited probability of withdrawal (XW) at 18 TFW, Kadena AB, Japan.
9 Dec 1970	At 18 TFW, Kadena AB, Japan, being prepared for transfer (PL).
15 Dec 1970	At Air Asia, Tainan, Taiwan, for contract depot work (WK).
26 Jan 1971	Returned (PL) to 18 TFW, Kadena AB, Okinawa, (AVH-16).
2 Feb 1971	Operationally ready (CC) at 18 TFW, Kadena AB, Okinawa.
20 Mar 1971	At 18 TFW, Kadena AB, Okinawa, being prepared for transfer (PL).
24 Mar 1971	Transferred (PL) to 23 TFW, McConnell AFB KS.
6 Apr 1971	Placed in flyable storage (PR) at 23 TFW, McConnell AFB KS.
23 Apr 1971	Operationally ready (CC) at 23 TFW, McConnell AFB KS.

16 Aug 1971	At 23 TFW, McConnell AFB KS being prepared for transfer (PL).
20 Aug 1971	Transferred (PL) to 113 TFG ANG, Andrews AFB MD.
22 Aug 1971	Operationally ready (CC) at 113 TFG ANG, Andrews AFB MD.
1 Aug 1972	In contract depot work (WM) by Dynalectron Corp (DYNZZ) at Andrews AFB MD. (AVH-18).
5 Aug 1972	Returned to 113 TFG ANG, Andrews AFB MD.
6 Sep 1972	In contract depot work (WM) by Dynalectron Corp (DYNZZ) at Andrews AFB MD.
11 Sep 1972	Returned to 113 TFG ANG, Andrews AFB MD.
13 Dec 1972	In contract depot maintenance (WK) by Fairchild Engine and Aircraft Corporation (FACCF) at Bob Sikes Municipal Airport, Crestview FL.
15 Jan 1973	Returned (PL) to 113 TFG ANG, Andrews AFB MD. (AVH-20).
19 Jan 1973	At 113 TFG ANG, Andrews AFB MD (CC).
14 Mar 1973	In depot maintenance (WO) by SM-ALC at McClellan AFB CA.
4 Jun 1973	Returned (PL) to 113 TFG ANG, Andrews AFB MD.
21 Jun 1973	At 113 TFG ANG, Andrews AFB MD (CC).
8 Jan 1974	In contract depot maintenance (WM) by Dynalectron Corporation (DYNZZ) at Andrews AFB MD. (AVH-22).
12 Jan 1974	At 113 TFG ANG, Andrews AFB MD (CC).
21 Mar 1974	In contract depot maintenance (WM) by Dynalectron Corporation (DYNZZ) at Andrews AFB MD.
26 Mar 1974	Operational (CC) at 113 TFG ANG, Andrews AFB MD.
30 Nov 1974	Assigned unit redesignated 113 TFW ANG, Andrews AFB MD.
5 Dec 1974	In contract depot maintenance (WM) by Dynalectron Corporation (DYNZZ) at Andrews AFB MD.
31 Dec 1975	At 113 TFW ANG, Andrews AFB MD (CC). (AVH-23).
15 May 1976	Displayed at Niagara Falls International Airport. (Dan Hagedorn photo, letter, 29 Apr 97).
14 Sep 1976	In depot maintenance by SM-ALC at Andrews AFB MD. 4,054.0 flying hours. (AVH-25 & AVH-26).
15 Sep 1976	At 113 TFW ANG, Andrews AFB MD. 4,054.0 flying hours.
18 Oct 1976	In depot maintenance by SM-ALC at Andrews AFB MD. 4,054.0 flying hours.
1 Nov 1976	At 113 TFW ANG, Andrews AFB MD. 4,054.0 flying hours.
23 Jun 1977	In contract depot maintenance by Dynalectron Corp. (DYNZZ) at Andrews AFB MD. 4,179.0 flying hours.
10 Sep 1978	At 113 TFW ANG, Andrews AFB MD. 4,380.0 flying hours.
15 Oct 1978	At 113 TFW ANG, Andrews AFB MD. 4,404.0 flying hours.
4 Aug 1979	In contract depot maintenance by Dynalectron Corp. (DYNZZ) at Andrews AFB MD. 4,450.0 flying hours. (AVH-27).
4 Sep 1979	At 113 TFW ANG, Andrews AFB MD. 4,450.0 flying hours.
20 Jun 1980	In depot maintenance at McClellan AFB CA. 4,555.7 flying hours. (GO33B 22 Jan 81).
1 Aug 1980	Returned to 113 TFW ANG, Andrews AFB MD. 4,571.3 flying hours.
24 Nov 1981	Transferred to 466 TFS AFRES, Hill AFB UT. 4,747.1 flying hours. (GO33B Dec 81).
19 Aug 1982	In depot maintenance at Ogden ALC, Hill AFB UT. 4,895.2 flying hours. (GO33B 1 Feb 83).
16 Sep 1982	At 466 TFS AFRES, Hill AFB UT. 4,912.4 flying hours.
4 Oct 1983	At 3280 TTA Group (ATC), Lackland AFB TX. (Possession code: TX. Inventory account: GB). 5,110.8 flying hours. (GO33B 9 Feb 84).
5 Oct 1983	Redesignated GF-105D at 3280 TTA Group (ATC), Lackland AFB TX. (Possession code: TX. Inventory account: GC). 5,110.8 flying hours.

F-105D-30RE 62-4242

Republic Production No: D-441 Production Sequence No: 521

Location: Displayed at Vance AFB, Enid, Oklahoma.

Aircraft Name(s)	Crew	Unit	Date	Description
April K	1 Lt. Thomas G. Ryan	44 TFS 355 TFW		
Miss Julie Girl	Capt. K. Lindell	44 TFS 388 TFW	May 69	In white on left fuselage. "Amazon Ace" in black with ace of spades on right fuselage.
Miss World		44 TFS 388 TFW	Jul 69	Blue globe on right fuselage.
Devil Woman	Maj. Gordy Lewis	44 TFS 388 TFW	Jul 69	In red on left fuselage.
Bachelor II	1Lt. Thomas G. Ryan	44 TFS 355 TFW	Apr 70	
Animal	1Lt. Thomas G. Ryan	44 TFS 355 TFW	Apr 70	On intakes.

Aircraft Chronology

5 Feb 1963	At MOAMA, Brookley AFB AL for depot work (WO). (ACA-88).
20 Feb 1963	Delivered to 18 TFW, Kadena AB, Okinawa.
6 Jan 1964	In depot work (WM) by field team from MOAMA at Kadena AB, Okinawa.
9 Jan 1964	At 18 TFW, Kadena AB, Okinawa.
1 Aug 1964	In contract depot work (WK) at Air Asia, Tainan, Taiwan. (AVH-1).
30 Sep 1964	In depot maintenance (WM) by field team from MOAMA at Kadena AB, Okinawa. (AVH-2).
1 Oct 1964	At 18 TFW, Kadena AB, Okinawa. Assigned crew chief: A1C W. A. Lindaberry. (18 TFW History, Jul–Dec 64, USAF microfilm MO496).
31 Jan 1965	At 18 TFW, Kadena AB, Okinawa. Assigned crew chief: A1C S. Riggs. (18 TFW History, Jan–Jun 65, USAF microfilm MO497).
17 May 1965	At Air Asia, Tainan, Taiwan, for contract depot work (WK). (AVH-4).
19 Sep 1965	Returned to 18 TFW, Kadena AB, Okinawa.

This plane spent the first eight years of its career in the Pacific beginning in 1963 at Kadena Air Base, Okinawa. In 1967 it transferred to Korat, Thailand, with the 388 Tactical Fighter Wing where, for the next two years, it flew combat missions with the 469 and 44 Tactical Fighter Squadrons. After moving with the 44th in 1969 to the 355 Tactical Fighter Wing at Takhli, it continued flying combat missions until it returned to Okinawa in 1971. Staying only three months with its original unit, the plane then spent a little over a year at McConnell Air Force Base, Kansas, before moving to the Virginia Air National Guard at Richmond. Its next transfer brought it to the Air Force Reserve unit at Tinker Air Force Base, Oklahoma, who flew it to England during their summer deployment in 1978. Its last assignment was with the Reserves at Hill Air Force Base, Utah, the last unit to fly the Thunderchief. It deployed with Hill's 466 Tactical Fighter Squadron to Denmark in the summer of 1981 and retired two years later. (Photograph by Ronald L. Shepard, 9 March 1998.)

Nov 1965	At 18 TFW, Kadena AB, Okinawa. Assigned crew chief: TSgt. C. Willis. (18 TFW History, Jul–Dec 65, USAF microfilm MO497).
2 May 1966	In depot work (WM) by SMAMA field team at Kadena AB, Okinawa. (AVH-5).
3 May 1966	At 18 TFW, Kadena AB, Okinawa.
30 Aug 1966	In depot work (WM) by SMAMA field team at Kadena AB, Okinawa.
2 Sep 1966	At 18 TFW, Kadena AB, Okinawa.
31 Dec 1966	While assigned to the 18 TFW, Kadena AB, Okinawa, the aircraft flew 39 hours during the month of December 1966 and had accumulated 1,004 flying hours. (18 TFW History, Jul–Dec 66, USAF microfilm MO498).
15 Mar 1967	While assigned to the 18 TFW, Kadena AB, Okinawa, the aircraft lost a piece of its left aileron during flight due to material failure. (18 TFW History, Jan–Mar 67, USAF microfilm MO498).
20 Apr 1967	In depot maintenance (WM) by SMAMA field team at Kadena AB, Okinawa. (AVH-8).
28 Apr 1967	At 18 TFW, Kadena AB, Okinawa.
31 May 1967	At 12 TFS, 18 TFW, Kadena AB, Okinawa. Aircraft had accumulated 1,114 flying hours. (18 TFW History, Apr–Jun 67, USAF microfilm MO499).
15 Jul 1967	Transferred to the 469 TFS, 388 TFW, Korat RTAB, Thailand. (AVH-8).
6 Oct 1967	In depot maintenance (WM) by SMAMA field team at Korat RTAB, Thailand.
9 Oct 1967	At 388 TFW, Korat RTAB, Thailand.
5 Mar 1968	In depot maintenance (WM) by SMAMA field team at Korat RTAB, Thailand. (AVH-10).
9 Mar 1968	At 388 TFW, Korat RTAB, Thailand.
16 Mar 1968	At Air Asia, Tainan, Taiwan, for contract depot maintenance (WK).
30 May 1968	Returned to 388 TFW, Korat RTAB, Thailand.
14 May 1968	In depot maintenance (WM) by SMAMA field team at Korat RTAB, Thailand.
15 May 1968	At 388 TFW, Korat RTAB, Thailand.
31 Oct 1968	Aircraft had accumulated 2,029.0 flying hours while assigned to the 388 TFW, Korat RTAB, Thailand. (388 TFW History, Oct–Dec 68, USAF microfilm NO585).
30 Jan 1969	Deployed to Takhli RTAB, Thailand, with 388 TFW during runway repairs at Korat RTAB, Thailand. (AVH-12).
31 Jan 1969	Flown on a strike mission in the Barrel Roll region of Laos by 44 TFS pilot, 388 TFW, while operating from Takhli RTAB, Thailand. (388 TFW History, Jan–Mar 69, USAF microfilm NO586).
13 Feb 1969	Flown on a strike mission in the Steel Tiger region of Laos by 44 TFS pilot, 388 TFW, while operating from Takhli RTAB, Thailand.
26 Feb 1969	Flown on a strike mission in the Steel Tiger region of Laos by 44 TFS pilot, 388 TFW, while operating from Takhli RTAB, Thailand.
1 Mar 1969	Returned to 388 TFW, Korat RTAB, Thailand. (AVH-12).
8 Mar 1969	At Air Asia, Tainan, Taiwan, for contract depot work (WK).
30 Apr 1969	Returned to 388 TFW, Korat RTAB, Thailand. While assigned to the 34 TFS, 388 TFW, Korat RTAB, Thailand, the aircraft had accumulated 2,315.9 flying hours. (388 TFW History, Apr–Jun 69, USAF microfilm NO586).
30 Jun 1969	While assigned to the 44 TFS, 388 TFW, Korat RTAB, Thailand, the aircraft flew 50.2 hours in the month of June 1969 and had accumulated 2,433.3 total flying hours.
19 Aug 1969	While assigned to the 44 TFS, 388 TFW, Korat RTAB, Thailand, the aircraft ground aborted due to inoperative nose wheel steering. (388 TFW History, Jul–Sep 69, Vol. III, USAF microfilm NO587).
10 Oct 1969	Transferred with the 44 TFS to the 355 TFW, Takhli RTAB, Thailand. (AVH-12).
23 Nov 1969	In depot maintenance (WM) by SMAMA at Takhli RTAB, Thailand.
29 Nov 1969	At 355 TFW, Takhli RTAB, Thailand.
4 Mar 1970	In depot work (WM) by SMAMA at Takhli RTAB, Thailand. (AVH-14).

11 Mar 1970	At 355 TFW, Takhli RTAB, Thailand.
1 Apr 1970	Combat damaged (VO) at 355 TFW, Takhli RTAB, Thailand.
3 Apr 1970	At 355 TFW, Takhli RTAB, Thailand, available for combat (CC).
31 May 1970	Aircraft assigned to D Flight, 44 TFS, 355 TFW, Takhli RTAB, Thailand. Pilot: 1Lt. Thomas G. Ryan. (44 TFS Aircraft Assignment Roster).
24 Sep 1970	At 355 TFW, Takhli RTAB, Thailand, being prepared for transfer (PL). (AVH-14)
29 Sep 1970	At Air Asia, Tainan, Taiwan, for contract depot maintenance (WK).
19 Jan 1971	Transferred (PL) to the 18 TFW, Kadena AB, Okinawa. (AVH-16).
26 Jan 1971	Operationally ready (CC) at 18 TFW, Kadena AB, Okinawa.
23 Mar 1971	At 18 TFW, Kadena AB, Okinawa, being prepared for transfer (PL).
25 Mar 1971	Operationally ready (CC) at 18 TFW, Kadena AB, Okinawa.
2 Apr 1971	At 18 TFW, Kadena AB, Okinawa, being prepared for transfer (PL).
3 Apr 1971	Transferred (PL) to the 23 TFW, McConnell AFB KS.
7 Apr 1971	Placed in flyable storage (PR) at 23 TFW, McConnell AFB KS.
4 May 1971	Operationally ready (CC) at 23 TFW, McConnell AFB KS.
1 Mar 1972	Carried on assignment roster for the 562 TFS, 23 TFW, at McConnell AFB KS. (Master 23 TFW Aircraft Assignment as of 1 March 1972).
10 May 1972	In contract depot maintenance (WK) by Fairchild Engine and Aircraft Corporation (FACCF) at Bob Sikes Municipal Airport, Crestview FL. (AVH-18).
7 Jun 1972	Returned to the 23 TFW, McConnell AFB KS.
1 Jul 1972	Assigned to the 561 TFS, McConnell AFB KS when the 23 TFW relocated to England AFB LA.
25 Jul 1972	Transferred to 192 TFG ANG, Byrd Field, Richmond VA.
21 Nov 1972	In contract depot work (WM) by Dynalectron Corp (DYNZZ) at Byrd Field, Richmond VA.
29 Aug 1972	Returned to 192 TFG ANG, Byrd Field, Richmond VA.
4 Apr 1973	In contract depot work (WM) by Dynalectron Corp (DYNZZ) at Byrd Field, Richmond VA (AVH-20).
6 Apr 1973	At 192 TFG ANG, Byrd Field, Richmond VA.
16 May 1973	In contract depot work (WM) by Dynalectron Corp (DYNZZ) at Byrd Field, Richmond VA.
17 May 1973	At 192 TFG ANG, Byrd Field, Richmond VA.
20 May 1973	In contract depot work (WM) by Dynalectron Corp (DYNZZ) at Byrd Field, Richmond VA.
13 Jun 1973	At 192 TFG ANG, Byrd Field, Richmond VA.
31 Jan 1974	In contract depot work (WM) by Dynalectron Corp (DYNZZ) at Byrd Field, Richmond VA. (AVH-22).
19 Feb 1974	At 192 TFG ANG, Byrd Field, Richmond VA.
13 Jan 1975	In contract depot work (WM) by Dynalectron Corp (DYNZZ) at Byrd Field, Richmond VA. (AVH-23).
7 Feb 1975	At 192 TFG ANG, Byrd Field, Richmond VA.
10 Feb 1975	In contract depot maintenance (WK) by Fairchild Engine and Aircraft Corporation (FACCF) at Bob Sikes Municipal Airport, Crestview FL.
11 Jul 1975	At 192 TFG ANG, Byrd Field, Richmond VA. (AVH-23 & AVH-24).
22 Feb 1976	In depot maintenance (WM) by SM-ALC at Byrd Field, Richmond VA. (AVH-24).
28 Sep 1976	At 192 TFG ANG, Byrd Field, Richmond VA. 4,181 flying hours.
1 Oct 1976	In contract depot maintenance (WK) by Fairchild Engine and Aircraft Corporation (FACCF) at Bob Sikes Municipal Airport, Crestview FL. 4,181.0 flying hours. (AVH-25 & AVH-26).
22 Dec 1977	Transferred to the 465 TFS AFRES, Tinker AFB OK. 4,187.0 flying hours.
10 Jun 1978	Deployed under "Coronet Oriole" with 465 TFS to Sculthorpe, England, from Tinker AFB OK. (British Aviation Review, Dec 1995).
23 Jun 1978	Returned from England to Tinker AFB OK.
25 May 1979	While assigned to the 465 TFS AFRES, Tinker AFB OK, the aircraft ground aborted due to a bad

voltage regulator that caused the AC generator to drop off line. (301 TFW History 1 Apr–30 Jun 1979, USAF microfilm 343832).

30 Jun 1979	While assigned to the 465 TFS AFRES, Tinker AFB OK, the aircraft flew 5.8 hours during the month of June 1979 and had accumulated a total of 4,480.5 flying hours. The assigned crew chief was Bradley. (301 TFW History, Apr–Jun 1979, USAF microfilm 34382).
21 Aug 1979	In contract depot maintenance (FACBM) at Tinker AFB OK. 4,480.5 flying hours. (AVH-27).
27 Aug 1979	At 465 TFS AFRES, Tinker AFB OK. 4,501.0 flying hours.
30 Jun 1980	In depot maintenance ("FACBM") Tinker AFB OK. 4,745.3 flying hours. (GO33B 22 Jan 81).
25 Jul 1980	At 465 TFS AFRES, Tinker AFB OK. 4,762.7 flying hours.
30 Jul 1980	Transferred to 466 TFS AFRES, Hill AFB UT. 4,762.7 flying hours.
24 Oct 1980	In depot maintenance at McClellan AFB, Sacramento CA. 4,809.2 flying hours.
19 Nov 1980	At 466 TFS AFRES, Hill AFB UT. 4,827.7 flying hours.
23 Jun 1981	In depot maintenance at Ogden ALC, Hill AFB UT. 4,945.8 flying hours. (GO33B Dec 81 & GO33B 1 Feb 83).
15 Aug 1981	Deployed under "Coronet Rudder" with 466 TFS to Skrydstrup, Denmark, from Hill AFB UT. (British Aviation Review, Dec 1995).
29 Aug 1981	Returned from Denmark to Hill AFB UT.
15 Jun 1983	At 466 TFS AFRES, Hill AFB UT. Inventory account "ZW"—School or museum. 5,344.2 flying hours. (GO33B 9 Feb 84).
23 Sep 1986	In USAF Museum account at Vance AFB OK. (AMARC Letter, 23 Sep 86).

F-105D-30RE 62-4253

Republic Production No: D-452 Production Sequence No: 532

Location: At the Kansas Air National Guard area, McConnell AFB, Wichita, Kansas.

Aircraft Name(s)	Crew	Unit	Date	Description
Thunder Bee	Capt. D. Nelson	333 TFS 355 TFW	Jul 69	Name on both intakes. Art on left fuselage with name in yellow and black stripes.
Rajin Cajun/Rych Bitch		333 TFS 355 TFW	Jan 70	On intakes.

Aircraft Chronology

6 Mar 1963	At MOAMA, Brookley AFB AL for depot work (WO) after production by Republic Aviation. Assigned (PL) to the 18 TFW at Kadena AB, Okinawa. (ACA-88).
24 Mar 1963	One of the last three F-105Ds delivered to the 18 TFW at Kadena AB, Okinawa.
22 Dec 1963	In depot maintenance (WM) by MOAMA field team at the 18 TFW, Kadena AB, Okinawa.
2 Jan 1964	Operational (CC) at the 18 TFW, Kadena AB, Okinawa.
29 Aug 1964	In contract depot work (WK) at Air Asia, Tainan, Taiwan. (AVH-1).
30 Sep 1964	At 18 TFW, Kadena AB, Okinawa. Assigned crew chief: TSgt. S. Pence. (18 TFW History, Jul–Dec 64, USAF microfilm MO496).
31 Jan 1965	At 18 TFW, Kadena AB, Okinawa. Assigned crew chief: TSgt. S. Pence. (18 TFW History, Jan–Jun 65, USAF microfilm MO497).

Arriving at Kadena Air Base, Okinawa, on 6 March 1963, this was one of the last F-105s that formed the initial 83-aircraft fleet of the 18 Tactical Fighter Wing. The plane remained with the 18th for the next five years, transferring to combat duties in July 1968 with the 355 Tactical Fighter Wing at Takhli, Thailand. When Takhli closed at the end of 1970, the plane moved on to McConnell Air Force Base where it joined the Kansas Air National Guard. After nine years in Kansas, it flew briefly with the Air Force Reserve units at Carswell Air Force Base, Texas, and Hill Air Force Base, Utah. It retired at Hill in November 1983 and found its way back to the Kansas Guard where it sits in a display of well restored planes formerly flown by that unit. (Photograph by author, 6 August 1995.)

18 Feb 1965	Crash damaged (WJ) at 18 TFW, Kadena AB, Okinawa. (AVH-4).
2 Mar 1965	At Air Asia, Tainan, Taiwan, for crash damage repair (WR).
26 Sep 1965	At 18 TFW, Kadena AB, Okinawa.
Nov 1965	At 18 TFW, Kadena AB, Okinawa. Assigned crew chief: A1C B. Mitchell. (18 TFW History, Jul–Dec 65, USAF microfilm MO497).
29 Apr 1966	At 18 TFW, Kadena AB, Okinawa. (AVH-5).
8 May 1966	At Korat RTAB, Thailand, with the 18 TFW.
16 Jun 1966	At Air Asia, Tainan, Taiwan, for contract depot work (WK).
23 Jun 1966	Returned to 18 TFW, Kadena AB, Okinawa.
21 Sep 1966	At 18 TFW, Kadena AB, Okinawa.
31 Dec 1966	While assigned to the 18 TFW, Kadena AB, Okinawa, the aircraft flew 19 hours during the month of December 1966 and had accumulated 824 flying hours. (18 TFW History, Jul–Dec 66, USAF microfilm MO498).
23 Apr 1967	At 18 TFW, Kadena AB, Okinawa. (AVH-8).
25 Sep 1967	In depot maintenance (WM) by SMAMA field team at Kadena AB, Okinawa.
31 Oct 1967	At 18 TFW, Kadena AB, Okinawa.
29 Jan 1968	At Osan AB, Korea, with the 18 TFW in response to the U.S.S. Pueblo incident. (AVH-10).
6 Mar 1968	At 18 TFW, Kadena AB, Okinawa.
15 Mar 1968	At Osan AB, Korea, with 18 TFW.
3 Jun 1968	At 18 TFW, Kadena AB, Okinawa.
4 Jun 1968	In depot maintenance (WM) by SMAMA field team at Kadena AB, Okinawa.
9 Jun 1968	At 18 TFW, Kadena AB, Okinawa.
17 Jul 1968	Transferred to 355 TFW, Takhli RTAB Thailand.
11 Oct 1968	In depot repair (WO & VN) by SMAMA at Takhli RTAB, Thailand.
1 Nov 1968	While assigned to the 355 TFW, Takhli RTAB, Thailand, aircraft had accumulated 1,458.2 flying hours. (355 TFW History, Oct–Dec 68, USAF microfilm NO466).
7 Nov 1968	At 355 TFW, Takhli RTAB, Thailand (VO).

2 Dec 1968	At 355 TFW, Takhli RTAB, Thailand (CC).
28 Feb 1969	While assigned to the 355 TFW, Takhli RTAB, Thailand, the aircraft flew 92.4 hours during the month of February 1969 and had accumulated 1,705.3 flying hours. (355 TFW History, Jan–Mar 69, Vol. II, USAF Microfilm NO467).
24 Mar 1969	In depot maintenance (WM) by SMAMA field team at Takhli RTAB, Thailand. (AVH-12).
25 Mar 1969	At 355 TFW, Takhli RTAB, Thailand.
8 Apr 1969	At Air Asia, Tainan, Taiwan, for contract depot work (WK).
2 Jun 1969	Returned to 355 TFW, Takhli RTAB, Thailand.
3 Dec 1969	In depot maintenance (WM) by SMAMA field team at Takhli RTAB, Thailand.
12 Dec 1969	At 355 TFW, Takhli RTAB, Thailand.
24 Oct 1970	At 355 TFW, Takhli RTAB, Thailand, being prepared for transfer (PL). (AVH-14).
27 Oct 1970	Transferred (PL) to 23 TFW, McConnell AFB KS.
4 Nov 1970	Placed in flyable storage (PR) at 23 TFW, McConnell AFB KS.
4 Jan 1971	At 23 TFW, McConnell AFB KS being prepared for transfer (PL).
26 Jan 1971	In depot work (WO) by SMAMA at McClellan AFB CA. (AVH-16).
17 Mar 1971	Transferred (PL) to 184 TFG ANG, McConnell AFB KS.
16 Dec 1972	In contract depot maintenance (WK) by Fairchild Engine and Aircraft Corporation (FACCF) at Bob Sikes Municipal Airport, Crestview FL. (AVH-18).
16 Jan 1973	Returned to 184 TFG ANG, McConnell AFB KS. (AVH-20).
17 Apr 1973	In depot maintenance (WO) by SM-ALC at McClellan AFB CA.
15 Aug 1973	Returned to 184 TFG ANG, McConnell AFB KS.
3 Jan 1974	Assigned to combat crew training duties (TF) at 184 TFG ANG, McConnell AFB KS.
27 Nov 1974	In contract depot work (WM) by Dynalectron Corporation (DYNZZ) at McConnell AFB KS. (AVH-22).
12 Dec 1974	At 184 TFTG ANG, McConnell AFB KS for combat crew training (TF).
28 Jan 1975	In contract depot work (WM) by Dynalectron Corporation (DYNZZ) at McConnell AFB KS. (AVH-23).
5 Feb 1975	At 184 TFTG ANG, McConnell AFB KS for combat crew training (TF).
1 Oct 1976	In depot maintenance by SM-ALC at McConnell AFB KS. 4,008.0 flying hours. (AVH-25 & AVH-26).
12 Oct 1976	At 184 TFG ANG, McConnell AFB KS for student and combat crew training (TF). 4,008.0 flying hours.
1 Mar 1978	At SM-ALC depot, McClellan AFB CA. 4,303.0 flying hours.
13 Apr 1978	At 184 TFG ANG, McConnell AFB KS for student and combat crew training (TF). 4,316.0 flying hours.
25 Apr 1978	At 184 TFG ANG, McConnell AFB KS for student and combat crew training (TF). 4,430.0 flying hours.
25 Apr 1978	At 184 TFG ANG, McConnell AFB KS. Possession code: BQ. 4,316.0 flying hours.
17 Aug 1979	In contract depot maintenance (DYNFW) at McConnell AFB KS. 4,723.5 flying hours. (AVH-27).
30 Aug 1979	At 184 TFG ANG, McConnell AFB KS for student and combat crew training (TF). 4,741.8 flying hours.
11 Aug 1980	At 457 TFS AFRES, Carswell AFB TX. 4,8481 flying hours. (GO33B 22 Jan 81).
26 Feb 1982	At 466 TFS AFRES, Hill AFB UT. 5,122.8 flying hours. (GO33B 1 Feb 83).
Nov 1983	Disposed of at Hill AFB UT. (Aviation News 19 Feb 1984).

F-105D-30RE 62-4259

Republic Production No: D-458 Production Sequence No: 538

Location: At Security Police Flightline Training Area #7, Lackland AFB, San Antonio, Texas.

Aircraft Name(s)	Crew	Unit	Date	Description
Cajun Queen	Maj. Ronald C. Senac	333 TFS 355 TFW	May 70	White letters on red background on both intakes.

Aircraft Chronology

29 Mar 1963	USAF production acceptance at Republic Aviation, Farmingdale NY. (ACA-88).
29 Mar 1963	Delivered to 4 TFW, Seymour Johnson AFB NC.
13 Mar 1964	At Eglin AFB FL with 4485 Test Wing.
25 Jun 1964	At 4 TFW, Seymour Johnson AFB NC.
1 Aug 1964	At 4485 TW TAC, Eglin AFB FL. (AVH-1).
23 Feb 1965	At 4 TFW, Seymour Johnson AFB NC. (AVH-4).
9 Aug 1965	At MOAMA, Brookley AFB AL for depot work (WO).
16 Dec 1965	Returned to 4 TFW, Seymour Johnson AFB NC.
22 Dec 1965	While assigned to the 4 TFW, Seymour Johnson AFB NC, the aircraft air aborted due to a landing gear solenoid that failed to operate. (4 TFW History, Jul–Dec 65, Vol. II, USAF microfilm MO292).
31 Dec 1965	While assigned to the 4 TFW, Seymour Johnson AFB NC, the aircraft flew 18.0 hours for the month of December 1965 and had 659.0 total flying hours. Assigned Crew Chief: TSgt. Emerson. (4 TFW History, Jul–Dec 65, Vol. II, USAF microfilm MO292).
24 Jun 1966	At SMAMA, McClellan AFB CA for depot work (WO). (AVH-5).
8 Jul 1966	Returned to 4 TFW, Seymour Johnson AFB NC.

This plane spent its first three years flying F-105 tests with the 4 Tactical Fighter Wing at Seymour Johnson Air Forced Base, North Carolina, and Eglin Air Force Base, Florida. In 1966 it transferred to the 41 Air Division at Yokota Air Base, Japan, and, for the next year, rotated to and from Osan Air Base, Korea, where it sat on alert with nuclear weapons. In August 1967, it was an attrition replacement to the 355 Tactical Fighter Wing at Takhli, Thailand, and flew the final phases of the Rolling Thunder bombing campaign over North Vietnam. When Takhli closed at the end of 1970, the plane transferred to the 18 Tactical Fighter Wing at Kadena Air Base, Okinawa. The 18th flew it in and out of Taegu Air Base, Korea, one of the forward bases used by the 18th following the U.S.S. Pueblo incident in January 1968. In 1972 the plane went from Okinawa to the Air Force Reserve's 465 Tactical Fighter Squadron at Tinker Air Force Base, Oklahoma, where it was severely damaged in a landing accident. Its last flying assignment, before retirement in 1983, was with the Reserve's 466 Tactical Fighter Squadron at Hill Air Force Base, Utah. (Photograph by author, 4 August 1997.)

31 Jul 1966	While assigned to the 4 TFW, Seymour Johnson AFB NC, the aircraft flew 25.7 hours for the month of July 1966 and had accumulated 865.1 flying hours. Assigned crew chief: SSgt. L. G. McClain. (4 TFW History, Jul–Dec 66, USAF microfilm MO293).
13 Sep 1966	At Air Asia, Tainan, Taiwan, for contract depot work from 6441 TFW. (AVH-5).
13 Nov 1966	At 41 AD, Yokota AB, Japan.
3 Jan 1967	At Osan AB, Korea, for nuclear weapon alert with the 41 AD. (AVH-8).
7 Apr 1967	At 41 AD, Yokota AB, Japan.
5 Jul 1967	At Osan AB, Korea, for nuclear weapon alert with the 41 AD.
28 Jul 1967	At 41 AD, Yokota AB, Japan.
23 Aug 1967	Transferred to the 355 TFW, Takhli RTAB, Thailand.
28 Aug 1967	Flown by Maj. Donald M. Russell (333 TFS, 355 TFW) on a combat mission that lasted 2.4 hours from Takhli RTAB, Thailand. (Maj. Russell's Individual Flight Record as of 31 Dec 67).
2 Sep 1967	In depot maintenance (WM) by SMAMA field team at Takhli RTAB, Thailand.
4 Sep 1967	At 355 TFW, Takhli RTAB, Thailand.
16 Sep 1967	In depot maintenance (WM) by SMAMA field team at Takhli RTAB, Thailand.
19 Oct 1967	At 355 TFW, Takhli RTAB, Thailand.
24 Oct 1967	At 355 TFW, Takhli RTAB, Thailand being prepared (PL) for delivery to depot.
30 Oct 1967	At Air Asia, Tainan, Taiwan, for contract depot work (WK).
6 Jan 1968	At 355 TFW, Takhli RTAB, Thailand. (AVH-10).
4 Feb 1968	In depot maintenance (WM) by SMAMA field team at Takhli RTAB, Thailand.
8 Feb 1968	At 355 TFW, Takhli RTAB, Thailand.
14 Jun 1968	In depot maintenance (WM) by SMAMA field team at Takhli RTAB, Thailand.
17 Jun 1968	At 355 TFW, Takhli RTAB, Thailand.
2 Oct 1968	At Air Asia, Tainan, Taiwan, for contract depot work (WK).
19 Nov 1968	Returned to 355 TFW, Takhli RTAB, Thailand.
30 Nov 1968	While assigned to the 355 TFW, Takhli RTAB, Thailand, the aircraft had accumulated 1,933.0 flying hours. (355 TFW History, Oct–Dec 68, USAF microfilm NO466).
28 Feb 1969	While assigned to the 355 TFW, Takhli RTAB, Thailand, the aircraft flew 8.7 hours during the month of February 1969 and had accumulated 2,137.3 flying hours. (355 TFW History, Jan–Mar 69, Vol. II, USAF Microfilm NO467).
3 Mar 1969	In depot maintenance (WM) by SMAMA RAM team at 355 TFW, Takhli RTAB, Thailand. Aircraft was the prototype for a depot modification to twenty-five 355 TFW aircraft that required 600 labor-hours per aircraft. (AVH-12 & 355 TFW History, Jan–Mar 69, USAF microfilm NO466).
15 Mar 1969	Depot modification completed and aircraft turned back over to 355 TFW, Takhli RTAB, Thailand.
6 Dec 1969	At Air Asia, Tainan, Taiwan, for contract depot work (WK).
11 Feb 1970	Returned to 355 TFW, Takhli RTAB, Thailand. (AVH-14).
10 Oct 1970	Transferred to 18 TFW, Kadena AB, Okinawa.
11 Feb 1971	At Air Asia, Tainan, Taiwan, for contract depot work (WK). (AVH-16).
9 Apr 1971	Returned to 18 TFW, Kadena AB, Okinawa.
20 Oct 1971	At Taegu AB, Korea, with 18 TFW.
12 Nov 1971	Returned to 18 TFW, Kadena AB, Okinawa.
30 Nov 1971	At Taegu AB, Korea, with 18 TFW.
3 Dec 1971	Returned to 18 TFW, Kadena AB, Okinawa.
16 Dec 1971	In depot maintenance (WM) by SMAMA at Kadena AB, Okinawa.
11 Apr 1972	Departed (PL) 18 TFW, Kadena AB, Okinawa, Japan. (AVH-18).
12 Apr 1972	Arrived at SM-ALC, McClellan AFB CA for depot work (WO).

18 Aug 1972	Transferred (PL) to 507 TFG AFRES, Tinker AFB OK.
29 Aug 1972	At 507 TFG AFRES, Tinker AFB OK (CC).
31 Mar 1973	Assigned to 507 CMTSQ AFRES, Tinker AFB OK. (AVH-20).
23 May 1973	At 507 CMTSQ AFRES, Tinker AFB OK.
24 Mar 1974	At 507 CMTSQ AFRES, Tinker AFB OK. Assignment code WN. (AVH-22).
May 1974	At 507 TFG AFRES, Tinker AFB OK. "During flight with pilot Jim Parker, right hand anti-spin valve failed closed. When gear was lowered the brakes were still locked. Aircraft slid down runway 35 at Tinker AFB blowing main tires. The plane ended up with left wing stuck in the ground about 3 feet deep with the left MLG inserted into the side of the fuselage. The nose gear went out the right side of the wheel well. Took us about 18 months to rebuild her. 'Boot legged' a lot of work to keep it as Class 'B'. Replaced the wing and other major parts." (Gabby Hays, former AFRES F-105 crew chief, e-mail, 18 Mar 1996).
28 Jun 1974	In depot maintenance (WM) by SM-ALC at Tinker AFB OK. (AVH-22).
5 Sep 1974	At 507 CMTSQ AFRES, Tinker AFB OK. In crash damage repair (WN).
16 Sep 1974	At 507 CMTSQ AFRES, Tinker AFB OK (CC).
16 Oct 1974	Assigned unit redesignated 507 CLMSQ AFRES, Tinker AFB OK (CC).
25 Mar 1975	In depot maintenance (WM) by SM-ALC at Tinker AFB OK. (AVH-23).
8 Apr 1975	At 507 CLMSQ AFRES, Tinker AFB OK. (AVH-23 & AVH-24).
12 Jun 1975	In depot maintenance (WM) by SM-ALC at Tinker AFB OK.
27 Jun 1975	At 507 CLMSQ AFRES, Tinker AFB OK.
16 Mar 1976	In depot maintenance (WM) by SM-ALC at Tinker AFB OK. (AVH-24).
26 Apr 1976	In contract depot work at Aero Corporation (AROLF), Moultrie GA. 3,926.0 flying hours. (AVH-25 & AVH-26).
24 Nov 1976	At 507 TFG AFRES, Tinker AFB OK. 3,926.0 flying hours.
11 Apr 1979	While assigned to the 465 TFS AFRES, Tinker AFB OK, the aircraft ground aborted due to no rudder movement with stability augmentation. (301 TFW History 1 Apr–30 Jun 1979, USAF microfilm 343832).
12 Apr 1979	While assigned to the 465 TFS AFRES, Tinker AFB OK, the aircraft ground aborted due to the 25" accumulator not holding pressure. (301 TFW History 1 Apr–30 Jun 1979, USAF microfilm 343832).
17 Apr 1979	While assigned to the 465 TFS AFRES, Tinker AFB OK, the aircraft ground aborted due to a faulty actuator causing the pilot's seat to stick. (301 TFW History 1 Apr–30 Jun 1979, USAF microfilm 343832).
12 May 1979	Deployed under "Coronet Palomino" with 465 TFS to Gioia Del Colle, Italy, from Tinker AFB OK. The aircraft flew 58.7 hours during the month of May 1979. The assigned crew chief was Carlson. (301 TFW History 1 Apr–30 Jun 1979, USAF microfilm 343832).
24 May 1979	Returned from Italy to Tinker AFB OK.
30 Jun 1979	While assigned to the 465 TFS AFRES, Tinker AFB OK, the aircraft flew 3.5 hours during the month of June 1979 and had accumulated a total of 4,561.7 flying hours. The assigned crew chief was Carlson. (301 TFW History, Apr–Jun 1979, USAF microfilm 34382).
5 Mar 1980	At McClellan AFB CA for depot maintenance. 4,7271 flying hours. (GO33B 24 Jun 80).
14 Apr 1980	At 465 TFS, Tinker AFB OK. 4,735.2 flying hours.
23 Jun 1980	In depot maintenance (FACBM) at Tinker AFB OK. 4,758.5 flying hours. (GO33B 22 Jan 81).
15 Jul 1980	At 465 TFS AFRES, Tinker AFB OK. 4,765.4 flying hours.
1 Oct 1980	Transferred to the 466 TFS AFRES, Hill AFB UT. 4,803.7 flying hours.
15 Dec 1980	In depot maintenance at Ogden ALC, Hill AFB UT. 4,858.3 flying hours.
24 Sep 1981	In depot maintenance at Ogden ALC, Hill AFB UT. 4,963.4 flying hours. (GO33B Dec 81 & GO33B 1 Feb 83).
8 Oct 1981	At 466 TFS AFRES, Hill AFB UT. 4,976.0 flying hours.

1 Dec 1982	In depot maintenance at Ogden ALC, Hill AFB UT. 5,179.7 flying hours. (GO33B 1 Feb 83).
16 Dec 1982	At 419 TFG AFRES, Hill AFB UT. 5,179.7 flying hours.
17 Dec 1982	At 466 TFS AFRES, Hill AFB UT. 5,186.1 flying hours. (GOB 9 Feb 84).
4 Oct 1983	At 3280 TTA Group (ATC), Lackland AFB TX. (Possession code: TX. Inventory account: GB). 5,263.1 flying hours.
5 Oct 1983	Redesignated GF-105D at 3280 TTA Group (ATC), Lackland AFB TX. (Possession code: TX. Inventory account: GC). 5,263.1 flying hours.

F-105D-31RE 62-4279

Republic Production No: D-478 Production Sequence No: 558

Location: At Security Police Flightline Training Area #7, Lackland AFB, San Antonio, Texas.

Aircraft Chronology

26 Mar 1963	USAF production acceptance from Republic Aviation, Farmingdale NY and delivery to MOAMA, Brookley AFB AL for depot work. (ACA-88).
31 Mar 1963	At MOAMA, Brookley AFB AL for depot work.
13 Apr 1963	Delivered to 8 TFW, Itazuke AB, Japan.
13 May 1964	Transferred to 41 AD, Yokota AB, Japan. (AVH-1).
21 Jul 1964	Transferred to 18 TFW, Kadena AB, Okinawa.
30 Sep 1964	At 18 TFW, Kadena AB, Okinawa. Assigned crew chief: A1C C. Gehring. (18 TFW History, Jul–Dec 64, USAF microfilm MO496).
31 Jan 1965	At 18 TFW, Kadena AB, Okinawa. Assigned crew chief: SSgt. C. Gehring. (18 TFW History, Jan–Jun 65, USAF microfilm MO497).
6 Apr 1965	At Tainan, Taiwan, for contract depot work (WK). (AVH-4).
21 Apr 1965	Returned to 18 TFW Kadena AB, Okinawa.
6 Dec 1965	At Tainan, Taiwan, for contract depot work (WK).
30 Nov 1965	At 18 TFW, Kadena AB, Okinawa. Assigned crew chief: SSgt. M. Maley. (18 TFW History, Jul–Dec 65, USAF microfilm MO497).
31 Dec 1966	While assigned to the 18 TFW, Kadena AB, Okinawa, the aircraft flew 29 hours during the month of December 1966 and had accumulated 878 flying hours. (18 TFW History, Jul–Dec 66, USAF microfilm MO498).
15 Feb 1967	At Air Asia, Tainan, Taiwan, for contract depot work (WK). (AVH-8).
24 Apr 1967	Returned to 18 TFW, Kadena AB, Okinawa, and assigned to 12 TFS. 910 flying hours. (18 TFW History, Apr–Jun 67, USAF microfilm MO498).
17 Sep 1967	In depot maintenance by SMAMA field team at Kadena AB, Okinawa. (AVH-18).
18 Sep 1967	At 18 TFW, Kadena AB, Okinawa.
23 Jan 1968	Deployed to Osan AB, Korea, with 18 TFW for U.S.S. Pueblo incident. (AVH-10).
8 Feb 1968	Returned to 18 TFW, Kadena AB, Okinawa.
19 Feb 1968	At Osan AB, Korea, with 18 TFW.
20 Mar 1968	Returned to 18 TFW, Kadena AB, Okinawa.
22 Mar 1968	At Osan AB Korea, with 18 TFW.

F-105D 62-4279 spent nine years in the Pacific beginning with its first assignment in April 1963 to the 8 Tactical Fighter Wing at Itazuke Air Base, Japan. A year later, when the 8th was discontinued and Itazuke became a forward operating base, the plane spent two months at Yokota Air Base, Japan, before going to the 18 Tactical Fighter Wing at Kadena Air Base, Okinawa. It was one of the first F-105s to respond to the U.S.S. Pueblo incident in January 1968 and spent the next three years flying in and out of three bases in South Korea from its home at Kadena. In August 1972, it transferred with its sister F-105D 62-4259 (described previously), to the Air Force Reserve's 465 Tactical Fighter Squadron at Tinker Air Force Base, Oklahoma. Its last three years were with the Reserve's 466 Tactical Fighter Squadron at Hill Air Force Base, Utah, who flew it on its NATO deployment to Denmark in August 1981. (Photograph by author, 4 August 1997.)

13 Jun 1968	At 18 TFW, Kadena AB, Okinawa.
28 Jun 1968	In depot maintenance (WM) by SMAMA at Kadena AB, Okinawa.
29 Jun 1968	At 18 TFW, Kadena AB, Okinawa.
16 Aug 1968	At Kwangju AB, Korea, with 18 TFW.
31 Aug 1968	Returned to 18 TFW, Kadena AB, Okinawa.
14 Jun 1969	At Air Asia, Tainan, Taiwan, for contract depot work (WK). (AVH-12).
9 Aug 1969	Returned to 18 TFW, Kadena AB, Okinawa.
18 Aug 1969	At Kwangju AB, Korea, with 18 TFW.
21 Aug 1969	Returned to 18 TFW, Kadena AB, Okinawa.
18 Oct 1969	In depot maintenance (WM) by SMAMA at Kadena AB, Okinawa.
21 Oct 1969	At 18 TFW, Kadena AB, Okinawa.
15 Dec 1969	At Air Asia, Tainan, Taiwan, for contract depot work (WK).
19 Feb 1970	Returned to 18 TFW, Kadena AB, Okinawa. (AVH-14).
24 Jun 1970	At Kwangju AB, Korea, with 18 TFW.
27 Jun 1970	Returned to 18 TFW, Kadena AB, Okinawa.
21 Oct 1970	At Kwangju AB, Korea, with 18 TFW.
24 Oct 1970	Returned to 18 TFW, Kadena AB, Okinawa.
26 Oct 1970	At Kwangju AB, Korea, with 18 TFW.
4 Nov 1970	Returned to 18 TFW, Kadena AB, Okinawa.
5 Feb 1971	At Air Asia, Tainan, Taiwan, for contract depot work (WK). (AVH-16).
23 Mar 1971	Returned to 18 TFW, Kadena AB, Okinawa.
28 Sep 1971	At Taegu AB, Korea, with 18 TFW.
1 Oct 1971	Returned to 18 TFW, Kadena AB, Okinawa.

22 Oct 1971	At Taegu AB, Korea, with 18 TFW.
29 Oct 1971	Returned to 18 TFW, Kadena AB, Okinawa.
3 Dec 1971	In depot work (WM) by SMAMA at Kadena AB, Okinawa.
10 Dec 1971	At 18 TFW, Kadena AB, Okinawa.
16 Apr 1972	Departed (PL) 18 TFW, Kadena AB, Okinawa, Japan. (AVH-18).
19 Apr 1972	Arrived at SM-ALC, McClellan AFB CA for depot work (WO).
18 Aug 1972	Transferred (PL) to 507 TFG AFRES, Tinker AFB OK.
29 Aug 1972	At (CC) 507 TFG AFRES, Tinker AFB OK.
19 Mar 1973	In depot maintenance (WM) by SM-ALC at Tinker AFB OK. (AVH-20).
21 Mar 1973	At (CC) 507 TFG AFRES, Tinker AFB OK.
31 Mar 1973	Assigned unit changed to 507 CMTSQ AFRES, Tinker AFB OK.
16 Apr 1974	In depot maintenance (WM) by SM-ALC at Tinker AFB OK. (AVH-22).
23 Apr 1974	At 507 CMTSQ AFRES, Tinker AFB OK.
16 Oct 1974	Assigned unit redesignated 507 CLMSQ AFRES, Tinker AFB OK.
27 Jan 1975	In depot maintenance (WM) by SM-ALC at Tinker AFB OK. (AVH-23).
14 Feb 1975	At 507 CLMSQ AFRES, Tinker AFB OK.
10 Jun 1975	In depot maintenance (WM) by SM-ALC at Tinker AFB OK. (AVH-23 & AVH-24).
31 Jul 1975	At 507 CLMSQ AFRES, Tinker AFB OK.
11 Mar 1976	In depot maintenance (WM) by SM-ALC at Tinker AFB OK. (AVH-24).
8 Apr 1976	At 507 TFG AFRES, Tinker AFB OK. 2,981 flying hours.
1 Aug 1976	In depot maintenance (DM) by SM-ALC at Tinker AFB OK. 2,983 flying hours.
4 Aug 1976	At 507 TFG AFRES, Tinker AFB OK. 2,983 flying hours.
24 Sep 1976	In contract depot maintenance (DK) by Fairchild Engine and Aircraft Corporation (FACCF) at Bob Sikes Municipal Airport, Crestview FL. 2,983 flying hours.
23 Aug 1978	In contract depot maintenance (DYNFW) at Tinker AFB OK. 3,171.0 flying hours. (AVH-26).
20 Oct 1978	At 465 TFS AFRES, Tinker AFB OK. 3,174.0 flying hours.
30 Jun 1979	While assigned to the 465 TFS AFRES, Tinker AFB OK, the aircraft flew 26.2 hours during the month of June 1979 and had accumulated a total of 3,362.7 flying hours. The assigned crew chief was Rodgers. (301 TFW History, Apr–Jun 1979, USAF microfilm 34382).
2 Apr 1980	In depot maintenance Fairchild Aircraft Corporation (FACBM) at Tinker AFB OK. 3,548.5 flying hours. (GO33B 24 Jun 80).
14 May 1980	At 465 TFS, Tinker AFB OK. 3,562.7 flying hours.
11 Aug 1980	In depot maintenance at McClellan AFB CA. 3,564.0 flying hours. (GO33B 22 Jan 81).
24 Sep 1980	At Hill AFB UT but still assigned to 465 TFS AFRES from Tinker AFB OK. 3,582.5 flying hours.
1 Oct 1980	Reassigned to 466 TFS AFRES, Hill AFB UT. 3,582.5 flying hours.
15 Aug 1981	Deployed under "Coronet Rudder" with 466 TFS to Skrydstrup, Denmark, from Hill AFB UT. (British Aviation Review, Dec 1995).
29 Aug 1981	Returned from Denmark to Hill AFB UT.
11 Feb 1982	In depot maintenance at Ogden ALC, Hill AFB UT. 3,767.4 flying hours. (GO33B 1 Feb 83).
4 Jun 1983	One of 24 F-105s flown on ceremonial final mission at Hill AFB UT. After mission, aircraft was one of seven delivered to 3280 TTA Group (ATC), Lackland AFB TX for security police flightline training. (Possession code: TX. Inventory account: GB). 4,031.6 flying hours. (GO33B 9 Feb 84).
5 Jun 1983	Redesignated GF-105D at 3280 TTA Group (ATC), Lackland AFB TX. (Possession code: TX. Inventory account: GC). 4,031.6 flying hours.

F-105D–31RE 62-4299

Republic Production No: D-498 Production Sequence No: 578

Location: At the Travis Air Force Museum, Travis AFB, Fairfield, California.

Aircraft Name(s)	Crew	Unit	Date	Description
Boss Hog		457 TFS AFRES		
Desert Fox		466 TFS AFRES	Apr 83	Fox with Arab head dress flying F-105D with yellow stripe and HI on tail. Yellow scarf streaming behind fox. Left fuselage.

Aircraft Chronology

19 Apr 1963	USAF production acceptance from Republic Aviation, Farmingdale NY. (ACA-88).
20 Apr 1963	Delivered to 355 TFW, George AFB CA.
20 Nov 1964	Transferred with the 355 TFW to McConnell AFB KS. (AVH-2).
10 Apr 1965	At SMAMA, McClellan AFB CA for depot work (WO). (AVH-4).
9 May 1965	Returned to the 355 TFW, McConnell AFB KS.
12 Jun 1965	Deployed to Korat RTAB, Thailand, with the 357 TFS, 355 TFW, from McConnell AFB KS. Assigned Crew Chief: SSgt. Schmidt. (18 TFW History, Jan–Jun 65, USAF microfilm MO497).
20 Oct 1965	Transferred to the 23 TFW, McConnell AFB KS. (AVH-4).
22 Oct 1965	At SMAMA, McClellan AFB CA for depot work (WO).
23 Nov 1965	At 23 TFW, McConnell AFB KS.
21 Jan 1966	At Yokota AB, Japan, with 355 TFW from 23 TFW. (AVH-5).
28 Feb 1966	At Osan AB, Korea, for nuclear weapon alert with 6441 TFW.
30 Apr 1966	At Air Asia, Tainan, Taiwan, for contract depot work (WK).
29 Jun 1966	At 6441 TFW, Yokota AB, Japan.
29 Aug 1966	At Air Asia, Tainan, Taiwan, for contract depot work (WK).
3 Dec 1966	At 41 AD, Yokota AB, Japan.
24 Feb 1967	In storage (XT) at 18 TFW, Kadena AB, Okinawa. (AVH-8).
28 Feb 1967	Operationally ready (CC) at 18 TFW, Kadena AB, Okinawa.
5 Apr 1967	In depot maintenance (WM) by SMAMA field team at Kadena AB, Okinawa.
17 Apr 1967	At 18 TFW, Kadena AB, Okinawa.
31 May 1967	At 12 TFS, 18 TFW, Kadena AB, Okinawa. Aircraft had accumulated 1,080 flying hours. (18 TFW History, Apr–Jun 67, USAF microfilm MO499).
23 Jan 1968	Deployed to Osan AB Korea, with 18 TFW for U.S.S. Pueblo incident. (AVH-10).
18 Feb 1968	Returned to 18 TFW, Kadena AB, Okinawa.
29 Feb 1968	At Osan AB, Korea, with 18 TFW.
18 Apr 1968	Returned to 18 TFW, Kadena AB, Okinawa.
22 Apr 1968	At Osan AB, Korea, with 18 TFW.
13 Jun 1968	At 18 TFW, Kadena AB, Okinawa.
3 Jul 1968	In depot maintenance (WM) by SMAMA at Kadena AB, Okinawa.
4 Jul 1968	At 18 TFW, Kadena AB, Okinawa.
28 Jul 1968	At Kwangju AB, Korea, with 18 TFW.
31 Aug 1968	Returned to 18 TFW, Kadena AB, Okinawa.

Delivered from Republic's production line in early 1963, this plane was initially assigned to the 355 Tactical Fighter Wing at George Air Force Base, California. In November 1964, it followed the 355th when the Wing moved to McConnell Air Force Base, Kansas. Beginning in June 1965, it flew combat missions with one of the Wing's squadrons on temporary duty at Korat, Thailand. It briefly returned to McConnell at the end of 1965, then spent all of 1966 flying from Yokota Air Base, Japan. In early 1967, it moved once again, this time to the 18 Tactical Fighter Wing in Okinawa. In January 1968, when the North Koreans captured the U.S.S Pueblo, the 18th sent the plane to South Korea to help dampen North Korea's aggression. Over the next three years, the plane cycled numerous times between Okinawa and bases in Korea, helping the 18th with its alert duties. When F-105Ds were withdrawn from combat duties in the Pacific at the end of 1970, the plane returned to McConnell and, in early 1971, transferred to the Virginia Air National Guard at Richmond. It's initial Guard assignment lasted only a little over a year when, in an unusual move, the plane returned to the active-duty Air Force to train pilots at Nellis Air Force Base, Nevada. Two years later, it moved back to a Guard unit, this time in Kansas, where it flew for the next five years. In March 1980, it joined the last of the F-105s that gathered at the Air Force Reserve unit at Hill Air Force Base, Utah, from where it flew to a well-deserved retirement in 1982. (Photograph by Donald Hilburn, 18 December 1996.)

28 May 1969	At Air Asia, Tainan, Taiwan, for contract depot work (WK). (AVH-12).
16 Jul 1969	Returned to 18 TFW, Kadena AB, Okinawa.
8 Sep 1969	At Kwangju AB, Korea, with 18 TFW.
10 Sep 1969	Returned to 18 TFW, Kadena AB, Okinawa.
4 Nov 1969	At Kwangju AB, Korea, with 18 TFW.
5 Nov 1969	Returned to 18 TFW, Kadena AB Okinawa.
15 Jan 1970	At Kwangju AB, Korea, with 18 TFW. (AVH-14).
18 Jan 1970	Returned to 18 TFW, Kadena AB, Okinawa.
11 Mar 1970	At Kwangju AB, Korea, with 18 TFW.
22 Mar 1970	Returned to 18 TFW, Kadena AB, Okinawa.
15 Apr 1970	At Kwangju AB, Korea, with 18 TFW.
30 Apr 1970	Returned to 18 TFW, Kadena AB, Okinawa.
1 May 1970	In depot work by SMAMA at Kadena AB, Okinawa.
13 May 1970	At 18 TFW, Kadena AB, Okinawa.
26 Aug 1970	At Kwangju AB, Korea, with 18 TFW.
7 Sep 1970	Returned to 18 TFW, Kadena AB, Okinawa.
3 Nov 1970	Transferred (PL) to 23 TFW, McConnell AFB KS.

12 Nov 1970	In flyable storage (PR) at 23 TFW, McConnell AFB KS.
4 Jan 1970	At 23 TFW, McConnell AFB KS being prepared for transfer (PL).
2 Mar 1971	In depot maintenance (WO) by SMAMA at McClellan AFB CA. (AVH-16).
30 Apr 1971	Transferred (PL) to 192 TFG ANG, Byrd Field, Richmond VA.
29 Sep 1971	In contract depot work (WM) by Dynalectron Corporation (DYNZZ) at Byrd Field, Richmond VA.
25 Oct 1971	At 192 TFG ANG, Byrd Field, Richmond VA.
4 May 1972	In contract depot work (WM) by Dynalectron Corporation (DYNZZ) at Byrd Field, Richmond VA. (AVH-18).
20 May 1972	At 192 TFG ANG, Byrd Field, Richmond VA.
23 Aug 1972	In depot maintenance (WO) by SM-ALC at McClellan AFB CA.
24 Aug 1972	At 192 TFG ANG, Byrd Field, Richmond VA.
27 Sep 1972	Transferred (PL) to 57 FWW TAC, Nellis AFB NV.
30 Sep 1972	Assigned to Combat Crew Training (TF) at 57 FWW TAC, Nellis AFB NV.
26 Nov 1972	Departed (PL) 57 FWW TAC, Nellis AFB NV.
27 Nov 1972	In contract depot maintenance (WK) by Fairchild Engine and Aircraft Corporation (FACCF) at Bob Sikes Municipal Airport, Crestview FL.
20 Dec 1972	Departed (PL) Bob Sikes Municipal Airport, Crestview FL.
26 Dec 1972	At 57 FWW TAC for combat crew training (TF). (AVH-20).
8 Feb 1973	In depot work (WM) by 916 CLSS from SM-ALC at Nellis AFB NV.
11 Jul 1973	Departed (PL) 57 FWW TAC, Nellis AFB NV.
12 Jul 1973	In contract depot maintenance (WK) by Fairchild Engine and Aircraft Corporation (FACCF) at Bob Sikes Municipal Airport, Crestview FL.
4 Jan 1974	At 57 FWW TAC, Nellis AFB NV for combat crew training (TF). (AVH-22).
9 Sep 1974	Reassigned to 184 TFTG ANG, McConnell AFB KS for combat crew training (TF).
7 Feb 1975	In contract depot work (WM) by Dynalectron Corporation (DYNZZ) at McConnell AFB KS. (AVH-23).
13 Feb 1975	At 184 TFTG ANG, McConnell AFB KS for combat crew training (TF).
21 Apr 1975	In contract depot work (WM) by Dynalectron Corporation (DYNZZ) at McConnell AFB KS. (AVH-23 & AVH-24).
30 Apr 1975	At 184 TFTG ANG, McConnell AFB KS for combat crew training (TF).
28 Sep 1976	In depot maintenance by SM-ALC at McConnell AFB KS. 3,125.0 flying hours. (AVH-25 & AVH-26).
4 Oct 1976	At 184 TFG ANG, McConnell AFB KS for student and combat crew training (TF). 3,125.0 flying hours.
21 Nov 1978	In depot maintenance by SM-ALC at McConnell AFB KS. 3,500.0 flying hours.
5 Dec 1978	In contract depot maintenance (DYNFW) at McConnell AFB KS. 3,500.0 flying hours.
24 Apr 1979	At 184 TFG ANG, McConnell AFB KS for student and combat crew training (TF). 3,500.0 flying hours. (AVH-27).
3 Oct 1979	In contract depot maintenance (DYNFW) at McConnell AFB KS. 3,571.5 flying hours.
12 Oct 1979	At 184 TFG ANG, McConnell AFB KS for student and combat crew training (TF). 3,571.5 flying hours.
12 Oct 1979	At 184 TFG ANG, McConnell AFB KS. 3,622.3 flying hours. (GO33B 24 Jun 80).
28 Mar 1980	Transferred to the 466 TFS AFRES, Hill AFB UT. 3,652.3 flying hours.
2 Jun 1980	In depot maintenance at Ogden ALC, Hill AFB UT. 3,655.9 flying hours. (GO33B 22 Jan 81).
1 Dec 1980	At 457 TFS AFRES, Carswell AFB TX. 3,689.5 flying hours.
26 Feb 1982	At 466 TFS AFRES, Hill AFB UT. 3,805.2 flying hours. (GO33B 1 Feb 83).

F-105D-31RE 62-4301

Republic Production No: D-500 Production Sequence No: 580

Location: At McClellan Aviation Museum, McClellan AFB, Sacramento, California.

Aircraft Name(s)	Crew	Unit	Date	Description
My Karma		466 TFS AFRES	Oct 83	Name in blue on both fuselage sides forward of cockpit. Red star on fuselage right side inscribed with "IL-28."

Aircraft Chronology

25 Apr 1963	USAF production acceptance from Republic Aviation, Farmingdale NY. Flown to MOAMA, Brookley AFB AL for depot work. (ACA-88).
26 Apr 1963	Delivered to the 8 TFW, Itazuke AB, Japan.
13 May 1964	Transferred to the 41 AD, Yokota AB, Japan. (AVH-1).
31 Aug 1964	At 41 AD Yokota AB, Japan. Assigned Crew Chief: SSgt. Kiyomi Noriye. (41 AD Monthly Maintenance Summary).
30 Apr 1965	At 6441 TFW, Yokota AB, Japan. Assigned Crew Chief: A1C Ferguson. (6441 TFW History, Apr–Jun 65, USAF microfilm PO231).
1 Apr 1965	At 6441 TFW, Yokota AB, Japan. (AVH-4).
28 Jun 1965	At Air Asia, Tainan, Taiwan, for contract depot work (WK).
7 Jul 1965	Returned to 6441 TFW, Yokota AB, Japan.
31 Aug 1965	At 6441 TFW, Yokota AB, Japan. Assigned Crew Chief: A1C Ferguson. (6441 TFW History, Jul–Dec 65, USAF microfilm PO232).
31 Jan 1966	At Takhli RTAB, Thailand, with 6441 TFW. (AVH-5).
7 Feb 1966	At Air Asia, Tainan, Taiwan, for contract depot work (WK).
25 Feb 1966	Returned to 6441 TFW, Yokota AB, Japan.
27 Apr 1966	At Takhli RTAB, Thailand, with 6441 TFW.
2 May 1966	Returned to Yokota AB, Japan.
27 Oct 1966	In depot maintenance (WM) by SMAMA field team at 6441 TFW, Yokota AB, Japan.
31 Oct 1966	Operationally ready (CC) at 6441 TFW, Yokota AB, Japan.
15 Nov 1966	Assigned unit redesignated 41 AD, Yokota AB, Japan.
18 Nov 1966	At Air Asia, Tainan, Taiwan, for contract depot work (WK).
12 Jan 1967	Returned to 41 AD, Yokota AB, Japan. (AVH-8).
12 Jun 1967	At Osan AB, Korea, with 41 AD for nuclear weapons alert.
14 Jul 1967	Returned to 41 AD, Yokota AB, Japan.
30 Oct 1967	At Osan AB, Korea, with 41 AD for nuclear weapons alert.
15 Nov 1967	Returned to 41 AD, Yokota AB, Japan.
18 Jan 1968	Assigned unit redesignated 347 TFW at Yokota AB, Japan. (AVH-10).
29 Jan 1968	Deployed to Osan AB Korea, with the 18 TFW for the U.S.S. Pueblo incident.
9 Apr 1968	Transferred to 18 TFW, Kadena AB, Okinawa.
10 Apr 1968	In depot maintenance by SMAMA at 18 TFW, Kadena AB, Okinawa.
11 Apr 1968	Returned to Osan AB, Korea, with 18 TFW.
24 May 1968	At 18 TFW, Kadena AB, Okinawa.

This plane spent its entire nine-year active-duty career in the Pacific. It arrived from production in April 1963 to Itazuke Air Base, Japan. A year later it moved to Yokota Air Base, Japan, where it remained until Yokota converted to F-4Ds in early 1968. It deployed to Korea when North Korea captured the U.S.S. Pueblo in January 1968. Afterward, it went to the 18 Tactical Fighter Wing at Kadena Air Base, Okinawa, who flew it in and out of Korea for the next four years. When it left active duty in 1972, it joined the Air Force Reserve squadron at Tinker Air Force Base, Oklahoma. It deployed to England with this unit in the summer of 1978 and to Italy the following year. In 1980, it moved to the 466 Tactical Fighter Squadron, the Reserve unit at Hill Air Force Base, Utah, who took it with them to Denmark during their NATO deployment in August 1981. It was one of the last "Ds" to fly when it landed at McClellan Air Force Base, California, on 16 January 1984. (Photograph by Norman Hamrah, 20 August 1997.)

27 May 1968 Returned to Osan AB, Korea, with 18 TFW.
11 Jun 1968 At 18 TFW, Kadena AB, Okinawa.
20 Feb 1969 At Kwangju AB, Korea, with 18 TFW. (AVH-12).
6 May 1969 Returned to 18 TFW, Kadena AB, Okinawa.
4 Jun 1969 At Air Asia, Tainan, Taiwan, for contract depot work (WK).
1 Aug 1969 Returned to 18 TFW, Kadena AB, Okinawa.
18 Aug 1969 At Kwangju AB, Korea, with 18 TFW.
21 Aug 1969 Returned to 18 TFW, Kadena AB, Okinawa.
10 Sep 1969 At Kwangju AB, Korea, with 18 TFW.
27 Aug 1969 Returned to 18 TFW, Kadena AB, Okinawa.
6 Oct 1969 At Air Asia, Tainan, Taiwan, for contract depot work (WK).
10 Dec 1969 Returned to 18 TFW, Kadena AB, Okinawa.
19 Feb 1970 At Kwangju AB, Korea, with 18 TFW. (AVH-14).
21 Feb 1970 Returned to 18 TFW, Kadena AB, Okinawa.
26 Aug 1970 At Kwangju AB, Korea, with 18 TFW.
3 Sep 1970 Returned to 18 TFW, Kadena AB, Okinawa.
24 Oct 1970 At Kwangju AB, Korea, with 18 TFW.
10 Nov 1970 Returned to 18 TFW, Kadena AB, Okinawa.
11 Jun 1971 At 18 TFW, Kadena AB, Okinawa, being prepared for transfer (PL). (AVH-16).
12 Jun 1971 At Air Asia, Tainan, Taiwan, for contract depot work (WK).
12 Jul 1971 Returned (PL) to 18 TFW, Kadena AB, Okinawa.
30 Nov 1971 At Taegu AB, Korea, with 18 TFW.
3 Dec 1971 Returned to 18 TFW, Kadena AB, Okinawa.
8 Dec 1971 In depot maintenance (WM) by SMAMA at Kadena AB, Okinawa.

11 Dec 1971	At 18 TFW, Kadena AB, Okinawa.
16 Apr 1972	Departed (PL) 18 TFW, Kadena AB, Okinawa. (AVH-18).
20 Apr 1972	Placed in inactive storage (XW) at SM-ALC, McClellan AFB CA.
30 Apr 1972	In depot work (WO) by SM-ALC at McClellan AFB CA.
18 Aug 1972	Transferred (PL) to the 507 TFG AFRES, Tinker AFB OK.
21 Sep 1972	At 465 TFS AFRES, Tinker AFB OK. Landed at Tinker with nose gear jammed up by the preflight/postflight checklist book. Pilot: Capt. Hammons. (Gabby Hays, AFRES F-105 crew chief, E-mail 18 Mar 1996).
31 Mar 1973	Assigned to 507 CMTSQ AFRES, Tinker AFB OK. (AVH-20).
3 Apr 1973	In depot work (WM) by SM-ALC at Tinker AFB OK.
4 Apr 1973	At 507 CMTSQ AFRES, Tinker AFB OK.
20 May 1974	In depot work (WM) by SM-ALC at Tinker AFB OK. (AVH-22).
24 May 1974	At 507 CMTSQ AFRES, Tinker AFB OK.
16 Oct 1974	Assigned unit redesignated 507 CLMSQ AFRES, Tinker AFB OK.
4 Apr 1975	In depot work (WM) by SM-ALC at Tinker AFB OK. (AVH-23 & AVH-24).
16 Apr 1975	At 507 CLMSQ AFRES, Tinker AFB OK.
30 May 1975	In depot work (WM) by SM-ALC at Tinker AFB OK.
7 Jul 1975	At 507 CLMSQ AFRES, Tinker AFB OK.
18 Feb 1976	In depot work (WM) by SM-ALC at Tinker AFB OK. (AVH-24).
22 Dec 1976	In depot work (DM) by SM-ALC at Tinker AFB OK. 3,315 flying hours.
3 Jan 1977	At 507 TFG AFRES, Tinker AFB OK. 3,330.0 flying hours. (AVH-25 & AVH-26).
1 Apr 1978	At 465 TFS AFRES, Tinker AFB OK. 3,617.0 flying hours.
10 Jun 1978	Deployed under "Coronet Oriole" with 465 TFS to Sculthorpe, England, from Tinker AFB OK. (British Aviation Review, Dec 1995).
23 Jun 1978	Returned from England to Tinker AFB OK.
12 May 1979	Deployed under "Coronet Palomino" with the 465 TFS AFRES to Gioia Del Colle, Italy, from Tinker AFB OK. (British Aviation Review, Dec 1995).
24 May 1979	Returned from Italy to Tinker AFB OK.
31 May 1979	While assigned to the 465 TFS AFRES, Tinker AFB OK, the aircraft flew 45.9 hours during the month of May 1979 and had accumulated 3,963.7 flying hours. The assigned crew chief was Riely. (301 TFW History 1 Apr–30 Jun 1979, USAF microfilm 343832).
30 Jun 1979	While assigned to the 465 TFS AFRES, Tinker AFB OK, the aircraft flew 2.7 hours during the month of June 1979 and had accumulated a total of 3,966.4 flying hours. The assigned crew chief was Riely. (301 TFW History, Apr–Jun 1979, USAF microfilm 34382).
22 May 1980	In depot maintenance at McClellan AFB CA. 4,123.9 flying hours. (GO33B 22 Jan 81).
3 Jul 1980	At 465 TFS AFRES, Tinker AFB OK. 4,137.0 flying hours.
30 Jul 1980	Transferred to 466 TFS AFRES, Hill AFB UT. 4,137.0 flying hours.
21 Oct 1980	In depot maintenance at Odgen ALC, Hill AFB UT. 4,174.1 flying hours.
13 Nov 1980	At 466 TFS AFRES, Hill AFB UT. 4,198.5 flying hours.
15 Aug 1981	Deployed under "Coronet Rudder" with 466 TFS to Skrydstrup, Denmark, from Hill AFB UT. (British Aviation Review, Dec 1995).
29 Aug 1981	Returned from Denmark to Hill AFB UT.
6 Oct 1981	In depot maintenance at Ogden ALC, Hill AFB UT. 4,418.5 flying hours. (GO33B Dec 81 & GO33B 1 Feb 83).
16 Nov 1981	At 466 TFS AFRES, Hill AFB UT. 4,418.5 flying hours.
7 Feb 1983	In depot maintenance at Ogden ALC, Hill AFB UT. 4,623.5 flying hours. (GO33B 9 Feb 84).

17 Feb 1983	At 466 TFS AFRES, Hill AFB, Hill AFB UT. 4,623.5 flying hours.
16 Jan 1984	Flown from Hill AFB UT to McClellan AFB CA for display at McClellan Aviation Museum. (Letter from McClellan Aviation Museum, Aug 1996).

F-105D-31RE 62-4318

Republic Production No: D-517 Production Sequence No: 597

Location: At Security Police Flightline Training Area #7, Lackland AFB, San Antonio, Texas.

Aircraft Name(s)	Crew	Unit	Date	Description
Iron Butterfly		357 TFS, 355 TFW	Jan 70	On fuselage below cockpit.

Aircraft Chronology

15 May 1963	USAF production acceptance from Republic Aviation, Farmingdale NY. (ACA-88).
23 May 1963	At MOAMA, Brookley AFB AL for depot work.
28 May 1963	Delivered to 8 TFW, Itazuke AB, Japan.
13 May 1964	Transferred to 41 AD, Yokota AB, Japan under "Project Clearwater." (AVH-1).
Aug 1964	At 41 AD Yokota AB, Japan. Assigned Crew Chief: SSgt. A. Melvin. (41 AD Monthly Maintenance Summary).
28 Oct 1964	At Air Asia, Tainan, Taiwan, for contract depot work. (AVH-2).
25 Nov 1964	Returned to Yokota AB, Japan.
13 Jan 1965	In contract depot work (WR) by field team from Air Asia at Yokota AB, Japan.
25 Feb 1965	At Air Asia, Tainan, Taiwan, for contract depot work (WK). (AVH-4).
11 Mar 1965	Returned to 41 AD, Yokota AB, Japan.
1 Apr 1965	Assigned unit redesignated 6441 TFW at Yokota AB, Japan.
April 1965	At 6441 TFW, Yokota AB, Japan. Assigned Crew Chief: A1C Ryman. (6441 TFW History, Apr–Jun 65, USAF microfilm PO231).
Aug 1965	At 6441 TFW, Yokota AB, Japan. Assigned Crew Chief: SSgt. Embry. (6441 TFW History, Jul–Dec 65, USAF microfilm PO232).
31 Jan 1966	Deployed to Takhli RTAB, Thailand, with the 6441 TFW (AVH-5).
25 Feb 1966	At Air Asia, Tainan, Taiwan, for contract depot work (WK).
10 Apr 1966	In depot maintenance (WM) by SMAMA field team at 6441 TFW, Yokota AB, Japan.
8 Sep 1966	Reassigned to the 355 TFW, Takhli RTAB, Thailand.
31 Jan 1967	While assigned to the 355 TFW at Takhli RTAB, Thailand, the aircraft had accumulated 883 flying hours. (355 TFW History, Jan–Jun 67, USAF microfilm NO462).
4 Feb 1967	At Air Asia, Tainan, Taiwan, for contract depot work (WK). (AVH-8).
6 Apr 1967	Returned to 355 TFW, Takhli RTAB, Thailand.
29 Jul 1967	In depot maintenance (WM) by SMAMA field team at Takhli RTAB, Thailand.
1 Aug 1967	At 355 TFW, Takhli RTAB, Thailand.
15 Sep 1967	In depot maintenance (WM) by SMAMA field team at Takhli RTAB, Thailand.
7 Oct 1967	One of four F-105Ds flown on Rolling Thunder mission RT56A-157 by pilots from the 357 TFS, 355

In its 20 years of service, F-105D 62-4318 accumulated over 6,300 flying hours, one of the longest flying Thunderchiefs ever. Its career began with its initial assignment to the 8 Tactical Fighter Wing at Itazuke Air Base, Japan, in May 1963, and ended in 1983 with the Air Force Reserve's 466 Tactical Fighter Squadron at Hill Air Force Base, Utah. For four years it flew combat missions over North Vietnam and Laos with the 355 Tactical Fighter Wing at Takhli, Thailand. While with the 355th, it was damaged in combat and repaired at least twice before it was withdrawn in October 1970 to McConnell Air Force Base, Kansas. It served with the Kansas Air National Guard at McConnell for six years and with the Washington DC Air National Guard at Andrews Air Force Base, Maryland, for another three. It arrived at Lackland Air Force Base, Texas, in November 1983. (Photograph by Pete A. Sanders, Jr., 16 June 1996.)

	TFW, Takhli RTAB, Thailand. They strafed the Hoa Lac helicopter dispersal area in North Vietnam at coordinates 21-05-00N and 105-23-50E. The pilot was Maj White. (National Archives gun camera film shot list, item 42718A).
22 Oct 1967	Flown by Capt. Gene I. Basel (354 TFS, 355 TFW) on a combat mission lasting 3.1 hours from Takhli RTAB, Thailand. (Capt. Basel's Individual Flight Record as of 31 Dec 67)
30 Nov 1967	While assigned to the 357 TFS, 355 TFW, Takhli RTAB, Thailand, the aircraft flew 39 sorties, the highest number of any F-105 in the squadron for the month. (355 TFW History, Oct Dec 67, USAF microfilm NO463).
21 Dec 1967	Flown by Capt. Gene I. Basel (354 TFS, 355 TFW) on a mission lasting 2.8 hours from Takhli RTAB, Thailand. (Capt. Basel's Individual Flight Record as of 31 Dec 67)
25 Jan 1968	In depot-level maintenance (WM) by SMAMA at 355 TFW, Takhli RTAB, Thailand. (AVH-10).
28 Jan 1968	At the 355 TFW, Takhli RTAB, Thailand.
6 May 1968	In depot-level maintenance (WM) at 355 TFW, Takhli RTAB, Thailand.
8 May 1968	Combat capable (CC) at the 355 TFW, Takhli RTAB, Thailand.
17 Aug 1968	While assigned to the 355 TFW, Takhli RTAB, Thailand, the aircraft received major combat damage to the left side of the fuselage and in the gun bay area. Several stringers and bulkheads were also torn. (355 TFW History, Jul–Sep 68, USAF microfilm NO465).
30 Nov 1968	While assigned to the 357 TFS, 355 TFW, Takhli RTAB, Thailand, the aircraft had accumulated 2,524.8 flying hours. (355 TFW History, Oct–Dec 68, USAF microfilm NO466).
14 Dec 1968	At Air Asia, Tainan, Taiwan, for contract depot work (WK). (AVH-10).
1 Feb 1969	Returned to 355 TFW, Takhli RTAB, Thailand. (AVH-12).
28 Feb 1969	While assigned to the 355 TFW, Takhli RTAB, Thailand, the aircraft flew 68.5 hours during the month

	of February 1969 and had accumulated 2,613.5 flying hours. (355 TFW History, Jan–Mar 69, Vol. II, USAF Microfilm NO467).
31 Mar 1969	While assigned to the 357 TFS, 355 TFW, Takhli RTAB, Thailand, the aircraft flew 104.3 hours for a Wing high for the month of March 1969. (355 TFW History, Jan–Mar 69, USAF microfilm NO466).
5 May 1969	While assigned to the 355 TFW, Takhli RTAB, Thailand, the aircraft received combat damage. It "... was hit by what appeared to be a 14.5 mm round during an AGM-12C missile pass in the 'E' sector of Southern Laos … . The round entered the underside of the right intake duct and the shrapnel caused extensive damage to the inside of the duct and the engine. 384 man-hours were required to repair the damage." (355 TFW History, Apr–Jun 69, Vol. III, USAF microfilm NO468).
7 May 1969	In depot work for combat damage (VM) by SMAMA field team at Takhli RTAB, Thailand. (AVH-12).
30 May 1969	At 355 TFW, Takhli RTAB, Thailand.
18 Mar 1970	At Air Asia, Tainan, Taiwan, for contract depot work (WK). (AVH-14).
4 Jun 1970	Returned to 355 TFW, Takhli RTAB, Thailand.
24 Oct 1970	At 355 TFW, Takhli RTAB, Thailand, being prepared for transfer (PL).
27 Oct 1970	Transferred (PL) to 23 TFW, McConnell AFB KS.
4 Nov 1970	In flyable storage (PR) at 23 TFW, McConnell AFB KS.
4 Jan 1971	At 23 TFW, McConnell AFB KS, being prepared for transfer (PL).
20 Jan 1971	Transferred (PL) to 184 TFG ANG, McConnell AFB KS. (AVH-16).
11 Feb 1971	Operationally ready (CC) at 184 TFG ANG, McConnell AFB KS.
30 Mar 1971	In depot work (WO) by SMAMA at McClellan AFB CA.
14 May 1971	Returned (PL) to 184 TFG ANG, McConnell AFB KS.
15 May 1971	Operationally ready (CC) at 184 TFG ANG, McConnell AFB KS.
30 May 1972	In contract depot maintenance (WK) by Fairchild Engine and Aircraft Corporation (FACCF) at Bob Sikes Municipal Airport, Crestview FL. (AVH-18).
22 Jun 1972	Returned to 184 TFG ANG, McConnell AFB KS.
20 May 1974	In contract depot maintenance (WK) by Fairchild Engine and Aircraft Corporation (FACCF) at Bob Sikes Municipal Airport, Crestview FL. (AVH-22).
8 Oct 1974	Returned to 184 TFTG ANG, McConnell AFB KS.
19 Nov 1975	In contract depot maintenance (WM) by Dynalectron Corporation (DYNZZ) at McConnell AFB KS. (AVH-23 & AVH-24).
2 Dec 1975	At 184 TFTG ANG, McConnell AFB KS for combat crew training (TF).
18 Feb 1977	In contract depot maintenance (DYNFW) at McConnell AFB KS. 5,272.0 flying hours. (AVH-25 & AVH-26).
11 Aug 1978	Transferred to 113 TFW ANG, Andrews AFB MD. 5,604.0 flying hours.
23 May 1979	In contract depot maintenance (WM) by Dynalectron Corporation (DYNZZ) at Andrews AFB MD. 5,605.0 flying hours. (AVH-27).
7 Jul 1979	At 113 TFG ANG, Andrews AFB MD. 5,605.0 flying hours.
9 Nov 1979	At Sacramento ALC, McClellan AFB CA for "domestic project" (DO). 5,621.2 flying hours.
2 Jan 1980	At 113 TFG ANG, Andrews AFB MD. 5,653.7 flying hours. (GO33B 24 Jun 80).
2 Nov 1981	At 466 TFS AFRES, Hill AFB UT. 5,944.5 flying hours. (GO33B Dec 81 & GO33B 1 Feb 83).
29 Nov 1983	One of 24 F-105s flown on ceremonial final mission at Hill AFB UT. After mission, aircraft was one of seven delivered to 3280 TTA Group (ATC), Lackland AFB TX for security police flightline training. (Possession code: TX. Inventory account: GB). 6,387.1 flying hours. (GO33B 9 Feb 84).
30 Nov 1983	Redesignated GF-105D at 3280 TTA Group (ATC), Lackland AFB TX. (Possession code: TX. Inventory account: GC). 6,387.1 flying hours.

F-105D-31RE 62-4328

Republic Production No: D-527 Production Sequence No: 607

Location: Displayed near the main gate at Arnold Air Force Base, Manchester, Tennessee.

Aircraft Chronology

22 Jun 1963	USAF production acceptance from Republic Aviation, Farmingdale NY. (ACA-88).
25 Jun 1963	At MOAMA, Brookley AFB AL, for depot work.
28 Jun 1963	Delivered to 8 TFW, Itazuke AB, Japan.
30 Jun 1964	Transferred to 18 TFW, Kadena AB, Okinawa.
31 Jan 1965	At 18 TFW, Kadena AB, Okinawa. Assigned crew chief: A1C B. Tattersall. (18 TFW History, Jan–Jun 65, USAF microfilm MO497).
Nov 1965	At 18 TFW, Kadena AB, Okinawa. Assigned crew chief: SSgt. W. Atkinson. (18 TFW History, Jul–Dec 65, USAF microfilm MO497).
25 Jun 1965	At Air Asia, Tainan, Taiwan, for contract depot work (WK). (AVH-4).
6 Jul 1965	Returned to 18 TFW, Kadena AB, Okinawa.
10 Jan 1966	At Air Asia, Tainan, Taiwan, for contract depot work (WK). (AVH-5).
2 Feb 1966	At 18 TFW, Kadena AB, Okinawa.
31 Dec 1966	While assigned to the 18 TFW, Kadena AB, Okinawa, the aircraft flew 25 hours during the month of December 1966 and had accumulated 1,047 flying hours. (18 TFW History, Jul–Dec 66, USAF microfilm MO498).
20 Jan 1967	At Air Asia, Tainan, Taiwan, for contract depot work (WK). (AVH-8).
25 Mar 1967	Returned to 18 TFW, Kadena AB, Okinawa.
11 Aug 1967	In depot maintenance by SMAMA field team at Kadena AB, Okinawa.
12 Aug 1967	At 18 TFW, Kadena AB, Okinawa.
29 Jan 1968	Deployed to Osan AB, Korea, with 18 TFW for U.S.S. Pueblo incident. (AVH-10).
24 Mar 1968	Returned to 18 TFW, Kadena AB, Okinawa.
25 Mar 1968	In depot-level maintenance (WM) by SMAMA at 18 TFW, Kadena AB, Okinawa.
26 Mar 1968	At 18 TFW, Kadena AB, Okinawa.
28 Mar 1968	Returned to Osan AB, Korea, with 18 TFW.
2 May 1968	At 18 TFW, Kadena AB, Okinawa.
9 May 1968	Returned to Osan AB, Korea, with 18 TFW.
10 Jun 1968	At 18 TFW, Kadena AB, Okinawa.
14 Jul 1968	At 18 TFW, Kadena AB in depot-level maintenance (WM).
15 Jul 1968	Operational (CC) at 18 TFW, Kadena AB, Okinawa.
2 Aug 1968	At Kwangju AB, Korea, with 18 TFW.
14 Sep 1968	Returned to 18 TFW, Kadena AB, Okinawa, for transfer (PL).
18 Sep 1968	Transferred (PL) to 388 TFW, Korat RTAB, Thailand.
21 Sep 1968	Operational (CC) at 388 TFW, Korat RTAB, Thailand.
31 Oct 1968	Aircraft had accumulated 1,561.9 flying hours while assigned to the 388 TFW, Korat RTAB, Thailand. (388 TFW History, Oct–Dec 68, USAF microfilm NO585).
31 Jan 1969	At Takhli RTAB, Thailand, with 388 TFW during runway repairs at Korat RTAB. (AVH-12).
12 Feb 1969	Flown on a strike mission in the Barrel Roll region of Laos by 44 TFS pilot, 388 TFW, while operating from Takhli RTAB, Thailand. (388 TFW History, Jan–Mar 69, USAF microfilm NO586).

This was another F-105D that spent its entire Air Force career in the Pacific. A year after its 1963 production delivery to Itazuke Air Base, Japan, the plane moved to the 18 Tactical Fighter Wing at Kadena Air Base, Okinawa. Except for six months in 1968 and 1969 when it flew combat missions with the 388 Tactical Fighter Wing from Korat, Thailand, the plane remained for the next eight years with the 18th at Kadena. In September 1972, it transferred to the Air Force Reserve's 465 Tactical Fighter Squadron at Tinker Air Force Base, Oklahoma. The 465th flew it on a NATO deployment to Italy in 1979. When the squadron converted to F-4Ds in 1980, the plane transferred to the 466 Tactical Fighter Squadron at Hill Air Force Base, Utah. The plane accompanied the 466th during their NATO deployment to Denmark in 1981. In early 1984, it was one of several Thunderchiefs the 466th flew to retirement at museums and air base gate guard duty—62-4328 going to Arnold Air Force Station in Tennessee. (Photograph by Bill Malerba, 25 July 1995.)

13 Feb 1969	Flown on a strike mission in the Steel Tiger region of Laos by 44 TFS pilot, 388 TFW, while operating from Takhli RTAB, Thailand.
17 Feb 1969	Flown on a strike mission in the Steel Tiger region of Laos by 44 TFS pilot, 388 TFW, while operating from Takhli RTAB, Thailand.
1 Mar 1969	Returned to 388 TFW, Korat RTAB, Thailand.
1 Apr 1969	At Air Asia, Tainan, Taiwan, for contract depot work (WK). (AVH-12).
30 Apr 1969	While assigned to the 34 TFS, 388 TFW, Korat RTAB, Thailand, the aircraft had accumulated 1,922.1 flying hours. (388 TFW History, Apr–Jun 69, USAF microfilm NO586).
17 May 1969	Transferred to 18 TFW, Kadena AB, Okinawa. (AVH-12).
7 Jun 1969	At Kwangju AB, Korea, with 18 TFW.
10 Jun 1969	Returned to 18 TFW, Kadena AB, Okinawa.
24 Jun 1969	At Kwangju AB, Korea, with 18 TFW.
9 Jul 1969	Returned to 18 TFW, Kadena AB, Okinawa.
18 Aug 1969	At Kwangju AB, Korea, with 18 TFW.
21 Aug 1969	Returned to 18 TFW, Kadena AB, Okinawa.
6 Oct 1969	At Kwangju AB, Korea, with 18 TFW.
8 Oct 1969	Returned to 18 TFW, Kadena AB, Okinawa.
6 Nov 1969	At Air Asia, Tainan, Taiwan, for contract depot work (WK).
19 Nov 1969	Returned to 18 TFW, Kadena AB, Okinawa.
17 Jan 1970	At 18 TFW, Kadena AB, Okinawa. (AVH-14).
5 Mar 1970	At Kwangju AB, Korea, with 18 TFW.
12 Mar 1970	Returned to 18 TFW, Kadena AB, Okinawa.
19 Mar 1970	At Kwangju AB, Korea, with 18 TFW.
19 Apr 1970	Returned to 18 TFW, Kadena AB, Okinawa.

5 Jul 1970	At Kwangju AB, Korea, with 18 TFW.
3 Aug 1970	Returned to 18 TFW, Kadena AB, Okinawa.
7 Oct 1970	At Kwangju AB, Korea, with 18 TFW.
4 Nov 1970	Returned to 18 TFW, Kadena AB, Okinawa.
8 Feb 1971	At Air Asia, Tainan, Taiwan, for contract depot work (WK). (AVH-16).
25 Mar 1971	Returned to 18 TFW, Kadena AB, Okinawa.
28 Sep 1971	At Taegu AB, Korea, with 18 TFW.
1 Oct 1971	Returned to 18 TFW, Kadena AB, Okinawa.
27 Nov 1971	In depot work (WO) by SMAMA at Kadena AB, Okinawa.
1 Dec 1971	At 18 TFW, Kadena AB, Okinawa.
16 Apr 1972	Departed (PL) 18 TFW, Kadena AB, Japan. (AVH-18).
25 Apr 1972	Placed in inactive storage (XW) at SM-ALC, McClellan AFB CA.
30 Apr 1972	In depot work (WO) by SM-ALC at McClellan AFB CA.
13 Sep 1972	Transferred (PL) to 507 TFG AFRES, Tinker AFB OK.
19 Sep 1972	At (CC) 507 TFG AFRES, Tinker AFB OK.
31 Mar 1973	Reassigned to 507 CMTSQ AFRES, Tinker AFB OK. (AVH-20).
8 Apr 1974	In depot maintenance (WM) by SM-ALC at Tinker AFB OK. (AVH-22).
26 Apr 1974	At 507 CMTSQ AFRES, Tinker AFB OK.
23 Sep 1974	In depot maintenance (WM) by SM-ALC at Tinker AFB OK.
19 Dec 1974	Reassigned to 507 CLMSQ AFRES, Tinker AFB OK.
13 Jun 1974	At 465 TFS AFRES, Tinker AFB OK. The canopy mechanism broke when the pilot landed and tried to open the canopy resulting in $35,000 damage.
21 Jul 1975	At 507 CLMSQ AFRES, Tinker AFB OK. (AVH-23 & AVH-24).
5 Apr 1976	In depot maintenance (DM) by SM-ALC at Tinker AFB OK. (AVH-24).
30 Apr 1976	At 507 TFG AFRES, Tinker AFB OK.
18 Oct 1976	In depot maintenance by SM-ALC at Tinker AFB OK. 3,540.0 flying hours. (AVH-25 & AVH-26).
1 Nov 1976	At 507 TFG AFRES, Tinker AFB OK. 3,540.0 flying hours.
25 Feb 1978	In SM-ALC depot at McClellan AFB CA. 3,811.0 flying hours. Possession Code: DO.
8 Sep 1978	In SM-ALC depot at McClellan AFB CA. 3,824.0 flying hours. Possession Codes: DO & DR.
28 Sep 1978	Returned to 465 TFS AFRES, Tinker AFB OK. 3,824.0 flying hours.
8 Mar 1979	In contract depot maintenance (FACBM) at Tinker AFB OK. 3,899.1 flying hours. (AVH-27).
14 Mar 1979	At 465 TFS AFRES, Tinker AFB OK. 3,899.1 flying hours.
12 May 1979	Deployed under "Coronet Palomino" with 465 TFS to Gioia Del Colle, Italy, from Tinker AFB OK. (British Aviation Review, Dec 1995).
24 May 1979	Returned from Italy to Tinker AFB OK.
28 Jun 1979	While assigned to the 465 TFS AFRES, Tinker AFB OK, the aircraft ground aborted due to no brakes with the anti skid on. (301 TFW History 1 Apr–30 Jun 1979, USAF microfilm 343832).
30 Jun 1979	While assigned to the 465 TFS AFRES, Tinker AFB OK, the aircraft flew 29.7 hours during the month of June 1979 and had accumulated a total of 4,003.3 flying hours. The assigned crew chief was named Lee. (301 TFW History, Apr–Jun 1979, USAF microfilm 34382).
30 Aug 1979	At 465 TFS AFRES, Tinker AFB OK. 4,028.0 flying hours. (AVH-27).
13 Nov 1980	Transferred to 466 TFS AFRES, Hill AFB UT. 4,342.8 flying hours. (GO33B 22 Jan 81).
15 Aug 1981	Deployed under "Coronet Rudder" with 466 TFS to Skrydstrup, Denmark, from Hill AFB UT. (British Aviation Review, Dec 1995).
29 Aug 1981	Returned from Denmark to Hill AFB UT.
30 Jun 1982	In depot maintenance at Odgen ALC, Hill AFB UT. 4,604.4 flying hours. (GO33B 1 Feb 83).

21 Jul 1982 At 466 TFS AFRES, Hill AFB UT. 4,604.4 flying hours.

1984 "The F-105 was flown to AEDC for the Center's first permanent aircraft display in early 1984. It was dedicated in memory of Lt. Gen. Robert M. Bond. General Bond, who died in service while Vice Commander of Air Force Systems Command, flew the F-105 as a test and combat pilot." (Air Classics Magazine, Jul 1990). General Bond "... died after ejecting near Tonopah, (Nevada), from an 'Air Force specially modified test aircraft' on Apr. 26, 1984. It was thought to be a MIG-23, possibly involved in testing against nascent U.S. stealth technologies and other countermeasures." (Aviation Week & Space Technology/April 17, 2000, page 33).

F-105D-31RE 62-4346

Republic Production No: D-545 Production Sequence No: 625

Location: At Security Police Flightline Training Area #7, Lackland AFB, San Antonio, Texas.

Aircraft Name(s)	Crew	Unit	Date	Description
Itazuke Express				Black letters on tail.
Good Golly Miss Molly	Col. Walker	469 TFS 388 TFW	1968	Blue letters with red and yellow background on fuselage side under wing.

This plane followed the pattern of F-105Ds delivered in 1963 by starting with the 8 Tactical Fighter Wing at Itazuke Air Base, Japan; transferring a year later to the 41 Air Division at Yokota Air Base, Japan; followed by duty with the 18 Tactical Fighter Wing at Kadena Air Base, Okinawa, and a combat tour in Thailand. However, 62-4346 is the only one of the thirteen Thunderchiefs being used today by the 343 Training Squadron that was assigned to the 388 Tactical Fighter Wing at Korat, one of the two F-105 bases in Thailand. During most of its six-month combat assignment with the 388th, the bombing of North Vietnam had been severely restricted so the plane flew missions over Laos. For its last three years in the Pacific, the plane returned to Kadena where it frequently rotated to bases in South Korea to support the 18 Tactical Fighter Wing's commitment resulting from the U.S.S. Pueblo incident. In April 1972, it was assigned directly from Kadena to the Air Force Reserve unit at Tinker Air Force Base, Oklahoma. It deployed in the summer of 1978 to Great Britain for a NATO exercise and, three years later, supported the Reserve's NATO deployment to Denmark from Hill Air Force Base, Utah. Its last flight was in June 1983 to Lackland Air Force Base, Texas. (Photograph by author, 4 August 1997.)

Aircraft Chronology

15 Jul 1963	USAF production acceptance from Republic Aviation, Farmingdale NY. (ACA-88).
16 Jul 1963	At MOAMA, Brookley AFB AL for depot work.
24 Jul 1963	Delivered to the 8 TFW, Itazuke AB, Japan.
13 May 1964	Transferred to 41 AD, Yokota AB, Japan, under "Project Clearwater." (AVH-1).
Aug 1964	At 41 AD, Yokota AB, Japan. Assigned Crew Chief: SSgt. R. Carmichael. (41 AD Monthly Maintenance Summary).
1 Apr 1965	Assigned unit redesignated 6441 TFW at Yokota AB, Japan. (AVH-4).
30 Apr 1965	At 6441 TFW, Yokota AB, Japan. Assigned Crew Chief: SSgt. Embry. (6441 TFW History, Apr–Jun 65, USAF microfilm PO231).
Aug 1965	At 6441 TFW, Yokota AB, Japan. Assigned Crew Chief: SSgt. Moore. (6441 TFW History, Jul–Dec 65, USAF microfilm PO232).
27 Dec 1965	At Air Asia, Tainan, Taiwan, for contract depot work (WK). (AVH-4).
20 Jan 1966	Returned to 6441 TFW, Yokota AB, Japan. (AVH-5).
16 Mar 1966	At Osan AB, Korea, with 6441 TFW for nuclear weapon alert.
31 May 1966	Returned to 6441 TFW, Yokota AB, Japan.
31 Oct 1966	In depot maintenance (WM) by SMAMA field team at 6441 TFW, Yokota AB, Japan.
2 Nov 1966	Reassigned to 41 AD, Yokota AB, Japan.
3 Jan 1967	At 41 AD, Yokota AB, Japan. (AVH-8).
9 Apr 1967	Transferred to 12 TFS, 18 TFW, Kadena AB, Okinawa. Aircraft had accumulated 739 flying hours. (18 TFW History, Apr–Jun 67, USAF microfilm MO498).
15 May 1967	At Air Asia, Tainan, Taiwan, for contract depot work (WK). Aircraft had accumulated 751 flying hours. (AVH-8 & 18 TFW History, Apr–Jun 67, USAF microfilm MO499).
15 Jul 1967	Returned to 18 TFW, Kadena AB, Okinawa.
13 Sep 1967	In depot maintenance (WM) by SMAMA field team at Kadena AB, Okinawa.
14 Sep 1967	At 18 TFW, Kadena AB, Okinawa.
29 Jan 1968	Deployed to Osan AB, Korea, with the 18 TFW for U.S.S. Pueblo incident. (AVH-10).
10 Mar 1968	Returned to 18 TFW, Kadena AB, Okinawa.
18 Mar 1968	At Osan AB, Korea, with 18 TFW.
11 Apr 1968	Returned to 18 TFW, Kadena AB, Okinawa.
12 Apr 1968	In depot-level maintenance (WM) by SMAMA at Kadena AB, Okinawa.
13 Apr 1968	At Osan AB, Korea, with 18 TFW.
11 Jun 1968	Returned to 18 TFW, Kadena AB, Okinawa.
6 Jul 1968	In depot-level maintenance (WM) at 18 TFW, Kadena AB, Okinawa.
7 Jul 1968	Operationally ready (CC) at 18 TFW, Kadena AB, Okinawa.
8 Sep 1968	At 18 TFW, Kadena AB, Okinawa, being prepared for transfer (PL).
9 Sep 1968	Transferred (PL) to 388 TFW, Korat RTAB, Thailand.
12 Sep 1968	Operational (CC) at 388 TFW, Korat RTAB, Thailand.
31 Oct 1968	Aircraft had accumulated 1,273.1 flying hours while assigned to the 388 TFW, Korat RTAB, Thailand. (388 TFW History, Oct–Dec 68, USAF microfilm NO585).
21 Dec 1968	Aircraft drag chute spilled on runway immediately upon landing from a combat mission while assigned to the 388 TFW, Korat RTAB, Thailand. (388 TFW History, Oct–Dec 68, USAF microfilm NO585).
29 Jan 1969	At 388 TFW, Korat RTAB, Thailand. (AVH-12).
2 Feb 1969	While assigned to the 388 TFW, Korat RTAB, Thailand, the aircraft was damaged during a combat mission by stores from the centerline MER striking the inboard leading edge of the left horizontal slab. The damage required 12 man hours to repair. (388 TFW History, Jan–Mar 69, USAF microfilm NO586).

8 Feb 1969	Flown on a strike mission in the Steel Tiger region of Laos by 44 TFS pilot, 388 TFW, while operating from Takhli RTAB, Thailand, during runway repairs at Korat RTAB.
15 Feb 1969	Flown on a strike mission in the Steel Tiger region of Laos by 44 TFS pilot, 388 TFW, while operating from Takhli RTAB, Thailand.
3 Mar 1969	Flown on a strike mission in the Steel Tiger region of Laos by 44 TFS pilot, 388 TFW, while operating from Takhli RTAB, Thailand. Aircraft recovered at Korat after sortie. (388 TFW History, Jan–Mar 69, USAF microfilm NO586).
28 Apr 1969	At Air Asia, Tainan, Taiwan, for contract depot work (WK). (AVH-12).
30 Apr 1969	While assigned to the 34 TFS, 388 TFW, Korat RTAB, Thailand, the aircraft had accumulated 1,652.6 flying hours. (388 TFW History, Apr–Jun 69, USAF microfilm NO586).
21 Jun 1969	Transferred to the 18 TFW, Kadena AB, Okinawa. (AVH-12).
24 Jul 1969	At Kwangju AB, Korea, with 18 TFW.
7 Aug 1969	Returned to 18 TFW, Kadena AB, Okinawa.
18 Aug 1969	At Kwangju AB, Korea, with 18 TFW.
21 Aug 1969	Returned to 18 TFW, Kadena AB, Okinawa.
10 Sep 1969	At Kwangju AB, Korea, with 18 TFW.
20 Sep 1969	Returned to 18 TFW, Kadena AB, Okinawa.
21 Sep 1969	At Kwangju AB, Korea, with 18 TFW.
22 Sep 1969	Returned to 18 TFW, Kadena AB, Okinawa.
23 Sep 1969	At Kwangju AB, Korea, with 18 TFW.
12 Oct 1969	Returned to 18 TFW, Kadena AB, Okinawa.
15 Nov 1969	In depot maintenance (WM) by SMAMA at Kadena AB, Okinawa.
21 Nov 1969	At 18 TFW, Kadena AB, Okinawa.
5 Feb 1970	At Kwangju AB, Korea, with 18 TFW. (AVH-14).
13 Feb 1970	Returned to 18 TFW, Kadena AB, Okinawa.
19 Feb 1970	At Air Asia, Tainan, Taiwan, for contract depot work (WK).
22 Apr 1970	Returned to 18 TFW, Kadena AB, Okinawa.
14 Aug 1970	At Kwangju AB, Korea, with 18 TFW.
27 Aug 1970	Returned to 18 TFW, Kadena AB, Okinawa.
14 Oct 1970	At Kwangju AB, Korea, with 18 TFW.
26 Oct 1970	Returned to 18 TFW, Kadena AB, Okinawa.
25 Mar 1971	At Air Asia, Tainan, Taiwan, for contract depot work (WK). (AVH-16).
28 Apr 1971	Returned to 18 TFW, Kadena AB, Okinawa.
28 Sep 1971	At Taegu AB, Korea, with 18 TFW.
1 Oct 1971	Returned to 18 TFW, Kadena AB, Okinawa.
22 Oct 1971	At Taegu AB, Korea, with 18 TFW.
29 Oct 1971	Returned to 18 TFW, Kadena AB, Okinawa.
11 Apr 1972	Departed (PL) 18 TFW, Kadena AB, Okinawa, Japan. (AVH-18).
12 Apr 1972	Arrived (PL) at 937 MALGP (AFRES), Tinker AFB OK.
20 May 1972	Assigned to 507 TFG AFRES, Tinker AFB OK.
24 Aug 1972	In contract depot maintenance (WK) by Fairchild Engine and Aircraft Corporation (FACCF) at Bob Sikes Municipal Airport, Crestview FL.
18 Sep 1972	Returned to 507 TFG AFRES, Tinker AFB OK.
31 Mar 1973	Assigned to 507 CMTSQ AFRES, Tinker AFB OK. (AVH-20).
11 Apr 1973	Departed (PL) 507 CMTSQ AFRES, Tinker AFB OK.
17 Apr 1973	In depot work (WO) by SM-ALC at McClellan AFB CA.

17 Dec 1973	Returned to 507 CMTSQ AFRES, Tinker AFB OK.
23 Apr 1974	In depot work (WO) by SM-ALC at Tinker AFB OK. (AVH-22).
6 May 1974	At 507 CMTSQ AFRES, Tinker AFB OK.
16 Oct 1974	Assigned unit redesignated 507 CLMSQ AFRES, Tinker AFB OK.
8 Apr 1975	In depot work (WO) by SM-ALC at Tinker AFB OK. (AVH-23 & AVH-24).
20 Apr 1975	At 507 CLMSQ AFRES, Tinker AFB OK.
9 Mar 1976	In depot work (WO) by SM-ALC at Tinker AFB OK. (AVH-24).
2 Apr 1976	At 507 TFG AFRES, Tinker AFB OK.
21 Apr 1977	At 507 TFG AFRES, Tinker AFB OK. 3,275.0 flying hours. (AVH-25 & AVH-26).
26 Jul 1977	In depot maintenance by SM-ALC at Tinker AFB OK. 3,275.0 flying hours.
10 Jun 1978	Deployed under "Coronet Oriole" with the 465 TFS to Sculthorpe, England, from Tinker AFB OK. (British Aviation Review, Dec 1995).
23 Jun 1978	Returned from England to Tinker AFB OK
25 Apr 1979	In contract depot maintenance (FACBM) at Tinker AFB OK. 3,684.4 flying hours. (AVH-27).
14 May 1979	At 465 TFS AFRES, Tinker AFB OK. 3,701.9 flying hours.
21 Jun 1979	While assigned to the 465 TFS AFRES, Tinker AFB OK, the aircraft air aborted due to fumes in the cockpit after the gear was retracted. The air conditioning package was changed. (301 TFW History 1 Apr–30 Jun 1979, USAF microfilm 343832).
30 Jun 1979	While assigned to the 465 TFS AFRES, Tinker AFB OK, the aircraft flew 2.9 hours during the month of June 1979 and had accumulated a total of 3,704.8 flying hours. The assigned crew chief was Nelson. (301 TFW History, Apr–Jun 1979, USAF microfilm 34382).
15 Oct 1980	At 466 TFS AFRES, Hill AFB UT. 4,099.0 flying hours. (GO33B 22 Jan 81).
10 Aug 1981	At 466 TFS AFRES, Hill AFB UT. 4,248.4 flying hours. (GO33B Dec 81 & GO33B 1 Feb 83).
15 Aug 1981	Deployed under "Coronet Rudder" with 466 TFS to Skrydstrup, Denmark, from Hill AFB UT. (British Aviation Review, Dec 1995).
29 Aug 1981	Returned from Denmark to Hill AFB UT.
4 Jun 1983	One of 24 F-105s flown on ceremonial final mission at Hill AFB UT. After the mission, the aircraft was one of seven delivered to 3280 TTA Group (ATC), Lackland AFB TX for security police flightline training. (Possession code: TX. Inventory account: GB). 4,597.7 flying hours. (GO33B 9 Feb 84).
5 Jun 1983	Redesignated GF-105D at 3280 TTA Group (ATC), Lackland AFB TX. (Possession code: TX. Inventory account: GC). 4,597.7 flying hours.

F-105D-31RE 62-4347

Republic Production No: D-546 Production Sequence No: 626

Location: Displayed on pylon near the South Gate at Hill AFB, Ogden, Utah.

Aircraft Name(s)	Crew	Unit	Date	Description
Wendy June II				
Little Lois Ann	Maj. Stanley Dunkley	333 TFS 355 TFW	Aug 67	On left fuselage
Calamity Jane II		333 TFS 355 TFW	Jan 70	On both intakes.
High Time Thud		466 TFS AFRES	Jun 82	On nose below windscreen side/ under intake.
Stardust 6		466 TFS AFRES	Oct 82	

Aircraft Chronology

23 Jul 1963	USAF production acceptance from Republic Aviation, Farmingdale NY. (ACA-88).
29 Jul 1963	Delivered to the 355 TFW, George AFB CA.
3 Jul 1964	Transferred with the 355 TFW to McConnell AFB KS. (AVH-1).
6 Aug 1964	One of 18 F-105Ds deployed on TDY to Yokota AB, Japan, with the 357 TFS, 355 TFW, from McConnell AFB KS, under "Operation One Buck Two" in response to the Gulf of Tonkin incident.
15 Dec 1964	Transferred on TDY to Kadena AB, Okinawa, with the 469 TFS, 355 TFW, from McConnell AFB KS. Assigned Crew Chief: TSgt. Green. (18 TFW History, Jan–Jun 65, USAF microfilm MO497).
3 Mar 1965	Transferred to the 354 TFS on TDY to Kadena AB, Okinawa, from the 355 TFW, McConnell AFB KS. Assigned Crew Chief: TSgt. Insani. (18 TFW History, Jan–Jun 65, USAF microfilm MO497).
30 May 1965	At Air Asia, Tainan, Taiwan, for contract depot work (WK). (AVH-4).
16 Jun 1965	Returned to Kadena AB, Okinawa, with the 421 TFS, 355 TFW, from McConnell AFB KS. Assigned Crew Chief: TSgt. Rock.
20 Feb 1966	At Air Asia, Tainan, Taiwan, for contract depot work (WK). (AVH-5).
12 Mar 1966	Transferred to the 355 TFW, Takhli RTAB, Thailand.
6 Jun 1966	At Air Asia, Tainan, Taiwan, for contract depot work (WK). Assigned to 6441 TFW.
9 Oct 1966	In depot repair for combat damage (VM) by SMAMA field team at Takhli RTAB, Thailand.
31 Jan 1967	While assigned to the 355 TFW at Takhli RTAB, Thailand, the aircraft had accumulated 1,535 flying hours. (355 TFW History, Jan–Jun 67, USAF microfilm NO462).
Jun 1967	Aircraft received battle damage while assigned to the 355 TFW, Takhli RTAB, Thailand. Aircraft flying hours: 1,901. (355 TFW History, Jul–Sep 67, USAF microfilm NO463).
2 Jun 1967	At 366 TFW, Da Nang AB, South Vietnam. Coded "CC." (AVH-8).
14 Aug 1967	Returned to 355 TFW, Takhli RTAB, Thailand. Assigned to the 333 TFS.
16 Aug 1967	In depot maintenance (WM) by SMAMA field team at Takhli RTAB, Thailand.
19 Aug 1967	At 355 TFW, Takhli RTAB, Thailand.
29 Aug 1967	Flown by Maj. Donald M. Russell (333 TFS, 355 TFW) on a combat mission that lasted 3.9 hours from Takhli RTAB, Thailand. (Maj. Russell's Individual Flight Record as of 31 Dec 67).
18 Oct 1967	Flown on Rolling Thunder mission RT56A-168 by Maj Robert L. Stirm from the 333 TFS, 355 TFW, Takhli RTAB, Thailand. The target was the Bak Le railroad segment 35 NM NE of Hanoi, North Vietnam, at coordinates 21-31-19N and 106-26-40E. (National Archives strike camera film shot list, item 42718A).
24 Oct 1967	Flown on Rolling Thunder mission RT56A-174 by Capt Ramon A. Horinek from the 357 TFS, 355 TFW, Takhli RTAB, Thailand. The target was Kep Airfield 33 NM NE of Hanoi, North Vietnam, at coordinates 21-23-26N and 106-15-58E.
31 Dec 1967	While assigned to the 357 TFS, 355 TFW, Takhli RTAB, Thailand, the aircraft flew 36 sorties in December 1967, the highest number of any F-105 in the squadron for the month. (355 TFW History, Oct–Dec 67, USAF microfilm NO463).
26 Apr 1968	In depot-level maintenance (WM) at 355 TFW, Takhli RTAB, Thailand. (AVH-10).
29 Apr 1968	At 355 TFW, Takhli RTAB, Thailand.
8 Jun 1968	In depot-level maintenance (WQ) at 355 TFW, Takhli RTAB, Thailand.
16 Jun 1968	Combat capable (CC) at the 355 TFW, Takhli RTAB, Thailand.
9 Sep 1968	At Air Asia, Tainan, Taiwan, for contract depot work (WK).
21 Oct 1968	Returned to 355 TFW, Takhli RTAB, Thailand.
1 Nov 1968	While assigned to the 355 TFW, Takhli RTAB, Thailand, aircraft had accumulated 2,982.8 flying hours. (355 TFW History, Oct–Dec 68, USAF microfilm NO466).
31 Nov 1968	While assigned to the 333 TFS, 355 TFW, Takhli RTAB, Thailand, the aircraft flew 115.4 hours in November 1968, the highest of the month for the Wing's F-105s. (355 TFW History, Oct–Dec 68, USAF microfilm NO465).

This "D" is the well-known "High Time Thud"—the F-105 that accumulated the most flying hours of all the Thunderchiefs. In its twenty-year career, its airframe logged over 6,700 hours. It spent six years in the Pacific with the 355 Tactical Fighter Wing, beginning in August 1964 with the first F-105 deployment from the Tactical Air Command in response to the North Vietnamese attack in the Gulf of Tonkin. This deployment began two years of temporary duty with three of the 355th's squadrons at Yokota Air Base, Japan, and Kadena Air Base, Okinawa. It moved to Takhli, Thailand, in March 1966 and stayed there until the base closed near the end of 1970. During its four years of combat flying from Takhli, the plane consistently set monthly sortie and flying-hour records, a tribute to the skilled care from its crew chiefs. When it went to the Kansas Air National Guard in 1971, it had reached over 4,000 hours, the design life of the F-105. The Kansans flew it another 2,000 hours before turning it over in 1980 to the 466 Tactical Fighter Squadron, the Air Force Reserve unit at Hill Air Force Base, Utah. When it retired three years later, the 466th placed it on a dramatic pylon mount and dedicated it to all Thunderchief crews who lost their lives flying the Thud. (Photograph by author, 25 March 1997.)

28 Feb 1969	While assigned to the 355 TFW, Takhli RTAB, Thailand, the aircraft flew 43.9 hours during the month of February 1969 and had accumulated 3,194.3 flying hours. (355 TFW History, Jan–Mar 69, Vol. II, USAF Microfilm NO467).
30 Jan 1969	In depot maintenance (WM) by SMAMA at Takhli AB, Thailand. (AVH-12).
9 Feb 1969	At 355 TFW, Takhli RTAB, Thailand.
28 Apr 1969	In depot maintenance (WM) by SMAMA at Takhli AB, Thailand.
22 May 1969	At 355 TFW, Takhli RTAB, Thailand.
20 Aug 1969	At Air Asia, Tainan, Taiwan, for contract depot work (WK).
10 Nov 1969	Returned to 355 TFW, Takhli RTAB, Thailand.
10 Dec 1969	In depot maintenance (WM) by SMAMA at Takhli AB, Thailand.
13 Dec 1969	At 355 TFW, Takhli RTAB, Thailand.
Jun 1970	While assigned to 333 TFS, 355 TFW, Takhli RTAB, Thailand, the aircraft accumulated 4,020 flying hours. Pilot: Maj. John Fail. (Thunderchief Worldwide Report, Vol. 5, No. 9, June 1970).
24 Oct 1970	At 355 TFW, Takhli RTAB, Thailand, being prepared for transfer (PL). (AVH-14).
27 Oct 1970	Transferred (PL) to 23 TFW, McConnell AFB KS.
4 Nov 1970	Placed in flyable storage (PR) at 23 TFW, McConnell AFB KS.
4 Jan 1971	At 23 TFW, McConnell AFB KS being prepared for transfer (PL).
17 Feb 1971	Transferred to 184 TFTG ANG, McConnell AFB KS. (AVH-16).
30 Mar 1971	In depot work (WO) by SMAMA at McClellan AFB CA.
18 May 1971	Returned to 184 TFTG ANG, McConnell AFB KS.
12 Dec 1972	In contract depot maintenance (WK) by Fairchild Engine and Aircraft Corporation (FACCF) at Bob Sikes Municipal Airport, Crestview FL. (AVH-18).
8 Jan 1973	Departed (PL) Fairchild Engine and Aircraft Corporation (FACCF) at Bob Sikes Municipal Airport, Crestview FL. (AVH-20).

16 Jan 1973	At 184 TFTG ANG, McConnell AFB KS.
25 Jun 1973	In contract depot maintenance (WM) by Dynalectron Corporation (DYNZZ) at McConnell AFB KS.
13 Jul 1973	At 184 TFTG ANG, McConnell AFB KS.
11 Oct 1973	In contract depot work (WK) at Fairchild Engine and Aircraft Corporation (FACCF) at Bob Sikes Municipal Airport, Crestview FL.
13 May 1974	At 184 TFTG ANG, McConnell AFB KS for combat crew training (TF). (AVH-22).
28 Mar 1975	In contract depot maintenance (WM) by Dynalectron Corporation (DYNZZ) at McConnell AFB KS. (AVH-23).
8 Apr 1975	At 184 TFTG ANG, McConnell AFB KS, for combat crew training (TF). (AVH-23 & AVH-24).
21 Dec 1976	In contract depot work by General Dynamics (DYNFW) with Possession Code "DK," at McConnell AFB KS. 5,604.0 flying hours. (AVH-25 & AVH-26).
28 Dec 1976	At 184 TFTG ANG, McConnell AFB KS. 5,604.0 flying hours.
17 Apr 1978	At 184 TFTG ANG, McConnell AFB KS. 5,892.0 flying hours.
27 Apr 1979	In contract depot maintenance (DYNFW) at McConnell AFB KS. 5,950.0 flying hours. (AVH-27).
25 May 1979	At 184 TFTG ANG, McConnell AFB KS for student and combat crew training (TF). 5,950.0 flying hours.
21 Aug 1979	In contract depot maintenance (DYNFW) at McConnell AFB KS. 5,975.4 flying hours.
24 Aug 1979	At 184 TFTG ANG, McConnell AFB KS, for student and combat crew training (TF). 6,000.7 flying hours.
24 Aug 1979	At 184 TFTG ANG, McConnell AFB KS. 6,044.5 flying hours. (GO33B 24 Jun 80).
28 Mar 1980	Transferred to the 466 TFS AFRES, Hill AFB UT. 6,070.9 flying hours.
15 Jul 1980	In depot maintenance at Ogden ALC, Hill AFB UT. 6,092.0 flying hours. (GO33B 22 Jan 81).
4 Aug 1980	At 466 TFS AFRES, Hill AFB UT. 6,111.4 flying hours.
30 Oct 1980	In depot maintenance at McClellan AFB CA. 6,148.1 flying hours.
1 Dec 1980	At 466 TFS AFRES, Hill AFB UT. 6,175.2 flying hours.
15 Aug 1981	Deployed under "Coronet Rudder" with 466 TFS to Skrydstrup, Denmark from Hill AFB UT. (British Aviation Review, Dec 1995).
29 Aug 1981	Returned from Denmark to Hill AFB UT.
3 Oct 1983	Aircraft flown on its last flight by the 419 TFW AFRES at Hill AFB UT. The aircraft accumulated a total of 6,730.5 flying hours, the highest time of any F-105. (Wings Magazine, Apr 1991).
25 Feb 1984	During the "Thud-Out" ceremonies hosted by the 419 TFW AFRES, at Hill AFB UT, the plane was mounted on a pylon and "... dedicated as a monument to all Air Force personnel who lost their lives while flying the Thunderchief ...." (Thud-Out Program Handout).

F-105D-31RE 62-4353

Republic Production No: D-552 Production Sequence No: 632

Location: At Security Police Flightline Training Area #7, Lackland AFB, San Antonio, Texas.

Aircraft Name(s)	Crew	Unit	Date	Description
Billie Fern/ Thunderchief		354 TFS 355 TFW		Name on both intakes. On fuselage below cockpits.
Thunderchief		354 TFS 355 TFW	May 70	Name in red. Storm cloud with yellow lightning bolt and profile of Indian chief's head. On gun access panel.
No Guts No Glory		466 TFS AFRES	Jul 82	Mouse with dream cloud of WW I airplane in shield.

Aircraft Chronology

30 Aug 1963	USAF production acceptance from Republic Aviation, Farmingdale NY. (ACA-88).
6 Sep 1963	At MOAMA, Brookley AFB AL, for depot work.
16 Sep 1963	Delivered to 8 TFW, Itazuke AB, Japan.
13 May 1964	Transferred to 41 AD, Yokota AB, Japan, under "Project Clearwater." (AVH-1).
1 Apr 1965	Assigned unit redesignated 6441 TFW at Yokota AB, Japan. (AVH-4).
30 April 1965	At 6441 TFW, Yokota AB, Japan. Assigned Crew Chief: TSgt. Halbash. (6441 TFW History, Apr–Jun 65, USAF microfilm PO231).
30 Apr 1965	At Air Asia, Tainan, Taiwan, for contract depot work (WK).
16 May 1965	Returned to 6441 TFW Yokota AB, Japan.
Aug 1965	At 6441 TFW, Yokota AB, Japan. Assigned Crew Chief: SSgt. Coughlin. (6441 TFW History, Jul–Dec 65, USAF microfilm PO232).
13 Jan 1966	At Air Asia, Tainan, Taiwan, for contract depot work (WK). (AVH-5).
7 Feb 1966	At 6441 TFW Yokota AB, Japan.
31 May 1966	At Osan AB, Korea, with 6441 TFW for nuclear weapon alert.
22 Sep 1966	In depot maintenance (WM) by SMAMA field team at 6441 TFW, Yokota AB, Japan.
24 Sep 1966	At Osan AB, Korea, with 6441 TFW for nuclear weapon alert.
3 Jan 1967	At Osan AB, Korea, with 41 AD for nuclear weapon alert. (AVH-8).
23 Mar 1967	Returned to 41 AD, Yokota AB, Japan.
25 Mar 1967	At Air Asia, Tainan, Taiwan, for contract depot work (WK).
1 Jun 1967	Transferred to 67 TFS, 18 TFW, Kadena AB, Okinawa. Aircraft had accumulated 915 flying hours.
9 Aug 1967	In depot maintenance (WM) by SMAMA field team at Kadena AB, Okinawa.
14 Sep 1967	At 18 TFW, Kadena AB, Okinawa.
15 Sep 1967	In depot maintenance (WM) by SMAMA field team at Kadena AB, Okinawa.
31 Oct 1967	At 18 TFW, Kadena AB, Okinawa.
8 Jan 1968	At Air Asia, Tainan, Taiwan, for contract depot work (WO). (AVH-10).
9 Jan 1968	Crash damaged (WJ) at 18 TFW, Kadena AB, Okinawa.
3 Feb 1968	At Air Asia, Tainan, Taiwan, for contract depot work (WK).
27 May 1968	Returned to 18 TFW, Kadena AB, Okinawa.
31 May 1968	At Osan AB, Korea, with 18 TFW.
10 Jun 1968	Returned to 18 TFW, Kadena AB, Okinawa.
12 Jun 1968	In depot work (WM) by SMAMA at 18 TFW, Kadena AB, Okinawa.
15 Jun 1968	At 18 TFW, Kadena AB, Okinawa.
17 Jul 1968	Transferred (PL) to 355 TFW, Takhli RTAB, Thailand.
21 Jul 1968	Operational (CC) at 355 TFW, Takhli RTAB, Thailand.
1 Nov 1968	While assigned to the 355 TFW, Takhli RTAB, Thailand, the aircraft had accumulated 1,498.9 flying hours. (355 TFW History, Oct–Dec 68, USAF microfilm NO466).
28 Feb 1969	While assigned to the 355 TFW, Takhli RTAB, Thailand, the aircraft flew 110.0 hours during the month of February 1969 and had accumulated 1,783.3 flying hours. (355 TFW History, Jan–Mar 69, Vol. II, USAF Microfilm NO467).
18 Mar 1969	In depot maintenance by SMAMA at Takhli RTAB, Thailand. (AVH-12).
19 Mar 1969	At 355 TFW, Takhli RTAB, Thailand.
19 Apr 1969	The aircraft was flown on a combat mission by Maj Eugene E. Cirillo, 333 TFS, 355 TFW, from Takhli RTAB, Thailand. It was his 165th and last combat mission. "... 0545 Briefing. Target was Route 8 where it exits North Vietnam through Ban Karai Pass into northern Laos. Objective was to cut the road. Call

F-105D 62-4353 was the fourth of Lackland's 343 Training Squadron's Thunderchiefs delivered from production in 1963 to the 8 Tactical Fighter Wing at Itazuke Air Base, Japan. It accompanied the three fighter squadrons from the 8 Tactical Fighter Wing to Yokota Air Base, Japan, when the 8th was discontinued under a program named "Project Clearwater." The 41 Air Division at Yokota used the plane for nuclear alert duties at Osan Air Base, Korea, and transferred it to the 18 Tactical Fighter Wing at Kadena Air Base, Okinawa, when Yokota converted to F-4s in 1967. The plane went to the 355 Tactical Fighter Wing at Takhli, Thailand, on 17 July 1968 to replace an F-105D lost in combat over North Vietnam a few days earlier. When Takhli began closing down at the end of 1970, the plane rested for a short while at McConnell Air Force Base, Kansas, and then, in 1971, went to the Virginia Air National Guard at Richmond. Its last unit was the Air Force Reserve's 466 Tactical Fighter Squadron at Hill Air Force Base, Utah, who, in August 1981, flew it on the NATO deployment to Denmark named "Coronet Rudder." It arrived at Lackland Air Force Base, Texas, in October 1983. (Photograph by author, 4 August 1997.)

sign: "Dolphin." It was a four ship flight. I was Lead, Maj. John Perkins was 2, Col. Sam McClurkin (Wing Vice CC) was 3, and Maj. Jim Howerton was 4. Ordnance on each aircraft was six Mark 117, 750-lb bombs with .125 fusing on the centerline station, two 450 gallon tanks on the inboards and a QRC Pod and an AIM-9 on the outboard stations. We cut the road, and did not sustain any battle damage. Pretty uneventful ..." (Gene Cirillo, e-mail 6 April 2000).

10 May 1969 At Air Asia, Tainan, Taiwan, for contract depot work (WK).

4 Jul 1969 Returned to 355 TFW, Takhli RTAB, Thailand.

1 Mar 1970 At Air Asia, Tainan, Taiwan, for contract depot work (WK). (AVH-14).

6 May 1970 Returned to 355 TFW, Takhli RTAB, Thailand.

28 Aug 1970 Combat damaged (VO) at 355 TFW, Takhli RTAB, Thailand.

29 Aug 1970 Combat ready (CC) at 355 TFW, Takhli RTAB, Thailand.

19 Oct 1970 Transferred (PL) to 23 TFW, McConnell AFB KS.

27 Oct 1970 Placed in flyable storage (PR) at 23 TFW, McConnell AFB KS.

4 Jan 1971 At 23 TFW, McConnell AFB KS being prepared for transfer (PL).

4 Mar 1971 In depot work (WO) by SMAMA at McClellan AFB CA. (AVH-16).

1 May 1971 Transferred to 192 TFG ANG, Byrd Field, Richmond VA.

28 Oct 1971 In contract depot maintenance (WO) by Dynalectron Corporation (DYNZZ) at Byrd Field, Richmond VA.

18 Nov 1971 At 192 TFG ANG, Byrd Field, Richmond VA.

25 May 1972 In contract depot maintenance (WK) by Fairchild Engine and Aircraft Corporation (FACCF) at Bob Sikes Municipal Airport, Crestview FL. (AVH-18).

28 Jun 1972 Returned to 192 TFG ANG, Byrd Field, Richmond VA.

12 Dec 1972 In contract depot maintenance (WO) by Dynalectron Corporation (DYNZZ) at Byrd Field, Richmond VA.

27 Jan 1973 At 192 TFG ANG, Byrd Field, Richmond VA. (AVH-20).

15 Mar 1973 In contract depot work (WM) by Dynalectron Corporation (DYNZZ) at Byrd Field, Richmond VA.

20 Mar 1973	At 192 TFG ANG, Byrd Field, Richmond VA.
23 Aug 1973	In contract depot work (WM) by Dynalectron Corporation (DYNZZ) at Byrd Field, Richmond VA.
25 Aug 1973	At 192 TFG ANG, Byrd Field, Richmond VA.
9 Oct 1973	In contract depot work (WM) by Dynalectron Corporation (DYNZZ) at Byrd Field, Richmond VA.
19 Oct 1973	At 192 TFG ANG, Byrd Field, Richmond VA.
28 Feb 1974	In contract depot maintenance (WK) by Fairchild Engine and Aircraft Corporation (FACCF) at Bob Sikes Municipal Airport, Crestview FL. (AVH-22).
23 Aug 1974	Returned to 192 TFG ANG, Byrd Field VA.
18 Sep 1975	In contract depot work (WM) by Dynalectron Corporation (DYNZZ) at Byrd Field, Richmond VA. (AVH-23 & AVH-24).
30 Jan 1976	At 192 TFG ANG, Byrd Field VA. (AVH-24).
12 Dec 1976	In contract depot work (WM) by Dynalectron Corporation (DYNZZ) at Byrd Field, Richmond VA. 3,600 flying hours.
6 Jan 1977	At 192 TFG ANG, Byrd Field VA. 3,663.0 flying hours. (AVH-25 & AVH-26).
6 Apr 1978	At 192 TFG ANG, Byrd Field VA. 3,819.0 flying hours. (AVH-26).
2 Jun 1978	At 192 TFG ANG, Byrd Field VA. 3,874.0 flying hours.
30 Jul 1979	In contract depot maintenance by Dynalectron Corporation (DYNZZ) at Byrd Field VA. 4,074.2 flying hours. (AVH-27).
16 Aug 1979	At 192 TFG ANG, Byrd Field VA. 4,074.2 flying hours.
21 Feb 1980	At McClellan AFB for depot maintenance. 4,097.4 flying hours. (GO33B 24 Jun 80).
14 Apr 1980	At 192 TFG ANG, Byrd Field VA. 4,110.7 flying hours.
15 May 1981	At 466 TFS AFRES, Hill AFB UT. 4,281.4 flying hours. (GO33B Dec 81 & GO33B 1 Feb 83).
15 Aug 1981	Deployed under "Coronet Rudder" with 466 TFS to Skrydstrup, Denmark from Hill AFB UT. (British Aviation Review, Dec 1995).
29 Aug 1981	Returned from Denmark to Hill AFB UT.
11 Oct 1983	One of 24 F-105s flown on ceremonial final mission at Hill AFB UT. After the mission, the aircraft was one of seven delivered to 3280 TTA Group (ATC), Lackland AFB TX, for security police flightline training. (Possession code: TX. Inventory account: GB). 4,769.1 flying hours. (GO33B 9 Feb 84).
12 Oct 1983	Redesignated GF-105D at 3280 TTA Group (ATC), Lackland AFB TX. (Possession code: TX. Inventory account: GC). 4,769.1 flying hours.

F-105D-31RE 62-4360

Republic Production No: D-559 Production Sequence No: 639

Location: Displayed outside at Heritage Museum, Tinker AFB, Oklahoma City, Oklahoma.

Aircraft Name(s)	Crew	Unit	Date	Description
12 O'clock High		469 TFS 388 TFW		Man drinking from bottle with arm around post in front of pub door. Under right wing.
Screaming Eagle	Col. John A. Nelson	44 TFS 388 TFW	Jun 69	In black on left fuselage.
Iron Duke	1Lt Allan V. Shulke	354 TFS 355 TFW	Jan 70	On both intakes in blue with red shadow behind letters.

This plane served at every F-105 base in the Pacific beginning in August 1963 when it arrived from production to the 8 Tactical Fighter Wing at Itazuke Air Base, Japan. When Itazuke closed a year later the plane moved to Yokota Air Base, Japan, where it cycled to Korea for nuclear weapon alerts. In January 1968, it transferred to Okinawa just in time to return to Korea in response to North Korea capturing the U.S.S. Pueblo. In September 1968, it began a steady diet of combat over North Vietnam and Laos when it served with the 388 Tactical Fighter Wing at Korat, Thailand, then moved the next year to Takhli, Thailand, with the 355 Tactical Fighter Wing. When Takhli began closing in October 1968, the plane returned to Okinawa where it stayed for the next four years until transferring directly to the Air Force Reserve at Tinker Air Force Base, Oklahoma. The Reserves kept it flying for the next seven years and took it with them for their 1978 NATO summer deployment to Great Britain. When it retired in 1980, it served for a few years as a battle damage repair trainer at McClellan Air Force Base, California, until the Reserves brought it back to Tinker where it is displayed today. (Photograph by Ronald L. Shepard, 30 April 1998.)

Aircraft Chronology

28 Aug 1963	USAF production acceptance from Republic Aviation, Farmingdale NY. (ACA-88).
29 Aug 1963	At MOAMA, Brookley AFB AL for depot work.
30 Aug 1963	Delivered to 8 TFW, Itazuke AB, Japan.
13 May 1964	Transferred to 41 AD, Yokota AB, Japan under "Project Clearwater" that deactivated the 8 TFW. (AVH-1).
Aug 1964	At 41 AD Yokota AB, Japan. Crew Chief: A1C B. Duncan. (41 AD Monthly Maint Summary).
Apr 1965	At 6441 TFW, Yokota AB, Japan. Assigned Crew Chief: SSgt. Brame. (6441 TFW History, Apr–Jun 65, USAF microfilm PO231).
1 Apr 1965	Assigned unit redesignated 6441 TFW at Yokota AB, Japan. (AVH-4).
1 Jun 1965	At Air Asia, Tainan, Taiwan, for contract depot work (WK).
23 Jun 1965	At Yokota AB, Japan, with the 23 TFW.
Aug 1965	At 6441 TFW, Yokota AB, Japan. Assigned Crew Chief: A1C Randolph. (6441 TFW History, Jul–Dec 65, USAF microfilm PO232).
17 Jan 1966	At Air Asia, Tainan, Taiwan, for contract depot work (WK) from the 23 TFW. (AVH-5).
26 Jan 1966	While at Tainan for contract depot work, aircraft transferred to 41 AD.
16 Feb 1966	At 6441 TFW, Yokota AB, Japan.
28 Apr 1966	While flying with the 355 TFW at Takhli RTAB, Thailand, the aircraft received combat damage consisting of a 10" x 3/4" tear from a projectile entering the wing root fairing. The shell broke a wire bundle clamp, cut several wires, and caused other damage. The projectile was found under the fairing. (355 TFW History, Jan–Jun 1966, USAF microfilm NO461).
7 May 1966	At Air Asia, Tainan, Taiwan, for contract depot work (WK).
22 May 1966	Returned to 6441 TFW, Yokota AB, Japan.
3 Nov 1966	In depot maintenance (WM) by SMAMA field team at 6441 TFW, Yokota AB, Japan.

5 Nov 1966	At 6441 TFW, Yokota AB, Japan.
15 Nov 1966	At Osan AB, Korea, for nuclear weapon alert with 6441 TFW.
3 Jan 1967	At 41 AD, Yokota AB, Japan (AVH-8).
8 Jan 1967	At Air Asia, Tainan, Taiwan, for contract depot work (WK).
13 Mar 1967	Returned to 41 AD, Yokota AB, Japan.
19 Jun 1967	At Osan AB, Korea, for nuclear weapon alert with 41 AD.
7 Jul 1967	At 41 AD, Yokota AB, Japan.
26 Jul 1967	At Osan AB, Korea, for nuclear weapon alert with 41 AD.
14 Aug 1967	At 41 AD, Yokota AB, Japan.
30 Aug 1967	At Osan AB, Korea, for nuclear weapon alert with 41 AD.
31 Oct 1967	At 41 AD, Yokota AB, Japan.
7 Nov 1967	At Osan AB, Korea, for nuclear weapon alert with 41 AD.
27 Nov 1967	At 41 AD, Yokota AB, Japan.
19 Jan 1968	Transferred to 18 TFW, Kadena AB, Okinawa. (AVH-10).
29 Jan 1968	Deployed to Osan AB, Korea, with 18 TFW for U.S.S. Pueblo incident.
22 Mar 1968	Returned to 18 TFW, Kadena AB, Okinawa.
23 Mar 1968	In depot-level maintenance (WM) by SMAMA at Kadena AB, Okinawa.
24 Mar 1968	Returned to Osan AB, Korea, with 18 TFW.
29 Apr 1968	At 18 TFW, Kadena AB, Okinawa.
8 May 1968	Returned to Osan AB, Korea, with 18 TFW.
11 Jun 1968	At 18 TFW, Kadena AB, Okinawa.
15 Jun 1968	In depot-level maintenance (WM) at Kadena AB, Okinawa.
18 Jun 1968	At 18 TFW, Kadena AB, Okinawa.
28 Jul 1968	At Kwangju AB, Korea, with 18 TFW.
3 Aug 1968	Returned to 18 TFW, Kadena AB, Okinawa.
9 Sep 1968	Transferred to 388 TFW, Korat RTAB, Thailand.
31 Oct 1968	Aircraft had accumulated 1,585.4 flying hours while assigned to the 388 TFW, Korat RTAB, Thailand. (388 TFW History, Oct–Dec 68, USAF microfilm NO585).
28 Nov 1968	At Air Asia, Tainan, Taiwan, for contract depot work (WK). (AVH-10).
9 Jan 1969	Returned to 388 TFW, Korat RTAB, Thailand. (AVH-12).
31 Jan 1969	At Takhli RTAB, Thailand, with 388 TFW during runway repairs at Korat RTAB, Thailand.
8 Feb 1969	Flown on a strike mission in the Steel Tiger region of Laos by 44 TFS pilot, 388 TFW, while operating from Takhli RTAB, Thailand. (388 TFW History, Jan–Mar 69, USAF microfilm NO586).
12 Feb 1969	Flown on a strike mission in the Steel Tiger region of Laos by 44 TFS pilot, 388 TFW, while operating from Takhli RTAB, Thailand.
13 Feb 1969	Flown on a strike mission in the Steel Tiger region of Laos by 44 TFS pilot, 388 TFW, while operating from Takhli RTAB, Thailand.
17 Feb 1969	Flown on a strike mission in the Steel Tiger region of Laos by 44 TFS pilot, 388 TFW, while operating from Takhli RTAB, Thailand.
19 Feb 1969	Flown on a strike mission in the Steel Tiger region of Laos by 44 TFS pilot, 388 TFW, while operating from Takhli RTAB, Thailand.
21 Feb 1969	Flown on a strike mission in the Steel Tiger region of Laos by 44 TFS pilot, 388 TFW, while operating from Takhli RTAB, Thailand.
22 Feb 1969	Flown on a strike mission in the Steel Tiger region of Laos by 44 TFS pilot, 388 TFW, while operating from Takhli RTAB, Thailand.
23 Feb 1969	Flown on a strike mission in the Steel Tiger region of Laos by 44 TFS pilot, 388 TFW, while operating

	from Takhli RTAB, Thailand. During second strike sortie of day, the aircraft diverted to Ubon RTAB, Thailand, due to an aircraft problem.
27 Feb 1969	Flown on a strike mission in the Steel Tiger region of Laos by 44 TFS pilot, 388 TFW, while operating from Takhli RTAB, Thailand.
2 Mar 1969	Returned to 388 TFW, Korat RTAB, Thailand. (AVH-12).
30 Apr 1969	While assigned to the 34 TFS, 388 TFW, Korat RTAB, Thailand, the aircraft had accumulated 1,913.8 flying hours. (388 TFW History, Apr–Jun 69, USAF microfilm NO586).
30 Jun 1969	While assigned to the 44 TFS, 388 TFW, Korat RTAB, Thailand, the aircraft flew 70.3 hours in the month of June 1969 and had accumulated 2,049.1 total flying hours.
27 Aug 1969	Transferred to 355 TFW, Takhli RTAB, Thailand. (AVH-12).
5 Sep 1969	Returned to 388 TFW, Korat RTAB, Thailand.
10 Oct 1969	Transferred again to 355 TFW, Takhli RTAB, Thailand.
10 Feb 1970	At Air Asia, Tainan, Taiwan, for contract depot work (WK). (AVH-14).
16 Apr 1970	Returned to 355 TFW, Takhli RTAB, Thailand.
30 May 1970	Aircraft assigned to D Flight, 44 TFS, 355 TFW, Takhli RTAB. Pilot: 1 Lt Davis. (44 TFS Aircraft Assignment Roster).
10 Oct 1970	Transferred to 18 TFW, Kadena AB, Okinawa. (AVH-14).
1 Nov 1970	At Kwangju AB, Korea, with 18 TFW.
4 Nov 1970	Returned to 18 TFW, Kadena AB, Okinawa.
18 Nov 1970	At Kwangju AB, Korea, with 18 TFW.
27 Nov 1970	Returned to 18 TFW, Kadena AB, Okinawa.
19 Apr 1971	At Air Asia, Tainan, Taiwan, for contract depot work (WK). (AVH-16).
26 May 1971	Returned (PL) to 18 TFW, Kadena AB, Okinawa.
25 Oct 1971	At Taegu AB, Korea ,with 18 TFW.
29 Oct 1971	Returned to 18 TFW, Kadena AB, Okinawa.
11 Nov 1971	At Taegu AB, Korea, with 18 TFW.
16 Nov 1971	Returned to 18 TFW, Kadena AB, Okinawa.
30 Nov 1971	In depot work (WM) by SMAMA at Kadena AB, Okinawa.
4 Dec 1971	At 18 TFW, Kadena AB, Okinawa.
26 Apr 1972	Departed (PL) 18 TFW, Kadena AB, Okinawa, Japan. (AVH-18).
27 Apr 1972	Arrived (PL) at 937 MALGP (AFRES), Tinker AFB OK.
20 May 1972	Assigned to 507 TFG (AFRES), Tinker AFB OK.
18 Sep 1972	In contract depot maintenance (WK) by Fairchild Engine and Aircraft Corporation (FACCF) at Bob Sikes Municipal Airport, Crestview FL.
16 Oct 1972	Returned to 507 TFG (AFRES), Tinker AFB OK.
5 Mar 1973	Departed (PL) 507 TFG (AFRES), Tinker AFB OK for depot work. (AVH-20).
8 Mar 1973	In depot maintenance (WO) by SM-ALC at McClellan AFB CA.
21 May 1973	Returned (PL) to 507 TFG (AFRES), Tinker AFB OK.
1 Jun 1973	Combat ready (CC) at 507 TFG (AFRES), Tinker AFB OK.
13 May 1974	In depot maintenance by SM-ALC at Tinker AFB OK. (AVH-22).
17 May 1974	At 507 CMTSQ AFRES, Tinker AFB OK.
16 Oct 1974	Assigned unit redesignated 507 CLMSQ AFRES, Tinker AFB OK.
16 Apr 1975	In depot maintenance (WM) by SM-ALC at Tinker AFB OK. (AVH-23 & AVH-24).
27 Apr 1975	At 507 CLMSQ AFRES, Tinker AFB OK.
11 May 1976	In depot maintenance (DM) by SM-ALC at Tinker AFB OK. 3,859 flying hours (AVH-24).

15 May 1976	At 507 TFG AFRES, Tinker AFB OK. 3,859 flying hours.
19 Aug 1976	In depot maintenance (DM) by SM-ALC at Tinker AFB OK. 3,932 flying hours.
1 Sep 1976	At 507 TFG AFRES, Tinker AFB OK. 3,969 flying hours.
28 Sep 1976	In depot work (DK) by ARDLF at Moultrie GA. 3,969 flying hours.
11 Jan 1977	At 507 TFG AFRES, Tinker AFB OK. 3,974.0 flying hours. (AVH-25 & AVH-26).
31 Jan 1977	In depot maintenance by SM-ALC at Tinker AFB OK. 3,974.0 flying hours.
1 Feb 1977	At 507 TFG AFRES, Tinker AFB OK. 3,974.0 flying hours.
13 Oct 1977	At 465 TFS AFRES, Tinker AFB OK. 4,147.0 flying hours. (AVH-26).
10 Jun 1978	Deployed under "Coronet Oriole" with 465 TFS to Sculthorpe, England, from Tinker AFB OK. (British Aviation Review, Dec 1995).
23 Jun 1978	Returned from England to Tinker AFB OK.
16 Jul 1978	In contract depot maintenance (DYNFW) at Tinker AFB OK. 4,374.0 flying hours. (AVH-26).
31 Jul 1978	At 465 TFS AFRES, Tinker AFB OK. 4,374.0 flying hours.
18 Apr 1979	While assigned to the 465 TFS AFRES, Tinker AFB OK, the aircraft ground aborted due to an inoperative anti skid valve. (301 TFW History 1 Apr–30 Jun 1979, USAF microfilm 343832).
5 Jun 1979	While assigned to the 465 TFS AFRES, Tinker AFB OK, the aircraft ground aborted due to the right 450 gallon tank pylon being cracked. (301 TFW History 1 Apr–30 Jun 1979, USAF microfilm 343832).
30 Jun 1979	While assigned to the 465 TFS AFRES, Tinker AFB OK, the aircraft flew 29.2 hours during the month of June 1979 and had accumulated a total of 4,559.6 flying hours. The assigned crew chief was Phillips. (301 TFW History, Apr–Jun 1979, USAF microfilm 34382).
31 Jul 1979	At 465 TFS AFRES, Tinker AFB OK. 4,481.4 flying hours. (AVH-27).
1 Nov 1979	In contract depot maintenance (FACBM), Tinker AFB OK. 4,623.7 flying hours.
5 Dec 1979	In depot maintenance (FACBM) at Tinker AFB OK. 4,650.4 flying hours. Allocated to museum (ZW). (GO33B 24 Jun 80 & GO33B 22 Jan 81).
9 Nov 1983	At 2951 CLSS, McClellan AFB CA for ABDR training. (HQ 2852 ABG/DADF letter 9 Nov 83).
22 May 1985	At 2951 CLSS, McClellan AFB CA for ABDR training. (HQ 2852 ABG/DADF letter 22 May 85).
23 Sep 1986	In USAF Museum account at Tinker AFB OK. (AMARC Letter, 23 Sep 86).

F-105D-31RE 62-4361

Republic Production No: D-560 Production Sequence No: 640

Location: On the flightline near the 121 ARW ANG at Rickenbacker Airport, Columbus, Ohio.

Aircraft Name(s)	Crew	Unit	Date	Description
Blinky III		388 TFW	Jul 68	
Mary Bee		34 TFS 388 TFW	Mar 69	In yellow and black block print on both fuselage sides.
Bonnie III		44 TFS 388 TFW	May 69	In black on left fuselage. Deleted by Jun 69.
Oscar Meyer		44 TFS 388 TFW	Jul 69	In red on right fuselage. Applied between 8–18 July 1969.
War Wagon	Capt. Bob Nesbitt	44 TFS 388 TFW	Aug 69	On right fuselage. Dark blue with green trim.

After spending its first three years in Japan, this "D" transferred in June 1966 to the 388 Tactical Fighter Wing at Korat, Thailand, where it survived three years of combat over North Vietnam. During February 1969, while the runway at Korat was being repaired, the plane flew missions over Laos from Takhli, Thailand. It continued to drop bombs on targets in Laos after the runway at Korat reopened but was damaged in its nose section by anti-aircraft gunfire during a mission in May 1969. After 300 hours of labor, maintenance technicians had the plane flying again. It stayed at Korat until October 1969 when it moved with the 44 Tactical Fighter Squadron to Takhli where it endured another year of combat with the 355 Tactical Fighter Wing. When Takhli closed in late 1970, the plane transferred to McConnell Air Force Base, Kansas, spending six months with the 23 Tactical Fighter Wing. It then moved across the base in March 1971 to the Kansas Air National Guard that, by this time, had became the only unit training F-105 pilots. On 9 September 1976, the plane reached 5,000 hours of flying time. It continued training pilots until January 1980 when it moved briefly to the Air Force Reserve unit at Tinker Air Force Base, Oklahoma, before transferring to the last unit to fly F-105s, the Reserve's 466 Tactical Fighter Squadron at Hill Air Force Base, Utah. In 1984, the plane flew its last sortie, landing at Columbus, Ohio, where it sat for the next 12 years near the entrance gate to the Defense Construction Supply Center. In June 1996, the Ohio Air National Guard moved the plane to its collection of other restored aircraft on the flight line at Rickenbacker Air Base outside Columbus. (Photograph by author, 5 June 1998.)

Aircraft Name(s)	Crew	Unit	Date	Description
Prudi's Pride	Capt. Bob Nesbitt	44 TFS 388 TFW	Sep 69	Blue letters with red trim on a white cloud with a black scorpion in the center on the left fuselage. Applied between 28 Sep–10 Oct 69.
Christie		44 TFS 355 TFW	Jan 70	On both intakes.
Yankee Peddler		127 TFS KANG	Apr 71	

Aircraft Chronology

30 Aug 1963	USAF production acceptance from Republic Aviation, Farmingdale NY. (ACA-88).
30 Aug 1963	Delivered to 8 TFW, Itazuke AB, Japan.
13 May 1964	Transferred to 41 AD, Yokota AB, Japan, under "Project Clearwater" that deactivated the 8 TFW. (AVH-1).
Aug 1964	At 41 AD Yokota AB, Japan. Crew Chief: SSgt. J. Ashley. (41 AD Monthly Maint. Summary).
22 Mar 1965	At Air Asia, Tainan, Taiwan, for contract depot work (WK). (AVH-4).
30 Apr 1965	At 6441 TFW, Yokota AB, Japan. Assigned Crew Chief: SSgt. Oakes. (6441 TFW History, Apr–Jun 65, USAF microfilm PO231).

31 Aug 1965	At 6441 TFW, Yokota AB, Japan. Assigned Crew Chief: SSgt. Goggans. (6441 TFW History, Jul–Dec 65, USAF microfilm PO232).
27 Nov 1965	At Air Asia, Tainan, Taiwan, for contract depot work (WK). (AVH-4).
16 Dec 1965	At Osan AB, Korea, for nuclear weapon alert with 6441 TFW. (AVH-5).
16 Mar 1966	At Takhli RTAB, Thailand, with 6441 TFW.
29 Apr 1966	In depot maintenance (WM) by SMAMA field team at Takhli RTAB with 6441 TFW.
1 May 1966	At Takhli RTAB, Thailand, with 6441 TFW.
19 May 1966	In depot maintenance (WM) by SMAMA field team at 6441 TFW, Yokota AB, Japan.
16 Jun 1966	Transferred to 388 TFW, Korat RTAB, Thailand.
31 May 1967	At Air Asia, Tainan, Taiwan, for contract depot work (WK). (AVH-8).
5 Aug 1967	Returned to 388 TFW, Korat RTAB, Thailand.
7 Oct 1967	In depot maintenance (WM) by SMAMA field team at Korat RTAB, Thailand.
8 Oct 1967	At 388 TFW, Korat RTAB, Thailand.
1 Dec 1967	One of nine F-105Ds flown on Rolling Thunder mission RT56A-212 by pilots from the 469 TFS, 388 TFW, Korat RTAB, Thailand. They bombed a target in Laos 7 NM SSE of Sam Neua at coordinates 20-19N and 104-00E. The pilot was Capt Dennis Jarvi. (National Archives strike camera film shot list, item 42649C).
25 Feb 1968	In depot maintenance (WM) by SMAMA at Korat RTAB, Thailand. (AVH-10).
28 Feb 1968	At 388 TFW, Korat RTAB, Thailand.
1 Jun 1968	In depot maintenance (WM) by SMAMA at Korat RTAB, Thailand.
3 Jun 1968	At 388 TFW, Korat RTAB, Thailand.
31 Aug 1968	Aircraft flew 108 hours during the month of August 1968 while assigned to the 388 TFW, Korat RTAB, Thailand. (388 TFW History, Jul–Sep 68, USAF microfilm NO585).
30 Sep 1968	Aircraft flew 81 hours during the month of September 1968 while assigned to the 388 TFW, Korat RTAB, Thailand. (388 TFW History, Jul–Sep 68, USAF microfilm NO585).
31 Oct 1968	Aircraft had accumulated 2,479.3 flying hours while assigned to the 388 TFW, Korat RTAB, Thailand. (388 TFW History, Oct–Dec 68, USAF microfilm NO585).
24 Dec 1968	At Air Asia, Tainan, Taiwan, for contract depot work (WK). (AVH-10).
31 Jan 1969	Returned to 388 TFW, Korat RTAB, Thailand. (AVH-12).
2 Feb 1969	At Takhli RTAB, Thailand, with 388 TFW during runway repairs at Korat RTAB, Thailand.
11 Feb 1969	Flown on a strike mission in the Steel Tiger region of Laos by 44 TFS pilot, 388 TFW, while operating from Takhli RTAB, Thailand. (388 TFW History, Jan–Mar 69, USAF microfilm NO586).
13 Feb 1969	Flown on a strike mission in the Steel Tiger region of Laos by 44 TFS pilot, 388 TFW, while operating from Takhli RTAB, Thailand.
18 Feb 1969	Flown on a strike mission in the Steel Tiger region of Laos by 44 TFS pilot, 388 TFW, while operating from Takhli RTAB, Thailand.
22 Feb 1969	Flown on a strike mission in the Steel Tiger region of Laos by 44 TFS pilot, 388 TFW, while operating from Takhli RTAB, Thailand.
23 Feb 1969	Flown on a strike mission in the Steel Tiger region of Laos by 44 TFS pilot, 388 TFW, while operating from Takhli RTAB, Thailand. During second sortie of the day, the aircraft diverted to Ubon RTAB due to an aircraft problem.
27 Feb 1979	Flown on a strike mission in the Steel Tiger region of Laos by 44 TFS pilot, 388 TFW, while operating from Takhli RTAB, Thailand.
2 Mar 1969	Returned from Takhli to the 388 TFW, Korat RTAB, Thailand.
30 Apr 1969	While assigned to the 34 TFS, 388 TFW, Korat RTAB, Thailand, the aircraft flew 57 hours in the month of April 1969 and had accumulated 2,782.3 total flying hours. (388 TFW History, Apr–Jun 69, USAF microfilm NO586).

26 May 1969	During a combat mission over Laos from the 388 TFW, the aircraft received combat damage that required 300 labor hours to repair. Antiaircraft shell fragments tore the gun compartment bulkhead and panels, damaged the forward gun mount, jammed the weapon, and gouged oxygen lines. (388 TFW History, Apr–Jun 69, USAF microfilm NO586).
30 Jun 1969	While assigned to the 44 TFS, 388 TFW, Korat RTAB, Thailand, the aircraft flew 77 hours in the month of June 1969 and had accumulated 2,927.3 total flying hours.
11 Aug 1969	In depot maintenance by SMAMA at Takhli RTAB, Thailand. (AVH-12).
18 Aug 1969	Returned to 388 TFW, Korat RTAB, Thailand.
10 Oct 1969	Transferred with the 44 TFS to the 355 TFW, Takhli RTAB, Thailand.
14 May 1970	At Air Asia, Tainan, Taiwan, for contract depot work (WK). (AVH-14).
30 May 1970	Aircraft assigned to D Flight, 44 TFS, 355 TFW, Takhli RTAB, Thailand. Pilot: Capt. Newhouse. (44 TFS Aircraft Assignment Roster).
24 Oct 1970	At 355 TFW, Takhli RTAB, Thailand, being prepared for transfer (PL). (AVH-14).
27 Oct 1970	Transferred (PL) to 23 TFW, McConnell AFB KS.
4 Nov 1970	Placed in flyable storage (PR) at 23 TFW, McConnell AFB KS.
4 Jan 1971	At 23 TFW, McConnell AFB KS being prepared for transfer (PL).
2 Feb 1971	In depot maintenance (WO) by SMAMA at McClellan AFB CA. (AVH-16).
20 Mar 1971	Transferred (PL) to 184 TFG ANG, McConnell AFB KS.
24 Mar 1971	Assigned unit redesignated 184 TFTG ANG, McConnell AFB KS.
14 Apr 1971	Operationally ready at 184 TFTG ANG, McConnell AFB KS.
11 Sep 1972	In contract depot maintenance (WK) by Fairchild Engine and Aircraft Corporation (FACCF) at Bob Sikes Municipal Airport, Crestview FL. (AVH-18).
10 Oct 1972	Returned to 184 TFG ANG, McConnell AFB KS.
13 Aug 1973	In contract depot work (WM) by Dynalectron Corporation (DYNZZ) at McConnell AFB KS. (AVH-20).
24 Aug 1973	At 184 TFG ANG, McConnell AFB KS.
3 Jan 1974	Assigned to combat crew training (TF) at 184 TFG ANG, McConnell AFB KS.
18 Jan 1974	In contract depot maintenance (WK) by Fairchild Engine and Aircraft Corporation (FACCF) at Bob Sikes Municipal Airport, Crestview FL. (AVH-22).
17 Jul 1974	Returned to 184 TFTG ANG, McConnell AFB KS.
14 Aug 1975	In contract depot work (WM) by Dynalectron Corporation (DYNZZ) at McConnell AFB KS. (AVH-23 & AVH-24).
26 Aug 1975	At 184 TFTG ANG, McConnell AFB KS for combat crew training (TF).
2 Sep 1976	In depot maintenance by SM-ALC at McConnell AFB KS. 5,000.0 flying hours. (AVH-25 & AVH-26).
9 Sep 1976	At 184 TFG ANG, McConnell AFB KS. 5,000.0 flying hours.
15 Jul 1977	In contract depot work (DYNFW) at McConnell AFB KS. 5,135.0 flying hours.
15 Jun 1978	At OC-ALC depot, Tinker AFB OK. 5,377.0 flying hours. (AVH-26).
10 Sep 1978	At OC-ALC depot, Tinker AFB OK. 5,391.0 flying hours.
1 Sep 1978	At 184 TFG ANG, McConnell AFB KS. 5,391.0 flying hours.
11 Jun 1979	In contract depot maintenance (DYNFW) at McConnell AFB KS. 5,559.5 flying hours. (AVH-27).
21 Jun 1979	At 184 TFG ANG, McConnell AFB KS. 5,595.1 flying hours.
11 Oct 1979	In contract depot maintenance (DYNFW) at McConnell AFB KS. 5,659.6 flying hours.
17 Oct 1979	At 184 TFG ANG for student and combat crew training (TF), McConnell AFB KS. 5,684.4 flying hours.
11 Jan 1980	Transferred to the 465 TFS AFRES, Tinker AFB OK. 5,711.0 flying hours. (GO33B 24 Jun 80).
3 Jul 1980	In depot maintenance at McClellan AFB CA. 5,819.1 flying hours. (GO33B 22 Jan 81).
11 Aug 1980	Returned to the 465 TFS AFRES, Tinker AFB OK. 5,838.0 flying hours.

1 Oct 1980	Transferred to the 466 TFS AFRES, Hill AFB UT. 5,842.3 flying hours.
1984	Flown by 419 TFW from Hill AFB UT to Port Columbus Airport, Ohio, and towed to Defense Construction Supply Center, Columbus, Ohio, for display in area behind main gate.
16 Jun 1996	Tail removed and aircraft towed from DCSC to Rickenbacker International Airport, Columbus, Ohio, for display by 121st Air Refueling Wing. Ron French, retired ANG technician, performed corrosion control and repainted the aircraft in Vietnam colors. (Dick Weimer, letter 15 Oct 1996).

F-105D-31RE 62-4375

Republic Production No: D-574 Production Sequence No: 654

Location: Displayed inside Hanger 602 at Combat Air Museum, Forbes Field, Topeka, Kansas.

Aircraft Name(s)	Crew	Unit	Date	Description
Kukhui		466 TFS AFRES	Oct 83	Yellow letters in front of palm tree.

Aircraft Chronology

21 Jun 1963	USAF production acceptance from Republic Aviation, Farmingdale NY. (ACA-88).
2 Oct 1963	At MOAMA, Brookley AFB AL for depot work.
8 Oct 1963	Delivered to 8 TFW, Itazuke AB, Japan.
13 May 1964	Transferred to 41 AD, Yokota AB, Japan under "Project Clearwater" that deactivated the 8 TFW. (AVH-1).
31 Aug 1964	At 41 AD Yokota AB, Japan. Crew Chief: SSgt. R. Stanhope. (41 AD Monthly Maintenance Summary).
27 Mar 1965	At Air Asia, Tainan, Taiwan, for contract depot work (WK), (AVH-4).
30 Apr 1965	At 6441 TFW, Yokota AB, Japan. Assigned Crew Chief: TSgt. R. Stanhope. (6441 TFW History, Apr–Jun 65, USAF microfilm PO231).
31 Aug 1965	At 6441 TFW, Yokota AB, Japan. Assigned Crew Chief: TSgt. R. Stanhope. (6441 TFW History, Jul–Dec 65, USAF microfilm PO232).
4 Oct 1965	Aircraft received the first F-105 phase inspection conducted at the 6441 TFW, Yokota AB, Japan. (6441 TFW History, Jul–Dec 65, USAF microfilm PO232).
4 Oct 1965	Deployed from Yokota AB, Japan, to Williamtown RAAF Base, New Castle, New South Wales, Australia, for "Pacific Concord I." (5th AF Safety Newsletter).
17 Oct 1965	The aircraft returned to Yokota AB, Japan, from Australia.
28 Oct 1965	At Air Asia, Tainan, Taiwan, for contract depot work (WK) and "Safety Pack II" modification. (AVH-4).
20 Dec 1965	Aircraft returned to Yokota AB, Japan.
19 Apr 1966	At 6441 TFW, Yokota AB, Japan. (AVH-5).
19 Sep 1966	In depot maintenance (WM) by SMAMA field team at 6441 TFW, Yokota AB, Japan.
15 Nov 1966	Assigned to 41 AD, Yokota AB, Japan.
3 Jan 1967	At Osan AB, Korea, with 41 AD for nuclear weapon alert. (AVH-8).
27 Feb 1967	At Air Asia, Tainan, Taiwan, for contract depot work (WK).
18 Apr 1967	Transferred to the 67 TFS, 18 TFW, Kadena AB, Okinawa. Aircraft had accumulated 916 flying hours. (18 TFW History, Apr–Jun 67, USAF microfilm MO498).
29 Jan 1968	Deployed to Osan AB, Korea, with 18 TFW for U.S.S. Pueblo incident. (AVH-10).

This "D" spent the first eight years of its career in the Pacific without being assigned to combat duties at Takhli or Korat in Thailand. When it left the Republic factory in 1963, it was one of the F-105s that replaced F-100s in the 8 Tactical Fighter Wing at Itazuke, Japan. When the 8th shut down in May 1964, the plane went with the wing's three squadrons to Yokota where it remained for the next four years. In October 1965, it was one of the first Thunderchiefs to visit Australia when it was the only "D" accompanying six two-seater "Fs" to a firepower demonstration. In 1967, when Yokota began converting to F-4s, the plane moved south to Kadena Air Base, Okinawa. Less than a year later it deployed to Osan Air Base, Korea, in response to the North Koreans capturing the U.S.S. Pueblo. The plane cycled between Okinawa and Korea for the next three years and then, in 1971, left the Pacific to spend a year at McConnell Air Force Base, Kansas. In 1972, it began its career with the Air Force Reserve when it moved to Tinker Air Force Base, Oklahoma. Its second Reserve assignment in 1980 sent it to Hill Air Force Base, Utah. This unit took the plane with them on their NATO deployment to Denmark in the Summer of 1981 and then retired it a couple of years later. The plane sat as a static display for a number of years in Knoxville, Tennessee, before moving to its current home in Topeka, Kansas. (Photograph by author, 7 August 1995.)

25 Mar 1968 Returned to 18 TFW, Kadena AB, Okinawa.
28 Mar 1968 In depot-level work (WM) at 18 TFW, Kadena AB, Okinawa.
29 Mar 1968 At 18 TFW, Kadena AB, Okinawa.
30 Mar 1968 At Osan AB, Korea, with 18 TFW.
28 May 1968 At 18 TFW, Kadena AB, Okinawa.
7 Jun 1968 At Osan AB, Korea, with 18 TFW.
11 Jun 1968 Returned to 18 TFW, Kadena AB, Okinawa.
3 Feb 1969 At Kwangju AB, Korea, with 18 TFW. (AVH-12).
11 Apr 1969 Returned to 18 TFW, Kadena AB, Okinawa.
22 May 1969 At Kwangju AB, Korea, with 18 TFW.
29 May 1969 Returned to 18 TFW, Kadena AB, Okinawa.
9 Jul 1969 At Kwangju AB, Korea, with 18 TFW.
22 Jul 1969 Returned to 18 TFW, Kadena AB, Okinawa.
6 Oct 1969 At Kwangju AB, Korea, with 18 TFW.

8 Oct 1969	Returned to 18 TFW, Kadena AB, Okinawa.
12 Jun 1970	At Air Asia, Tainan, Taiwan, for contract depot work (WK). (AVH-14).
31 Aug 1970	Returned to 18 TFW, Kadena AB, Okinawa.
10 Nov 1970	At Kwangju AB, Korea, with 18 TFW.
18 Nov 1970	Returned to 18 TFW, Kadena AB, Okinawa.
5 Mar 1971	At Air Asia, Tainan, Taiwan, for contract depot work (WK). (AVH-16).
12 Apr 1971	Returned (PL) to 18 TFW, Kadena AB, Okinawa.
14 Apr 1971	Operationally ready (CC) at 18 TFW, Kadena AB, Okinawa.
8 Jun 1971	At 18 TFW, Kadena AB, Okinawa, being prepared for transfer (PL).
12 Jun 1971	Transferred (PL) to 23 TFW, McConnell AFB KS.
1 Oct 1971	In depot work (WO) by SMAMA at McClellan AFB CA.
1 Mar 1972	Carried on assignment roster for the 562 TFS, 23 TFW, at McConnell AFB KS. (Master 23 TFW Aircraft Assignment as of 1 March 1972).
11 Jul 1972	Assigned to the 561 TFS at McConnell AFB KS when the 23 TFW relocated to Egland AFB LA. (AVH-18).
25 Jul 1972	Transferred to 507 TFG AFRES, Tinker AFB OK.
18 Aug 1972	In contract depot maintenance (WK) by Fairchild Engine and Aircraft Corporation (FACCF) at Bob Sikes Municipal Airport, Crestview FL.
11 Sep 1972	Returned to 507 TFG AFRES, Tinker AFB OK.
31 Mar 1973	Transferred to 507 CMTSQ AFRES, Tinker AFB OK. (AVH-20).
26 Apr 1973	In depot maintenance (WM) by SM-ALC field team at Tinker AFB OK.
27 Apr 1973	At 507 CMTSQ AFRES, Tinker AFB OK.
17 Sep 1973	In depot maintenance (WM) by SM-ALC field team at Tinker AFB OK.
2 Oct 1973	At 507 CMTSQ AFRES, Tinker AFB OK.
24 Jan 1974	In depot maintenance (WM) by SM-ALC field team at Tinker AFB OK. (AVH-22).
21 Feb 1974	At 507 CMTSQ AFRES, Tinker AFB OK.
10 Sep 1974	In contract depot maintenance (WK) by Fairchild Engine and Aircraft Corporation (FACCF) at Bob Sikes Municipal Airport, Crestview FL.
13 Dec 1974	Returned to 507 CLMSQ AFRES, Tinker AFB OK.
1 May 1975	In depot maintenance (WM) by SM-ALC field team at Tinker AFB OK. (AVH-23 & AVH-24).
9 May 1975	At 507 TFG AFRES, Tinker AFB OK. 2,923 flying hours.
22 Sep 1976	In contract depot maintenance (DK) by Fairchild Engine and Aircraft Corporation (FACCF) at Bob Sikes Municipal Airport, Crestview FL. 2,923 flying hours. (AVH-24)
17 Aug 1977	At 507 TFG AFRES, Tinker AFB OK. 2,925.0 flying hours. (AVH-25 & AVH-26).
9 May 1978	In depot maintenance by SM-ALC at Tinker AFB OK. 3,022.0 flying hours. (AVH-26).
11 Aug 1978	At 465 TFS AFRES, Tinker AFB OK. 3,074.0 flying hours.
23 Aug 1978	At 465 TFS AFRES, Tinker AFB OK. 3,140.9 flying hours. (AVH-27).
25 Jan 1979	In depot maintenance by Sacramento ALC, Tinker AFB OK. 3,171.8 flying hours.
8 Feb 1979	At 465 TFS AFRES, Tinker AFB OK. 3,171.8 flying hours.
30 Jun 1979	While assigned to the 465 TFS AFRES, Tinker AFB OK, the aircraft flew 6.3 hours during the month of June 1979 and had accumulated a total of 3,269.1 flying hours, the lowest time of any of the 465th's F-105Ds. The assigned crew chief was Augilar. (301 TFW History, Apr–Jun 1979, USAF microfilm 34382).
17 Mar 1980	In depot maintenance (FACBM) at Tinker AFB OK. 3,436.3 flying hours. (GO33B 24 Jun 80).
24 Mar 1980	At 465 TFS AFRES, Tinker AFB OK. 3,449.7 flying hours.
20 Dec 1980	Transferred to the 466 TFS AFRES, Hill AFB UT. 3,646.7 flying hours. (GO33B 22 Jan 81).

15 1981	Deployed under "Coronet Rudder" with 466 TFS to Skrydstrup, Denmark, from Hill AFB UT. (British Aviation Review, Dec 1995).
29 Aug 1981	Returned from Denmark to Hill AFB UT.
11 Jan 1982	In depot maintenance at Ogden ALC, Hill AFB UT. 3,785.1 flying hours. (GO33B 1 Feb 83).
11 Feb 1982	At 466 TFS AFRES, Hill AFB UT. 3,793.1 flying hours.
1988	On static display at Professional Military Education Center, McGee Tyson Airport, Knoxville ANG Base, Knoxville TN.
Aug 1992	Relocated to Combat Air Museum, Topeka KS.

F-105D-31RE 62-4383

Republic Production No: D-582 Production Sequence No: 662

Location: At March Field Museum, March Air Reserve Base, Riverside, California.

Aircraft Name(s)	Crew	Unit	Date	Description
Fire Bug		465 TFS AFRES	May 77	On left nose gear door.

Like many of the other F-105s produced in early 1963, "383's" first assignment was with the 8 Tactical Fighter Wing at Itazuke Air Base, Japan. When the 8th was discontinued in May 1964, the plane moved to the 41 Air Division at Yokota, Japan. It had a brief spell of combat in late 1965 from Takhli, Thailand, but returned to Yokota until its transfer in November 1966 to the F-105 Replacement Training Unit program at McConnell Air Force Base, Kansas. During the next two years, the plane accompanied four of the 23 Tactical Fighter Wing's RTU deployments to George Air Force Base, California. When the 23rd gave up F-105s in July 1972, the plane continued training pilots for a short while at Nellis Air Force Base, Nevada, and then passed on to the Air Force Reserve's 465 Tactical Fighter Squadron at Tinker Air Force Base, Oklahoma. It picked up the name *"Fire Bug"* when it was damaged by an in-flight engine fire in August 1976. In the summer of 1978, the Reserves flew it on its NATO deployment to Great Britain. A year later, it accompanied the 465th to Italy. When the 465th converted to F-4s, "383" transferred to the Reserve's sister unit at Hill Air Force Base, Utah, from where it found its way to retirement at the March Air Force Base museum in California. (Photograph by author, 31 October 1996.)

Aircraft Chronology

April 1963	Delivered from production to the 8 TFW, Itazuke AB, Japan.
13 May 1964	Transferred to 41 AD, Yokota AB, Japan, under "Project Clearwater" that deactivated the 8 TFW. (ACA-88 & AVH-1).
31 Aug 1964	At 41 AD Yokota AB, Japan. Crew Chief: TSgt. C. Green. (41 AD Monthly Maint. Summary).
30 Apr 1965	At 6441 TFW, Yokota AB, Japan. Assigned Crew Chief: SSgt. Putman. (6441 TFW History, Apr–Jun 65, USAF microfilm PO231).
1 Apr 1965	At 6441 TFW, Yokota AB, Japan. (AVH-4).
28 Jun 1965	At Air Asia, Tainan, Taiwan, for contract depot work (WK).
12 Jul 1965	At 6441 TFW, Yokota AB, Japan.
9 Oct 1965	At Air Asia, Tainan, Taiwan, for contract depot work (WK).
6 Dec 1965	At Takhli RTAB, Thailand, with the 6441 TFW.
16 Mar 1966	At 6441 TFW, Yokota AB, Japan. (AVH-5).
16 May 1966	In depot maintenance (WM) by SMAMA field team at Takhli RTAB with 6441 TFW.
17 May 1966	At 6441 TFW, Yokota AB, Japan.
14 Aug 1966	At MOAMA, Brookley AFB AL for depot work.
19 Nov 1966	Transferred to the 23 TFW, McConnell AFB KS.
24 Nov 1966	In depot maintenance (WM) by SMAMA field team at 23 TFW, McConnell AFB KS.
29 Nov 1966	At 23 TFW, McConnell AFB KS.
9 Mar 1967	Crash damaged (WJ) at 23 TFW, McConnell AFB KS. (AVH-8).
6 Apr 1967	Operational (CC) at 23 TFW, McConnell AFB KS.
4 Aug 1967	Deployed to George AFB CA with the 561 TFS, 23 TFW, for air-to-air gunnery training for RTU class 68AR.
29 Sep 1967	At George AFB CA with the 562 TFS, 23 TFW, for air-to-air gunnery training for RTU class 68BR, "The Many Splendored Studs."
13 Oct 1967	Returned to 23 TFW, McConnell AFB KS.
12 Mar 1968	Deployed to George AFB CA with the 562 TFS, 23 TFW, for air-to-air gunnery training for RTU Class 68HR. (AVH-10).
28 Mar 1968	Returned to 23 TFW, McConnell AFB KS.
14 May 1968	Deployed to George AFB CA with the 560 TFS, 23 TFW, for air-to-air gunnery training for RTU Class 68JR.
29 May 1968	Returned to 23 TFW, McConnell AFB KS.
10 Apr 1970	At SMAMA, McClellan AFB CA for depot work (WO) (AVH-14).
17 Jul 1970	Returned to 23 TFW, McConnell AFB KS.
3 Feb 1971	At 23 TFW, McConnell AFB KS being prepared for transfer (PL). (AVH-16).
5 Feb 1971	In contract depot maintenance (WK) by Fairchild Engine and Aircraft Corporation (FACCF) at Bob Sikes Municipal Airport, Crestview FL.
4 Mar 1971	Returned (PL) to 23 TFW, McConnell AFB KS.
1 Mar 1972	Carried on assignment roster for the 562 TFS, 23 TFW, at McConnell AFB KS. (Master 23 TFW Aircraft Assignment as of 1 March 1972).
26 Jun 1972	In contract depot maintenance (WK) by Fairchild Engine and Aircraft Corporation (FACCF) at Bob Sikes Municipal Airport, Crestview FL. (AVH-18).
2 Jul 1972	Returned to 23 TFW, McConnell AFB KS.
27 Jul 1972	Reassigned to 57 FWW TAC, Nellis AFB NV for combat crew training (TF).
2 Mar 1973	At 57 FWW TAC, Nellis AFB NV for combat crew training (TF). (AVH-20).

24 May 1973	Departed (PL) 57 FWW TAC, Nellis AFB NV.
30 May 1973	Transferred (PL) to 507 CMTSQ AFRES, Tinker AFB OK.
5 Jun 1973	At 507 CMTSQ AFRES, Tinker AFB OK.
10 Sep 1973	In contract depot maintenance (WK) by Fairchild Engine and Aircraft Corporation (FACCF) at Bob Sikes Municipal Airport, Crestview FL.
29 Jan 1974	Returned to 507 CMTSQ AFRES, Tinker AFB OK. (AVH-22).
11 Feb 1974	In depot maintenance by SM-ALC at Tinker AFB OK.
21 Feb 1974	At 507 CMTSQ AFRES, Tinker AFB OK.
18 Jun 1974	In depot maintenance by SM-ALC at Tinker AFB OK.
8 Aug 1974	At 507 CMTSQ AFRES, Tinker AFB OK.
16 Oct 1974	Assigned unit redesignated 507 CLMSQ AFRES, Tinker AFB OK.
14 Feb 1975	In depot maintenance by SM-ALC at Tinker AFB OK. (AVH-23).
27 Feb 1975	At 507 CLMSQ AFRES, Tinker AFB OK.
12 May 1975	In contract depot maintenance (WK) by Fairchild Engine and Aircraft Corporation (FACCF) at Bob Sikes Municipal Airport, Crestview FL. (AVH-23 & AVH-24.
20 May 1975	Returned to 507 CLMSQ AFRES, Tinker AFB OK.
8 Aug 1975	In depot maintenance (WM) by SM-ALC at Tinker AFB OK.
25 Aug 1975	At 507 CLMSQ AFRES, Tinker AFB OK.
9 Mar 1976	In depot maintenance (WM) by SM-ALC at Tinker AFB OK. (AVH-24).
25 Mar 1976	At 507 TFG AFRES, Tinker AFB OK. 3,389 flying hours.
18 Aug 1976	At 507 TFG AFRES, Tinker AFB OK. In-flight fire when turbine exit guide vane came loose on burner light. Pilot: Coakley. Fire burned through the aft section, cutting hydraulic lines for speed brakes, severed the bleed actuation lines for eye-lid actuators. Pilot jettisoned the external tanks and barely got her back on the ground in one piece. We did some real quick "cosmetic work" and ran down to Keesler AFB MS to "borrow" the aft section from a D going on a stick from the Washington DC ANG. Got written off as a high "C." (Gabby Hays, former AFRES F-105 crew chief, e-mail, 18 Mar 96).
25 Jul 1977	At 507 TFG AFRES, Tinker AFB OK. 3,605.0 flying hours. (AVH-25 & AVH-26).
9 May 1978	In depot maintenance by SM-ALC at Tinker AFB OK. 3,755.0 flying hours. (AVH-26).
17 May 1978	At 465 TFS AFRES, Tinker AFB OK. 3,806.0 flying hours.
10 Jun 1978	Deployed under "Coronet Oriole" with 465 TFS to Sculthorpe, England, from Tinker AFB OK. (British Aviation Review, Dec 1995).
23 Jun 1978	Returned from England to Tinker AFB OK.
12 May 1979	Deployed under "Coronet Palomino" with 465 TFS AFRES to Gioia Del Colle, Italy, from Tinker AFB OK. (301 TFW History 1 Apr–30 Jun 1979, USAF microfilm 343832).
24 May 1979	Returned from Italy to Tinker AFB OK.
31 May 1979	While assigned to the 465 TFS AFRES, Tinker AFB OK, the aircraft flew 45.4 hours during the month of May 1979 and had accumulated 4,114.6 flying hours. The assigned crew chief was SSgt. James T. Carmen.
5 Jun 1979	In contract depot maintenance (FACBM) at Tinker AFB OK. 4,069.2 flying hours. (AVH-27).
11 Jun 1979	At 465 TFS AFRES, Tinker AFB OK. 4,114.6 flying hours.
30 Jun 1979	While assigned to the 465 TFS AFRES, Tinker AFB OK, the aircraft flew 2.8 hours during the month of June 1979 and had accumulated a total of 4,117.4 flying hours. It was in work by a contract field team for TCTO 1288. The assigned crew chief was SSgt. James T. Carmen. (301 TFW History, Apr–Jun 1979, USAF microfilm 34382).
17 Dec 1979	In depot maintenance by Sacramento ALC at Tinker AFB OK. 4,190.1 flying hours. (AVH-27).
4 Feb 1980	At 465 TFS AFRES, Tinker AFB OK. 4,231.9 flying hours. (GO33B 24 Jun 80).

9 Nov 1980	Transferred to 466 TFS AFRES, Hill AFB UT. 4,449.7 flying hours. (GO33B 22 Jan 81).
3 Jun 1981	At 466 TFS AFRES, Hill AFB UT. 4,548.8 flying hours. (GO33B Dec 81 & GO33B 1 Feb 83).
Jan 1984	Dropped from the USAF inventory and transferred to the March Field museum.

F-105D-31RE 62-4387

Republic Production No: D-586 Production Sequence No: 666

Location: On static display at Lackland AFB, Texas.

Aircraft Name(s)	Crew	Unit	Date	Description
Eve of Destruction		34 TFS 388 TFW	Jun 67	
Sweet Bippy		354 TFS 355 TFW	Jun 69	On intake.
Devil's Angel/ Grim Reaper	1Lt Chuck deVlaming	354 TFS 355 TFW	May 70	Winged skeleton below cockpit on gun access panel. Name on left intake.
Grim Reaper		354 TFS 355 TFW	Oct 70	
The Hog		457 TFS AFRES	Oct 81	
The Hawk		466 TFS AFRES	Sep 83	

Aircraft Chronology

May 1963	Delivered from production to the 8 TFW, Itazuke AB, Japan.
13 May 1964	Transferred under "Project Clearwater" from 8 TFW, Itazuke AB, Japan, to 41 AD Yokota AB, Japan. (ACA-88 & AVH-1).
31 Aug 1964	At 41 AD Yokota AB, Japan. Crew Chief: SSgt. J. Hancock. (41 AD Monthly Maintenance Summary, August 1964).

This is the last of the surviving "Ds." Delivered in May 1963 to the 8 TFW at Itazuke Air Base, Japan, it survived four years of combat over North Vietnam and Laos flying from both Korat and Takhli in Thailand where it was shot up and repaired at least three times. After seven years in the Pacific, it came home to McConnell Air Force Base where, after being stored for a short while, it joined the Kansas Air National Guard. In February 1980, it moved to the Air Force Reserve's 457 Tactical Fighter Squadron at Carswell Air Force Base, Texas, one of the few Thunderchiefs this unit flew that was not a T-Stick II. As did many F-105 survivors, it retired in 1983 from the Reserve's 466 Tactical Fighter Squadron at Hill Air Force Base, Utah. (Photograph by author, 3 August 1997.)

1 Apr 1965	At 6441 TFW, Yokota AB, Japan. (AVH-4).
6 Apr 1965	In contract depot maintenance (WK) at Air Asia, Tainan, Taiwan.
22 Apr 1965	Returned to 6441 TFW, Yokota AB, Japan.
30 Apr 1965	At 6441 TFW, Yokota AB, Japan. Assigned Crew Chief: TSgt. Green. (6441 TFW History, Apr–Jun 65, USAF microfilm PO231).
31 Aug 1965	At 6441 TFW, Yokota AB, Japan. Assigned Crew Chief: SSgt. Clover. (6441 TFW History, Jul–Dec 65, USAF microfilm PO232).
25 Jan 1966	In contract depot maintenance (WK) at Air Asia (AAITT), Tainan, Taiwan. (AVH-5).
31 Jan 1966	Operating from Takhli RTAB, Thailand, with the 6441 TFW, Yokota AB, Japan.
23 May 1966	Returned to 6441 TFW, Yokota AB, Japan.
16 Jun 1966	Reassigned to the 388 TFW, Korat RTAB, Thailand.
22 Jul 1966	In crash damage repair (WN) at 388 TFW, Korat RTAB, Thailand.
20 Aug 1966	Combat capable (CC) at 388 TFW, Korat RTAB, Thailand.
5 Feb 1967	In depot work (WK) at Air Asia (AAITT), Tainan, Taiwan. (AVH-8).
15 Apr 1967	Returned (PL) to 388 TFW, Korat RTAB, Thailand.
8 Aug 1967	In depot maintenance (WM) by SMAMA field team at Korat RTAB, Thailand.
13 Aug 1967	Combat capable (CC) at 388 TFW, Korat RTAB, Thailand.
24 Aug 1967	Aircraft was flown by 1Lt David B. Waldrop III (44 TFS, 388 TFW) from Korat RTAB, Thailand, on a combat mission that lasted 3.3 hours. (Lt. Waldrop's Individual Flight Record as of 24 Feb 1968).
3 Oct 1967	One of two F-105Ds flown on Rolling Thunder mission RT56A-153 by pilots from the 469 TFS, 388 TFW, Korat RTAB, Thailand. They bombed a target 17 NM NNE of Haiphong, North Vietnam, at coordinates 20-09N and 106-46E. The pilot was Capt Long. (National Archives strike camera film shot list, item 42649B).
13 Oct 1967	In depot maintenance (WM) by SMAMA field team at Korat RTAB, Thailand.
14 Oct 1967	Combat capable (CC) at 388 TFW, Korat RTAB, Thailand.
16 Oct 1967	One of four F-105Ds flown on Rolling Thunder mission RT56A-166 by pilots from the 469 TFS and the 34 TFS, 388 TFW, Korat RTAB, Thailand. They bombed the Dai Loi railroad yard near Bac Ninh, North Vietnam, at coordinates 21-12-40N and 106-05-27E. The pilot was Maj Blakeslee from the 34 TFS. (National Archives strike camera film shot list, item 42649B).
1 Dec 1967	One of nine F-105Ds flown on Rolling Thunder mission RT56A-212 by pilots from the 469 TFS, 388 TFW, Korat RTAB, Thailand. They bombed a target in Laos 7 NM SSE of Sam Neua at coordinates 20-19N and 104-00E. The pilot was Maj James D. Murray. (National Archives strike camera film shot list, item 42649C).
9 Dec 1967	One of three F-105Ds flown on Rolling Thunder mission RT56A-220 by pilots from the 34 TFS, 388 TFW, Korat RTAB, Thailand. They bombed a target in Laos at coordinates 20-31-16N and 102-54-47E. The pilot was Capt Crane.
14 Dec 1967	One of seven F-105Ds flown on Rolling Thunder mission RT56A-225 by pilots from the 34 TFS and 44 TFS, 388 TFW, Korat RTAB, Thailand. They bombed the Hanoi railroad and highway bridge in North Vietnam at coordinates 20-02N and 105-51E. The pilot was Capt Morgan from the 34 TFS.
13 Feb 1968	In depot maintenance (WM) by SMAMA field team at Korat RTAB, Thailand. (AVH-10).
15 Feb 1968	Combat capable (CC) at 388 TFW, Korat RTAB, Thailand.
7 Mar 1968	In battle damage repair (MV) by SMAMA field team at Korat RTAB, Thailand.
23 Mar 1968	Combat capable (CC) at 388 TFW, Korat RTAB, Thailand.
16 May 1968	In depot maintenance (WM) by SMAMA field team at Korat RTAB, Thailand.
18 May 1968	Combat capable (CC) at 388 TFW, Korat RTAB, Thailand.
6 Nov 1968	At 388 TFW, Korat RTAB, Thailand, being prepared for transfer (PL).
8 Nov 1968	Transferred (PL) to the 355 TFW, Takhli RTAB, Thailand. Aircraft had accumulated 2,573.1 flying hours. (AVH-10 & 355 TFW History, Oct–Dec 68, USAF microfilm NO466).

12 Nov 1968	Combat capable (CC) at 355 TFW, Takhli RTAB, Thailand.
16 Nov 1968	At 355 TFW, Takhli RTAB, Thailand, being prepared for transfer (PL).
18 Nov 1968	Transferred (PL) to Air Asia, Tainan, Taiwan, for contract depot work (WK).
4 Jan 1969	Returned (PL) to 355 TFW, Takhli RTAB, Thailand. (AVH-12).
28 Feb 1969	While assigned to the 355 TFW, Takhli RTAB, Thailand, the aircraft flew 74.4 hours during the month of February 1969 and had accumulated 2,707.1 flying hours. (355 TFW History, Jan–Mar 69, Vol. II, USAF Microfilm NO467).
7 Jun 1969	While assigned to the 355 TFW, Takhli RTAB, Thailand, the aircraft was damaged in combat (VJ). It was "… hit by an unknown size round … during the pull-off from a strafe pass against military structures in the 'H' sector of Laos. The damage was to the bottom of the aft fuselage and caused loss of the utility hydraulic system. The pilot had delivered eight M-117 bombs and observed no enemy defenses in the area. Two hundred labor hours were required to repair the damage. (355 TFW History, Apr–Jun 69, Vol. III, USAF microfilm NO468 & AVH-12).
15 Jun 1969	Combat capable (CC) at 355 TFW, Takhli RTAB, Thailand.
26 Sep 1969	In battle damage repair (VO) by 355 TFW, Takhli RTAB, Thailand.
30 Oct 1969	Combat capable (CC) at 355 TFW, Takhli RTAB, Thailand.
30 Jan 1970	At 355 TFW, Takhli RTAB, Thailand, being prepared for transfer (PL). (AVH-14).
1 Feb 1970	Transferred (PL) to Air Asia (AAITT) at Tainan, Taiwan, for contract depot work (WK).
1 Apr 1970	Depot work completed at Air Asia (AAITT), Tainan, Taiwan. Aircraft being prepared for transfer (PL).
10 Apr 1970	Returned (PL) to 355 TFW, Takhli RTAB, Thailand.
14 Apr 1970	Combat capable (CC) at 355 TFW, Takhli RTAB, Thailand.
19 Oct 1970	Transferred (PL) to the 23 TFW, McConnell AFB KS shortly before the 355 TFW was discontinued and Takhli RTAB, Thailand, closed. (AVH-14).
27 Oct 1970	Under "Project Bighorn," aircraft was placed in flyable storage (PR) at McConnell AFB KS.
4 Jan 1971	At 23 TFW, McConnell AFB KS being prepared for transfer (PL).
19 Feb 1971	In depot work (WO) by SMAMA, McClellan AFB CA. (AVH-16).
31 Mar 1971	Transferred (PL) to 184 TFG ANG, McConnell AFB KS.
29 Nov 1971	In depot work (WO) by SMAMA, McClellan AFB CA.
26 Sep 1972	At 184 TFG ANG, McConnell AFB KS. (AVH-18).
9 Nov 1972	In contract depot work (WK) by Fairchild Engine and Aircraft Corporation (FACCF) at Bob Sikes Airport, Crestview FL.
13 Dec 1972	Returned to 184 TFG ANG, McConnell AFB KS.
27 Aug 1973	In depot work (WM) by Dynalectron Corporation (DYNZZ) at McConnell AFB KS. (AVH-20).
7 Sep 1973	Combat capable (CC) at 184 TFG ANG at McConnell AFB KS.
3 Jan 1974	At 184 TFG ANG at McConnell AFB KS for combat crew training (TF).
20 Feb 1974	In contract depot work (WK) by Fairchild Engine and Aircraft Corporation (FACCF) at Bob Sikes Airport, Crestview FL. (AVH-22).
14 Aug 1974	Returned to 184 TFTG ANG at McConnell AFB KS for combat crew training (TF).
16 Aug 1974	In depot work (WM) by Dynalectron Corporation (DYNZZ) at McConnell AFB KS.
23 Aug 1974	At 184 TFTG ANG at McConnell AFB KS for combat crew training (TF).
17 Jul 1975	In depot maintenance (WM) by Dynalectron Corporation (DYNZZ) at McConnell AFB KS. (AVH-23 & AVH-24).
1 Aug 1975	At 184 TFTG ANG at McConnell AFB KS for combat crew training (TF).
5 Sep 1979	In contract depot maintenance (CM) by General Dynamics (DYNFW) at McConnell AFB KS. 5,536.1 flying hours. (AVH-27).
28 Sep 1979	At 184 TFG ANG, McConnell AFB KS for combat crew training (TF). 5,591.2 flying hours. (GO33B 22 Jan 81).

20 Feb 1980	Transferred to 457 TFS AFRES, Carswell AFB TX. 5,618.3 flying hours.
31 Aug 1981	In contract depot maintenance (DM) by General Dynamics (DYNFW), at Carswell AFB TX. 5,766.5 flying hours. (GO33B Dec 81).
28 Sep 1981	At 457 TFS AFRES, Carswell AFB TX. 5,790.7 flying hours.
26 Feb 1982	Transferred to the 466 TFS AFRES, Hill AFB UT. 5,817.9 flying hours. (GO33B 1 Feb 83).

F-105G–1RE 62-4416

Republic Production No: F-5 Production Sequence No: 695

Location: At Palmdale Plant 42 Heritage Airpark, Palmdale, California.

Aircraft Name(s)	Crew	Unit	Date	Description
Barney Google				
Wyatt's Weasel				
Jinkin-Mutha				
Thor's Thunder				
Red River Raider				
Little Steveie		13 TFS 388 TFW	Jun 67	Boy's face and letters on nose gear door.

The fifth F-105F produced and the oldest of the surviving two-seat Thunderchiefs, this plane was delivered to the 4 Tactical Fighter Wing in January 1964. During its early service period at Eglin AFB, Florida, it was the first "F" to be modified with the Wild Weasel III equipment. After a brief stint training Wild Weasel pilots at Nellis, the plane arrived for its first combat tour at Korat, Thailand, in late 1966. It remained at Korat for a year and then moved to Kadena Air Base, Okinawa, during the Spring and Summer of 1968. Its second combat tour began in October 1968 with the 355 Tactical Fighter Wing at Takhli, Thailand, where, a year later, it upgraded from an "F" to a "G." When Takhli began closing in late 1970, the plane moved back to Korat where, on 20 November 1970, it supported the raid to rescue prisoners from the Son Tay prison camp. After returning to the United States in July 1973, it spent its last seven years with the 35 Tactical Fighter Wing at George Air Force Base, California. In August 1978, the plane deployed with the 561 Tactical Fighter Squadron to Denmark where it was severely damaged during a test flight when its wing tanks broke off. After ten days of repairs in Denmark, the plane flew back to George. It was its last flight. The plane remained grounded for two years and was then put on static display at George in July 1980 as a memorial to F-105 pilots. When George closed in 1992, the plane was towed to a hanger for storage. In October 1998, it was trucked to Palmdale, California. (Photograph by author, 5 December 1999.)

Aircraft Name(s)	Crew	Unit	Date	Description
Snuffy Smith		12 TFS 18 TFW	Jul 68	Cartoon figure holding baby in blanket.
Vegetable (SEA)		561 TFS 835 AD	Dec 72	
Sam Slayer		562 TFS 35 TFW	Jul 80	Name in black and yellow curving above gun bay door and mailed fist crushing SAM under left windscreen.

Aircraft Chronology

27 Nov 1963	USAF production acceptance from Republic Aviation, Farmingdale NY. (ACA-88).
5 Jan 1964	Delivered to 4 TFW, Seymour Johnson AFB NC.
13 Mar 1964	At Eglin AFB FL with the 4 TFW.
2 May 1964	At 4485 TW, Eglin AFB FL. (AVH-1).
18 Aug 1964	Returned to 4 TFW, Seymour Johnson AFB NC.
17 Sep 1964	At 4485 TW, Eglin AFB FL.
16 Apr 1965	Returned to 4 TFW, Seymour Johnson AFB NC for periodic inspection. (AVH-4).
30 Apr 1965	While possessed by the 4 TFW, Seymour Johnson AFB NC, but assigned to the 333 TFS at TAWC, Eglin AFB FL, the aircraft was flown 1.7 hours during the month of April 1965 and had accumulated a total of 395.7 flying hours. (4 TFW History, Jan–Jun 65, Vol. II, USAF microfilm MO292).
4 Jun 1965	At 4485 TW, Eglin AFB FL. (AVH-4).
30 Jun 1965	Returned to 4 TFW, Seymour Johnson AFB NC.
8 Jul 1965	In depot work (WO) by MOAMA, Brookley AFB AL.
3 Aug 1965	Returned to 4 TFW, Seymour Johnson AFB NC.
30 Nov 1965	While assigned to the 4 TFW, Seymour Johnson AFB NC, the aircraft flew 30.1 hours for the month of November 1965 and had 549.0 total flying hours. Assigned Crew Chief: SSgt. Nyland. (4 TFW History, Jul–Dec 65, Vol. II, USAF microfilm MO292).
4 Dec 1965	In depot work (WO) for installation of Wild Weasel III equipment by SMAMA, McClellan AFB CA. (AVH-4).
6 Jan 1966	At SMAMA, McClellan AFB CA for test (EI) and depot work (WO). (AVH-5).
16 Jan 1966	First test flight at Eglin AFB FL as prototype "EF-105F," the first F-105F modified for Wild Weasel III program. After five test missions, the aircraft and five others were flown to McClellan AFB CA to fix problems. ("Wild Weasel The SAM Suppression Story" by Larry Davis).
1 Feb 1966	At SMAMA, McClellan AFB CA for test (EI). (AVH-5).
12 Mar 1966	Returned to Eglin AFB FL for further Wild Weasel III testing. ("Wild Weasel The SAM Suppression Story" by Larry Davis).
15 Jun 1966	At 4520 CCTW, Nellis AFB NV for combat crew training (TF). (AVH-5).
31 Aug 1966	Reassigned to 4525 FWW, Nellis AFB NV for combat crew training (TF).
Oct 1966	Transferred to 388 TFW, Korat RTAB, Thailand. (George AFB Hi-Desert Flyer, 11 Jul 1980).
5 Jun 1967	In depot maintenance (WM) by SMAMA field team at Korat RTAB, Thailand. (AVH-8).
11 Jun 1967	At 44 TFS, 388 TFW, Korat RTAB, Thailand.
31 Aug 1967	At Air Asia, Tainan, Taiwan, for contract depot maintenance (WK).
11 Nov 1967	Returned to 44 TFS, 388 TFW, Korat RTAB, Thailand.
7 Dec 1967	In depot maintenance (WM) by SMAMA field team at Korat RTAB, Thailand.
8 Dec 1967	At 34 TFS, 388 TFW, Korat RTAB, Thailand.
2 Feb 1968	Transferred to 18 TFW, Kadena AB, Okinawa. (AVH-10).
6 Feb 1968	At Osan AB, Korea, from 18 TFW in response to U.S.S. Pueblo crisis.

10 Mar 1968	At 18 TFW, Kadena AB, Okinawa.
20 Mar 1968	At Osan AB, Korea, from 18 TFW.
8 May 1968	At 18 TFW, Kadena AB, Okinawa.
10 May 1968	At Osan AB, Korea, from 18 TFW.
12 Jun 1968	At 18 TFW, Kadena AB, Okinawa.
11 Jul 1968	In depot maintenance by SMAMA at 18 TFW, Kadena AB, Okinawa.
12 Jul 1968	At 18 TFW, Kadena AB, Okinawa.
30 Aug 1968	At Kwangju AB, Korea, from 18 TFW.
31 Aug 1968	At 18 TFW, Kadena AB, Okinawa.
28 Oct 1968	Transferred to 355 TFW, Takhli RTAB, Thailand.
1 Nov 1968	While assigned to the 355 TFW, Takhli RTAB, Thailand, aircraft had accumulated 1,790.9 flying hours. (355 TFW History, Oct–Dec 68, USAF microfilm NO466).
28 Feb 1969	While assigned to the 355 TFW, Takhli RTAB, Thailand, the aircraft flew 66.6 hours during the month of February 1969 and had accumulated 2,022.5 flying hours. (355 TFW History, Jan–Mar 69, Vol. II, USAF Microfilm NO467).
7 Mar 1969	At 355 TFW, Takhli RTAB, Thailand. (AVH-12).
8 Mar 1969	At Air Asia, Tainan, Taiwan, for contract depot work (WK).
6 May 1969	Returned to 355 TFW, Takhli RTAB, Thailand.
18 Dec 1969	Designated F-105G at 355 TFW, Takhli RTAB, Thailand.
24 Sep 1970	Assigned to Detachment 1, 12 TFS, 18 TFW, at Korat RTAB, Thailand, (AVH-14).
1 Nov 1970	Reassigned to the 6010 WWS, 388 TFW, Korat RTAB, Thailand.
20 Nov 1970	One of the five F-105Gs flown to support the Son Tay raid by the 6010 WWS from the 388 TFW, Korat RTAB, Thailand. During the raid, the plane fired two AGM-45 Shrike missiles at North Vietnamese SAM sites. (Bob Kronebusch, e-mail, 9 Feb 1998).
21 Nov 1970	After the Son Tay mission, landed at Udorn RTAB, Thailand, to refuel before returning to Korat.
19 Mar 1971	At the 388 TFW, Korat RTAB, Thailand being prepared (PL) for transfer to depot. (AVH-16).
21 Mar 1971	In depot work (WO) by SMAMA at McClellan AFB CA.
19 Nov 1971	Returned to Korat RTAB, Thailand, with the 388 TFW.
26 Nov 1971	In depot maintenance (WM) at 388 TFW, Korat RTAB, Thailand.
27 Nov 1971	Operational (CC) at 388 TFW, Korat RTAB, Thailand.
1 Dec 1971	Reassigned to the 17 WWS, 388 TFW, Korat RTAB, Thailand. (George AFB Hi-Desert Flyer, 11 Jul 1980).
23 Oct 1972	Assigned to the 561 TFS (TAC TDY) at Korat RTAB, Thailand. (AVH-18).
27 Dec 1972	In depot maintenance (WM) by SM-ALC at Korat RTAFB, Thailand.
29 Dec 1972	Returned to the 561 TFS at Korat RTAB, Thailand.
2 Jul 1973	Reassigned to 35 TFW from George AFB CA while at Korat RTAB, Thailand. (AVH-20).
14 Sep 1973	One of 12 F-105Gs transferred (PL) to the 35 TFW (TAC) at George AFB CA from Korat RTAB, Thailand.
19 Sep 1973	At (CC) 35 TFW, George AFB CA.
20 Feb 1974	In depot maintenance (WM) by SM-ALC at George AFB CA. (AVH-22).
1 Mar 1974	At 35 TFW, George AFB CA.
24 May 1974	At Shaw AFB SC with 35 TFW.
7 Jun 1974	Returned to 35 TFW, George AFB CA.
5 Sep 1974	In depot maintenance (WO) by SM-ALC at McClellan AFB CA.
21 Feb 1975	In depot repair (WR) by SM-ALC at McClellan AFB CA. (AVH-23)
14 Mar 1975	Returned to 35 TFW, George AFB CA.

20 Jun 1978	At Eglin AFB FL with 35 TFW from George AFB CA. 5,525.0 flying hours. (AVH-26).
27 Jun 1978	At 35 TFW TAC, George AFB CA. 5,525.0 flying hours.
9 Aug 1978	Aircraft deployed with the 561 TFS under "Coronet Sparrow "to Karup AB, Denmark, as one of 12 F-105Gs from the 35 TFW, George AFB CA. It had accumulated 5,540.0 flying hours. While in Denmark, the aircraft was damaged during a functional check flight to confirm that a flight control problem from an earlier sortie had been fixed. The FCF was flown with empty wing tanks and, during flight, the tanks collapsed and damaged the aircraft. The aircraft remained an additional ten days at Karup for repairs after the other F-105Gs returned to George on 9 Sep 1978. F-105G 63-8285 remained behind with 62-4416. (Mary Head, former 35 TFW F-105G crew chief, e-mail message, 16 July 1998).
17 Sep 1978	After the 35 TFW chief of maintenance approved a one-time flight, the aircraft, along with 63-8285, returned to George AFB CA with 13 "red X" conditions. 5,543.0 flying hours. Assigned crew chiefs were John Taylor and Mike Strysko.
11 Oct 1978	In depot maintenance by SM-ALC at George AFB CA. 5,579.0 flying hours.
9 Jul 1979	At 35 TFW, George AFB CA for aircrew training (TF). 5,579.0 flying hours. (AVH-27).
8 Nov 1979	At 35 TFW, George AFB CA assigned to combat duties (CC).
1 Feb 1980	In contract depot maintenance ("DYNFW") at George AFB CA. 5,579.0 flying hours. (GO33B 24 Jun 80).
27 May 1980	At 35 TFW TAC, George AFB CA. 5,579.0 flying hours. (GO33B 22 Jan 81).
12 Jul 1980	Aircraft was placed on static display near building 701 at George AFB CA during the "Thunderchief Sawadee" hosted by the 35 TFW commemorating the retirement of the F-105 from USAF active duty. "...Kept at George AFB CA as a memorial to former Thud pilots." (George AFB Hi-Desert Flyer, July 11, 1980 & "Wild Weasels," page 42, by Frank Mormillo).
15 Dec 1992	USAF inactivated the 35 TFW and closed George AFB CA. Aircraft parked in Building 862, engine run-up hanger ("Hush House"). (William E. Blomendale, Station Manager, World Maintenance Company, interview, 1 Nov 1996).
21 Nov 1995	Static display sponsorship transferred from the USAF to the Victor Valley Economic Development Authority. (AMARC/LG-3 Static Report 5/3/96).
24 Aug 1998	Static display sponsorship transferred to the city of Palmdale CA. (Rebecca Garza, AMARC, e-mail, 1 Sep 1999).
20 Oct 1998	Placed on static display at Palmdale CA. (Carol Seidel, Assistant City Manager, telephone interview 19 Mar 99).

F-105F-1RE 62-4417

Republic Production No: F-6 Production Sequence No: 696

Location: At Flaugausstellung Leo Und Peter Junior museum near Trier, Germany.

Aircraft Chronology

16 Dec 1963	USAF production acceptance (PP) from Republic Aviation, Farmingdale NY. (ACA-88).
20 Dec 1963	Delivered to 4520 CCTW, Nellis AFB, NV for combat crew training (TF).
2 May 1965	At 4520 CCTW, Nellis AFB NV for combat crew training (TF). (AVH-4).
24 Jan 1966	At SMAMA, McClellan AFB CA for depot work (WO). (AVH-5).
22 Feb 1966	At 4520 CCTW, Nellis AFB NV for combat crew training (TF).

This two-seat F-105F was built as a trainer and remained a trainer throughout its nineteen years of flying service. In December 1963, it went from factory production at Republic Aviation to Nellis Air Force Base, Nevada, where it flew for the next four years. It transferred to McConnell Air Force Base, Kansas, in October 1967 and stayed there for twelve years, first with the 23 Tactical Fighter Wing and then with the Kansas Air National Guard. After a short stay with the Georgia Air National Guard, it flew to storage at Davis-Monthan Air Force Base, Arizona, in February 1982. Two years later it was shipped to Camp New Amsterdam, Holland, where it continued as a trainer for seven more years, this time for teaching sheet metal mechanics to repair battle damaged airframes. In 1991, it was sent to the scrap yard at Soesterberg Air Base, Holland, and then purchased by a German aviation museum where it is displayed today. (Photograph by Donald Hilburn, 4 November 1995.)

31 Aug 1966	Reassigned to 4525 FWW, Nellis AFB NV for combat tactics development (CB).
14 Nov 1966	In depot maintenance at Nellis AFB NV.
18 Nov 1966	At 4525 FWW, Nellis AFB NV for combat tactics development.
2 Feb 1967	In depot maintenance (WM) by SMAMA field team at Nellis AFB NV. (AVH-8).
6 Feb 1967	At 4520 CCTW, Nellis AFB NV for aircrew training (TF).
4 Aug 1967	In depot maintenance (WM) by SMAMA field team at Nellis AFB NV.
6 Oct 1967	At 4520 CCTW, Nellis AFB NV for aircrew training (TF).
25 Oct 1967	Transferred to 23 TFW, McConnell AFB KS.
15 Nov 1967	Assigned to combat crew training (TF) at 23 TFW, McConnell AFB KS.
23 Jan 1968	Deployed to George AFB CA with the 561 TFS, 23 TFW, for air-to-air gunnery training for RTU Class 68FR. (AVH-10).
3 Feb 1968	Returned to 23 TFW, McConnell AFB KS for combat crew training (TF).
8 Apr 1968	An depot-level maintenance (WM) by SMAMA at McConnell AFB KS.
17 May 1968	At 23 TFW, McConnell AFB KS for combat crew training (TF).
18 Jun 1968	Assigned to combat duties (CC) at 23 TFW, McConnell AFB KS.
6 Apr 1969	In depot maintenance at SMAMA, McClellan AFB CA. (AVH-12).
28 Apr 1969	Returned to 23 TFW, McConnell AFB KS.
17 Oct 1969	In depot maintenance (WO) at SMAMA, McClellan AFB CA.
23 Jan 1970	Returned to 23 TFW, McConnell AFB KS. (AVH-14).
11 Dec 1970	Assigned to combat crew training (TF) at 23 TFW, McConnell AFB KS.
28 Jan 1971	Transferred (PL) to 184 TFG ANG, McConnell AFB KS. (AVH-16).
24 Mar 1971	Assigned unit redesignated 184 TFTG ANG, McConnell AFB KS.
15 Apr 1971	In depot maintenance (WO) at SMAMA, McClellan AFB CA.
11 Jun 1971	Returned to 184 TFTG ANG, McConnell AFB KS.

24 Apr 1972	In contract depot maintenance (WK) by Fairchild Engine and Aircraft Corporation (FACCF) at Bob Sikes Municipal Airport, Crestview FL. (AVH-18).
23 May 1972	Returned to 184 TFTG ANG, McConnell AFB KS.
29 May 1973	In contract depot maintenance (WM) by Dynalectron Corporation (DYNZZ) at McConnell AFB KS (AVH-20).
1 Jun 1973	At 184 TFTG ANG, McConnell AFB KS.
25 Oct 1973	In contract depot maintenance (WM) by Dynalectron Corporation (DYNZZ) at McConnell AFB KS.
2 Nov 1973	At 184 TFTG ANG, McConnell AFB KS.
11 Dec 1973	In depot maintenance (WO) by SM-ALC at McClellan AFB CA.
25 Mar 1974	In depot maintenance (WR) by SM-ALC at McClellan AFB CA. (AVH-22).
2 Apr 1974	Returned to 184 TFTG ANG, McConnell AFB KS.
10 Sep 1974	In contract depot maintenance (WM) by Dynalectron Corporation (DYNZZ) at McConnell AFB KS.
12 Sep 1974	At 184 TFTG ANG, McConnell AFB KS.
10 Sep 1975	In contract depot maintenance (WM) by Dynalectron Corporation (DYNZZ) at McConnell AFB KS. (AVH-23 & AVH-24).
24 Sep 1975	At 184 TFTG ANG, McConnell AFB KS for combat crew training (TF).
13 Jun 1979	In contract depot maintenance (DYNFW) at McConnell AFB KS. 4,256.0 flying hours. (AVH-27).
13 Aug 1979	At 184 TFG ANG, McConnell AFB KS. 4,277.6 flying hours.
13 Aug 1979	At 184 TFG ANG McConnell AFB KS. 4,316.6 flying hours. (GO33B 24 Jun 80).
6 Feb 1980	Transferred to the 116 TFW ANG, Dobbins AFB GA. 4,333.6 flying hours.
1 Feb 1982	Flown to storage at MASDC, Davis-Monthan AFB AZ. 4,735.9 flying hours. (MASDC Aircraft Status Directory 30 Jun 84 & GO33B 1 Feb 83).
20 Dec 1982	Still in storage at MASDC, Davis-Monthan AFB AZ. 4,754.2 flying hours.
17 Oct 1984	Removed from MASDC storage for use as ABDR trainer at Camp New Amsterdam, The Netherlands. (John Coon's list, 24 Mar 87).
22 May 1985	At 32 TFS, Camp New Amsterdam, The Netherlands, for ABDR training. (HQ 2852 ABG/DADF Letter 22 May 85).
Dec 1991	Sent to scrap yard at Soesterberg AB, The Netherlands, after being used for ABDR training.
	Purchased as scrap by private museum in Germany.

F-105F–1RE 62-4418

Republic Production No: F-7 Production Sequence No: 697

Location: On a concrete pad near 18 Wing headquarters, Kadena AB, Japan.

Aircraft Name(s)	Crew	Unit	Date	Description
Killer Ace		149 TFS VA ANG		Ace of spades pierced by knife.

Aircraft Chronology

1964	Delivered to 4520 CCTW, Nellis AFB, NV.
19 Jun 1965	At 4520 CCTW, Nellis AFB NV for combat crew training (TF). (AVH-4).

11 Dec 1965	In depot maintenance (WO) at SMAMA, McClellan AFB CA.
17 Jan 1966	At 4520 CCTW, Nellis AFB NV for combat crew training (TF). (AVH-5).
8 Sep 1966	At 355 TFW, Takhli RTAB, Thailand.
13 Oct 1966	Returned to 4520 CCTW, Nellis AFB NV for combat crew training (TF).
20 Apr 1967	In depot maintenance (WM) by SMAMA field team at McConnell AFB KS. (AVH-8).
21 Apr 1967	At 4520 CCTW, Nellis AFB NV for combat crew training (TF).
22 Aug 1967	In depot maintenance (WM) by SMAMA field team at Nellis AFB NV.
29 Aug 1967	At 4520 CCTW, Nellis AFB NV for combat crew training (TF).
2 Sep 1967	In depot maintenance (WM) by SMAMA field team at Nellis AFB NV.
7 Sep 1967	At 4520 CCTW, Nellis AFB NV for combat crew training (TF).
25 Oct 1967	Transferred to 23 TFW, McConnell AFB KS.
27 Nov 1967	Assigned to combat crew training (TF) at 23 TFW, McConnell AFB KS.
8 Dec 1967	Deployed to George AFB CA to join the 560 TFS from 23 TFW conducting air-to-air gunnery training for F-105 RTU class 68ER.
22 Dec 1967	Returned to 23 TFW, McConnell AFB KS.
16 Apr 1968	Deployed to George AFB CA with the 563 TFS from 23 TFW conducting air-to-air gunnery training for F-105 RTU class 68IR. (AVH-10).
9 May 1968	Returned to 23 TFW, McConnell AFB KS for combat crew training (TF).
10 May 1968	In depot maintenance (WM) at McConnell AFB KS.
17 May 1968	At 23 TFW, McConnell AFB KS for combat crew training (TF).
15 May 1969	In depot maintenance (WO) at SMAMA, McClellan AFB CA. (AVH-12).
18 Jun 1969	Returned to 23 TFW, McConnell AFB KS.
23 Oct 1969	In depot maintenance (WO) at SMAMA, McClellan AFB CA.
5 Feb 1970	Returned to 23 TFW, McConnell AFB KS. (AVH-14).
11 Feb 1970	Assigned to combat crew training (TF) at 23 TFW, McConnell AFB KS.
5 Jun 1970	At 23 TFW, McConnell AFB KS.
9 Feb 1971	While assigned to the 23 TFW, McConnell AFB KS, a pilot inadvertently activated the explosive tail hook bolt on the ground resulting in an explosive safety incident. (23 TFW History Jan–Mar 71, USAF microfilm MO556).
4 Jun 1971	In depot maintenance (WO) by SMAMA at McClellan AFB CA. (AVH-16).
13 Jul 1971	Transferred (PL) to 184 TFTG ANG, McConnell AFB KS.
22 May 1972	In contract depot maintenance (WK) by Fairchild Engine and Aircraft Corporation (FACCF) at Bob Sikes Municipal Airport, Crestview FL. (AVH-18).
20 Jun 1972	Returned to 184 TFTG ANG, McConnell AFB KS.
3 May 1973	In contract depot maintenance (WK) by Dynalectron Corporation (DYNZZ) at McConnell AFB KS. (AVH-20).
11 May 1973	At 184 TFTG ANG, McConnell AFB KS.
2 Nov 1973	In contract depot maintenance (WK) by Dynalectron Corporation (DYNZZ) at McConnell AFB KS.
12 Nov 1973	At 184 TFTG ANG, McConnell AFB KS.
3 Jan 1974	Assigned to combat crew training (TF) at 184 TFG ANG, McConnell AFB KS.
1 Apr 1974	In depot work (WO & WR) by SMAMA at McClellan AFB CA. (AVH-22).
25 Jun 1974	Returned to 184 TFTG ANG, McConnell AFB KS.
9 Oct 1974	In contract depot maintenance (WK) by Dynalectron Corporation (DYNZZ) at McConnell AFB KS.
21 Oct 1974	At 184 TFTG ANG, McConnell AFB KS.
11 Nov 1975	In contract depot maintenance (WM) by Dynalectron Corporation (DYNZZ) at McConnell AFB KS. (AVH-23 & AVH-24).

In 1964, this "F" went to Nellis Air Force Base, Nevada, to train pilots. For a brief period in 1966 it was on the roster of the 355 Tactical Fighter Wing at Takhli, Thailand, but returned to Nellis to continue its pilot training duties. In late 1967, the plane transferred to McConnell Air Force Base, Kansas, where it continued to train pilots for the next twelve years. During its last three years, it served with the Virginia and Georgia Air National Guard units before ending up as a battle damage repair trainer at Hill Air Force Base, Utah. After three years of being patched by student sheet metal mechanics it was shipped to Kadena Air Base, Okinawa, where its display is a reminder of the Thunderchief heritage of the 18th Wing. (USAF photograph from MSgt. James A. Allender, Historian, 18th Wing, June 1995.)

18 Nov 1975	At 184 TFTG ANG, McConnell AFB KS for combat crew training (TF).
17 Sep 1976	In contract depot maintenance by Dynalectron Corporation (DYNZZ) at McConnell AFB KS. 3,625.0 flying hours. (AVH-25 & AVH-26).
27 Sep 1976	At 184 TFTG ANG, McConnell AFB KS. 3,625.0 flying hours.
19 Jan 1979	At 116 TFW ANG, Dobbins AFB GA. 4,156.0 flying hours. (AVH-27).
23 Mar 1979	Returned to 184 TFTG ANG for student and combat crew training at McConnell AFB KS. 4,213.1 flying hours.
20 Apr 1979	In contract depot maintenance (DYNFW) at McConnell AFB KS. 4,247.6 flying hours.
13 Jun 1979	At 184 TFTG ANG for student and combat crew training (TF) at McConnell AFB KS. 4,254.9 flying hours.
30 Aug 1979	In contract depot maintenance (DYNFW) at McConnell AFB KS. 4,283.0 flying hours.
13 Sep 1979	At 184 TFG ANG for student and combat crew training (TF) at McConnell AFB KS. 4,283.0 flying hours.
13 Sep 1979	At 184 TFG, ANG McConnell AFB KS. 4,324.3 flying hours. (GO33B 24 Jun 80).
28 Dec 1979	At 192 TFG, ANG Byrd Field, Richmond VA. 4,324.3 flying hours.
25 Sep 1980	At 116 TFW ANG, Dobbins AFB GA. 4,452.0 flying hours. (GO33B 22 Jan 81).
1 Oct 1980	At 192 TFG, ANG Byrd Field, Richmond VA. 4,454.0 flying hours.
15 Oct 1981	At 116 TFW ANG, Dobbins AFB GA. 4,578.9 flying hours. (GO33B Dec 81 & GO33B 1 Feb 83).
6 Dec 1982	At 116 TFW ANG, Dobbins AFB GA. 4,834.5 flying hours. Transferred to Hill AFB UT. Inventory account "ZD"—Test to Destruction. (GO33B 9 Feb 84 & 116 TFW History, Jan–Dec 1982, USAF microfilm 45509).
9 Nov 1983	At 2952 CLSS, Hill AFB UT for ABDR training. (HQ 2852 ABG/DADF Letter 9 Nov 83).
22 May 1985	At 2952 CLSS, Hill AFB UT allocated to "local base museum." (2852 ABG/DAFD letter 22 May 85).

2 Jun 1986	Declared excess to the needs of the 2952 CLSS at Hill AFB UT and responsibility for aircraft transferred to the Hill AFB Heritage Foundation. (2952 CLSS/LGM letter 2 Jun 86).
21 Dec 1987	Aircraft arrived for static display at Kadena AB, Japan, from Hill AFB UT. (MSgt. James A. Allender, 18th Wing Historian).
1988	Aircraft placed on display at Kadena AB, Japan, after preparation by base maintenance personnel.
Late 1993	Aircraft repainted from gray to camouflage by 18th Wing Corrosion Control shop personnel.
Spring 1995	Aircraft had paint touched up and was placed on new concrete pad at Kadena AB, Okinawa.

F-105G-1RE 62-4425

Republic Production No: F-14 Production Sequence No: 704

Location: Parked in front of Robert Meachen American Legion Post 325, Blissfield, Michigan.

Aircraft Name(s)	Crew	Unit	Date	Description
Kloyjai	Capt. Jim Boyd/Capt. Kim Pepperell	17 WWS 388 TFW	Dec 72	On intakes

Aircraft Chronology

16 Jan 1964	USAF production acceptance from Republic Aviation, Farmingdale NY. (ACA-88).
18 Jan 1964	Delivered to 4 TFW, Seymour Johnson AFB, NC.
13 Mar 1964	At 4485 Test Wing TAC, Eglin AFB FL.
16 Apr 1964	At 4 TFW, Seymour Johnson AFB NC. (AVH-1).
12 May 1964	At 4485 Test Wing TAC, Eglin AFB FL.
1 Dec 1964	At 4 TFW, Seymour Johnson AFB NC. (AVH-2).
22 Apr 1965	At 4485 Test Wing TAC, Eglin AFB FL. (AVH4).
11 Jun 1965	Returned to 4 TFW, Seymour Johnson AFB, NC.
27 Aug 1965	In contract depot maintenance (WK) by Republic Fairchild (RACFA) at Crestview FL.
5 Oct 1965	Transferred to 4520 CCTW, Nellis AFB NV for aircrew training (TF).
31 Mar 1966	In depot work (WO) by SMAMA, McClellan AFB CA. (AVH-5).
13 Apr 1966	Returned to 4520 CCTW, Nellis AFB NV for aircrew training (TF).
1 Oct 1966	In depot work (WO) by SMAMA, McClellan AFB CA.
17 Oct 1966	Reassigned to 4525 FWW, Nellis AFB NV for aircrew training (TF).
25 Apr 1967	In depot work for combat damage (VM) by SMAMA field team at Udorn RTAB, Thailand. (AVH-8).
1 Nov 1967	Returned to 4525 FWW, Nellis AFB NV for aircrew training (TF).
31 Jan 1968	At Osan AB, Korea, with 4525 FWW from Nellis AFB NV in response to the U.S.S. Pueblo incident. (AVH-10).
21 Jul 1968	At Kadena AB, Okinawa, with 4525 FWW for depot-level maintenance (WM) by SMAMA.
26 Jul 1968	Returned to Osan AB, Korea, with 4525 FWW.
28 Jul 1968	At Kwangju AB, Korea, with 4525 FWW.
31 Aug 1968	At Kadena AB, Okinawa, with 4525 FWW.
2 Nov 1968	Transferred to 18 TFW, Kadena AB, Okinawa.
21 Jan 1969	At 18 TFW, Kadena AB, Okinawa. (AVH-12).

On 29 December 1972, this plane flew the final F-105G Wild Weasel mission of the Vietnam war. Its service began eight years earlier when it was delivered as an "F" from factory production to the 4 Tactical Fighter Wing at Seymour Johnson Air Force Base, North Carolina. In October 1965, the plane transferred to Nellis Air Force Base, Nevada, to train pilots. In January 1968, it flew to South Korea shortly after the North Koreans captured the Navy intelligence ship, U.S.S. Pueblo. Over the next two years, during the aftermath of the Pueblo crisis, it bounced between Okinawa and South Korea with the 18 Tactical Fighter Wing where it acquired its "G" designation. In May 1971, it moved to Korat, Thailand, and the 388 Tactical Fighter Wing until the Air Force involvement in the war over North Vietnam ended in 1973. After returning from South East Asia, the plane became one of the Weasels that gathered at George Air Force Base, California, with the 35 Tactical Fighter Wing who flew it for the next six years. It then passed on to the Georgia Air National Guard where it was badly damaged in a landing accident. The Guard repaired the damage and then retired the plane a few years later. After serving for several years as a battle damage repair trainer at Wright Patterson Air Force Base, Ohio, it moved up the road to guard the front lawn of an American Legion hall in a small town in southern Michigan. (Photograph by author, 11 August 1995.)

3 Feb 1969	At Kwangju AB, Korea, with 18 TFW.
29 Apr 1969	Returned to 18 TFW, Kadena AB, Okinawa.
3 Jun 1969	At Kwangju AB, Korea, with 18 TFW.
15 Jun 1969	Returned to 18 TFW, Kadena AB, Okinawa.
24 Jun 1969	At Kwangju AB, Korea, with 18 TFW.
1 Jul 1969	Returned to 18 TFW, Kadena AB, Okinawa.
5 Aug 1969	At Kwangju AB, Korea, with 18 TFW.
10 Aug 1969	Returned to 18 TFW, Kadena AB, Okinawa.
11 Aug 1969	At Kwangju AB, Korea, with 18 TFW.
30 Nov 1969	Returned to 18 TFW, Kadena AB, Okinawa.
12 Dec 1969	At Kwangju AB, Korea, with 18 TFW.
8 Feb 1970	Returned to 18 TFW, Kadena AB, Okinawa. (AVH-14).
9 Feb 1970	Redesignated F-105G at 18 TFW, Kadena AB, Okinawa.
17 Feb 1970	In depot maintenance (WM) by SMAMA at Kadena AB, Okinawa.

22 Mar 1970	At 18 TFW, Kadena AB, Okinawa.
9 Apr 1970	At Kwangju AB, Korea, with 18 TFW.
29 Apr 1970	Returned to 18 TFW, Kadena AB, Okinawa.
13 Dec 1970	At Kwangju AB, Korea, with 18 TFW.
18 Sep 1970	Returned to 18 TFW, Kadena AB, Okinawa.
20 Oct 1970	In depot work (WO) by SMAMA at McClellan AFB CA.
27 May 1971	Transferred (PL) to 388 TFW, Korat RTAB, Thailand. (AVH-16).
10 Nov 1971	In depot work (WM) at 388 TFW, Korat RTAB, Thailand.
15 Nov 1971	Operationally ready (CC) at 388 TFW, Korat RTAB, Thailand.
28 Aug 1972	In depot work by SM-ALC at Korat RTAB, Thailand. (AVH-18).
14 Sep 1972	Returned to 388 TFW, Korat RTAB, Thailand.
21 Sep 1972	In depot work by SM-ALC at Korat RTAB, Thailand.
25 Sep 1972	Returned to 388 TFW, Korat RTAB, Thailand.
29 Dec 1972	While assigned to the 17 WWS, 388 TFW, Korat RTAB, Thailand, the aircraft flew on the final Wild Weasel mission of "Linebacker II." The crew was Capt. Jimmy Boyd, pilot, and Capt. Kim Pepperell, EWO. ("Wild Weasel, The SAM Suppression Story," by Larry Davis).
8 Sep 1973	Transferred (PL) to 35 TFW TAC, George AFB CA. (AVH-20).
12 Sep 1973	At (CC) 35 TFW TAC, George AFB CA.
1 Mar 1974	In depot maintenance by SM-ALC at McClellan AFB CA. (AVH-22).
14 Jun 1974	Returned to 35 TFW, George AFB CA.
16 Aug 1974	In depot maintenance (WM) by SM-ALC at George AFB CA.
22 Aug 1974	At 35 TFW, George AFB CA.
17 Aug 1977	In depot maintenance (WO & WR) by SM-ALC at George AFB CA. 4,245.0 flying hours. (AVH-25 & AVH-26).
26 Aug 1977	At 35 TFW TAC, George AFB CA. 4,248.0 flying hours.
6 Apr 1978	At OC-ALC depot, Tinker AFB OK. (Possession Code: DR). 4,299.0 flying hours. (AVH-26).
25 Apr 1978	At 35 TFW TAC, George AFB CA. 4,299.0 flying hours.
22 Jun 1978	At MacDill AFB FL with 35 TFW TAC. 4,422.0 flying hours.
11 Jul 1978	At Nellis AFB NV with 35 TFW TAC. 4,422.0 flying hours.
21 Jul 1978	At 35 TFW TAC, George AFB CA. 4,437.0 flying hours.
9 Aug 1978	Deployed with 561 TFS under "Coronet Sparrow "to Karup AB, Denmark, from 35 TFW, George AFB CA. 4,437.0 flying hours.
6 Sep 1978	Returned to 35 TFW TAC, George AFB CA. 4,454.0 flying hours.
30 Sep 1978	At 35 TFW TAC, George AFB CA. 4,505.0 flying hours.
25 Apr 1979	In depot maintenance by Sacramento ALC at George AFB CA. 4,614.0 flying hours. (AVH-27).
19 Sep 1979	At 35 TFW TAC, George AFB CA. 4,626.0 flying hours.
19 Sep 1979	Transferred to 116 TFG ANG, Dobbins AFB GA. 4,626.0 flying hours.
11 Dec 1979	At 116 TFG ANG, Dobbins AFB GA. 4,616.7 flying hours.
30 Jun 1980	In depot maintenance (DYNFW) at Dobbins AFB GA. 4,765.7 flying hours. (GO33B 22 Jan 81).
22 Jul 1980	At 116 TFG ANG, Dobbins AFB GA. 4,765.7 flying hours.
24 Aug 1981	At 116 TFG ANG, Dobbins AFB GA. 4,855.8 flying hours. (GO33B Dec 81 & GO33B 1 Feb 83).
1981/1982	The aircraft was severely damaged during a night landing at Dobbins AFB GA. Pilot, 1Lt Mark Woodhouse, and EWO, Capt. Bill Bryan, "... impacted the runway almost vertically ... landing at over 200 knots." The afterburner petals were crushed, the ventral fin shoved into the aircraft and engine, the fuel dump torn off and the nose gear almost destroyed when the plane slammed down onto the runway. In repairing the aircraft, the ANG swapped the damaged aft section with the good one from F-105G

	63-8345 that had been grounded by wing cracks. (SMSgt. Jerry L. Powell, 116 BW GA ANG, e-mail 27 July 2000).
31 Dec 1982	While assigned to the 128 TFS ANG, Dobbins AFB GA, the aircraft flew 17.9 hours during the month of December 1982 and had accumulated 5,038.0 flying hours. (116 TFW History, Jan–Dec 1982, USAF microfilm 45509).
11 Jan 1983	At 116 TFG ANG, Dobbins AFB GA. 5,039.7 flying hours. (GO33B 9 Feb 84).
9 Nov 1983	At 401 CLSS, Wright-Patterson AFB OH for ABDR training. (HQ 2852 ABG/DADF letter 9 Nov 83).
22 May 1985	At 401 CLSS, Wright-Patterson AFB OH for ABDR training. (HQ 2852 ABG/DADF letter 22 May 85).
15 Jun 1987	AMARC transfer documents signed with American Legion Post 325, Blissfield MI for AF Static Display Program.
11 Jul 1987	Arrived at Blissfield MI for static display.

F-105G–1RE 62-4427

Republic Production No: F-16 Production Sequence No: 706

Location: Displayed outside at Pima Air Museum, Tucson, Arizona.

Aircraft Name(s)	Crew	Unit	Date	Description
Damn Okie		561 TFS, 23 TFW		

Aircraft Chronology

9 Jan 1964	Delivered from production to the 4 TFW, Seymour Johnson AFB NC. (ACA-88).
13 Mar 1964	At the 4485 TW TAC, Eglin AFB FL. (ACA-88 & AVH-1).
2 Oct 1964	At 4 TFW, Seymour Johnson AFB NC. (AVH-2).
23 Oct 1964	At 4485 TW, Eglin AFB FL for "Operation South Shores."
23 Feb 1965	At 4 TFW, Seymour Johnson AFB NC. (AVH-4).
30 Apr 1965	While assigned to the 4 TFW, Seymour Johnson AFB NC, the aircraft flew 17.5 hours for the month of April 1965 and had 347.0 total flying hours. Assigned Crew Chief: TSgt. Schumate. (4 TFW History, Jan–Jun 65, Vol. II, USAF microfilm MO292).
8 Jul 1965	At MOAMA, Brookley AFB AL for depot work (WO). (AVH-4).
3 Aug 1965	Returned to 4 TFW, Seymour Johnson AFB NC.
30 Nov 1965	While assigned to the 4 TFW, Seymour Johnson AFB NC, the aircraft flew 40.8 hours for the month of November 1965 and had 526.4 total flying hours. Assigned Crew Chief: TSgt. Ottinger. (4 TFW History, Jul–Dec 65, Vol. II, USAF microfilm MO292).
10 Dec 1965	At McClellan AFB CA for depot work. ("Safety Pack II"). (AVH-4).
13 Jan 1966	At 23 TFW, McConnell AFB KS. (AVH-5).
20 Oct 1966	At SMAMA, McClellan AFB CA for depot work (WO). ("Wild Weasel III" Modification).
18 Nov 1966	Reassigned to 4525 FWW, Nellis AFB NV. 779 flying hours.
8 Feb 1967	At 4525 FWW, Nellis AFB NV for combat crew training (TF). (AVH-8).
31 Jan 1968	Deployed to Osan AB, Korea, with 4525 FWW in response to the U.S.S. Pueblo incident. (AVH-10).

Beginning in January 1964, this "F" spent its entire service with units of the Tactical Air Command. In its first eight years, it began at Seymour Johnson Air Force Base, North Carolina, moved to Nellis Air Force Base, Nevada, and transferred several times between Nellis and McConnell Air Force Base, Kansas. The plane accompanied a Wild Weasel deployment from Nellis to South Korea when North Korea captured the U.S.S. Pueblo in January 1968. In April 1972, it made another combat deployment from McConnell to Korat, Thailand. Less than a year after it returned to McConnell, it transferred to its last unit, the 35 Tactical Fighter Wing at George Air Force Base, California, where it stayed for seven years. In July 1980, due to advancing age and cracked wings, it retired to the Boneyard at Davis-Monthan Air Force Base, Arizona. Four years later it was towed through the storage yard's back fence for display at the adjoining Pima Air and Space Museum. (Photograph by author, 2 May 1996.)

1 Feb 1968 — Returned to 4525 FWW, Nellis AFB NV for combat crew training (TF).

24 Mar 1969 — In depot maintenance (WO) at SMAMA, McClellan AFB CA. (AVH-12).

3 Jun 1969 — Returned to 4525 FWW, Nellis AFB NV for combat crew training (TF).

15 Oct 1969 — Transferred to 57 FWW, Nellis AFB NV for combat crew training (TF).

18 Nov 1969 — In depot maintenance (WM) by SMAMA at Nellis AFB NV.

21 Nov 1969 — At 57 FWW, Nellis AFB NV for combat crew training (TF).

9 Jun 1970 — Designated F-105G at 57 FWW, Nellis AFB NV. (AVH-14).

4 Nov 1970 — Transferred to 23 TFW, McConnell AFB KS.

16 Nov 1970 — In contract depot work (WK) at Bob Sikes Airport, Crestview FL.

28 Dec 1970 — Returned to 57 FWW, Nellis AFB NV.

4 Jan 1971 — At 57 FWW, Nellis AFB NV for combat crew training (TF). (AVH-16).

5 Apr 1972 — Departed (PL) 57 FWW, Nellis AFB NV. (AVH-18).

6 Apr 1972 — Transferred to the 561 TFS, McConnell AFB KS.

13 Apr 1972 — Deployed with the 561 TFS from McConnell AFB KS under "Constant Guard I" to Korat RTAB, Thailand.

24 Aug 1972 — Departed (PL) Korat RTAB, Thailand.

26 Aug 1972 — Returned to the 561 TFS at McConnell AFB KS.

30 Jun 1973 — Reassigned to 35 TFW TAC, George AFB CA. (AVH-20).

22 May 1974 — At 35 TFW TAC, George AFB CA. (AVH-22).

29 Aug 1974 — In depot maintenance (WM) by SM-ALC at George AFB CA.

5 Sep 1974 — At 35 TFW, George AFB CA.

26 Nov 1974 — While assigned to the 35 TFW at George AFB CA, the aircraft was involved in a flying safety incident. The cable tension on the stabilator control system was found to be out of adjustment. (35 TFW History, 1 Oct–31 Dec 1974, USAF microfilm 30591).

21 Aug 1975	In depot work (WO) by SM-ALC at McClellan AFB CA. (AVH-23 & AVH-24).
14 Nov 1975	In crash damage repair (WR) by SM-ALC at McClellan AFB CA.
12 Dec 1975	Returned to 35 TFW, George AFB CA.
6 Oct 1976	At MacDill AFB FL with the 35 TFW. 3,683 flying hours. (AVH-24).
19 Oct 1976	Returned to 35 TFW, George AFB CA. 3,683 flying hours.
6 Apr 1977	In depot maintenance by SM-ALC at George AFB CA. 3,829.0 flying hours. (AVH-25 & AVH-26).
8 Apr 1977	At 35 TFW TAC, George AFB CA. 3,829.0 flying hours.
17 Mar 1978	Aircraft had flight restrictions at George AFB CA due to cracks in main landing gear wing rib found during inspection required by TCTO 1F-105-1281. "...Restricted to 47,500 lb. gross takeoff weight, 10 knots crosswind component, 4 G's symmetrical and 2.5 G's rolling." (35 TFW/MA memo).
30 Sep 1978	At 35 TFW TAC, George AFB CA. 4,145.0 flying hours.
5 Feb 1979	In depot maintenance by Sacramento ALC at George AFB CA. 4,156.3 flying hours. (AVH-27).
1 Jun 1979	At 35 TFW TAC, George AFB CA for student and combat crew training (TF). 4,179.4 flying hours.
13 Jun 1979	Combat assigned (CC) at 35 TFW TAC, George AFB CA. 4,179.4 flying hours.
14 Jul 1980	Delivered to MASDC, Davis-Monthan AFB AZ. ("Inviolate storage"—XS). 4,364.2 flying hours. (GO33B 22 Jan 81).
20 Dec 1982	In storage at MASDC, Davis Monthan AFB AZ. ("Low probability of withdrawal"—XX). Corrected flying hours: 4,371.6. (GO33B 1 Feb 83).
21 Jun 1984	Removed from AMARC storage for Pima Air Museum. (AMARC List 24 Mar 87).

F-105G-1RE 62-4428

Republic Production No: F-17 Production Sequence No: 707

Location: A gate guard at the entrance to RAF Croughton, Northamptonshire, Great Britain.

Aircraft Name(s)	Crew	Unit	Date	Description
June Bug	Capt. Bill Bryant/ Capt. Harvey Campbell	44 TFS 388 TFW	Jun 68	Dark blue letters in silver cloud on left fuselage.
Rum Runner		44 TFS 388 TFW	Jul 68	Black yellow and blue letters & black bomb with shark's mouth carrying case of booze on its back below right wing.
Red Ball		561 TFS Det. 1	Jan 73	Name in red letters on left intake (TDY at Korat)

Aircraft Chronology

28 Jan 1964	USAF production acceptance (PP) from Republic Aviation, Farmingdale NY. (ACA-88).
6 Feb 1964	Delivered to 355 TFW, George AFB, CA.
5 Aug 1964	Transferred with the 355 TFW to McConnell AFB KS. (AVH-1).
13 Apr 1965	In depot maintenance (WO) by SMAMA, McClellan AFB CA. (AVH-4).
2 May 1965	Returned to the 355 TFW, McConnell AFB KS.
15 May 1965	Transferred to 4520 CCTW, Nellis AFB NV.

21 Jul 1965	Assigned to aircrew training (TF) at 4520 CCTW, Nellis AFB NV.
13 Dec 1965	In depot maintenance (WO) by SMAMA, McClellan AFB CA.
11 Jan 1966	Returned to 4520 CCTW, Nellis AFB NV for aircrew training (TF). (AVH-5).
18 Nov 1966	In depot work (WM) by SMAMA field team at Nellis AFB NV.
22 Nov 1966	At 4520 CCTW, Nellis AFB NV for aircrew training (TF).
10 Mar 1967	In depot maintenance (WO) by SMAMA, McClellan AFB CA. (AVH-8).
10 Apr 1967	In transfer status (PL) at 4525 FWW, Nellis AFB NV.
12 Jun 1967	Transferred to 388 TFW, Korat RTAB, Thailand.
1 Jul 1967	Assigned to 388 TFW, Korat RTAB, Thailand, as attrition replacement. (388 TFW History, Apr–Dec 67, USAF microfilm NO583).
28 Aug 1967	In depot maintenance (WM) by SMAMA field team at Korat RTAB, Thailand. (AVH-8).
4 Sep 1967	At 388 TFW, Korat RTAB, Thailand.
3 Dec 1967	At Air Asia, Tainan, Taiwan, for contract depot work (WK).
4 Feb 1968	Returned to 388 TFW, Korat RTAB, Thailand. (AVH-10).
4 Apr 1968	In depot maintenance (WM) by SMAMA at Korat RTAB, Thailand.
16 Apr 1968	At 388 TFW, Korat RTAB, Thailand.
17 May 1968	In depot maintenance (WM) by SMAMA at Korat RTAB, Thailand.
18 May 1968	At 388 TFW, Korat RTAB, Thailand.
31 Oct 1968	Aircraft had accumulated 1,772.9 flying hours while assigned to the 388 TFW, Korat RTAB, Thailand. (388 TFW History, Oct–Dec 68, USAF microfilm NO585).
31 Jan 1969	Flown on an Iron Hand mission in the Steel Tiger region of Laos by a 44 TFS Wild Weasel crew from Korat RTAB, Thailand. Returning from the mission, the aircraft recovered at Takhli RTAB, Thailand, beginning a 30-day deployment of the 388 TFW due to runway repairs at Korat. (AVH-12 & 388 TFW History, Jan–Mar 69, USAF microfilm NO586).
1 Feb 1969	One of ten F-105F Wild Weasels flown on an Iron Hand mission in the Steel Tiger region of Laos by a 44 TFS crew, 388 TFW, while operating from Takhli RTAB, Thailand. (388 TFW History, Jan–Mar 69, USAF microfilm NO586).
2 Feb 1969	Flown on an Iron Hand and Commando Nail mission in the Steel Tiger region of Laos by a 44 TFS crew, 388 TFW, while operating from Takhli RTAB, Thailand.
3 Feb 1969	Flown on a mission in the Steel Tiger region of Laos by a 44 TFS crew, 388 TFW, while operating from Takhli RTAB, Thailand.
5 Feb 1969	Flown on an Iron Hand mission in the Steel Tiger region of Laos by a 44 TFS crew, 388 TFW, while operating from Takhli RTAB, Thailand.
6 Feb 1969	Flown on an Iron Hand mission in the Steel Tiger region of Laos by a 44 TFS crew, 388 TFW, while operating from Takhli RTAB, Thailand.
7 Feb 1969	Flown on a mission in the Steel Tiger region of Laos by a 44 TFS crew, 388 TFW, while operating from Takhli RTAB, Thailand.
9 Feb 1969	Flown on an Iron Hand mission in Route Pack I of North Vietnam by a 44 TFS crew, 388 TFW, while operating from Takhli RTAB, Thailand.
17 Feb 1969	Flown on a strike mission in the Steel Tiger region of Laos by a 44 TFS crew, 388 TFW, while operating from Takhli RTAB, Thailand.
25 Feb 1969	One of two F-105 Wild Weasels flown on a strike mission in the Steel Tiger region of Laos by 44 TFS crews, 388 TFW, while operating from Takhli RTAB, Thailand.
2 Mar 1969	Returned to 388 TFW, Korat RTAB, Thailand. (AVH-12).
7 Apr 1969	At Air Asia, Tainan, Taiwan, for contract depot work (WK).
30 Apr 1969	While assigned to the 44 TFS, 388 TFW, Korat RTAB, Thailand, the aircraft flew 4 hours in the month of April 1969 and had accumulated 2,018.4 total flying hours. (388 TFW History, Apr–Jun 69, USAF microfilm NO586).

This "G" started life as a two-seat trainer at George Air Force Base, California, followed by a year at McConnell Air Force Base, Kansas, when the 355 Tactical Fighter Wing moved there from George in the summer of 1964. It then spent two more years as a trainer at Nellis Air Force Base, Nevada. When it arrived at Korat, Thailand, in June 1967, it went to combat as a Wild Weasel aircraft knocking out missile sites in North Vietnam and Laos. In October 1969, it was one of eleven Wild Weasel birds transferred with the 44 Tactical Fighter Squadron to its original unit, the 355 Tactical Fighter Wing now at Takhli, Thailand. In September 1970, after getting the modifications for the APR-35 radar warning receiver and the equipment for the Standard ARM missile at Takhli, it was designated a "G" but did not get the ALQ-105 radar-jamming blisters on its fuselage at this time. The plane returned to the States in September 1970, shortly before Takhli closed. It was assigned to the 561 Tactical Fighter Squadron at McConnell and, when the 561st' deployed under "Constant Guard I," went back to Korat in April 1972. It returned to McConnell four months later. It probably got its jamming pod blisters in April 1973 while it was in the depot at McClellan Air Force Base, California. In June 1973, when the 561st joined the rest of the Wild Weasel units at the 35 Tactical Fighter Wing at George, the plane moved back to the same base that received it from production nine years earlier. It stayed there for five years, going on a NATO deployment to Denmark in 1977, and then transferred to the Georgia Air National Guard where it remained for the next five years until it retired to the Arizona "Boneyard" in 1983. About two years later it was removed from storage and shipped to Upper Heyford, England, where it was used as a battle damage repair trainer. After a series of transfers, it ended up at an Air Force communication station in Croughton, England, as a POW/MIA memorial. It is marked with an erroneous "63-" instead of the correct "62-" in its tail number. (USAF photograph from Pamela Robbins, 100th Air Refueling Wing Public Affairs Office, August 1996.)

30 May 1969	Returned to 388 TFW, Korat RTAB, Thailand. (AVH-12).
30 Jun 1969	While assigned to the 44 TFS, 388 TFW, Korat RTAB, Thailand, the aircraft flew 50.7 hours in the month of June 1969 and had accumulated 2,080.6 total flying hours. (388 TFW History, Apr–Jun 69, USAF microfilm NO586).
19 Aug 1969	While assigned to the 44 TFS, 388 TFW, Korat RTAB, Thailand, the aircraft ground aborted due to a landing gear hydraulic leak. (388 TFW History, Jul–Sep 69, Vol. III, USAF microfilm NO587).
10 Oct 1969	One of 11 Wild Weasel F-105Fs transferred with the 44 TFS to the 355 TFW at Takhli RTAB, Thailand. (AVH-12).
18 Dec 1969	Redesignated F-105G at 355 TFW, Takhli RTAB, Thailand.
16 Feb 1970	In depot maintenance (WM) by SMAMA at Takhli RTAB, Thailand. (AVH-14).
6 Mar 1970	At 355 TFW, Takhli RTAB, Thailand.
26 Sep 1970	At 355 TFW, Takhli RTAB, Thailand, being prepared for transfer (PL).
28 Sep 1970	In depot maintenance (WO) by SMAMA at McClellan AFB CA.
14 Mar 1971	Transferred (PL) to 23 TFW, McConnell AFB KS. (AVH-16).
1 Mar 1972	Carried on assignment roster for the 561 TFS, 23 TFW, at McConnell AFB KS. (Master 23 TFW Aircraft Assignment as of 1 March 1972).

11 Apr 1972	At Korat RTAB, Thailand, with the 561 TFS from McConnell AFB KS under "Constant Guard I." (AVH-18).
24 Aug 1972	Departed (PL) Korat RTAFB, Thailand.
25 Aug 1972	Arrived at McConnell AFB KS with the 561 TFS that was assigned directly to the 832 Air Division.
3 Nov 1972	In contract depot maintenance (WK) by Fairchild Engine and Aircraft Corporation (FACCF) at Bob Sikes Municipal Airport, Crestview FL.
30 Nov 1972	Returned (PL) to 561 TFS, 832 Air Division, McConnell AFB KS.
10 Mar 1973	At 561 TFS, 832 Air Division, McConnell AFB KS. (AVH-20).
6 Apr 1973	In depot work (WO) by SM-ALC at McClellan AFB CA.
19 Jun 1973	Returned (PL) to 561 TFS, 832 Air Division, McConnell AFB KS.
30 Jun 1973	Transferred to the 35 TFW TAC, George AFB CA.
26 Jun 1974	In depot work (WO & WR) by SM-ALC at McClellan AFB CA. (AVH-22).
7 Nov 1974	Returned to 35 TFW, George AFB CA.
20 Jan 1975	In depot work (WM) by SM-ALC at George AFB CA. (AVH-23).
23 Jan 1975	At 35 TFW, George AFB CA.
4 Mar 1976	In depot work (WM) by SM-ALC at George AFB CA. (AVH-24).
5 Mar 1976	At 35 TFW, George AFB CA. 4,314 flying hours.
12 Aug 1977	Deployed under "Coronet Club" with 563 TFS to Karup AB, Denmark, from 35 TFW, George AFB CA. 4,458 flying hours. (AVH-25 & British Aviation Review, Dec 1995).
30 Aug 1977	Returned from Denmark to George AFB CA.
28 Mar 1978	At Seymour Johnson AFB NC with the 35 TFW. 4,533.0 flying hours. (AVH-26).
21 Mar 1978	Returned to the 35 TFW, George AFB CA. 4,544.0 flying hours.
16 Jun 1978	In depot maintenance (DM) by SM-ALC at George AFB CA. 4,614.0 flying hours.
27 Jun 1978	At the 35 TFW, George AFB CA. 4,614.0 flying hours.
10 Jul 1978	At the 35 TFW, George AFB CA. Aircraft being ferried (BQ) by Air Training Command. 4,626.0 flying hours.
31 Jul 1978	At the 35 TFW, George AFB CA. 4,626.0 flying hours.
13 Sep 1978	Transferred to the 116 TFW ANG at Dobbins AFB GA. 4,627 flying hours.
31 Oct 1979	At the 116 TFW ANG, Dobbins AFB GA. 4,766.3 flying hours.
7 Jun 1980	At SM-ALC, McClellan AFB CA for depot work (DO). 4,891.5 flying hours. (GO33B 24 Jun 80).
15 Jul 1980	Returned to the 116 TFW ANG, Dobbins AFB GA. 4,913.0 flying hours.
23 Sep 1980	In contract depot maintenance (DM) by General Dynamics (DYNFW) at Dobbins AFB GA. 4,928.3 flying hours.
16 Oct 1980	At 116 TFW ANG, Dobbins AFB GA. 4,928.3 flying hours.
20 Oct 1980	In contract depot maintenance (DM) by General Dynamics (DYNFW) at Dobbins AFB GA. 4,928.3 flying hours.
5 Dec 1980	At 116 TFW ANG, Dobbins AFB GA. 4,928.3 flying hours.
31 Dec 1982	While assigned to the 128 TFS AFRES, Dobbins AFB GA, the aircraft flew 12.4 hours during the month of December 1982 and had accumulated 5,276.7 flying hours. (116 TFW History, Jan–Dec 1982, USAF microfilm 45509).
3 Jan 1983	Sent to MASDC storage (XX), Davis-Monthan AFB AZ. 5,280 flying hours. (GO33B Dec 83 & MASDC Aircraft Status Directory, 30 Jun 84).
5 Dec 1984	Removed from MASDC storage to RAF Upper Heyford UK. (John Coon).
22 May 1985	At 48 TFW RAF Lakenheath and 20 TFW RAF Upper Heyford, UK for ABDR training. (HQ 2852 ABG/DADF letter 22 May 85).
Oct 1993	Removed as POW/MIA display at RAF Upper Heyford, UK after USAF left Upper Heyford. Aircraft sent to RAF Croughton as ABDR trainer. (British Aviation Review).

1995	Aircraft "... on display at entrance to RAF Croughton, a USAF communications base in Northamptonshire." (David Wilton, British Aviation Research Group, letter dated 12 May 1996).

F-105G-1RE 62-4432

Republic Production No: F-21 Production Sequence No: 711

Location: In AMARC storage on "Celebrity Row," Davis-Monthan AFB, Tucson, Arizona.

Aircraft Chronology

31 Jan 1964	USAF production acceptance (PP) at Republic Aviation, Farmingdale NY. (ACA-88).
7 Feb 1964	At MOAMA, Brookley AFB, Alabama, for depot work (WO).
20 Feb 1964	One of the first two F-105F's (along with 62-4424) delivered to the 36 TFW, Bitburg AB, Germany. (History of 36 TFW, USAF microfilm MO627).
28 Feb 1964	Combat ready (CC) at the 36 TFW, Bitburg AB, Germany. (ACA-88).
8 Jan 1965	At the 36 TFW, Bitburg AB, Germany. Assigned Crew Chief: SSgt. Donald G. Nelson (36 OMS Special Order 31, signed by Maj. Hoyt S. Vandenberg, Jr., Commander).
10 Jan 1965	At Wheelus AB, Libya, for aircrew weapons delivery training with the 36 TFW. (AVH4).
28 Mar 1965	Returned to the 36 TFW, Bitburg AB, Germany.
29 Jul 1965	In contract depot work (WK) by CASA at Madrid, Spain.
27 Nov 1965	Returned to the 36 TFW, Bitburg AB, Germany.
13 Jan 1966	At the 36 TFW, Bitburg AB, Germany. (AVH-5).
26 Jan 1966	Transferred to the 23 TFW, McConnell AFB KS.
8 Jun 1966	In depot work (WO) by MOAMA at Brookley AFB AL.
14 Jun 1966	Returned to the 23 TFW, McConnell AFB KS.
22 Sep 1966	In depot work (WO) by MOAMA at Brookley AFB AL.
23 Nov 1966	In receiving inspection (PL) by the 23 TFW, McConnell AFB KS after return from the depot.
25 Nov 1966	Combat ready (CC) at the 23 TFW, McConnell AFB KS.
2 Jun 1967	In depot maintenance (WM) by SMAMA at McConnell AFB KS. (AVH-8).
10 Jun 1967	Combat ready (CC) at the 23 TFW, McConnell AFB KS.
3 Nov 1967	At the 23 TFW, McConnell AFB KS being prepared for transfer (PL).
17 Jan 1968	In depot work (WO) by SMAMA at McClellan AFB CA. Probably modified to "Combat Martin" configuration. (AVH-10).
16 Feb 1968	Transferred (PL) to the 355 TFW, Takhli RTAB, Thailand.
27 Feb 1968	Combat ready (CC) at the 355 TFW, Takhli RTAB, Thailand.
30 Apr 1968	In depot maintenance (WM) by SMAMA field team at Takhli RTAB, Thailand.
5 May 1968	Combat ready (CC) at the 355 TFW, Takhli RTAB, Thailand.
2 Jul 1968	At the 355 TFW, Takhli RTAB, Thailand, being prepared for transfer (PL).
3 Jul 1968	In contract depot work (WK) by Air Asia, Tainan, Taiwan.
10 Sep 1968	Returned (PL) to the 355 TFW, Takhli RTAB, Thailand.
18 Sep 1968	Combat ready (CC) at the 355 TFW, Takhli RTAB, Thailand.

This Wild Weasel "G" began life in February 1964 as one of the first two-seat "Fs" delivered to the 36 Tactical Fighter Wing at Bitburg, Germany. It remained with the 36th for two years before transferring to the 23 Tactical Fighter Wing at McConnell Air Force Base, Kansas, where it stayed for two more years. In January 1968, while at the depot in California, it became one of ten "Fs" modified for the Combat Martin mission, having its rear seat removed and a communications jammer installed. After its modification in February 1968, it was one of the five Combat Martin "Fs" initially assigned to the 355 Tactical Fighter Wing at Takhli, Thailand, where it's intended use was to jam MiG radio communications over North Vietnam. However, shortly after its arrival at Takhli, President Johnson limited bombing to the southern region of North Vietnam where MiGs weren't a threat to American planes. Deprived of its primary mission, the plane remained at Takhli as a single-seat bomber for eighteen months and then moved to the 18 Tactical Fighter Wing at Kadena Air Base, Okinawa, where it stayed for only a year before being given back to the 23rd at McConnell. Due to its rear cockpit being unusable, the 23rd put the aircraft in flyable storage for much of the next two years. Finally, in April 1972, the plane returned to the depot where the Combat Martin equipment was removed and the plane modified as a "G." It then began an eight-year period as a Wild Weasel trainer, first at Nellis Air Force Base, Nevada, then at George Air Force Base, California. Its last assignment was with the Georgia Air National Guard who flew it for a little over a year before retiring it to the Arizona Boneyard in December 1982. (Photograph by Colonel Walter W. Saeger, Jr., 24 January 1999.)

1 Nov 1968 While assigned to the 354 TFS, 355 TFW, Takhli RTAB, Thailand, the aircraft had accumulated 1,529.5 flying hours. (355 TFW History, Oct–Dec 68, USAF microfilm NO466).

23 Dec 1968 In work (VO) by the 355 TFW at Takhli RTAB, Thailand. (AVH-10).

27 Dec 1968 Combat ready (CC) at the 355 TFW, Takhli RTAB, Thailand.

28 Feb 1969 While assigned to the 355 TFW, Takhli RTAB, Thailand, the aircraft flew 64.3 hours during the month of February 1969 and had accumulated 1,771.6 flying hours. (355 TFW History, Jan–Mar 69, Vol. II, USAF Microfilm NO467).

10 Sep 1969 At the 355 TFW, Takhli RTAB, Thailand, being prepared for transfer (PL). (AVH-12).

14 Sep 1969 Transferred (PL) to the 18 TFW, Kadena AB, Okinawa.

24 Sep 1969 Combat ready (CC) at the 18 TFW, Kadena AB, Okinawa.

2 Oct 1969 At Kwangju AB, Korea, with the 18 TFW.

3 Oct 1969 Returned to the 18 TFW, Kadena AB, Okinawa.

29 Nov 1969 At Kwangju AB, Korea, with the 18 TFW.

4 Dec 1969 Returned to the 18 TFW, Kadena AB, Okinawa.

5 Dec 1969 At Kwangju AB, Korea, with the 18 TFW.

22 Dec 1969 Returned to the 18 TFW, Kadena AB, Okinawa.

26 Dec 1969 At Kwangju AB, Korea, with the 18 TFW.

28 Dec 1969	Returned to the 18 TFW, Kadena AB, Okinawa.
2 Jan 1970	At Kwangju AB, Korea, with the 18 TFW.
3 Jan 1970	Returned to the 18 TFW, Kadena AB, Okinawa.
5 Jan 1970	At the 18 TFW, Kadena AB, Okinawa, being prepared for transfer (PL). (AVH-14).
6 Jan 1970	In depot maintenance (WM) by SMAMA field team at Kadena AB, Okinawa.
16 Jan 1970	Returned (PL) to the 18 TFW, Kadena AB, Okinawa.
1 May 1970	At Kwangju AB, Korea, with the 18 TFW.
23 Jun 1970	Returned to the 18 TFW, Kadena AB, Okinawa.
23 Sep 1970	At Kwangju AB, Korea, with the 18 TFW.
9 Oct 1970	Returned to the 18 TFW, Kadena AB, Okinawa.
2 Nov 1970	At the 18 TFW, Kadena AB, Okinawa, being prepared for transfer (PL).
3 Nov 1970	Transferred (PL) to the 23 TFW, McConnell AFB KS.
12 Nov 1970	Placed in flyable storage (PR) at the 23 TFW, McConnell AFB KS.
2 Feb 1971	In contract depot work (WK) by Fairchild Engine and Aircraft Corporation (FACCF) at Bob Sikes Airport, Crestview FL. (AVH-16).
10 Mar 1971	Returned to flyable storage (PR) at the 23 TFW, McConnell AFB KS.
4 Oct 1971	At the 23 TFW, McConnell AFB KS being processed for transfer (PL).
8 Oct 1971	In depot work (WO) by SMAMA at McClellan AFB CA.
1 Mar 1972	Assigned to 561 TFS, 23 TFW at McConnell AFB KS. Still carried as having Combat Martin configuration. (Master 23 TFW Aircraft Assignment as of 1 March 1972).
18 Apr 1972	In depot work (WO) to upgrade the aircraft from a Combat Martin "F" to an F-105G by SM-ALC at McClellan AFB CA. (AVH-18).
4 May 1972	Transferred (PL) as an F-105G to the 57 FWW, Nellis AFB NV for combat crew training (TF).
17 Oct 1972	At the 57 FWW, Nellis AFB NV being prepared for transfer (PL).
19 Oct 1972	In contract depot work (WK) by Fairchild Engine and Aircraft Corporation (FACCF) at Bob Sikes Airport, Crestview FL.
14 Nov 1972	Returned (PL) to the 57 FWW, Nellis AFB NV for combat crew training (TF).
14 Feb 1973	In depot maintenance (WM) by SM-ALC at Nellis AFB NV. (AVH-20).
16 Feb 1973	At the 57 FWW, Nellis AFB NV for combat crew training (TF).
25 Sep 1973	In depot maintenance (WM) by SM-ALC at Nellis AFB NV.
18 Oct 1973	At the 57 FWW, Nellis AFB NV for combat crew training (TF).
20 Oct 1973	In depot maintenance (WM) by SM-ALC at Nellis AFB NV.
29 Oct 1973	At the 57 FWW, Nellis AFB NV for combat crew training (TF).
3 Dec 1973	In depot maintenance (WM) by SM-ALC at Nellis AFB NV.
21 Dec 1973	At the 57 FWW, Nellis AFB NV for combat crew training (TF).
31 Jan 1973	Delivered (PL) to Republic Aviation, Farmingdale NY for contract depot work (WK). (AVH-22).
14 May 1973	Transferred to SM-ALC, McClellan AFB CA for engineering tests (EI).
13 Jun 1973	Returned to the 57 FWW, Nellis AFB NV for combat crew training (TF).
26 Jun 1975	In depot work (WO) by SM-ALC at McClellan AFB CA. (AVH-23 & AVH-24).
26 Sep 1975	In depot repair (WR) by SM-ALC at McClellan AFB CA.
22 Oct 1975	Transferred to the 35 TFW, George AFB CA for combat crew training (TF).
14 Apr 1977	In depot maintenance (DM) by SM-ALC at George AFB CA. Aircraft had accumulated 3,284.0 flying hours. (AVH-25 & AVH-26).
17 Mar 1978	Aircraft had flight restrictions at George AFB CA due to cracks in main landing gear wing rib found during inspection required by TCTO 1F-105-1281. "...Restricted to 47,500 lb. gross takeoff weight, 10 knots crosswind component, 4 G's symmetrical and 2.5 G's rolling." (35 TFW/MA memo).

22 May 1979	At OC-ALC, Tinker AFB OK, for a "domestic project" (DO). 3,596.5 flying hours (AVH-27).
7 Jun 1979	Returned to the 35 TFW, George AFB CA. 3,596.5 flying hours.
23 Jun 1980	In depot maintenance by SM-ALC at George AFB CA. 3,663.6 flying hours. (GO33B 24 Jun 80).
4 Feb 1980	In contract depot maintenance (DM) by DYNFW at George AFB CA. 3,618.8 flying hours. (GO33B 22 Jan 81).
3 Mar 1980	At the 35 TFW, George AFB CA. 3,629.1 flying hours.
15 Sep 1981	Transferred to the 116 TFW, Georgia ANG, Dobbins AFB GA. 3,770.0 flying hours. (GO33B Dec 81).
1 Dec 1982	Flown from the 116 TFW ANG, Dobbins AFB GA, to MASDC storage, Davis-Monthan AFB AZ. 3,969 flying hours. (MASDC Aircraft Status Directory, 30 Jun 84 & GO33B 1 Feb 1983).
24 Jan 1999	One of 13 F-105s still in AMARC storage, Davis-Monthan AFB AZ. (DOO3AF762 Part 1, 29 Apr 96).

F-105G-1RE 62-4438

Republic Production No: F-27 Production Sequence No: 717

Location: Displayed outside at Museum of Aviation, Robins AFB, Warner Robins, Georgia.

Aircraft Chronology

11 Feb 1964	USAF production acceptance from Republic Aviation, Farmingdale NY. (ACA-88).
7 Mar 1964	Delivered to 4520 CCTW, Nellis AFB NV for combat crew training (TF).

For its first eleven years, this two-seater trained pilots at two bases, moving several times between Nellis Air Force Base, Nevada, and McConnell Air Force Base, Kansas. During the second of its three assignments to Nellis, the plane was upgraded to a "G" after which it served as a Wild Weasel trainer. In July 1975, the plane transferred to the 35 Tactical Fighter Wing at George Air Force Base, California. The wing flew it to Denmark during a NATO summer deployment in 1977, and, three years later, passed it on to the Georgia Air National Guard who flew it until 1983. Its last flight was a short hop from Dobbins Air Force Base to Robins Air Force Base in Georgia where it served for a year as a battle damage repair trainer. The Air Force Museum then allocated it to the growing aviation museum at Robins where it is displayed today. (Photograph by author, 1 January 1996.)

12 Jun 1965	At 4520 CCTW, Nellis AFB NV for aircrew training (TF). (AVH-4).
22 Dec 1965	At SMAMA, McClellan AFB CA for depot work (WO).
19 Jan 1966	At 4520 CCTW, Nellis AFB NV for student and combat crew training (TF). (AVH-5).
6 Aug 1966	Transferred to 23 TFW, McConnell AFB KS.
26 May 1967	In depot maintenance (WM) by SMAMA field team at McConnell AFB KS. (AVH-8).
30 May 1967	At 23 TFW, McConnell AFB KS.
12 Dec 1967	At SMAMA, McClellan AFB CA for depot work (WO).
11 Jan 1968	Returned to 23 TFW, McConnell AFB KS. (AVH-10).
23 Jan 1968	Deployed to George AFB CA with the 561 TFS, 23 TFW, for air-to-air gunnery training for RTU Class 68FR.
27 Jan 1968	Returned early to 23 TFW, McConnell AFB KS.
3 Feb 1968	Rejoined the 561 TFS, 23 TFW at George AFB for air-to-air gunnery training for RTU Class 68FR.
8 Feb 1968	Returned to 23 TFW, McConnell AFB KS.
12 Mar 1968	Deployed to George AFB CA with the 562 TFS, 23 TFW, for air-to-air gunnery training for RTU Class 68HR.
28 Mar 1968	Returned to 23 TFW, McConnell AFB KS.
3 Jun 1968	Transferred to 4525 FWW, Nellis AFB NV for combat tactics development (CB).
14 May 1969	At 4525 FWW, Nellis AFB NV for combat crew training (TF). (AVH-12).
26 Jun 1969	At SMAMA, McClellan AFB CA for depot maintenance (WO).
15 Sep 1969	Returned to 4525 FWW, Nellis AFB NV.
7 Oct 1969	Assigned to 4525 FWW, Nellis AFB NV for Combat Tactics Development (CB).
15 Oct 1969	Reassigned to 57 FWW, Nellis AFB NV for Combat Tactics Development (CB).
9 Jun 1970	Designated F-105G at 57 FWW, Nellis AFB NV. (AVH-14).
26 Aug 1970	At 57 FWW, Nellis AFB NV for Wild Weasel combat crew training (TF).
15 Jan 1971	At 57 FWW, Nellis AFB NV being prepared (PL) for transfer to the depot. (AVH-16).
21 Jan 1971	In depot work (WO) by SMAMA at McClellan AFB CA.
12 May 1971	Returned (PL) to 57 FWW, Nellis AFB NV.
14 May 1971	At 57 FWW, Nellis AFB NV for combat crew training (TF).
6 Apr 1972	Departed (PL) 57 FWW, Nellis AFB NV. (AVH-18).
7 Apr 1972	Transferred to 23 TFW, McConnell AFB KS.
12 Apr 1972	Transferred back to 57 FWW, Nellis AFB NV for combat crew training (TF).
16 Aug 1972	In contract depot maintenance (WK) by Fairchild Engine and Aircraft Corporation (FACCF) at Bob Sikes Municipal Airport, Crestview FL.
8 Sep 1972	Returned to 57 FWW, Nellis AFB NV for combat crew training (TF).
26 Jan 1973	In depot maintenance by SM-ALC field team from McClellan AFB CA at Nellis AFB NV (AVH-20).
30 Jan 1973	At 57 FWW, Nellis AFB NV for combat crew training (TF).
19 Jun 1973	In depot work (WO) by SM-ALC at McClellan AFB CA.
21 Sep 1973	Returned (PL) to 57 FWW, Nellis AFB NV.
26 Sep 1973	At 57 FWW, Nellis AFB NV for combat crew training (TF).
17 May 1974	In depot work (WO & WR) by SM-ALC at McClellan AFB CA. (AVH-22).
23 Sep 1974	Returned to 57 FWW, Nellis AFB NV for combat crew training (TF).
21 Oct 1974	In depot work (WM) by SM-ALC at Nellis AFB NV.
8 Nov 1974	At 57 FWW, Nellis AFB NV for combat crew training (TF).
26 Dec 1974	In depot work (WM) by SM-ALC at Nellis AFB NV.
9 Jan 1975	At 57 FWW, Nellis AFB NV for combat crew training (TF). (AVH-23).

16 Jan 1975	In contract depot maintenance (WK) by Fairchild Engine and Aircraft Corporation (FACCF) at Bob Sikes Municipal Airport, Crestview FL.
27 Jun 1975	Returned to 57 FWW, Nellis AFB NV for combat crew training (TF). (AVH-23 & AVH-24).
17 Jul 1975	Transferred to 35 TFW, George AFB CA for Wild Weasel combat crew training (TF).
12 Aug 1977	Deployed under "Coronet Club" to Karup AB, Denmark, with the 562 TFS, 35 TFW TAC. 3,475.0 flying hours. (AVH-25 & AVH-26).
30 Aug 1977	Returned from Denmark to George AFB CA.
23 Jan 1978	At 35 TFW TAC, George AFB CA. 3,578.0 flying hours. (AVH-26)
17 Mar 1978	Aircraft had flight restrictions at George AFB CA due to cracks in main landing gear wing rib found during inspection required by TCTO 1F-105-1281. "…Restricted to 47,500 lb. gross takeoff weight, 10 knots crosswind component, 4 G's symmetrical and 2.5 G's rolling." (35 TFW/MA memo).
15 Sep 1978	At OC-ALC depot at Tinker AFB OK. 3,748.0 flying hours.
14 Dec 1978	In depot maintenance by OC-ALC, Tinker AFB OK. 3,765.0 flying hours. (AVH-27).
19 Jan 1979	At 35 TFW TAC, George AFB CA for student and combat crew training (TF). 3,765.0 flying hours.
27 Jul 1979	In depot maintenance by Sacramento ALC at George AFB CA. 3,830.4 flying hours.
23 Sep 1979	Combat assigned (CC) at 35 TFW TAC, George AFB CA. 3,857.4 flying hours.
30 Jul 1980	At 35 TFW, George AFB CA. 3,939.5 flying hours. (GO33B 22 Jan 81).
31 Jul 1980	Transferred to 116 TFW ANG, Dobbins AFB GA. 3,939.5 flying hours.
31 Dec 1982	While assigned to the 128 TFS AFRES, Dobbins AFB GA, the aircraft flew 15.6 hours during the month of December 1982 and had accumulated 4,327.6 flying hours. (116 TFW History, Jan–Dec 1982, USAF microfilm 45509).
12 Apr 1983	At 116 TFW ANG, Dobbins AFB GA. 4,353.9 flying hours. (GO33B 9 Feb 84).
Summer 1983	Last flight. Delivered from Dobbins AFB GA to Robins AFB GA by pilot Capt. Chris Smisson, 116 TFW, GA ANG. (Interview with Maj. Jim Carter, USAF Ret.).
9 Nov 1983	At 2955 CLSS, Robins AFB GA for ABDR training. (HQ 2852 ABG/DADF Letter 9 Nov 83).
13 Jul 1984	Declared by 2955 Combat Logistic Support Squadron (AFLC), Robins AFB GA as " … excess to our Aircraft Battle Damage Repair (ABDR) training requirements…" and offered to the USAF Museum for "… static display purposes." (2955 CLSS/CC letter).
31 Jul 1984	Directed by USAF Museum to be transferred to Warner Robins ALC for static display. (DD Form 1149, "Requisition and Invoice/Shipping Document").
22 May 1985	Still at 2955 CLSS, Robins AFB GA for ABDR training. (HQ 2852 ABG/DADF Letter 22 May 85).

F-105G-1RE 62-4440

Republic Production No: F-29 Production Sequence No: 719

Location: Displayed inside Aerospace Museum, Hill AFB, Ogden, Utah.

Aircraft Name(s)	Crew	Unit	Date	Description
Zero		17 WWS 388 TFW	Dec 72	Name on left intake.

Aircraft Chronology

19 Feb 1964	USAF production acceptance (PP) from Republic Aviation, Farmingdale NY. (ACA-88).
11 Mar 1964	Delivered to the 4 TFW, Seymour Johnson AFB NC.

It its nineteen years of flying, this "G" served in six units and deployed five times to four different countries. Its career began in 1964 with the 4 Tactical Fighter Wing at Seymour Johnson Air Force Base, North Carolina. The plane went with the 4th during its six-month deployment to Turkey in 1964 and 1965. It then moved to Nellis Air Force Base, Nevada, where it trained pilots for two years followed by five more years of pilot training at McConnell Air Force Base, Kansas. It joined the 388 Tactical Fighter Wing at Korat, Thailand, in November 1972 in time to participate in "Linebacker II" , the final bombing campaign of the Vietnam war. During its next assignment with the 35 Tactical Fighter Wing at George Air Force Base, California, it deployed twice for NATO "Coronet" exercises. It went to Germany in 1976 and to Denmark a year later. The 35th turned the plane over to the Georgia Air National Guard in October 1979 who also used it for its 1980 "Coronet" deployment to Turkey, the country the plane visited on its first overseas trip fifteen years earlier. The Guard retired it in 1983, flying it to Hill Air Force Base, Utah, where it served as a battle damage repair trainer for a few years before being restored for display at the Hill Aerospace Museum. (Photograph by author, 25 March 1997.)

17 Nov 1964 Deployed to Incirlik AB, Turkey, with the 335 TFS, 4 TFW, from Seymour Johnson AFB NC. (AVH-4).

30 Apr 1965 On TDY at Incirlik AB, Turkey, with the 334 TFS from the 4 TFW, Seymour Johnson AFB NC. (4 TFW History, Jan–Jun 65, Vol. II, USAF microfilm MO292).

2 May 1965 Returned to 4 TFW, Seymour Johnson AFB NC. (AVH-4).

26 Aug 1965 At Crestview FL for contract depot work (WK) by Republic Aviation (RACFA).

30 Sep 1965 Transferred to 4520 CCTW, Nellis AFB NV for combat crew training (TF).

21 Feb 1966 At SMAMA, McClellan AFB for depot work (WO). (AVH-5).

17 Mar 1966 At 4520 CCTW, Nellis AFB NV for aircrew training (TF).

20 Jul 1967 In depot maintenance (WM) by SMAMA field team at Nellis AFB NV. (AVH-8).

24 Jul 1967 At 4520 CCTW, Nellis AFB NV for aircrew training (TF).

12 Oct 1967 In depot maintenance (WM) by SMAMA field team at Nellis AFB NV.

16 Oct 1967 At 4520 CCTW, Nellis AFB NV for aircrew training (TF).

14 Nov 1967 Transferred to 23 TFW, McConnell AFB KS for combat crew training (TF).

27 Jan 1968 Joined the 561 TFS, 23 TFW, already deployed to George AFB CA for air-to-air gunnery training for RTU Class 68FR. (AVH-10).

8 Feb 1968 Returned to 23 TFW, McConnell AFB KS for combat crew training (TF).

11 Apr 1968 At SMAMA, McClellan AFB CA for depot work (WO).

3 May 1968 Returned to 23 TFW, McConnell AFB KS.

7 May 1968	In depot maintenance (WM) by SMAMA at McConnell AFB KS.
10 May 1968	At 23 TFW, McConnell AFB KS.
20 Aug 1968	With 4525 FWW, Nellis AFB NV for combat tactics development (CB).
4 Oct 1968	At 23 TFW, McConnell AFB KS for combat tactics development (CB).
11 Oct 1968	At 23 TFW, McConnell AFB KS for combat crew training (TF).
14 May 1970	At 23 TFW, McConnell AFB KS for combat crew training (TF). (AVH-14).
14 Aug 1970	In depot maintenance (WO) at SMAMA, McClellan AFB CA.
2 Mar 1971	At 23 TFW, McConnell AFB KS for combat crew training (TF). (AVH-16).
16 Mar 1971	In depot maintenance (WK) by Fairchild Engine and Aircraft Corporation (FACCF) at Bob Sikes Municipal Airport, Crestview FL.
6 Apr 1971	Returned (PL) to 23 TFW, McConnell AFB KS for combat crew training (TF).
10 May 1971	Assigned to combat duties (CC) at 23 TFW, McConnell AFB KS.
1 Mar 1972	Assigned to 561 TFS, 23 TFW, at McConnell AFB KS. (Master 23 TFW Aircraft Assignment as of 1 March 1972).
22 Mar 1972	In depot work (WO) by SMAMA at McClellan AFB CA. (AVH-18).
15 Aug 1972	Redesignated "F-105G" at SMAMA, McClellan AFB CA
29 Aug 1972	Returned to 561 TFS under the 832 Air Division, McConnell AFB KS.
30 Aug 1972	In depot maintenance (WK) by Fairchild Engine and Aircraft Corporation (FACCF) at Bob Sikes Municipal Airport, Crestview FL.
20 Sep 1972	Returned to 561 TFS, 832 AD, McConnell AFB KS.
13 Oct 1972	In transient maintenance (WL) at Hickam AFB HI.
17 Nov 1972	Transferred to 17 WWS, 388 TFW, Korat RTAB, Thailand.
20 Jan 1973	Combat capable (CC) at 17 WWS, 388 TFW, Korat RTAB, Thailand. (AVH-20).
16 Jul 1974	In depot work (WM & WR) by SM-ALC field team at Korat RTAB, Thailand. (AVH-22).
26 Jul 1974	Combat capable (CC) at 17 WWS, 388 TFW PACAF, Korat RTAB, Thailand.
29 Oct 1974	Transferred to 35 TFW TAC, George AFB CA.
14 May 1975	At 35 TFW TAC, George AFB CA. (AVH-23 & AVH-24).
11 Sep 1975	In depot repair (WR) by SMAMA at McClellan AFB CA.
17 Dec 1975	Returned to 35 TFW TAC, George AFB CA.
30 Aug 1976	Deployed with 562 TFS under "Coronet Yankee" to Spangdahlem AB, Germany, from the 35 TFW, George AFB CA. 3,629 flying hours. (British Aviation Review, Dec 1995 & AVH-24).
20 Sep 1976	Returned from Germany to 35 TFW, George AFB CA. 3,639 flying hours. (AVH-24).
6 Oct 1976	At MacDill AFB FL with the 35 TFW. 3,639 flying hours.
19 Oct 1976	Returned to 35 TFW, George AFB CA. 3,639 flying hours.
12 Aug 1977	Deployed to Karup AB, Denmark, under "Coronet Club" with 562 TFS, 35 TFW, from George AFB CA. 3,838.0 flying hours. (AVH-25 & AVH-26).
30 Aug 1977	Returned from Denmark to George AFB CA.
17 Mar 1978	Aircraft had flight restrictions at George AFB CA due to cracks in main landing gear wing rib found during inspection required by TCTO 1F-105-1281. "…Restricted to 47,500 lb. gross takeoff weight, 10 knots crosswind component, 4 G's symmetrical and 2.5 G's rolling." (35 TFW/MA memo).
10 Jul 1978	In depot maintenance by SM-ALC at George AFB CA. 4,098.0 flying hours.
20 Jul 1978	At 35 TFW TAC, George AFB CA. 4,098.0 flying hours.
25 Oct 1978	At Eglin AFB FL with 35 TFW from George AFB CA. 4,119.0 flying hours.
7 Nov 1978	At 35 TFW TAC, George AFB CA. 4,119.0 flying hours.
4 Jun 1979	In depot maintenance by Sacramento ALC at George AFB CA. 4,243.1 flying hours. (AVH-27).
7 Oct 1979	Transferred to 116 TFW ANG, Dobbins AFB GA. 4,269.8 flying hours.

28 Apr 1980	At 116 TFW ANG, Dobbins AFB GA. 4,347.9 flying hours. (GO33B 22 Jan 81).
24 Sep 1980	Deployed to Murted AB, Turkey, via Torrejon AB, Spain, with 128 TFS, GANG under "Coronet Power." (British Aviation Review, Dec 1995).
12 Oct 1980	Returned from Turkey to Dobbins AFB GA.
18 May 1981	At 116 TFW ANG, Dobbins AFB GA. 4,569.2 flying hours. (GO33B Dec 81 & GO33B 1 Feb 83).
6 Dec 1982	At 116 TFW ANG, Dobbins AFB GA. 4,817.6 flying hours. Transferred to Hill AFB UT for ABDR program. (GO33B 9 Feb 84 & 116 TFW History, Jan–Dec 1982, USAF microfilm 45509).
9 Nov 1983	At 2952 CLSS, Hill AFB UT for ABDR training. (HQ 2852 ABG/DADF Letter 9 Nov 83).
22 May 1985	At 2952 CLSS, Hill AFB UT allocated to "local base museum." (HQ 2852 ABG/DAFD letter 22 May 85).
16 May 1986	Moved to the Hill AFB Museum after having been painted and marked as a Wild Weasel. (OO-ALC/XRH letter 20 May 86).

F-105G-1RE 62-4444

Republic Production No: F-33 Production Sequence No: 723

Location: Displayed outside at Empire State Aerosciences Museum, Scotia, New York.

Aircraft Chronology

14 Mar 1964	USAF production acceptance from Republic Aviation, Farmingdale NY. (ACA-88).
19 Mar 1964	Delivered to 4520 CCTW, Nellis AFB NV for combat crew training (TF).
6 Apr 1964	At 4520 CCTW, Nellis AFB NV for combat crew training (TF). (AVH-1).
11 Apr 1966	At SMAMA, McClellan AFB for depot work (WO). (AVH-5).
16 May 1966	Returned to 4520 CCTW, Nellis AFB NV for aircrew training (TF).
22 Feb 1967	In depot maintenance (WM) by SMAMA field team at Nellis AFB NV. (AVH-8).
27 Feb 1967	At 4520 CCTW, Nellis AFB NV for aircrew training (TF).
2 Oct 1967	In depot maintenance (WM) by SMAMA field team at Nellis AFB NV.
9 Oct 1967	At 4520 CCTW, Nellis AFB NV for aircrew training (TF).
25 Oct 1967	Transferred to 23 TFW, McConnell AFB KS for combat crew training (TF).
7 Dec 1967	Joined the 560 TFS, 23 TFW, already deployed to George AFB CA for air-to-air gunnery training for RTU Class 68ER.
22 Dec 1967	Returned to 23 TFW, McConnell AFB KS for combat crew training (TF).
19 Feb 1968	In depot maintenance (WM) by SMAMA at McConnell AFB KS for "Combat Martin" modification that removed rear seat and installed a MiG communication jammer. (AVH-10).
23 Feb 1968	At 23 TFW, McConnell AFB KS for combat crew training (TF).
6 Mar 1968	At 23 TFW, McConnell AFB KS being prepared for transfer (PL).
25 Mar 1968	Transferred (PL) to 355 TFW, Takhli RTAB, Thailand. One of five Combat Martin F-105Fs assigned to Takhli.
20 Jun 1968	In depot maintenance (WM) by SMAMA at Takhli RTAB, Thailand.
30 Jun 1968	At 355 TFW, Takhli RTAB, Thailand.
30 Nov 1968	While assigned to the 357 TFS, 355 TFW, Takhli RTAB, Thailand, the aircraft had accumulated 1,688.4 flying hours. (355 TFW History, Oct–Dec 68, USAF microfilm NO466).

21 Jan 1969	In depot maintenance (WM) by SMAMA at Takhli RTAB, Thailand. (AVH-12).
7 Feb 1969	At 355 TFW, Takhli RTAB, Thailand.
28 Feb 1969	While assigned to the 355 TFW, Takhli RTAB, Thailand, the aircraft flew 54.1 hours during the month of February 1969 and had accumulated 1,851.5 flying hours. (355 TFW History, Jan–Mar 69, Vol. II, USAF Microfilm NO467).
5 Jun 1969	At Air Asia, Tainan, Taiwan, for contract depot maintenance (WK). (AVH-12).
28 Jul 1969	Returned to 355 TFW, Takhli RTAB, Thailand.
30 Aug 1969	Transferred to 18 TFW, Kadena AB, Okinawa.
2 Oct 1969	At Kwangju AB, Korea, with 18 TFW.
3 Oct 1969	Returned to 18 TFW, Kadena AB, Okinawa.
30 Oct 1969	At Kwangju AB, Korea, with 18 TFW.
31 Oct 1969	Returned to 18 TFW, Kadena AB, Okinawa.
4 Nov 1969	At Kwangju AB, Korea, with 18 TFW.
5 Nov 1969	Returned to 18 TFW, Kadena AB, Okinawa.
11 Nov 1969	At Kwangju AB, Korea, with 18 TFW.
12 Nov 1969	Returned to 18 TFW, Kadena AB, Okinawa.
12 Dec 1969	At Kwangju AB, Korea, with 18 TFW.
18 Dec 1969	Returned to 18 TFW, Kadena AB, Okinawa.
21 Dec 1969	At Kwangju AB, Korea, with 18 TFW.
16 Jan 1970	Returned to 18 TFW, Kadena AB, Okinawa. (AVH-14).
19 Jan 1970	In depot work (WM) by SMAMA at Kadena AB, Okinawa.
22 Jan 1970	At 18 TFW, Kadena AB, Okinawa.
11 Feb 1970	At Kwangju AB, Korea, with 18 TFW.
5 Mar 1970	Returned to 18 TFW, Kadena AB, Okinawa.
23 Jun 1970	At Kwangju AB, Korea, with 18 TFW.
14 Aug 1970	Returned to 18 TFW, Kadena AB, Okinawa.
7 Sep 1970	At Kwangju AB, Korea, with 18 TFW.
25 Sep 1970	Returned to 18 TFW, Kadena AB, Okinawa.
26 Sep 1970	Transferred to 23 TFW, McConnell AFB KS.
8 Mar 1971	Placed in flyable storage (PR) at 23 TFW, McConnell AFB KS. (AVH-16).
21 May 1971	Operationally ready (CC) at 23 TFW, McConnell AFB KS.
24 May 1971	In contract depot maintenance (WK) by Fairchild Engine and Aircraft Corporation (FACCF) at Bob Sikes Municipal Airport, Crestview FL.
11 Jun 1971	Returned (PL) to 23 TFW, McConnell AFB KS.
16 Jun 1971	Operationally ready (CC) at 23 TFW, McConnell AFB KS.
20 Jul 1971	Placed in flyable storage (PR) at 23 TFW, McConnell AFB KS.
20 Oct 1971	In depot maintenance (WO) by SMAMA at McClellan AFB CA.
1 Mar 1972	Assigned to 561 TFS, 23 TFW, at McConnell AFB KS. Still carried as having "Combat Martin" configuration. (Master 23 TFW Aircraft Assignment as of 1 March 1972).
24 April 1972	In depot work (WO) by SM-ALC at McClellan AFB CA. Combat Martin equipment removed and aircraft modified to an F-105G Wild Weasel. (AVH-18).
5 May 1972	Transferred (PL) to the 57 FWW, Nellis AFB NV for combat crew training (TF).
16 Jun 1972	At the 57 FWW, Nellis AFB NV being prepared for transfer (PL).
26 Jun 1972	Transferred (PL) to the 388 TFW, Korat RTAB, Thailand.
15 Jul 1972	Combat capable (CC) at the 388 TFW, Korat RTAB, Thailand.

Known by its crew chiefs as "Many Fours," 62-4444 started as a trainer at Nellis Air Force Base, Nevada, in March 1964. It remained at Nellis until October 1967 when it moved to McConnell Air Force Base, Kansas, to continue pilot training. However, four months later, it became one of ten F-105Fs modified for "Combat Martin" with a MiG communications jammer in the rear cockpit instead of an ejection seat. On 25 March 1968, it joined four other "Combat Martin" planes at Takhli, Thailand, just before the bombing halt of North Vietnam on 1 April 1968. The halt made the plane's "Combat Martin" mission unnecessary. It stayed with the 355 Tactical Fighter Wing at Takhli for sixteen months and then moved to the 18 Tactical Fighter Wing at Kadena Air Base, Okinawa, who flew it for a year to and from its alert base in Korea. After it returned to McConnell in September 1970, it transferred in and out of flyable storage. Finally, while at the depot in April 1972, the unusable "Combat Martin" gear was removed and the plane converted to a Wild Weasel F-105G. In June 1972, it returned to Vietnam combat for the final phase of the war with the 388 Tactical Fighter Wing at Korat, Thailand. It joined the 35 Tactical Fighter Wing Wild Weasel training program at George Air Force Base, California, in October 1974. Over the next five years, the 35th fought increasing fatigue cracks in the plane's wings before giving it to the Georgia Air National Guard who flew it an additional four years. In 1983, they retired it as a battle damage repair trainer for the New York Air National Guard. (Photograph by author, 15 August 1995.)

3 Jan 1973	In depot maintenance (WM) by SM-ALC field team at Korat RTAB, Thailand. (AVH-20).
10 Jan 1973	At 388 TFW, Korat RTAB, Thailand.
23 Jan 1973	In depot maintenance (WM) by SM-ALC field team at Korat RTAB, Thailand.
24 Jan 1973	At 388 TFW, Korat RTAB, Thailand.
5 Feb 1973	In depot maintenance (WM) by SM-ALC field team at Korat RTAB, Thailand.
9 Feb 1973	At 388 TFW, Korat RTAB, Thailand.
29 Jul 1974	In depot maintenance (WM) by SM-ALC field team At Korat RTAB. (AVH-22).
12 Aug 1974	At 388 TFW, Korat RTAB.
29 Oct 1974	Transferred to the 35 TFW, George AFB CA.
24 Apr 1975	In depot work (WO) by SM-ALC at McClellan AFB CA. (AVH-23 & AVH-24).
31 Jul 1975	In crash damage repair (WR) by SM-ALC at McClellan AFB CA.
21 Aug 1975	Returned to 35 TFW, George AFB CA.
7 Jul 1977	In depot maintenance by SM-ALC at George AFB CA. 4,068.0 flying hours. (AVH-25 & AVH-26).
12 Jul 1977	At 35 TFW TAC, George AFB CA. 4,068.0 flying hours.
27 Feb 1978	At OC-ALC depot, Tinker AFB OK. 4,117.0 flying hours. (AVH-26).
11 Mar 1978	At 35 TFW TAC, George AFB CA. 4,117.0 flying hours.

17 Mar 1978	Aircraft had flight restrictions at George AFB CA due to cracks in main landing gear wing rib found during inspection required by TCTO 1F-105-1281. "...Restricted to 47,500 lb. gross takeoff weight, 10 knots crosswind component, 4 G's symmetrical and 2.5 G's rolling." (35 TFW/MA memo).
Sept 1978	While at the 35 TFW, George AFB CA, the aircraft flew a sortie in which A1C Mary C. "Chris" Kollhoff, rode in the rear cockpit as a reward for being selected the wing's Crew Chief of the Month. She became the first female crew chief to ride in an F-105 (she was crew chief of F-105G 63-8274). Capt. James L. "Jimmy" Boyd from the 561 TFS was the pilot. (Mary Kollhoff Head, e-mail, 15 July 1998).
31 Oct 1978	In depot maintenance by SM-ALC at George AFB CA. 4,252.0 flying hours.
28 Mar 1979	At 35 TFW TAC, George AFB CA. 4,256.2 flying hours. (AVH-27).
28 Mar 1979	Transferred to 116 TFW ANG, Dobbins AFB GA. 4,256.2 flying hours.
16 Oct 1979	In contract depot maintenance (DYNFW) at McConnell AFB KS. 4,365.3 flying hours.
24 Oct 1979	At 116 TFW ANG, Dobbins AFB GA. 4,365.3 flying hours.
22 May 1981	At 116 TFW ANG, Dobbins AFB GA. 4,528.0 flying hours. (GO33B Dec 81 & GO33B 1 Feb 83).
31 Dec 1982	While assigned to the 128 TFS AFRES, Dobbins AFB GA, the aircraft flew 15.5 hours during the month of December 1982 and had accumulated 4,855.1 flying hours. (116 TFW History, Jan–Dec 1982, USAF microfilm 45509).
14 Jan 1983	At 116 TFW ANG, Dobbins AFB GA. 4,858.4 flying hours. (GO33B 9 Feb 84).
9 Nov 1983	At 174 TFW ANG, Hancock Field NY for ABDR training. (HQ 2852 ABG/DADF letter 9 Nov 83).
22 May 1985	At 174 TFW ANG, Hancock Field NY for ABDR training. (HQ 2852 ABG/DADF letter 22 May 85).

F-105G–1RE 62-4446

Republic Production No: F-35 Production Sequence No: 725

Location: On concrete pads near the billeting office at Spangdahlem AB, Germany.

Aircraft Name(s)	Crew	Unit	Date	Description
Sneaky Pete		13 TFS 388 TFW	Jun 67	Cowboy with two holsters on fuselage side below wing.
Mostes	Lt. Col. Herb Sherrill/ Maj. Red Hargis	44 TFS 388 TFW	Jun 69	In black old English script on left fuselage.
Linda Lou	Lt. Col. Herb Sherrill/ Maj. Red Hargis	44 TFS 388 TFW	Aug 69	In red with black trim on right fuselage.
The Silent Majority	Capt. T. J. Brown/ Capt. J. K. Thomas	354 TFS 355 TFW	Apr 70	In white old English script on fuselage below cockpits. Also three bombs (red, white & blue). "Pat" & "Linda" in white script on canopy bows.

Aircraft Chronology

28 Feb 1964	USAF production acceptance from Republic Aviation, Farmingdale NY. (ACA-88).
7 Mar 1964	Delivered to 23 the TFW, McConnell AFB KS.
1 Mar 1965	Deployed with the 561 TFS, 23 TFW, from McConnell AFB KS to 6441 TFW, Yokota AB, Japan

	under Operation "One Buck Nine." Assigned Crew Chief: TSgt. Tolotti. (6441 History Apr–Jun 65, USAF microfilm PO231 & AVH-4).
27 May 1965	Returned to 23 TFW, McConnell AFB KS. (AVH-4).
15 Jul 1965	Transferred to 4520 CCTW, Nellis AFB NV.
20 Sep 1965	At Republic Fairchild (RACFA), Crestview FL for contract depot work (WK).
2 Nov 1965	Returned to 4520 CCTW, Nellis AFB NV for combat crew training (TF).
9 Oct 1966	At SMAMA, McClellan AFB CA for depot work (WO). (AVH-5).
28 Oct 1966	Reassigned to 4525 FWW, Nellis AFB NV for student and combat crew training (TF).
2 Jan 1967	Transferred to 388 TFW, Korat RTAB, Thailand. Configured as a Ryan's Raiders aircraft (Commando Nail) with modified ASG-19 radar. Radar modification performed by 388th Avionics Maintenance Squadron at Korat RTAB. After receiving combat damage, the aircraft was later de-modified during depot repair. (AVH-8 & 388 TFW History, Apr–Dec 1967, USAF microfilm NO583).
13 May 1967	In depot maintenance (VM) by SMAMA field team at Korat RTAB, Thailand.
17 May 1967	At 388 TFW, Korat RTAB, Thailand.
26 May 1967	In depot maintenance (VM) by SMAMA field team at Korat RTAB, Thailand.
31 May 1967	Combat ready (CC) 388 TFW, Korat RTAB, Thailand.
31 Jul 1967	Combat damaged (VO) at 388 TFW, Korat RTAB, Thailand.
Aug 1967	Repairs for combat damage completed. Required major structural repair in the bomb bay area. (388 TFW History, Apr–Dec 67, USAF microfilm NO584).
25 Aug 1967	Operationally ready (CC) at the 388 TFW, Korat RTAB, Thailand. (AVH-8).
30 Sep 1967	In depot maintenance (WM) by SMAMA field team at Korat RTAB, Thailand.
5 Oct 1967	At 388 TFW, Korat RTAB, Thailand.
31 Oct 1967	In depot maintenance for combat damage (VM) by SMAMA field team at Udorn RTAB, Thailand.
26 Dec 1967	At 388 TFW, Korat RTAB, Thailand.
3 Feb 1968	At Air Asia, Tainan, Taiwan, for contract depot work (WK). (AVH-10).
10 Apr 1968	Returned to 388 TFW, Korat RTAB, Thailand.
8 May 1968	In depot maintenance (WM) by SMAMA field team at Korat RTAB, Thailand.
9 May 1968	At 388 TFW, Korat RTAB, Thailand.
26 Jun 1968	In depot maintenance (WM) by SMAMA field team at Korat RTAB, Thailand.
15 Jul 1968	At 388 TFW, Korat RTAB, Thailand.
14 Aug 1968	In depot maintenance (WM) by SMAMA field team at Korat RTAB, Thailand.
16 Aug 1968	At 388 TFW, Korat RTAB, Thailand.
31 Oct 1968	Aircraft had accumulated 1,579.2 flying hours while assigned to the 388 TFW, Korat RTAB, Thailand. (388 TFW History, Oct–Dec 68, USAF microfilm NO585).
31 Jan 1969	Deployed to Takhli RTAB, Thailand with the 44 TFS, 388 TFW, during runway repairs at Korat RTAB, Thailand. (AVH-12 & 388 TFW History, Jan–Mar 69, USAF microfilm NO586).
1 Feb 1969	Flown on an Iron Hand mission in the Steel Tiger region of Laos by a 44 TFS crew while the 388 TFW operated from Takhli RTAB, Thailand. (388 TFW History, Jan–Mar 69, USAF microfilm NO586).
2 Feb 1969	Flown on an Iron Hand mission in the Steel Tiger region of Laos by a 44 TFS crew while the 388 TFW operated from Takhli RTAB, Thailand.
4 Feb 1969	Flown on two missions in the Steel Tiger region of Laos by 44 TFS crews, 388 TFW, while operating from Takhli RTAB, Thailand.
5 Feb 1969	Flown on a mission in the Steel Tiger region of Laos by a 44 TFS crew, 388 TFW, while operating from Takhli RTAB, Thailand.
6 Feb 1969	Flown on an Iron Hand mission in the Steel Tiger region of Laos by a 44 TFS crew, 388 TFW, while operating from Takhli RTAB, Thailand.

For the first ten years of its service, this aircraft was heavily involved in the war in South East Asia. In March 1965, a year after it was delivered to the 23 Tactical Fighter Wing at McConnell Air Force Base, Kansas, it deployed to Yokota Air Base, Japan, to back up Yokota's combat operations at Takhli, Thailand. After a year and a half training pilots at Nellis Air Force Base, Nevada, the plane transferred to Korat, Thailand, with the 388 Tactical Fighter Wing. The wing maintenance organization modified the plane's radar to support the "Commando Nail" night bombing mission. However, when the plane was damaged in combat, the modification was removed. During the month of February 1969, while the runway at Korat was being resurfaced, the plane flew missions over Laos from Takhli, Thailand, with the 388th's 44 Tactical Fighter Squadron. In October 1969, when the 44th transferred to the 355 Tactical Fighter Wing, the plane moved permanently to Takhli. In December 1969, it was modified at Takhli from an F-105F to a Wild Weasel "G." Near the end of 1970, when Takhli began closing, the plane was damaged once again and sent to the depot in California for repairs. In September 1971, it returned to combat at Korat where it remained until 1974 when the Air Force ended its Thailand involvement in the Vietnam war. On its return to the States, the plane went to the 35 Tactical Fighter Wing at George Air Force Base, California, the only Air Force unit then flying the F-105 Wild Weasels. The 35th took the plane with them on their NATO exercise to Denmark in August 1978 and then transferred it to the Georgia Air National Guard in 1980. Two years later, after the plane had accumulated over 5,000 flying hours, the Guard retired it to storage in Arizona. In late 1984, the plane was shipped to Incirlik Air Base, Turkey, where it served as a battle damage repair trainer. In 1988, after restoration, it was displayed as a POW/MIA memorial at Spangdahlem Air Base, Germany, the former base for the 49 Tactical Fighter Wing that flew F-105s in the early 1960s. (Photograph by Donald Hilburn, 4 November 1995.)

7 Feb 1979 Flown on a mission in the Steel Tiger region of Laos by a 44 TFS crew, 388 TFW, while operating from Takhli RTAB, Thailand.

8 Feb 1969 Flown on a mission in the Steel Tiger region of Laos by a 44 TFS crew, 388 TFW, while operating from Takhli RTAB, Thailand.

9 Feb 1969 Flown on an Iron Hand mission in the Steel Tiger region of Laos by a 44 TFS crew, 388 TFW, while operating from Takhli RTAB, Thailand.

11 Feb 1969 Flown on a mission in the Steel Tiger region of Laos by a 44 TFS crew, 388 TFW, while operating from Takhli RTAB, Thailand.

13 Feb 1969 Flown on a local mission from Takhli RTAB, Thailand, by a 44 TFS crew, 388 TFW.

15 Feb 1969 Flown on two missions in the Steel Tiger region of Laos by 44 TFS crews, 388 TFW, while operating from Takhli RTAB, Thailand.

16 Feb 1969 Flown on an Iron Hand mission in Route Pack I of North Vietnam by a 44 TFS crew, 388 TFW, while operating from Takhli RTAB, Thailand. Aircraft also flew a second Iron Hand mission in the Steel Tiger region of Laos.

27 Feb 1969 Flown on a strike mission in the Steel Tiger region of Laos by a 44 TFS crew, 388 TFW, while operating from Takhli RTAB, Thailand.

28 Feb 1969 Flown on a strike mission in the Steel Tiger region of Laos by a 44 TFS crew, 388 TFW, while operating from Takhli RTAB, Thailand.

1 Mar 1969 Recovered at Korat RTAB, Thailand, after flying a strike mission in the Steel Tiger region of Laos by a 44 TFS crew, 388 TFW, after taking off from Takhli RTAB, Thailand.

30 Apr 1969 While assigned to the 44 TFS, 388 TFW, Korat RTAB, Thailand, the aircraft flew 78.4 hours for the

month of April 1969 and had accumulated 1,909.6 total flying hours. (388 TFW History, Apr–Jun 69, USAF microfilm NO586).

21 Jun 1969 At Air Asia, Tainan, Taiwan, for contract depot work (WK). (AVH-12).

30 Jun 1969 While assigned to the 44 TFS, 388 TFW, Korat RTAB, Thailand, the aircraft flew 31.5 hours in the month of June 1969 and had accumulated 1,992.2 total flying hours. (388 TFW History, Apr–Jun 69, USAF microfilm NO586).

13 Aug 1969 Returned to 388 TFW, Korat RTAB, Thailand. (AVH-12).

10 Oct 1969 Transferred with the 44 TFS to the 355 TFW, Takhli RTAB, Thailand.

18 Dec 1969 Redesignated as F-105G at 355 TFW, Takhli RTAB, Thailand.

12 Mar 1970 In depot work (WM) by SMAMA at Takhli RTAB, Thailand. (AVH-14).

29 Mar 1970 At 355 TFW, Takhli RTAB, Thailand.

19 Aug 1970 At 355 TFW, Takhli RTAB, Thailand. Assignment status "WN."

21 Sep 1970 In depot work for crash damage (WR) by SMAMA field team at Takhli RTAB, Thailand.

9 Nov 1970 In storage (XT) at SMAMA, McClellan AFB CA. (AVH-16).

13 Jan 1971 In depot work (WO) by SMAMA at McClellan AFB CA.

14 Sep 1971 Transferred (PL) to 388 TFW, Korat RTAB, Thailand.

2 Oct 1971 Combat capable (CC) at 388 TFW, Korat RTAB, Thailand.

16 Oct 1972 In depot work (WO) by SM-ALC at McClellan AFB CA.

1 Nov 1972 Returned to 388 TFW, Korat RTAB, Thailand.

10 Jan 1973 In depot work (WM) by SM-ALC field team at Korat RTAB, Thailand. (AVH-20).

24 Jan 1973 At 388 TFW, Korat RTAB, Thailand.

3 Jul 1974 In depot work (WM & WR) by SM-ALC at Korat RTAB, Thailand. (AVH-22).

12 Jul 1974 At 388 TFW PACAF, Korat RTAB, Thailand.

29 Oct 1974 Transferred to 35 TFW TAC, George AFB CA.

21 Apr 1975 In depot maintenance (WM) by SM-ALC at George AFB CA. (AVH-23 & AVH-24).

22 Apr 1975 At 35 TFW TAC, George AFB CA.

16 Dec 1975 In depot work (WO) by SM-ALC at McClellan AFB CA.

22 Apr 1976 In depot work (DR) by SM-ALC at McClellan AFB CA. (AVH-24).

10 May 1976 Returned to 35 TFW, George AFB CA.

6 Oct 1976 At MacDill AFB FL with the 35 TFW. 4,241 flying hours.

19 Oct 1976 Returned to 35 TFW, George AFB CA.

8 Apr 1977 In depot maintenance by SM-ALC at George AFB CA. 4,368.0 flying hours. (AVH-25 & AVH-26).

20 Mar 1978 In depot maintenance by SM-ALC at George AFB CA. 4,545.0 flying hours. (AVH-26).

14 Apr 1978 At 35 TFW TAC, George AFB CA. 4,545.0 flying hours.

9 Aug 1978 Deployed with 562 TFS under "Coronet Sparrow "to Karup AB, Denmark, from 35 TFW, George AFB CA. 4,680.0 flying hours.

6 Sep 1978 Returned from Denmark to 35 TFW TAC, George AFB CA. 4,687.0 flying hours.

2 Oct 1978 At 35 TFW TAC, George AFB CA. 4,744.0 flying hours.

28 Apr 1980 At 116 TFG ANG, Dobbins AFB GA. 4,347.9 flying hours. (GO33B 24 Jun 80).

9 Jul 1980 In depot maintenance (DYNFW) at George AFB CA. 4,979.9 flying hours. (GO33B 22 Jan 81).

9 Oct 1980 At 35 TFW, George AFB CA. 4,985.9 flying hours.

9 Oct 1980 Transferred to 116 TFG ANG, Dobbins AFB GA. 4,885.9 flying hours.

22 Jul 1982 Sent to storage at MASDC, Davis-Monthan AFB AZ. ("High probability of withdrawal"—XV). 5,124.6 flying hours. (GO33B 1 Feb 83).

20 Dec 1982 MASDC storage code changed to "XX" (Low probability of withdrawal). 5,129.3 flying hours.

31 Oct 1984	Removed from MASDC storage.
22 May 1985	At 39 CAMS, Incirlik AB, Turkey, for ABDR training. (HQ 2852 ABG/DADF Letter 22 May 85).
9 May 1988	Static display dedication at Spangdahlem AB, Germany, in remembrance of POWs/MIAs in SEA.

F-105F-1RE 63-8261

Republic Production No: F-38 Production Sequence No: 728

Location: Parked on the grass at All Flags Heritage Park, Camp Robinson, Little Rock, Arkansas.

Aircraft Name(s)	Crew	Unit	Date	Description
Boss Hoss				Horse's head with bridle above name in black letters.

Aircraft Chronology

18 Feb 1964	USAF Production acceptance from Republic Aviation, Farmingdale NY. (ACA-89).
17 Apr 1964	At MOAMA, Brookley AFB AL for depot work. (AVH-1).
3 May 1964	Delivered to 18 TFW, Kadena AB, Okinawa.
Sep 1964	At 18 TFW, Kadena AB, Okinawa. Assigned crew chief: SSgt. E. Baker. (18 TFW History, Jul–Dec 64, USAF microfilm MO496).
31 Jan 1965	At 18 TFW, Kadena AB, Okinawa. Assigned crew chief: A1C R. Hannula. (18 TFW History, Jan–Jun 65, USAF microfilm MO497).
27 Mar 1965	At Air Asia, Tainan, Taiwan, for contract depot work (WK). (AVH-4).
9 Apr 1965	Returned to 18 TFW, Kadena AB, Okinawa.
28 Aug 1965	At Itazuke AB, Japan, for depot work (WM) by AFLC field team.
20 Nov 1965	At Air Asia, Tainan, Taiwan, for contract depot work (WK).
11 Dec 1965	Returned to 18 TFW, Kadena AB.
10 Nov 1966	In depot maintenance (WM) by SMAMA field team at 18 TFW, Kadena AB, Okinawa. (AVH-5).
14 Nov 1966	At 18 TFW, Kadena AB, Okinawa.
31 Dec 1966	While assigned to the 18 TFW, Kadena AB, Okinawa, the aircraft flew 26 hours during the month of December 1966 and had accumulated 866 flying hours. (18 TFW History, Jul–Dec 66, USAF microfilm MO498).
9 Apr 1967	At 18 TFW, Kadena AB, Okinawa. (AVH-8).
31 May 1967	At 12 TFS, 18 TFW, Kadena AB, Okinawa. Aircraft had accumulated 967 flying hours. (18 TFW History, Apr–Jun 67, USAF microfilm MO499).
11 Aug 1967	Being prepared for transfer (PL) at 18 TFW, Kadena AB, Okinawa. (AVH-8).
31 Aug 1967	Transferred to 23 TFW, McConnell AFB KS.
13 Nov 1967	In depot maintenance (WO) by SMAMA at McClellan AFB CA.
2 Feb 1968	Returned to (PL) 23 TFW, McConnell AFB KS. (AVH-10).
5 Feb 1968	At 23 TFW, McConnell AFB KS for combat crew training (TF).
3 May 1968	In depot maintenance (WM) by SMAMA at McConnell AFB KS.
7 May 1968	At 23 TFW, McConnell AFB KS for combat crew training (TF).
19 Jun 1968	Reassigned to combat duties (CC) at 23 TFW, McConnell AFB KS.

During its first seven years, this "F" served in only two Air Force wings then spent its last thirteen years flying with three different Air National Guard and Air Force Reserve units. While most of its contemporaries were turned into Wild Weasel birds, this plane remained a straight two-seat trainer for its whole career. Delivered in May 1964 to the 18 Tactical Fighter Wing at Kadena Air Base, Okinawa, it transferred three years later to the 23 Tactical Fighter Wing at McConnell Air Force Base, Kansas. In March 1971, it went to the Virginia Air National Guard who turned it over in February 1974 to the Air Force Reserve at Carswell Air Force Base, Texas—one of the few F-105s this unit flew that wasn't a Thunderstick II-modified F-105D. The plane accompanied the Carswell squadron on its 1979 summer deployment to Italy and then, in February 1982, moved to a sister Reserve squadron at Hill Air Force Base, Utah. In February 1984, it was one of the planes flown during the "Thud Out" F-105 retirement ceremony at Hill. Its rear-seat pilot was Col. Merlyn Dethlefsen, who had been awarded a Medal of Honor as an F-105F Wild Weasel pilot during the Vietnam war. One of the last Thunderchiefs to take to the air, the plane made its final flight from Hill to Little Rock, Arkansas, on 3 March 1984. (Photograph by author, 17 May 1995.)

21 May 1970	At 23 TFW, McConnell AFB KS (CC). (AVH-14).
11 Dec 1970	Assigned to combat crew training (TF) at 23 TFW, McConnell AFB KS.
19 Jan 1971	At 23 TFW, McConnell AFB KS being prepared for transfer (PL) to depot. (AVH-16).
21 Jan 1971	In depot work (WO) by SMAMA at McClellan AFB CA.
5 Mar 1971	Transferred (PL) to 192 TFG ANG, Byrd Field, Richmond VA.
28 Jun 1971	In depot work (WO) by SMAMA at McClellan AFB CA.
26 Jan 1972	Returned to 192 TFG ANG, Byrd Field, Richmond VA. (AVH-18).
26 Aug 1972	In depot maintenance (WK) by Fairchild Engine and Aircraft Corporation (FACCF) at Bob Sikes Municipal Airport, Crestview FL.
27 Sep 1972	Returned to 192 TFG ANG, Byrd Field, Richmond VA.
24 Mar 1973	In contract depot maintenance (WM) by Dynalectron Corporation (DYNZZ) at Byrd Field, Richmond VA. (AVH-20).
29 Mar 1973	At 192 TFG ANG, Byrd Field, Richmond VA.
27 Jun 1973	In contract depot maintenance (WM) by Dynalectron Corporation (DYNZZ) at Byrd Field, Richmond VA.
30 Jun 1973	At 192 TFG ANG, Byrd Field, Richmond VA.
26 Feb 1974	Transferred to 506 CMTSQ AFRES, Carswell AFB TX. (AVH-22).
25 Nov 1974	Assigned unit redesignated 457 TFS AFRES, Carswell AFB TX. 3,438 flying hours. (AVH-22 & AVH-24).
31 Aug 1976	In depot work (DO & DR) by SM-ALC at McClellan AFB CA. 3,450 flying hours. (AVH-24).
13 Sep 1976	Returned to 457 TFS AFRES, Carswell AFB TX. 3,450 flying hours.
14 Aug 1977	Deployed under "Coronet Poker" with 457 TFS to Norvenich, Germany, from Carswell AFB TX. (British Aviation Review, Dec 1995).
27 Aug 1977	Returned from Germany to Carswell AFB TX.
5 Apr 1978	At 457 TFS AFRES, Carswell AFB TX. 3,739.0 flying hours. (AVH-26).
5 Mar 1979	In contract depot maintenance (FACBM) at Tinker AFB OK. 4,039.2 flying hours. (AVH-27).

9 Apr 1979	At 457 TFS AFRES Carswell AFB TX. 4,055.7 flying hours.
12 May 1979	Deployed under "Coronet Palomino" with 457 TFS to Gioia Del Colle, Italy, from Carswell AFB TX. (British Aviation Review, Dec 1995).
24 May 1979	Returned from Italy to Carswell AFB TX.
30 Jun 1979	While assigned to the 457 TFS AFRES, Carswell AFB TX, the aircraft flew 23.1 hours during the month of June 1979 and had accumulated 4,150.6 flying hours. (301 TFW History, Apr–Jun 1979, USAF microfilm 34382).
15 Oct 1979	In contract depot maintenance (DYNFW) at Carswell AFB TX. 4,236.6 flying hours.
23 Oct 1979	At 457 TFS AFRES Carswell AFB TX. 4,236.6 flying hours.
26 Feb 1980	In depot maintenance (DYNFW) at Carswell AFB TX. 4,313.3 flying hours. (GO33B 24 Jun 80).
25 Mar 1980	At 457 TFS AFRES, Carswell AFB TX. 4,327.4 flying hours.
13 Jun 1980	At 457 TFS AFRES, Carswell AFB TX. 4,344.4 flying hours. (GO33B 22 Jan 81).
23 Jun 1980	At 457 TFS AFRES, Carswell AFB TX. 4,359.8 flying hours.
6 Oct 1980	In depot maintenance (DYNFW) at Carswell AFB TX. 4,388.4 flying hours.
26 Feb 1982	At 466 TFS AFRES, Hill AFB UT. 4,658.7 flying hours. (GO33B 1 Feb 83).
28 Feb 1983	In depot maintenance at Ogden ALC, Hill AFB UT. 4,838.7 flying hours. (GO33B 9 Feb 84).
14 Mar 1983	At 466 TFS AFRES, Hill AFB UT. 4,845.2 flying hours.
25 Feb 1984	One of three F-105F's flown in the Thud-Out ceremony at Hill AFB UT. Pilot: Maj. Frank Bernard. "Backseat Honoree": Col. Merlyn Dethlefsen (USAF, Ret).
3 Mar 1984	Last flight from Hill AFB UT to Little Rock AFB AR, the next to last Thunderchief to fly. The pilot was Maj. Kent "Supe" Clark with Mr. Theodore W. Van Geffen as the rear seat passenger. (Theo Van Geffen, e-mail to the RATNET, 27 Feb 1999).

F-105G–1RE 63-8266

Republic Production No: F-43 Production Sequence No: 733

Location: Parked on ramp at Mid-America Air Museum, Liberal, Kansas.

Aircraft Name(s)	Crew	Unit	Date	Description
Can't Mack It To It		561 TFS Det. 1 (TDY to Korat)		
White Lightning		17 WWS 388 TFW	Dec 72	Name inside lightning flash on left intake.

Aircraft Chronology

25 Mar 1964	USAF production acceptance from Republic Aviation, Farmingdale NY. (ACA-89).
27 Mar 1964	Delivered to 4520 CCTW, Nellis AFB NV. (AVH-1).
24 Mar 1965	At SMAMA, McClellan AFB CA for depot work (WO). (AVH-4).
15 Apr 1965	At 4520 CCTW, Nellis AFB NV for combat crew training.
12 Oct 1965	At SMAMA, McClellan AFB CA for depot work (WO).
30 Nov 1965	At 4520 CCTW, Nellis AFB NV for combat crew training (TF).
6 Aug 1966	Reassigned to 23 TFW, McConnell AFB KS. (AVH-5).
22 Apr 1967	In depot maintenance (WM) by SMAMA field team at McConnell AFB KS. (AVH-8).

27 Apr 1967 At 23 TFW, McConnell AFB KS.

31 May 1967 Deployed to George AFB CA to join the 563 TFS from the 23 TFW providing air-to-air gunnery training for F-105 RTU class 67IR, "The Reluctant Hog-Herders."

14 Jul 1967 Returned to 23 TFW, McConnell AFB KS.

9 Aug 1967 In depot maintenance (WM) by SMAMA field team at McConnell AFB KS.

10 Aug 1967 At 23 TFW, McConnell AFB KS.

31 Aug 1967 In depot maintenance (WM) by SMAMA field team at McConnell AFB KS.

1 Sep 1967 At 23 TFW, McConnell AFB KS.

18 Dec 1967 In depot maintenance (WO) by SMAMA at McClellan AFB CA.

18 Jan 1968 Returned to 23 TFW, McConnell AFB KS. (AVH-10).

30 Jan 1968 Transferred to the 4525 FWW, Nellis AFB NV for combat crew training (TF).

15 Oct 1969 Reassigned to 57 FWW, Nellis AFB NV for combat crew training (TF). (AVH-12).

29 Jul 1970 At 57 FWW, Nellis AFB NV. (AVH-14).

4 Aug 1970 In depot maintenance (WO) by SMAMA at McClellan AFB CA.

3 Mar 1971 Designated as an F-105G while in depot maintenance (WO) by SMAMA at McClellan AFB CA. (AVH-16).

25 May 1971 Transferred (PL) to 17 WWS, 388 TFW, Korat RTAB, Thailand.

24 Nov 1971 At 388 TFW (CC), Korat RTAB, Thailand.

11 Nov 1972 In depot work (WM) by SM-ALC at Korat RTAB, Thailand. (AVH-18).

21 Nov 1972 Returned to 388 TFW, Korat RTAB, Thailand.

7 Sep 1973 Aircraft left the 388 TFW, Korat RTAB, Thailand, for the 35 TFW, George AFB CA. After leaving Korat enroute to George, the aircraft experienced engine vibration and the crew diverted to Johnston Atoll where the engine was changed. Pilot: Capt. John R. Baker. (Airpower Magazine, May 1998, page 36.)

14 Sep 1973 Arrived (PL) at 35 TFW TAC, George AFB CA. (AVH-20).

2 Oct 1973 In depot maintenance (WO) by SM-ALC at McClellan AFB CA.

2 Oct 1973 Returned to 35 TFW TAC, George AFB CA.

25 Jan 1974 In depot maintenance (WR) by SM-ALC at McClellan AFB CA. (AVH-22).

11 Feb 1974 Returned to 35 TFW TAC, George AFB CA.

12 Aug 1974 In depot maintenance (WM) by SM-ALC at George AFB CA.

16 Aug 1974 At 35 TFW TAC, George AFB CA.

31 Mar 1975 In depot maintenance (WM) by SM-ALC at George AFB CA. (AVH-23).

14 Apr 1975 At 35 TFW TAC, George AFB CA. (AVH-23 & AVH-24).

30 Aug 1976 Deployed with 561 TFS under "Coronet Yankee" to Spangdahlem AB, Germany, from 35 TFW, George AFB CA. 4,210 flying hours. (British Aviation Review, Dec 1995 & AVH-24).

20 Sep 1976 Returned to 35 TFW TAC, George AFB CA. 4,220 flying hours. (AVH-24).

6 Oct 1976 At MacDill AFB FL with the 35 TFW. 4,220 flying hours.

19 Oct 1976 Returned to 35 TFW TAC, George AFB CA. 4,220 flying hours.

21 Feb 1978 At OC-ALC depot, Tinker AFB OK. 4,541.0 flying hours. (AVH-26).

25 May 1978 At 35 TFW TAC, George AFB CA. 4,650.0 flying hours.

10 Jul 1978 At 35 TFW TAC, George AFB CA. 4,654.0 flying hours.

31 Jul 1978 At 35 TFW TAC, George AFB CA. 4,658.0 flying hours.

30 Sep 1978 At 35 TFW TAC, George AFB CA. 4,687.0 flying hours.

30 Oct 1979 At 35 TFW TAC, George AFB CA. 4,827.3 flying hours. (AVH-27).

19 Feb 1980 In depot maintenance (DYNFW) at George AFB CA. 4,898.8 flying hours. (GO33B 24 Jun 80).

This F-105G 63-8266 spent from March 1964 to March 1971 as a trainer at Nellis Air Force Base, Nevada, and McConnell Air Force Base, Kansas. After the depot in California turned it into a Wild Weasel "G," it went to war in May 1971 with the 388 Tactical Fighter Wing at Korat, Thailand. It transferred in September 1973 to its last organization, the 35 Tactical Fighter Wing at George Air Force Base, California, who flew it to Germany during its 1976 NATO summer deployment. The 35th retired it with nearly 5,000 flying hours on its airframe in December 1982. It was pulled from storage in the early 1990s and given to the Mid-America Air Museum in Liberal, Kansas, down the road from its earlier base in Wichita. (Photograph by author, 6 August 1995.)

29 Feb 1980	At 35 TFW, George AFB CA. 4,898.8 flying hours.
1 Jul 1980	Delivered to MASDC storage (XV—"High probability of withdrawal") at Davis-Monthan AFB AZ. 4,932.4 flying hours. (GO33B 22 Jan 81).
20 Dec 1982	MASDC storage code changed to "XX" (Low probability of withdrawal). 4,943.9 flying hours. (GO33B 1 Feb 83).
1988	In storage at AMARC, Davis-Monthan AFB AZ. Allocated to Mid-America Air Museum.
14 Nov 1990	Removed from AMARC storage for Mid-America Air Museum, Liberal KS. (AMARC Report D003A/B, 22 Feb 91).
1 Sep 1992	Arrived at Mid-America Air Museum, Liberal KS.

F-105G–1RE 63-8274

Republic Production No: F-51 Production Sequence No: 741

Location: At the Glen L. Martin Aviation Museum, Baltimore, Maryland.

Aircraft Name(s)	Crew	Unit	Date	Description
The Great Speckled Bird		44 TFS 388 TFW	Jul 68	Black letters over crow carrying missile under its wing. On fuselage below left wing.

Aircraft Chronology

30 Apr 1964	USAF production acceptance from Republic Aviation, Farmingdale NY. (ACA-89).
6 May 1964	At MOAMA, Brookley AFB AL for depot work (WO).

27 Jun 1964	Delivered to 41 AD, Yokota AB, Japan. (AVH-1).
August 1964	At 41 AD Yokota AB, Japan. Crew Chief: SSgt. E. Cosper. (41 AD Monthly Maintenance Summary).
1 Apr 1965	Owning unit redesignated 6441 TFW, Yokota AB, Japan. (AVH-4).
30 April 1965	At 6441 TFW, Yokota AB, Japan. Assigned Crew Chief: SSgt. Johnson. (6441 TFW History, Apr–Jun 65, USAF microfilm PO231).
17 Jun 1965	At Air Asia, Tainan, Taiwan, for contract depot work (WK).
3 Jul 1965	Returned to 6441 TFW, Yokota AB, Japan.
Aug 1965	At 6441 TFW, Yokota AB, Japan. Assigned Crew Chief: SSgt. Johnson. (6441 TFW History, Jul–Dec 65, USAF microfilm PO232).
30 Sep 1965	At Air Asia, Tainan, Taiwan, for contract depot work (WK) and Safety Pack II Modification. (AVH-4).
18 Oct 1965	Returned to 6441 TFW, Yokota AB, Japan.
31 May 1966	At Osan AB, Korea, with the 6441 TFW for nuclear weapon alert. (AVH-5).
6 Jun 1966	At Air Asia, Tainan, Taiwan, for contract depot work (WK).
15 Jun 1966	Returned to 6441 TFW, Yokota AB, Japan.
15 Nov 1966	Assigned to 41 AD, Yokota AB, Japan.
3 Jan 1967	At 41 AD, Yokota AB, Japan. (AVH-8).
22 Jun 1967	In depot work (WK) by SMAMA at Yokota AB, Japan. Modified for Ryan's Raiders (Commando Nail) mission.
24 Jun 1967	At 41 AD, Yokota AB, Japan.
18 Oct 1967	In depot maintenance (WM) at Kadena AB, Okinawa, by AFLC field team from SMAMA.
31 Oct 1967	Transferred to 18 TFW, Kadena AB, Okinawa.
9 Jan 1968	In depot maintenance (WM) at Kadena AB, Okinawa, by AFLC field team from SMAMA. (AVH-10).
7 Feb 1968	At 18 TFW, Kadena AB, Okinawa.
14 Feb 1968	Transferred to 388 TFW, Korat RTAB, Thailand.
27 Apr 1968	In depot maintenance (WM) by SMAMA at Korat RTAB, Thailand.
10 May 1968	At 388 TFW, Korat RTAB, Thailand.
17 Oct 1968	Aircraft drag chute failed to deploy when landing from a combat mission while assigned to the 388 TFW, Korat RTAB, Thailand. (388 TFW History, Oct–Dec 68, USAF microfilm NO585).
31 Oct 1968	Aircraft had accumulated 1,546.6 flying hours while assigned to the 388 TFW, Korat RTAB, Thailand. (388 TFW History, Oct–Dec 68, USAF microfilm NO585).
15 Nov 1968	Aircraft drag chute failed to deploy when landing from a combat mission while assigned to the 388 TFW, Korat RTAB, Thailand. (388 TFW History, Oct–Dec 68, USAF microfilm NO585).
8 Dec 1968	Departed (PL) 388 TFW, Korat RTAB, Thailand. (AVH-10).
18 Dec 1968	In transient maintenance (WL) at 6486 ABW, Hickam AFB HI.
9 Jan 1969	Transferred to 23 TFW, McConnell AFB KS for combat crew training (TF). (AVH-12).
21 Apr 1969	In depot maintenance (WM) by field team from SMAMA at McConnell AFB KS.
22 Apr 1969	At 23 TFW, McConnell AFB KS for combat crew training (TF).
6 Apr 1971	In depot maintenance (WK) by Fairchild Engine and Aircraft Corporation (FACCF) at Bob Sikes Municipal Airport, Crestview FL. (AVH-16).
27 Apr 1971	Returned to 23 TFW, McConnell AFB KS for combat crew training (TF).
10 May 1971	Assigned combat duties (CC) at 23 TFW, McConnell AFB KS.
26 Nov 1971	In depot work (WO) by SMAMA at McClellan AFB CA.
1 Mar 1972	Carried on assignment roster for the 561 TFS, 23 TFW, at McConnell AFB KS as having "Combat Nail" configuration. (Master 23 TFW Aircraft Assignment as of 1 March 1972).
17 May 1972	Designated F-105G while in depot work by SM-ALC at McClellan AFB CA. (AVH-18).
15 Jun 1972	Transferred to 57 FWW, Nellis AFB NV for combat crew training (TF).

Produced in April 1964, it was delivered to its first unit, the 41st Air Division at Yokota AB, Japan, in June 1964. It transferred to the 18 Tactical Fighter Wing at Kadena Air Base, Okinawa, in October 1967 and then to the 388 Tactical Fighter Wing at Korat, Thailand, in February 1968 where it flew combat missions with the 44 Tactical Fighter Squadron. In January 1969, it moved for combat crew training to the 23 Tactical Fighter Wing at McConnell Air Force Base, Kansas. In May 1972, while in the depot at McClellan Air Force Base, California, the plane was one of the last of the 61 "Fs" upgraded to an F-105G. Coming out of the depot in June 1972, it was assigned to the 57 Fighter Weapons Wing at Nellis Air Force Base, Nevada, for Wild Weasel crew training. It then moved to the 35 Tactical Fighter Wing at George Air Force Base, California, in July 1975 after all Wild Weasel training transferred there. In August 1977, it deployed for three weeks to Karup Air Base, Denmark, with George's 563 Tactical Fighter Squadron. In October 1980, it moved to its last unit, the Georgia Air National Guard's 128 Tactical Fighter Squadron at Dobbins Air Force Base. After accumulating a little over 4,100 flying hours, it made its last flight in May 1983 from Dobbins to Patuxent River Naval Air Station, Maryland. It was one of 14 F-105Fs and F-105Gs that were barged up Chesapeake Bay from "Pax River" to be used as targets for missile tests at the Army's Aberdeen Proving Grounds. In June 1996, it escaped destruction when it was lifted by helicopter from Aberdeen to its present location at the Glen L. Martin museum outside Baltimore, Maryland. (Photograph by Linda L Brothers via Jack W. Brothers, August 1996.)

8 Jul 1972	In depot maintenance (WK) by Fairchild Engine and Aircraft Corporation (FACCF) at Bob Sikes Municipal Airport, Crestview FL.
3 Aug 1972	Returned to 57 FWW, Nellis AFB NV for combat crew training (TF).
24 Jan 1973	In depot maintenance (WM) by SM-ALC at Nellis AFB NV. (AVH-20).
26 Jan 1973	At 57 FWW, Nellis AFB NV for combat crew training (TF).
6 Nov 1973	In depot maintenance (WM) by SM-ALC at Nellis AFB NV.
29 Nov 1973	At 57 FWW, Nellis AFB NV for combat crew training (TF).
11 Jan 1974	In depot maintenance (WM) by SM-ALC at Nellis AFB NV. (AVH-22).
16 Jan 1974	At 57 FWW, Nellis AFB NV for combat crew training (TF).
11 Aug 1974	In depot maintenance (WM) by SM-ALC at Nellis AFB NV.
27 Aug 1974	At 57 FWW, Nellis AFB NV for combat crew training (TF).
14 Apr 1975	In depot maintenance (WO & WR) by SM-ALC at McClellan AFB CA. (AVH-23).
31 Jul 1975	Transferred to 35 TFW, George AFB CA for combat crew training (TF).
7 Oct 1976	At MacDill AFB FL with the 35 TFW. 3,240 flying hours. (AVH-24).
20 Oct 1976	Returned to 35 TFW, George AFB CA. 3,240 flying hours.
8 Apr 1977	In depot maintenance (DM) by SM-ALC at George AFB CA. 3,357 flying hours. (AVH-25).
12 Apr 1977	At 35 TFW, George AFB CA. 3,357 flying hours.
12 Aug 1977	Deployed under "Coronet Club" with 563 TFS to Karup AB, Denmark, from 35 TFW, George AFB CA. 3,412 flying hours. (British Aviation Review, Dec 1995).
30 Aug 1977	Returned from Denmark to George AFB CA.
29 Feb 1978	In depot maintenance (DM) by SM-ALC at George AFB CA. (AVH-26).
5 Mar 1978	At 35 TFW, George AFB CA. 3,515.0 flying hours.
3 Oct 1978	At 35 TFW, George AFB CA. 3,715.0 flying hours.
9 Apr 1979	At OC-ALC Tinker AFB OK for domestic project (DO). 3,762.6 flying hours. (AVH27).

19 Oct 1979	Returned to 35 TFW, George AFB CA. 3,782.0 flying hours.
12 Dec 1979	In depot maintenance (DM) by SM-ALC at George AFB CA.
2 Jan 1980	At 35 TFW TAC, George AFB CA. 3,710.9 flying hours. (GO33B Dec 80)
26 Jun 1980	In depot maintenance by SM-ALC at George AFB CA. 3,798.5 flying hours. (GO33B 24 Jun 80).
9 Oct 1980	At 35 TFW TAC, George AFB CA. 3,805.5 flying hours.
9 Oct 1980	Transferred to 116 TFW ANG, Dobbins AFB GA. 3,805.5 flying hours.
21 May 1981	At 116 TFW ANG, Dobbins AFB GA. 3,811.3 flying hours. (GO33B Dec 81).
31 Dec 1982	While assigned to the 128 TFS AFRES, Dobbins AFB GA, the aircraft flew 16.9 hours during the month of December 1982 and had accumulated 4,136.4 flying hours. (116 TFW History, Jan–Dec 1982, USAF microfilm 45509).
4 Feb 1983	At 116 TFW ANG, Dobbins AFB GA. 4,141.9 flying hours. Assigned to US Army (ZL). (GO33B 9 Feb 84).
17 May 1983	Last flight from 128 TFS ANG, Dobbins AFB GA to Patuxent River NAS MD for delivery to the U.S. Army's Aberdeen Proving Ground MD. (John Coon).
	Towed on a barge by tugboat from Patuxent River NAS to Aberdeen Range MD as target for munitions tests.
20 Jun 1996	Transported from Aberdeen MD to Glen L. Martin Aviation Museum, Baltimore MD. Aft section lifted by helicopter. (Mr. Jack Brothers, Museum Member, letter 20 Jul 1996).

F-105G-1RE 63-8276

Republic Production No: F-53 Production Sequence No: 743

Location: On a pedestal at History Park, Nellis AFB, Las Vegas, Nevada.

Aircraft Name(s)	Crew	Unit	Date	Description
Angel/ The Beno Bitch	1Lt Emerson B. Taylor	4519 CCTS 23 TFW	May 69	First name below left wing, second name and reclining nude below right. "Bitch" in red forms woman's body.

Aircraft Chronology

16 Apr 1964	USAF production acceptance from Republic Aviation, Farmingdale NY. (ACA-89 & AVH-1).
20 Apr 1964	At MOAMA, Brookley AFB AL for depot work (WO).
2 May 1964	Delivered to 18 TFW, Kadena AB, Okinawa.
30 Sep 1964	At 18 TFW, Kadena AB, Okinawa. Assigned crew chief: SSgt. J. Lohman. (18 TFW History, Jul–Dec 64, USAF microfilm MO496).
31 Jan 1965	At 18 TFW, Kadena AB, Okinawa. Assigned crew chief: A1C R. Nyhus. (18 TFW History, Jan–Jun 65, USAF microfilm MO497).
8 Apr 1965	At Air Asia, Tainan, Taiwan, for contract depot work (WK). (AVH-4).
24 Apr 1965	Returned to 18 TFW, Kadena AB, Okinawa.
6 Nov 1966	In depot maintenance (WM) by SMAMA field team at 18 TFW, Kadena AB, Okinawa. (AVH-5).
10 Nov 1966	At 18 TFW, Kadena AB, Okinawa.
31 Dec 1966	While assigned to the 18 TFW, Kadena AB, Okinawa, the aircraft flew 16 hours during the month of

This plane began its service in May 1964 when it was delivered to the 18 Tactical Fighter Wing at Kadena Air Base, Okinawa. It remained at Kadena for the next four years except for an eight-month period in 1967 when it transferred to Yokota Air Base, Japan. It spent most of 1968 flying combat missions with the 388 Tactical Fighter Wing from Korat, Thailand. In December 1968, it moved to McConnell Air Force Base, Kansas, to train pilots heading for war in South East Asia. After a short stay at Nellis Air Force Base, Nevada, in 1970, it found its way to the depot at McClellan Air Force Base, California, where it upgraded to a Wild Weasel "G" in December 1972. In February 1973, it joined the 561 Tactical Fighter Squadron at McConnell, a self-contained Wild Weasel unit with a detachment at Korat still supporting the war in Vietnam. In June 1973, with the war winding down, the 561st gathered its F-105Gs at McConnell and then transferred to the 35 Tactical Fighter Wing at George Air Force Base, California, where the plane spent its last eight years. It was one of six Wild Weasels flown on a NATO exercise with the 35th to Spangdahlem Air Base, Germany, in 1976 and was one of the 18 planes accompanying the 35th on a similar exercise to Denmark two years later. The 35th was the last active-duty Air Force unit to fly the F-105 and retired "276" in July 1980 when the wing ceased flying Thunderchiefs. Eight years later, the plane left storage for display at Nellis. (Photograph by author, 5 December 1999.)

	December 1966 and had accumulated 870 flying hours. (18 TFW History, Jul–Dec 66, USAF microfilm MO498).
22 Mar 1967	Transferred from the 12 TFS, 18 TFW, Kadena AB, Okinawa, to the 41 AD, Yokota AB, Japan. Aircraft had accumulated 921 flying hours. (AVH-8 & 18 TFW History, Jan–Mar 67, USAF microfilm MO498).
23 Jun 1967	In depot maintenance (WK) by SMAMA field team at Yokota AB, Japan. Modified for Ryan's Raiders (Commando Nail) mission.
26 Jun 1967	At 41 AD, Yokota AB, Japan.
31 Oct 1967	In depot maintenance (WM) by SMAMA field team at 18 TFW, Kadena AB, Okinawa.
9 Nov 1967	Transferred to 18 TFW, Kadena AB, Okinawa.
23 Jan 1968	In depot maintenance (WM) by SMAMA at Kadena AB, Okinawa. (AVH-10).
31 Jan 1968	At 18 TFW, Kadena AB, Okinawa.
3 Feb 1968	At 18 TFW, Kadena AB, Okinawa being prepared for transfer (PL).
14 Feb 1968	Transferred (PL) to 388 TFW, Korat RTAB, Thailand.
3 Jun 1968	In depot-level maintenance (WM) by SMAMA at 388 TFW, Korat RTAB, Thailand.
5 Jun 1968	Operational (CC) at 388 TFW, Korat RTAB, Thailand.
8 Jul 1968	In depot-level maintenance (WM) at 388 TFW, Korat RTAB, Thailand.
24 Jul 1968	At 388 TFW, Korat RTAB, Thailand.
31 Oct 1968	Aircraft had accumulated 1,462.1 flying hours while assigned to the 388 TFW, Korat RTAB, Thailand. (388 TFW History, Oct–Dec 68, USAF microfilm NO585).
8 Dec 1968	At 388 TFW, Korat RTAB, Thailand, being prepared for transfer (PL). (AVH-10).
14 Dec 1968	Transferred (PL) to 23 TFW, McConnell AFB KS for combat crew training (TF).

2 May 1969	At 23 TFW, McConnell AFB KS. (AVH-12).
6 May 1969	In depot maintenance (WO) at SMAMA McClellan AFB CA.
27 May 1969	Returned to 23 TFW, McConnell AFB KS.
10 May 1970	Assigned to 57 FWW, Nellis AFB NV. (AVH-14).
25 Jun 1970	In depot repair (WJ) at 57 FWW, Nellis AFB NV.
4 Aug 1970	Placed in storage (XT) at SM-ALC, McClellan AFB CA.
1 Feb 1972	In depot work (WR) by SM-ALC at McClellan AFB CA. (AVH-18).
19 Dec 1972	Modified to an F-105G Wild Weasel configuration while at SM-ALC, McClellan AFB CA.
16 Feb 1973	Transferred (PL) to 561 TFS, 832 Air Division, McConnell AFB KS. (AVH-20).
23 Feb 1973	At 561 TFS, 832 Air Division, McConnell AFB KS.
30 Jun 1973	Transferred with the 561 TFS to the 35 TFW, George AFB CA.
20 Aug 1973	While flying in formation with a refueling tanker, the aircraft experienced sluggish control. After landing, the cause was traced to a chafed left trailing edge flap flex shaft. This condition was caused by a clamp improperly installed by maintenance. (35 TFW History, 1 Jul–30 Sep 73, USAF microfilm 24233).
11 Mar 1974	In depot maintenance (WM) by SM-ALC at George AFB CA. (AVH-22).
18 Mar 1974	At 35 TFW, George AFB CA.
26 Oct 1974	On static display for the 35 TFW's Open House, "Salute to the High Desert," at George AFB CA. (Photo in 35 TFW History, Oct–Dec 74, USAF microfilm 30591).
26 Sep 1975	In depot repair (WR & WO) by SM-ALC at McClellan AFB CA. (AVH-23 & AVH-24).
6 Jan 1976	Returned to 35 TFW, George AFB CA. (AVH-24).
30 Aug 1976	One of six F-105Gs that deployed with the 561 TFS under "Coronet Yankee" to Spangdahlem AB, Germany, from 35 TFW, George AFB CA. 2,605 flying hours. (British Aviation Review, Dec 1995 & AVH-24).
20 Sep 1976	Returned to 35 TFW, George AFB CA. 2,613 flying hours. (AVH-24).
6 Oct 1976	At MacDill AFB FL with the 35 TFW. 2,613 flying hours.
19 Oct 1976	Returned to 35 TFW, George AFB CA. 2,613 flying hours
31 Jan 1978	In depot maintenance by SM-ALC at George AFB CA. 2,909.0 flying hours. (AVH-26).
1 Mar 1978	At 35 TFW TAC, George AFB CA 2,914.0 flying hours.
17 Mar 1978	Aircraft had flight restrictions at 35 TFW, George AFB CA due to cracks in main landing gear wing rib found during inspection required by TCTO 1F-105-1281. "…Restricted to 47,500 lb. gross takeoff weight, 10 knots crosswind component, 4 G's symmetrical and 2.5 G's rolling." (35 TFW/MA memo).
17 Apr 1978	In depot maintenance by SM-ALC at George AFB CA. 2,914.0 flying hours.
9 Aug 1978	One of 18 F-105Gs that deployed with the 562 TFS under "Coronet Sparrow "to Karup AB, Denmark, from 35 TFW, George AFB CA. 3,015.0 flying hours.
7 Sep 1978	Returned to 35 TFW TAC, George AFB CA. 3,026.0 flying hours. Assigned crew chief was A1C Mary C. "Chris" Kollhoff. (Mary Kollhoff Head, e-mail, 15 July 1998).
16 May 1979	At 35 TFW TAC, George AFB CA. 3,166.0 flying hours. (AVH-27).
8 Nov 1979	In depot maintenance by Sacramento ALC at George AFB CA. 3,244.4 flying hours.
14 Nov 1979	At 35 TFW TAC, George AFB CA. 3,244.4 flying hours.
22 Jul 1980	Delivered to MASDC ("Inviolate storage"—XS), Davis Monthan AFB AZ. 3,326.1 flying hours. (GO33B 22 Jan 81).
20 Dec 1982	MASDC storage code changed to "XX" (Low probability of withdrawal). 3,326.8 flying hours. (GO33B 1 Feb 83).
27 Apr 1988	Removed from AMARC and shipped to Nellis AFB for static display. 3,328 flying hours. (AMARC Report D003A/B, 6 May 94).

F-105G–1RE 63-8278

Republic Production No: F-55 Production Sequence No: 745

Location: At Veterans Memorial Park, V.A. Medical Center, Mather AFB, Sacramento, California.

Aircraft Chronology

17 Apr 1964	USAF production acceptance from Republic Aviation, Farmingdale NY. (ACA-89 & AVH-1).
23 Apr 1964	At MOAMA, Brookley AFB AL for depot work.
30 Sep 1964	At 18 TFW, Kadena AB, Okinawa. Assigned crew chief: TSgt. R. Johnson. (18 TFW History, Jul–Dec 64, USAF microfilm MO496).
31 Jan 1965	At 18 TFW, Kadena AB, Okinawa. Assigned crew chief: SSgt. J. Shew. (18 TFW History, Jan–Jun 65, USAF microfilm MO497).
28 Apr 1965	At Air Asia, Tainan, Taiwan, for contract depot work (WK). (AVH-4).
14 May 1965	At 18 TFW, Kadena AB, Okinawa.
18 Oct 1965	At Air Asia, Tainan, Taiwan, for contract depot work (WK)
4 Nov 1965	At 18 TFW, Kadena AB, Okinawa. Assigned Crew Chief: SSgt. D. Broyles.
29 Dec 1965	At 6441 TFW, Yokota AB, Japan. (AVH-5).
15 Jan 1966	At 18 TFW, Kadena AB, Okinawa.
31 Dec 1966	While assigned to the 18 TFW, Kadena AB, Okinawa, the aircraft flew 10 hours during the month of December 1966 and had accumulated 870 flying hours. (18 TFW History, Jul–Dec 66, USAF microfilm MO498).
31 May 1967	At 18 TFW, Kadena AB, Okinawa. (AVH-8).

This "G" retired in July 1980 with fewer than 3,500 flying hours on its airframe, relatively low for an F-105. The plane accumulated nearly half of its flying time during the first four and a half years of assignments beginning in April 1964 with the 18 Tactical Fighter Wing, at Kadena Air Base, Okinawa. After leaving Kadena, it flew night bombing "Commando Nail" missions for most of 1968 with the 388 Tactical Fighter Wing at Korat, Thailand. At the end of the year, it transferred to the 23 Tactical Fighter Wing at McConnell Air Force Base, Kansas. The plane was at the depot in California for the first six months of 1972 where it upgraded to a "G" Wild Weasel. It began training Wild Weasel crews at Nellis Air Force Base, Nevada, in July 1972, but after three months, wound up in depot field-team repair for the next six months. It joined its final unit, the 35 Tactical Fighter Wing, at George Air Force Base, California, in July 1975. The plane accompanied the 35th on a deployment to Denmark in August 1977. In March 1978, it suffered from wing cracks that restricted its flying until the cracks could be repaired. The 35th retired it about two years later. After five years in storage, the plane was shipped for static display to Mather Air Force Base, California. Before it closed, Mather was the Air Force training center for navigators, many of whom probably flew in this plane's rear cockpit as Wild Weasel Electronic Warfare Officers. (Photograph by Gene Cirillo, 6 April 2000.)

8 Nov 1967	In depot maintenance (WM) by SMAMA field team at Kadena AB, Okinawa. Modified for Ryan's Raider (Commando Nail) mission.
17 Nov 1967	At 18 TFW, Kadena AB, Okinawa.
5 Feb 1968	In depot maintenance by SMAMA at Kadena AB, Okinawa. (AVH-10).
26 Feb 1968	At 18 TFW, Kadena AB, Okinawa.
4 Mar 1968	Transferred (PL) to the 388 TFW, Korat RTAB, Thailand.
14 Jun 1968	In depot-level maintenance at 388 TFW, Korat RTAB, Thailand.
16 Jun 1968	Operational at 388 TFW, Korat RTAB, Thailand.
10 Aug 1968	In depot-level maintenance (WM) by SMAMA at 388 TFW, Korat RTAB, Thailand.
12 Aug 1968	Operational (CC) at 388 TFW, Korat RTAB, Thailand.
31 Oct 1968	Aircraft had accumulated 1,476.5 flying hours while assigned to the 388 TFW, Korat RTAB, Thailand. (388 TFW History, Oct–Dec 68, USAF microfilm NO585).
8 Dec 1968	At 388 TFW, Korat RTAB, Thailand, being prepared for transfer (PL). (AVH-10).
20 Dec 1968	Transferred (PL) to 23 TFW, McConnell AFB KS for combat crew training (TF).
10 May 1971	In depot maintenance (WK) by Fairchild Engine and Aircraft Corporation (FACCF) at Bob Sikes Municipal Airport, Crestview FL. (AVH-16).
25 May 1971	Returned to 23 TFW, McConnell AFB KS. Assigned to combat duties (CC).
11 Jan 1972	In depot work (WO) by SM-ALC at McClellan AFB CA. (AVH-18).
1 Mar 1972	Aircraft still had a Combat Nail configuration as an F-105F assigned to the 561 TFS, 23 TFW, at McConnell AFB KS. (Master 23 TFW Aircraft Assignment as of 1 March 1972).
1 Jul 1972	Modified to an F-105G Wild Weasel configuration while at SM-ALC, McClellan AFB CA. (AVH-18).
28 Jul 1972	Transferred (PL) to 57 FWW, Nellis AFB NV for combat crew training (TF).
10 Oct 1972	In crash damage repair (WJ) by SM-ALC field team at Nellis AFB NV.
2 Mar 1973	Still in depot work (WM) by SM-ALC at Nellis AFB NV. (AVH-20).
11 Apr 1973	At 57 FWW, Nellis AFB NV for combat crew training (TF).
17 May 1973	In depot work (WO) by SM-ALC at McClellan AFB CA.
13 Jul 1973	Returned (PL) to 57 FWW, Nellis AFB NV.
18 Jul 1973	At 57 FWW, Nellis AFB NV for combat crew training (TF).
29 Aug 1974	In depot maintenance (WM) by SM-ALC at Nellis AFB NV. AVH-22).
10 Sep 1974	At 57 FWW, Nellis AFB NV for combat crew training (TF).
25 Jul 1975	Transferred to 35 TFW, George AFB CA for combat crew training (TF). (AVH-23 & AVH-24).
8 Aug 1975	In depot work (WO & WR) by SM-ALC at McClellan AFB CA.
4 Nov 1975	Returned to 35 TFW, George AFB CA for combat crew training (TF).
20 May 1976	At 35 TFW, George AFB CA for combat crew training (TF). 2,970 flying hours. (AVH-24).
4 Oct 1976	At 35 TFW, George AFB CA. Possession code: BQ. 2,973 flying hours.
2 Nov 1976	In depot maintenance (WK) by Fairchild Engine and Aircraft Corporation (FACCF) at Bob Sikes Municipal Airport, Crestview FL. 2,973 flying hours.
21 Jul 1977	In contract depot maintenance (DYNFW) at George AFB CA. 2,984.0 flying hours. (AVH-25 & AVH-26).
28 Jul 1977	At 35 TFW TAC, George AFB CA. 2,984.0 flying hours.
12 Aug 1977	Deployed under "Coronet Club" to Karup AB, Denmark, with the 563 TFS, 35 TFW, from George AFB CA. 2,991.0 flying hours.
30 Aug 1977	Returned from Denmark to George AFB CA.
17 Mar 1978	Aircraft had flight restrictions at George AFB CA due to cracks in main landing gear wing rib found during inspection required by TCTO 1F-105-1281. "...Restricted to 47,500 lb. gross takeoff weight, 10 knots crosswind component, 4 G's symmetrical and 2.5 G's rolling." (35 TFW/MA memo).

24 Mar 1978	In depot maintenance by SM-ALC at George AFB CA. 3,055.0 flying hours.
30 Mar 1978	At 35 TFW TAC, George AFB CA. 3,055.0 flying hours.
5 Apr 1978	In depot maintenance by SM-ALC at George AFB CA. 3,055.0 flying hours.
22 Sep 1978	At 35 TFW TAC, George AFB CA. 3,092.0 flying hours.
16 May 1979	At 35 TFW TAC, George AFB CA. 3,196.6 flying hours. (AVH-27).
4 Feb 1980	At 562 TFS, 35 TFW, George AFB CA. 3,358.1 flying hours. (GO33B 24 Jun 80).
29 Jul 1980	Delivered to MASDC ("Inviolate storage"—XS), Davis-Monthan AFB AZ. 3,458.1 flying hours. (GO33B 22 Jan 81).
20 Dec 1982	MASDC storage code changed to "XX" (Low probability of withdrawal). 3,462.8 flying hours. (GO33B 1 Feb 83).
Jan 1985	Sent from MASDC storage to Mather AFB CA for static display. (Theodore Van Geffen, "Thudologist," e-mail on 30 Aug 1997). "The 453rd FTS EWO School instructors and students brought it up from the Boneyard.... They went down there on their own time, dismantled it, had it trucked up to a hanger at Mather, and in their off time put it back together and painted it. They put Dethlefsen's name and mine on the cockpits and put it in their Heritage Park (with a few other A/C). This was done to honor the efforts of the EWO School graduates who had served in the Weasel program." (Mike Gilroy, e-mail to the Weasel Net, 20 Jan 00).
6 Nov 1996	Aircraft identified for transfer to AMARC's Conditional Donation Program to be loaned to a veteran's organization. (Tom Brewer, USAF Museum, telephone interview).
25 Mar 1997	Aircraft transferred to Sacramento County for display at the Veterans Hospital at Mather AFB. (Rebecca Garza, AMARC, e-mail, 1 Sep 1999).
1998	Aircraft moved to the parking ramp at Mather AFB, CA. (Rancho Cordova Grapevine Independent, 24 May 2000, page 1).
May 2000	Aircraft towed two miles to the Mather VA Medical Center for display at the Veterans Memorial Park that was established on 24 May 2000.

F-105G-1RE 63-8285

Republic Production No: F-62 Production Sequence No: 752

Location: At Site 5, Munitions Storage Area, Davis-Monthan AFB, Tucson, Arizona.

Aircraft Name(s)	Crew	Unit	Date	Description
Porky	Maj. Al McLean/Capt. Frank Gorg	44 TFS 388 TFW	Dec 68	On right fuselage.
Honey	Maj. Robert J. Reisenwitz	333 TFS 355 TFW	Jan 70	Name on both intakes.
Peggy II		561 TFS Det. 1 (TDY to Korat)	Apr 72	On intake.

Aircraft Chronology

21 May 1964	USAF production acceptance from Republic Aviation, Farmingdale NY. (ACA-89 & AVH-1).
22 May 1964	At MOAMA, Brookley AFB AL for depot work (WO).
31 May 1964	Delivered to 18 TFW, Kadena AB , Okinawa.
Sep 1964	At 18 TFW, Kadena AB, Okinawa. Assigned crew chief: SSgt. A. Bernabei. (18 TFW History, Jul–Dec 64, USAF microfilm MO496).
31 Jan 1965	At 18 TFW, Kadena AB, Okinawa. Assigned crew chief: SSgt. J. Lohman. (18 TFW History, Jan–Jun 65, USAF microfilm MO497).

9 Apr 1965	At Air Asia, Tainan, Taiwan, for contract depot work (WK). (AVH-4).
25 Apr 1965	At 18 TFW, Kadena AB, Okinawa.
26 Aug 1965	At Itazuke AB, Japan, for depot maintenance by AFLC field team from SMAMA.
Nov 1965	At 18 TFW, Kadena AB, Okinawa. Assigned crew chief: SSgt. J. Lohman. (18 TFW History, Jul–Dec 65, USAF microfilm MO497).
14 Jan 1966	At SMAMA, McClellan AFB CA for depot work (WO). (AVH-5).
12 Feb 1966	Reassigned to 4520 CCTW, Nellis AFB NV for combat crew training (TF).
3 Mar 1966	At SMAMA, McClellan AFB CA for depot work (WO).
5 Apr 1966	Returned to 4520 CCTW, Nellis AFB NV for combat crew training (TF).
9 Nov 1966	In depot maintenance (WM) by SMAMA field team at 4520 CCTW, Nellis AFB NV.
14 Nov 1966	At 4520 CCTW, Nellis AFB NV for combat crew training (TF).
20 Jan 1967	In depot maintenance (WO) by SMAMA at McClellan AFB CA. (AVH-8).
7 Mar 1967	Transferred to 388 TFW, Korat RTAB, Thailand. (AVH-8). Configured as a Ryan's Raiders aircraft (Commando Nail) with modified ASG-19 radar. Radar modification performed by 388 Avionics Squadron at Korat RTAB, Thailand. (388 TFW History, Apr–Dec 1967, USAF microfilm NO583).
31 May 1967	At Korat RTAB, Thailand, aircraft modified for updated Wild Weasel III (ER-142) equipment. (388 TFW History, Apr–Dec 1972, USAF microfilm NO583).
1 Jun 1967	In depot maintenance (WM) by SMAMA field team at Korat RTAB, Thailand. (AVH-8).
3 Jun 1967	At 388 TFW, Korat RTAB, Thailand.
4 Oct 1967	In depot maintenance (WM) by SMAMA field team at Korat RTAB, Thailand.
5 Oct 1967	At 388 TFW, Korat RTAB, Thailand.
24 May 1968	In depot-level maintenance (WM) by SMAMA at 388 TFW, Korat RTAB. (AVH-10).
4 Jun 1968	At Air Asia, Tainan, Taiwan, for contract depot work (WK).
2 Aug 1968	Returned to 388 TFW, Korat RTAB, Thailand.
25 Sep 1968	In depot-level maintenance (WM) at Korat RTAB, Thailand.
27 Sep 1968	One of four aircraft modified with the Bistatic Aided Strike System (BASS) at the 388 TFW, Korat RTAB, Thailand. (388 TFW History, Jul-Sep 68, USAF microfilm NO585).
4 Oct 1968	At 388 TFW, Korat RTAB, Thailand. (AVH-10).
11 Oct 1968	Aircraft drag chute failed to deploy when landing from a combat mission while assigned to the 388 TFW, Korat RTAB, Thailand. (388 TFW History, Oct–Dec 68, USAF microfilm NO585).
31 Oct 1968	Aircraft had accumulated 1,934.0 flying hours while assigned to the 388 TFW, Korat RTAB, Thailand. (388 TFW History, Oct–Dec 68, USAF microfilm NO585).
31 Jan 1969	Deployed to Takhli RTAB, Thailand, with the 44 TFS, 388 TFW, during runway repairs at Korat RTAB, Thailand. Aircraft flown on an Iron Hand mission in the Steel Tiger region of Laos by a 44 TFS crew. (388 TFW History, Jan–Mar 69, USAF microfilm NO586 & AVH-12).
4 Feb 1979	Flown on a mission in the Steel Tiger region of Laos by a 44 TFS crew while the 388 TFW operated from Takhli RTAB, Thailand.
5 Feb 1969	Flown on a mission in the Steel Tiger region of Laos by a 44 TFS crew while the 388 TFW operated from Takhli RTAB, Thailand.
6 Feb 1969	Flown on an Iron Hand mission in the Steel Tiger region of Laos by a 44 TFS crew while the 388 TFW operated from Takhli RTAB, Thailand.
7 Feb 1969	Flown on a mission in the Steel Tiger region of Laos by a 44 TFS crew while the 388 TFW operated from Takhli RTAB, Thailand. Flew a second Iron Hand mission also in the Steel Tiger region of Laos.
11 Feb 1969	Flown on a local test hop by a 44 TFS crew while the 388 TFW operated from Takhli RTAB, Thailand.
14 Feb 1969	Flown on a mission in the Steel Tiger region of Laos by a 44 TFS crew while the 388 TFW operated from Takhli RTAB, Thailand.
15 Feb 1969	Flown on an Iron Hand mission in the Steel Tiger region of Laos by a 44 TFS crew while the 388 TFW operated from Takhli RTAB, Thailand.

This Wild Weasel "G" survived seven years of continuous Vietnam combat. After its factory acceptance as an F-105F in May 1964, it flew for three years at Kadena Air Base, Okinawa, and Nellis Air Force Base, Nevada. In March 1967, it joined the 388 Tactical Fighter Wing at Korat, Thailand, where it was modified with an improved radar scope to fly "Commando Nail" night bombing missions. In September 1968, it became one of four "Fs" at Korat that received the Bistatic-Aided Strike System, an unsuccessful, short-lived experiment in locating ground radar sites. The plane flew fourteen combat missions over Laos with the 44 Tactical Fighter Squadron that deployed temporarily to Takhli, Thailand, during February 1969 while the runway at Korat was resurfaced. It then moved permanently to Takhli in October 1969 when the 44th transferred to the 355 Tactical Fighter Wing. During its first two months at Takhli, the plane was further modified from an "F" to a "G" Wild Weasel. When Takhli began closing in late 1970, the plane returned to Korat. The plane stayed at Korat until the F-105Gs came home to the 35 Tactical Fighter Wing at George Air Force Base, California, the primary Air Force unit still flying Wild Weasels. The 35th took the plane on its NATO summer deployment to Denmark in 1978 and then retired it two years later. (Photograph by Lieutenant Colonel Judith Breeding, 25 May 1997.)

17 Feb 1969 Flown on an Iron Hand mission in the Steel Tiger region of Laos by a 44 TFS crew while the 388 TFW operated from Takhli RTAB, Thailand.

18 Feb 1969 Flown on an Iron Hand mission in the Steel Tiger region of Laos by a 44 TFS crew while the 388 TFW operated from Takhli RTAB, Thailand.

19 Feb 1969 Flown on an Iron Hand mission in the Steel Tiger region of Laos by a 44 TFS crew while the 388 TFW operated from Takhli RTAB, Thailand.

20 Feb 1969 One of four F-105Fs flown on an Iron Hand mission in the Steel Tiger region of Laos by a 44 TFS crew while the 388 TFW operated from Takhli RTAB, Thailand.

21 Feb 1969 One of two F-105Fs flown on an Iron Hand mission in the Steel Tiger region of Laos by a 44 TFS crew while the 388 TFW operated from Takhli RTAB, Thailand.

22 Feb 1969 One of two F-105Fs flown on an Iron Hand mission in the Steel Tiger region of Laos by a 44 TFS crew while the 388 TFW operated from Takhli RTAB, Thailand.

1 Mar 1969 Returned to the 388 TFW, Korat RTAB, Thailand. (AVH-12).

23 Mar 1969 In depot maintenance (WM) by SMAMA at Takhli RTAB, Thailand.

11 Apr 1969 Returned to 388 TFW, Korat RTAB, Thailand.

30 Apr 1969 While assigned to the 44 TFS, 388 TFW, Korat RTAB, Thailand, the aircraft flew 6 hours in the month of April 1969 and had accumulated 2,218.4 total flying hours. (388 TFW History, Apr–Jun 69, USAF microfilm NO586).

30 Jun 1969 While assigned to the 44 TFS, 388 TFW, Korat RTAB, Thailand, the aircraft flew 59.1 hours in the month of June 1969 and had accumulated 2,306.2 total flying hours.

6 Sep 1969 While assigned to the 388 TFW, Korat RTAB, Thailand, the aircraft drag chute failed on landing. The cockpit handle come out resulting in the door failing to open. (388 TFW History, Jul–Sep 69, Vol. III, USAF microfilm NO587).

12 Sep 1969 While assigned to the 388 TFW, Korat RTAB, Thailand, the aircraft drag chute failed due to the door not opening. The pilot had to catch the barrier.

24 Sep 1969	While assigned to the 388 TFW, Korat RTAB, Thailand, the aircraft drag chute failed due to the door not opening. The pilot had to catch the barrier.
10 Oct 1969	Transferred with the 44 TFS to the 355 TFW, Takhli RTAB, Thailand. (AVH-12).
19 Oct 1969	In depot maintenance (WM) by SMAMA at Takhli RTAB, Thailand.
24 Nov 1969	At 355 TFW, Takhli RTAB, Thailand.
18 Dec 1969	Redesignated F-105G at 355 TFW, Takhli RTAB, Thailand.
12 Oct 1970	At Korat RTAB, Thailand, with Detachment 1 of the 12 TFS from the 18 TFW. (AVH-14).
1 Nov 1970	Assigned to the 6010 WWS at the 388 TFW, Korat RTAB, Thailand.
23 Dec 1970	At the 388 TFW, Korat RTAB, Thailand. (John Tomany, e-mail, 8 Dec 1997).
7 May 1971	At 388 TFW, Korat RTAB, Thailand, being prepared for transfer (PL) to depot. (AVH-16).
8 May 1971	In depot work (WO) by SMAMA at McClellan AFB CA.
8 Jan 1972	Returned (PL) to 388 TFW, Korat RTAB, Thailand. (AVH-18).
8 Mar 1972	Crash damaged (WJ) at 388 TFW, Korat RTAB, Thailand.
4 Apr 1972	In depot work for crash damage (VN) by SMAMA field team at Korat RTAB, Thailand.
19 Jun 1972	Returned to 388 TFW, Korat RTAB, Thailand.
14 Sep 1972	In depot work (WM) by SMAMA field team at Korat RTAB, Thailand.
30 Sep 1972	Returned to 388 TFW, Korat RTAB, Thailand.
23 Oct 1972	Assigned to 561 TFS (TAC) at Korat RTAB, Thailand.
2 Jul 1973	Assigned to 35 TFW (TAC) while at Korat RTAB, Thailand. (AVH-20).
8 Sep 1973	Transferred to 35 TFW, George AFB CA.
24 Jan 1974	In depot maintenance (WM) by SM-ALC at George AFB CA. (AVH-22).
29 Jan 1974	At 35 TFW, George AFB CA.
8 Feb 1974	In depot maintenance (WM) by SM-ALC at George AFB CA.
14 Feb 1974	At 35 TFW, George AFB CA.
4 Oct 1977	In depot maintenance (WM) by SM-ALC at George AFB CA.
7 Oct 1974	At 35 TFW, George AFB CA.
3 Mar 1976	In depot maintenance (WO) by SM-ALC at McClellan AFB CA. (AVH-24).
14 Jun 1976	In depot maintenance (DR) by SM-ALC at McClellan AFB CA. 4,682 flying hours.
21 Jun 1973	Returned to 35 TFW, George AFB CA. 4,741 flying hours.
12 Apr 1977	In depot maintenance by SM-ALC at George AFB CA. 4,781.0 flying hours. (AVH-25 & AVH-26).
14 Apr 1977	At 35 TFW TAC, George AFB CA. 4 ,781.0 flying hours.
22 Aug 1977	At Eglin AFB FL with 35 TFW TAC, George AFB CA. 4,843.0 flying hours.
17 Mar 1978	Aircraft had flight restrictions at George AFB CA due to cracks in main landing gear wing rib found during inspection required by TCTO 1F-105-1281. "...Restricted to 47,500 lb. gross takeoff weight, 10 knots crosswind component, 4 G's symmetrical and 2.5 G's rolling." (35 TFW/MA memo).
9 Aug 1978	Deployed with 562 TFS under "Coronet Sparrow "to Karup AB, Denmark, from 35 TFW, George AFB CA. 5,018.0 flying hours.
17 Sep 1978	Returned to 35 TFW TAC, George AFB CA. 5,038.0 flying hours.
4 Oct 1978	At 35 TFW TAC, George AFB CA. 5,084.0 flying hours.
25 Oct 1978	At Eglin AFB FL with 35 TFW, George AFB CA. 5,084.0 flying hours.
7 Nov 1978	At 35 TFW TAC, George AFB CA. 5,084.0 flying hours.
1 Dec 1978	In depot maintenance by SM-ALC at George AFB CA. 5,099.7 flying hours.
27 Dec 1978	At 35 TFW TAC, George AFB CA. 5,121.1 flying hours. (AVH-27).
2 Jan 1980	In depot maintenance (DYNFW) at George AFB CA. 5,247.7 flying hours. (GO33B 24 Jun 80).
28 Feb 1980	At 35 TFW, George AFB CA. 5,289.1 flying hours.

2 Sep 1980	Sent to storage at MASDC (FK022), Davis-Monthan AFB AZ. 5,350 flying hours. (MASDC Aircraft Status Directory, 30 Jun 84).
20 Dec 1982	Still in storage at MASDC, Davis-Monthan AFB AZ. ("Low probability of withdrawal"—XX). 5,350.3 flying hours. (GO33B 1 Feb 83).
7 Mar 1990	Removed from AMARC storage and towed to 355 TFW, Davis-Monthan AFB AZ for static display. 5,350 flying hours. (AMARC Report D003A/B, 3 Aug 90).

F-105F-1RE 63-8287

Republic Production No: F-64 Production Sequence No: 754

Location: At Octave Chanute Aerospace Museum, Rantoul, Illinois.

Aircraft Chronology

15 May 1964	USAF production acceptance from Republic Aviation, Farmingdale NY. (ACA-89 & AVH-1).
20 May 1964	At MOAMA, Brookley AFB AL for depot work (WO).
31 May 1964	Delivered to 18 TFW, Kadena AB, Japan.
30 Sep 1964	At 18 TFW, Kadena AB, Okinawa. Assigned crew chief: A1C R. Tew, Jr. (18 TFW History, Jul–Dec 64, USAF microfilm MO496).
31 Jan 1965	At 18 TFW, Kadena AB, Okinawa. Assigned crew chief: A1C R. Tew, Jr. (18 TFW History, Jan–Jun 65, USAF microfilm MO497).
5 Apr 1965	At Air Asia, Tainan, Taiwan, for contract depot work (WK). (AVH-4).
18 Apr 1965	At 18 TFW, Kadena AB, Okinawa.
22 Oct 1965	At Air Asia, Tainan, Taiwan, for contract depot work (WK).
10 Nov 1965	Returned to 18 TFW, Kadena AB, Okinawa. Assigned crew chief: SSgt. J. Jones.
13 Nov 1966	In depot maintenance (WM) by SMAMA field team at Kadena AB, Okinawa. (AVH-5).
16 Nov 1966	At 18 TFW, Kadena AB, Okinawa.
31 Dec 1966	While assigned to the 18 TFW, Kadena AB, Okinawa, the aircraft flew 17 hours during the month of December 1966 and had accumulated 898 flying hours. (18 TFW History, Jul–Dec 66, USAF microfilm MO498).
4 May 1967	While assigned to the 18 TFW, Kadena AB, Okinawa, the aircraft's left 450 gallon fuel tank separated in flight due to the failure of the front and rear bulkhead attachment fittings. (18 TFW History, Apr–Jun 67, USAF microfilm MO499).
1 Jun 1967	At 18 TFW, Kadena AB, Okinawa. (AVH-8).
11 Aug 1967	At 18 TFW, Kadena AB, Okinawa being readied for transfer (PL).
31 Aug 1967	Transferred to 23 TFW, McConnell AFB KS.
24 Oct 1967	In depot maintenance (WO) by SMAMA, McClellan AFB CA.
11 Mar 1968	Returned (PL) to 23 TFW, McConnell AFB KS for combat crew training (TF). (AVH-10).
14 May 1968	Deployed to George AFB CA with the 560 TFS, 23 TFW, for air-to-air gunnery training for RTU Class 68JR.
29 May 1968	Returned to 23 TFW, McConnell AFB KS for combat crew training.
24 Apr 1970	At 23 TFW, McConnell AFB KS. (AVH-14).
13 Oct 1970	In depot maintenance (WM) by OCAMA at McConnell AFB KS.

After being one of three F-105Fs flown for the "Thud-Out" retirement ceremony at Hill Air Force Base, Utah, in February 1984, this plane was the last F-105s in the air before it landed at Chanute on 10 March 1984. It started life 20 years earlier when it was delivered to Kadena Air Base, Okinawa, in May 1964. In August 1967, it moved to McConnell Air Force Base, Kansas, and then, in March 1973, joined the 465 Tactical Fighter Squadron—the Air Force Reserve unit at Tinker Air Force Base, Oklahoma. The 465th flew it to Great Britain during their NATO deployment in June 1978, and, eleven months later, took it with them on their deployment to Italy. While in Italy, the plane was badly damaged when a landing gear bolt failed shortly after touchdown and the plane skidded down the runway. The plane was left in Italy until July 1978 when a repair team from Tinker patched it up and flew it home. In October 1980, it transferred to the Reserve unit at Hill Air Force Base, Utah, who flew it on their NATO deployment to Denmark in August 1981 and, then for its last mission, during their "Thud-Out" three years later. (Photograph by author, 9 August 1995.)

18 Jan 1971	At 23 TFW, McConnell AFB KS for combat crew training (TF). (AVH-16).
10 May 1971	Assigned operational duties (CC) at 23 TFW, McConnell AFB KS.
18 May 1971	At 23 TFW, McConnell AFB KS being prepared (PL) for transfer to depot.
19 May 1971	In depot work (WO) by SMAMA at McClellan AFB CA.
16 Feb 1972	In storage (XW) at McClellan AFB CA. (AVH-18).
17 Apr 1972	In depot work (WO) by SM-ALC at McClellan AFB CA.
12 July 1972	Transferred (PL) to the 507 TFG AFRES, Tinker AFB, OK.
25 Jul 1972	Operational (CC) at the 507 TFG AFRES, Tinker AFB, OK.
31 Mar 1973	At 507 CMTSQ AFRES, Tinker AFB OK. (AVH-20).
24 Apr 1973	In depot maintenance (WM) by SM-ALC at Tinker AFB OK.
8 Jun 1973	Returned to 507 CMTSQ AFRES, Tinker AFB OK.
26 Sep 1973	In depot maintenance (WM) by SM-ALC at Tinker AFB OK.
4 Oct 1973	Returned to 507 CMTSQ AFRES, Tinker AFB OK.
28 Jun 1974	In depot maintenance (WM) by SM-ALC at Tinker AFB OK. (AVH-22).
11 Jul 1974	At 507 CMTSQ AFRES, Tinker AFB OK.
16 Oct 1974	Assigned unit redesignated 507 CLMSQ AFRES, Tinker AFB OK.
12 Jun 1975	At 507 CLMSQ AFRES, Tinker AFB OK. (AVH-23 & AVH-24).

6 Oct 1975 In depot maintenance (WM) by SM-ALC at Tinker AFB OK.

5 Nov 1975 At 507 TFG AFRES, Tinker AFB OK. 2,773 flying hours.

20 Sep 1976 In depot maintenance (DK) by Fairchild Engine and Aircraft Corporation (FACCF) at Bob Sikes Municipal Airport, Crestview FL. 2,775 flying hours.

10 Jun 1978 Deployed under "Coronet Oriole" with the 465 TFS to Sculthorpe, England, from Tinker AFB OK. (British Aviation Review, Dec 1995).

23 Jun 1978 Returned from England to Tinker AFB OK.

10 Oct 1978 At 465 TFS AFRES, Tinker AFB OK. 3,085.0 flying hours. (AVH-26).

11 May 1979 Deployed under "Coronet Palomino" with the 465 TFS to Gioia del Colle, Italy, from the 465 TFS AFRES, Tinker AFB OK. While in Italy, the aircraft was damaged during landing due to a failure of the right main gear side brace link bolt. "The right gear collapsed about 2,000 feet from touchdown, the left tire blew, and the aircraft drifted off the runway. The pilot and the passenger (a flight surgeon) egressed without incident. The right wing tip, right drop tank, ventral fin, horizontal stabilizer, left main wheel and wheel well were damaged." The plane did not return home with the squadron on 25 May 1979. In July, a team of 18 members of the 507 TFG from Tinker AFB, led by SMSgt Barry L. McMillen, returned to Italy to repair the damage. (301 TFW History, Apr–Jun 1979, USAF microfilm 34382).

30 Jun 1979 While assigned to the 465 TFS AFRES, Tinker AFB OK, the aircraft had accumulated a total of 3,332.1 flying hours, the lowest time of any of the 465th's F-105Fs. The assigned crew chief was Oden. (301 TFW History, Apr–Jun 1979, USAF microfilm 34382).

2 Oct 1979 In contract depot maintenance (FACBM) at Tinker AFB OK. 3,369.3 flying hours. (AVH-27).

4 Dec 1979 At 465 TFS AFRES, Tinker AFB OK. 3,380.5 flying hours.

29 Apr 1980 In depot maintenance (FACBM) at Tinker AFB OK. 3,411.6 flying hours. (GO33B 24 Jun 80 & 22 Jan 81).

11 Aug 1980 At 465 TFS AFRES, Tinker AFB OK. 3,422.9 flying hours.

1 Oct 1980 Transferred to the 466 TFS AFRES, Hill AFB UT. 3,422.9 flying hours.

15 Aug 1981 Deployed under "Coronet Rudder" with 466 TFS to Skrydstrup, Denmark, from Hill AFB UT. (British Aviation Review, Dec 1995).

29 Aug 1981 Returned from Denmark to Hill AFB UT.

25 Feb 1984 One of three F-105F's flown in the "Thud-Out" ceremony at Hill AFB UT. Pilot: Lt. Col. James "Gringo" Webster. "Backseat Honoree": Col. Thomas "Zipgun" Coady. The Thud-Out program said that Col. Coady was the "... high combat time F-105 pilot in the Air Force. He has 1,850 hours—1000 in combat."

10 Mar 1984 The last Thunderchief to fly when Capt. Joe Gelinger flew it with an empty rear seat from Hill AFB UT for display at Chanute AFB IL. (Mr. Theo Van Geffen, e-mail to the RATNET, 27 Feb 1999).

F-105G-1RE 63-8296

Republic Production No: F-73 Production Sequence No: 763

Location: At Heritage Park, England Industrial Air Park & Community, Alexandria, Louisiana.

Aircraft Chronology

21 May 1964 USAF production acceptance from Republic Aviation, Farmingdale NY. (ACA-89 & AVH-1).

26 May 1964 At MOAMA, Brookley AFB AL for depot work (WO).

Delivered to Yokota Air Base, Japan, in June 1964, this was one of five "Fs" (and one "D") Yokota flew to Australia in October 1965 for a joint exercise with the Air Forces of Australia and New Zealand. Three months later the plane began training pilots at McConnell Air Force Base, Kansas, and then, in November 1966, relocated to Nellis Air Force Base, Nevada, to train Wild Weasel crews. The plane remained at Nellis until 1 February 1968 when it deployed from Nellis' 4525 Fighter Weapons Wing to Osan Air Base, Korea. Its deployment was in response to North Korea capturing the U.S.S. Pueblo eight days earlier. For the next nine months, still assigned to Nellis, it flew between Korea and Kadena Air Base, Okinawa. In November 1968, it joined the 18 Tactical Fighter Wing at Kadena where it continued for another year flying in and out of Korea. In November 1969, it began a combat tour with the 355 Tactical Fighter Wing at Takhli, Thailand, where it was upgraded to a "G" Wild Weasel. During 1970 and 1971, it moved four times before settling in for another combat tour in February 1972, this time with the 388 Tactical Fighter Wing at Korat, Thailand. When it came home in September 1972, it spent much of the next two years at McConnell and the depot in California. In January 1974, it was assigned from McConnell to the 35 Tactical Fighter Wing at George Air Force Base, California. In July 1974, the plane returned once again to the 388th at Korat. Three months later, it was one of the last twelve Thunderchief Wild Weasels to leave Korat, closing 10 years of continuous F-105 participation in the Vietnam war. The 35th at George flew the plane for the next six years, retiring it in July 1980. (Photograph by John Coon, 27 August 1998.)

27 Jun 1964	Delivered to 41 AD, Yokota AB, Japan. (AVH-1).
August 1964	At 41 AD Yokota AB, Japan. Crew Chief: A1C A. Ferguson. (41 AD Monthly Maintenance Summary).
5 Mar 1965	At Air Asia, Tainan, Taiwan, for contract depot work (WK). (AVH-4).
28 Mar 1965	Returned to 41 AD, Yokota AB, Japan.
1 Apr 1965	Assigned unit redesignated 6441 TFW, Yokota AB, Japan.
April 1965	At 6441 TFW, Yokota AB, Japan. Assigned Crew Chief: TSgt. Jeffers. (6441 TFW History, Apr–Jun 65, USAF microfilm PO231).
Aug 1965	At 6441 TFW, Yokota AB, Japan. Assigned Crew Chief: SSgt. Oakley. (6441 TFW History, Jul–Dec 65, USAF microfilm PO232).
4-17 Oct 65	Deployed from Yokota AB, Japan to Williamtown RAAF Base, New Castle, New South Wales, Australia, for "Pacific Concord I."
26 Jan 1966	Reassigned to 23 TFW, McConnell AFB KS. (AVH-5).
10 Mar 1966	At 23 TFW, McConnell AFB KS.
11 Oct 1966	At SMAMA, McClellan AFB CA for depot work (WO).
3 Nov 1966	Reassigned to 4525 FWW, Nellis AFB NV.
8 Feb 1967	At 4525 FWW, Nellis AFB NV for combat crew training (TF). (AVH-8).

1 Feb 1968	Deployed to Osan AB, Korea, with 4525 FWW in response to the U.S.S. Pueblo incident. (AVH-10).
26 Jul 1968	At Kadena AB, Okinawa, with 4525 FWW.
16 Aug 1968	At Kwangju AB, Korea, with 4525 FWW.
31 Aug 1968	Returned to Kadena AB, Okinawa, with 4525 FWW.
2 Nov 1968	Transferred to 18 TFW, Kadena AB, Okinawa.
3 Feb 1969	At Kwangju AB, Korea, with 18 TFW. (AVH-12).
15 May 1969	Returned to 18 TFW, Kadena AB, Okinawa.
22 May 1969	At Kwangju AB, Korea, with 18 TFW.
23 May 1969	Returned to 18 TFW, Kadena AB, Okinawa.
5 Jun 1969	At Kwangju AB, Korea, with 18 TFW.
9 Jul 1969	Returned to 18 TFW, Kadena AB, Okinawa.
10 Jul 1969	At Kwangju AB, Korea, with 18 TFW.
12 Jul 1969	Returned to 18 TFW, Kadena AB, Okinawa.
25 Sep 1969	At Kwangju AB, Korea, with 18 TFW.
12 Oct 1969	Returned to 18 TFW, Kadena AB, Okinawa.
12 Nov 1969	Transferred to 355 TFW, Takhli RTAB, Thailand.
18 Dec 1969	Redesignated F-105G at 355 TFW, Takhli RTAB, Thailand.
6 Jan 1970	At 355 TFW, Takhli RTAB, Thailand. (AVH-14).
8 Jan 1970	In depot work (WO) at McClellan AFB CA.
16 May 1970	Transferred to 23 TFW, McConnell AFB KS for combat crew training (TF).
9 Jun 1970	At 23 TFW, McConnell AFB KS (TF).
15 Mar 1971	At 388 TFW, Korat RTAB, Thailand. (AVH-16).
18 Jun 1971	In contract depot (WK) at Air Asia, Tainan, Taiwan.
5 Aug 1971	Transferred to 18 TFW, Kadena AB, Okinawa.
8 Nov 1971	In depot work (WM) by SMAMA at Kadena AB, Okinawa.
17 Nov 1971	At 18 TFW, Kadena AB, Okinawa.
16 Feb 1972	At 388 TFW, Korat RTAB, Thailand. (AVH-18).
1 Aug 1972	In depot work (WM) by SM-ALC at Korat RTAB, Thailand.
7 Aug 1972	In crash damage status (WJ) at 388 TFW, Korat RTAB, Thailand.
9 Aug 1972	In depot work (WM) by SM-ALC at Korat RTAB, Thailand.
12 Sep 1972	At 388 TFW, Korat RTAB, Thailand. Combat capable (CC) status.
12 Sep 1972	In depot work (WM) by SM-ALC at Korat RTAB, Thailand.
15 Sep 1972	At 388 TFW, Korat RTAB, Thailand. Combat capable (CC) status.
29 Sep 1972	Departed (PL) Korat RTAB, Thailand.
30 Sep 1972	Arrived at SM-ALC, McClellan AFB CA for storage (XW).
24 Oct 1972	In depot work (WO) by SM-ALC at McClellan AFB CA.
27 Dec 1972	Transferred (PL) to the 561 TFS, McConnell AFB KS.
4 Jan 1973	At 561 TFS, McConnell AFB KS. (AVH-20).
12 Feb 1973	In depot maintenance (WM) by SM-ALC at McConnell AFB KS.
12 Mar 1973	At 561 TFS, McConnell AFB KS.
27 Apr 1973	In depot maintenance (WO) by SM-ALC at McClellan AFB CA.
15 Aug 1973	In test (EI) by SM-ALC at McClellan AFB CA.
24 Jan 1974	Transferred to 35 TFW TAC, George AFB CA. (AVH-22).
3 Jul 1974	Transferred to 388 TFW PACAF, Korat RTAB, Thailand.

29 Oct 1974	Returned to 35 TFW TAC, George AFB CA.
6 Jan 1976	In depot maintenance (WO) by SM-ALC at McClellan AFB CA. (AVH-24).
7 Jan 1976	Returned to 35 TFW TAC, George AFB CA. 3,247 flying hours.
14 Apr 1977	In depot maintenance by SM-ALC at George AFB CA. 3,317.0 flying hours. (AVH-25 & AVH-26).
20 Jun 1978	At Eglin AFB FL with 35 TFW from George AFB CA. 3,591.0 flying hours. (AVH-26).
27 Jun 1978	At 35 TFW TAC, George AFB CA. 3,591.0 flying hours.
18 Jul 1978	At Nellis AFB NV with 35 TFW from George AFB CA. 3,617.0 flying hours.
21 Jul 1978	At 35 TFW TAC, George AFB CA. 3,617.0 flying hours.
14 Apr 1980	In depot maintenance (DYNFW) at George AFB CA. 3,915.2 flying hours. (GO33B 24 Jun 80).
1 May 1980	At 35 TFW, George AFB CA. 3,915.2 flying hours.
14 Jul 1980	Delivered to MASDC ("Inviolate storage"—XS), Davis-Monthan AFB AZ. 3,942.9 flying hours. (GO33B 22 Jan 81).
20 Dec 1982	MASDC storage code changed to "XX" (Low probability of withdrawal). 3,945.6 flying hours. (GO33B 1 Feb 83).
5 Nov 1985	Removed from MASDC storage for display at England AFB LA. (John Coon).

F-105G-1RE 63-8300

Republic Production No: F-77 Production Sequence No: 767

Location: At Le Bourget Museum, Paris, France.

Aircraft Chronology

13 Jul 1964	Delivered after production to 49 TFW, Spangdahlem AB, Germany. (AVH-1).
6 Jul 1965	At CASA, Getafe, Spain, for contract depot work (WK). (AVH-4).
23 Jul 1965	At 49 TFW, Spangdahlem AB, Germany.
2 Aug 1965	At CASA, Madrid, Spain, for contract depot work (WK).
28 Feb 1966	Returned to 49 TFW, Spangdahlem AB, Germany. (AVH-5).
27 Oct 1966	At Wheelus AB, Libya, with 49 TFW for weapons delivery training.
23 Nov 1966	Returned to 49 TFW, Spangdahlem AB, Germany.
10 Jan 1967	At 49 TFW, Spangdahlem AB, Germany, being readied for transfer. (AVH-8).
13 Jan 1967	Transferred to 23 TFW, McConnell AFB KS.
23 Feb 1967	In depot maintenance (WO) by MOAMA, Brookley AFB AL.
3 Mar 1967	Returned to 23 TFW, McConnell AFB KS.
8 May 1967	In depot maintenance (WM) by SMAMA field team at McConnell AFB KS.
11 May 1967	At 23 TFW, McConnell AFB KS.
27 Jun 1967	In depot maintenance (WM) by SMAMA field team at McConnell AFB KS.
30 Jun 1967	At 23 TFW, McConnell AFB KS.
16 Sep 1967	In depot maintenance (WM) by SMAMA field team at McConnell AFB KS.
18 Sep 1967	At 23 TFW, McConnell AFB KS.
29 Sep 1967	Deployed to George AFB CA with 562 TFS, 23 TFW, for air-to-air gunnery training for F-105 RTU Class 68 BR, "The Many Splendored Studs."

13 Oct 1967	Returned to 23 TFW, McConnell AFB KS.
11 Dec 1967	In depot maintenance (WM) by SMAMA field team at McConnell AFB KS.
30 Jan 1968	Returned to 23 TFW, McConnell AFB KS. (AVH-10).
1 Feb 1968	At SMAMA, McClellan AFB CA for depot work (WO).
24 Feb 1968	At 23 TFW, McConnell AFB KS.
12 Mar 1968	Deployed to George AFB CA with the 562 TFS, 23 TFW, for air-to-air gunnery training for RTU Class 68HR.
28 Mar 1968	Returned to 23 TFW, McConnell AFB KS.
29 Oct 1968	In depot repair (WR) by SMAMA at McConnell AFB KS. (AVH-12).
14 Nov 1968	At Fairchild Republic, Farmingdale NY for crash damage repair (WR).
10 Oct 1969	In depot maintenance by SMAMA, McClellan AFB CA.
27 Jan 1970	At 57 FWW, Nellis AFB NV for combat crew training (TF). (AVH-14).
3 Jun 1970	Transferred (PL) to the 23 TFW, McConnell AFB KS.
8 Jun 1970	Redesignated an F-105G at the 23 TFW, McConnell AFB KS (CC).
15 Mar 1971	Transferred to the 17 WWS, 388 TFW, Korat RTAB, Thailand. (AVH-16).
3 May 1971	In contract depot work (WK) at Air Asia, Tainan, Taiwan.
6 Jun 1971	Returned to 388 TFW, Korat RTAB, Thailand.
15 Jun 1972	Departed (PL) 388 TFW, Korat RTAB, Thailand. (AVH-18).
20 Jun 1972	Transferred (PL) to 57 FWW, Nellis AFB NV for combat crew training (TF).
15 Aug 1972	In depot maintenance (WK) by Fairchild Engine and Aircraft Corporation (FACCF) at Bob Sikes Municipal Airport, Crestview FL.
11 Sep 1972	Returned to 57 FWW, Nellis AFB NV for combat crew training (TF).
27 Feb 1973	In depot work (WO) by SM-ALC, McClellan AFB CA. (AVH-20).
1 Jun 1973	Returned (PL) to 57 FWW, Nellis AFB NV.
6 Jun 1973	At 57 FWW, Nellis AFB NV for combat crew training (TF).
22 Jul 1974	In depot work (WO) by SM-ALC, Nellis AFB NV. (AVH-22).
2 Aug 1974	At 57 FWW, Nellis AFB NV for combat crew training (TF).
10 Oct 1974	In depot work (WO) by SM-ALC, Nellis AFB NV.
11 Oct 1974	At 57 FWW, Nellis AFB NV for combat crew training (TF).
21 Jul 1975	Transferred to 35 TFW, George AFB CA for combat crew training (TF). (AVH-23 & AVH-24).
22 Oct 1975	In depot work (WO & WR) by SM-ALC at McClellan AFB CA.
12 Feb 1976	Returned to 35 TFW, George AFB CA. (AVH-24).
30 Aug 1976	Deployed with 562 TFS under "Coronet Yankee" to Spangdahlem AB, Germany, from 35 TFW, George AFB CA. 3,506 flying hours. (British Aviation Review, Dec 1995 & AVH-24).
20 Sep 1976	Returned to 35 TFW, George AFB CA. 3,526 flying hours. (AVH-24).
6 Oct 1976	At MacDill AFB FL with the 35 TFW. 3,526 flying hours.
19 Oct 1976	Returned to 35 TFW, George AFB CA. 3,526 flying hours.
7 Jul 1977	At 35 TFW TAC, George AFB CA. 3,731.0 flying hours. (AVH-25 & AVH-26).
12 Aug 1977	Deployed under "Coronet Club" to Karup AB, Denmark, with 563 TFS, 35 TFW, from George AFB CA. 3,731.0 flying hours.
30 Aug 1977	Returned from Denmark to George AFB CA.
17 Mar 1978	Aircraft had flight restrictions at George AFB CA due to cracks in main landing gear wing rib found during inspection required by TCTO 1F-105-1281. "…Restricted to 47,500 lb. gross takeoff weight, 10 knots crosswind component, 4 G's symmetrical and 2.5 G's rolling." (35 TFW/MA memo).
19 May 1978	In depot maintenance by SM-ALC at George AFB CA. 3,871.0 flying hours. (AVH-26).

In its sixteen years of flying, this "G" belonged to five different fighter wings. The 49 Tactical Fighter Wing at Spangdahlem, Germany, received it as an "F" from production in July 1964. Two and a half years later, when the 49th converted to F-4Ds, the plane moved to the 23 Tactical Fighter Wing's Replacement Training Unit at McConnell Air Force Base, Kansas. In 1970, it went briefly to Nellis Air Force Base, Nevada, then back to McConnell where it upgraded to a "G" Wild Weasel. In March 1971, the plane began fifteen months of combat duties with the 388 Tactical Fighter Wing at Korat, Thailand. It returned to Nellis in June 1972 where it stayed as a Wild Weasel trainer for the next two years. When Nellis closed its Wild Weasel training program in 1975, the plane transferred to the 35 Tactical Fighter Wing at George Air Force Base, California. The plane returned to its first base at Spangdahlem during the 35th's NATO deployment in 1976 and a year later deployed with the 35th to Denmark. In July 1980, five years and one day after it moved to George, the 35th retired it to Arizona. Six years later, it was removed from storage and flown on a C-5A to Germany then trucked to Paris' Le Bourget museum where it was restored and put on display in 1993. (Photograph from Musee de L'Air et de L'Espace/Le Bourget, 1993.)

13 Jun 1978	At 35 TFW TAC, George AFB CA. 3,999.0 flying hours.
30 Sep 1978	At 35 TFW TAC, George AFB CA. 4,072.0 flying hours.
5 Oct 1979	In depot maintenance by Sacramento ALC at George AFB CA. 4,175.3 flying hours. (AVH-27).
9 Nov 1979	At 35 TFW TAC, George AFB CA. 4,191.1 flying hours.
22 Jul 1980	Delivered to MASDC ("Inviolate storage"—XS), Davis Monthan AFB AZ. 4,265.6 flying hours. (GO33B 22 Jan 81).
20 Dec 1982	MASDC storage code changed to "XX" (Low probability of withdrawal). 4,266.3 flying hours. (GO33B 1 Feb 83).
8 Apr 1986	Given to the Musee de l'Air et de l'Espace by the United States Air Force . (Musee de l'air et de l'espace letter, 23 May 1997).
22 Apr 1986	Shipped to Ramstein AB, Germany, via C-5A for transportation to Paris, France. (British Aviation Review, Dec 1995 & Musee de l'air et de l'espace letter, 23 May 1997).
5 Oct 1986	Shipped by truck provided by French Air Force from Ramstein AB, Germany, to Le Bourget, France.
1987–1993	Restored by "Les Ailes Anciennes—Ile de France."
1993	Placed on display at Musee de L'Air et de L'Espace/Le Bourget, Paris, France.

F-105G–1RE 63-8320

Republic Production No: F-97 Production Sequence No: 787

Location: Inside the Air Force Museum at Wright-Patterson AFB, Dayton, Ohio.

Aircraft Name(s)	Crew	Unit	Date	Description
Takhli Avenger		333 TFS, 355 TFW		
Ione		333 TFS, 355 TFW		
The Trol		333 TFS, 355 TFW		
Baby Bear's Lair	Capt. John Manning	333 TFS, 355 TFW		
Cooter	Maj. Wallace/ Capt. Hoynacki	333 TFS, 355 TFW	Jan 70	Name on both intakes. White owl and moon on left fuselage. Two MiG kills below cockpit.
Bam Bam		561 TFS Det. 1	Aug 73	On wing root. (TDY to Korat).
Hanoi Hustler	Lt. Col. Rich Simons	562 TFS, 35 TFW	Feb 80	In red on fuselage side under 3 red stars.

Displayed at the Air Force Museum since 1980, this F-105G, with its extensive combat history, is one of the best known Thunderchiefs. It was produced as an "F" in July 1964. It served first at Spangdahlem Air Base in Germany, then moved to McConnell Air Force Base, Kansas, and Nellis Air Force Base, Nevada, before arriving for combat duty in November 1967 with the 355 Tactical Fighter Wing at Takhli, Thailand. Within its first two months at Takhli, two pilots flying the plane claimed MiG kills, none of which was officially credited due to lack of sufficient evidence. As described in its detailed chronology, an error in historical record keeping during this period is apparently the reason why the plane acquired its third MiG-kill star. Two years later, in December 1969, while still at Takhli, the plane was designated an F-105G. In September 1970, as Takhli was closing, "320" moved to Korat, Thailand, and was assigned to Detachment 1 of the 12 Tactical Fighter Squadron and then to the 6010 Wild Weasel Squadron. In 1971, the plane returned to the States for depot work but, in April 1972, it arrived once again at Korat to participate in the "Linebacker" bombing raids against North Vietnam. In September 1973, it was one of the last twelve F-105Gs to leave Korat and the Vietnam war. That month it joined the 35 Tactical Fighter Wing at George Air Force Base, California, where it remained for the next seven years. The 35th flew it on their NATO deployments to Denmark in 1977 and 1978 and, on 23 February 1980, retired it to the Air Force Museum. (Photograph by author, 7 June 1998.)

Aircraft Chronology

30 Jul 1964	USAF production acceptance from Republic Aviation, Farmingdale NY. (AVH-1)
6 Aug 1964	At MOAMA, Brookley AFB AL for depot work (WO).
13 Aug 1964	Delivered to 49 TFW, Spangdahlem AB, Germany.
31 Jul 1965	At CASA Madrid, Spain, for contract depot work (WK). (AVH-4).
3 Dec 1965	At 49 TFW, Spangdahlem AB, Germany. (AVH-5).
15 Nov 1966	Transferred to 23 TFW, McConnell AFB KS.
10 Jan 1967	At MOAMA, Brookley AFB AL for depot work (WO). (AVH-8).
18 Jan 1967	At 23 TFW, McConnell AFB KS.
23 Apr 1967	At SMAMA, McClellan AFB CA for depot work (WO).
1 Jun 1967	Transferred to 4525 FWW, Nellis AFB NV.
5 Jun 1967	At Eglin AFB FL, with 4525 FWW.
2 Jul 1967	Returned to 4525 FWW, Nellis AFB NV.
13 Nov 1967	Transferred (PL) to 355 TFW, Takhli RTAB, Thailand.
26 Nov 1967	Operational (CC) at 333 TFS, 355 TFW, Takhli RTAB, Thailand.
5 Dec 1967	Aircraft flown by Capt. Phillip M. Drew (pilot) and Maj. William H. Wheeler (EWO) from the 357 TFS, 355 TFW, on a combat mission lasting 3.3 hours from Takhli RTAB, Thailand. (Capt. Drew's and Maj. Wheeler's Individual Flight Records as of 24 Feb 1968).
15 Dec 1967	Aircraft flown by Maj. William M. Dalton (pilot) and Maj. James L. Graham (EWO) from the 333 TFS, 355 TFW, on a combat mission lasting 3.4 hours from Takhli RTAB, Thailand. (Maj. Dalton's and Maj. Graham's Individual Flight Records, as of 30 Nov 1968).
Nov/Dec 1967	MiG kill claimed by Maj. George O. Guss, 333 TFS, 355 TFW, Takhli RTAB, Thailand. "... Maj. ... Guss cleared the aircraft wings of ordnance and jettisoned the racks in preparation for a dogfight with a flight of four MiG-17s. A MiG flew straight into the ejected rack and was destroyed." Date not certain. (MiG kill not officially granted). (USAF Museum Friends Bulletin, Vol. 3, No. 1, Spring 1980). "The story about me downing a MiG with ejection racks happened on my first flight over North Vietnam. I was #2 in our flight of two F-105F's when four MiG-17's jumped us. My leader tried to turn with them which was impossible. One of them was firing and he couldn't get enough lead. The other three were beginning to move under me which didn't look good. At that time, I pushed what we called the 'master panic button' that jettisoned everything on the plane—bombs, pylons and rockets—and went for the deck. My leader looked back and saw a ball of fire and thought I had been hit. He swears he saw an airplane go down. All I know is I had a full load and they had a lot of garbage to dodge." (Letter from Lt. Col. George O. Guss, USAF Ret, to Rick Versteeg posted on Thud Ridge Web site.)
19 Dec 1967	Aircraft flown by Maj. Robert R. Huntley with EWO Capt. Ralph W. Stearman, 354 TFS, 355 TFW, from Takhli RTAB, Thailand, on an Iron Hand support mission five miles west of Phuc Yen airfield. Call sign: "Otter 1." They encountered several MiG-17's and fired at one hitting it. They claimed credit for a MiG kill, but, after a two-year investigation, the claim was disallowed by Seventh Air Force's Enemy Aircraft Claims Evaluation Board. Instead, MiG kills were awarded to two other members of the flight, Otter 2 and Otter 3. Otter 2 was Maj. William M. Dalton (pilot) and Maj. James L. Graham (EWO) flying F-105F 63-8329. (In some histories, this crew is erroneously credited with the MiG kill while flying 63-8320, accounting for this plane's third MiG-kill star). However, they shared their MiG kill with an F-4D (Nash 1) flying MIGCAP. Otter 3 was Capt. Phillip M. Drew (pilot) and Maj. William H. Wheeler (EWO) in F-105F 63-8317. Excerpts from Maj. Huntley's Statement of MiG Engagement: "... At this time I saw another MiG at my 11 o'clock position in a left turn diving toward me. I pulled hard into a left climbing turn to establish a head-on firing pass. During the climb, I selected Dive on the Sight Mode Selector switch which gave me a fixed sight. ... As I was climbing thru approximately 2500 feet, I fired at the MiG while still on a head-on pass and at about 2000 slant range (Photo #1). I observed my 20mm HEI impacting in the fuselage area and saw him start trailing heavy black smoke (Photo #2). ... I observed the MiG until he passed through approximately 1500 feet ... and at no time did he attempt to roll out his bank angle or pull out of the dive. ... Suddenly my

peripheral vision caught another MiG trailing black smoke in a steep left turning spiral dive approximately a mile south of the MiG I had shot at (Photo #3). I was unable to actually see the disabled MiGs impact the ground. … Analysis of strike camera (KA71) film … clearly shows the MIG-17 burning furiously." (Aces & Aerial Victory, pages 73 & 74; and "Statement of MIG Engagement—19 Dec 67," by Maj. Robert R. Huntley).

11 Jan 1968 At 355 TFW, Takhli RTAB, Thailand. (AVH-10).

13 Jan 1968 At Air Asia, Tainan, Taiwan, for contract depot maintenance (WK).

18 Mar 1968 Returned to 355 TFW, Takhli RTAB, Thailand.

3 May 1968 In depot-level maintenance (WM) at 355 TFW, Takhli RTAB, Thailand.

5 May 1968 Operational (CC) at 355 TFW, Takhli RTAB, Thailand.

9 May 1968 In depot-level maintenance (WM) at 355 TFW, Takhli RTAB.

20 May 1968 Operational (CC) at 355 TFW, Takhli RTAB, Thailand.

1 Nov 1968 While assigned to the 355 TFW, Takhli RTAB, Thailand, aircraft had accumulated 1,588.4 flying hours. (355 TFW History, Oct–Dec 68, USAF microfilm NO466).

28 Feb 1969 While assigned to the 355 TFW, Takhli RTAB, Thailand, the aircraft flew 68.7 hours during the month of February 1969 and had accumulated 1,813.4 flying hours. (355 TFW History, Jan–Mar 69, Vol. II, USAF Microfilm NO467).

28 Aug 1969 In depot maintenance (WM) by SMAMA at Takhli RTAB, Thailand. (AVH-12).

25 Sep 1969 At 355 TFW, Takhli RTAB, Thailand.

18 Dec 1969 Redesignated F-105G at 355 TFW, Takhli RTAB, Thailand.

24 Sep 1970 Assigned to Detachment 1 of the 12 TFS, 18 TFW, at Korat RTAB, Thailand. (AVH-14).

1 Nov 1970 Reassigned to the 6010 WWS, 388 TFW, Korat RTAB, Thailand.

23 Dec 1970 At the 388 TFW, Korat RTAB, Thailand. (John Tomany, e-mail, 8 Dec 97).

25 Aug 1971 In depot work (WO) by SMAMA at McClellan AFB CA. (AVH-16).

1 Mar 1972 Carried on assignment roster for the 561 TFS, 23 TFW, at McConnell AFB KS. (Master 23 TFW Aircraft Assignment as of 1 March 1972).

7 Apr 1972 Arrived (PL) at Takhli RTAB, Thailand, with 388 TFW. (AVH-18).

10 Apr 1972 Assigned to 388 TFW (PACAF), Korat RTAB, Thailand.

23 Oct 1972 Assigned to 561 TFS under TAC TDY (TAO) at Korat RTAB, Thailand.

22 Dec 1972 In depot maintenance (WM) by SM-ALC at Korat RTAB, Thailand.

29 Dec 1972 Returned to 561 TFS under TAC TDY (TAO) at Korat RTAB, Thailand.

2 Jul 1973 Assigned to 35 TFW under TAC TDY (TAO) at Korat RTAB, Thailand. (AVH-20).

8 Sep 1973 Transferred (PL) to 35 TFW, TAC, George AFB CA.

12 Sep 1973 At 562 TFS, 35 TFW, TAC, George AFB CA.

31 Jan 1974 In depot maintenance (WM) by SM-ALC at George AFB CA. (AVH-22).

8 Feb 1974 At 35 TFW TAC, George AFB CA.

6 Sep 1974 In depot maintenance (WM) by SM-ALC at George AFB CA.

15 Sep 1974 At 35 TFW, TAC, George AFB CA.

26 Jun 1975 In depot repair (WR) by SM-ALC at McClellan AFB CA. (AVH-23 & AVH-24).

3 Feb 1976 Returned to 35 TFW, TAC, George AFB CA.

8 Jul 1977 In depot maintenance by SM-ALC at George AFB CA. 5,245.0 flying hours. (AVH-25 & AVH-26).

15 Jul 1977 At 35 TFW, TAC, George AFB CA. 5,263.0 flying hours.

12 Aug 1977 One of 18 F-105Gs deployed from the 35 TFW, George AFB CA to Karup AB, Denmark, under Exercise "Coronet Club." Assigned to the 561 TFS. 5,275.0 flying hours.

30 Aug 1977 Returned from Denmark to George AFB CA.

10 Jul 1978 At 35 TFW TAC, George AFB CA. 5,479.0 flying hours. (AVH-26).

31 Jul 1978	At 35 TFW TAC, George AFB CA. 5,496.0 flying hours.
9 Aug 1978	One of 12 F-105Gs deployed from the 35 TFW, George AFB CA to Karup AB, Denmark, under Exercise "Coronet Sparrow." Assigned to the 562 TFS. 5,496.0 flying hours.
6 Sep 1978	Returned to 35 TFW TAC, George AFB CA. 5,499.0 flying hours.
4 Oct 1978	At 35 TFW TAC, George AFB CA. 5,557.0 flying hours.
25 Oct 1978	At Eglin AFB FL from 35 TFW, George AFB CA. 5,557.0 flying hours.
8 Nov 1978	Returned to 35 TFW TAC, George AFB CA. 5,557.0 flying hours.
21 Dec 1979	At 35 TFW TAC, George AFB CA. 5,750.3 flying hours. (AVH-27).
26 Dec 1979	In contract depot maintenance (DYNFW) at George AFB CA. 5,755.8 flying hours. (GO-33. 24 Jun 1980).
1 Feb 1980	At 35 TFW, George AFB CA. 5,765.1 flying hours.
18 Feb 1980	In depot maintenance (DYNFW) at George AFB CA. 5,765.9 flying hours.
23 Feb 1980	Last flight from the 35 TFW, George AFB CA to Wright-Patterson AFB, OH by 562 TFS pilot, Maj. Jimmy Boyd with EWO, Capt. Gary Crystal.
24 Feb 1980	Transferred to the USAF Museum. 5,765.9 flying hours.

F-105F–1RE 63-8331

Republic Production No: F-108 Production Sequence No: 798

Location: Displayed at the Pacific Coast Air Museum, Santa Rosa, California.

Aircraft Name(s)	Crew	Unit	Date	Description
Double Trouble		457 TFS AFRES	Jun 81	Stenciled in black on nose gear door.

Aircraft Chronology

28 Aug 1964	USAF production acceptance from Republic Aviation, Farmingdale NY. (AVH-1).
1 Sep 1964	Delivered to 4 TFW TAC, Seymour Johnson AFB NC.
17 Nov 1964	Deployed from Seymour Johnson AB NC to Incirlik AB, Turkey, with the 335 TFS, 4 TFW. (AVH-4).
16 Feb 1965	Aircraft reassigned to the 334 TFS from 4 TFW that replaced the 335 TFS at Incirlik AB, Turkey. (4 TFW History, Jan–Jun 65, Vol. II, USAF microfilm MO292).
30 Apr 1965	On TDY at Incirlik AB, Turkey, with the 334 TFS from the 4 TFW, Seymour Johnson AFB NC.
16 May 1965	Returned to 4 TFW, Seymour Johnson AFB NC when the 336 TFS replaced the 334 TFS at Incirlik AB, Turkey. (AVH-4).
20 Aug 1964	In depot maintenance (WM) at Republic Aviation facility, Crestview FL.
20 Sep 1965	Returned to 4 TFW, Seymour Johnson AFB NC.
30 Nov 1965	While assigned to the 4 TFW, Seymour Johnson AFB NC, the aircraft flew 28.9 hours for the month of November 1965 and had 501.1 total flying hours. Assigned Crew Chief: SSgt. Ragsdale. (4 TFW History, Jul–Dec 65, Vol. II, USAF microfilm MO292).
5 Dec 1965	Transferred to 4520 CCTW, Nellis AFB NV. (AVH-4).
31 Dec 1965	Aircraft was one of five on loan to Nellis AFB NV from the 4 TFW, Seymour Johnson AFB NC. (4 TFW History, Jul–Dec 65, Vol. II, USAF microfilm MO292).
31 Jan 1966	Returned to 4 TFW, Seymour Johnson AFB NC. (AVH-5).

This "F" began as a two-seat trainer in August 1964 and remained a trainer for its 18 years of service. It was one of the few "Fs" that did not see combat in South East Asia and so had a relatively uneventful career. Two months after receiving it from factory production, its first unit, the 4 Tactical Fighter Wing at Seymour Johnson Air Force Base, North Carolina, flew it in November 1964 to Incirlik Air Base, Turkey. They kept the plane at their NATO alert operation at Incirlik for six months. In December 1965, the 4th loaned it to Nellis Air Force Base, Nevada, for that unit's pilot training program. When the 4th converted to F-4Ds in late 1966, the plane moved to the F-105 pilot training program at McConnell Air Force Base, Kansas. In 1973, it joined the 465 Tactical Fighter Squadron—the Air Force Reserve unit at Tinker Air Force Base, Oklahoma. This squadron flew it on its NATO deployment to Great Britain in June 1978 and to Italy the next year. A year later, they passed it on to the Air Force Reserve's 457 Tactical Fighter Squadron at Carswell Air Force Base, Texas. After flying it for two years, the 457th sent the plane to the "Boneyard" in February 1982. In the mid-1980s it came out of storage as one of two planes given for static display to the USAF Combat Ammunition Center, a tenant at the Sierra Army Depot in California. When this Air Force unit moved from the Army depot, they left their Thunderchiefs at Sierra (its location in the photograph). In June 1999, the plane moved to an air museum in Santa Rosa, California. (U.S. Army photograph by Larry Rogers, Public Affairs, 15 March 1997.)

20 Jul 1966	In depot work (WO) by MOAMA, Brookley AFB AL.
26 Jul 1966	Returned to 4 TFW, Seymour Johnson AFB NC.
31 Jul 1966	While assigned to the 4 TFW, Seymour Johnson AFB NC, the aircraft flew 25.0 hours for the month of July 1966 and had accumulated 732.3 flying hours. Assigned crew chief: SSgt. J. L. Ashley. (4 TFW History, Jul–Dec 66, USAF microfilm MO293).
14 Nov 1966	Transferred (PL) to 23 TFW, McConnell AFB KS. (AVH-5).
16 Nov 1966	Combat capable (CC) at 23 TFW, McConnell AFB KS.
1 Mar 1967	In depot work (WM) by SMAMA at McConnell AFB KS. (AVH-8).
6 Mar 1967	Combat capable (CC) at 23 TFW, McConnell AFB KS.
29 Sep 1967	Deployed to George AFB CA with the 562 TFS from the 23 TFW, McConnell AFB KS to support gunnery training for F-105 RTU Class 68BR, "The Many Splendored Studs."
13 Oct 1967	Returned to 23 TFW, McConnell AFB KS.
25 Apr 1969	In depot work (WO) by SMAMA, McClellan AFB CA. (AVH-12).
20 May 1969	Returned (PL) to 23 TFW, McConnell AFB KS.
21 May 1969	Combat capable (CC) at 23 TFW, McConnell AFB KS.
22 Dec 1969	At 23 TFW, McConnell AFB KS being prepared for transfer (PL).
23 Dec 1969	In depot work (WO) by SMAMA, McClellan AFB CA.
20 Mar 1970	Returned (PL) to 23 TFW, McConnell AFB KS. (AVH-14).
24 Mar 1970	Combat capable (CC) at 23 TFW, McConnell AFB KS.
8 Jan 1971	At 23 TFW, McConnell AFB KS being prepared for transfer (PL). (AVH-16).
12 Jan 1971	In depot maintenance (WK) by Fairchild Engine and Aircraft Corporation (FACCF) at Bob Sikes Municipal Airport, Crestview FL.
9 Feb 1971	Returned to (PL) to 23 TFW, McConnell AFB KS.

11 Feb 1971	Combat capable (CC) at 23 TFW, McConnell AFB KS.
1 Mar 1972	Carried on assignment roster with the 562 TFS, 23 TFW, at McConnell AFB KS. (Master 23 TFW Aircraft Assignment as of 1 March 1972).
1 Jul 1972	Reassigned to the 561 TFS at McConnell AFB KS when the 23 TFW relocated to England AFB LA and converted to A-7Ds. (AVH-18).
13 Jul 1972	In depot maintenance (WK) by Fairchild Engine and Aircraft Corporation (FACCF) at Bob Sikes Municipal Airport, Crestview FL.
21 Aug 1972	Transferred to the 507 TFG AFRES, Tinker AFB OK.
6 Nov 1972	At 507 TFG AFRES, Tinker AFB OK being prepared for transfer (PL).
13 Nov 1972	Transferred back to the 561 TFS at McConnell AFB KS.
17 Nov 1972	Combat capable (CC) with the 561 TFS at McConnell AFB KS.
11 Jan 1973	Transferred (PL) to 507 TFG AFRES, Tinker AFB OK. (AVH-20).
31 Mar 1973	Reassigned to 507 CMTSq AFRES, Tinker AFB OK.
20 May 1973	In depot maintenance (WM) by SMAMA at Tinker AFB OK.
23 May 1973	Combat capable (CC) at 507 CMTSq AFRES, Tinker AFB OK.
3 Dec 1973	In depot maintenance (WM) by SMAMA at Tinker AFB OK.
20 Feb 1974	Combat capable (CC) at 507 CMTSq AFRES, Tinker AFB OK. (AVH-22).
28 Mar 1974	In depot work (WO) by SMAMA at McClellan AFB CA.
23 Jul 1974	Returned to 507 CMTSq AFRES, Tinker AFB OK.
18 Oct 1974	In depot maintenance (WM) by SMAMA at Tinker AFB OK.
12 Nov 1974	Combat capable at 507 CLMSq AFRES, Tinker AFB OK.
7 Jul 1975	In depot maintenance (WM) by SMALC at Tinker AFB OK. (AVH-23 & AVH-24).
16 Jul 1975	Combat capable at 507 TFG AFRES, Tinker AFB OK. 3,497 flying hours. (AVH-24).
3 Jun 1976	At 507 TFG AFRES, Tinker AFB OK. 3,700 flying hours. (AVH-25 & AVH-26).
19 Sep 1976	In depot maintenance (DM) by SM-ALC at Tinker AFB OK. 4,068 flying hours.
2 Oct 1976	At 465 TFS AFRES, Tinker AFB OK. 4,068 flying hours.
10 Jun 1978	Deployed under "Coronet Oriole" with 465 TFS AFRES to Sculthorpe, England, from Tinker AFB OK. (British Aviation Review, Dec 95).
23 Jun 1978	Returned from England to Tinker AFB OK.
12 Feb 1979	In contract depot maintenance (DM) by Fairchild Baltimore (FACBM) at Tinker AFB OK. 4,149.3 flying hours. (AVH-27).
14 Mar 1979	At 465 TFS AFRES, Tinker AFB OK. 4,154.2 flying hours.
12 May 1979	Deployed under "Coronet Palomino" with the 465 TFS AFRES to Gioia Del Colle, Italy, from Tinker AFB OK. (British Aviation Review, Dec 95).
24 May 1979	Returned from Italy to Tinker AFB OK.
31 May 1979	While assigned to the 465 TFS AFRES, Tinker AFB OK, the aircraft flew 57.7 hours during the month of May 1979 and had accumulated 4,253.7 flying hours. The assigned crew chief was Sullivan. (301 TFW History 1 Apr–30 Jun 1979, USAF microfilm 343832).
20 Jun 1979	In "Domestic Project" (DO) by OC-ALC at Tinker AFB OK. 4,253.7 flying hours. (AVH-27).
30 Jun 1979	While assigned to the 465 TFS AFRES, Tinker AFB OK, the aircraft was not flown during the month of June 1979 because it was in Analytical Condition Inspection (ACI). It had accumulated a total of 4,253.7 flying hours, the highest time of any of the 465th's F-105Fs. The assigned crew chief was Sullivan. (301 TFW History, Apr–Jun 1979, USAF microfilm 34382).
14 Dec 1979	At OC-ALC, Tinker AFB OK for "Domestic Project" (DO). 4,253.7 flying hours. (GO33B 24 Jun 80).
1 Jun 1980	Transferred to 457 TFS AFRES, Carswell AFB TX. 4,301.7 flying hours. (GO33B 22 Jan 81).
26 Nov 1980	In depot maintenance at General Dynamics, Ft. Worth TX (DYNFW). 4,397.7 flying hours.

1 Jun 1981	In depot maintenance at General Dynamics, Ft. Worth TX (DYNFW). 4,470.1 flying hours. (GO33B Dec 81).
13 Jun 1981	At 457 TFW AFRES, Carswell AFB TX. 4,518.2 flying hours.
11 Feb 1982	Sent to "inviolate" storage (XS) at MASDC, Davis-Monthan AFB AZ. 4,611.3 flying hours. (GO33B 1 Feb 83).
20 Dec 1982	MASDC storage code changed to "XX" (Low probability of withdrawal). 4,617.0 flying hours.
1985/1986	One of two F-105s removed from MASDC (now renamed "AMARC") for display at the Air Force Combat Ammunition Center (AFCOMAC), Sierra Army Depot, Herlong CA.. Following a study initiated by Lt Gen Leo Marquez, Hq USAF DCS Logistics and Engineering, the Air Force established AFCOMAC at Sierra on 1 November 1985 as a munitions assembly procedures training school. The aircraft was parked outside for static display and marked with tail code "JE" that had been used by the 44 TFS when the squadron was assigned to the 388 TFW at Korat RTAB, Thailand, from 1967 to 1969.
1 Oct 1992	The Air Force directed that AFCOMAC relocate from Sierra Army Depot to Beale AFB CA. The organization left their two static-display F-105s at Sierra and they became U.S. Army property.
9 June 1999	The aircraft was disassembled and transported by truck from Sierra Army Depot to the Pacific Coast Air Museum, Santa Rosa CA. The aircraft was saved from being sold as scrap when Mr. Al Reddick, owner of Advanced Aviation Services Co., Reno NV, arranged for the Army to transfer possession of both F-105s at Sierra to the U.S. Navy at NAS Fallon NV. This plane was then transferred to the museum. Mr. Don Ricchi, museum volunteer, was assigned as its crew chief. (Telephone interviews, 15 September 1999 with Mr. Butch Causey, museum director, and 8 October 1999 with Mr. Al Reddick.)

F-105G-1RE 63-8336

Republic Production No: F-113 Production Sequence No: 803

Location: At the airport in Reno, Nevada.

Aircraft Name(s)	Crew	Unit	Date	Description
The Virginian		44 TFS 388 TFW		Black letters and black pilot's head with helmet below right wing.
Patience		17 WWS 388 TFW	Apr 73	Name on left intake.

Aircraft Chronology

12 Sep 1964	USAF production acceptance from Republic Aviation, Farmingdale NY. (AVH-1).
13 Sep 1964	Delivered to 23 TFW, McConnell AFB KS.
30 Apr 1965	In depot maintenance (WO) by SMAMA, McClellan AFB CA. (AVH-4).
19 May 1965	Returned to 23 TFW, McConnell AFB KS.
15 Jul 1965	Transferred to 4520 CCTW, Nellis AFB CA for combat crew training (TF).
20 Dec 1965	In depot maintenance (WO) by SMAMA, McClellan AFB CA.
18 Jan 1966	Returned to 4520 CCTW, Nellis AFB CA for combat crew training (TF). (AVH-5).
27 Mar 1967	Assigned to the 4525 Fighter Weapons Wing, Nellis AFB NV for combat crew training (TF). (AVH-8).
31 Mar 1967	Reassigned to the 4520 CCTW, Nellis AFB NV for combat crew training (TF).
18 Aug 1967	In depot maintenance (WM) by a field team from SMAMA at Nellis AFB NV.

This is the second F-105 abandoned by its Air Force sponsor at the Army's Sierra Depot. However, unlike its companion, this "G" had an extensive combat career and was one of the last Thunderchiefs to leave South East Asia at the end of the war. For its first four years, the plane served as a trainer at McConnell Air Force Base, Kansas, and at Nellis Air Force Base, Nevada. In March 1968, it joined the 388 Tactical Fighter Wing at Korat, Thailand, where it was one of the 388th's five two-seaters modified for "Combat Martin." This program removed the rear seat and, in its place, installed a radio jammer intended to interrupt North Vietnamese ground control communications with their MiG interceptors. However, within two weeks of the plane's arrival at Korat, the U. S. restricted combat flying around Hanoi, the primary operating arena for MiGs, making the Combat Martin jamming equipment unnecessary. The 388th removed the gear from the rear cockpit and, for the next year, flew the plane as a single-seat bomber which complicated the fighter wing's flight scheduling. After a brief stay with the 355 Tactical Fighter Wing, at Takhli, Thailand, the plane passed to the 18 Tactical Fighter Wing at Kadena Air Base, Okinawa. In November 1970, the plane moved back to McConnell. A year later it entered the depot where it was converted to a Wild Weasel "G." With its newly restored and upgraded two-seat capability, the plane returned to Korat where, once again, it flew combat missions over North Vietnam. It remained at Korat until October 1974 when the Wild Weasel Thunderchiefs came home to the 35 Tactical Fighter Wing at George Air Force Base, California. The 35th flew the plane for the next four years. In November 1978, they gave it to the Georgia Air National Guard's 128 Tactical Fighter Squadron who flew it for another four years. The 128th took it on their NATO deployment to Turkey in 1980 and retired it to Arizona two years later. In the mid-1980s it came out of storage as the second of two planes given for static display to the USAF Combat Ammunition Center, a tenant at the Sierra Army Depot in Herlong, California (the plane's location in the photograph). In July 1999, the plane moved to the airport in Reno, Nevada. (U.S. Army photograph by Larry Rogers, Sierra Army Depot, Public Affairs, 15 March 1997.)

23 Aug 1967	At 4520 CCTW, Nellis AFB NV for combat crew training (TF).
18 Aug 1967	Being prepared for transfer (PL) from the 4520 CCTW, Nellis AFB CA.
25 Oct 1967	Transferred (PL) to the 23 TFW, McConnell AFB KS.
27 Oct 1967	Combat capable (CC) at the 23 TFW, McConnell AFB KS.
3 Nov 1967	Deployed to George AFB CA with the 563 TFS from the 23 TFW, McConnell AFB KS to support gunnery training for F-105 RTU Class 68DR.
22 Nov 1967	Returned to 23 TFW, McConnell AFB KS.
27 Nov 1967	At 23 TFW, McConnell AFB KS for combat crew training (TF).
5 Feb 1968	In depot maintenance (WM) by SMAMA at McConnell AFB KS. (AVH-10).
19 Feb 1968	At 23 TFW, McConnell AFB KS for combat crew training (TF).
26 Feb 1968	At 23 TFW, McConnell AFB KS being prepared for transfer (PL).
14 Mar 1968	Assigned to 388 TFW, Korat RTAB, Thailand. The second F-105F assigned to the 388 TFW configured for "Combat Martin" with the rear seat removed and a QRC-128 UHF jammer installed in the rear cockpit. (388 TFW History, Jan–Mar 68, USAF microfilm NO584).
24 Apr 1968	In depot maintenance (WM) by SMAMA field team at Korat RTAB, Thailand. (AVH-10).
26 Apr 1968	Combat capable (CC) at 388 TFW, Korat RTAB, Thailand.
20 May 1968	In depot maintenance (WM) by SMAMA field team at Korat RTAB, Thailand.
24 May 1968	Combat capable (CC) at 388 TFW, Korat RTAB, Thailand.

6 Aug 1968	In depot maintenance (WM) by SMAMA field team at Korat RTAB, Thailand.
8 Aug 1968	Combat capable (CC) at 388 TFW, Korat RTAB, Thailand.
27 Oct 1968	Aircraft received major combat damage in the aft section and speed brake petals while assigned to the 388 TFW, Korat RTAB, Thailand. The pilot was Maj. Vandevender. An estimated 400 maintenance hours were required for repairs. (388 TFW History, Oct–Dec 68, USAF microfilm NO585).
25 Nov 1968	Combat capable (CC) at 388 TFW, Korat RTAB, Thailand. (AVH-10).
21 Dec 1968	In depot maintenance (WM) by SMAMA field team at Korat RTAB, Thailand.
6 Jan 1969	Combat capable (CC) at 388 TFW, Korat RTAB, Thailand. (AVH-12).
31 Jan 1969	Began operating from Takhli RTAB, Thailand with the 388 TFW while the runway at Korat RTAB, Thailand, was being repaired.
3 Feb 1969	Flown on a mission in the Steel Tiger region of Laos by a 44 TFS crew while the 388 TFW operated from Takhli RTAB, Thailand. (388 TFW History, Jan–Mar 69, USAF microfilm NO586).
5 Feb 1969	Flown on an Iron Hand mission in the Steel Tiger region of Laos by a 44 TFS crew while the 388 TFW operated from Takhli RTAB, Thailand.
6 Feb 1969	Flown on an Iron Hand mission in the Steel Tiger region of Laos by a 44 TFS crew while the 388 TFW operated from Takhli RTAB, Thailand.
8 Feb 1969	Flown on a local mission by a 44 TFS crew while the 388 TFW operated from Takhli RTAB, Thailand.
10 Feb 1969	Flown on an Iron Hand mission in the Steel Tiger region of Laos by a 44 TFS crew while the 388 TFW operated from Takhli RTAB, Thailand.
11 Feb 1969	Flown on a strike mission in the Steel Tiger region of Laos by a 44 TFS crew while the 388 TFW operated from Takhli RTAB, Thailand.
12 Feb 1969	Flown on a strike mission in the Steel Tiger region of Laos by a 44 TFS crew while the 388 TFW operated from Takhli RTAB, Thailand.
13 Feb 1969	Flown on a local mission by a 44 TFS crew while the 388 TFW operated from Takhli RTAB, Thailand.
14 Feb 1969	Flown on two strike missions in the Steel Tiger region of Laos by 44 TFS crews while the 388 TFW operated from Takhli RTAB, Thailand.
16 Feb 1969	Flown on an Iron Hand mission in the Steel Tiger region of Laos by a 44 TFS crew while the 388 TFW operated from Takhli RTAB, Thailand.
18 Feb 1969	Flown on a strike mission in the Steel Tiger region of Laos by a 44 TFS crew while the 388 TFW operated from Takhli RTAB, Thailand.
19 Feb 1969	Flown on a strike mission in the Steel Tiger region of Laos by a 44 TFS crew while the 388 TFW operated from Takhli RTAB, Thailand.
23 Feb 1969	Flown on a strike mission in the Steel Tiger region of Laos by a 44 TFS crew while the 388 TFW operated from Takhli RTAB, Thailand.
25 Feb 1969	Flown on a strike mission in the Steel Tiger region of Laos by a 44 TFS crew while the 388 TFW operated from Takhli RTAB, Thailand.
26 Feb 1969	Flown on a strike mission in the Steel Tiger region of Laos by a 44 TFS crew while the 388 TFW operated from Takhli RTAB, Thailand.
28 Feb 1969	Flown on a strike mission in the Steel Tiger region of Laos by a 44 TFS crew while the 388 TFW operated from Takhli RTAB, Thailand.
2 Mar 1969	Returned to 388 TFW, Korat RTAB, Thailand, after runway repairs were completed. (AVH-12).
24 Apr 1969	In depot maintenance (WM) by SMAMA field team at Korat RTAB, Thailand.
30 Apr 1969	While assigned to the 44 TFS, 388 TFW, Korat RTAB, Thailand, the aircraft flew 37 hours in the month of April 1969 and had accumulated 1,867.0 total flying hours. (388 TFW History, Apr–Jun 69, USAF microfilm NO586).
18 May 1969	At 388 TFW, Korat RTAB, Thailand, being prepared for transfer (PL) after conversion of the 34 TFS at Korat to F-4Es.
20 May 1969	Transferred to the 355 TFW, Takhli RTAB, Thailand.

25 Sep 1969	At 355 TFW, Takhli RTAB, Thailand, being prepared for transfer (PL).
29 Sep 1969	Transferred (PL) to the 18 TFW, Kadena AB, Okinawa.
7 Oct 1969	Combat capable (CC) at 18 TFW, Kadena AB, Okinawa.
30 Oct 1969	In contract depot work (WK) by Air Asia (AAITT) at Tainan, Taiwan.
12 Jan 1970	Returned to the 18 TFW, Kadena AB, Okinawa. (AVH-14).
16 Jan 1970	In depot maintenance (WM) by SMAMA field team at Kadena AB, Okinawa.
18 Jan 1970	Combat capable (CC) at 18 TFW, Kadena AB, Okinawa.
5 Mar 1970	At Kwangju AB, Korea, with the 18 TFW.
30 Apr 1970	Returned to the 18 TFW, Kadena AB, Okinawa.
20 May 1970	At Kwangju AB, Korea, with the 18 TFW.
27 Jan 1970	Returned to the 18 TFW, Kadena AB, Okinawa.
14 Oct 1970	At Kwangju AB, Korea, with the 18 TFW.
22 Oct 1970	Returned to the 18 TFW, Kadena AB, Okinawa.
3 Nov 1970	Transferred (PL) to 23 TFW, McConnell AFB KS.
12 Nov 1970	Placed in flyable storage (PR) at 23 TFW, McConnell AFB KS.
7 May 1971	Combat capable (CC) at 23 TFW, McConnell AFB KS. (AVH-16).
11 Mar 1971	In depot maintenance (WK) by Fairchild Engine and Aircraft Corporation (FACCF) at Bob Sikes Municipal Airport, Crestview FL.
2 Jun 1971	Returned (PL) to 23 TFW, McConnell AFB KS.
20 Jul 1971	Placed in flyable storage (PR) at 23 TFW, McConnell AFB KS.
21 Dec 1971	At 23 TFW, McConnell AFB KS being prepared for transfer (PL).
23 Dec 1971	In depot work (WO) by SMAMA, McClellan AFB CA to be upgraded from an F-105F to an F-105G.
1 Mar 1972	Carried on assignment roster for the 561 TFS, 23 TFW, at McConnell AFB KS as having "Combat Martin" configuration. (Master 23 TFW Aircraft Assignment as of 1 March 1972).
29 Jun 1972	Redesignated F-105G at SM-ALC, McClellan AFB CA. (AVH-18).
11 Aug 1972	Transferred (PL) to 17 WWS, 388 TFW, Korat RTAB, Thailand, to participate in Wild Weasel missions over North Vietnam during "Operation Linebacker I."
27 Sep 1972	In depot maintenance (WM) by field team from Warner Robins AMA at Korat RTAB, Thailand.
18 Oct 1972	Combat capable (CC) at 17 WWS, 388 TFW, Korat RTAB, Thailand.
22 Jan 1973	In depot maintenance (WM) by field team from SM- AMA at Korat RTAB, Thailand. (AVH-20).
24 Jan 1973	Combat capable (CC) at 17 WWS, 388 TFW, Korat RTAB, Thailand.
29 Oct 1974	One of ten F-105Gs transferred to the 35 TFW TAC, George AFB CA when the 17 WWS at Korat RTAB, Thailand, inactivated. (AVH-22).
23 Jan 1975	In depot maintenance (WM) by SM-ALC at George AFB CA. (AVH-23).
3 Feb 1975	At 35 TFW TAC, George AFB CA.
17 May 1975	Combat capable (CC) at 35 TFW TAC, George AFB CA. (AVH-24).
6 Nov 1976	Badly damaged by engine fire and a crash landing at Holloman AFB NM. Assigned to the 49 TFW. Assignment code: BL. 3,466 flying hours. Aircraft was "... later trucked to George AFB CA in five crates. More than 12,000 man-hours , $230,000, and parts from two F-105s in the scrap heap went into the rebuilding job, with MSgt. William E. Poole, quality assurance representative, working 18 months with technicians from Dynalectron Corporation. Col. James Jones and Capt. Jimmy Boyd took the aircraft on its 'maiden' flight' ... " from George AFB after a two-year reconstruction. (AVH-24 & Air Force Times, October 9, 1978, pg 38).
1 Mar 1977	In depot maintenance (DM) by SM-ALC at George AFB CA. 3,500 flying hours. (AVH-25 & AVH-26).
17 Mar 1978	In contract depot maintenance at 35 TFW, George AFB CA. (35 TFW/MA memo).
29 Aug 1978	At 35 TFW, George AFB CA. 3,497 flying hours. (AVH-26).

30 Sep 1978	At 35 TFW, George AFB CA. 3,498 flying hours. Possession code: "BQ," Ferried Aircraft.
2 Nov 1978	The fifth F-105G transferred from the 35 TFW, George AFB CA to the 116 TFW Georgia ANG, Dobbins AFB GA. (116 TFW History, Oct–Dec 1978, USAF microfilm 33958). Aircraft had accumulated 3,498 flying hours. (AVH-26).
8 Aug 1979	In contract depot maintenance (DK) by Fairchild Engine and Aircraft Corporation (FACCF) at Bob Sikes Municipal Airport, Crestview FL. 3,569.2 flying hours. (AVH-27).
2 Mar 1980	In contract depot maintenance (WK) by Fairchild Engine and Aircraft Corporation (FACCF) at Bob Sikes Municipal Airport, Crestview FL. 3,370.3 flying hours. (GO33B 24 Jun 80).
3 Mar 1980	Returned to 116 TFG ANG, Dobbins AFB GA. 3,370.3 flying hours.
24 Sep 1980	Deployed to Murted AB, Turkey, via Torrejon AB, Spain, with 128 TFS, GANG, under "Coronet Power." (British Aviation Review, Dec 1995).
12 Oct 1980	Returned from Turkey to Dobbins AFB GA.
23 Apr 1982	Sent to MASDC storage, Davis-Monthan AFB AZ. 4,001.7 flying hours. (GO33B 1 Feb 83).
1985/1986	One of two F-105s removed from MASDC (now renamed "AMARC") for display at the Air Force Combat Ammunition Center (AFCOMAC), Sierra Army Depot, Herlong CA. Following a study initiated by Lt Gen Leo Marquez, Hq USAF DCS Logistics and Engineering, the Air Force established AFCOMAC on 1 November 1985 as a munitions assembly procedures training school and a tenant at Sierra. The aircraft was parked outside for static display and marked with serial number "63-8332" and tail code "JB" that had been used by the 17 WWS when the squadron was assigned to the 388 TFW at Korat RTAB, Thailand, from 1972 to 1974.
1 Oct 1992	The Air Force directed that AFCOMAC relocate from Sierra Army Depot to Beale AFB CA. The organization left their two static-display F-105s at Sierra and they became U.S. Army property.
July 1999	The aft section of the aircraft was disconnected and the two sections of the plane were transported from Sierra Army Depot to the airport at Reno, Nevada, by an Army National Guard CH-47D "Chinook" helicopter during sling-load training by Detachment 1, Company G, 140th Aviation (the "Mustangs") from Stead, NV. The aircraft was saved from being sold as scrap when Mr. Al Reddick, owner of Advanced Aviation Services Co., Reno NV, arranged for the Army to transfer possession of both F-105s at Sierra to the U.S. Navy at NAS Fallon NV. (Telephone interview with Mr. Al Reddick, 8 October 1999.)

F-105F–1RE 63-8343

Republic Production No: F-120 Production Sequence No: 810

Location: Parked on the ramp of the Cavanaugh Flight Museum, Addison, Texas.

Aircraft Chronology

17 Sep 1964	USAF production acceptance from Republic Aviation, Farmingdale NY. (AVH-1).
18 Sep 1964	Delivered to 23 TFW, McConnell AFB KS.
26 Oct 1964	One of 19 F-105s (16 F-105Ds and 3 F-105Fs) flown by 561 TFS, 23 TFW, in "Operation Goldfire I" at Olathe Naval Air Station KS. (23 TFW Unit History 1/6/64–1/6/68. USAF microfilm MO554).
12 Nov 1964	Returned from "Goldfire I" to McConnell AFB KS.
12 Mar 1965	At McClellan AFB CA from 23 TFW for depot work (WO). (Safety Pack I Modification). (AVH-4).
13 Apr 1965	Returned to 23 TFW, McConnell AFB KS.

Apr 1965	Deployed on TDY to Kadena AB, Okinawa, with the 421 TFS, 355 TFW, from McConnell AFB KS. Assigned Crew Chief: SSgt. C. Smith. (18 TFW History, Jan–Jun 65, USAF microfilm MO497).
12 May 1965	On TDY at Takhli RTAB, Thailand, with the 563 TFS, 23 TFW. Supported from Yokota AB, Japan.
3 Aug 1965	Transferred to 4520 CCTW, Nellis AFB NV for combat crew training.
4 Jan 1966	At SMAMA. McClellan AFB CA for depot work (WO). (Safety Pack II Modification). (AVH-5).
10 Feb 1966	At 4520 CCTW, Nellis AFB NV for aircrew training (TF).
6 Feb 1967	In depot maintenance (WM) by SMAMA field team at Nellis AFB NV. (AVH-8).
9 Feb 1967	At 4520 CCTW, Nellis AFB NV for aircrew training (TF).
27 Mar 1967	Reassigned to 4525 FWW, Nellis AFB NV for aircrew training (TF).
4 Apr 1967	Returned to 4520 CCTW, Nellis AFB NV for aircrew training (TF).
23 Aug 1967	In depot maintenance (WM) by SMAMA field team at Nellis AFB NV.
28 Aug 1967	At 4520 CCTW, Nellis AFB NV for aircrew training (TF).
20 Dec 1967	Transferred to 23 TFW, McConnell AFB KS for aircrew training (TF).
16 Apr 1968	Deployed to George AFB CA with the 563 TFS, 23 TFW, for air-to-air gunnery training for F-105 RTU class 68IR. (AVH-10).
18 Apr 1968	At 23 TFW McConnell AFB KS for combat crew training (TF).
15 May 1968	In depot maintenance (WM) by SMAMA at McConnell AFB KS.
17 May 1968	At 23 TFW McConnell AFB KS for combat crew training (TF).
21 Apr 1969	In depot maintenance (WO) at SMAMA, McClellan AFB CA. (AVH-12).
13 May 1969	Returned to 23 TFW, McConnell AFB KS.
24 Jul 1970	In depot maintenance (WO) at SMAMA, McClellan AFB CA. (AVH-14).
24 Nov 1970	Returned to 23 TFW, McConnell AFB KS.
4 May 1971	In contract depot maintenance (WK) by Fairchild Engine and Aircraft Corporation (FACCF) at Bob Sikes Municipal Airport, Crestview FL. (AVH-16).
27 May 1971	Returned to 23 TFW, McConnell AFB KS.
1 Mar 1972	Carried on assignment roster with the 562 TFS, 23 TFW, at McConnell AFB KS. (Master 23 TFW Aircraft Assignment as of 1 March 1972).
22 Jun 1972	Departed 23 TFW, McConnell AFB KS. (AVH-18).
23 Jun 1972	In contract depot maintenance (WK) by Fairchild Engine and Aircraft Corporation (FACCF) at Bob Sikes Municipal Airport, Crestview FL.
26 Jul 1972	Transferred to 57 FWW, Nellis AFB NV for combat crew training (TF).
22 Feb 1973	In depot work (WM) by SM-ALC at Nellis AFB NV. (AVH-20).
23 Feb 1973	Returned to 57 FWW, Nellis AFB NV for combat crew training (TF).
31 Aug 1973	In depot maintenance (WO) by SM-ALC at McClellan AFB CA.
21 Dec 1973	Returned to 57 FWW, Nellis AFB NV for combat crew training (TF).
31 Mar 1974	At 57 FWW, Nellis AFB NV for combat crew training (TF). (AVH-22).
24 Jul 1975	Transferred to 35 TFW, George AFB CA for combat crew training (TF). (AVH-23 & AVH-24).
5 Nov 1975	Transferred to 113 TFW ANG, Andrews AFB MD.
3 Jan 1976	At 113 TFW ANG, Andrews AFB MD.
15 Jan 1976	Transferred back to 35 TFW, George AFB CA for combat crew training (TF).
5 Aug 1977	In depot maintenance by SM-ALC at George AFB CA. 3,648.0 flying hours. (AVH-25 & AVH-26).
19 Aug 1977	At 35 TFW TAC, George AFB CA. 3,667.0 flying hours.
8 Jan 1978	In depot maintenance by SM-ALC at George AFB CA. 3,733.0 flying hours. (AVH-26).
17 Mar 1978	Aircraft grounded at George AFB CA due to cracks in main landing gear wing rib found during inspection required by TCTO 1F-105-1281. (35 TFW/MA memo).

This "F" is in temporary custody of the Cavanaugh Flight Museum, near Dallas, Texas. It arrived at the 23 Tactical Fighter Wing, McConnell Air Force Base, Kansas, in September 1964. In May 1965, it flew combat missions with the 563 Tactical Fighter Squadron at Takhli, Thailand, on temporary duty from McConnell. When the 563rd returned home in early August 1965, the plane went to Nellis Air Force Base, Nevada, where it began the first of several pilot-training assignments over the next fourteen years. In 1980, it moved to the Air Force Reserve's 457 Tactical Fighter Squadron at Carswell Air Force Base, Texas. While with the 457th, the plane developed a persistent fuel leak that the squadron could not fix. They retired the plane in the early 1980s and it became part of the aircraft collection parked outside the General Dynamics plant adjacent to Carswell. After the company gave up its collection in the early 1990s, their F-105F was stored in a hanger at Addison Airport, north of Dallas. In 1994, an aircraft restoration company, even though they did not own it, attempted unsuccessfully (and unrealistically) to restore the plane to flying condition for demonstrations at airshows. In 1996, the Aviation Heritage Museum that had acquired the General Dynamics collection, loaned the plane to the Cavanaugh Flight Museum adjacent to the Addison Airport. At some point, the names of two F-105 pilots killed in the Vietnam war were added to its canopy rails. "Capt. Ned Miller," the name on the front canopy, died on 12 November 1965 when his F-105D exploded over Thailand due to a bomb fuze malfunction enroute to North Vietnam. "Capt. Don C. Wood," the name on the rear canopy, died on 16 January 1966 when anti-aircraft fire shot down his F-105D over Laos. (Photograph by author, 13 July 1995.)

17 Apr 1978	At 35 TFW TAC, George AFB CA. 3,733.0 flying hours.
4 Aug 1978	In depot maintenance by SM-ALC at George AFB CA. 3,847.0 flying hours.
4 Oct 1978	At 35 TFW TAC, George AFB CA. 3,867.0 flying hours.
12 Jun 1979	In depot maintenance by Sacramento ALC at George AFB CA. 3,934.8 flying hours. (AVH-27).
3 Aug 1979	At 35 TFW TAC, George AFB CA for student and combat crew training (TF). 3,947.6 flying hours.
11 Jul 1980	At 457 TFS AFRES, Carswell AFB TX. 4,075.7 flying hours. (GO33B 22 Jan 81).
12 Jun 1981	At 457 TFS AFRES, Carswell AFB TX. 4,099.6 flying hours. (GO33B Dec 81 & GO33B 1 Feb 83).
20 Sep 1981	At 457 TFS AFRES, Carswell AFB TX. 4,101.9 flying hours. Aircraft experienced a fuel leak that the unit could not repair. Despite many hours of troubleshooting and several test flights, the leak persisted until the plane retired. (CMSgt. Charlie Ashley, 301 Maint. Sq., Interview, Aug 1995).
1986	At Southwest Museum outside General Dynamics plant at Fort Worth TX. (Flypast #54, Jan 1986)

May 1994	In hanger at Addison Airport TX. Being worked on by company named "Sierra Hotel" that was attempting to restore aircraft to flyable condition for airshows. (Telephone interview with David Strait).
12 Jul 1995	Parked on ramp near Million Air FBO, Addison Airport, Addison TX. Awaiting disposition by Aviation Heritage Museum. Lacked engine and several aft fuselage parts. "TH" tail code. Names on canopy rails: Front—"Capt. Ned Miller." Rear—"Capt. Don C. Wood." (Personal visit & interview with Mr. Ed Petrushka, Museum Director).
10 May 1996	Parked on ramp at Cavanaugh Flight Museum, Addison TX. Still awaiting disposition by Aviation Heritage Museum. (Benjamin Kristy, Curator, Cavanaugh Flight Museum).

F-105G-1RE 63-8345

Republic Production No: F-122 Production Sequence No: 812

Location: Stored by the Air National Guard at Robins AFB, Warner-Robins, Georgia.

Aircraft Name(s)	Crew	Unit	Date	Description
The Buckeye Avenger	Capt. Marty Noel/ Capt. Jim Weaver	561 TFS	Nov 72	Outline of Ohio & name in red on top of C/L pylon; later on left intake.

Aircraft Chronology

28 Sep 1964	USAF production acceptance from Republic Aviation, Farmingdale NY. (AVH-1).
1 Oct 1964	Delivered to 355 TFW, McConnell AFB KS. (AVH-2).
16 Mar 1965	At SMAMA, McClellan AFB CA for depot work (WO). (AVH-4).
11 Apr 1965	Returned to 355 TFW, McConnell AFB KS.
20 Oct 1965	Transferred to 23 TFW, McConnell AFB KS.
20 May 1966	At MOAMA, Brookley AFB AL for depot work (WO). (AVH-5).
26 May 1966	Returned to 23 TFW, McConnell AFB KS.
18 Oct 1966	At SMAMA, McClellan AFB CA for depot work (WO).
14 Nov 1966	Transferred to 4525 FWW, Nellis AFB NV.
31 May 1967	At 4525 FWW, Nellis AFB NV for combat crew training (TF). (AVH-8).
31 Jan 1968	At Osan AB, Korea, with 4525 FWW in response to the U.S.S. Pueblo incident. (AVH-10).
28 Jul 1968	At Kwangju AB, Korea, with 4525 FWW.
5 Aug 1968	At Kadena AB, Okinawa, for depot-level work (WM) by SMAMA field team.
11 Aug 1968	Returned to Kwangju AB, Korea, with 4525 FWW.
31 Aug 1968	At Kadena AB, Okinawa, with 4525 FWW.
2 Nov 1968	Transferred to 18 TFW, Kadena AB, Okinawa.
3 Feb 1969	At Kwangju AB, Korea, with 18 TFW. (AVH-12).
10 May 1969	Returned to 18 TFW, Kadena AB, Okinawa.
15 May 1969	At Kwangju AB, Korea, with 18 TFW.
24 Jun 1969	Returned to 18 TFW, Kadena AB, Okinawa.
1 Jul 1969	At Kwangju AB, Korea, with 18 TFW.
15 Jul 1969	Returned to 18 TFW, Kadena AB, Okinawa.

During its career, this "G" made four trips to Asia and one to Europe. After production in October 1964, it joined the 355 Tactical Fighter Wing at McConnell Air Force Base, Kansas. When the 355th moved to Takhli a year later, the plane transferred to the 23 Tactical Fighter Wing also at McConnell. The 4525 Fighter Weapons Wing at Nellis Air Force Base, Nevada, acquired it in November 1966. In January 1968, the plane accompanied Wild Weasel crews from Nellis who abruptly deployed to Osan, Korea, when the North Koreans captured the U.S.S. Pueblo. For the next two years, the plane traveled between Korea for alert duties and Okinawa for maintenance. In November 1969, the plane rejoined the 355th now flying combat from Takhli, Thailand. During its two and a half months at Takhli, it upgraded to a "G," then in June 1970, moved back to the 23rd at McConnell. Less than a year later, the plane flew across the Pacific to Korat, Thailand, for Wild Weasel missions with the 388 Tactical Fighter Wing. In 1972, it joined the 561 Tactical Fighter Squadron at McConnell. This Wild Weasel unit flew the plane on its fourth trip to Asia when they deployed to Korat in October 1972 for the final phases of the Vietnam war. In November 1972, the plane returned to McConnell, transferring in June 1973 to the 35 Tactical Fighter Wing at George Air Force Base, California. The 35th flew the plane to Denmark in August 1977, and, in February 1969, transferred it to the Air National Guard at Dobbins Air Force Base, Georgia. The Georgia Guard retired it less than a year later due to cracked wings. The Guard swapped its good tail section with a damaged one from F-105G 62-4425 before putting 63-8345 on display at Dobbins (its location in the photo). In Apr 1996, the Guard moved south to Robins Air Force Base to fly the B-1B. They retrieved their static displays at Dobbins in May 2000 and stored them until they can be restored for display in their new home. (Photograph by John Coon, 28 August 1998.)

18 Aug 1969	At Kwangju AB, Korea, with 18 TFW.
21 Aug 1969	Returned to 18 TFW, Kadena AB, Okinawa.
2 Oct 1969	At Kwangju AB, Korea, with 18 TFW.
3 Oct 1969	Returned to 18 TFW, Kadena AB, Okinawa.
6 Oct 1969	At Kwangju AB, Korea, with 18 TFW.
8 Oct 1969	Returned to 18 TFW, Kadena AB, Okinawa.
12 Nov 1969	Transferred to 355 TFW, Takhli RTAB, Thailand.
18 Dec 1969	Redesignated F-105G at 355 TFW, Takhli RTAB, Thailand.
31 Jan 1970	In depot work (WO) at SMAMA, McClellan AFB CA. (AVH-14).
23 Jun 1970	Transferred to 23 TFW, McConnell AFB KS.
12 Jan 1971	At 23 TFW, McConnell AFB KS being prepared for transfer (PL) to depot. (AVH-16).
16 Jan 1971	In depot maintenance (WK) by Fairchild Engine and Aircraft Corporation (FACCF) at Bob Sikes Municipal Airport, Crestview FL.
9 Feb 1971	Returned to 23 TFW, McConnell AFB KS.
15 Mar 1971	Transferred (PL) to 388 TFW, Korat RTAB, Thailand.

11 Dec 1971	Parked on flightline at Nakhon Phanom RTAB, Thailand, with tail code "ZB" (17 WWS). Aircraft was loaded with two AGM-45s on outboard pylons and an AGM-78 on right inboard pylon with tanks on centerline and left inboard pylons. (Ted Fandel record card).
6 Jul 1972	Departed (PL) 388 TFW, Korat RTAB, Thailand. (AVH-18).
25 Jul 1972	Transferred to 57 FWW, Nellis AFB NV for combat crew training (TF).
11 Aug 1972	In depot maintenance (WK) by Fairchild Engine and Aircraft Corporation (FACCF) at Bob Sikes Municipal Airport, Crestview FL.
6 Sep 1972	Returned to 57 FWW, Nellis AFB NV for combat crew training (TF).
14 Aug 1972	Transferred to 561 TFS (TAC), McConnell AFB KS.
22 Oct 1972	Deployed with 561 TFS to Korat RTAB, Thailand, under "Constant Guard I."
6 Nov 1972	Returned to 561 TFS, McConnell AFB KS with stops at Guam, Hickam, and Nellis. Crew was Capt. Marty Noel, pilot, and Capt. Jim Weaver, EWO. (Marty Noel, e-mail, 4 Nov 1999).
14 Feb 1973	At 561 TFS, McConnell AFB KS. (AVH-20).
28 Mar 1973	In depot maintenance (WO) by SM-ALC at McClellan AFB CA.
29 Jun 1973	Transferred (PL) to 35 TFW, George AFB CA.
29 Mar 1974	In depot maintenance (WM) by SM-ALC at George AFB CA. (AVH-22).
5 Apr 1974	At 35 TFW, George AFB CA.
24 May 1974	At Shaw AFB SC with 35 TFW from George AFB CA.
7 Jun 1974	Returned to 35 TFW, George AFB CA.
15 Sep 1974	In depot maintenance (WM) by SM-ALC at George AFB CA.
21 Sep 1974	At 35 TFW, George AFB CA.
17 May 1976	In depot work (DO & DR) by SM-ALC at McClellan AFB CA. 4,059 flying hours. (AVH-24).
2 Sep 1976	Returned to 35 TFW, George AFB CA. 4,087 flying hours.
12 Aug 1977	Deployed with 561 TFS under "Coronet Club" to Karup AB, Denmark, from the 35 TFW, George AFB CA. 4,246.0 flying hours. (AVH-25 & AVH-26).
30 Aug 1977	Returned from Denmark to George AFB CA.
17 Mar 1978	Aircraft had flight restrictions at George AFB CA due to cracks in main landing gear wing rib found during inspection required by TCTO 1F-105-1281. "...Restricted to 47,500 lb. gross takeoff weight, 10 knots crosswind component, 4 G's symmetrical and 2.5 G's rolling." (35 TFW/MA memo).
25 Sep 1978	In depot maintenance by SM-ALC at George AFB CA. 4,572.0 flying hours.
4 Oct 1978	At 35 TFW TAC, George AFB CA. 4,578.0 flying hours.
6 Dec 1978	In depot maintenance by SM-ALC at George AFB CA. 4,587.4 flying hours.
20 Feb 1979	Transferred to the 116 TFW ANG, Dobbins AFB GA. 4,603.0 flying hours.
2 Nov 1979	In contract depot maintenance (DYNFW) at McConnell AFB KS. 4,705.0 flying hours.
19 Nov 1979	At 116 TFW ANG, Dobbins AFB GA. 4,705.0 flying hours.
28 Nov 1979	At 116 TFG ANG, Dobbins AFB GA. 4,708.2 flying hours. Aircraft grounded due to wing cracks. Being assigned to a museum (ZW). (GO33B 24 Jun 80).
1981/1982	Tail section swapped with the one from F-105G 62-4425 that had been damaged in a night landing accident at Dobbins AFB GA. Aircraft placed on a pedestal for display marked with "425's" tail number in honor of USAF instructor pilot Major Jimmy "Stache" Boyd who flew "425" in SEA. (SMSgt Jerry L. Powell, 116 BW GA ANG, e-mail 27 July 2000).
11 May 2000	Aircraft disassembled and removed from its pedestal at Dobbins and trucked to Robins AFB GA. Stored pending restoration and display at the GA ANG area of the 116 Bomb Wing (B-1Bs) at Robins.

F-105F-1RE 63-8357

Republic Production No: F-134 Production Sequence No: 824

Location: Displayed by Musee du Chateau de Savigny in Savigny-les-Beaune near Dijon, France.

Aircraft Chronology

27 Oct 1964	USAF production acceptance from Republic Aviation, Farmingdale NY. (AVH-2).
30 Oct 1964	Delivered to 355 TFW, McConnell AFB, KS.
13 Apr 1965	At SMAMA, McClellan AFB CA for depot work (WO). (AVH-4).
1 May 1965	Returned to 355 TFW, McConnell AFB, KS.
18 May 1965	Transferred to 4520 CCTW, Nellis AFB NV.
21 Jul 1965	Assigned to combat crew training (TF) at 4520 CCTW, Nellis AFB NV.
20 Dec 1965	At SMAMA, McClellan AFB CA for depot work (WO).
18 Jan 1966	At 4520 CCTW, Nellis AFB NV for aircrew training (TF). (AVH-5).
12 Jan 1967	In depot work (WM) by SMAMA field team at Nellis AFB NV. (AVH-8).
17 Jan 1967	At 4520 CCTW, Nellis AFB NV for aircrew training (TF).
27 Aug 1967	In depot work (WM) by SMAMA field team at Nellis AFB NV.
25 Oct 1967	At 4520 CCTW, Nellis AFB NV for aircrew training (TF).
20 Dec 1967	Transferred to 23 TFW, McConnell AFB KS for combat crew training (TF).
23 Jan 1968	Deployed to George AFB CA with the 561 TFS, 23 TFW, for air-to-air gunnery training for RTU Class 68FR. (AVH-10).
4 Feb 1968	Returned to 23 TFW, McConnell AFB KS for combat crew training (TF).
21 Apr 1968	Joined the 563 TFS, 23 TFW, already deployed to George AFB CA for air-to-air gunnery training for RTU Class 68IR.
9 May 1968	Returned to 23 TFW, McConnell AFB KS for combat crew training (TF).
29 Sep 1969	In depot maintenance (WO) at SMAMA, McClellan AFB CA. (AVH-12).
6 Jan 1970	Returned to 23 TFW (PL), McConnell AFB KS. (AVH-14).
14 Jan 1970	At 23 TFW, McConnell AFB KS for combat crew training (TF).
12 Jan 1971	In contract depot maintenance (WK) by Fairchild Engine and Aircraft Corporation (FACCF) at Bob Sikes Municipal Airport, Crestview FL. (AVH-16).
5 Feb 1971	Returned (PL) to 23 TFW, McConnell AFB KS.
9 Feb 1971	Assigned to aircrew training (TF) at 23 TFW, McConnell AFB KS.
11 Feb 1971	Assigned to combat duties (CC) at 23 TFW, McConnell AFB KS.
26 May 1971	While assigned to the 23 TFW, McConnell AFB KS, for unknown causes the aircraft lost the DART tow target during takeoff. The aircraft was not damaged. (23 TFW History, Apr–Jun 71, USAF microfilm MO556).
30 Jun 1971	Transferred (PL) to 113 TFG ANG, Andrews AFB MD.
6 Jul 1971	Operationally ready (CC) at 113 TFG ANG, Andrews AFB MD.
17 May 1972	In depot maintenance (WO) by SM-ALC, McClellan AFB CA. (AVH-18).
2 Oct 1972	Returned (PL) to 113 TFG ANG, Andrews AFB MD.
16 Apr 1973	In contract depot maintenance (WM) by Dynalectron Corporation (DYNZZ) at Andrews AFB MD. (AVH-20).
17 Apr 1973	At 113 TFG ANG, Andrews AFB MD.
18 Jun 1973	In contract depot maintenance (WM) by Dynalectron Corporation (DYNZZ) at Andrews AFB MD.

This "F" is another two-seat Thunderchief that remained a trainer all its career. After delivery to the 355 Tactical Fighter Wing in October 1964, it stayed only a few months at McConnell Air Force Base, Kansas, before moving to Nellis Air Force Base, Nevada. It returned to McConnell in December 1967, this time with the 23 Tactical Fighter Wing. In June 1971, it transferred to the DC Air National Guard at Andrews Air Force, Maryland, who flew it for the next ten years. The Guard retired it to desert storage in July 1981. Four years later it was shipped to Hahn Air Base, Germany, as a battle-damage repair trainer. At some point, it was sold as scrap from Hahn to a private aviation museum in Germany who later traded it to another private museum in France. (Photograph by Peter Yearsley, 16 June 1999.)

2 Jul 1973	At 113 TFG ANG, Andrews AFB MD.
12 Jul 1973	In contract depot maintenance (WM) by Dynalectron Corporation (DYNZZ) at Andrews AFB MD.
27 Jul 1973	At 113 TFG ANG, Andrews AFB MD.
24 Oct 1973	In depot maintenance (WO & WR) by SM-ALC at McClellan AFB CA.
27 Feb 1974	Returned to 113 TFG ANG, Andrews AFB MD. (AVH-22).
30 Nov 1974	Assigned unit redesignated 113 TFW ANG, Andrews AFB MD.
13 Feb 1975	In contract depot maintenance (WM) by Dynalectron Corporation (DYNZZ) at Andrews AFB MD. (AVH-23).
24 Feb 1975	At 113 TFW ANG, Andrews AFB MD.
9 Mar 1977	In depot maintenance by SM-ALC at Andrews AFB MD. 3,164.0 flying hours. (AVH-25 & AVH-26).
16 Mar 1977	At 113 TFW ANG at Andrews AFB MD. 3,164.0 flying hours.
16 Nov 1978	At 113 TFW ANG at Andrews AFB MD. 3,564.0 flying hours. (AVH-26).
27 Apr 1979	In contract depot maintenance by Dynalectron Corporation (DYNZZ) at Andrews AFB MD. 3,579.8 flying hours. (AVH-27).
13 Jul 1979	At 113 TFW ANG Andrews AFB MD. 3,583.3 flying hours.
10 Jul 1981	Sent to storage at MASDC, Davis-Monthan AFB AZ. 3,882 flying hours. (MASDC Aircraft Status Directory, 30 Jun 84).

20 Dec 1982 Still in storage at MASDC, Davis-Monthan AFB AZ, (XX- Low probability of withdrawal). 3,856.2 flying hours. (GO33B 1 Feb 83).

24 Oct 1984 Removed from MASDC storage and shipped to Hahn AB, Germany, as ABDR trainer. (John Coon's list, 24 Mar 87).

22 May 1985 At 50 TFW, Hahn AB, Germany, for ABDR training. (HQ 2852 ABG/DADF Letter 22 May 85).

Turned in to salvage yard at Hahn AB, Germany.

Purchased as scrap for display at private museum (Flaugausstellung Leo Und Peter Junior) in Hermeskeil, Germany.

24 Aug 1995 Traded by museum in Hermeskeil, Germany, to private museum in Savigny-les-Beaune near Dijon, France. (David Wilton, BARG, in letter to author, 1 Jul 1996).

F-105G–1RE 63-8363

Republic Production No: F-140 Production Sequence No: 830

Location: Possessed by the Texas Air Museum in San Antonio, Texas.

Aircraft Chronology

30 Dec 1964 USAF production acceptance from Republic Aviation, Farmingdale NY. (AVH-2).

31 Dec 1964 At MOAMA, Brookley AFB AL for depot work. (AVH-4).

15 Jan 1965 Delivered to 18 TFW, Kadena AB, Okinawa.

31 Jan 1965 At 18 TFW, Kadena AB, Okinawa. Assigned crew chief: A1C J. Argot. (18 TFW History, Jan–Jun 65, USAF microfilm MO497).

18 May 1965 At Air Asia, Tainan Airport, Taiwan, for contract depot work (WK).

3 Jun 1965 Returned to 18 TFW, Kadena AB, Okinawa.

6 Oct 1965 At Air Asia (AAITT) Tainan Airport, Taiwan, for contract depot work (WK).

26 Oct 1965 Returned to 18 TFW, Kadena AB, Okinawa.

30 Nov 1965 At 18 TFW, Kadena AB, Okinawa. Assigned crew chief: A1C J. Argot. (18 TFW History, Jul–Dec 65, USAF microfilm MO497).

2 Jun 1966 At Air Asia (AAITT) Tainan Airport, Taiwan, for contract depot work (WK). (AVH-5).

14 Jun 1966 Returned to 18 TFW, Kadena AB, Okinawa.

20 Oct 1966 In depot maintenance (WM) by SMAMA at Kadena AB, Okinawa.

24 Oct 1966 At 18 TFW, Kadena AB, Okinawa.

31 Dec 1966 While assigned to the 18 TFW, Kadena AB, Okinawa, the aircraft flew 19 hours during the month of December 1966 and had accumulated 642 flying hours. (18 TFW History, Jul–Dec 66, USAF microfilm MO498).

19 Sep 1967 In depot maintenance (WM) by SMAMA at Kadena AB, Okinawa. (AVH-8).

20 Sep 1967 At 18 TFW, Kadena AB, Okinawa.

25 Sep 1967 In depot maintenance (WM) by SMAMA at Kadena AB, Okinawa.

6 Oct 1967 At 18 TFW, Kadena AB, Okinawa.

30 Nov 1967 In depot maintenance (WM) by SMAMA at Kadena AB, Okinawa.

6 Dec 1967 At 18 TFW, Kadena AB, Okinawa.

29 Jan 1968 In depot maintenance (WM) by SMAMA at Kadena AB, Okinawa. (AVH-10).

F-105F 63-8363 went from Republic's production line to Kadena Air Base, Okinawa, in January 1965, the next-to-last new F-105 the 18 Tactical Fighter Wing received. It remained with the 18th for three years and transferred as a Wild Weasel attrition replacement to the 388 Tactical Fighter Wing at Korat, Thailand. It stayed at Korat throughout 1968 but, two months after President Johnson halted the bombing of North Vietnam, transferred to McConnell Air Force Base, Kansas, where it supported the 23 Tactical Fighter Wing's Replacement Training Unit. The 23rd flew the plane until January 1972 then transferred it to the depot to become an F-105G. In September 1972, it went to Nellis Air Force Base, Nevada, where it trained Wild Weasel pilots for South East Asia. In July 1975, after the Vietnam war ended, 63-8363 joined the rest of the Wild Weasel Thunderchiefs at the 35 Tactical Fighter Wing at George Air Force Base, California. In the summer of 1977, it was one of eighteen "Gs" the 35th deployed to Denmark for a two-week NATO exercise. In April 1979, the 35th turned the plane over to the Georgia Air National Guard at Dobbins Air Force Base outside Atlanta. It returned to George as a representative of the Georgia Guard in the summer of 1980 for the F-105 "Sawadee," a party and ceremony commemorating the departure of the last F-105 from active duty. It served with the Georgia Guard until November 1982 when it flew to the "Boneyard" at Davis-Monthan Air Force Base, Arizona. It stayed in desert storage until August 1985 when it was shipped to San Antonio, Texas. For years, it was parked at Brooks Air Force Base as an Aircraft Battle Damage Repair trainer for the Combat Logistics Support Squadron at Kelly Air Force Base. On the day it was scheduled for destruction in 1997, it escaped the scrap yard when the Texas Air Museum acquired it for eventual display at one of their locations. (Photograph by Dr. Carroll Brown, 31 May 1998.)

2 Feb 1968	At 18 TFW, Kadena AB, Okinawa.
21 Feb 1968	Transferred (PL) to 388 TFW, Korat RTAB, Thailand.
22 Feb 1968	Combat capable (CC) at 388 TFW, Korat RTAB, Thailand. (388 TFW History, Jan–Mar 68, USAF microfilm NO584).
24 May 1968	In depot maintenance (WM) by SMAMA at Korat RTAB, Thailand. (AVH-10).
26 May 1968	At 388 TFW, Korat RTAB, Thailand.
27 Jul 1968	In depot maintenance (WM) by SMAMA at Korat RTAB, Thailand.
21 Aug 1968	At 388 TFW, Korat RTAB, Thailand.
9 Dec 1968	At 388 TFW, Korat RTAB, Thailand, being prepared for transfer (PL).
20 Dec 1968	Transferred to (PL) 23 TFW, McConnell AFB KS.
3 Jan 1969	At 23 TFW, McConnell AFB KS for combat crew training (TF). (AVH-12).
10 May 1971	Assigned to combat duties (CC) at 23 TFW, McConnell AFB KS. (AVH-16).
25 May 1971	At 23 TFW, McConnell AFB KS being prepared for transfer (PL).
27 May 1971	In contract depot work (WK) by Fairchild Engine and Aircraft Corporation (FACCF) at Bob Sikes Municipal Airport, Crestview FL.
18 Jun 1971	Returned (PL) to 23 TFW, McConnell AFB KS.
23 Jun 1971	Combat capable (CC) at 23 TFW, McConnell AFB KS.

19 Jan 1972	At 23 TFW, McConnell AFB KS being prepared for transfer (PL). (AVH-18).
1 Mar 1972	Carried on assignment roster for the 561 TFS, 23 TFW, at McConnell AFB KS as having "Combat Nail" configuration. (Master 23 TFW Aircraft Assignment as of 1 March 1972).
20 Jan 1972	In depot work (WO) by SM-ALC at McClellan AFB CA. Modified from F-105F to F-105G.
12 Sep 1972	Transferred (PL) as F-105G to 57 FWW, Nellis AFB NV for combat crew training (TF).
2 Nov 1972	At 57 FWW, Nellis AFB NV being prepared for transfer to depot (PL).
3 Nov 1972	In contract depot work (WK) by Fairchild Engine and Aircraft Corporation (FACCF) at Bob Sikes Municipal Airport, Crestview FL.
30 Nov 1972	Returned (PL) to 57 FWW, Nellis AFB NV for combat crew training (TF).
20 Feb 1973	In depot maintenance (WM) by SM-ALC at Nellis AFB NV. (AVH-20).
21 Feb 1973	At 57 FWW, Nellis AFB NV for combat crew training (TF).
31 Mar 1973	In depot work (WQ) by SM-ALC at Nellis AFB NV.
31 May 1973	At 57 FWW, Nellis AFB NV being prepared for transfer (PL).
1 Jun 1973	In depot work (WO) by SM-ALC at McClellan AFB CA.
23 Aug 1973	Returned (PL) to 57 FWW, Nellis AFB NV.
28 Aug 1973	At 57 FWW, Nellis AFB NV for combat crew training (TF).
10 Sep 1974	In depot maintenance (WM) by SM-ALC at Nellis AFB NV. (AVH-22).
28 Mar 1975	At 57 FWW, Nellis AFB NV for combat crew training (TF). (AVH-23).
17 Jul 1975	Transferred to the 35 TFW, George AFB CA for combat crew training (TF). (AVH-23 & AVH-24).
8 Aug 1977	Deployed with 561 TFS under "Coronet Club" to Karup AB, Denmark, from 35 TFW, George AFB CA. 3,038 flying hours. (British Aviation Review, Dec 95 & AVH-25).
30 Aug 1977	Returned from Denmark to George AFB CA.
13 Mar 1978	At Seymour Johnson AFB NC with the 35 TFW from George AFB CA. 3, 153.0 flying hours. (AVH 26).
21 Mar 1978	Returned to the 35 TFW, George AFB CA. 3,166.0 flying hours.
20 Jun 1978	At Eglin AFB FL with the 35 TFW from George AFB CA. 3,354 flying hours.
27 Jun 1978	Returned to the 35 TFW, George AFB CA. 3,354.0 flying hours.
7 Jul 1978	At Nellis AFB NV with the 35 TFW, George AFB CA. 3,354.0 flying hours.
21 Jul 1978	Returned to the 35 TFW, George AFB CA. 3,374.0 flying hours.
25 Sep 1978	In depot maintenance (DM) by SM-ALC at George AFB CA. 3,4070 flying hours.
19 Oct 1978	At 35 TFW, George AFB CA. 3,414.0 flying hours.
10 Jan 1979	In depot maintenance (DM) by SM-ALC at George AFB CA. 3,436.0 flying hours. (AVH-27).
24 Apr 1979	At 13:00 hours possessed by the 35 TFW, George AFB CA. At 14:00 hours, transferred to the 116 TFW ANG, Dobbins AFB GA. 3,437.9 flying hours.
27 Sep 1979	In depot maintenance by SM-ALC at Dobbins AFB GA. 3,482.7 flying hours.
12 Oct 1979	At 116 TFW ANG, Dobbins AFB GA. 3,482.7 flying hours.
13 Dec 1979	In contract depot maintenance by General Dynamics (DYNFW) at Dobbins AFB GA. 3,482.7 flying hours.
6 Mar 1980	At 116 TFG ANG, Dobbins AFB GA. 3,482.7 flying hours. (GO33B 24 Jun 80).
12 Jul 1980	With the 116 TFG ANG at George AFB CA for the retirement ceremony of the F-105 from the active duty USAF. (Airpower Magazine, Jan 81).
1 Nov 1982	Sent to MASDC storage, Davis-Monthan AFB AZ. 3,890.2 flying hours, later corrected to 3,908.3 flying hours. Inventory account: "XV"—Recommended Reclamation, later changed to "XX"—Low Probability of Withdrawal. (MASDC Aircraft Status Directory, 30 Jun 84 & GO33B 1 Feb 83 and 9 Feb 84).
21 Aug 1985	Withdrawn from MASDC storage to Brooks AFB TX for ABDR training.
5 May 1997	Allocated to Texas Air Museum, Rio Hondo, Texas. (John Houston, Director Texas Air Museum, telephone interview, 15 May 1997).

4 Aug 1997	Aircraft to remain stored in San Antonio TX pending decision on permanent location by Texas Air Museum. (Telephone interview with John Tosh, Texas Air Museum).

F-105F-1RE 63-8365

Republic Production No: F-142 Production Sequence No: 832

Location: Parked at Tinker AFB, Oklahoma.

Aircraft Chronology

30 Nov 1964	USAF production acceptance from Republic Aviation, Farmingdale NY. (AVH-2).
30 Nov 1964	Delivered to the 18 TFW, Kadena AB, Okinawa.
5 Jan 1965	At MOAMA, Brookley AFB AL for depot work (WO). (AVH-4).
31 Jan 1965	At 18 TFW, Kadena AB, Okinawa. Assigned crew chief: A1C L. Schmitt. (18 TFW History, Jan–Jun 65, USAF microfilm MO497).
23 Mar 1965	At Air Asia, Tainan, Taiwan, for contract depot work (WK).
6 Apr 1965	Returned to 18 TFW, Kadena AB, Okinawa.
16 Aug 1965	At Air Asia, Tainan, Taiwan, for contract depot work (WK).
19 Sep 1965	Returned to 18 TFW, Kadena AB, Okinawa.
30 Nov 1965	At 18 TFW, Kadena AB, Okinawa. Assigned crew chief: SSgt. F. Amidon. (18 TFW History, Jul–Dec 65, USAF microfilm MO497).

F-105F 63-8365 was the next to the last F-105 built and has languished for years in a storage yard at Tinker Air Force Base, Oklahoma. It started its career in November 1964 with the 18 TFW at Kadena Air Base, Okinawa, where it stayed until it transferred in August 1967 to the 23 Tactical Fighter Wing at McConnell Air Force Base, Kansas. It supported McConnell's F-105 Replacement Training Unit program until July 1972 when the 23rd moved to England Air Force Base, Louisiana, to fly A-7s. The plane then transferred to the Reserve's 465 Tactical Fighter Squadron at Tinker. During its years with the 465th, it deployed to Europe three times on a series of CORONET exercises for NATO. When the 465th converted to F-4Ds in 1980, "365" moved to their sister Reserve unit, the 466 Tactical Fighter Squadron at Hill Air Force Base, Utah. The 466th was the last unit to fly F-105s and, in early 1984, the first Reserve unit to convert to F-16As. The plane arrived at Tinker sometime between March 1983 and April 1984 where it was used for Battle Damage Repair training. It is shown awaiting disposition by the Air Force Museum. (Photograph by Ronald L. Shepard, 1 April 1998.)

22 Jun 1966	At 18 TFW, Kadena AB, Okinawa. (AVH-5).
24 Oct 1966	In depot maintenance (WM) by SMAMA field team at Kadena AB, Okinawa.
28 Oct 1966	At 18 TFW, Kadena AB, Okinawa.
31 Dec 1966	While assigned to the 18 TFW, Kadena AB, Okinawa, the aircraft flew 10 hours during the month of December 1966 and had accumulated 644 flying hours. (18 TFW History, Jul–Dec 66, USAF microfilm MO498).
13 Mar 1967	While assigned to the 18 TFW, Kadena AB, Okinawa, the aircraft lost the DART gunnery target with part of the tow adapter during flight. The cause of the incident was undetermined. (18 TFW History, Jan–Mar 67, USAF microfilm MO498).
22 Mar 1967	Transferred from the 12 TFS, 18 TFW, Kadena AB, Okinawa, to the 41 AD, Yokota AB, Japan. Aircraft had accumulated 694 flying hours. (AVH-8 & 18 TFW History, Jan–Mar 67, USAF microfilm MO498).
14 Aug 1967	Transferred to the 23 TFW, McConnell AFB KS. (AVH-8).
9 Sep 1967	In depot maintenance (WM) by SMAMA field team at McConnell AFB KS.
12 Sep 1967	At 23 TFW, McConnell AFB KS.
3 Oct 1967	In depot maintenance (WM) by SMAMA field team at McConnell AFB KS.
1 Nov 1967	At 23 TFW, McConnell AFB KS.
27 Nov 1967	Assigned to combat crew training (TF) at 23 TFW, McConnell AFB KS.
7 Dec 1967	Joined the 560 TFS, 23 TFW, at George AFB CA conducting air-to-air gunnery training for F-105 RTU Class 68ER.
22 Dec 1967	Returned to 23 TFW, McConnell AFB KS for combat crew training (TF).
31 Jan 1968	At 560 TFS, 23 TFW. Crew Chief: SSgt. Robert E. Anderson selected as Wing Crew Chief of the Month. Aircraft flew 33 sorties and 54 flying hours. (23 TFW History, Jan–Jun 68, USAF microfilm MO554).
31 Mar 1968	At 23 TFW, McConnell AFB KS. (AVH-10).
1 Apr 1968	In depot maintenance (WM) by SMAMA at McConnell AFB KS.
4 Apr 1968	At 23 TFW, McConnell AFB KS.
14 May 1968	Deployed to George AFB CA with the 560 TFS, 23 TFW, for air-to-air gunnery training for RTU Class 68JR.
29 May 1968	Returned to 23 TFW, McConnell AFB KS.
9 Sep 1969	In depot maintenance (WO) at SMAMA, McClellan AFB CA. (AVH-12).
10 Dec 1969	Returned to 23 TFW, McConnell AFB KS.
16 Jan 1971	At 23 TFW, McConnell AFB KS for combat crew training (TF). (AVH-16).
10 May 1971	Assigned combat duties (CC) at 23 TFW (PL), McConnell AFB KS.
1 Mar 1972	Carried on assignment roster for the 561 TFS, 23 TFW, at McConnell AFB KS. (Master 23 TFW Aircraft Assignment as of 1 March 1972).
1 Jul 1972	At 561 TFS, McConnell AFB KS being prepared for transfer (PL) after 23 TFW moved to England AFB LA. (AVH-18).
7 Jul 1972	Arrived (PL) at 507 TFG AFRES, Tinker AFB OK.
12 Jul 1972	In contract depot maintenance (WK) by Fairchild Engine and Aircraft Corporation (FACCF) at Bob Sikes Municipal Airport, Crestview FL.
7 Aug 1972	Returned to 507 TFG AFRES, Tinker AFB OK.
23 Feb 1973	In depot maintenance (WM) by SM-ALC at Tinker AFB OK. (AVH-20).
12 Jul 1973	Assigned to 507 CMTSQ AFRES, Tinker AFB OK.
2 Aug 1973	In depot work (WO) by SM-ALC at McClellan AFB CA.
27 Nov 1973	Returned to 507 CMTSQ AFRES, Tinker AFB OK.
16 Oct 1974	Assigned unit redesignated 507 CLMSQ AFRES, Tinker AFB OK. (AVH-22).
13 May 1975	In depot maintenance (WM) by SM-ALC at Tinker AFB OK. (AVH-23 & AVH-24).
27 May 1975	At 507 CLMSQ AFRES, Tinker AFB OK.

29 Aug 1975	In depot maintenance (WM) by SM-ALC at Tinker AFB OK.
18 Sep 1975	At 507 CLMSQ AFRES, Tinker AFB OK.
13 Apr 1976	In depot maintenance (DM) by SM-ALC at Tinker AFB OK. (AVH-24).
10 May 1976	At 507 TFG AFRES, Tinker AFB OK.
Aug 1977	At 507 TFG AFRES, Tinker AFB OK. "During a Stan Eval visit, pilot, Lt. Col. Durnbaugh, landed a "little high" and drove the V-fin up through the belly and caused some other associated aft section damage." (Gabby Hays, former AFRES F-105 crew chief, e-mail, 18 Mar 96).
14 Aug 1977	Deployed under "Coronet Poker" with 465 TFS to Norvenich, Germany, from Tinker AFB OK. (British Aviation Review, Dec 1995).
27 Aug 1977	Returned from Germany to Tinker AFB OK.
6 Nov 1977	At 465 TFS AFRES, Tinker AFB OK. 3,915.3 flying hours. (AVH-26).
10 Jun 1978	Deployed under "Coronet Oriole" with 465 TFS to Sculthorpe, England, from Tinker AFB OK. (British Aviation Review, Dec 1995).
23 Jun 1978	Returned from England to Tinker AFB OK.
9 Nov 1978	At 465 TFS AFRES, Tinker AFB OK. 3,915.3 flying hours. (AVH-27).
14 Mar 1979	At 465 TFS AFRES, Tinker AFB OK. 3,948.5 flying hours.
12 May 1979	Deployed under "Coronet Palomino" with 465TFS to Gioia Del Colle, Italy, from Tinker AFB OK. (British Aviation Review, Dec 1995).
24 May 1979	Returned from Italy to Tinker AFB OK.
31 May 1979	While assigned to the 465 TFS, Tinker AFB OK, the aircraft flew 52.1 hours during the month of May 1979, the most hours for the month of any of the squadron's F-105s. The crew chief was Larry Reed. (301 TFW History 1 Apr–30 Jun 1979, USAF microfilm 343832).
30 Jun 1979	While assigned to the 465 TFS AFRES, Tinker AFB OK, the aircraft flew 22.6 hours during the month of June 1979 and had accumulated a total of 4,050.0 flying hours. (301 TFW History, Apr–Jun 1979, USAF microfilm 34382).
22 Jul 1979	In contract depot maintenance (FACBM) at Tinker AFB OK. 4,027.4 flying hours. (AVH-27).
25 Sep 1979	At 465 TFS AFRES, Tinker AFB OK. 4,074.4 flying hours.
20 Nov 1980	At 466 TFS AFRES, Hill AFB UT. 4,323.3 flying hours. (GO33B 22 Jan 81).
2 Dec 1980	In depot maintenance at Ogden ALC, Hill AFB UT. 4,323.3 flying hours.
15 Aug 1981	Deployed under "Coronet Rudder" with 466 TFS to Skrydstrup, Denmark, from Hill AFB UT. (British Aviation Review, Dec 1995).
29 Aug 1981	Returned from Denmark to Hill AFB UT.
30 Nov 1982	At Ogden ALC, Hill AFB UT for ground test (EJ). 4,620.5 flying hours. (GO33B 1 Feb 83).
4 Mar 1983	At 466 TFS, Hill AFB UT. 4,620.5 flying hours. (GO33B 9 Feb 84).

F-105F–1RE 63-8366

Republic Production No: F-143 Production Sequence No: 833

Location: Displayed on a pedestal near the main gate at McConnell AFB, Wichita, Kansas.

Aircraft Chronology

27 Dec 1964	USAF production acceptance from Republic Aviation, Farmingdale NY. (AVH-4).
29 Dec 1965	At MOAMA, Brookley AFB AL for depot work (WO).

21 Jan 1965	Delivered to 41 AD, Yokota AB, Japan.
1 Apr 1965	Assigned unit redesignated 6441 TFW at Yokota AB, Japan. (AVH-4).
30 Apr 1965	At 6441 TFW, Yokota AB, Japan. Assigned Crew Chief: SSgt. Clover. (6441 TFW History, Apr–Jun 65, USAF microfilm PO231).
4 Jun 1965	At Air Asia, Tainan, Taiwan, for contract depot work (WK). (AVH-4).
19 Jun 1965	At 6441 TFW, Yokota AB, Japan.
Aug 1965	At 6441 TFW, Yokota AB, Japan. Assigned Crew Chief: TSgt. May. (6441 TFW History, Jul–Dec 65, USAF microfilm PO232).
1 Sep 1965	At Itazuke AB, Japan, for depot maintenance by AFLC field team from SMAMA. (AVH-4).
6 Sep 1965	Returned to 6441 TFW, Yokota AB, Japan.
19 Oct 1965	At Air Asia, Tainan, Taiwan, for contract depot work (WK) and Safety Pack II Modification.
8 Nov 1965	Returned to 6441 TFW, Yokota AB, Japan.
31 Jan 1966	At Osan AB, Korea, with 6441 TFW for nuclear weapon alert. (AVH-5).
16 Mar 1966	Returned to 6441 TFW, Yokota AB, Japan.
15 Nov 1966	At Osan AB, Korea, with 41 AD for nuclear weapon alert.
3 Jan 1967	At 41 AD, Yokota AB, Japan. (AVH-8).
10 Aug 1967	Transferred to 23 TFW, McConnell AFB KS.
25 Sep 1967	In depot maintenance (WM) by SMAMA field team at McConnell AFB KS.
27 Sep 1967	At 23 TFW, McConnell AFB KS.
27 Nov 1967	Assigned to combat crew training (TF) at 23 TFW, McConnell AFB KS.
15 Jan 1968	At 23 TFW, McConnell AFB KS. (AVH-10).
23 Jan 1968	Deployed to George AFB CA with the 561 TFS, 23 TFW, for air-to-air gunnery training for F-105 RTU Class 68FR.
8 Feb 1968	Returned to 23 TFW, McConnell AFB KS.
18 Mar 1968	In depot maintenance by SMAMA at McConnell AFB KS.
21 Mar 1968	At 23 TFW, McConnell AFB KS.
Dec 1969	Aircraft out of commission for maintenance. (23 TFW History, Jan–Mar 70, USAF microfilm MO555).
11 Mar 1970	Repairs to the upper portion of the bomb bay completed by 23 FMS at McConnell AFB KS.
24 May 1970	At 23 TFW, McConnell AFB KS (CC). (AVH-14).
25 May 1970	In depot work by SMAMA, McClellan AFB CA.
1 Sep 1970	Transferred (PL) to 57 FWW, Nellis AFB NV.
4 Sep 1970	At 57 FWW, Nellis AFB NV for combat crew training (TF).
8 Feb 1971	In contract depot maintenance (WK) by Fairchild Engine and Aircraft Corporation (FACCF) at Bob Sikes Municipal Airport, Crestview FL. (AVH-16).
11 Mar 1971	Returned to 57 FWW, Nellis AFB NV for combat crew training (TF).
30 Mar 1972	Departed (PL) 57 FWW, Nellis AFB NV. (AVH-18).
31 Mar 1972	Transferred (PL) to 23 TFW, McConnell AFB KS.
15 May 1972	In contract depot maintenance (WK) by Fairchild Engine and Aircraft Corporation (FACCF) at Bob Sikes Municipal Airport, Crestview FL.
6 Jun 1972	Returned to 23 TFW, McConnell AFB KS.
1 Jul 1972	Assigned to 561 TFS (TAC), McConnell AFB KS when the 23 TFW moved to England AFB LA.
19 Jul 1972	Transferred to 184 TFTG ANG, McConnell AFB KS.
21 May 1973	In contract depot maintenance (WM) by Dynalectron Corporation (DYNZZ) at McConnell AFB KS. (AVH-20).
25 May 1973	At 184 TFTG ANG, McConnell AFB KS.

This "F" marked the end of the line for the F-105 as it was the last Thunderchief produced. It began its career at Yokota Air Base, Japan, in January 1965 where it flew in and out of Osan Air Base, Korea, to sit alert with nuclear weapons under its wings. In 1967, it began 12 years of pilot training when it transferred to the 23 Tactical Fighter Wing at McConnell Air Force Base, Kansas. It moved several times between McConnell and Nellis Air Force Base, Nevada, and finally settled down with the Kansas Air National Guard at McConnell in 1972. The Guard retired it in 1979 and placed it on a concrete pedestal to guard the main gate at McConnell. (Photograph by author, 7 August 1995.)

23 Jul 1973	Transferred (PL) to 57 FWW TAC, Nellis AFB NV.
26 Jul 1973	At 57 FWW TAC, Nellis AFB NV for combat crew training (TF).
24 Sep 1973	In depot maintenance (WM) by 916 CLSS at Nellis AFB NV.
10 Oct 1973	At 57 FWW TAC, Nellis AFB NV for combat crew training (TF).
11 Dec 1973	Transferred back to 184 TFTG ANG, McConnell AFB KS.
3 Jan 1974	At 184 TFTG ANG, McConnell AFB KS for combat crew training (TF).
15 Jul 1974	In contract depot maintenance (WM) by Dynalectron Corporation (DYNZZ) at McConnell AFB KS. (AVH-22).
17 Jul 1974	At 184 TFTG ANG, McConnell AFB KS for combat crew training (TF).
26 Aug 1974	In contract depot maintenance (WM) by Dynalectron Corporation (DYNZZ) at McConnell AFB KS.
12 Sep 1974	At 184 TFTG ANG, McConnell AFB KS for combat crew training (TF).
20 Sep 1974	In contract depot maintenance (WM) by Dynalectron Corporation (DYNZZ) at McConnell AFB KS.
15 Oct 1974	At 184 TFTG ANG, McConnell AFB KS for combat crew training (TF).
15 Jan 1975	In depot work (WO) by SM-ALC at McClellan AFB CA. (AVH-23).
19 May 1975	In depot work (WR) by SM-ALC at McClellan AFB CA. (AVH-23 & AVH-24).
30 May 1975	Returned to 184 TFTG ANG, McConnell AFB KS for combat crew training (TF).
17 Apr 1978	At 184 TFTG ANG, McConnell AFB KS. 3,556.0 flying hours. (AVH-26).
22 May 1978	At 184 TFTG ANG, McConnell AFB KS. 3,610.0 flying hours.
24 May 1978	At SM-ALC depot, McClellan AFB CA. 3,615.0 flying hours.
22 Sep 1978	Returned to 184 TFTG ANG, McConnell AFB KS. 3,615.0 flying hours.
16 Oct 1979	At 184 TFTG ANG, McConnell AFB KS. 3,839.9 flying hours. Being transferred to museum (ZW). (AVH-27 & GO33B 24 Jun 80).

Appendix 1

The Thunderchief Tour

To make it easier to visit the planes detailed in Part II, Appendix 1 lists them under the name of the state or country where they are located.

Alabama

1	YF-105B	54-0102	In the Aircraft Pavilion at the USS Alabama Battleship Museum, Mobile.
2	F-105D	61-0176	Displayed outside with Maxwell AFB Collection, Maxwell AFB, Montgomery.

Arkansas

3	F-105F	63-8261	Parked on the grass at All Flags Heritage Park, Camp Robinson, Little Rock.

Arizona

4	F-105D	61-0086	Displayed outside as "Big Sal" at the Pima Air Museum, Tucson.
5	F-105D	61-0159	Displayed outside at Warrior Park, Davis-Monthan AFB, Tucson.
6	F-105G	62-4427	Displayed outside at the Pima Air Museum, Tucson.
7	F-105G	62-4432	Displayed on AMARC's "Celebrity Row," Davis-Monthan AFB, Tucson.
8	F-105G	63-8285	Displayed at Site 5, Munitions Storage Area, Davis-Monthan AFB, Tucson.

California

9	F-105B	57-5803	At March Field Museum, March Air Reserve Base, Riverside.
10	F-105B	57-5837	At Castle Air Museum, Atwater.
11	F-105D	61-0146	Parked at South Base for the AFFTC Museum, Edwards AFB, Rosamond.
12	F-105D	62-4299	"Desert Fox" at the Travis Air Force Museum, Travis AFB, Fairfield.
13	F-105D	62-4301	At the McClellan Aviation Museum, McClellan AFB, Sacramento.

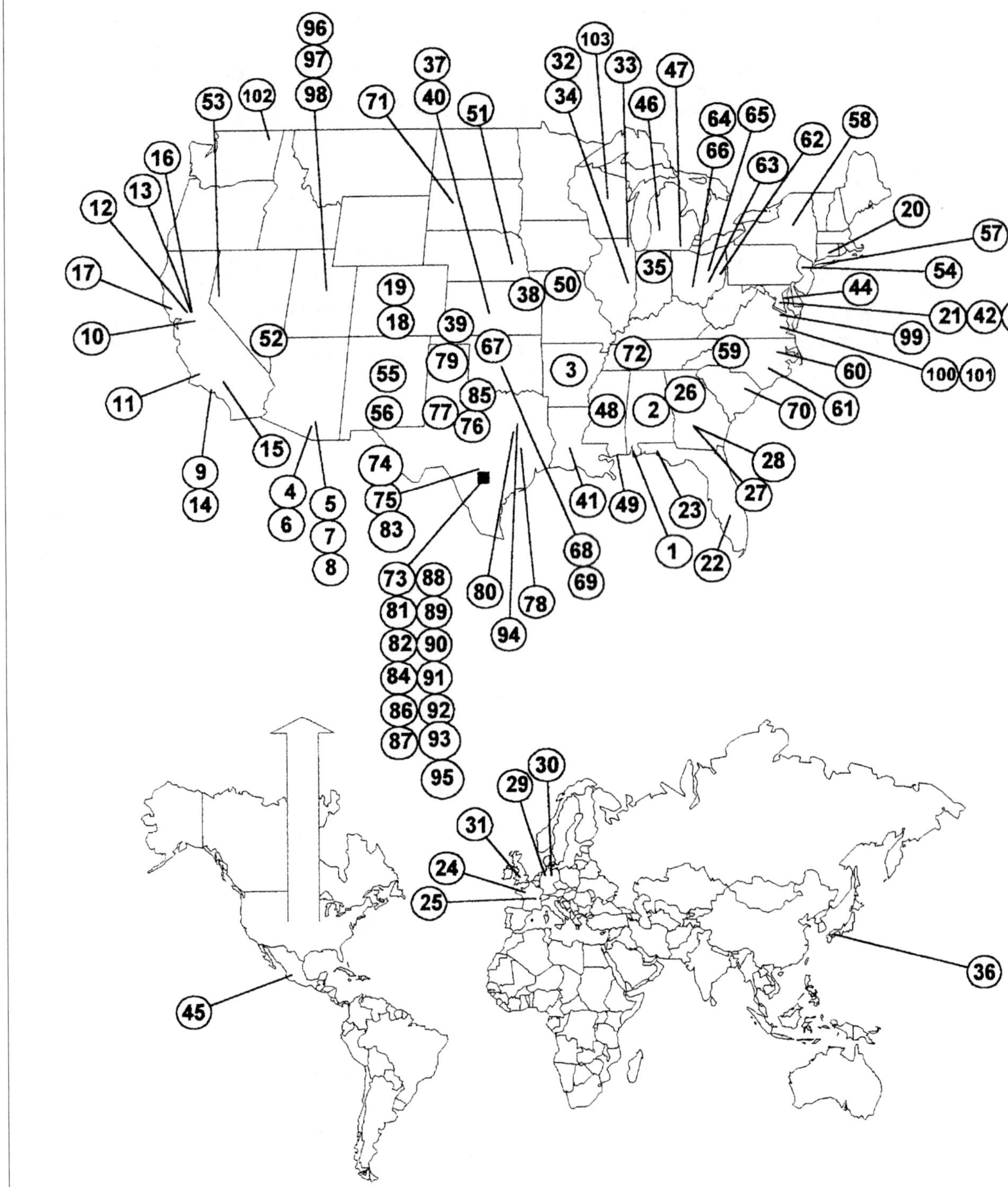

The numbers on this pin map correlate with the plane's number in the geographic listing.

14	F-105D	62-4383	At the March Field Museum, March Air Reserve Base, Riverside.
15	F-105G	62-4416	At Palmdale Plant 42 Heritage Airpark, Palmdale.
16	F-105G	63-8278	Displayed near the VA Hospital at Mather AFB, Sacramento.
17	F-105F	63-8331	Displayed at the Pacific Coast Air Museum, Santa Rosa.

Colorado

18	F-105D	60-0482	On the quadrangle at the Air Force Academy, Colorado Springs.
19	F-105D	60-0508	Inside the Wings Over Rockies Air & Space Museum (Lowry AFB), Denver.

Connecticut

20	F-105B	57-5778	Displayed inside the New England Air Museum, Windsor Locks.

District of Columbia

21	F-105D	61-0138	Displayed outside on a pedestal near the main gate at Bolling AFB.

Florida

22	F-105B	57-5820	Displayed outside at the Florida Military Aviation Museum, Fort Meade.
23	F-105D	58-1155	Displayed inside the USAF Armament Museum, Eglin AFB, Shalimar.

France

24	F-105G	63-8300	Displayed outdoors at Le Bourget Museum, Paris.
25	F-105F	63-8357	At the Musee du Chateau de Savigny in Savigny-les-Beaune near Dijon.

Georgia

26	F-105D	61-0164	Displayed as "59-1746" at Hunter Park in the city of Douglasville.
27	F-105G	62-4438	Displayed outside at Museum of Aviation, Robins AFB, Warner Robins.
28	F-105G	63-8345	Stored by the 116 BW ANG, Robins AFB, Warner Robins.

Germany

29	F-105F	62-4417	At the Flaugausstellung Leo Und Peter Junior museum near Trier.
30	F-105G	62-4446	Displayed outside near the billeting office at Spangdahlem AB.

Great Britain

31	F-105G	62-4428	Displayed as a gate guard at the entrance to RAF Croughton, Northamptonshire.

Illinois

32	F-105B	54-0104	Displayed outside the Octave Chanute Aerospace Museum, Rantoul.
33	F-105D	61-0099	Displayed by the Air Classics Museum at Sugar Grove Airport, Aurora.
34	F-105F	63-8287	Parked outside hanger at the Octave Chanute Aerospace Museum, Rantoul.

Indiana

35	F-105D	61-0088	Displayed outside at the Heritage Museum Park, Grissom ARB, Peru.

Japan

36	F-105F	62-4418	Displayed outside near 18 Wing headquarters, Kadena AB, Okinawa.

Kansas

37	F-105D	62-4253	Displayed at the Kansas Air National Guard area, McConnell AFB, Wichita.
38	F-105D	62-4375	Displayed inside Hanger 602 at the Combat Air Museum, Forbes Field, Topeka.
39	F-105G	63-8266	Displayed outside parked on ramp at the Mid-America Air Museum, Liberal.
40	F-105F	63-8366	Displayed outside on pedestal near the main gate at McConnell AFB, Wichita.

Louisiana

41	F-105G	63-8296	At Heritage Park, England Industrial Air Park & Community, Alexandria.

Maryland

42	F-105D	60-0445	Stored at the National Air & Space Museum, Silver Hill.
43	F-105D	61-0041	Displayed by the 113 TFW DC ANG at Andrews AFB.
44	F-105G	63-8274	Displayed outside at the Glen L. Martin Aviation Museum, Baltimore.

Mexico

45	F-105B	57-5784	Displayed outside at the Planetario Severo Diaz Galindo, Guadalajara.

Michigan

46	F-105B	57-5793	At the Yankee Air Museum, Willow Run Airport, Belleville.
47	F-105G	62-4425	Parked in front of the Robert Meachen American Legion Post 325, Blissfield.

Mississippi

48	F-105D	60-0455	T-Stick II. Parked in front of Harry H. Graves American Legion Post 1, Jackson.
49	F-105D	60-0535	Displayed on a pedestal at Keesler AFB, Biloxi.

Missouri

50	F-105B	57-5817	Displayed on four steel pylons at the municipal airport entrance, Chillicothe.

Nebraska

51	F-105D	61-0069	At the SAC Museum, Ashland.

Nevada

52	F-105G	63-8276	Displayed outside on a pedestal at History Park, Nellis AFB, Las Vegas.
53	F-105G	63-8336	At the airport, Reno.

New Jersey

54	F-105B	57-5776	Displayed on a pedestal in the ANG area at McGuire AFB, Trenton.

New Mexico

55	F-105D	61-0107	On a pedestal at the National Atomic Museum, Kirtland AFB, Albuquerque.
56	F-105D	61-0145	Displayed outside at Veteran's Square, Holloman AFB, Alamogordo.

New York

57	F-105B	57-5783	Inside Hanger 4 at the Cradle of Aviation Museum, Mitchel Field, Garden City.
58	F-105G	62-4444	Displayed outside at the Empire State Aerosciences Museum, Scotia.

North Carolina

59	F-105B	54-0107	Displayed by the Sabre Society at Hickory Municipal Airport, Hickory.
60	F-105D	61-0056	Displayed on a steel pylon at Seymour Johnson AFB, Goldsboro.
61	F-105D	61-0165	Displayed near the main gate at Pope AFB, Fayetteville.

Ohio

62	F-105B	57-5792	At the municipal airport, Zanesville.
63	F-105D	59-1771	Displayed outside at the AMVETS Post 2256, Circleville.
64	F-105D	60-0504	*Memphis Belle II* inside Air Force Museum, Wright-Patterson AFB, Dayton.
65	F-105D	62-4361	On the flightline by the 121 ARW ANG at Rickenbacker Airport, Columbus.
66	F-105G	63-8320	"Bam Bam" inside the Air Force Museum at Wright-Patterson AFB, Dayton.

Oklahoma

67	F-105D	62-4242	Displayed at Vance AFB, Enid.
68	F-105D	62-4360	*Iron Duke* outside the Heritage Museum, Tinker AFB, Oklahoma City.
69	F-105F	63-8365	Parked inside a fenced storage yard at Tinker AFB, Oklahoma City.

South Carolina

70	F-105B	57-5819	Displayed at the Poinsett Electronic Combat Range, Shaw AFB, Sumpter.

South Dakota

71	F-105B	57-5839	At the South Dakota Air and Space Museum, Ellsworth AFB, Rapid City.

Tennessee

72	F-105D	62-4328	Displayed outside near the main gate at Arnold Air Force Base, Manchester.

Texas

73	JF-105	54-0105	Photo nose. Displayed at Lackland AFB Annex, San Antonio
74	F-105B	57-5789	At the USAF Ground Combat Skills School, Camp Bullis, San Antonio.

75	F-105B	57-5835	At the USAF Ground Combat Skills School, Camp Bullis, San Antonio.
76	F-105D	59-1738	At Linear Air Park, Texas Museum of Military History, Dyess AFB, Abelene.
77	F-105D	59-1739	Displayed outside at American Airpower Heritage Museum, Midland.
78	F-105D	60-0500	T-Stick II. At the Pate Museum of Transportation, Cresson.
79	F-105D	61-0093	Displayed outside at the Texas Air Museum, Caprock Chapter, Slaton.
80	F-105D	61-0100	T-Stick II. Displayed outside at NAS Ft. Worth Joint Reserve Base, Ft. Worth.
81	F-105D	61-0106	At the Security Police Flightline Training Area #7, Lackland AFB, San Antonio.
82	F-105D	61-0108	At the Security Police Flightline Training Area #7, Lackland AFB, San Antonio.
83	F-105D	61-0110	T-Stick II. At the USAF Ground Combat Skills School, Camp Bullis, San Antonio.
84	F-105D	61-0115	At the Security Police Flightline Training Area #7, Lackland AFB, San Antonio.
85	F-105D	61-0175	Displayed outside on a pedestal at Sheppard AFB, Wichita Falls.
86	F-105D	61-0199	At the Security Police Flightline Training Area #7, Lackland AFB, San Antonio.
87	F-105D	62-4228	At the Security Police Flightline Training Area #7, Lackland AFB, San Antonio.
88	F-105D	62-4259	At the Security Police Flightline Training Area #7, Lackland AFB, San Antonio.
89	F-105D	62-4279	At the Security Police Flightline Training Area #7, Lackland AFB, San Antonio.
90	F-105D	62-4318	At the Security Police Flightline Training Area #7, Lackland AFB, San Antonio.
91	F-105D	62-4346	At the Security Police Flightline Training Area #7, Lackland AFB, San Antonio.
92	F-105D	62-4353	At the Security Police Flightline Training Area #7, Lackland AFB, San Antonio.
93	F-105D	62-4387	On static display at Lackland AFB, San Antonio.
94	F-105F	63-8343	Parked outside on the ramp of the Cavanaugh Flight Museum, Addison.
95	F-105G	63-8363	Stored by the Texas Air Museum in San Antonio.

Utah

96	F-105D	59-1743	*Arkansas Traveler* outside the Aerospace Museum, Hill AFB, Ogden.
97	F-105D	62-4347	Displayed outside on a pylon near the South Gate at Hill AFB, Ogden.
98	F-105G	62-4440	Displayed inside at the Aerospace Museum, Hill AFB, Ogden.

Virginia

99	F-105D	61-0050	Displayed on a column at Byrd Field, Richmond.
100	F-105D	61-0073	Displayed outside at the Airpower Park and Museum, Hampton.
101	F-105D	61-0188	Displayed on a pylon at TAC Memorial Park, Langley AFB, Hampton.

Washington

102	F-105B	57-5823	On display at the Heritage Museum, Fairchild AFB, Spokane.

Wisconsin

103	F-105B	57-5838	*Xanadu* at the Wisconsin ANG Museum, Volk Field, Tomah.

Appendix 2

To the Glue Factory

The one hundred three F-105s whose histories are detailed in Part II of this book were not the only Thunderchiefs to survive their operational careers. One hundred eighteen others also passed on to retirement. However, those in this group were less fortunate since most, but not all, have been scrapped—the aviation equivalent of the glue factory. Appendix 2 identifies these planes and their fates.

While reviewing this list, notice that some were previously displayed; others have been allocated for future display; and a few, with the right combination of organization and circumstance, could be resurrected.

YF-105A 54-0099 Last flight 24 February 1960. Scrapped at Edwards AFB, California.

YF-105B 54-0100 1998—Scrapped at McClellan AFB, Sacramento, California.

When YF-105B 54-0100, the third F-105 built, retired from its test duties in the early 1960s, the depot at McClellan Air Force Base, California, modified the nose so it resembled an F-105D and mounted it on a pedestal where it sat for years slowly rusting away until it was removed and stored as shown here. It was scrapped in 1998 at the direction of the Air Force Museum (photograph by Norman Hamrah, 11 June 1997).

YF-105B 54-0103 June 1967—After USAF write-off, last used by the Naval EOD (Explosive Ordnance Disposal) School, Indian Head, Maryland.

F-105B 54-0109 1965—Scrapped after last assignment as a ground instructional trainer at the 3320 MSG Amarillo AFB, Texas.

F-105B 54-0110 1960—Scrapped as obsolete after last assignment to Brookley AFB, Alabama.

F-105B 54-0111 23 Jan 1961—Scrapped after last assignment to Brookley AFB, Alabama.

JF-105 54-0108 1 September 1962—"Photo nose." Scrapped after being in crash damage repair at Brookley AFB, Alabama.

JF-105 54-0112 1977—"Photo nose." Scrapped after last assignment as ground instructional aircraft at Chanute AFB, Illinois.

F-105B 57-5779 27 Feb 1985—Removed from AMARC (storage number FK032) to be used as a target for weapons studies at the New Mexico Institute of Mining & Technology, Socorro, New Mexico, where it was scrapped.

F-105B 57-5780 27 Feb 1985—Removed from AMARC (storage number FK027) to be used as a target for weapons studies at the New Mexico Institute of Mining & Technology, Socorro, New Mexico, where it was scrapped.

F-105B 57-5782 27 Feb 1985—Former T-Bird. Removed from AMARC (storage number FK033) to be used as a target for weapons studies at the New Mexico Institute of Mining & Technology, Socorro, New Mexico, where it was scrapped.

F-105B 57-5787 27 Feb 1985—Former T-Bird. Removed from AMARC (storage number FK026) to be used as a target for weapons studies at the New Mexico Institute of Mining & Technology, Socorro, New Mexico, where it was scrapped.

F-105B 57-5795 1985—Probably scrapped after being use by 2953 CLSS (Combat Logistics Support Squadron) for ABDR (Aircraft Battle Damage Repair) training at OC-ALC, Tinker Air Force Base, Oklahoma.

F-105B 57-5797 Jan 1997—Scrapped at Kelley AFB, Texas, after use for ABDR training by the 2954 CLSS at Brooks AFB, Texas.

This broken aft section was all that remained of F-105B 57-5797 when photographed at Brooks Air Force Base, Texas, in July 1996 (Steve Hester photograph via John Coon).

The Planes of Fame Museum in Chino, California, bought this F-105B carcass from a scrap dealer in Sacramento, California, intending to restore it for their collection. The plane is missing its aft section and has been stripped of all markings that could identify its tail number. A penciled message on its fuselage indicates it had been used for ABDR training at McClellan Air Force Base. Records show that two F-105Bs were at McClellan for this purpose—57-5812 and 57-5816 (see below). This derelict is most probably one of these. 57-5812 was the plane that Brigadier General Joseph H. Moore flew on 11 December 1959 when he set a world speed record (photograph by author, 31 October 1996).

F-105B 57-5804	May 1985—Probably scrapped after use by the 2953 CLSS for ABDR training at OC-ALC, Tinker Air Force Base, Oklahoma.
F-105B 57-5808	23 Jul 1987—Sold as scrap from AMARC (storage number FK024) to Kotz Metal, Tucson, Arizona.
F-105B 57-5812	1985—Scrapped after use by 2951 CLSS for ABDR training at SM-ALC, McClellan AFB, California. Its forward fuselage is possibly the one at Planes of Fame Museum, Chino, California.
F-105B 575813	Nov/Dec 1995—Scrapped after use by the 2954 CLSS for ABDR training at Kelly AFB, Texas.
F-105B 57-5814	Former Thunderbird aircraft, "T-Bird 1." Scrapped sometime after 1986 after being displayed for several years at the airport in Salt Lake City, Utah.
F-105B 57-5815	1985—Probably scrapped after being used by 2953 CLSS for ABDR training at OC-ALC, Tinker Air Force Base, Oklahoma.
F-105B 57-5816	1985—Scrapped after use by 2951 CLSS for ABDR training at SM-ALC, McClellan AFB, California. Its forward fuselage is possibly the one at the Planes of Fame Museum, Chino, California.
F-105B 57-5826	29 Apr 1980—Sold as scrap to Consolidated Aircraft Sales from MASDC (storage number FK007) at Davis-Monthan AFB, Tucson, Arizona.
F-105B 57-5829	1985—Probably scrapped after being used by 2953 CLSS for ABDR training at OC-ALC, Tinker Air Force Base, Oklahoma.
F-105B 57-5833	May 1985—Scrapped after being used by the 2953 CLSS for ABDR training at OC-ALC, Tinker Air Force Base, Oklahoma.
F-105B 57-5834	6 Oct 1980—Flown from Hill AFB, Utah, to Wright-Patterson AFB, Ohio, for ABDR training with the 401 CLSS. Scrapped in 1991.
F-105D 58-1147	26 Mar 1968—Scrapped at McClellan AFB, California.

F-105D 58-1159	1 Apr 1985—Removed from AMARC (storage number FK052) to be used as a target for weapons studies at the New Mexico Institute of Mining & Technology, Socorro, New Mexico, where it was scrapped.
F-105D 58-1167	1 May 1973—Scrapped at McClellan AFB, California.
F-105D 58-1172	1976—Probably scrapped at Naval EOD School, Indian Head, Maryland.
F-105D 58-1173	26 Apr 1985—Removed from AMARC (storage number FK043) to be used as a target for weapons studies at the New Mexico Institute of Mining & Technology, Socorro, New Mexico, where it was scrapped.
F-105D 59-1731	19 Aug 1996—Purchased as scrap from AMARC (storage number FK040) for restoration and future display at Gateway Fighter & Aircraft Museum, St. Louis, Missouri.
F-105D 59-1732	1 Apr 1985—Removed from AMARC (storage number FK039) to be used as a target for weapons studies at the New Mexico Institute of Mining & Technology, Socorro, New Mexico, where it was scrapped.
F-105D 59-1733	14 Jun 1984—Sold as scrap from MASDC (storage number FK004) to Allied Aircraft Sales, Tucson, Arizona.
F-105D 59-1759	2 Jan 1999—Still at AMARC (storage number FK054), Davis-Monthan Air Force Base, Tucson, Arizona.
F-105D 59-1769	2 Apr 1980—Sold as scrap from MASDC (storage number FK003) to Allied Aircraft Sales, Tucson, Arizona.
F-105D 59-1774	26 Feb 1997—Removed from AMARC (storage number FK035) and transported to Airburst Range, Peterson AFB, Colorado, for use as a target.
F-105D 59-1822	15 Jul 1999—Removed from AMARC storage for shipment to the American Air Museum in Great Britain.
F-105D 60-0423	Nov 1967—Combat damaged at Korat, Thailand, and written off at McClellan AFB, California.
F-105D 60-0438	14 Jun 1984—Sold as scrap from MASDC (storage number FK002) to Allied Aircraft Sales, Tucson, Arizona.
F-105D 60-0449	15 Jun 1984—Sold for scrap from MASDC (storage number FK005) at Davis-Monthan AFB, Arizona.
F-105D 60-0452	19 Aug 1996—Purchased as scrap from AMARC (storage number FK061) for restoration and future display at Gateway Fighter & Aircraft Museum, St. Louis, Missouri.
F-105D 60-0458	26 Apr 1985—T-Stick II. Removed from AMARC (storage number FK076) to be used as a target for weapons studies at the New Mexico Institute of Mining & Technology, Socorro, New Mexico, where it was scrapped.
F-105D 60-0464	27 Feb 1985—T-Stick II. Removed from AMARC (storage number FK078) to be used as a target for weapons studies at the New Mexico Institute of Mining & Technology, Socorro, New Mexico, where it was scrapped.
F-105D 60-0465	1 Apr 1985—T-Stick II. Removed from AMARC (storage number FK079) to be used as a target for weapons studies at the New Mexico Institute of Mining & Technology, Socorro, New Mexico, where it was scrapped.
F-105D 60-0471	2 Jan 1999—T-Stick II. Still at AMARC (storage number FK070), Davis-Monthan AFB, Tucson, Arizona.
F-105D 60-0480	19 Feb 1970—T-Stick II. Write-off by the 457 TFS at Carswell Air Force Base, Texas, due to wing cracks. Parts used on other aircraft and the remainder placed as a target on the range at Ft. Hood, Texas.
F-105D 60-0492	2 Jan 1999—Still at AMARC (storage number FK045), Davis-Monthan AFB, Tucson, Arizona.
F-105D 60-0493	27 Feb 1985—T-Stick II. Removed from AMARC (storage number FK072) to be used as a target for weapons studies at the New Mexico Institute of Mining & Technology, Socorro, New Mexico, where it was scrapped.
F-105D 60-0496	1985—Scrapped after use for ABDR training by the 2951 CLSS at McClellan AFB, California.

F-105D 59-1759 flew combat with the 355 and 388 Tactical Fighter Wings from 1967 to 1970. Its last unit was the DC Air National Guard who retired it on 10 July 1981. MASDC gave it storage number FK054 (photograph by Col. Walter W. Saeger, Jr., 2 January 1999).

F-105D 59-1822 was known as the "*Polish Glider*" when flown by Major Donald J. Kutyna from the 44 Tactical Fighter Squadron at Takhli, Thailand, in 1970. Its last unit was the Virginia Air National Guard who named it "*Super Hog*" and retired it on 22 March 1981 due to wing cracks. When photographed, it had AMARC storage number FK030 and was awaiting shipment to the American Air Museum at Duxford, England (photograph by Col. Walter W. Saeger, Jr., 2 January 1999).

Last flown by the Air Force Reserve's 457 Tactical Fighter Squadron from Carswell Air Force Base, Texas, T-Stick II F-105D 60-0471 retired to storage on 13 November 1981. It was given MASDC number FK070 (photograph by Col. Walter W. Saeger, Jr., 2 January 1999).

The remains of F-105D 60-0496 rests between two other scrapped carcasses, in a field at McClellan Air Force Base, California. The plane was a 1967 combat veteran with the 388 Tactical Fighter Wing at Korat, Thailand (photograph by Norman Hamrah, 6 November 1997).

F-105D 60-0492 was last flown by the Virginia Air National Guard who named it *"Ye Old War Horse"* and put it out to pasture on 17 July 1981. It received storage number FK045 (photograph by Col. Walter W. Saeger, Jr., 2 January 1999).

F-105D 60-0498 — 1 Apr 1985—Removed from AMARC (storage number FK036) to be used as a target for weapons studies at the New Mexico Institute of Mining & Technology, Socorro, New Mexico, where it was scrapped.

F-105D 60-0514 — 1 Apr 1985—Removed from AMARC (storage number FK069) to be used as a target for weapons studies at the New Mexico Institute of Mining & Technology, Socorro, New Mexico, where it was scrapped.

F-105D 60-0517 — 26 Apr 1985—T-Stick II. Removed from AMARC (storage number FK071) to be used as a target for weapons studies at the New Mexico Institute of Mining & Technology, Socorro, New Mexico, where it was scrapped.

F-105D 60-0519 — 14 Jun 1984—Sold as scrap from MASDC (storage number FK011) to Allied Aircraft Sales, Tucson, Arizona.

F-105D 60-0525 — 9 Sep 1985—Removed from AMARC (storage number FK073) as a target for the bombing range at Peterson Air Force Base, Colorado.

F-105D 60-0527 — 1 Apr 1985—T-Stick II. Removed from AMARC (storage number FK073) to be used as a target for weapons studies at the New Mexico Institute of Mining & Technology, Socorro, New Mexico, where it was scrapped.

F-105D 60-0528 — 26 Apr 1985—T-Stick II. Removed from AMARC (storage number FK074) to be used as a target for weapons studies at the New Mexico Institute of Mining & Technology, Socorro, New Mexico, where it was scrapped.

F-105D 60-0533 — 27 Feb 1985—T-Stick II. Removed from AMARC (storage number FK085) to be used as a target for weapons studies at the New Mexico Institute of Mining & Technology, Socorro, New Mexico, where it was scrapped.

F-105D 60-5385	2 Jan 1999—Still at AMARC (storage number FK042), Davis-Monthan AFB, Tucson, Arizona.
F-105D 61-0044	May 1997—T-Stick II. Scrapped at Brooks AFB, Texas, after use for ABDR training by the 2954 CLSS at Kelly AFB, Texas.
F-105D 61-0061	26 Apr 1985—Removed from AMARC (storage number FK067) to be used as a target for weapons studies at the New Mexico Institute of Mining & Technology, Socorro, New Mexico, where it was scrapped.
F-105D 61-0063	1 Apr 1985—T-Stick II. Removed from AMARC (storage number FK081) to be used as a target for weapons studies at the New Mexico Institute of Mining & Technology, Socorro, New Mexico, where it was scrapped.
F-105D 61-0064	26 Apr 1985—T-Stick II. Removed from AMARC (storage number FK077) to be used as a target for weapons studies at the New Mexico Institute of Mining & Technology, Socorro, New Mexico, where it was scrapped.
F-105D 61-0065	1985—Scrapped at McClellan AFB, California.
F-105D 61-0071	5 May 1995—Sent from AMARC (storage number FK049) to the range as a target at Holloman AFB, Alamogordo, New Mexico.
F-105D 61-0074	27 Feb 1985—T-Stick II. Removed from AMARC (storage number FK084) to be used as a target for weapons studies at the New Mexico Institute of Mining & Technology, Socorro, New Mexico, where it was scrapped.
F-105D 61-0075	26 Apr 1985—T-Stick II. Removed from AMARC (storage number FK064) to be used as a target for weapons studies at the New Mexico Institute of Mining & Technology, Socorro, New Mexico, where it was scrapped.
F-105D 61-0076	26 Apr 1985—T-Stick II. Removed from AMARC (storage number FK083) to be used as a target for weapons studies at the New Mexico Institute of Mining & Technology, Socorro, New Mexico, where it was scrapped.
F-105D 61-0080	16 Sep 1985—T-Stick II. Removed from AMARC (storage number FK059) and placed as a target on the bombing range near Peterson Air Force Base, Colorado.
F-105D 61-0084	26 Apr 1985—T-Stick II. Removed from AMARC (storage number FK075) to be used as a target for weapons studies at the New Mexico Institute of Mining & Technology, Socorro, New Mexico.
F-105D 61-0096	1 Apr 1985—T-Stick II. Removed from AMARC (storage number FK082) to be used as a target for weapons studies at the New Mexico Institute of Mining & Technology, Socorro, New Mexico, where it was scrapped.
F-105D 61-0129	1981—Scrapped at NAS Patuxent River, Maryland.
F-105D 61-0134	14 Jun 1984—Sold as scrap from MASDC (storage number FK010) to Allied Aircraft Sales, Tucson, Arizona.
F-105D 61-0152	1980—Probably scrapped at Tinker AFB, Oklahoma.
F-105D 61-0154	1 Apr 1985—Removed from AMARC (storage number FK057) to be used as a target for weapons studies at the New Mexico Institute of Mining & Technology, Socorro, New Mexico, where it was scrapped.
F-105D 61-0161	7 Feb 1985—T-Stick II. Removed from AMARC (storage number FK060) to be used as a target for weapons studies at the New Mexico Institute of Mining & Technology, Socorro, New Mexico, where it was scrapped.
F-105D 61-0166	27 Feb 1985—Removed from AMARC (storage number FK038) to be used as a target for weapons studies at the New Mexico Institute of Mining & Technology, Socorro, New Mexico, where it was scrapped.
F-105D 61-0167	26 Apr 1985—Removed from AMARC (storage number FK047) to be used as a target for weapons studies at the New Mexico Institute of Mining & Technology, Socorro, New Mexico, where it was scrapped.
F-105D 61-0170	1 Apr 1985—Removed from AMARC (storage number FK063) to be used as a target for weapons studies at the New Mexico Institute of Mining & Technology, Socorro, New Mexico, where it was scrapped.

F-105D 60-5385 was named *"Fireball Express"* by the Virginia Air National Guard's 149 Tactical Fighter Squadron. They retired it to MASDC on 29 May 1981 where it was given storage number FK042. MASDC allocated it for "tri-service testing" of preservation coatings (photograph by Col. Walter W. Saeger, Jr., 2 January 1999).

F-105D 61-0183	15 Jun 1984—Sold as scrap from MASDC (storage number FK001) to Allied Aircraft Sales, Tucson, Arizona.
F-105D 61-0204	14 Jun 1984—Sold as scrap from MASDC (storage number FK009) to Allied Aircraft Sales, Tucson, Arizona.
F-105D 61-0212	1 Apr 1985—Removed from AMARC (storage number FK037) to be used as a target for weapons studies at the New Mexico Institute of Mining & Technology, Socorro, New Mexico, where it was scrapped.
F-105D 62-4246	14 Jun 1984—Sold as scrap from MASDC (storage number FK006) to Allied Aircraft Sales, Tucson, Arizona.
F-105D 62-4291	12 Aug 1983—Removed from MASDC (storage number FK053) and shipped to Clark AB, Philippines, for ABDR training. Probably scrapped after eruption of Mount Pinatubo in June 1991.
F-105D 62-4311	24 May 1973—Written off after use as a ground instructional aircraft while in contract work at Republic Aviation, Farmingdale, New York.
F-105D 62-4344	23 Nov 1994—Sold as scrap from AMARC (storage number FK051) to AMCEP Inc., Tucson, Arizona.
F-105D 62-4365	26 Apr 1985—Removed from AMARC (storage number FK031) to be used as a target for weapons studies at the New Mexico Institute of Mining & Technology, Socorro, New Mexico, where it was scrapped.
F-105D 62-4411	27 Feb 1985—Removed from AMARC (storage number FK041) to be used as a target for weapons studies at the New Mexico Institute of Mining & Technology, Socorro, New Mexico, where it was scrapped.
F-105F 62-4413	30 Oct 1984—Removed from MASDC (storage number FK065) for use by the 2953 CLSS for ABDR training at Tinker AFB, Oklahoma. Scrapped by June 1989.
F-105F 62-4414	30 Oct 1984—Removed from MASDC (storage number FK066) for use by the 2953 CLSS for ABDR training at Tinker AFB, Oklahoma. Scrapped by June 1989.
F-105G 62-4422	1983—Barged from Patuxent River NAS, Maryland, to Aberdeen Range for use as a target for Army munitions tests.

F-105G 63-8316 is pushed by a tug boat up Chesapeake Bay from Patuxent River Naval Air Station to Aberdeen Proving Grounds, Maryland. This plane was one of fifteen Thunderchief Wild Weasels the Georgia Air National Guard flew in May 1983 from Dobbins Air Force Base, Georgia, to retirement at "Pax" River (Bill Malerba archive photograph).

F-105G 62-4423	1983—Barged from Patuxent River NAS, Maryland, to Aberdeen Range for use as a target for Army munitions tests.
F-105F 62-4433	1983—Barged from Patuxent River NAS, Maryland, to Aberdeen Range for use as a target for Army munitions tests.
F-105G 62-4434	13 Dec 1984—Removed from MASDC (storage number FK013) and shipped to RAF Lakenheath, Great Britain, for use as an ABDR trainer. Scrapped on 28 May 1996 when no museum in Great Britain could afford to transport it.
F-105G 62-4439	1983—Barged from Patuxent River NAS, Maryland, to Aberdeen Range for use as a target for Army munitions tests.
F-105G 62-4442	6 Feb 1985—Removed from AMARC (storage number FK090) and shipped to Aviano AB, Italy, for use as an ABDR trainer. Scrapped at Aviano in Oct 1991.
F-105G 63-8265	20 Mar 1985—Removed from MASDC (storage number FK092) to Torrejon AB, Spain, for ABDR training. Scrapped at Torrejon in July 1991
F-105G 63-8275	1983—Barged from Patuxent River NAS, Maryland, to Aberdeen Range for use as a target for Army munitions tests.
F-105F 63-8288	26 Feb 1997—Removed from AMARC (storage number FK012) for use as a target on the Airburst Range, Peterson AFB, Colorado.
F-105G 63-8291	15 Oct 1976—Written off due to wing cracks at McClellan AFB, California.
F-105G 63-8292	26 Mar 1985—Removed from MASDC (storage number FK094) for ABDR training at Torrejon AB and Zaragoza AB, Spain. Scrapped at Torrejon in January 1992.
F-105F 63-8294	Nov 1985—Removed from AMARC (storage number FK029) and shipped to Clark AB, Philippines, for ABDR training. Probably scrapped after the eruption of Mount Pinatubo in June 1991.
F-105F 63-8299	1983—Barged from Patuxent River NAS, Maryland, to Aberdeen Range for use as a target for Army munitions tests.
F-105G 63-8303	3 Feb 1986—Removed from MASDC (storage number FK023) for ABDR training at Incirlik AB, Turkey. Scrapped at Incirlik in July 1992

Missing its right wing and many other parts, F-105G 63-8305 appeared ready for the glue factory a few months before it was sold as scrap. A 1972 Vietnam combat veteran at Korat, Thailand, it was last flown by the 35 Tactical Fighter Wing from George Air Force Base, California, who retired it on 1 July 1980 (photograph by Col. Walter W. Saeger, Jr., 2 January 1999).

F-105F 63-8362 on 12 March 1994 at Coleman Barracks near Mannheim, Germany. When the plane belonged to the Virginia Air National Guard in the 1970s, it was called *Do It with Finesse* and sported a colorful drawing below its left wing of a gladiator striking a missile with a spiked ball on a chain. As the photo on the next page shows, the panel has been cut out of the fuselage (Leslie Sargent photograph via John Coon).

F-105G 63-8304	1983—Barged from Patuxent River NAS, Maryland, to Aberdeen Range for use as a target for Army munitions tests.
F-105G 63-8305	1999—Sold as scrap from AMARC (storage number FK015), to Fritz Enterprises, Taylor, Michigan.
F-105G 63-8306	1983—Barged from Patuxent River NAS, Maryland, to Aberdeen Range for use as a target for Army munitions tests.
F-105G 63-8307	21 Aug 1985—Removed from AMARC (storage number FK021) and sent as ABDR trainer to Brooks AFB, Texas, where it was scrapped in 1997.
F-105F 63-8309	5 Jul 1995—Scrapped after use for ABDR training by the 2955 CLSS at Robins AFB, Georgia. Previously displayed at Robins AFB museum.

This photo of F-105F 63-8362 at Coleman Barracks near Mannheim, Germany, shows the missing fuselage panel below the left wing (Leslie Sargent photograph via John Coon).

F-105G 63-8313	1983—Barged from Patuxent River NAS, Maryland, to Aberdeen Range for use as a target for Army munitions tests.
F-105G 63-8316	1983—Barged from Patuxent River NAS, Maryland, to Aberdeen Range for use as a target for Army munitions tests.
F-105G 63-8319	1983—Barged from Patuxent River NAS, Maryland, to Aberdeen Range for use as a target for Army munitions tests.
F-105F 63-8325	1985—Probably scrapped after being used by 2951 CLSS for ABDR training at SM-ALC, McClellan AFB, California.
F-105G 63-8328	1983—Barged from Patuxent River NAS, Maryland, to Aberdeen Range for use as a target for Army munitions tests.
F-105G 63-8332	1983—Barged from Patuxent River NAS, Maryland, to Aberdeen Range for use as a target for Army munitions tests.
F-105G 63-8339	1985—Probably scrapped at Robins AFB, Georgia.
F-105G 63-8351	Nov 1978—Scrapped at George AFB, California.
F-105G 63-8355	1983—Barged from Patuxent River NAS, Maryland, to Aberdeen Range for use as a target for Army munitions tests.
F-105F 63-8362	1994—Abandoned at Coleman Barracks Army Air Field, Mannheim, Germany, after use by the U.S. Army for helicopter sling-load training.

Index